8-16-99

The Handbook of
Contemporary Hospitality
Management Research

Dedication

For Penny
my one and only love

The Handbook of Contemporary Hospitality Management Research

Edited by

BOB BROTHERTON

JOHN WILEY & SONS, LTD
Chichester · New York · Weinheim · Brisbane · Singapore · Toronto

Other Wiley Editorial Offices

John Wiley & Sons, Inc., 605 Third Avenue,
New York, NY 10158-0012, USA

WILEY-VCH Verlag GmbH, Pappelallee 3,
D-69469 Weinheim, Germany

Jacaranda Wiley Ltd, 33 Park Road, Milton,
Queensland 4064, Australia

John Wiley & Sons (Asia) Pte Ltd, 2 Clementi Loop #02-01,
Jin Xing Distripark, Singapore 129809

John Wiley & Sons (Canada) Ltd, 22 Worcester Road,
Rexdale, Ontario M9W 1L1, Canada

Library of Congress Cataloging-in-Publication Data
The handbook of contemporary hospitality management research / edited
   by Bob Brotherton.
       p.   cm.
     Includes bibliographical references and index.
     ISBN 0-471-98395-0 (cloth)
     1. Hospitality industry—Management.   2. Hospitality industry—
Research—Handbooks, manuals, etc.   I. Brotherton, Bob.
TX911.3.M27H373   1999
647.94'068—dc21   98-39462
                                                          CIP

British Library Cataloguing in Publication Data

A catalogue record for this book is available from the British Library

ISBN 0-471-98395-0

Typeset in 10/12 pt Times by Mathematical Composition Setters Ltd, Salisbury.
Printed and bound in Great Britain by Bookcraft (Bath) Limited, Midsomer Norton, Somerset.

This book is printed on acid-free paper responsibly manufactured from sustainable forestry,
in which at least two trees are planted for each one used in paper production.

Contents

Contributors

Michael Baker, Department of Management Studies, University of Surrey, Guildford, Surrey, GU2 5XH

Gerald L. Barlow, Department of Management, University of Central England, Perry Barr, Birmingham, B42 2SU

Tom Baum, The Scottish Hotel School, University of Strathclyde, Curran Building, 94 Cathedral Street, Glasgow G4 0LG, Scotland

Maureen Brookes, School of Hotel and Restaurant Management, Oxford Brookes University, Gipsy Lane Campus, Headington, Oxford OX3 0BP

Bob Brotherton, Department of Hospitality and Tourism Management, Manchester Metropolitan University, Hollings Faculty, Old Hall Lane, Manchester M14 6HR

Francis Buttle, Manchester Business School, Booth Street West, Manchester, M15 6PB

David Edgar, Department of Hospitality, Tourism and Leisure Management, Glasgow Caledonian University, Park Drive, Glasgow G3 6LP, Scotland

Martin Friel, Department of Hotel and Tourism Management, University of Buckingham, Buckingham MK18 1EG

Alan Fyall, Napier University, Craighouse Campus, Craighouse Road, Edinburgh EH10 5LG, Scotland

David Gilbert, Department of Management Studies, University of Surrey, Guildford, Surrey, GU2 5XH

Frank Go, Centre for Tourism Management, Erasmus University Rotterdam, PO Box 1738, Burg, Oudla an 50, 3062 PA Rotterdam, The Netherlands

Anne Hampton, Department of Hotel and Tourism Management, University of Buckingham, Buckingham, MK18 1EG

Nigel Hemmington, School of Hotel and Restaurant Management, Oxford Brookes University, Gipsy Lane Campus, Headington, Oxford OX3 0BP

Haydn Ingram, Department of Management Studies, University of Surrey, Guildford, Surrey, GU2 5XH

Stephanie Jameson, Faculty of Cultural and Education Studies, Leeds Metropolitan University, Calverley Street, Leeds, LS1 3HE

Stuart Jauncey, School of Hotel and Restaurant Management, Oxford Brookes University, Gipsy Lane Campus, Headington, Oxford OX3 0BP

Nick Johns, Research Centre of Bornholm, Stenbrudsvej 55, 3730 Nexc, Denmark

Peter Jones, Department of Management Studies, University of Surrey, Guildford, Surrey, GU2 5XH

Conrad Lashley, Faculty of Cultural and Education Studies, Leeds Metropolitan University, Calverley Street, Leeds, LS1 3HE

David Litteljohn, Department of Hospitality, Tourism and Leisure Management, Glasgow Caledonian University, Park Drive, Glasgow, G3 6LP, Scotland

Andrew Lockwood, Department of Management Studies, University of Surrey, Guildford, Surrey, GU2 5XH

Rosemary Lucas, Department of Hospitality and Tourism Management, Manchester Metropolitan University, Hollings Faculty, Old Hall Lane, Manchester M14 6HR

Michael Olsen, Department of Hospitality and Tourism Management, Virginia Polytechnic, 362 Wallace Hall, Blacksburg, VA 240661-0429, USA

Angela Roper, School of Hotel and Restaurant Management, Oxford Brookes University, Gipsy Lane Campus, Headington, Oxford OX3 0BP

Silvia Sussmann, Department of Management Studies, University of Surrey, Guildford, Surrey, GU2 5XH

Stephen Taylor, The Scottish Hotel School, University of Strathclyde, Curran Building, 94 Cathedral Street, Glasgow G4 0LG, Scotland

Rhodri Thomas, Faculty of Cultural and Education Studies, Leeds Metropolitan University, Calverley Street, Leeds LS1 3HE

Richard Thomas, Southampton Institute of Higher Education, East Park Terrace, Southampton SO14 0YN

Eliza Ching-Yick Tse, Department of Hospitality and Tourism Management, Virginia Polytechnic, 362 Wallace Hall, Blacksburg, VA 240661-0429, USA

Sandra Watson, Napier University, Craighouse Campus, Craighouse Road, Edinburgh, EH10 5LG, Scotland

Susan Welch, Faculty of Cultural and Education Studies, Leeds Metropolitan University, Calverley Street, Leeds LS1 3HE

Roy C. Wood, The Scottish Hotel School, University of Strathclyde, Curran Building, 94 Cathedral Street, Glasgow G4 0LG, Scotland

Preface

In research terms Hospitality Management is a relatively new 'discipline' which has traditionally looked to other, longer-established discipline specialisms for its research perspectives and methods. However, over the last ten to fifteen years a considerable body of hospitality management research has been conducted by a wide range of researchers, with the output from this research effort largely available only through the laborious process of accessing it via the wide range of diverse journal and conference paper sources it has been published in. Unfortunately the combination of these two sets of factors has led to a situation where no specific and comprehensive hospitality management research text is currently available for students, academic researchers and practitioners. The consequence of this has been that academic colleagues, students and practitioners have had no alternative but to turn to the general business/management, and/or specific discipline-based, research texts for assistance with methodological issues. In addition, colleagues have also faced an often difficult and increasingly time-consuming search to find a coherent point of reference for their research plans and activities because of the increasing range of diverse outlets used to publish the contemporary hospitality management research output. Therefore, in the light of the increasing quantity and quality of research in the hospitality management field there is a clear need for a comprehensive handbook of this nature.

In designing this handbook one feature which experience suggests is very important to hospitality management students, academics and practitioners is the contextualisation of 'generic' material to their chosen field of study or employment. Therefore, this text has been designed with this feature in mind. The 'methodology' chapters in Part One utilise examples drawn from contemporary hospitality management research to illustrate the application of the philosophical issues and alternative research approaches and methods. Similarly, the 'state of the art' chapters in Part Two are firmly rooted in the type of contemporary research related to each hospitality management specialism. In addition, as the chapter authors are drawn from amongst the leading figures in contemporary hospitality management research, the handbook as a whole provides an authoritative, and demonstrably applied, commentary on each of the areas it covers.

The first two chapters in Part One, by Roy Wood, Stephen Taylor and David Edgar, are primarily concerned with exploring basic philosophical and methodological issues and choices available to the hospitality management researcher and reflect a variety of critical debates regarding such choices. The main purpose of these chapters is to sensitise the reader to the nature, substance and importance of these fundamental issues, and to encourage him or her to confront the epistemological and ontological questions and choices which these discussions raise. Each of these chapters explores the background and basis of the philosophical issues it deals with and illuminates the key issues, and their implications for alternative philosophical choices, by reference to, and discussion of, the use of such perspectives in recent research studies conducted within the field of hospitality management. This provides readers with an opportunity not only to familiarise themselves with the generic nature of the philosophical issues, but also to relate these issues to their primary context of interest—hospitality management research.

Chapters 3 and 4, by David Litteljohn, Angela Roper, Maureen Brookes and Anne Hampton, explore different approaches which may be adopted to conduct research. The purpose of these chapters is to provide the reader with a critical awareness and understanding of the fundamental nature, suitability and applicability of these different approaches, and a clear exposition of the perspectives and techniques utilised to implement them effectively. The basis and advantages/disadvantages of each approach are discussed in relation to both general methodological issues and the actual or potential application of the approach to particular types of research issues and questions in the hospitality management field. This discussion, particularly the latter element, is conducted through reference to, and use of, actual examples drawn from contemporary hospitality management research studies. Again it is this aspect which strongly differentiates these chapters from those on the same issues to be found in general business/management research texts and gives the material its unique identity and value to the handbook's target readership.

Chapters 5–10 clearly focus upon a range of alternative 'methods' and 'techniques' available to the researcher. Rosemary Lucas explores a number of methodological issues associated with survey research, whilst Peter Jones, Bob Brotherton, Conrad Lashley and Stuart Jauncey do likewise for experimental, case study, comparative, action, and observational research respectively. These provide a background for the final set of chapters in Part One which focus on the issues related to the use of a range of specific techniques associated with these methods. Thus, Chapters 11–16 find David Gilbert and Andrew Lockwood dealing with critical incident technique; Francis Buttle exploring measurement issues; Nigel Hemmington discussing sampling considerations; Alan Fyall and Richard Thomas contributing a useful discussion on the application of quantitative data analysis techniques; Anne Hampton providing a qualitative foil for the previous chapter; and Tom Baum dealing with an often neglected aspect of the research process—the presentation of research findings. The aim of these chapters is essentially to explore and explain the methods and techniques through which the various research 'approaches' may be operationalised and implemented. Each of them addresses this aim through a discussion of the underlying methodological issues and the use of actual examples, drawn from a range of contemporary hospitality management research studies, to illustrate the application of these methods to particular questions and studies.

The chapters in Part Two of the handbook are designed to provide the reader with a critical 'state of the art' review of hospitality management research in each of the specialisms. They explore the predominant paradigms and themes utilised in contemporary research studies in each specialism and provide the reader with a clear indication of the major types of approaches and themes which have been adopted in the particular specialism. In addition they also focus upon the specific nature of the type of research studies which have been undertaken in the specialism. The 10 'hospitality management specialism' chapters in Part Two cover a wide range, though clearly not the entire field, of the key areas in which contemporary hospitality management researchers are involved. Perhaps the most notable omission here is that of marketing. The original design for the text did incorporate such a chapter, but unfortunately the author contracted to write it did not deliver and it was decided not to delay publication by seeking an alternative author at the eleventh hour. However, if a second edition of the handbook is to be produced in the future a chapter on marketing will be included. Finally, the concluding chapter reflects upon a number of the key issues raised in Parts One and Two, and attempts to focus attention on some of the recurring themes and future questions which hospitality management researchers will need to address if this field of research is to develop further in the future.

In approaching the end of this Preface I would like to offer a heartfelt thank you to a number of people who have helped to bring this project to fruition. In the first instance I would like to thank Dr Iain Stevenson who, although he has now left John Wiley & Sons, had the vision and sufficient belief in the value of this work to commission it in the first place. I would also like to thank his successor at John Wiley & Sons, Claire Plimmer, and all her colleagues who have largely left me alone to get on with the job of producing the copy but were always available to offer support when things didn't always go to plan! Similarly, as this large project comes to fruition, it would be remiss of me not to record my sincere thanks to my wife Penny, who has endured the loneliness which the long periods of time I have spent writing or editing this work have created with as much cheerful fortitude as possible. The support and encouragement she has provided has been invaluable and greatly appreciated.

However, there is no doubt that the largest thank you must go to the enormous cast of authors who contributed the chapters for this volume. Without the willingness of these colleagues to find the time and energy, within their already busy lives, to research and write the chapters, this handbook would not exist. I am immensely grateful to all the contributing authors, both individually and collectively, for providing copy and responding so positively to my editorial comments and suggestions. There is no doubt in my mind that all the contributors associated with this venture can be justifiably proud of both their individual contribution and the final volume as a whole. I would also like to extend my thanks to the management, colleagues and students at Blackpool and The Fylde College, particularly the Head of Hospitality Management (Sean Mooney) for keeping much of the daily detritus from reaching my desk, who have all been extremely supportive and helpful during the process of completing this project. Finally, as is usual in ventures of this nature, it should be noted that the responsibility for any deficiencies, errors and omissions in this text lie with myself and all the value must be attributed to the contributing authors.

Bob Brotherton

Part One:
Philosophies, Approaches and Methods

1 Traditional and alternative research philosophies

ROY C. WOOD

When academics start talking about traditional and alternative research philosophies it is a good time for the uninitiated to dive for cover. Frequently, debates about this distinction are ill-informed, selective and sterile. Indeed, this chapter will argue the point that the very premise of a distinction between traditional and alternative research philosophies is flawed. In so doing, it is important to emphasise that the approach taken here is essentially 'idealised' in nature. Put another way, the discussion that follows is highly pragmatic in representing the *typical* arguments that surround questions of what constitute 'traditional' and 'alternative' research philosophies and methods. One consequence of this is that the pluralism of so-called 'alternative' approaches characteristic of research in social and management sciences is expressed in only a very limited way. For example, there is no discussion of the many interfaces which exist between research philosophy, ideology and methodology, such as feminist critiques of research philosophy and 'feminist' research methodologies. Nor is the undoubted pluralism of 'alternative' research philosophies afforded detailed examination in terms of the impact such philosophies have on the choice of research method(s) and the production of research findings. There is no shortage of both introductory (Gilbert, 1993) and more complex (Denzin and Lincoln, 1994) accounts of such issues, but in flagging those areas that do not receive detailed consideration in what follows, it is important to emphasise that the advantage of pursuing an 'idealised' approach to research methodology derives from the clarity it lends to the book's main focus—research into hospitality and the hospitality industry. Specifically, in postulating an initial distinction between 'traditional' and 'alternative' research philosophies, it is possible to draw an (albeit simplistic) landscape of the strengths and weaknesses of research in the field. This chapter therefore embraces a necessary compromise whereby idealised oversimplification of the nature of 'research' facilitates discussion of the current status and sophistication of 'hospitality' research.

Some 'types' of research

At the most general level, everyday discourse on research tends to operate on the basis of simple bipolarities. Thus it is not uncommon to hear 'commonsense' conversations about the distinctions between 'pure and applied', 'primary and secondary', 'theoretical

The Handbook of Contemporary Hospitality Management Research, Edited by Bob Brotherton.
© 1999 John Wiley & Sons Ltd.

and empirical', and 'descriptive and explanatory' research. What do these terms mean? In terms of pure and applied research, pure research is that which has no obvious practical implications, no obvious *use* value beyond contributing to a particular area of intellectual endeavour. Pure research may produce knowledge that *is* ultimately put to some practical use but the major motivation of those conducting pure research is to seek to contribute to the canon of knowledge in a particular area for its own sake. Applied research is, by way of contrast, problem-oriented, directed towards solving some particular intellectual puzzle that has practical implications. Both pure and applied research can lead to the uncovering of new knowledge and new 'facts' about a phenomenon or phenomena.

Turning to primary and secondary research, primary research is a term that usually refers to research which involves the collection of original data using an accepted methodology, in contrast to secondary research which normally implies an activity whereby no new original data is generated but where the research project draws on existing ('secondary') sources alone. Of course, most forms of investigative work usually include secondary research: where original primary data is collected, secondary research to establish what prior work has been undertaken in a particular area is a necessary precursor to research design. A corollary of the distinction between primary and secondary research is, as implied in the preceding remarks, that between primary and secondary data. Primary data is generally that which is collected specifically in pursuit of particular research objectives: it is 'new' and original data. Secondary data is 'the rest'—books, statistical reports from government and other agencies, documents and so on.

Following from the distinction between primary and secondary research, that between theoretical and empirical is a little more complex. In essence, theoretical research is where research activity contributes to the study of a particular area of intellectual enquiry. It can involve the collection of original data, but outside the natural sciences, theoretical research has more abstract and contemplative connotations and may entail acts of interpretation and reinterpretation of existing data to extend understanding of phenomena. Empirical research is a term employed to describe the collection of original data for analysis. In this sense, empirical research is synonymous with primary research. The literal meaning of the term 'empirical' is 'based on observation or experiment, not on theory' (*The Oxford Minidictionary*, 1991 edition) though, of course, observations, experiments and data can make a contribution to theory just as data arguably must be interpreted using a theoretical framework.

The final distinction often encountered in the literature on research methodology is that between descriptive and explanatory research. Descriptive research is largely concerned with questions of what, when, where and who, whereas explanatory research goes beyond this and is concerned with why and how questions. Descriptive research is thus essentially informational in character. It may involve the collection of original data for analysis but its main purpose is to establish a factual 'picture' of the object of study. Explanatory research is directed towards exploring the relationships between concepts and phenomena and explaining the causality and/or interdependency between these.

All the above distinctions share a particular explanatory utility in that they shed light upon the nuances of argument which arise in debates about so-called 'traditional' and 'alternative' research philosophies. In this context, the two terms are more specifically interpreted as postulating a further distinction—that between 'positivism' and 'interpretative' research (e.g. Easterby-Smith, Thorpe and Lowe, 1991). This, as it were, is the mother of all other distinctions and consideration of the two terms frames the areas of our concern here.

Positivism

In their *Collins Dictionary of Sociology*, Jary and Jary (1995) identify three principal definitions of positivism in general usage. These are:

- Positivism as a doctrine or belief that the only true knowledge is scientific in character, describing the interrelationships between real, observable phenomena (whether social or physical).
- Positivism as an approach which assumes that the (research) methods of the natural sciences (for example, measurement and the search for general laws of causation) can be applied unproblematically to the study of social phenomena.
- The pejorative corollary of the second definition above, where social scientists are seen as erroneously seeking to apply scientific methods to social scientific phenomena.

In respect of the final point above, an illuminating recent comment on the nature of positivism is offered by Wacquant (1993: 495) who notes somewhat acidly that positivism ' ... has become a term of polemical indictment, if not abuse, in contemporary social science ... [.] And, like ideology, it has assumed a multiplicity of meanings so that there are nearly as many definitions of positivism as there are critics of it ... '. Positivism, then, has become a dirty word for some, and despite many facets is viewed by its critics as seeking to apply scientific research methods to the study of social (including management) phenomena in order to establish explanatory laws in an objective, unbiased, 'value-free' manner. Positivism embraces a number of assumptions which may crudely be summarised as follows:

- There exists a 'real world' of social and physical phenomena.
- This real world is objective and tangible (that is, most people would agree on what constitutes the 'real world' of phenomena).
- This world can be analysed (researched) in an objective fashion in order to increase understanding of the phenomena of which it is comprised.
- The methods employed in such research are (should be) objective and impartial as well as immune from the influence of human values and beliefs (value-free).
- If research is undertaken objectively, then the gradual accumulation of knowledge should enable accurate description of the nature and behaviour of such phenomena, including the interrelationships between phenomena in terms of cause and effect, dependency and interdependency and so on: in short, the findings of research should be capable of explanatory generalisation.

The main expression of the positivist approach to research is the hypothetico-deductive method which is generally believed to govern the procedures of natural-scientific investigation. Natural scientists (chemists, biologists, physicists) are said to view the world as being external, 'out there', and enjoying a real existence which is beyond being misconstrued by humans. Accordingly, the rational investigation of the real world of phenomena will ultimately yield universal truths about their character and behaviour.

In this view, the scientist begins with a phenomenon to study and generates ideas about its character and behaviour. These ideas are crystallised into a hypothesis which is a statement about the qualities or behaviour of a phenomenon that is advanced for testing. In testing the hypothesis, most commonly in the natural sciences by experimentation, the researcher seeks to establish whether the hypothesis-statement is factually sustainable. The manner in which a hypothesis is tested will to a degree be dictated by the theoretical and/or conceptual framework(s) within which the scientist operates. The extension and consolidation of these frameworks will result from the outcome of experimentation, i.e. hypothesis testing. The demonstration and rejection of hypotheses both contribute to establishing the logical consistency and parameters of the frameworks employed by effectively detailing what is or is not to be regarded as legitimate scientific knowledge.

At this point, it is useful to make a distinction between the verification and falsification of the hypothesis. In classical hypothetico-deductive research, the investigator ought to *verify* the hypothesis, that is to show that the hypothesis is true. However, an alternative view closely associated with the philosopher Karl Popper is that hypotheses should be subjected to the process of falsification, that is a process designed, crudely speaking, to show that a hypothesis is wrong or false. The example usually marshalled to illustrate this point concerns black swans. Consider the assertion that 'all swans are white'. How can this assertion be shown to be true or false? One answer would be to verify the assertion by counting all swans. But, even if this were possible, how would the researcher know that they had counted all swans? More significantly, even if all the swans observed were white, it would not necessarily hold true that all future swans would be white. In many, if not all, cases, it is impossible to verify a hypothesis completely. It is, however, much easier to falsify one since it requires only one contrary piece of evidence to refute the assertions of a hypothesis—in this case, the observation of one black swan.

The purpose of the hypothetico-deductive method is data collection directed towards the testing of a hypothesis with the result that the hypothesis is accepted or rejected. If the hypothesis is new, and it is accepted, then this is, technically, a contribution to theory. If it is rejected, a further new hypothesis or hypotheses may be formed and the test process begins again. If (and when) a theory or theories are sufficiently sophisticated, then laws pertaining to the phenomenon which the theory or theories purport to circumscribe may be derived from the body of theoretical knowledge and used to predict the future behaviour of the phenomenon.

A useful development of this view is offered by Gilbert (1993: 25–26) who notes that theories comprise one or more hypotheses each of which in turn is made up of concepts linked by relationships. Gilbert employs the classic example of Emile Durkheim's 'theory' of suicide to illustrate this point. The French sociologist Durkheim postulated that economic crises have a causal effect on suicide rates. Here, Gilbert argues, 'economic conditions' and 'the suicide rate' are concepts linked by a relationship. Given that a theory is intended to constitute a body of knowledge capable of describing (explaining) the nature of a phenomenon and its behaviour, it will almost certainly be the case that at the heart of a theory will be a series of propositions (concepts) linked by relationships of a causal nature.

All theories must be capable of being tested and a number of hypotheses could be derived from the suicide example to test Durkheim's theory. One candidate would be:

'Changes in economic conditions cause (have an effect on) rates of suicide'. There are limitations to such a hypothesis because of the vagaries of the terms 'changes', 'economic conditions' and 'rates of suicide'. The hypothesis is imprecise. To adequately test the hypothesis, we would have to select certain investigative methods, i.e. select an appropriate research methodology or methodologies. It is generally held that 'good' methodology satisfies three principal criteria, being (McNeill, 1990: 14–16):

- reliability
- validity
- representativeness and generalisability.

To talk of methodological principles is to talk primarily of the means of data collection and the use of data. In this sense, it is possible for illustrative purposes to frame a number of questions pertaining to the items listed above, questions which illuminate the significance of each for sound methodology. These are as follows:

- Is the method of data collection reliable and are the conclusions drawn from it equally reliable, that is, consistent with the data?
- Was the data collected (a) valid data to collect; (b) collected in a valid way using an appropriate technique or techniques; and (c) on the basis of (a) and (b) congruent with the conclusions drawn from it?
- Was the data collected representative in the sense of being typical, thus allowing for (a) the generalisation/extrapolation of research conclusions beyond the boundaries of the subject studied; and (b) replication of results by other researchers?

It is worth noting that these questions, and the very concepts of reliability, validity and representativeness/generalisability, are a reflection of the imperatives of the positivist tradition. Nevertheless, they have meaning and significance beyond research conducted in the positivist tradition and, in the broadest sense, are general and generalised criteria for the appraisal of research technique, though this does not mean they can be regarded as unproblematic, as we shall see.

It will be recalled from the earlier discussion that if theories comprise one or more hypotheses each of which constitutes concepts linked by relationships, then to test a theory it is necessary to compare the predictions made by the theory with measurements of those parts of the real world to which the theory applies. In practice, this means measuring the concept or concepts that go to make up the theory. The problem is that concepts, being essentially abstract in nature, cannot be measured directly. Concepts must be operationalised, that is, for each concept there must be some indicator, normally a method of measurement, which stands for the concept and is accepted as allowing for the inference of accurate measurement of the concept. These indicators must also be *valid* in that they accurately measure the concept, and *reliable* in the sense that they are consistent from one measurement to the next (Gilbert, 1993).

As researchers we begin with a theory, for example the theory of suicide proposed by Durkheim. Here, there are concepts—'economic conditions' and 'suicide'—linked by a relationship, a causal relationship in that changes in the suicide rates are held to be affected by changes in economic conditions. From these observations, hypotheses can be derived for the purposes of testing the general theory. For example, the previously noted and imprecise hypothesis that 'Changes in economic conditions have an effect on rates of suicide' requires the concepts to be operationalised. We would therefore search for some adequate and meaningful indicator of 'economic conditions' and 'suicide rates'. In making our selection (assuming that some element of choice is possible), we would have to be confident that the indicators chosen were both valid (measuring accurately the concept(s) concerned) and reliable (consistent from one measurement to the next). How would we do this?

There are, in fact, no easy or exact answers to these questions (which is why Durkheim's theory of suicide, while ambitious, has been found wanting). One area of agreement might be that the indicators we use will invariably be secondary measurements, for example government data. But what then? The number of potential measures of economic conditions (however defined—and definition is a problem here) are considerable and include unemployment levels, economic growth, gross domestic product, the rate of inflation and so on. All of these measurements themselves are the product of data collection and measurement, thus compounding the problem of reliability and validity. As far as suicide rates are concerned, we may again be reliant upon official statistics which may not reflect a 'true' picture of the suicide rate because of cases of unexplained death, cases where motives for suicide are unclear and which have led officials to classify a death as something other than suicide, and so on. The problem is compounded when we consider the problems of representativeness and generalisability.

The discussion of the reliability and validity of data offered so far has concentrated on issues related to the *internal* consistency of each. A harder test of the reliability and validity of data and research relates to their explanatory power. This is increased the more likely it is believed that the research findings are (a) applicable to subjects beyond the sample studied; and (b) replicable—i.e. reproducible—by other researchers. Applicability in this context is simply another way of asking if the data is both representative and generalisable. If the data from a piece of research is representative, there is a high probability that it is generalisable (together with the findings drawn from data analysis). Representative in this context therefore refers to an appraisal of the reliability and validity of data relative to its generalisability. As Raimond (1993) notes, representativeness and generalisability are inherently bound up with an assessment of whether the conclusions of a piece of research are based on a wide enough range of cases or are subject specific. In management research, investigations are often small-scale, qualitative and interpretive in nature.

Representativeness and generalisability are thus very much (arguably very much more than reliability and validity) positivist in their assumptions about the nature of research and the 'real world' of phenomena, and their application as standards to certain types of research might be inappropriate. In short, there are certain types of activity which we describe as 'research' which may not meet the criteria of representativeness and generalisability. For many positivists such work should not be regarded as in any way meaningful research. One possible way out of this dilemma is to appeal to the 'test' of replicability, to claim that other researchers using similar methods in the same or similar context will produce the same or similar results. This is a valid stance in many cases. The literature on hotel and catering occupations with specific reference to waiting-on-tables shows without exception that whether in the UK or USA, in hotels or stand-alone restaurants, in the case of large or small hotels, or in the case of men and women, waiting staff engage in activities such as petty theft and that the motives they advance for engaging in such activities are consistent in nature.

Positivism has many critics. This is not to say that such critics are opposed to the creation of general explanatory theories (though some might think this to be an impossible goal) or to objectivity in research. Rather, they are united in a profound suspicion that positivist approaches (including the hypothetico-deductive method) to research are inappropriate to the study of social phenomena because social phenomena are the products of human action, and the study of people and their actions is not amenable to the research techniques most closely associated with positivism. At the most obvious level, for ethical reasons it is not possible to experiment on people to any great extent or with any breadth of purpose. A more potent criticism is that people are directed, capable of making choices: they are not inanimate and their behaviour is not readily understood in terms of simple causal factors. Rather, human behaviour is to a large degree constructed through shared meanings, and to study such behaviour effectively it is necessary to identify, understand and interpret such meanings.

A further major objection to positivism in general and the hypothetico-deductive method in particular concerns the actual status of both as methods of investigation as opposed to the characteristics that are *attributed* to each. The main issue here is the extent to which positivism and the hypothetico-deductive method *are* objective and value-free. Some critics argue that true value-freedom is impossible to attain since any (human) decision about what to study and how something should be studied is necessarily ideological, reflecting the interests and values of the person or people making these kinds of choices. In this view, no decisions of this kind are ever entirely neutral.

A related and powerful objection to so-called scientific method is that, like value-freedom, 'scientific method' is a sanitised and idealised model of what actually goes on in reality. In other words scientific research is *not* conducted solely according to the standards of scientific method. The main impetus for this view comes from the work of sociologists of science who have shown that in controversial scientific research where the outcome of experiments designed to test specific hypotheses is contentious, scientists frequently resort to extra-scientific means to attempt to resolve their disputes. Such means often take the form of what many lay people would understand as examples of *unscientific* behaviour, including activities like questioning the integrity or competence of rival researchers. A key point to emerge from many studies that have been undertaken of controversial scientific research is that what comes to count as scientific knowledge is the simultaneous product of both scientific method (as construed in the discussion so far) and rhetorical consensus—that is, agreement as to what will be accepted and acceptable as scientific knowledge.

Understandably, many natural scientists and others feel uncomfortable, even downright hostile to such a view. All other things being equal, when one switches a light switch to the 'on' position, there is a reasonable expectation that the light fitting it is intended to activate will function accordingly. Electricity in this context is an accomplishment of science—an understanding of the nature of electrical power and its applications to lighting. In such circumstances, how can *this* science be a *social* construct—it is real, tangible, and if not quite 'natural', flows from an understanding of certain natural associations between scientific processes? This is a good question. Much sociology of science has been conducted in what its practitioners call an 'empirical relativist' manner, whereby scientific knowledge is seen as being 'produced' in the same fashion as any other kind of knowledge. Sociologists working in this tradition do not for the most part seek to deny the existence of a 'natural' scientific world but argue, as indicated above, that scientific processes are essentially social ones. The problems with this approach to science and scientific method are considerable. Many 'empirical relativist' studies of scientific controversy have focused on areas where resolution of the controversy has been negative (the claims of potential knowledge-makers being rejected) or open-ended (where the dispute has fizzled out without conclusion). Negative or non-outcomes pose a problem of analytic symmetry for empirical relativists because the methods embodied in such an approach should ideally explain 'successful' science also without resorting to commentaries couched in terms of part of the natural order being uncontroversial—put crudely, the natural world is either natural or not. The *strength* of this approach (and, incidentally, the many other philosophical and sociological approaches to science) is that it debunks those myths about the purity of science and scientific research being conducted in an atmosphere of objective neutrality.

The present author's own limited involvement in the sociology of science in the early 1980s involved study of a controversy in nutrition and physiology. Around 70 scientists, mostly based in the UK, were engaged in a debate started by a small group of their number about the causes of obesity. These researchers argued that obesity could be caused not only, as scientific orthodoxy maintained, by excessive food energy intake relative to energy output, but by the absence of (or failure in) a special kind of body tissue that 'burned off' excess calories. In other words, some fat people were fat because they lacked this special tissue or it did not work properly. Whatever the merits of the scientific case, these claims were hotly contested, and in interviews with the leading protagonists it became clear that much of the debate centred not on 'scientific' issues but on personality issues. Enough (confidential) taped material was collected from the protagonists to fuel a substantial legal case of defamation! The idea that science was about 'the facts' just did not bear close scrutiny as politics and personalities intruded into the debate. Some 15 years later, medical–scientific orthodoxy still proclaims the causes of obesity as rooted in too much energy intake and too little energy output. What is fascinating about this orthodoxy is that it is rarely expressed in such neutral terms. Rather, it is linked to moral imperatives, to societal values. Thus, too much energy intake and too little energy output is more usually couched in terms of too much food and too little exercise. Scientific research in the field barely supports this point, and there are many alternative views that have been largely dismissed. The strength of the orthodox view should surely descend (according to the positivist model of science as value-neutral) from evidence garnered in the natural world. That it has to link its case to certain moral and value judgements suggests, rightly or wrongly, that the science involved is far from certain.

Despite this, contemporary philosophy and sociology of science currently face a backlash from such eminent figures as University of London Professor Lewis Wolpert, who at the time of writing has a column in *The Independent on Sunday* newspaper in which he occasionally berates the *lack* of contribution that philosophers and sociologists have made to an understanding of science. Not only is this an instance of positivism in science reasserting itself, it is a reflection of the fragility of science—and of scientists—who resort to blunt denial, the least scientific of all intellectual defences.

Interpretive research

The positivist approach to the study of the social and management world has been, and continues to be, influential, where the limitations of experimentation as an expression of positivism's commitment to objectivity have been recognised, and experimentation replaced to a large degree by the survey method as the principal means of data collection. If experimentation is the expression of positivist objectivity in the natural sciences, then in the social and management sciences this role has been fulfilled by the social survey, often entailing the collection of data (for example, through questionnaires) and the analysis of such data according to the rigours of the hypothetico-deductive method as expressed in statistical testing. As already suggested, however, there has been a retreat from positivism in these areas of enquiry. Further, while the influence of positivist approaches on social research should not be underestimated or denied, alternative approaches have always been present, especially in the disciplines that make up the social sciences. The late flowering of management as an academic discipline beyond merely a body of prescriptive knowledge on 'how to manage' has meant that these alternatives have to some extent been defining of approaches to management research.

These 'alternative' approaches to research generally constitute different *methods* of collecting and analysing data but sometimes vary more fundamentally in that they involve collecting different kinds of data from those normally associated with the positivist tradition. This is why they tend to be grouped under the heading of 'interpretative' or 'phenomenological' research approaches. It is appropriate here to consider some of their shared general characteristics. It will be recalled that key objections to 'applying' the positivist approach to the study of social behaviour and phenomena include the following observations:

- Social behaviour and phenomena are the product of human action which is of a variable rather than a fixed nature (though capable of considerable patterning).
- Human action and behaviour is predicated on the articulation of shared meanings.
- To achieve an effective understanding of human action, the social researcher (including the management researcher) must seek to identify, understand and interpret such meanings.
- Human actions are directed and rarely value-neutral in content or motivation.

The elements of this list can be usefully elaborated as follows (see Easterby-Smith, Thorpe and Lowe, 1991, for a more developed account). First the interpretative research tradition has, as one of its central tenets, a deep-seated scepticism of the positivist view of the 'real world of phenomena' as external and objective. In particular, the social world is seen as socially constructed on the basis of shared meanings which are subjective. The social world is also prone to greater variations than the natural world: while humans do exhibit regular, systematic patterns of behaviour (like certain molecules), these patterns cannot be assumed to be fixed forever. This leads to a second element of the interpretive approach, namely the unavoidable involvement of the researcher in the observation process. The social researcher being a part of the wider social structures which he or she studies can strive for (and often achieve) objectivity in the broadest positivist sense, but can never divorce themselves entirely from the subjectively constructed social contexts of which they are a part. A corollary of this and the first point is, of course, the previously mentioned view that 'scientific' research in the positivist tradition is itself far from objective in the sense that any human observer of natural, as well as social, phenomena brings to their observations certain values and beliefs that must, by definition, impinge upon their interpretation of those phenomena. The third characteristic of interpretive research then is the focus on meanings rather than facts alone.

The central practical problem for interpretive research is how to access the meanings of those under scrutiny. At a general level, all other things being equal, in any given society a degree of meaning will, as noted earlier, always be shared. For the most part, however, interpretive researchers do not study 'society in general' and the researcher's membership of society is so much 'noise' that has to be controlled to allow effective focus on the topics concerned. At the same time, when a group or collectivity of subjects is being studied, the researcher has to absorb a degree of the collectivity's culture and sense of social reality. Researchers may also have to acquire some forms of technical knowledge special to the collectivity being studied in order to maximise the chances of coming to understand the shared meanings of the subjects.

Types of interpretive research

Discussion of interpretive research is further complicated by the distinction often drawn between quantitative (usually employed to mean 'positivist', i.e. scientific or quasi-scientific method) and qualitative (interpretive) research. For many social scientists, however, 'interpretive' research is one broad school of qualitative research. A somewhat crude way around the complexities of semantics in this context is to focus on what may consensually be agreed to constitute the key 'qualitative' research *methods*. Elaboration of these (see Table 1.1) is not the remit of the present discussion. Many are discussed elsewhere in this volume. In the hospitality and tourism contexts, also useful to consult are the volumes by Ritchie and Goeldner (1994) (which is exhaustive and aimed at academic and other research practitioners) and Clark *et al.* (1997) (at the other end of the spectrum, intended as a first 'primer'). For an exhaustive general account of qualitative research pitched at a fairly complex level, Denzin and Lincoln (1994) is largely unbeatable. The concern here is with the significance of these methods as 'alternatives' to 'traditional' methodologies. In this respect we can make two preliminary observations.

First, the apparent diversity and number of qualitative/interpretive methods can be seen to reflect a certain ingenuity, evolved over time, in the development of methodological strategies for explaining human values and actions. This does not mean, however, that the plethora of techniques gives researchers a wider choice. Many qualitative techniques are suited only to particular research situations or scenarios. Indeed, as a general rule, many commentators have pointed out that a selection of particular techniques can be placed on a 'quantity continuum' (see Figure 1.1) where, by implication, qualitative techniques cease to be valid, reliable and generalisable (to which list we can add capable of manipulation) the more subjects one requires to study. It is in this

Table 1.1   Key qualitative research methods

Interviewing	Case studies
Ethnography and observation	Alternative analysis
Biographical method	Observation analysis
Narrative, content and semiotic analysis	Vignettes
Critical incident techniques	Psychographic analysis
Focus and nominal group techniques	Delphi technique

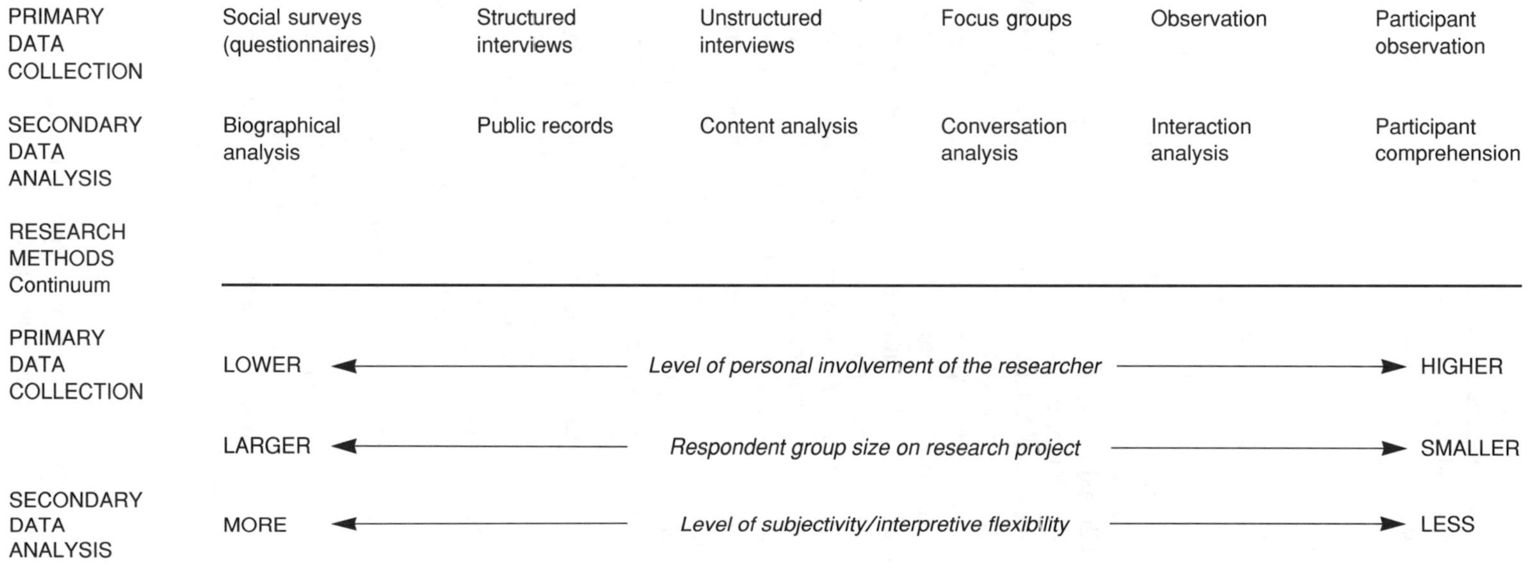

	Social surveys (questionnaires)	Structured interviews	Unstructured interviews	Focus groups	Observation	Participant observation
PRIMARY DATA COLLECTION	Social surveys (questionnaires)	Structured interviews	Unstructured interviews	Focus groups	Observation	Participant observation
SECONDARY DATA ANALYSIS	Biographical analysis	Public records	Content analysis	Conversation analysis	Interaction analysis	Participant comprehension

RESEARCH METHODS Continuum

PRIMARY DATA COLLECTION	LOWER ◄——— Level of personal involvement of the researcher ———► HIGHER
	LARGER ◄——— Respondent group size on research project ———► SMALLER
SECONDARY DATA ANALYSIS	MORE ◄——— Level of subjectivity/interpretive flexibility ———► LESS

Figure 1.1 Methods of data collection showing a continuum of research methods and techniques relative to respondent group size and researcher's level of involvement (after Worsley, 1977)

latter realm that 'traditional' or positivist techniques come into their own. This association between subject-quantity and method-suitability is arguably another artificial distinction. Why should a thousand interviews on the topic of interest be any less reliable than a questionnaire? Provided the proprieties are observed in respect of the validity, reliability and generalisability of data the answer is, of course, that they are not. Yet, the ease with which questionnaires can be manipulated via the conversion of qualitative to quantitative elements would give any sensible researcher pause for thought in selecting a research instrument.

The crucial issue here, then, is that of 'fitness to purpose'. The selection of a research instrument must balance consideration of reliability, validity and generalisability against the nature of the research problem, its complexity and sensitivity, and in fact often requires the researcher to make a choice between, in particular, low and high generalisability. A small-scale study of, say, hotel general managers' attitudes towards trade unions may be conducted using depth interviews which provide reliable (consistent) and valid data which cannot be generalised to all hotel managers but may form the basis of speculative comment (see Aslan and Wood, 1993, for precisely this scenario).

Secondly, the observation was made at the start of this chapter that the very distinction between 'traditional' and 'alternative' positivist/interpretive research methods was flawed. This can now be clearly shown pursuant upon contemplation of the variety of research techniques falling under the 'qualitative' heading. When presented in this fashion there appears a startling imbalance between the traditional/positivist and the alternative/interpretive–qualitative in favour of the latter. Having ruled out all but non-invasive human experimentation, 'traditional' research methods amount to little more than the questionnaire-based social survey. Even here, however, there is an epistemological problem, for the social survey method combines both qualitative and quantitative elements. Indeed, as intimated earlier, social survey method involves qualitative judgements about qualitative concepts that are, in analysis, converted into quantitative data (at least, this is the normal understanding of the use to which the social survey method is put).

By the same token, many of the techniques listed in Table 1.1 often generate data which can be treated quantitatively as well as qualitatively. For techniques such as content analysis, which entails the appraisal of regularities of particular variables in texts and other media, the quantitative is an intrinsic aspect of a method which is normally extrapolated to qualitative assessments of those variables. In short, therefore, any discussion of distinctions between traditional/positivist/quantitative and alternative/interpretive/qualitative research methods at the level of methodology alone, is pretty fruitless. Rather, to examine whether such a distinction has any operational significance it is necessary to supply a historiographical context which, by definition, would allow assessment of the manner in which research methodologies have *actually* been deployed. Since the object of interest in the present context is 'hospitality' research, it is to this area that the final part of the discussion in this chapter turns.

Hospitality research

For all intents and purposes, hospitality research has hitherto been defined in terms of investigation of aspects of the hotel and catering industry, a sector which cross-cuts private and public sector organisations in most economies. Taylor and Edgar (1996) draw on Litteljohn (1990) to identify the following three characteristic approaches to hospitality research:

- *The natural and physical sciences approach* whereby tangible elements of hospitality are examined from the perspectives of one of the natural/physical science disciplines.
- *The hospitality management approach* which draws on a variety of (usually management) disciplines to explore what are perceived to be the unique characteristics of the hospitality industry.
- *The hospitality studies approach* where the hospitality industry, while being perceived as unique, is seen to be amenable to investigation in all its dimensions from a much wider range of disciplines, including the social sciences.

This typology is necessarily artificial but it accurately reflects a core tradition in hospitality research, namely the utilisation of various disciplinary perspectives to address managerial 'problems' in the hospitality industry, an industry which is seen to be unique and in this uniqueness to require particular epistemological and methodological configurations in order to adequately analyse its constituent characteristics and activities.

This last point represents one of the great shibboleths of the hospitality research community and is, of course, complete poppycock. The hospitality industry is only unique in so far as any industry or economic sector possesses unique characteristics. The actual idea that a unique industry requires unique methodologies to generate unique insights (see Slattery, 1983; Wood, 1988) is fatally flawed—what would such a theory of knowledge look like? How is it possible? The idea is so silly, so naive, that it beggars belief. And yet such a belief remains strong—if abstractly so—in the hospitality research community despite even Litteljohn's imprecations which clearly point in another direction. For the purposes of this discussion, it is sufficient to note that one consequence of this belief is that it has generated a considerable insularity among hospitality researchers in terms of their approach to research problems. Solutions to such problems tend to be sought in terms of the particular or unique characteristics of the industry even when such problems are investigated from an established disciplinary base. Indeed, in conceptual terms, research in hospitality is stilted and underdeveloped precisely because of a failure, to paraphrase Doyle's illustrious detective Sherlock Holmes, to make theory fit the facts, rather than facts the theory.

A similar point is made by Taylor and Edgar (1996) in their landmark reflection of the state of hospitality research. One consequence of the dearth of conceptual research in hospitality resulting from an insular 'uniqueness' approach is the predominance of traditional, quantitative research studies. Using the UK Council for Hospitality Management Education (CHME) annual research conference as a template, Taylor and Edgar (1996: 213–214) estimate that for the four symposia of 1992–1995 the predominant research approach, using Litteljohn's typology, was 'hospitality management', representing a mean (unweighted) at 62% of contributions over the period. For 'research technique', quantitative methods predominated, accounting for an unweighted average of 50% of contributions over the period. This is perhaps the most interesting data in Taylor and Edgar's study for the purpose of the present discussion. The authors speculate that in respect of research techniques, the primacy of quantitative techniques in original studies can be accounted for in terms of 'the links to vocational education and the perceived need for speedy and "solid" results' (1996: 214). To this we might add the observation that in seeking to emulate the methods of the natural sciences, it is not uncommon to find new subject areas and fields adopting 'positivist' methodologies in research as these can most readily convey an aura of seriousness and legitimacy. Indeed, Taylor and Edgar make a similar observation, suggesting that one test of a field of study's maturity is the extent to which the preoccupation with positivist methodology is sacrificed to greater variety in the use of qualitative and 'mixed' techniques. By this standard, hospitality research is yet far from mature.

Taylor and Edgar undoubtedly have a point. Building on their criteria for 'maturity', they further suggest that evidence of a variety of research methods employed in a field of study would be linked by a shift to a 'hospitality studies' approach as defined by Litteljohn (1990). While a useful heuristic device, in their desire to ensure internal consistency in their argument, on this point they court the insularity of which they are properly critical. This is because Litteljohn's model is used as a starting *and* finishing point for Taylor and Edgar's critique whereas Litteljohn's model is itself incomplete. A fourth 'approach' can readily be added to the model and this would be the approaches of (principally social science) researchers to the study of hospitality phenomena from *outside* the environment of hotel management schools. Although it has developed in a piecemeal fashion, such research is, in quality and quantity, both substantial and agenda-setting. Some of it predates the systematic development of hotel management schools in the education systems of the advanced industrial nations, but the majority of output reflects the occasional 'contextual' (often one-off) intrusion into the study of hospitality by many individual scholars firmly located in disciplines like sociology, social anthropology, industrial relations and economics, and is wholly contemporaneous with the development of hospitality research within hotel schools.

This research output has two main features. First, the majority of it all falls broadly within what could at present be termed employee/human resource management. Secondly, taken as a body, this scholarship adopts overwhelmingly qualitative research methods where it involves original empirical research (see Wood, 1997, for a review). As is the case with social science research in general, the most commonly employed 'methods' are the depth interview and ethnography (including participant observation). An interesting aspect of this research is the extent to which it has failed to significantly influence output from researchers located in hotel schools. This is an example of insularity writ large. The research in question benefits from being informed by, and located within, a broad social scientific tradition. Though piecemeal in origin, it builds to a coherent and consistent whole, establishing empirical linkages on a great many fronts. Yet hospitality research, in whatever dimension of the Litteljohn (1990) model it is construed, has failed to engage with this work. Indeed, it has not been uncommon for 'mainstream' hospitality researchers to dismiss this work on the grounds that these scholars have an inadequate understanding of the 'unique' nature of the hospitality industry (e.g. Slattery, 1983).

Such a position is no longer tenable, if it ever was. The broad field of tourism and hospitality is attracting more and more attention from researchers outside the 'hotel school' research community. In an important sense, much of this interest evidences a process of 'separate development'. As Taylor and Edgar (1996: 215) note, a recent study of the internationalisation of the hotel industry contains no references to work by hotel school-based researchers. The phenomenon is increasingly being repeated. Thus the sociologist John Urry (1990), in one of the most influential books on tourism ever written, discusses the hospitality sector without evidencing any noticeable awareness of a significant proportion of the research literature emanating from 'hospitality researchers'. In turn, Urry's book has become a major reference point for other social scientists writing on the hospitality industry, often to bizarre effect (see Adkins, 1996, for a worrying example of the genre). Nevertheless, it must be conceded that for so long as there is a failure by hospitality researchers to address qualitative and conceptual issues, the gap is likely to be filled by those who draw on the hospitality industry if only to illustrate a wider theoretical agenda. That such an agenda may well come to represent a normative reference point for analysis of the hospitality sector emphasises the need for hospitality researchers to engage more actively with wider issues of theory and method in the broad areas of management and social science.

Conclusion

This chapter has sought to investigate some of the issues attendant on differentiating between 'traditional' and 'alternative' research methods. Such a distinction has limited utility for an understanding of the variety of available techniques or their application. More significantly, in the final part of the chapter, an effort has been made to consider the relevance of such a distinction to the practice of hospitality research. It is here that the greater significance of the division between positivist and interpretive research methods becomes apparent. If Taylor and Edgar (1996) are correct—and the weight of evidence suggests they are—then we can assert with some confidence that hospitality-centred research (that undertaken by the community of scholars located for the most part in advanced schools of hotel management) is largely 'positivist' in orientation.

A greater complication, however, is that this research dominates the field in terms of *quantity*. A large gap therefore exists in qualitative, but more importantly, *conceptual* research. This points up an important discontinuity with the natural sciences where a positivistic approach to methodology is firmly linked to conceptual schema. These schema themselves may make certain (sometimes questionable) assumptions about the 'natural' world but this is hardly the point. Rather, the procedures of the natural sciences encapsulate a complete epistemology, a theory of knowledge, centred on hypothesis testing directed towards theory building. In hospitality research, to draw a crude analogy, we have the jelly without the cream. That is, hospitality research appears condemned to a solitary existence in terms of asserting methodological priorities over conceptual development. In this sense it is unsurprising that hospitality research has little appeal to scholars more generally, as for the most part it consists of a body of individual studies that may or may not be utilised as a resource to illustrate broader and bigger themes and ideas but which, taken as an oeuvre *qua* oeuvre, consists of little more than a disconnected set of investigations with few if any linkages to a coherent body of theory.

One danger arising from this critique of hospitality research is the promotion of the idea that 'more' conceptual research will reduce some of these problems. This is not what is being advocated here—at least not quite. The current limitations of hospitality research relate strongly to concepts of 'appropriate' methodology, certainly, but a more fundamental problem, enshrined in Litteljohn's (1990) model, is the absence of any significant agreement as to the character and characteristics of hospitality. Construed by hospitality researchers for the most part as the hospitality *industry*, this is a limiting view which detracts from clarification of the nature of hospitality as a cultural phenomenon. The point has been clearly recognised by social scientists in their incursions into the field of tourism. Tourism is not simply an industry but a set of social–psychological attitudes that embrace diverse and varied understandings of the role of tourist activity within society and over time (Selwyn, 1996). A similar point has been made in respect of the nature of hospitality (Wood, 1994). The challenge for 'hospitality research' is thus less whether it follows a positivist or interpretive route in investigation than whether it is able to effectively clarify the very nature of the phenomenon it purports to study.

References

Adkins, L (1996) *Gendered Work: Sexuality, Family and the Labour Market*, Buckingham: Open University Press.

Aslan, A and Wood, R C (1993) 'Trade unions in the hotel and catering industry: the views of hotel managers', *Employee Relations*, **15**(2), 61–69.

Clark, M, Riley, M J, Wilkie, E and Wood, R C (1997) *Researching and Writing Dissertations in Hospitality and Tourism*, London: International Thomson Business Press.

Denzin, N K and Lincoln, Y S (Eds) (1994) *Handbook of Qualitative Research*, London: Sage.

Easterby-Smith, M, Thorpe, R and Lowe, A (1991) *Management Research: An Introduction*, London: Sage.

Gilbert, N (Ed.) (1993) *Researching Social Life*, London: Sage.

Jary, D and Jary, J (Eds) (1995) *Collins Dictionary of Sociology*, Glasgow: HarperCollins, 2nd Edition.

Litteljohn, D (1990) 'Hospitality research: philosophies and progress' *in* Teare, R, Moutinho, H and Morgan, N (Eds), *Managing and Marketing Services in the 1990's*, London: Cassell, 209–232.

McNeill, P (1990) *Research Methods*, London: Routledge.

Raimond, P (1993) *Management Projects: Design, Research and Presentation*, London: Chapman and Hall.

Ritchie, J R B and Goeldner, C (Eds) (1994) *Travel, Tourism and Hospitality Research: a Handbook for Managers and Researchers*, New York and Chichester: John Wiley, 2nd Edition.

Selwyn, T (1996) 'Introduction' *in* Selwyn, T (Ed.), *The Tourist Image: Myths and Myth Making in Tourism*, Chichester: John Wiley, 1–32.

Slattery, P (1983) 'Social scientific methodology and hospitality management', *International Journal of Hospitality Management*, **2**(1), 9–14.

Taylor, S and Edgar, D (1996) 'Hospitality research; the Emperor's new clothes', *International Journal of Hospitality Management*, **13**(3), 211–217.

Urry, J (1990) *The Tourist Gaze*, London: Sage.

Wacquant, L J D (1993) 'Positivism' *in* Outhwaite, W and Bottomore, T (Eds), *The Blackwell Dictionary of Twentieth-Century Social Thought*, Oxford: Blackwell, 495–498.

Wood, R C (1988) 'Against Social Science?', *International Journal of Hospitality Management*, **7**(3), 239–250.

Wood, R C (1994) 'Some theoretical perspectives on hospitality' *in* Seaton, A V *et al.* (Eds), *Tourism: The State of the Art*, Chichester: John Wiley, 737–742.

Wood, R C (1997) *Working in Hotels and Catering*, London: International Thomson Business Press, 2nd Edition.

Worsley, P (1977) *Introducing Sociology*, Harmondsworth: Penguin.

2 Lacuna or lost cause? Some reflections on hospitality management research

STEPHEN TAYLOR AND DAVID EDGAR

> ... hospitality management research is on a slow train headed nowhere. (with apologies to Daft and Buenger, 1990: 82)

Introduction

This chapter discusses some key issues regarding hospitality management research. As the opening quote suggests, it will be argued that significant scope exists for the development of this activity in terms of both its pace and its direction. While considerable progress may have been made in recent years, in terms of both the quantity and quality of research, the field has yet to reach a state of maturity (Taylor and Edgar, 1996). Throughout the academic world increasing pressures are being exerted upon higher education systems. One such pressure is that research has become considered an increasingly important activity during the 1990s for hospitality management academics. For example, in the USA, academics must publish if they are to secure tenure, while in the UK, academics have seen the introduction of the Research Assessment Exercise (RAE)—held every four years—which ties government research funding to the quality and quantity of published institutional research output. Research is therefore a topic which has become central to the working lives of many hospitality academics in the USA, the UK and elsewhere. Given these developments, it is perhaps surprising that there has been limited reflection on this activity within hospitality management.

Reflection upon hospitality management research is the focus of what follows. It is argued that progress in this area has been hampered through a failure to address certain key issues. At the most fundamental level is the current lack of any clear articulation of what is meant by the term hospitality management. How can academics teach and research in an area for which no clear theoretical/conceptual basis has been established? Perhaps this is a trivial issue. After all, thousands of people study hospitality management throughout the world. Hospitality faculties undertake and publish research in numerous journals and books. How then can one suggest that there is a 'pressing need' to question (and answer) the nature of its existence? It is suggested here that the historical failure to address such fundamentals explicitly is hampering meaningful progress in the area of hospitality management research.

The Handbook of Contemporary Hospitality Management Research, Edited by Bob Brotherton.
© 1999 John Wiley & Sons Ltd.

Accordingly, an effort is made to address such questions as 'what is the role of hospitality management research?' and 'what should be the scope of this research?'. In a text devoted to the 'how?' one should undertake research in hospitality management, it would seem desirable to address the 'why?' and the 'what?' dimensions at the outset. These questions could be viewed as *the* basic philosophical questions in respect of hospitality management research. There are, however, other philosophical issues that all researchers (regardless of their subject matter) should be aware of and should have given some thought to. This concerns the debates surrounding research philosophy and its relationship to research methodology. Consequently, the second half of this chapter is devoted to an examination of research philosophy and makes an attempt to explore its role in the context of hospitality management research. The chapter closes with some suggestions for progressing activity in this increasingly vital area of hospitality management education.

The philosophy of hospitality management research

Our starting point is a discussion of the philosophy of hospitality management research, i.e. what are its fundamental principles or primary elements? This is philosophy with a small 'p', so to speak. What follows is predicated on a belief that progress in hospitality management research requires the creation of a coherent framework to guide its future development. This requires that two main issues are addressed. First, there is a need for broad agreement as to the role (purpose) of research activity in hospitality management. Without a clear objective (i.e. a destination) it will be difficult for hospitality research to progress or indeed to measure if it has progressed. The second requirement is the need to agree and decide upon the scope (content) of hospitality research. In the absence of such coherency, hospitality management research will continue to develop in an *ad hoc* manner with no real direction available to guide the considerable human resource engaged in this activity. Given the lack of a clear articulation as to the theoretical underpinnings or conceptual domain of hospitality management, this chapter cannot attempt to provide a detailed map for researchers of what is still uncharted terrain. Instead, what is offered here is more akin to a compass that hopefully—by providing *some* direction in such an uncertain environment—will facilitate progress and perhaps even contribute to the task of mapping hospitality management.

What is the role of hospitality management research?

Within hospitality management there has been limited discussion on the topic of research and its role within hospitality education. Where it has arisen, typically it has been as part of the wider debate on hospitality theory and education (e.g. Nailon, 1982; Slattery, 1983). A rare exception is Litteljohn (1990: 211) who suggested that hospitality research has four main aims:

1. To develop insights into areas of hospitality and the discipline of hospitality.
2. To underpin the content and direction of academic courses.
3. To encourage the development of best-practice techniques in industry.
4. To stimulate further research by dissemination and experimentation.

That research should underpin teaching in hospitality (aim 2) is generally widely accepted, and for many hospitality academics this is possibly considered to be its most practical or relevant purpose. Litteljohn suggested that hospitality research performs a positivist role (under aim 1) and a normative role (under aim 3). In the case of the former—positivist research—this refers to research that seeks to describe existing behaviour/phenomena, i.e. 'what is'. A wide range of research activity in hospitality would fall under this category. For example, it would include research into service delivery systems, industry employment practices, strategic planning systems, financial control procedures, marketing activities and so on.

The second role suggested concerns normative research. Here the purpose of research is not to describe (although this invariably would be the starting point for this type of research) but to *prescribe* particular behaviour(s), i.e. say 'what should be'. Therefore research output is geared towards informing practitioners (or indeed, other researchers) how they should behave in relation to the issue under consideration. Implicit in this role is the view that the current behaviour under scrutiny is in some way 'sub-optimal' and that a key objective of hospitality research should be to improve 'industry performance', however this might be defined.

Given hospitality management's applied nature, it seems entirely consistent that research activity should embrace the purposes of both describing actual industry behaviour and prescribing new behaviours. There is, however, one difficulty with Litteljohn's first aim above, and that is the description of hospitality management as a discipline *per se*. It would perhaps be more useful and accurate to describe hospitality management as an area of professional study (see Shaw and Nightingale, 1995). Hospitality management education has demonstrated a tendency, as Wood (1988) has argued, to pursue a process of eclectic rationalisation of the content of social studies components in a way that is a threat to their ultimate intellectual coherency, while lacking any substantive academic justification for doing so. A parallel concern with respect to research must be advanced here.

Taking Litteljohn's aim 4 above, this is somewhat ambiguous, particularly in terms of what is meant by experimentation in this context. On the other hand, the need to disseminate research findings is critical if such activity is to inform both other researchers and industry practitioners. Arguably, this needs to take place on a much less myopic basis than hitherto. The somewhat artificial boundaries frequently imposed between hospitality management and more general management research seem increasingly difficult to justify, if indeed they ever were justifiable. It has been argued that this situation needs to be reconsidered to facilitate a wider dissemination process in *both* directions (see Taylor and Edgar, 1996). Where the level of dissemination of research output is insufficient, two things are likely to happen. First, research output will be fragmented and piecemeal in that it will typically consist of many isolated studies that neither draw upon nor contribute to one another. The second likely outcome is that the activities of practitioners are unlikely to be influenced to any great extent by this research output.

A case of conceptual malnutrition?   That the above situation describes current hospitality research output (Taylor and Edgar, 1996) can be attributed to the absence of any clear definition of 'hospitality management' and, directly related to this, the ubiquitous belief among many hospitality academics that hospitality is somehow 'different'.

Unfortunately, this position is adopted in complete absence of any articulation of a substantive case which supports such a stance. It is difficult to see that this has had any positive impact upon hospitality education and research. Rather, it has served to perpetuate the field's high degree of insularity and provided little or no tangible gains in respect of its longer-term development. The reality, as Wood (1988: 248) has pointed out, is 'that much of what is known about hospitality and the hospitality industry is derived from research firmly located in one or other tradition of mainstream social theory'. In essence, this is symptomatic of what might be described as a condition akin to 'conceptual malnutrition' in hospitality management.

In a later contribution, which explored a range of theoretical perspectives on hospitality, Wood (1994: 741) further underlined this situation when he cited Burgess (1982) who, it was suggested, implied the 'need for more detailed analysis of the concept [i.e. hospitality] at the abstract, theoretical level'. In supporting the utility of such an endeavour, Wood (1994: 741–742) goes on to add:

> This is a sensible prescription and one, furthermore, that might yield sufficiently valuable insights that can be put to good use in advancing research in the field more generally as well as repelling criticisms—both real and those arising from academic snobbery—directed at the legitimacy of hospitality *management* as an independent field of enquiry [emphasis in original].

Progress towards generating these vital conceptual insights on hospitality might, at long last, be forthcoming. There are now signs of what could be considered some activity within the field that might challenge its historical insularity or even finally provide some grounds for its justification! This is reflected in the recent initiative (in 1997) by a diverse group of UK hospitality academics which seeks to finally address the fundamental question 'what is hospitality?'. The answer to this question is likely to have significant implications for both the direction and the nature of future research activity in hospitality management. Nonetheless, for some, let us call them the 'hospitality pragmatists', such philosophical deliberations are merely distractions from the real solution to hospitality research's apparently moribund state. For them progress lies in a clear and direct course of action.

One UK academic, Jones (1997: 5), has recently argued the case for adopting a 'hospitality management paradigm' based upon operations management on the grounds that hospitality management, as he defined it, 'has at its heart the concept of managing processes'. Jones (1997: 15) also argued that a major shortcoming in hospitality research is the 'very limited empiricism to date', and while acknowledging that 'there are few established frames of reference' he suggested that too much 'effort has been put into articulating theories, building models and developing concepts rather than testing hypotheses'. For others, such views will be considered to be 'operations imperialism' and a complete failure to recognise that progress in hospitality management research has been impeded, not by a lack of empiricism, but by a lack of substantive theory building (i.e. hospitality management is currently atheoretical). This state of affairs can be seen to reside in the continuing failure to articulate a meaningful concept of hospitality management. Opponents to Jones' solution to this shortcoming might argue that it really is a case of putting the proverbial cart before the horse!

Notwithstanding these recent developments, the present state of affairs, with limited debate on the research activity in hospitality, has had considerable impact upon the nature of hospitality research output. For example, it has typically resulted in a situation whereby the perceived primary requirement for hospitality researchers (see Slattery, 1983; Litteljohn, 1990) has been the need to highlight the immediate relevance of their research—what might be best described as the 'tyranny of relevance' (Taylor and Edgar, 1996)—thus meeting their responsibility to practitioners, while simultaneously maintaining some gloss of academic credibility (albeit, at best, restricted to factions of the hospitality research community?). Related to this situation, one suspects, is the apparently widespread belief among most practitioners and many hospitality academics, that the theoretical dimension is the antithesis of the practical one. Such a situation is similar to that identified by Hunt (1991: 4) as existing in the marketing field:

> Almost all marketing practitioners, most marketing academicians, and, sadly, too many marketing researchers perceive theoretical and practical as being at the opposite ends of a continuum. This perception leads to the conclusion that as any analysis becomes theoretical, it must become less practical.

However, it is worth reminding colleagues both in academia and in industry disposed to such a view, that Keynes (1936) suggested:

> Practical men, who believe themselves to be quite exempt from any intellectual influences, are usually the slaves of some defunct economist. Madmen in authority, who hear voices in the air, are distilling their frenzy from some academic scribbler of a few years back.

Types of research in hospitality   In discussing the role of research in hospitality management the use, this far, of the term 'research' tends to suggest that its meaning is unproblematic. However, as the discussion in Chapter 1 has highlighted, this is unlikely to be the case as the term 'research' is a blanket descriptor for a wide range of different activities. Since this text is about undertaking hospitality management research, a clearer articulation of which types of research should be undertaken within hospitality would seem essential. As Wood has indicated in the previous chapter, the dichotomous distinctions between 'pure and applied' or 'theoretical and empirical' research have limited practical value. In this section, there is an attempt to examine the types of research that are applicable to those researching within hospitality management. In doing so the conventional wisdom that 'basic' research (as defined below) has no role within hospitality management research is challenged.

When attempting to tackle a similar issue in the context of marketing management research, Hunt (1991) and Myers, Greyser and Massey (1979) differentiated between basic research, problem-solving research and what the latter refer to as problem-oriented research. In the case of 'basic' research one seeks to increase the general knowledge base of a field, whereas in the case of 'problem-solving' research the focus is upon a particular company's problem in a given situation. This distinction perhaps usefully delineates between what is typically seen as academic research and consultancy projects. The difference between 'problem-orientated' research, which Hunt (1991) saw as a subclass of basic research, and 'basic' research itself is that the former is normative-driven and the latter positive-driven. Myers, Greyser and Massey (1979), on the other hand, somewhat unhelpfully suggested that 'problem-oriented' research lies between the other two types of research. However, it is this perceived middle-ground positioning that might well make this type of research attractive to hospitality researchers.

Within hospitality, the recent contribution by Shaw and Nightingale (1995: 86), which drew upon Boyer's (1990) model of scholarship (which consists of discovery,

integration, application and teaching), adopted the position that 'basic' research is
something which does not concern hospitality researchers:

> The Boyer model is especially appealing to hospitality higher education. As pro-
> fessional schools, the scholarship focus is on integration, application, and teach-
> ing. Generally speaking, hospitality faculty are not true basic researchers and
> thus, discovery should play only a minor role, if any.

Such a view is consistent with that expressed by Slattery (1983: 11) who stated 'once
the theory is selected and studied the scholar can then experiment with its application to
hospitality management … applying social scientific theories to the hospitality industry
is … about developing hospitality versions of the theories'. This, once again, reflects
the historical insularity evident in hospitality management education.

The stance generally adopted can be viewed as suggesting that hospitality research is
essentially the 'scholarship of integration' (Shaw and Nightingale, 1995)—which
reflects its interdisciplinary or multidisciplinary base—and the 'scholarship of application' or, as reflected in much current hospitality research, what might be described as
the 'scholarship of contextualisation' (Taylor and Edgar, 1996). One suspects that the
majority view would concur with that expressed above and, indeed, they *might* be
correct. While it is possible to have considerable sympathy for Shaw and Nightingale's
(1995) stance, the implied interpretation of basic research offered suggests a perspective that is perhaps too narrow and ultimately unhelpful to hospitality academics and
practitioners.

To explain why this is likely to be the case, it is worth highlighting one or two implications attached to adopting this very narrow perspective of basic research (i.e. the
scholarship of discovery) and its lack of relevance, as suggested by Shaw and
Nightingale (1995). A clear consensus appears to exist that hospitality research should
focus upon practical and relevant output that serves the needs of practitioners, i.e.
problem solving (see Slattery, 1983; Litteljohn, 1990). If one accepts this view as representing the fundamental *raison d'être* of hospitality research, how then does one
resolve the potential situation where an important industry problem cannot be tackled
with the current level of knowledge, as has arisen uniquely within the hospitality industry and no other industry? Claims of impossibility require care as they would have
potentially serious implications for the continuing justification for the degree of specialised educational provision for the industry. On this basis, there is justification for
the view that basic research—as defined here—should be recognised as an important
area of activity for hospitality researchers.

To sum up, it is suggested that the purpose of hospitality research is fundamentally
threefold. First, research seeks to uncover and make sense of existing patterns of behaviour and phenomena within the hospitality industry. Second, research is undertaken to
identify new and better ways of managing within the hospitality industry. Lastly, and
facilitated by the previous two purposes, research is undertaken to enable hospitality
faculty—what many perhaps see as their primary role—to educate future practitioners
through ensuring that they are equipped with the latest knowledge and thinking in relation to the task of managing hospitality provision. Viewed in this way, the role of hospitality management research, be it of a problem-solving, a problem-oriented, or a basic
research nature, is central to the task of hospitality education.

What is the scope of hospitality management research?

Having discussed the role or purpose of hospitality research (i.e., the why?), a related issue is the determination of the content or scope of this research (i.e., the what?). At the outset it is important to note that any such deliberations are somewhat hampered by the absence of a clear consensus as to 'what is hospitality?'. Nonetheless, building upon the arguments above, it is possible to make some progress by suggesting how one might go about delineating the appropriate content of hospitality management research. Very closely related to this task is the framing and agreement of the content of the hospitality curricula. Not surprisingly, given the absence of any consensus on the nature of hospitality, there is, as Litteljohn (1990: 216) observed:

> ... no recognised body of knowledge for the study of hospitality. Consensus centres on the interdisciplinary nature of management in the area. However, as exhibited by the course content of hotel and catering degree programmes in the UK, there is considerable disagreement on appropriate areas of content.

Some useful direction as to how to resolve this situation may be gained by drawing upon other areas of social science. For example, the marketing field, in response to this very issue of scope, has developed its *'Three Dichotomies Model'* (Hunt, 1976). Building upon earlier observations made by Kotler (1972), this model uses three categorical dichotomies:

1. Profit sector/non-profit sector
2. Micro/macro
3. Positive/normative

which yield eight classes overall in the schema. Could such an approach be usefully adapted for hospitality management? A tentative, and very incomplete, example of how this might look is shown in Figure 2.1. The profit/non-profit dimensions are excluded on the basis that this distinction is likely to be unhelpful given the convergence upon private sector practices. This is replaced with an intermediate (i.e. meso) level of analysis which recognises and delineates the sectors (e.g. hotels, restaurants, contract catering, etc.) of which the hospitality industry consists.

RESEARCH FOCUS/PURPOSE

	POSITIVIST	NORMATIVE
MICRO	1	2
MESO	3	4
MACRO	5	6

LEVEL OF ANALYSIS

Figure 2.1   The six 'quadrants' model of hospitality management

Thus under quadrant 1 (extending the meaning of 'quadrant' here to mean a sixth part), the focus would be upon carrying out research at the level of the individual firm, i.e. the micro-level, in order to be able to report upon *how firms are actually behaving*, i.e. it is descriptive, be it in terms of, for instance, their production techniques (e.g. food production methods) or their management practices (e.g. training approaches, marketing activities, etc.). Under quadrant 2, the focus is still the level of the individual firm but the objective is to inform firm practice as to *how they should behave* (i.e. it is prescriptive) to optimise performance, however we might choose to define this. Under quadrants 3 and 4, the focus is at sector level (this can be further sub-divided as required, e.g. restaurants: fine dining, ethnic, fast food, public houses, and so on) and the concern is therefore meso-level issues. Once again, this would be from both the positive (descriptive) and normative (prescriptive) perspectives—quadrants 3 and 4 respectively—but this time focusing upon the activities and phenomena at the intermediate aggregation of industry sector. A similar situation prevails with quadrants 5 and 6 but this time the focus is the industry as a whole, i.e. the macro-level.

If some basic consensus could be reached as to *which* topics fall within the scope of hospitality management, then a useful analytical framework might be available to guide both research and teaching activity in the field. Additionally, one also begins to develop a platform for rational debate as to the nature and extent to which hospitality actually is different from other areas of academic endeavour. It is worth noting, however, that the positive/normative dichotomy and some other aspects of the model are not entirely uncontroversial among marketers. Whether it has anything to offer hospitality is for hospitality academics to decide. The criteria of *analytical usefulness, pedagogical soundness and conceptual robustness* (Hunt, 1976) would be useful in determining whether it can have a role to play in contributing to the development of hospitality management as an academic field.

Philosophy and research methodology

> And strange to tell, among that Earthen Lot
> Some could articulate, while others not:
>   And suddenly one more impatient cried—
> 'Who *is* the Potter, pray, and who the Pot?'
>
>   (Omar Khayyám: *Rubá'iyát LX*)

The focus of this section of the chapter shifts the discussion to research philosophy at the generic level and develops some of the points introduced in Chapter 1. Consideration is given to certain key debates within the philosophy of science and their import for hospitality management research. As will be seen, these debates effectively concern answering the last line of Khayyám's Rubá'iyát above. While what follows might appear at first to concern somewhat esoteric issues, they are ones that any researcher should be familiar with as they impact directly upon the 'how' of the research process.

Philosophy and research

The novice researcher can be confronted by a bewildering range of meanings and positions in relation to research activity. As the previous chapter highlighted, quite different philosophical positions are adopted by those who advocate a *positivist* approach (who essentially see people as 'pots') and those advocating an *interpretive* approach (who view people to be more akin to 'potters'). It is important to note that it is impossible to 'prove' that either of these two positions is superior, on whichever criteria one attempts to operationalise such a measure. For as Hughes (1990: 5–6) pointed out, this ' … is not an empirical question but one requiring philosophical and logical argument and debate in which the very presuppositions of knowledge, as a general issue, are of concern. Philosophical questions are to be resolved by reason, not by empirical inquiry'. Fundamentally, each position is based upon certain beliefs as to the nature of the world that surrounds the holder of that view. Each of these 'worldviews' can be described as *inquiry paradigms* which 'define for inquirers what it is they are about, and what falls within and outside the limits of legitimate inquiry' (Guba and Lincoln, 1994: 108).

In this chapter a certain degree of intellectual precision will be forgone by adopting the simplifying assumption that there exist only two competing inquiry paradigms: the positivist and the interpretive. In actuality, there are considerable shades of grey not only between these two paradigms but also *within* each. This is especially true of the interpretive paradigm which is still evolving. The advantage of this sleight of hand is that it facilitates the development of a framework that distils the essence of each paradigm—highlighting their key philosophical differences and the implications of these for research methodology—that will be subsequently utilised to examine hospitality management research. Implicit in this approach is an assertion that a grasp of these metaphysical issues is fundamental to an understanding of research methodology.

Inquiry paradigms: a question of metaphysics

When we talk of a paradigm—the basic set of beliefs (i.e. metaphysics) that guide action—we are referring to human constructions of first principles that cannot be established as to their ultimate truthfulness. A paradigm can be viewed as consisting of three main elements: ontology, epistemology and methodology (Denzin and Lincoln, 1994). When we speak of *ontology* we are concerned with the nature of reality. Is reality something immutable, 'out there—a truth', waiting to be discovered? Or is it something that is socially constructed, a product of the human intellect, that results in the existence of multiple realities, sometimes conflicting and capable of changing over time? In the case of *epistemology*, the issue is how do we know the world and what is the relationship between the inquirer and what can be known? For example, is it (i) possible to observe the external world directly, neutrally and objectively to uncover knowledge, or is it (ii) the case that the observer and the subject of inquiry must interact to create knowledge? *Methodology* is the means by which we gain knowledge about the world. It deals with the issue of how we can go about the task of finding out what we believe to be true.

A moment's reflection upon the preceding paragraph will reveal an important relationship between the three elements of ontology, epistemology and methodology. Simply put, the belief about the nature of the world (ontology) adopted by an inquirer will influence their belief as to the nature of knowledge in that world (epistemology) which in turn will influence the inquirer's belief as to how that knowledge can be uncovered (methodology). That is, 'every research tool or procedure is inextricably embedded in commitments to particular versions of the world [i.e. ontology] and to knowing that world [i.e. epistemology]' (Hughes, 1990: 11). The critical point to be made here is that interpretive research is not merely a case of employing different methods of data collection and analysis to that of positivists. It is about differences in purpose, that is, it is about *differences in philosophy* (Schwandt, 1994). It is these basic differences in each of the two philosophical positions that are examined below.

The positivist paradigm

> You see but you do not observe.
> It is a capital mistake to theorise before one has data.
>
> (Sir Arthur Conan Doyle, *The Memoirs of Sherlock Holmes, The Crooked Man*)

The positivist's ontology can be described as 'naive realism' whereby there is the belief as to a 'real' reality which is apprehendable. This position is slightly modified by those who subscribe to 'postpositivism' and embrace 'critical realism' (Cook and Campbell, 1979). Here reality is seen as being 'real' but this can only be imperfectly and probabilistically apprehendable (Guba and Lincoln, 1994). This revised position reflects the shift from verificationism to falsificationism mentioned in the previous chapter. Realism therefore assumes, as Burrell and Morgan (1979: 4) put it, that reality ' … exists "out there", ontologically it is prior to the existence and consciousness of any single being. The realist considers the social world to have an existence which is as hard and concrete as the natural world'. For the positivist, knowledge is seen to reflect discovered 'truths', typically taking the form of generalisations, sometimes expressed as cause and effect laws.

Central to this ontology are the issues of reductionism and determinism. Reductionism means that positivists ignore the subjective aspects of human behaviour by assuming that this consists of automatic responses to external stimuli. People's behaviour is therefore viewed in a deterministic fashion and this is seen as being no different from a beaker of water heated by a Bunsen burner (external stimuli) which boils at 100°C (automatic response). No recognition is given to the existence of the internal logic and interpretative processes that shape human action. Such assumptions imply that given identical conditions and stimuli the actions of every human will also be identical.

Epistemology in positivism is embodied in the assumption of a 'dualism' between subject and object. Here, inquirers make the assumption that it is possible for them (the 'subject') to separate themselves from what is to be researched (the 'object'). Thus knowledge, independent of the observer, can be gleaned that, through use of rigorous methodology, remains uncontaminated by the act of observation. It has been argued that two of the most significant characteristics of positivist epistemology are the assertions that science is concerned only with directly observable phenomena and with the hypothetico-deductive testing of theories (Keat and Urry, 1975; Giddens, 1979). Based upon the prior assumptions implicit in dualism, the positivist compares his or her observations with the theory postulated. If these observations and the theory correspond, then the theory is true; if not, it is false and the theory is rejected.

This 'correspondence theory of truth' leads to an additional assumption in the positivist's epistemology, namely, that there is a 'theory-neutral observational language' available to direct that observation and the consequent empirical testing of theory (Gill and Johnson, 1991). Critics of positivism at this juncture point to what they see as a fundamental flaw, or contradiction, in positivist epistemology. This resides in their assertion that the act of observation is theory-laden and it is impossible to separate theory from interpretation and data (Hanson, 1958). Thus, there can be no theory-neutral language of observation which, in turn, makes the assumption of dualism—at the heart of the positivist's epistemology based upon correspondence theory—extremely dubious (see Gill and Johnson, 1991: 132–137, for a detailed consideration of this issue).

The interpretive paradigm

> All theory, dear friend is grey, but the golden tree of actual life springs ever green. (Goethe, 1832)

Whereas the positivist paradigm adopts ontological realism, the interpretive paradigm's philosophical position is described as being one of ontological *nominalism*. At the heart of this difference is the view that 'there is an ontological discontinuity between human beings and it-beings [i.e. other animals and physical objects] ... Persons are distinguished from things in that persons *experience* the world, whereas things behave in the world' (Laing, 1967: 53, emphasis added). Nominalism is a 'worldview' where what is considered to be 'an external objective reality' is seen to be brought into existence only through human cognition. In other words, reality is a social construction and therefore has no existence independent of human actors. Fundamentally, this results in the belief as to the existence of 'multiple, apprehendable, and sometimes conflicting social realities that are the products of human intellects' (Guba and Lincoln, 1994: 111).

The interpretive approach asserts that, unlike 'it-beings', human action is the result of subjective interpretations of the external world. Thus the *raison d'être* of interpretivists is to understand (this is referred to as *verstehen*) how people make sense of the outside world. This is of central importance because explanation of human action is seen to be shaped by this subjective process. Such action is considered to have purpose and meaning only in the context of this process of sense-making and is not governed by external stimuli as positivists claim. The fundamental basis for rejecting positivism for many social scientists is therefore a belief that human action cannot be viewed as being the product of a deterministic cause and effect relationship where a dependent variable (i.e. human action) is shaped by various external, independent variables (i.e. stimuli). Thus, the interpretivist rejects reductionism by according human subjectivity a central role as an influence upon human behaviour and therefore critical to its explanation.

The development of the interpretivists' ontology, and consequently their epistemological stance, can be seen as a reaction to a number of perceived problems associated with the quantification of the positivists. This includes what is seen as the tendency to 'context strip' through focusing upon a few selected key variables. By ignoring the wider context, in an attempt to increase theoretical rigour, positivists effectively weaken the relevance of their findings, it is argued. Additionally, there is seen to be a difficulty with the 'etic' (outsider) theory imposed by the positivists' *a priori*, deductive approach to theory building which may have little or no correspondence with the 'emic' (insider) view. For interpretivists, to overcome this issue, it is essential that theory is *grounded* through the process of induction and observation. This position sees useful theory building to reside in an inductive process that, through systematic empirical research, is more likely to align data and theory (see Glaser and Strauss, 1967, for an influential articulation of this position). Such an approach is seen as providing access to the 'emic' view and therefore avoids the problem of imposing an external logic upon a situation which may have little or no meaning to the 'reality' of the individuals or groups being studied.

The epistemological position adopted by interpretivists, as argued earlier, must necessarily reflect their ontological stance. It is characterised as being 'transactional and subjectivist' where the investigator (subject) and object are interactively linked. This means that findings are effectively created through the process of investigation (Guba and Lincoln, 1994). As these authors note (1994: 110), this position removes the traditional distinction between ontology and epistemology, as what can be known is context specific to the extent that it reflects 'the interaction between a *particular* investigator and a *particular* object or group' (emphasis in original). For positivists, this inherent subjectivity is considered to be a complete anathema to the pursuit of 'proper science'. However, for the interpretivist, given their ontological stance, it is seen as entirely natural that the values of the investigator mediate research findings which are created by the process of interaction that constitutes the research activity.

Impact of the philosophical paradigms upon methodology   It was stated earlier that the ontological and epistemological positions adopted by a researcher will directly influence the methodological approach adopted. So, for example, in the case of the positivists, as noted by Gill and Johnson (1991: 126), 'if we accept the philosophical assumptions of positivism and its consequent epistemological prescriptions, we are invariably drawn towards the exclusive utilization of nomothetic methodology'. This results in an emphasis being given to deductive research that seeks to provide explanation through an analysis of causal relationships and through covering laws. This involves the generation and use of quantitative data which are subject to either physical or statistical controls in order to facilitate hypothesis testing. The need to adopt a highly structured research methodology is seen as being essential due to the emphasis placed by positivists upon replicability. Accordingly, the research methods typically employed by the positivists are laboratory experiments, quasi-experiments and surveys.

Within hospitality management research, nomothetic methodology is well represented by the survey method (for a recent and *very* rare example of experimental research in hospitality, see Jones, 1996a). Indeed, surveys are deployed with such frequency that one is led to question the extent to which active consideration of other possible approaches is undertaken. However, if a positivist ontology is dominant among hospitality researchers, as is argued later, then, given hospitality's largely social scientific nature, such an outcome is perhaps not too surprising. For example, research in the area of customer satisfaction (see Oh and Parks (1997) for a review of research in this area and the closely related topic of service quality) has typically emphasised survey-based approaches. Since most theory here is derived from cognitive psychology, where experiments and quasi-experiments have been widely used, this situation is largely to be expected. Research in the USA into the sources of customer satisfaction, e.g. Lewis and Pizam (1981), Lewis (1983), Lewis and Klein (1987), Knutson (1988), Barsky (1992), and Barsky and Labagh (1992), has typically utilised secondary data largely derived from hotel guest survey questionnaires and guest comment cards. However, this is not the only feasible methodology for this type of research, as demonstrated by the UK-based study by Callan (1994) of customer satisfaction determinants. This utilised a more inductive approach through the use of extensive guest interviews and focus groups. (The difference between US- and UK-based hospitality management research is touched upon in more detail below.)

Additional examples of nomothetic methodology are readily found in other areas of hospitality management research. For instance, it has typically dominated research in hospitality strategic management (see Olsen, 1996, for a recent review of research in this area). Singh and Gu's (1994) US-based study of diversification and performance of food service firms provides another example of the use of secondary data in hospitality research (in this instance drawn from Standard and Poor's *COMPUSTAT II* business database). This research involved the analysis of 73 food service firms using a number of non-parametric statistical tests in an effort to measure the relationship(s) between diversification strategies and firm performance and stability. A typical example of survey-based research is Elwood-Williams and Tse's (1995) study of entrepreneurial types and strategy deployed. This was based upon a random sample of 1000 restaurant entrepreneurs (yielding a response rate of 15%) extracted from 56,000 qualifying restaurants held on Dun and Bradstreet's USA database. The resulting data was subjected to discriminant analysis in an effort to detect relationships between entrepreneurial type and strategy type. Phillips' (1996) UK-based study of the relationship between strategic planning and hotel performance provides a detailed example of the survey-based approach to research. It demonstrates the classical progression from literature review, the development of research question(s) and the subsequent operationalisation of variables through to data collection and analysis.

For the interpretivist, their ontological/epistemological stance results in their embracing ideographic methods which emphasise an inductive approach that focuses upon the subjective accounts of human actors. The process of explanation requires that researchers immerse themselves in the research context in order to develop the necessary understanding (*verstehen*) of these subjective accounts. The emphasis is therefore upon the generation and use of qualitative data. Control is not imposed in the same manner as by the positivists. Rather, there is an attempt to 'blend in' and thus minimise any reaction to the researcher's presence in the natural environment of the subjects under investigation. Similarly, a minimum level of structure is imposed upon the research methodology in order to support the commitment to explanation via understanding the subjective interpretation of actors' behaviour through qualitative data and this need to blend into the research context. This is seen as being essential in the light of the inductive approach embraced which stresses the need for developing grounded theory based upon empirical observation. Consequently, the interpretivist is likely to use action research, case studies and ethnography as their principal research methods.

As will be discussed below, the interpretive approach is not common among hospitality researchers. That said, some good examples of research utilising ideographic methodologies do exist in hospitality management research. Undoubtedly, the classic piece of research here is William Foote Whyte's 'The social structure of the restaurant' (1947) which reports on interviews and participant-observation studies carried out in 12 restaurants in Chicago over a period of 14 months. It provides an excellent example, within the context of measuring 'social structure', of the limitations of quantitative measures and the need to supplement these with a more qualitative approach. Whyte's closing thoughts on 'statistics versus the case study' are as relevant today as they were 50 years ago. A much more recent example of the participant-observation approach, this time based in a UK hotel, is the research by Prosser and Worsfold (1995). In order to overcome earlier difficulties experienced in attempting to identify and evaluate the informal social relations among employees as an outsider, Prosser reports how she gained employment as a waitress in a large hotel (i.e. an insider) in an effort to undertake her research. Additionally, this researcher also highlights some of the data collection challenges associated with such a covert approach.

Other good examples of ideographic methods in hospitality research—albeit once again, predominantly concerning sociological analyses of hospitality labour (see Lennon and Wood (1989) for a useful overview)—include Saunders' (1982) research on hotel head porters, research by Whyte and Hamilton (1964) and Shamir (1975) on the work of hotel receptionists and chambermaids, research by Prus and Vassilakopoulos (1979) on the facilitating role of male desk-clerks in prostitution in hotels, and Gabriel's (1988) examination of catering workers' perspectives on their 'working lives' in a range of operational contexts; while research on table waiting is well represented by a number of qualitative studies (e.g. Bowey, 1976; Mars, Bryant and Mitchell, 1979; Mars and Nicod, 1984). Given the nature of most of these studies (attempts to develop theory based upon the 'emic' perspectives of employees), it is difficult to see how nomothetic methodologies could possibly have provided viable alternative approaches.

Research philosophy in hospitality management

> A thing exists … if a world without it can't function normally. (Robert Pirsig, *Zen and the Art of Motorcycle Maintenance*)

The preceding section has emphasised the main philosophical differences between the two principal research schools of thought and the subsequent implications for the research methodologies employed. Although this provides an admittedly simplistic overview of issues which have been the subject of numerous weighty and learned tomes, it does sensitise readers to some of the key philosophical issues. So armed, attention is now turned to examining research philosophy in hospitality management research. While what follows represents a very personal interpretation of the 'current state-of-the-art' in hospitality management research, it is an honest one. The extent to which it is a 'true and accurate' reflection of hospitality research is for others to decide for themselves. In true interpretivist fashion, recognition is given to the likely existence of multiple and sometimes conflicting realities in respect of this issue.

Previously, the authors (Taylor and Edgar, 1996) have argued that hospitality management research was some considerable way from being 'mature', despite assertions to the contrary (Litteljohn, 1990). Since then, others have supported this 'lack of maturity thesis' (Jones, 1996b). Therefore, it would appear uncontroversial, as a starting point, to state that depending on your viewpoint, hospitality management research is at worst embryonic and at best developing. That it exists is not questioned—it clearly does, given the existence of specialist journals and research conferences (see Jones, 1996b: 6–7)—but its precise nature is open to debate. On this basis, an attempt is made to ascertain the nature of current hospitality management research. In doing so, the philosophical position of hospitality researchers has been inferred from the methodology employed. Such an approach is justified on the grounds, as discussed earlier, that a researcher's ontological stance influences their epistemological position which in turn determines their methodological approach. Logically, then, it should be feasible to infer a researcher' s ontology (be it explicit or implicit) from the methodology deployed in a given piece of research.

In an earlier contribution to this topic, the authors (Taylor and Edgar, 1996) analysed the output of the Council of Hospitality Management Education's (CHME) annual research conferences (the main UK hospitality research conference) from 1992 to 1995 and categorised these into four research methodologies/approaches. These were (i) *quantitative*, i.e. nomothetic methodologies; (ii) *qualitative*, i.e. ideographic methodologies; (iii) *mixed method*, i.e. a combination of (i) and (ii); and finally (iv) *conceptual*, i.e. papers with no empirical content. In crude terms, the contention is that the existence of positivism in hospitality will be evidenced by an emphasis upon quantitative research, while interpretivism will be evidenced by the utilisation of qualitative approaches and arguably, to a lesser extent, by the adoption of mixed methods. Below, this original analysis is extended (geographically) by repeating this exercise for papers published in the *Hospitality Research Journal* (*HRJ*—now the *Journal of Hospitality and Tourism Research*) over the same time period. These papers were overwhelmingly written by US-based academics and thus provide a reasonable benchmark of methodological approaches among hospitality researchers in this region. These findings are reproduced in Tables 2.1 and 2.2.

As can be seen from both tables, positivism would appear to be the dominant philosophy, as quantitative methodologies are the most frequently deployed empirical approach by UK- and US-based hospitality researchers. Interestingly, the US-based group are almost exclusively oriented towards positivism, while in the UK an

Table 2.1 Percentage of papers presented at CHME research conferences by research method, 1992–1995

	Research methodology			
Year	Quantitative	Qualitative	Mixed method	Conceptual
1992	52%	3%	8%	37%
1993	54%	7%	12%	27%
1994	49%	6%	16%	29%
1995	43%	9%	15%	33%

Source: Taylor and Edgar (1996). Reproduced with permission.

Table 2.2 Percentage of papers published in the *Hospitality Research Journal* by research method, 1992–1995

	Research methodology			
Year	Quantitative	Qualitative	Mixed method	Conceptual
1992	44%	0%	6%	50%
1993	21%	4%	0%	75%
1994	65%	0%	0%	35%
1995	82%	0%	9%	9%

interpretivist philosophy is evident among a minority of researchers. The 1993 volume of the *HRJ* can largely be ignored as being atypical since it contained a large special issue with conceptual papers focusing upon future scenarios in the hospitality industry, mainly written by non-academics. That approximately a third of the UK papers (the volume of US papers is more variable here but broadly comparable) are of a conceptual nature could be seen as indicative of efforts by hospitality researchers to undertake theory building. In the absence of a detailed examination of the content of these contributions it is difficult to comment further on this work. However, the atheoretical nature of hospitality management research alluded to earlier, coupled with the highly fragmented nature of output, suggests that these conceptual contributions are likely to be largely concerned with the contextualisation of theories developed in other academic fields.

In the case of the data from the 'empirical' categories, it is suggested that two things can be deduced from these basic findings. First, that the majority of hospitality researchers, whether consciously or not, subscribe to a positivist epistemological position. If this is not the case, then it would appear that they are utilising inappropriate methodologies in relation to an interpretivist ontology in their research efforts. Second, there is evidence that although interpretivist approaches are rare in hospitality research, this is less true within a UK context. This is unlikely to surprise many hospitality academics who recognise that such differences exist between these two national groupings. Indeed, recognition of such a difference has moved one prominent UK hospitality academic to go so far as to describe much US-based research in the field as the rigorous analysis of the fatuous! The authors, while not entirely unsympathetic to this viewpoint, consider the situation to be more complex than this, although it does highlight that two quite distinct research traditions exist when comparing UK and US hospitality management academics.

Of course, the differences between US and UK academics are not unique to hospitality management research. In fact, the differences are minor when compared, say, to the differences between marketing management research in both countries. The reasons for this situation are complex, but in simple terms they reside in the widespread belief in US academia that serious research must exhibit the highest degree of methodological rigour and that this is to be achieved through adopting the positivism of 'big science'. Accordingly, it is not surprising that ideographic methodologies rarely feature in US-based management journals. In UK management journals, while there is a greater degree of 'methodological pluralism', positivist approaches still tend to dominate, albeit frequently in a less extreme (i.e. methodologically rigorous) form. However, in relation to UK-based hospitality research, it would be misleading to overstate the extent to which interpretivist research approaches are utilised.

There is some evidence in hospitality management research that the interpretivist position is beginning to gain its advocates. Such is the current stage of development that this is currently evidenced mainly by papers that are written with the express purposes of introducing readers to the nature of the interpretivist position and the arguments which support or justify it. There are two recent examples of just this: one in a UK-based journal (Connell and Lowe, 1997) and the other in a US-based journal (Hughes, 1997). In the first of these, Connell and Lowe put the case for generating grounded theory from qualitative data within tourism and hospitality management research (see Connell (1997) for a write-up of the output generated by this approach on the topic of international franchising). The second paper, by Hughes (1997: 14), put the case for the use of ethnography in hospitality research and argued that its maturity in research terms has been impeded by the existence of a 'positivist epistemology and a sociology of regulation'.

While in no way demeaning these papers, the interesting point is the fact that these articles were published at all. Each essentially provides largely generic accounts of basic aspects of interpretive research. This, it is suggested, is indicative of two things. First, that interpretivist approaches are recognised as being novel in hospitality management research. Second, that while journals might be seen as signalling a willingness to consider output generated by such methodologies, they perceive a need to sensitise the community to the value of such research. This, coupled with the data in Tables 2.1 and 2.2, suggests that research generated by ideographic methodologies must be considered to be a minority activity within hospitality management. Although available evidence (e.g. Table 2.1), might be considered to suggest a trend towards more research of this type, it seems safe to predict that nomothetic methodologies driven by a positivist epistemology will continue to dominate hospitality research for the foreseeable future. The critical question is whether such a bias is ultimately a desirable one for future progress in hospitality management research.

Conclusions: progressing hospitality management research

> Alice laughed, 'there's no use trying' she said, 'one *can't* believe impossible things'. 'I dare say you haven't had much practice' said the queen. (Lewis Carroll, *Through the Looking-Glass*)

This chapter has offered a number of reflections upon hospitality management research. It has been suggested that there are two key philosophical dimensions that need to be addressed. The first of these concerns the need to articulate the philosophy of hospitality management research. The continuing failure to do so, it was suggested, will provide a serious impediment to progress in the area due to the absence of clear objectives and consequently the development of a strategy for their achievement. The second aspect examined concerned the wider issue of research philosophy. It has been argued that, since a researcher's ontological/epistemological position influences the research methodologies they deploy, it is important that hospitality researchers have a grasp of the philosophical aspects of the research process. Such a grasp can help researchers make more informed choices as to selecting an appropriate research methodology to match both their personal philosophical position and the nature of their research study. Some concluding thoughts on these two philosophical dimensions in the context of progressing hospitality management research are offered below.

It was argued that progress in hospitality management research has been hampered through the lack of a clear conceptualisation as to the nature of hospitality management. This deficiency has resulted in there being no clear agreement as to what should be either the purpose (i.e. 'the why?') or the content (i.e. 'the what?') of research activity within this area. While a search for a 'grand theory of hospitality management' is probably neither feasible nor desirable, the development of a robust conceptual domain to provide a clear direction for the activities of hospitality researchers and for delineating research in hospitality from other areas of research does appear overdue. The discussion above regarding the role and scope of hospitality research is intended to contribute, albeit modestly, to such an endeavour. If this current lacuna in hospitality is not addressed then it is difficult to see that hospitality management research can ultimately be anything other than a lost cause. However, such a *dénouement* is far from certain *if* appropriate action, along the lines suggested above, is forthcoming in the near future.

The second dimension of philosophy discussed in the chapter concerned basic issues relating to the philosophy of science. In any text devoted to the topic of research methodology it would seem essential that readers are conversant with the fundamental debates relating to ontology and epistemology. Only then can *informed* choices regarding research methodology be made. Within hospitality management there would appear to have been little or no explicit dialogue concerning research philosophy. Nonetheless, the limited evidence presented above indicates that hospitality management research is currently dominated by the presence of studies of a positivist nature. This is true of both UK- and US-based research. However, there is evidence in the UK that the interpretivist position is beginning to gain some ground. It is unlikely, given the very strong tradition of positivism and the institutionalisation of 'high methodological rigour' within most areas of US academia, that interpretivist-based research will increase to any great extent in this region. While of interest, these findings should not divert one's attention from what is perhaps the chapter's key message regarding research philosophy. That is, that these 'strategic' aspects of research (i.e. ontology and epistemology) are of critical importance because it is only through developing a sound grasp of these that hospitality management researchers can become truly effective users of the 'implementation' aspects of research, i.e. research methodology.

References

Barsky, J.D. (1992) 'Customer satisfaction in the hotel industry: Meaning and measurement', *Hospitality Research Journal*, **16**, 51–73.

Barsky, J.D. and Labagh, R. (1992) 'A strategy for customer satisfaction', *Cornell Hotel and Restaurant Administration Quarterly*, October, 32–40.

Bowey, A.M. (1976) *The sociology of organizations*, Hodder and Stoughton: London.

Boyer, E.L. (1990) *Scholarship reconsidered: Priorities of the professoriate*, Princeton University Press: Princeton, NJ.

Burgess, J. (1982) 'Perspectives on gift exchange and hospitable behaviour', *International Journal of Hospitality Management*, **1**, 49–57.

Burrell, G. and Morgan, G. (1979) *Sociological paradigms and organizational analysis*, Heinemann: London.

Callan, R.J. (1994) 'Development of a framework for the determination of attributes used for hotel selection—indications from focus group and in-depth interviews', *Hospitality Research Journal*, **18** (2), 53–74.

Connell, J. (1997) 'International hotel franchise relationships—UK franchisee perspectives', *International Journal of Contemporary Hospitality Management*, **9**, 215–220.

Connell, J. and Lowe, A. (1997) 'Generating grounded theory from qualitative data: The application of inductive methods in tourism and hospitality management research', *Progress in Tourism and Hospitality Research*, **3**, 165–173.

Cook, T. and Campbell, D.T. (1979) *Quasi-experimentation: Design and analysis issues for field settings*, Rand McNally: Chicago.

Daft, R.L. and Buenger, V. (1990) Hitching a ride on a fast train to nowhere: The past and future of strategic management research. In Fredrickson, J.W. (ed.), *Perspectives on strategic management*, 81–101, Harper Business: New York.

Denzin, N.K. and Lincoln, Y.S. (eds) (1994) *Handbook of qualitative research*, 1–18, Sage: London.

Elwood-Williams, C. and Tse, E.C.-Y. (1995) 'The relationship between strategy and entrepreneurship: the US restaurant sector', *International Journal of Contemporary Hospitality Management*, **7** (1), 22–26.

Gabriel, Y. (1988) *Working lives in catering*, Routledge & Kegan Paul: London and New York.

Giddens, A. (ed.) (1979) *Positivism and sociology*, Heinemann: London.

Gill, J. and Johnson, P. (1991) *Research methods for managers*, Paul Chapman Publishing: London.

Glaser, B.G. and Strauss, A.L. (1967) *The discovery of grounded theory: strategies for qualitative research*, Aldine: Chicago.

Guba, E.G. and Lincoln, Y.S. (1994) Competing paradigms in qualitative research. In Denzin, N.K. and Lincoln, Y.S. (eds), *Handbook of qualitative research*, 105–117, Sage: London.

Hanson, N.R. (1958) *Patterns of discovery*, Cambridge University Press: Cambridge.

Hughes, J.A. (1990) *The philosophy of social research*, Longman: London.

Hughes, J.C. (1997) 'Sociological paradigms and the use of ethnography in hospitality research', *Journal of Hospitality and Tourism Research*, **21** (1), 14–27.

Hunt, S.D. (1976) 'The nature and scope of marketing', *Journal of Marketing*, **40**, July, 17–28.

Hunt, S.D. (1991) *Modern marketing theory: Critical issues in the philosophy of marketing science*, South-Western Publishing Co.: Cincinnati, OH.

Jones, P. (1996a) 'Experimental research in hospitality operations: The case of waiting lines', *Proceedings of the Fifth Annual CHME Research Conference*, Nottingham Trent University: Nottingham.

Jones, P. (1996b) 'Hospitality research—where have we got to?', *International Journal of Hospitality Management*, **15** (1), 5–10.

Jones, P. (1997) 'Towards a hospitality management paradigm', unpublished paper.

Keat, R. and Urry, J. (1975) *Social theory as science*, Routledge: London.

Keynes, J.M. (1936) *The general theory of employment, interest and money*, Macmillan: London.

Knutson, B.J. (1988) 'Ten laws of customer satisfaction', *Cornell Hotel and Restaurant Administration Quarterly*, **29**, 14–17.

Kotler, P. (1972) Defining the limits of marketing. In Becker, B.W. and Becker, H. (eds), *Marketing education and the real world, 1972 Fall Conference Proceedings*, American Marketing Association: Chicago, IL.

Laing, R.D. (1967) *The politics of experience and the birds of paradise*, Penguin: Harmondsworth.

Lennon, J.J. and Wood, R.C. (1989) 'The sociological analysis of hospitality labour and the neglect of accommodation workers', *International Journal of Hospitality Management*, **8** (3), 227–235.

Lewis, R.C. (1983) 'Getting the most from marketing research', *Cornell Hotel and Restaurant Administration Quarterly*, November, 81–85.

Lewis, R.C. and Klein, D.M. (1987) The measurement of gaps in service quality. In Czepiel, J.A., Congram, C.A. and Shanahan, J. (eds), *The services challenge: Integrating for competitive advantage*, American Marketing Association: Chicago, IL.

Lewis, R.C. and Pizam, A. (1981) 'Guest surveys: A missed opportunity', *Cornell Hotel and Restaurant Administration Quarterly*, November, 37–44.

Litteljohn, D. (1990) Hospitality research: Philosophies and progress. In Teare, R., Moutinho, L. and Morgan, N. (eds), *Managing and marketing services in the 1990s*, Cassell: London.

Mars, G. and Nicod, M. (1984) *The world of waiters*, George Allen and Unwin: London.

Mars, G., Bryant, P. and Mitchell, P. (1979) *Manpower problems in the hotel and catering industry*, Saxon House: Farnborough.

Myers, J.G., Greyser, S.A. and Massey, W.F. (1979) 'The effectiveness of marketing's "R&D" for marketing management: An assessment', *Journal of Marketing*, **43**, January, 17–29.

Nailon, P. (1982) 'Theory in hospitality management', *International Journal of Hospitality Management*, **1** (3), 135–143.

Oh, H. and Parks, S.C. (1997) 'Customer satisfaction and service quality: A critical review of the literature and research implications for the hospitality industry', *Hospitality Research Journal*, **20** (3), 35–64.

Olsen, M.D. (1996) Research in strategic management in the hospitality industry. Hospitality management: state of the art, CHME sponsored global internet conference. http://www.mcb.co.uk/services/conferen/apr96/hospitality/olsen/touchsto.htm.

Phillips, P.A. (1996) 'Strategic planning and business performance in the quoted UK hotel sector: Results of an exploratory study', *International Journal of Hospitality Management*, **15** (4), 347–362.

Prosser, J. and Worsfold, P. (1995) Qualitative research and the quality of hospitality research, Paper presented at the Fourth Annual CHME Research Conference, Norwich Hotel School, 19–20 April.

Prus, R.C. and Vassilakopoulos, S. (1979) 'Desk clerks and hookers—hustling in a "shady" hotel', *Urban Life*, **8**, 52–71.

Saunders, K.C. (1982) *Head hall porters*, 2nd edn, Middlesex Polytechnic Research Monograph.

Schwandt, T.A. (1994) Constructivist, interpretivist approaches to human inquiry. In Denzin, N.K. and Lincoln, Y.S. (eds), *Handbook of qualitative research*, 118–137, Sage: London.

Shamir, B. (1975) A study of working environments and attitudes to work of employees in a number of British hotels, Unpublished Doctoral Thesis, London School of Economics.

Shaw, M. and Nightingale, M. (1995) 'Scholarship reconsidered: Implications for hospitality education', *Hospitality Research Journal*, **18** (3)/**19** (1), 81–93.

Singh, A. and Gu, Z. (1994) 'Diversification, financial performance, and stability of foodservice firms', *Hospitality Research Journal*, **18** (2), 3–18.

Slattery, P. (1983) 'Social scientific methodology and hospitality management', *International Journal of Hospitality Management*, **2** (1), 9–14.

Taylor, S. and Edgar, D. (1996) 'Hospitality research: The emperor's new clothes?', *International Journal of Hospitality Management*, **15** (3), 211–227.

Whyte, E.F. and Hamilton, E.L. (1964) *Action research in management*, Irwin: New York.

Whyte, W.F. (1947) 'The social structure of the restaurant', *American Journal of Sociology*, **54**, 302–310.

Wood, R.C. (1988) 'Against social science?', *International Journal of Hospitality Management*, **7** (3), 239–250.

Wood, R.C. (1994) Some theoretical perspectives on hospitality. In Seaton, A.V. (ed.), *Tourism: The State of the Art*, 737–742, John Wiley: Chichester.

3 Researching organisations from the outside

DAVID LITTELJOHN AND ANGELA ROPER

Section 1: Introduction

This chapter deals with gaining information on organisations where no consent is required from the organisation: what is here termed 'researching organisations from the outside'. Inevitably the chapter deals with the use of secondary sources. However, many hospitality, tourism and leisure operations offer opportunities for *incognito* entry without having to gain permission from the organisation or involving moral or ethical considerations in the collection or publication of data so obtained.

This type of data may be treated as preparatory to launching a programme of primary research. On the other hand, it might represent the only information that for whatever reason was available on an organisation. In this latter case, therefore, it is used as a basis for analysis in its own right. While the chapter does not deal with a research topic in itself, it could be of help to any work which requires study of organisations. It may help avoid cases where researchers rush into primary data collection without sufficient knowledge of an organisation's make-up and operations.

Presentation style of the chapter is in two forms: conversations between two researchers, and the use of Exhibits to provide further backup information on the topics discussed by the two researchers. Pierre is currently a full-time PhD researcher in a hospitality management department. He shares some methodology classes with part-time MBA students one evening a week. Here he has met Susan, an Area Manager for an international contract catering firm. She is approaching the end of her MBA and is about to commence her final project. Often Pierre and Susan with other students have a meal or a drink after their class. It is during these times when the authors have been able to overhear their conversation. In the course of these conversations Pierre and Susan learn the importance of understanding the full operational and strategic dimensions of the organisations in their projects. Why, and how, they come to this conclusion is the subject of this chapter.

In making their conversations accessible to a wider audience the authors have restructured the discussions for the sake of clarity and continuity. Pierre and Susan have agreed to these changes, and careful attention has been paid in transcribing Pierre's contribution to smooth out any unintended meanings springing from his developing knowledge of English: apologies for any that the authors have missed.

The Handbook of Contemporary Hospitality Management Research, Edited by Bob Brotherton.
© 1999 John Wiley & Sons Ltd.

By following the issues raised by the researchers you will:

- appreciate the importance of organisational contexts;
- understand researching features of organisations from external sources;
- identify sources available in researching organisation from the outside.

The chapter should be of help to anyone who wants to learn about specific organisations, or to contextualise knowledge within organisations. It is aimed at multiple audiences of researchers: undergraduates, postgraduates and those involved in professional development and lifelong learning projects. No previous specialist knowledge is necessary for tackling the subject matter.

The chapter begins by exploring definitions of organisations and reasons for adopting an organisational focus in hospitality management research. The next section provides a framework for categorising organisations. Later sections give guidelines on how to collect information on organisations.

Exhibit 3.1   Summarised curriculum vitae: Pierre and Susan*

Pierre Ledoux

Age: 26

Presently	PhD research student, United University, Newcastle, UK (currently second year)
Undergraduate education	
	Maitrisée d'Administration Commerciale, Paris Institute, Paris, France
Work experience	Shift supervisor, Café Rouge, Oxford, UK (6 months full-time)
	Retail sales assistant, Printemps, Paris, France (3 years part-time)

Susan Plender

Age: 33

Presently	Area manager, North England and Scotland Healthcare Division, PRoper Contract Catering—part of Trafalgar Group plc (currently in the third year of a part-time MBA course)
Undergraduate education	
	BA (Hons) Hotel and Catering Business, Business School, University of Kirklees, UK

Work experience since qualifying

Second promotion	Unit manager, various contracts in Industrial Division, PRoper Contract Catering
First promotion	Deputy unit manager, various contracts in Educational Division, PRoper Contract Catering
Initial position	Graduate management trainee, PRoper Contract Catering

Other work experience

Trainee manager, Bass Taverns, Leeds (6 months work placement)

Reception shift leader, Cambridge Marriott, Boston, USA

*These fictitious curriculum vitae are for contextual information only.

Section 2: Getting started

This section emphasises that many, possibly the majority of, hospitality management research projects are applied in nature. They have as their focus the performance of hospitality management and related organisations. This centrality of organisations is important to remember in framing research projects and assessing consequential information requirements.

Scene: The University's student refectory soon after the beginning of the semester

Susan and Pierre are in the dimly lit room. Their intense gaze into their coffee cups indicates that they are doing a lot of hard thinking. Susan has just confided in Pierre that she is experiencing a problem in deciding on her research topic. It wasn't easy confiding in someone she didn't know very well, but maybe exchanging some ideas might get her away from the brickwall that rises up whenever she thinks of her MBA dissertation proposal.

'I was hoping that I could use some of this Human Resources material that we're tackling at the moment: the empowerment area is absolutely fascinating ... and I keep reading articles in *European Contracting* on how HRM policy provides the future for creating efficient organisation structures and satisfied employees.'

'I see ...,' replied Pierre, sounding slightly suspicious, '... and have you thought how you might actually make that into a project which would be logical and rigorous? Have you talked to a lecturer yet?'

'What do you mean, "logical and rigorous"? That's OK for your doctorate, but I'm only doing an MBA project—there is a difference.'

'You're right in one sense,' said Pierre, 'I suppose mine does require more depth and research. Still, both your project and mine have to be *meaningful*.' Like a lecturer without any overhead projector he seemed to be emphasising a word to make some kind of point which wasn't immediately apparent to his audience. It was now Susan's turn to look suspicious.

'I mean ...,' Pierre went on, 'to present your findings in a way that makes sense and makes some kind of contribution to the knowledge or management practice in the area. *Meaningful*' (again the inflection was on the word) 'in the sense that your conclusions reflect some sort of progression from the right type of aims and objectives. And these have to be based on a reasonable knowledge of the subject area and your own resources—like access to information, and your own expertise—rather than just rewriting a range of material produced by different authors.'

Susan played with the sugar bowl in front of her. She knew research wasn't meant to be easy, but she hadn't really given it much more thought till now. 'Well, yes, I suppose you just can't include any old thing that's vaguely related to the topic area. I got marked down for that in that corporate strategy essay I had to write where I basically wrote about Porter and not much else.'

Susan looked across the rather messy eating and sitting area they were in. Most tables hadn't been cleaned recently and overflowing ashtrays lent a rather depressing air to the surroundings. 'Yes, and Andy has mentioned that it must be useful to the organisation.' Pierre looked quizzical. 'Andy?' Susan clarified, 'Oh, yes, Andy Trisslov, my new Area General Manager. He says that if I'm doing my MBA dissertation within the organisation he's quite prepared to help me but that he wants to see some benefit to the organisation coming from my work.'

'Well, you always need an organisational focus of some sort in hospitality management. It is a vocational area, after all. There is very little in hospitality management that doesn't have some immediate relationship to an organisation. ... Not that research is necessarily like consultancy ... that is looking at problems in a much more specific way and producing an immediate answer. I mean, if your research is in a very general area—like philosophy—you could say that whatever you're doing has got a value in itself. And even in other vocational areas like medicine or law, research may be in a quite general topic and have little immediate relevance to organisations. In hospitality management, however, the whole point of increasing knowledge could be seen to be aimed at making organisations work more effectively.' Pierre was practically red with the exertion of talking in English for such a long time.

'True,' said Susan, 'everything has some relevance to the bottom line.' She wondered if the mess in the cafeteria was the consequence of some madcap profit-seeking consultancy project ... or whether this was what people actually wanted and were prepared to pay for.

'Humm ... I'm not sure that I quite agree with the way you've expressed it.' Pierre was trying hard to explain some thoughts he had when preparing a seminar paper for his supervisor almost a year previously. 'Expressions like "bottom line", "profitability" and even "organisation" imply something that is quite permanent and measurable, but ... .'

'... But profit is measurable and observable. There are rules and regulations for working out profit and ... .'

'And the rules and regulations in the UK are different than in my own country of France. Also,' Pierre went on, 'you must be aware of the arguments that people have about what profits are and might be. Look what happens in takeover battles, for instance—and as organisations grow and contract they too change, as do the people in them who run the organisation and are employed by it. So what might appear to be a "fact" about an organisation isn't such a fact after all.'

As Susan's employers had been on the receiving end of an unsuccessful hostile bid a few years previously, she knew what he meant. During the company's defence the Finance Director had contacted her several times and asked for revisions of her past trading figures and 'minor' reclassification of her projected revenue and cost figures.

Pierre went on, 'Look at this place.' Susan declined his invitation. She could achieve a vivid enough picture if she closed her eyes and just sniffed at the passing mix of stale smells. 'Some of the students are doing a project on how this place is run and have to suggest improvements in the way it's operated. They were being so naive! They started gathering student views on the quality of service, the menu, the fittings and so on, then made a report to the Refectory Manager as if he had responsibility for everything! Just because the refectory is in the University they assumed that it was being run by the University itself. It was skewing up the whole way they were examining the operations.'

Susan knew better. Operations in the refectory were run by one of her company's competitors. 'Yes ... I see what you mean. Things are not always what they may seem at first. The students really needed to find out what at least two organisations need out of the situation—the University and the catering contractor. Probably they need to work all that out before they even begin to survey the students' catering demands.'

'Correct ...' assented Pierre, smiling, Gallic charm taking an upper hand now that his point had got home, '... perhaps we should go for a drink of something stronger now? The Student Association Bar isn't run on quite such strict profit targets.'

'OK' Susan agreed. 'So long as you don't keep on about how that's another organisation in the University's complex internal dynamics.' Pierre stared back. 'Sometimes I think you are taking fun of me' – and then he wondered if he'd said what he meant!

Susan hadn't heard him properly, however. She had already begun to think about her dissertation in terms of having a theoretical base, and a direct input into management of her organisation. Perhaps she could combine Service Marketing methods with different views at a particular catering site: those of the contractor, those of the client organisation and those of the customers. Pierre was ahead of her. He was opening the doors to the bar, and loud music would ensure that their discussion in the place wasn't likely to be so academic ...

Exhibit 3.2   Management and hospitality research: the centrality of organisations

Management involves 'handling people, technology, information, physical resources and finance to improve organisational effectiveness'. Management research, while encompassing these areas, extends to consider organisations and the broad contexts in which they operate, so that it relates to 'managers and their problems, and the process of management in developing, operating and controlling organisations (private, public and voluntary) in their economic, social and political contexts' (Commission on Management Research, 1994).

To relate this to hospitality environments, the definition could be adapted to the following:

Hospitality management research relates to investigating the issues faced by managers in hospitality and the processes involved in developing, operating, controlling and relating hospitality organisations (private, public and voluntary) in their economic, social and political contexts.

Management research draws on many disciplines, depending on the nature of the topic under study. Any project may involve several approaches, coming from such traditional academic areas as economics, sociology and psychology and/or newer ones like accounting and finance, marketing and human resources. Other areas, for example design, may involve disciplines from science and engineering. While the choice of discipline base is wide, it is important not to treat problems at a level of generality. A careful choice must be made of the disciplines used. Each will have strengths and weaknesses: strengths, since the discipline will have developed ways of analysing problems and a record of scholarship in the area; a developed framework, however, may present a weakness if it does not relate well to the problem, or the context, under investigation.

Successful hospitality management provides analysis, insight and ideas for action that will help hospitality managers and academics and those who relate to them understand and manage organisations in the industry, and possibly managers in other areas, more effectively.

Some themes that the Commission on Management Research (1994) propose as important for research are external change, organisational change, managerial roles, innovation, competitiveness, and internationalisation.

Section 3: Understanding organisations

This section emphasises the need to fully understand the nature and relationships that may be implied by the organisation type (e.g. ownership characteristics, divisional structure) so that the activities of managers within organisations may be understood, as can the organisation's relationship to markets and, more generally, to the wider environment.

Scene: The lounge of 'The Ferret and Paddle'

Several weeks later, Pierre and Susan have met again after their Wednesday lecture. This time the class have decided to adjourn to a nearby public house, which the parent retail company has recently refurbished at a cost of £200,000.

Susan looked up as Pierre brought over the drinks. Without waiting to be offered the cheese and onion crisps she had requested, she smiled and said '... so to continue what I was telling you in the lecture break, my company has this week formally *agreed* to be taken over by an organisation that is into all sorts of businesses. What it knows about contract catering could be written on a matchbox! And after all that fuss they made last time about their growth potential and need for independence.'

'What does it mean for you and your position there—is your role to change?' asked Pierre apprehensively.

'Too early to know', and in spite of her confidence, Susan shivered. 'I guess when you are in the middle of organisational change, it is scary ... but doesn't it show how organisations are really dynamic? I know that this pub, for example, has had several owners.'

When he had arrived in England Pierre hadn't known many people and had enjoyed observing quaint British habits second-hand—hence his familiarity with the pub. 'It was owned by a brewer when I first started coming here. The tenants—a landlord and his wife—were nice. Then they were replaced by a manager appointed from the parent brewing group—she must have been appointed when the theme of the place changed, you know, to be more up-market! Drink prices changed, I remember—more expensive for a poor research student! Now, and that is only a few months later, the brewing company has consolidated to become only a producer of beer and its pubs have been sold to a company that just owns and operates pubs and restaurants. But all the time the name of the pub has remained the same!'

'Anything else changed? ... Have they changed the drink choice and the prices again?'

Pleased he'd caught her attention Pierre went on: 'Well, recent changes have been minimal ... opening hours are longer and of course there is yet another new manager! The beer brands are the same, I think—maybe someone told me there is an agreement with the last owning company to just supply beer now. But of course I am not the manager—he may have different views on the subject; things we cannot see so easily. Changes in ownership may particularly have an impact upon the outlook of the company ... which goes back to my original point. Your own firm may change now that it is part of a different type of enlarged organisation. Your past employers used to concentrate on their "core" but from what you have told me, the organisation is now multinational as well as multi-product.' He felt on the table for his pint of beer, as he held her gaze, proud of his mastery of English but feeling he had earned a rest.

Susan was grateful that Pierre had stopped to have a gulp of his beer. It let her come back into the conversation. 'Hang on a minute, Pierre—too technical for me—multinational, multi-product. Have you swallowed a management textbook?'

Pierre blushed. She was quite assertive. 'Well, the new owner—Bludirk's? It has operations in several countries, eh?' 'Yes, as many as 40 countries.'

Satisfied that his points were being made for him, Pierre nevertheless decided they should be underlined. 'So it is multinational—it owns and operates income generating assets in several countries. It is also multi-product because you said that it is into all sorts of businesses and not previously into contract catering—*your* main problem with them as an owner, I think?'

'Yes. What do they know about our business? They have gold mines, cruise ships, luxury hotels, car dealerships, and they own newspapers, would you believe!'

'Exactly my point.'

Susan thought that the tone of his voice was getting just a bit smug. 'They are into multi-products, or multi-services to be more specific! Their goals may be different from your past owner's. Maybe they will leave your company ... now a subsidiary, I suppose ... to get on with what you know but maybe they will want you to achieve better profitability ... or maybe they will interfere and see the synergies that they can gain across their business world-wide ... maybe their gold mines and other businesses may be able to use your catering services! Perhaps knowing nothing about the contract catering businesses means that some of their executives will view what you do—your strategy, for example—very differently from what you've been used to. Presumably they will want you to be more internationally diverse?'

Susan now attacked the cheese and onion crisps. It might all come to this: change, change and change. Unsettling and exciting at the same time. 'Yes, yes, I see what you are saying—the difference in ownership may mean they view our operations very differently—could be good, for me, or bad! I may be able to go into the cruise ship business!'

She went on, 'In terms of what you are saying I suppose PRoper Contract Catering has also been multi-site, at least—all those hundreds of contracts we have throughout the country. ... My organisation has always had to cope with, and understand, different types of businesses—like clients and suppliers in the trade. And, yes, we do have different ways of negotiating when we're setting up contracts. Of course, I see these differences even more when the contract begins—there are many different types of situations to deal with. I remember once when I was a Unit Manager that I had to be aware of the politics in my own company as well as that of the client firm when I was deciding on issues such as when to open the restaurant, what to offer on the menu and even the facilities that we could give to our catering staff in the client's premises. Now ... well, look at your University's catering ... remember we discussed before how the manager has to be aware of the aims and goals of the University, as well as those of his employer, the contracting company. In a wider sense, he has to be aware of the broader environment in education because this affects what happens to student numbers, what they have to spend, and so on ...'.

'Head blowing, isn't it!' Pierre's colloquial English wasn't always quite up to scratch. 'When you had all those ideas for your project, which must be applied to your own company, I bet you never would have realised the complexity—organisations are dynamic and living things, aren't they? In addition there are so many different types—differences affecting their missions, goals, ways of doing business and employing people, etcetera etcetera. ... Time for another beer? My head hurts from this conversation!'

'*Your* conversation, you mean!' Susan said, with only half a smile on her face. 'Before you go for a drink—I'll take a multinational/multi-product vodka and tonic this time please—well, this discussion has been interesting. Our talks and my company's merger have made me realise that I must take a more holistic view (I am learning big words on the course!) of my company. I'll have to read the staff magazine when it comes round, and the company report. I always thought of those as not relating to my day-to-day job—in fact, if I knew more about the organisation I might view things a bit differently, and now of course I have to understand the firm that we have merged with—find out about its policies, its different subsidiaries, and so on!'

'Really, now what I could tell you about some hospitality and tourism companies in Europe you would not believe! Listen, after your vodka ... I am really hungry, have you got time for something to eat?'

'Sure,' said Susan, 'first drink, then eat. But we don't need to talk shop all the time, you know. I have got more than one topic of conversation!'

Later, at Bruno's Trattoria ...

Pierre looked at his tossed salad, and then at Susan. 'How's your lasagne? It worries me, eating out with a caterer. You all must be really demanding customers.'

'Its fine. Me a demanding customer? ... No, not really. I'm glad to be sitting at the table and not serving at one. Now, you were saying earlier, about juicy stories about European companies ... .'

Pierre looked bashful. 'Well, it's no big deal really.' He had been more interested in seeing more of Susan than talking about research topics. 'It was just to say that, of course, companies may be distinctive depending upon their origin. When I did my Maitrisée I studied companies in France. Many appear to be very different in their outlook to firms over here, even though they operate in similar markets.'

Susan finished chewing a mouthful of lasagne. 'Umm ... interesting. So I suppose I should have an open mind about a new German parent company. It's a bit like that lecturer said last week: I have "culturally tinted glasses" and that there are differences between how I view the world and how managers from the new owning company might see it. It should be interesting at our next Managers' Conference, if we still have them!'

Pierre recovered from his earlier bashfulness. 'Yes, I suppose the lecturer was talking about internal factors in the company. But there are also external factors which stakeholders in the company may be interested in. For example, the type of ownership. In the UK you have many public limited companies; in Europe there are more privately owned or family operated companies on the one hand, and also there are still quite a few public ones—though governments are now selling off a lot.'

'Yes, I see your point', Susan said. 'And you can think of other reasons why companies might be different. People talk nowadays about the difference in British Airways since it became privatised. It is now profit-driven. I noticed on my flight to LA that the staff were more customer-friendly too because I last flew with the company over ten years ago. They must have gone to some training programme—the British Airways Charm School!'

'Ten years is a long time between flights … don't you fly more often than that? Even on holiday?' asked Pierre.

'No, I have been more into travelling by car through Europe. My last boyfriend and I spent all our holidays travelling around and pitching the tent wherever we found ourselves!'

Pierre's attention changed from his pizza to his new friend opposite. 'You said ex-boyfriend?…'

Exhibit 3.3 Some major categories of organisations related to hospitality

Commercial sector	Public sector	Voluntary non-profit sector
• sole trader	• government department	• charity
• partnership	• local authority	• association
• private company	• direct service organisation	• society
• public limited company	• quasi-autonomous	• trust
subsidiary	government organisation	• co-operative
• (ultimate) holding		• consortium/consortium
company		member*
• strategic alliance		• (political) party
• strategic partner		• pressure group
• joint venture		• professional organisation
• owner		• (trade) union
• operator		
• tenant		
• licensor/licensee		
• franchisor/franchisee		
• management contractor		
• lessor/lessee		
• consortium/consortium		
member*		

*A consortium is essentially a term used to indicate joint activities between a number of organisations towards a specified end. They usually (but not necessarily) draw their membership from either the commercial sector or the voluntary sector. While they often work through non-profit-making arrangements, there are no rules about this.

Section 4: Learning about organisations

This section provides the reader with an appreciation that researchers often rely on many sources of information about organisations. This may be for a number of reasons: to decide which organisations are suitable for their research; to be able to describe the organisation appropriately before gaining access; to know how, and to whom, access should be obtained. Hospitality organisations, by nature of their customer orientation, allow access into at least some of their areas relatively easily. This opportunity can be used as a resource by researchers.

Scene: An Indian restaurant in the High Street

Another Wednesday night. It was so cold out that Susan has persuaded Pierre to go directly to the restaurant. She was feeling a bit down—there was still a lot of uncertainty at work. Also she had an assessment to finish for the MBA. She had wanted an

Indian meal 'because', she told Pierre, 'my life needs spicing up!' Pierre had chosen 'Bobo's Polo Club'.

'It seemed to take for ages to serve us, didn't it?' Susan rather snapped the sentence out. She thought it better to follow up with something more conciliatory. 'Anyway, how is your research going? I have had a crazy week, meeting my new boss and other people in my new, expanded team.'

'It's going OK. But I am having problems getting access to the companies that I need to use for my fieldwork.'

'When you say "access", do you mean getting formal permission from someone to undertake your fieldwork in their company? Is it possible to get your data from another route?'

'What do you mean?' Pierre was genuinely puzzled. '… Take another popadom or I will eat them all.'

'It makes a change for *me* to be telling *you* about research. There are ways and means, you know, to get information about an organisation. For example, since we've known each other we've visited a few restaurants and bars. We have gathered an awful lot of data on them—even as casual customers. We might not have recorded it properly, but I dare say we could have, if we'd had a purpose and developed a proper way of collecting information.'

'OK … so tonight we know the size of this restaurant and that it serves Indian food. We also know it is an owner-operated outlet because we know the son of the owner—Vijay, on the MBA. That's about it.'

Susan smiled. 'Well, you could be more imaginative. I thought all French were supposed to be intuitive! Don't you think research is a bit like detective work? How to gather evidence, how to interpret it, who to question. Well, surely, we could gather some "evidence" about this restaurant from the "outside", so to speak.'

For much of the rest of the night Pierre followed Susan as she developed her theory. Menus provided information about target markets, she said, particularly when different lunch and dinner pricing strategies were added in. Average spends for meals were soon suggested. Opening times, from the notice at the entrance, further provided an idea of markets served. Numbers of waiters observed provided staff-to-cover ratios (from which Susan began working out the staff running costs of the business); beer mats gave an idea of suppliers used by the restaurant. When she began to develop a theme about how the decor of the restaurant catered for customers' 'colonial assumptions' about India, Pierre felt she was verging into areas wider than just management … 'The decor—this tells you that some theming is going on here—all these lengths of silk and beautiful sari fabric. The artefacts from different parts of India—maps, lanterns, and so on.'

Pierre felt that she had definitely lost the place in relation to the topic they should be exploring—gaining access to particular organisations. Susan let him make his point.

'Hum … look further', Susan commanded. 'The chairs and carpets are quite new. The restaurant must have been refurbished lately … perhaps changed hands? There is nothing to say that it is a chain restaurant, is there? No branded items, signs? What's that over there? There … that sign that says "Curry Club of Great Britain". It's part of a wider organisation then, probably a consortium. You know, a number of businesses— usually independents—which combine in order to establish joint marketing activities and purchasing arrangements. …'

'But perhaps,' continued Susan, once Pierre had stopped her in full flow and reminded her of his worries, 'if you knew a lot about the organisation before you contacted them you'd know whom to speak to. Getting useful access into an organisation means that you have to target your enquiry. And also, if you know enough about the organisation, you're not so likely to ask what managers think are simple questions that make you, in their eyes, look like an idiot!' To test her theory further, they decided that they were researching in the area of human relations.

'In that case one obvious thing to analyse from the outside are the staff. It is obvious, even as a customer, that service training levels leave much to be desired. We were waiting over 25 minutes for our main courses to arrive—is it a kitchen problem too, do you think?' She further observed: 'Look how the waiting staff seem to really hover over those people when they are ready to pay … see that guy over there. He keeps asking that couple if they want extra coffee. He's really all over them—strange they get attention now, when their food took so long to be served. Perhaps staff are reliant on tips to make up wages. On the other hand, maybe that is too much supposition.'

'I suppose that is a problem … how far do we go without going direct to the organisation? If we questioned staff about their working conditions, for instance, are we not then "inside" the organisation? We would be stepping over this "outside" line. …,' Susan went on, with a faraway look in her eyes; as Pierre studied her he wasn't quite sure what exactly she was referring to. She continued, 'I think that there must be some boundaries around investigating from the outside. Research must be ethical, after all. If one participates—you could get a job here, for instance, Pierre—then your involvement in the research project should surely be explained up-front to the organisation. Where to draw the line is a problem, though.'

Pierre decided to be straightforward: 'Susan, sometimes you analyse too much.' He spoke quickly, as though he had to say this before he forgot. 'Organisations are important to our work in management. What we need to do is to gain a complete view as to what organisations are, what they are doing and so on. It would obviously be fantastic to go to one place to get all this information. But these places don't exist, within the organisation or outside it. I thought that the point you were making is that all the time we can learn about organisations. And learn to interpret what managers inside the organisation tell us about their operations. I still have problems in gaining access, of course, and my research does rely on talking to managers "on the inside"—but I suppose if I know a lot about their organisation before I get there I might be able to get more out of them. Isn't that one of your points?'

'OK, OK, OK' Susan faced the onslaught by rummaging in her handbag and taking out her purse. 'We'll see how long they take to deal with our bill. No, not you … this is my treat … after all, you're opening my eyes so much!'

Scene: At the Salsa Club next week—before the music begins!

Pierre thanked the gods that it was student night at the club. The tequila was on promotion too, so he would be able to afford more than just a few drinks. Better get the shop talk over first though. He gave Susan his complete attention as he asked her: 'OK—now this detecting thing—researching from the "outside"—how does this relate to your research, Sue? You have access to your organisation, don't you—how can you research from the outside as an insider? You're already a manager, after all.'

'Good point. Let me think while having another sip of my Margarita! Well, during my marketing class last semester we talked about mystery customer schemes—that is researching from the outside, isn't it?—getting an external perspective on how the company is doing. I know our hotel division—yes, I now read company information, Pierre!—uses inspectors to evaluate the company's hotels and compare them to competitors. I have also discovered that, before the Trafalgar Group launched their take-over bid, they enlisted consultants to assess the company—to check out things. I suppose that you could call them "take-over detectives".' Pierre's brow furrowed. 'But this is other people looking at your organisation, from the outside. How can you gain an outside perspective yourself in your research and still make your findings relevant to PRoper Contract Catering—or should I say Trafalgar Contract Catering?'

Susan raised her voice, perhaps because the music was getting a bit louder, 'Please! We still have the same name—we have an established brand as PRoper. But your point about insiders—I appreciate the problems of gaining an external view. I suppose I am well and truly engrossed in the internal politics of the company—even more so when my job may be on the line with the new ownership situation.'

'Given that you have been talking about basing your project upon strategic management,' Pierre was keen to help out, 'could you not begin by evaluating your competitors? That would mean researching from the outside, at least at the start. But it has a direct bearing on your company and its future. You could try to find out what they thought about you as a competitor?'

Susan was keen to find a way to start her research. After all, several weeks had gone by and there was a gnawing feeling that she should soon be completing that project proposal form. And yet …

'Good idea, the competitor analysis thing, finding out about what they think about us. But, something is worrying me … it could be a little unethical, though, don't you think, if I try to get information from them without telling them who I am? I mean, approaching them with a false ID, going undercover. Wouldn't that be overstepping the mark? On the other hand I suppose that if I used information openly available to me as a customer—like we did last week at Vijay's restaurant—or as any interested person, that wouldn't matter.'

Pierre felt that, not for the first time, Susan had come round only slowly. Why did she always get hold of the wrong end of the baton first? 'Susan, I would not like to see you arrested! Researching from the outside, because we've defined it as getting access to information which should not be formally sanctioned by the company, does not mean that you should attempt to use unauthorised means to get it! There exist so many sources which hold information about companies, as well as other organisations which may have knowledge about them because of their working relationships.'

'That's a point! It could be interesting talking to suppliers as well! If I was up-front with them about my position in the firm, I don't see why they wouldn't give me some information on their views about us as a customer.'

Pierre nodded, but pointed out, 'Yes, but they may not tell you the truth—they may think that you might try to renegotiate any deal or contract.'

'Ummm, see what you mean. I'll have to think it through. But the views of suppliers and, as Michael Porter, the great management guru, puts it, other "value chain members", may be interesting to assess. They are external to my company but are part of its operating environment.'

The barperson brought the two tequilas that Pierre had ordered. Pierre paid, and returned to the discussion. 'OK, enough about your research—can we talk about mine, please? I have to meet with my professor tomorrow and she will want some answers. I'll discuss some of the ideas we have had—the external detective bit. I mentioned to her that I had a college friend who worked for a hospitality consultancy firm. I did suggest contacting him for some information about the firms I want to study—she'll want to know if I've followed through.'

Susan sipped her drink. 'I am surprised at you Pierre! You haven't been listening to your own advice. Wouldn't that be an underhand method of getting information—it would mean your friend breaking his client's confidence.'

'OK, Mademoiselle Clever, getting assistance through my friend, Hugh, could "bastardise" my research findings a little. As a consultant it must be difficult balancing the roles of insider/outsider. You are of course right. It would be unfair to ask him to help me. On the other hand, he may be able to tell me who in the firm I could talk to.'

'There does seem to be a lack of clarity differentiating the two roles of insider/outsider. Whichever approach you take does seem to present its own methodological and, possibly, ethical issues. I never realised that research methodology could be such a complex area. It is the course I have probably found most interesting!'

Pierre put down his drink emphatically. The salsa music had just been raised a couple of hundred decibels. 'Is it really the subject or the good company you get in these classes you like most?' he shouted above the music. 'Lets dance!'

Exhibit 3.4   Using sources outside the organisation to explain the organisation

Below are two examples of researching organisations from the outside. The first is where, through necessity, the researcher has had to adopt an outside perspective. The second is more within the tradition of much social and historical study, where the nature of the research topic makes it impossible to go to the circumstances or individuals concerned.

Researching the Walt Disney Company from the outside
Bryman (1995) provides an overview of the literature on the Disney organisation and its importance to contemporary culture. Of significance is the fact that the material for this book was sourced totally externally. This is explained by the author in the preface as follows:

> This book's origins derive from the realization some time ago, following a trip to Disney World, that various people had written about the Disney theme parks. They had apparently found them significant. It struck me that it would be a good idea to examine these writings to see what the various authors made of the parks, and to produce a short article on my findings … But I soon became aware that there was a sizeable literature on Walt Disney, on his organization, and on the theme parks as well, and that it would be useful to consider the three in tandem. (p. viii)

(*continued*)

The author did not have any assistance from the Walt Disney Company, and his work is therefore completely independent of the company. This was partially planned. However, the author at one point did attempt to enter the organisation, although only to visit the Disney Archives in California in order to examine their repository of writings on the theme park. His entry to the archive was, however, rebuffed by someone in as they said 'paralegal': emphasising just how sensitively some organisations may guard their privacy (p. ix). From this experience Bryman discovered that many other researchers had encountered difficulty in gaining access—providing one reason why researching from the outside was, at the time, the most appropriate approach to adopt.

This example of organisational research undertaken by such an eminent social scientist illustrates the validity of researching organisations from an 'outside' perspective. Bryman presents fascinating insights into the founder (and his successors), the organisation and its theme parks, in particular, using only external reports and references. He is also skilful in viewing the company as objectively as possible, given their rejection of both his request for access to records and people inside the organisation and his later inquiry for photographs of buildings in the theme parks.

There are examples over the years of hospitality organisations which have a reputation for tight organisational secrecy and difficulty in obtaining access. Researchers should find it worth remembering to remain impartial when experiencing attitudes such as those encountered by Bryman.

Evaluating the emergence and historical development of the hospitality industry

In order to help rectify an absence of historical analysis in the hospitality industry, Nickson (1996) discusses the key role played by several famous 'hotel men' in the emergence and growth of some of the more prominent hospitality multinationals. He argues that current developments and debates in the contemporary hospitality industry can to some extent be understood and explained by examining the past. He subsequently reviews the biographies or autobiographies of Charles Forte, Conrad Hilton, Kemmons Wilson (the founder of Holiday Inn) and J.W. Marriott.

Reviewing these works facilitates discussion of key issues, such as 'strategies for internationalization and the rationale behind early cross-border expansion in the hotel industry: standardization versus differentiation; the role (or lack of it) of trade unions in the hotel industry; and the importance of paternalism in the management and organization of the emergent early hospitality multinationals' (Nickson, 1996, p. 178). In methodological terms, this review of selected 'hotel men' illustrates the usefulness of biographies or autobiographies as sources of secondary inquiry which are arguably an underrated source of information used in hospitality management research. However, it is worth remembering the often biased and propagandist nature of such sources, and the use of such data must be tempered with the usual warnings about the validity and reliability of data.

Postscript

As Keith Macdonald and Colin Tipton point out (in Chapter 10 of Gilbert, 1993), while there is a natural tendency to concentrate on documents, there are wider sources than this: for example, 'songs, buildings, statues, novels ... tell us something about the values, interests and purposes of those who commissioned or produced them'. Thus there is no reason why researching organisations from the outside is necessarily document- and library-bound. While these are key to the process they do not exclude other possibilities.

Exhibit 3.5 Organisational dynamics

Contemporary organisational scholars, such as Stacey (1996), see strategic management as a process where managers:

- discover in an intuitive rather than analytical way;
- make unconscious automatic choices rather than consciously intentional ones; and
- carry those choices in a reflective, automatic way rather than a deliberate one (Stacey, 1996, p. 8).

An organisation can therefore be viewed as a complex human system and, as Senge (1990) notes:

> The art of systems thinking lies in being able to recognise increasingly (dynamically) complex and subtle structures, ... amid the wealth of details, pressures and cross-currents that attend all real management settings. In fact, the essence of mastering systems thinking as a management discipline lies in seeing patterns where others see only events and forces react. (quoted in Stacey, p. 297)

Being an outsider, stepping back from such a system therefore has its advantages.

Our character, Susan, is obviously heavily embroiled in the internal dynamics of her firm. She is what we may term 'internalised', just as any of us are in our own organisational contexts, for example as students, lecturers, or researchers in a University setting. If she researched other organisations than her own from an external perspective then she might provide interesting insights into the operation of her own organisation.

Exhibit 3.6 Researching corporate culture and performance from the outside

---

Two professors, John Kotter and James Hesketh, supported by the Division of Research at the Harvard Business School, collaborated over a four-year period on an organisational research project. They conducted four studies, the ultimate purpose of which was to determine whether there was a relationship between corporate culture and long-term economic performance and, if there was, to:

- clarify the nature of that relationship;
- explore why it exists; and
- determine whether it can be exploited to augment corporate performance.

Their methodology involved mailing questionnaires to the six top officers in 207 US companies. This survey asked executives about the strengths of their competitors' corporate cultures (not their own) during the late 1970s and early 1980s. With the information collected from the survey they constructed 'culture strength indexes' by computing an average response for each firm.

In a second survey they solicited the assistance of financial analysts who were interviewed by a research assistant working on behalf of the Harvard professors. This stage focused upon 24 firms and in most instances analysts were chosen who knew at least two of the sample firms. Respondents were asked how they would describe the corporate culture of the particular firms' they were familiar with and how this corporate culture might have assisted in the firms economic performance over the long term.

Finally, to test the validity of their findings and these 'culture strength indexes' they then visited seven of the firms and talked this time to 'insiders'.

Section 5: Sources of information on organisations

Sources of information on organisations are many and varied. Some have been mentioned in earlier sections. This section shows major written sources which may be available to researchers. In bringing these sources together, some sector (and even industry) general sources have been introduced, as they may provide general information by which industry norms/comparators may be found. Also it is possible that some of these more general sources will, from time to time, include detail on specific organisations.

Scene: A conference room in a 120-bedroomed, four-star hotel

Susan nudged Pierre whom she thought was looking unusually smart in a lounge suit, white shirt and tie. Pierre felt unusually uncomfortable. The suit was one thing, but not the main one. It was the surroundings. They weren't the academic ones that he was used to: organised library shelves, rooms with numbers, an office which, if not tidy, was organised enough to find most things in under 15 minutes. Susan nudged Pierre again. 'Don't look so fidgety', she ordered.

They were in the lounge of one of those business/conference hotels on the edge of town. Add a swimming pool, a mini-gym and a weekend bargain break brochure and Pierre knew you had the recipe for a hundred other establishments within a couple of hours' drive from this hotel. Susan wasn't quite so contemplative. She tugged on Pierre's sleeve as she edged herself up to join a group of men who had just come into the room.

'It's Jonathan, of PerForm, the hospitality consultants', she whispered into Pierre's ear at almost the same time as she introduced herself to Jonathan. '… Yes, we met a couple of years ago. You were doing a survey on managers' perceptions of performance for that study that some banks were financing. What did become of it?'

Jonathan looked as though he had been brought up in smart suits. 'Oh, I've still got a few copies kicking about … I think that the clients lost a bit of interest as it neared completion—it was coming out with variables other than finance as being important. Not quite their cup of tea! I can send you a copy if you like. But it was never officially published.'

'I'd be more than grateful', Susan said quickly. 'You see, I'm doing a project as part of my MBA. It's on performance in organisations. The survey would act as useful background, though I wouldn't actually refer to it.'

'Sure thing, Patricia.' Susan winced: he had confused her with someone else. He went on. 'You should speak to Gerry Tomlinson there. He's from Newhouse and Farrel, the up-market restaurant group. I did some consultancy for him about a year ago. I know it's confidential, but you might be able to convince him that you're in a different enough field not to worry about your seeing the survey, as long as you keep the results to yourself. … Actually, he's speaking on the subject at an Association meeting in a few weeks' time. You might find out quite a bit if you go.'

Susan scribbled down the details that he was giving her on people, organisations and telephone numbers. She gave Jonathan her card, pointing out *'Susan* Plender'—Pierre was pleased to see that the relationship seemed purely professional—Jonathan hadn't given her *his* telephone number!

Later, that same evening …

'… So you see, Pierre,' Susan said, 'it was very useful coming. I made several contacts with managers in organisations and I got reminded of that evening the local branch of the Association are going to be running. I'll meet other people who may be able to help me out there as well.'

'Good for you. While you were networking I made an interesting contact too. With a young lady, as it happens. She used to have quite a senior position in one of my research sample companies. She explained the background to the thinking behind the cost-cutting exercise they started three years ago. It'll be very useful information, because their current chief finance executive has only been in the organisation six months. …' Susan's eyes narrowed. 'Unfortunately,' Pierre went on, 'it's all unofficial; I won't be able to use it directly in my research, but it will help me interviewing the finance man. It's annoying that I didn't get her phone number to check out his information, though …'

Susan relaxed, and asked Pierre if they shouldn't be on their way, and let the hotel staff get on with clearing the function room.

Section 6: Identifying and using written and electronic sources of information on organisations

The aim of this section is to extend the information in the previous section by explaining a range of sources which may be accessed for information about an organisation. It does not attempt to be definitive: for example it does not deal with practical areas such as establishing the credit rating of companies or look generally to an organisation's artefacts (e.g. specific consumer promotions material).

Susan sat in the library. Trying to get information about companies on a systematic basis was not exactly straightforward. At least she had some more guidance than was possessed by many of her fellow students—the handout that Pierre had prepared as his own *aide-memoire* on sources of information (see Exhibit 3.7), while he was away from town. To a certain extent it had helped her: from a starting point of practically zero, she had amassed great volumes of information on ten organisations which she had previously identified as being relevant for her initial project sample.

Yet data was not directly comparable. For example, while financial data in company annual reports was produced on a standard basis, other text and details were, as Pierre would say, 'over all the place'. One year a Chairman might make a statement about how many catering contracts the firm had and were negotiating for. The next year, there was no such information—though the overall turnover figure was supplemented by a geographical analysis of sales. However, as the actual number of contracts was not mentioned for the period, it was difficult to relate the operations of the first year to the next. It was simplistic, she supposed, to think that all she needed to do was to collect the data together. While industry sector reports were useful in providing 'snapshots' of a number of companies and trends in a specific sector at any one time, Susan sometimes had questions as to where they got their data or in other cases how current it was. Sometimes it seemed they included some information which was not very reliable …

Pierre suddenly appeared from behind the Social Studies (Gender Issues) bookstack. He grinned and said in a soft voice, so as not to disturb other students: 'Did my notes help you, Susan? You look a bit worried.'

'Welcome back. How did the interviews for your fieldwork go? In answer to your question—in some ways your handout has helped too well! I've got masses of information, but ...', she lowered her voice as a nearby student, engrossed in some government statistics on employment trends, smiled at her good-naturedly but with an implication that private study, not conversation, was the main aim of the library, '... it just seems that there is too much information, coming from too many sources. These US websites in particular are fantastic—the amount of information they have, and the links to other sites they provide. Yet the amount of data I have is overwhelming, and often there is conflicting information too.'

'Conflicting information, yes, I know. Well,' whispered Pierre, 'we are talking about organisations, not bacteria that we can put under a microscope. A lot of people provide information on organisations, for a whole lot of different reasons. You will be dealing with problems of validity and reliability, I think. I guess the point is that you cannot come up with an ideal description of an organisation just from getting a lot of details. I remember in my research I got three different totals for corporate room stock for a hotel company—all of which related to the same year!'

Pierre explained that he had to compare corporately owned room stock for a number of hotel chains. He had accessed a wide number of sources in his searches, including hotel directories, articles in both professional and trade journals and, thirdly, company annual reports. 'Initially I had thought that the hotel directories were the best sources. After all, you could write and get up-to-date directories. They might not all refer to precisely the same day but at least they would refer to the same year. Good enough for my purposes! But I soon found that there were disagreements among my sources for several companies. I eventually found out that these were franchising companies. While the directories listed all hotels in the franchise system, not all were owned by the corporate brand holder. I could have been counting two different things if I was not careful—corporately owned rooms and those owned by the franchisors. Once I was aware of this problem I was able to avoid it: I went to the companies themselves and was very lucky to telephone people in the organisation who would help me—at least I knew what kind of question to ask!' Said in a whisper, Susan found this quite conspiratorial and exciting. It was good to have Pierre's advice again.

He went on: 'Actually, having just finished my first interviews with company personnel, I can say that the previous work I did on building up company profiles proved most useful. For example, because I knew about the franchising issue in some organisations, I was able to interview in a lot more depth about their strategies in franchising, in particular how franchising affects their accounting policies towards valuing their brand names. It is fascinating, and something that I had never before thought relevant. So I have proved that working on the outside does have some important pay-offs. Now let me see how we can solve your problem together.'

Over the next few hours the two friends decided on the main organisational variables that Susan needed information on from her contracting companies. These covered such factors as total sales, profits, gross operating margins, numbers of staff, ratios of staff to contracts to sales, and so on. On the companies' client base, they decided to have a box for comments on the geographical distribution of contracts because there was no standard format or interval by which the companies could be compared. They adopted a similar approach for the type of markets they served, under headings of *industrial and commercial*, *educational*, *transport related*, *retail shopping* and *leisure/tourism attractions*. However, other information on corporate ownership (such as ultimate holding company and subsidiaries) was much easier to get as it was a legal requirement to register this, so it was available in a number of industry surveys.

'Make sure that you source all this information in your tables', Pierre reminded Susan. 'It would be very annoying for you if you asked company executives to verify something that they know is wrong and you can't tell them where it came from. It is *you* they will blame for bad information!'

Susan pondered the emerging framework below her. At last she felt that she was getting somewhere. Now she could compare her sample on a number of different variables in a reasonably systematic way. There were some blanks, of course, which she would have to try and fill—or maybe that was always going to be a weakness within the 'researching from the outside' approach. Ah, well, nothing was ever going to be perfect.

They had better leave the library soon, Susan thought, but not until she had verified a few more details in the company directories that were in the reference section. Perhaps Pierre would take her out for a drink.

Exhibit 3.7 Sources of information: some examples of printed and electronic sources and types of information on particular organisations

Publications produced by commercial organisations and consortia, produced for external or internal consumption	Publications produced by the public sector	Trade, professional associations and other not-for-profit
Annual reports, interim reports	Annual reports; promotional material and explanatory leaflets/application forms on schemes operated.	Annual reports; year books
Corporate brochures, directories (e.g. hotel guides), Web sites	Newsletters, bulletins, Web sites	Promotional material and explanatory leaflets/application forms on schemes operated; office holders and special group (e.g. committees) memberships; Web sites
In-company newsletters, Web pages	Tourist boards: e.g. research reports; industry surveys such as occupancy	Newsletters, membership lists
Franchise agreements		Technical advice/guidance notes
Customer promotion material, including:	Strategy documents (often consultative), financial statements	Minutes of committee meetings
Press releases, company briefings	Tender documents, minimum service agreements	Promotion, consultative information, including Web pages, newsgroups
Advertisements in press: customer, staff (e.g. recruitment)	Advertisements in press: customer, staff (e.g. recruitment)	Advertisements in press: customer, staff (e.g. recruitment)
Full range of internal documents and specifications of management information systems	Records/minutes of meetings, internal memoranda, etc.; specification of management information systems	Internal records

(continued)

Commercial organisations: privately and publicly owned

The larger the organisation the more attention it is likely to attract; however, the scope and frequency of legally required documentation to be lodged in the public domain will be affected by the nature of the organisation (e.g. a limited partnership, a public limited company). 'Hot spots' of activity may appear in the press at such times as presentation of accounts and announcements of interim levels of payments to shareholders and, more exceptionally, at times of major change (e.g. major development programmes, takeovers).

Public and statutory organisations in the UK

Public organisations are discussed in the press in much the same way as private organisations. They also produce a range of internal and external information of much the same nature as their commercial counterparts. There may be more significant discussion about them, though not necessarily on a regular basis, in the parliamentary procedures as reported in *Hansard* (the official report of these procedures).

Regulatory bodies (for example, Oftel) issue reports on a regular basis, and it is likely that consumer organisations also publish reports from time to time.

Examples of other statutory organisations are Tourist Boards (national/regional), statutory training organisations (e.g. Hospitality Training Foundation), Race Relations, Equal Opportunities, Arbitration and Conciliation Advisory Services: see Butcher (1991). For research in other countries, researchers are advised to search for a similar type of publication as a starting point.

Voluntary and other not-for-profit organisations

These produce prospectuses for attracting members and raising funds for general operations and for specific projects. In addition there is specialist data recorded by the Charities Commission: for an overview of aims and membership see directories such as that of the Association of Independent Tour Operators. They may also produce manuals, reports and newsletters for members.

Examples are the Hotel and Catering International Management Association, the Association of Leisure and Amenity Management, and the Tourism Society. For a good source of initial information about these organisations, including contact details, see Ramscar (1995).

Information supplied about organisations available in the public domain

Suppliers and others related to industries and sectors

A range of organisations collect information about industry players from a variety of sources. Thus media watchers collect information about advertising spends by organisation, while others collate information lodged in the public domain, such as financial data, but provide them in an easily digestible form.

Examples are Neilson Media Expenditure Analysis Limited (MEAL) and Extel (share movements, etc). Specialist database providers include FAME (Financial Access Made Easy) and Jordan's. Industry suppliers such as American Express also finance reports such as Business Travel and Airlines (through data provided on their Global Distribution Systems).

Government departments and quangos often contain information about sectors in general and specific organisations within sectors. Thus Monopolies and Mergers Commission reports may contain significant amounts of information obtained from organisations but not usually in the public domain. The *London* (and, for Scotland, *Edinburgh*) *Gazette* contains information about bankruptcies.

Press sources

Press sources often cover the workings of organisations from a relatively general point of view. In this respect the trade press will tend to be more focused, regular and detailed in their coverage of organisations related to a particular sector. The coverage may be organisation or issues based. An example in the latter case would be where an article dealt with approaches to marketing strategies used by fast food brands.

Some publications have Web pages and some of these will allow searches by company name or nature of issue (e.g. *Financial Times* at http://www.ft.com).

Academic sources

Refereed journals will usually contain only general information about specific companies as these may not be identified at all (e.g. many individual companies within one sample) or, if in a case study, may have a hidden identity (e.g. 'Company X'). Use of management abstracts (hospitality, tourism and leisure as well as less sectorally specific management abstracts) will provide a useful start in gaining relevant articles, though they do not usually yield much when searching by specific organisation names.

Other sources

There are a range of other sources that may be used for obtaining information about a sector. Pressure groups will have information on sectors and even individual organisations. Thus the Low Pay Unit may publicise information on rates of pay and conditions of service; consultants who have worked with different organisations will invariably have personal information about individuals they may have worked with in organisations, and sometimes may even publish some work that they have previously provided for a particular client (with their permission). Former employees may be another source, as are biographies and autobiographies.

From time to time management researchers may find they have access to documents which are produced by organisations for internal consumption. There is no strong rule which can be given as to whether this type of information can legitimately be used in the research or not. Usually it is assumed that the producer of the data would have to be approached, and their permission gained. As well as the ethical issues referred to in the chapter, there could also be issues of copyright. If the information is produced by a government department or a statutory organisation, the conditions of the Official Secrets Act (1911), as amended, may apply. Researchers should exercise extreme care in all cases that this type of information is used only once all relevant factors have been carefully considered.

Section 7: Conclusion

This section reflects on the content of the chapter.

The concluding scene is an up-market hotel function suite, full of people of all ages. It is a year since their first meeting. Pierre and Susan have had an eventful day. It is late and they really want to go home. But the band has struck up and they feel they will disappoint their friends if they don't have a waltz or two.

'Well,' said Susan as Pierre led her round the dance floor, 'we've made it. Through all that doubt and uncertainty. What to think, what to say, how to say it ... research can be so daunting! And now you've got your doctorate and I've got my MBA! It's good to be here at the Graduation Ball. But let me tell you, Dr Ledoux, five minutes more on this floor and I'll just drop. You'll have to get me home soon.'

Pierre smiled and wondered why she was so keen to leave; after all it wasn't every day you could decide to forget all about research and organisations ...

This chapter started from the premise that organisations are complex, changing phenomena. This is particularly the case as traditional lines of demarcation between public and private sector break down through policies which, in essence, commercialise many activities previously considered to be the domain of large, centrally controlled, government departments and agencies. Businesses too are adapting to changing environments. Currently many are concentrating on core activities and have introduced contracting support for other functions.

Because of limited space the chapter has emphasised the differentiated nature of organisations and identified some of the main sources available. It has not dealt greatly with the quality of the information obtained. However, the criteria of objectivity, reliability and time-frames touched upon in Section 6 must be considered fully in order to judge the utility of a source and its contents. Additional to this is the need to obtain complete information on organisations when coming to conclusions which are appropriate to their operations, structure and contexts.

However, commercially and officially sensitive areas often make it difficult or impossible to obtain data on a variety of subjects when researching a particular issue. Time constraints may also make it difficult to make sufficient meaningful contacts in organisations. Hence the researcher may have to be satisfied with using either information which has been obtained from outside the organisation, or information which the organisation itself produces for outside consumption. Wherever this is the case the researcher should explain the limitations of the data and, if relevant, why the research has had to rely on this source and why 'inside' sources were not available.

It has also been the emphasis of the chapter to concentrate on researching large organisations, rather than smaller ones. In an industry which is largely populated by small businesses it could be claimed that this is an omission. It is—but there is another chapter in this volume which deals specifically with the topic. The logic of this chapter is that many potential managers will enter larger organisations and therefore are excited about the prospect of knowing more about how they operate.

References

Bryman A (1995) *Disney and his Worlds*, Routledge, London

Butcher D (1991) *Official Publications in Britain*, Second edition, Library Association Publishing, London

Commission on Management Research (1994) *Building Partnerships—Enhancing the Quality of Management Research*, Economic and Social Research Council, Swindon

Gilbert N (1993) *Researching Social Life*, Sage, London

Kotter J P and Hesketh J L (1992) *Corporate Culture and Performance*, Free Press, New York.

Nickson D (1996) 'Colourful stories or historical insight?—A review of the auto/biographies of Charles Forte, Conrad Hilton, J W Marriott and Kemmons Wilson', *Fifth Annual CHME Research Conference*, Nottingham Trent University, Nottingham, UK, pp 176–190.

Ramscar J (ed.) (1995) *Association and Professional Bodies in the U.K.*, 14th edition, Gale Research, Detroit

Senge P M (1990) *The Fifth Discipline: The Art of Practice of the Learning Organisation*, Doubleday, New York

Stacey R (1996) *Strategic Management and Organisational Dynamics*, Second edition, Pitman Publishing, London

4 Interdisciplinary research: the team advantage!

MAUREEN BROOKES, ANNE HAMPTON AND ANGELA ROPER[1]

Introduction

As authors, we could not have summarised the ideas presented in this chapter better than Grau and Borchgrevink (1993: 68) who state that:

> We are rarely faced with problems, concerns, or opportunities that have their origin or solution in a singular intellectual discipline. As such, why do we approach teaching and research from the perspective of a singular intellectual discipline? In doing so, we create artificial limitations in our investigations and disseminations of relevant phenomena.

This chapter suggests that undertaking hospitality management research using a multi-disciplinary or interdisciplinary approach should generate more realistic findings than taking a single discipline perspective.

The environment in which hospitality management research takes place is diverse in terms of the sector being investigated, the geographical situation, the ownership and structure of the organisation, and the level of service and product provision. As the industry is also dependent on the financial health of other industries, it is essential that there is an understanding of the business climate in which hospitality firms operate (Shaw and Nightingale, 1995). Thus, the nature of such a disparate industry influences the methodological approaches used, the geographic focus of the research, the disciplines which may be appropriate for understanding the research problem, and the types of people who will be interested in the research process and its outcomes.

It is argued that hospitality should not be viewed as a single discipline, but as a grouping of disciplines which interrelate and assist our understanding of the hospitality industry. We support Shaw and Nightingale (1995) when they suggest that hospitality's knowledge base draws on multiple disciplines in management as well as related fields in the behavioural and social sciences. Given the increasing international focus of hospitality, Dunning's (1989) call for increased interdisciplinarity in international business is also pertinent. In addition, Doherty and Roper (1998) have called for closer collaboration between faculty members from different disciplines in teaching postgraduate courses in international hospitality management.

---

[1] All authors contributed equally to this chapter.

The Handbook of Contemporary Hospitality Management Research, Edited by Bob Brotherton.
© 1999 John Wiley & Sons Ltd.

This chapter begins by exploring the concept of an academic discipline and gives examples of the attributes of certain managerial disciplines applicable to issues being investigated in hospitality management research. It then contrasts multidisciplinary and interdisciplinary approaches to research and argues the superior contribution that the latter can make. As much interdisciplinary research is undertaken by a team, the practical aspects of researching in groups are considered.

We have tried to write this chapter with a range of readers in mind. Students at all levels who may be undertaking research for a group assignment, or as part of an integrated course or project, practitioners on special project teams or taskforces, and academic researchers seeking a more holistic approach to their work should all find this chapter both stimulating and valuable. Many of the ideas presented are based on the authors' own personal experiences of, and reflections on, researching in an interdisciplinary team.

What is a discipline?

There continues to be much debate about the nature and distinguishing features of an academic discipline. For example, a continuing discourse between hospitality management researchers centres around whether the concept of hospitality is either a scholarly discipline or 'an area of professional study' (Taylor and Edgar, 1996). The controversy about the characteristics of the hospitality concept is outside this particular chapter but as an illustration it serves to demonstrate that the notion of an academic discipline is not altogether straightforward.

A discipline has several different aspects. Although dated, King and Brownell's (1966) account of an academic discipline embraces a range of elements: a community, a network of communities, a tradition, a particular set of values and beliefs, a domain, a mode of enquiry and a conceptual structure. Other authors specify only certain factors, presenting disciplines either as being characterised by their own body of concepts, methods and fundamental aims (Toulmin 1972) or as being defined unequivocally as organised social groupings (Whitley, 1984). However, most commentators on the subject give equal emphasis to both aspects, concluding that disciplines are both a structure of knowledge or content and a social organisation. In other words, disciplines have their own aims, body of concepts and methods as well as their own social organisation. Becher (1989: 20) summarises this perhaps more succinctly when he explains that:

> the attitudes, activities and cognitive styles of groups of academics representing [or students studying in-depth] a particular discipline are closely bound up with the characteristics and structures of the knowledge domains with which groups are professionally concerned.

The same author goes on to describe those academics representing, or students studying, a particular discipline as an academic 'tribe'. A discipline can therefore be seen to have its own 'culture', defined by Hofstede (1994: 180) as 'the collective programming of the mind which distinguishes the members of one group or category of people from another' and as such will have a recognisable identity and set of attributes, namely idols, artefacts and a distinctive language. Although these are aspects relevant to all cultural phenomena, it is interesting to apply these characteristics to reiterate several disciplines in the management or business field. Although managerial disciplines share similar structural elements—they are all housed in the same academic department or school, a Business or Management School, for example (or they may all be incorporated into a business/management degree programme)—they must all have, to varying extents, organisational validity and they can also be viewed as disciplines in their own right.

Managerial functions such as cost and management accounting and marketing also apply to all sectors of the hospitality industry. As subject areas they often form part of hospitality management courses and are applied to issues being investigated in hospitality management research. The identities and attributes of these two functional/ subject areas may be manifest in the following ways:

- *Idols*:   Marketers view Theodore Levitt or Philip Kotler as their idols and, particularly in the UK, Colin Drury could be an icon of cost and management accountants.
- *Artefacts*:   Examples of promotional material, such as advertisements, posters, and copies of the mission statements of companies and institutions (such as the Chartered Institute of Marketing or the American Marketing Association) held in high esteem may adorn the walls of a marketer's office; whilst the cost accountant commonly fills shelves with copies of company reports and accounts and other statistical reports.

These, possibly crude, illustrations indicate some of the parameters of a discipline 'tribe' or community. It is, however, through the medium of language that some of the more fundamental distinctions emerge. This is a complex area involving in-depth research into 'disciplinary discourse', an area that Becher (1987) has spent ten years investigating, which is far longer than we have had to complete this chapter. However, on a superficial level it is interesting to speculate that in terms of appraisal the marketer may commend a piece of work as 'analytical' whilst a cost accountant will look for correctly operationalised numerical examples to illustrate the solution to a problem.

Thus, members of a disciplinary community share a 'mind-set', or particular view on the world. They also share distinctive norms, behaviours and regulatory mechanisms designed to maintain their existence. For managers in industry their professional backgrounds will have much influence upon their strategic choices (Roper, Brookes and Hampton, 1997), whilst for academics discipline 'conditioning' is perpetuated by the fact that:

> disciplines publish in their own professional journals which are rarely read by colleagues in the next corridor of the university building. (Hofstede, writing in the foreword for Usunier's (1993) text on international marketing, p. xi)

The individual variety of these two illustrative management disciplines—cost and management accounting and marketing—may further be summarised in an unrefined way by presenting a gallery of simplified stereotypes. This approach has been used by us in our postgraduate teaching when we have raised questions to a range of overseas students about the impressions they have formed of professionals in certain discipline (or, in industrial terms, functional) areas. Given the diverse cultural, educational and work experience backgrounds of the student group, their caricatures of the two professional groups display great similarity. The students pinpointed a number of contrasts (in a pictorial format) summarised as follows:

- *Marketers*:   display a flamboyant working dress sense, may drive some type of sports car and are constantly on their mobile phone.

- *Accountants*:   exhibit a more conservative image, often wear 'grey' pinstriped suits and glasses, and invariably are working at a computer or with a calculator.

Although slightly trivial, these stereotypes do establish that the two subjects in question are discernibly different. When questioning professionals themselves in these two areas about their view of each other, very distinct stereotypical caricatures are also likely to be painted.

Despite the various artefacts and stereotypes that assist in making clear distinctions between disciplines, it is suggested that there are benefits to be gained from working across these disciplines, in both academia and business. Recently, there has been a move towards the use of teams and group work in both industry and teaching. Fox and Faver (1982) report the growth of collaborative work and publications with two or more authors over past decades. This increase has been attributed to a number of organisational and institutional factors, including patterns of funded research, the maturation of disciplines and the increasing professionalisation of scholarship and science. On an individual level, collaboration is stimulated by such factors as the desire to join resources, divide labour, alleviate social isolation, and maintain motivation to work.

Collaborative work can help to reduce some anxieties inherent in research, although it may produce other concerns for those collaborating. Furthermore, Getty (1996) reports on a study investigating the reasons why groups tend to reach superior decisions compared to individuals working alone. It showed that the grouping of individual judgements improves the chances of success due to the cancellation of individual errors and that the interaction found in group activities improves the outcome. This move towards greater collaboration and the associated benefits is just one of the factors leading to greater value being placed upon multi- and interdisciplinary work.

Distinctions between multidisciplinary and interdisciplinary research

Generally, multidisciplinary and interdisciplinary are terms which are used interchangeably; however, there are marked conceptual and pragmatic distinctions between them. In multidisciplinary research only the subject of the research is the same, whilst the philosophy of the researchers may be completely different. For example, a team of researchers investigating the complex role of a hotel unit-level general manager may consist of an operations specialist, an accountant, a marketing specialist and a human resource management expert. In this case, they are all interested in the role of the general manager, but will be influenced by their own functional interests and will also bring different research philosophies to the research design. The language of the disciplines would remain with each subject specialist and there would be little integration or synthesis of concepts or ideas. In terms of the research design the different disciplines may place greater emphasis on different methods. As a generalisation, operations may wish to use critical incident analysis, the accountant may prefer a quantitative questionnaire, whilst the human resource specialist may favour more qualitative in-depth interviews. Thus, the subject of the research is the only linking mechanism and every researcher brings with them the research methods most commonly used in their own disciplines, and their own personal preferences and experiences of using specific methods. Furthermore, the research findings are likely to be interpreted individually by each specialist. The analysis of the findings will remain separate and appear to be compartmentalised. Multidisciplinary research would therefore provide a range of approaches towards a given subject but would lack the more unified approach of interdisciplinary research.

Interdisciplinary research examines a subject from different perspectives simultaneously. In the given example, the group of experts would work with each other to develop objectives and methodologies which were relevant and of interest to them all. They may therefore decide to investigate the skills necessary for a general manager to function efficiently and effectively. In addition, the research method would be discussed and refined to accommodate all discipline requirements. It is the development of this more unified approach and the researchers' willingness to be open-minded and interested in what each discipline may contribute towards the subject of investigation that leads to truly interdisciplinary research.

It is through this continuous and open process that a conceptually interlinked approach is developed. The process is not an easy one. It involves the team members being willing to discuss their own subject theories and concepts with the other members in order to develop a joint understanding of all the disciplines and what each may contribute to an understanding of the subject of investigation. The ability to develop each other's trust and to build on self-confidence is vital throughout: thus a holistic and synergistic understanding is achieved. The holistic nature permeates through the whole approach to research from the design of the research instrument to the analysis and evaluation of the findings. One way in which the fully integrated, holistic understanding is manifested is through the development of a meta-language. The research team are all able to fully comprehend each other in terms of discipline-specific jargon, and may even develop a language which is used to support the synergistic understanding they have developed.

A useful definition of interdisciplinary research, which also sums up many of the key points discussed here, is provided by Jack Nilles (in Benton, 1976: 37):

> The joint, co-ordinated and *continuously* integrated research done by experts with different disciplinary backgrounds, working together and producing reports, papers, recommendations and/or plans which are so tightly and thoroughly interwoven that the specific contribution of each research tends to be obscured by a joint product.

Benton (1976) adds to this through his discussion of why synergy and synthesis are such important factors in achieving interdisciplinarity. He particularly stresses the value of good communication structures and practices being developed to encourage interdisciplinary projects in organisations. We believe that in addition to the necessary communication links across disciplines, departments and functions, it is essential to develop researchers' understanding of what is involved in interdisciplinary research and the benefits of adopting such an approach that will lead to an increase in its use. The distinctive features of each approach are outlined in Exhibit 4.1.

Why interdisciplinary?

There are a number of reasons why it is appropriate for hospitality management

Exhibit 4.1 Summary of the differences between multidisciplinary and interdisciplinary research

MULTIDISCIPLINARY RESEARCH	INTERDISCIPLINARY RESEARCH
Only the subject of the research is the same, e.g. time allocation of general managers	Examines a subject from different perspectives simultaneously
The philosophy of researchers is different	Research is more unified in its philosophy
Each discipline uses its own concepts and methods	A conceptually interlinked approach is developed
The approach to research may be different	Holistic, synergistic, understanding is achieved
Results can only be interpreted by each separate discipline	Results will be jointly analysed
Each discipline employs its own language	A meta-language is developed

researchers to be considering the issue of multidisciplinary and interdisciplinary studies at this point in time. These reasons include the change in focus of the hospitality industry to a more holistic approach to business (Taylor and Edgar, 1996), evolutionary developments of hospitality research, and the recognition in hospitality education of the need for a more holistic approach. (This last point is evidenced in the pragmatic nature of GNVQ teaching, including realistic work settings, and by the use of integrated subjects and projects on degree programmes.) Further, Litteljohn (1990) suggests that strong interdisciplinary teams should be able to mount complex research and consultancy projects and to respond better to the needs of the industry. This may assist in the development of links between academic research and industry, as the very nature of an interdisciplinary approach may be more relevant to both parties. It may also be important in industry's willingness to fund research.

Interdisciplinary research is not a new phenomenon, however. A number of authors have been advocating the need for using either a multidisciplinary, or preferably an interdisciplinary, approach for some time, for example Benton (1976), Dymsza (1984), Litteljohn (1990) and Slattery (1983). There is also a need to bridge the gap between academic research and the value of research to practitioners. Many of the advantages of both multi- and interdisciplinary research are associated with the benefits of working in a team. The effective use of teams will achieve the following (Jolliffe, 1991):

- improve communication, making it multidirectional
- promote better use of human resources
- generate more creativity by allowing more minds to build on ideas
- create better leadership development
- improve job satisfaction
- promote creative tension

- reduce stress
- reduce isolation
- improve flows of information
- generate a more co-operative spirit.

Many researchers would welcome the benefits of working in a team listed here. When these benefits are combined with the advantages of interdisciplinarity, as discussed earlier, there is powerful evidence which supports the superiority of interdisciplinary practices in research.

Despite our own preferences towards an interdisciplinary approach, we recognise that even multidisciplinary studies develop and improve the depth of understanding in the issues surrounding hospitality research.

Interdisciplinary research in practice

Benton (1976) identified the most important factor related to interdisciplinarity as team-work and, although not always the case, much interdisciplinary research is undertaken by a team of researchers collaborating on a specific project that crosses disciplinary boundaries (see, for example, Exhibit 4.2).

This section of the chapter addresses some of the issues that must be given consideration in interdisciplinary collaborative research from the initial stages through to publication of research findings.

Research beginnings

In an interdisciplinary project the research topic may be the brainchild of one particular person or the result of a group effort. In either case there is a recognition that the research spans the boundaries of different disciplines, but there may be different implications for the project. A research proposal from a single source may result in that person assuming ownership of the project despite its interdisciplinary characteristics. If the research 'idea' is grounded in the particular discipline of the project founder, one must consider whether the research would be truly interdisciplinary, particularly if the

---

Exhibit 4.2   Gendered employment in hospitality in four European countries

This research project investigates women's employment in the hospitality industry in four European countries: Spain, France, Italy and the United Kingdom. It is being carried out by an established interdisciplinary research team of academics specialising in the areas of Human Resource Management, European Studies and Law. All have an established interest in women's employment, but come from different academic backgrounds and have different skills and knowledge to contribute.

In addition, the main research team have co-ordinated a network of researchers and academic partners interested in working on the topic in the four European countries. There are plans also to extend the project to include collaboration with academic colleagues in Finland and Bulgaria. These links build on prior research and teaching contacts.

For further information on this project, contact Liz Doherty, School of Hotel and Restaurant Management, Oxford Brookes University, Gipsy Lane Campus, Headington, Oxford, OX3 0BP, UK; liz@hrm.brookes.ac.uk.

methodology adopted is also embedded within that single disciplinary culture. A research proposal that begins collaboratively, however, may lead to a more democratic approach—one purported to be more effective for interdisciplinary research in the long run (King *et al.*, 1991).

Team formation

Through its inception, a collaborative research proposal may result in a ready-made research team. With a student project or company taskforce, the selection of the research team may be outside the control of the actual researchers. At other times a research team will need to be actively selected, particularly in the case of a singularly developed research proposal.

There are numerous factors to be considered in research team formation. It must be decided whether priority should be given to researchers who have complementary knowledge, especially if there is a deficiency in certain disciplines that are crucial to the research, or to team members who have complementary group skills (see, for example, Belbin, 1996). Laverty and Fawcett (1987) claim that strong, well-organised effective groups usually contain a variety of different sub-groups and individuals. Webster (1995) warns that disciplines have a rigour and depth that interdisciplinary adventures easily lose, and it is therefore very important that the researchers have a thorough grounding in their own discipline before undertaking interdisciplinary research. Fox and Faver (1982) advise that if researchers are complementary in knowledge and personal factors there is provision for enhancing one's own personal knowledge, an important factor in the development of interdisciplinary research teams.

Whatever the criteria for team selection, the diversity of the researchers (whether disciplinary, cultural, personal, etc.) is a factor that has a bearing on the dynamics of the team. For instance, if research members are recruited for their disciplinary expertise, there may be strong and opposing opinions within a research team as a result of different disciplinary mind-sets and cultures. As the size of the research team increases, so too will the diversity and thus the greater the potential for conflict. One possible consideration is that some researchers take responsibility for more than one discipline, an approach that would increase the interdisciplinary aspect of the project. A further possibility is to bring certain team members on board for their expertise in advisory roles only at relevant stages.

Roles and responsibilities

In these early stages of the research careful thought must be given to the roles and the responsibilities of all group members. Tomkins, Rosenberg and Colville (1991) advise that there must be a clear recognition of why each member has joined the research project and the risks each faces in terms of peer assessment and academic/career development. They recommend the use of an internal contract to focus on potential misunderstanding from the beginning of the project, especially when more than one discipline is involved. Students particularly are recommended to set explicit ground rules (see, for example, Gibbs and Habeshaw, 1994) regarding responsibilities and time commitments. Specific regulations on majority agreements and whether a certain minimum number of people need to be present to make a decision are also useful points to consider formalising before the project gets underway.

Even if a democratic approach is adopted, it may be advisable to plan for one member of the group to assume a leadership role if only for co-ordination and control purposes. According to Tomkins, Rosenberg and Colville (1991: 267):

> the need for establishing a means of controlling the project probably needs more delicate and explicit treatment when one has a mix of disciplinary backgrounds and activities in the team, than the relatively straightforward scheduling process which is probably adequate in most single-discipline projects.

When deciding on the nature of the leadership role, consideration needs to be given to the standing of all team members at whatever stage of educational achievement or hierarchical position in an organisation. It is important to realise that the person with the highest standing may not necessarily be the best person to assume a leadership role. Furthermore, if this person assumes the leadership role, it may lead to deference to his or her opinion in group decision making and a bias towards his or her specific discipline. Leadership roles could, of course, change at different stages in a research project.

Communication and co-ordination

Benton's (1976) early research on interdisciplinary projects indicates that it is possible to have teamwork and synergism without extensive communication of one particular type. However, even with well-established ground rules, there are potential problems that may be encountered in interdisciplinary research, especially in the early stages. Tomkins, Rosenberg and Colville (1991) report on the ambiguous nature of communication which can occur at the outset of any research project, especially one involving more than one discipline. Feelings of uncertainty and a reluctance to admit lack of knowledge and understanding of other disciplines and their languages contribute to initial problems and it is important to create trust between team members.

The difficulty for members of different academic faculties to communicate and interact professionally when undertaking interdisciplinary work in academic institutions is reported by Schratz (1993). Successful collaboration may require researchers to counter certain traditional academic styles and develop alternative skills and practices. Becher (1987) likens this questioning of one's accepted disciplinary ideology to heresy, thus increasing one's reluctance to interact across disciplines.

Co-ordinating meetings to keep the research progressing becomes a time-consuming process in itself, owing to the conflicting schedules of different members of any research team. Finding suitable meeting times and places is often a difficult task for students, particularly when there is a large research group. When meetings become difficult, King et al. (1991) suggest the use of the 'assertive memo' which specifies when and what type of action is wanted and what will occur if no response is received. When meetings are held, consideration should be given to developing agendas for chaired meetings that are clear-cut and suit the availability of different team members. Attention should be paid to keeping accurate minutes of meetings to inform those unable to attend of decisions taken and action required.

Time constraints and conflicting schedules create the need to 'task out' areas of research work. One possible difficulty with this approach is group members 'going off on their own tangent' and trying to fit individual pieces of work back into the interdisciplinary project. King *et al.* (1991) point out, however, that some tasks remain discipline specific depending on the nature of the research, and 'tasking out' work offers many advantages when faced with deadlines.

However, the benefits of teamwork outweigh some of these problems of interaction and co-ordination for companies. Exhibit 4.3 outlines positive and negative issues arising from the formation of special project teams and taskforces.

Data collection

One important aspect of interdisciplinary research is the potential for vast volumes of material to be generated. Therefore, it becomes necessary early in the project to establish responsibility for the collection and dissemination of secondary research data. It may also prove beneficial to have the task of data collection fall to one person to maintain consistency in the approach undertaken and avoid duplication of effort.

A definite process for distributing relevant material to team members should be established. If the circulation is on a discipline-specific basis then one must question

---

Exhibit 4.3   Special project teams and taskforces

Special project teams are often created to oversee the completion of a special activity (setting up a new technological process, bringing out a new product, starting up a new venture, consummating a merger with another company, seeing through the completion of a government contract, supervising the construction and opening of a new plant). They are especially suitable for one-of-a-kind situations with a finite life expectancy when the normal organisation is not equipped to achieve the same results in addition to regular duties. Companies with matrix organisational structures often create these separate, largely self-sufficient work groups which comprise a range of managers or representatives drawn from across functional, product and regional divisions.

There are a range of strengths and weaknesses associated with the operation of special project teams or taskforces. The strengths include:

- activity sharing and skills transfer;
- encouragement of co-operation, consensus building, conflict resolution and co-ordination of related activities;
- creation of checks and balances among competing viewpoints.

Weaknesses might comprise:

- complex to manage;
- 'transactions logjam'—due to need for communication and consensus;
- action turns into paralysis—need to check with others and get clearance;
- much time and psychic energy get eaten up in meetings and communicating back and forth;
- sizeable transaction costs and longer decision-making times.

However, overall the benefits of conflict resolution, consensus building and co-ordination outweigh these weaknesses. The interdisciplinary nature of project teams also means that there is a high rate of innovation.

Source: Adapted from Thompson and Strickland (1996: 264–266).

whether the research is truly interdisciplinary or whether it is only multidisciplinary. Consideration should therefore be given to circulating data across disciplinary boundaries. This approach will also provide different interpretations of data and potentially greater insight into the material. It may also help overcome discipline-specific language barriers and aid in the development of a meta-language. However, distributing all articles to all team members can become a very time-consuming process and the adoption of an intermediary approach may prove to be the most effective. For instance, data could be distributed across disciplines for review by some researchers and a précis circulated to all team members.

A database for recording information and the corresponding précis should be contemplated due to the logistics of storing all data. The development of key words to back up the database entries can also aid in the development of a meta-language and the adoption of a holistic approach.

Developing a research framework

Tomkins, Rosenberg and Colville (1991) advise that it is better to import a research paradigm from one discipline rather than merge research philosophies to produce new interdisciplinary paradigms. However, as people from different disciplines have different traditions and ways of thinking, and even describe the most elemental of matters differently (Webster, 1995), potential problems may arise when members try to import a research paradigm from another discipline. A research framework should, therefore, be developed that will work across the different disciplines and is acceptable to all team members.

Undertaking primary research/fieldwork

Primary research or fieldwork may not be relevant to all research projects, but if it is to be undertaken there are three main areas of contemplation, particularly if the research is to be done within a hospitality organisation. Gaining access to a company, to a specific and perhaps unfamiliar section of a company, or to the people within is the first concern. Access may be better negotiated by certain team members on the basis of personal attributes which may reflect their disciplinary background and/or their personality. In addition, there may be more credence to certain disciplines regarding research validity (e.g. marketing), or alternatively more reluctance to grant access for certain disciplines (e.g. finance).

The next point to reflect upon is which team members will actually undertake the fieldwork. In a truly interdisciplinary research team, all the members should theoretically be able to undertake fieldwork in any of the disciplinary domains. With conflicting schedules and heavy time constraints, this approach offers the greatest flexibility. It is important to note, however, that a consistent image should be presented by whichever members of the research team are conducting the fieldwork. Tomkins, Rosenberg and Colville (1991) point out that various members may react differently to the influence an organisation has over the research, resulting in possible aggravation for all involved.

What constitutes research time and thus what is relevant, ethical and/or usable data is the final point of deliberation in fieldwork. Different disciplines may have different views on these issues and therefore clarification may be necessary before undertaking fieldwork.

Analysis of data and presentation of findings

Disciplinary differences may become apparent in the interpretation and analysis of data. Different team members have different philosophical points of view and it is the philosophical school of thought that influences how they interpret events (Przeclawski, 1993). Although Tomkins, Rosenberg and Colville (1991) warn that these differing interpretations can lead to extra strain within a team, different interpretations are advantageous in interdisciplinary research where a holistic view is required. The use of a meta-language would be useful to express a holistic view based on a shared perspective of all the disciplines concerned.

Finding suitable journals and forums for the presentation and dissemination of academic research is another area of deliberation. Choice of the most suitable journals that reflect the interdisciplinary findings is often difficult (Riddick, De Schriver and Weissinger, 1984) as very often academic journals mirror the direction of a particular discipline's research (Van Doren and Heit, 1973). Furthermore there are often differing restrictions and practices between disciplines which must be taken into account prior to undertaking any writing. For instance, Becher (1987) reports on the differences in structure, length and terminology between journals of different disciplines and these issues may become evident if parts of articles are 'tasked out' amongst the research team. Many academic conferences, conventions and symposia also frequently have a single disciplinary focus. One example of a conference that has been conceived with interdisciplinarity in mind is summarised in Exhibit 4.4.

Exhibit 4.4   Presenting at interdisciplinary conferences

Finding suitable forums for the presentation and dissemination of interdisciplinary research findings can often prove a difficult task. One of the exceptions, however, is the European Institute of Retailing and Services Studies (EIRASS) Conference held in conjunction with the Canadian Institute of Retailing and Services Studies (CIRASS).

The conference is designed to stimulate participants to present and discuss their latest research proposals and findings in order to improve and disseminate their research endeavours and create an opportunity for networking. Recognising that the general field of retailing and consumer services tends to be split into various regionally- and disciplinary-based areas, the organisers of the CIRASS/EIRASS conferences attempt to bring these networks together to discuss theories, methodologies and empirical research findings of mutual interest.

At the latest annual conference, papers were invited on topics as diverse as consumer choice behaviour, retail and service strategy, geographical information systems, location analysis and land use planning, and human resource management. As a result conference delegates were representative of schools of hospitality management, marketing, architecture, planning, geography, tourism, economics, agricultural business and fashion, etc. Furthermore the conference attracted participants from a diverse range of countries including Australia, The Netherlands, Africa, Brazil, Malaysia, Canada and the United Kingdom. As a result, delegates are given the opportunity to learn more about their particular areas of research interest from different disciplinary perspectives.

Source: CIRASS/EIRASS (1997).

Consideration must also be given to potential problems in joint authorship both for academics and for students submitting or presenting group coursework for assessment. Researchers should consider equity in contribution, a factor that may be included in the ground rules set at the beginning of the project. The practice of certain members of the team publishing within their own discipline on the research project may also need to be considered under a jointly owned project, although this may prove difficult as the research is embedded in an interdisciplinary system that may not be deemed appropriate to a particular discipline.

Conclusion

Disciplinarity can be viewed on a continuum from a traditional single-discipline approach to that of a truly interdisciplinary one. Along the continuum there may be a point at which a hybrid of multi- and interdisciplinarity exists. In reality logistical, intellectual and/or professional, personal and ethical issues may inhibit a fully unified approach. In our experience (see Exhibit 4.5), achieving the interdisciplinary ideal could be viewed as an evolutionary process and experiential learning plays an important

---

Exhibit 4.5 What makes a successful international hotel group?

The authors of this chapter are drawn from the membership of an interdisciplinary research team who are investigating what makes a successful international hotel group. Although the team all reside in hospitality and tourism schools or divisions, we each represent very different managerial discipline bases, namely strategic, marketing, financial and human resource management.

The first stage of the study involved a survey to identify the performance measures utilised by international hotel groups. We then reviewed the factors that were reported to lead to success in each of our respective disciplinary/functional areas. At this stage of the process we were criticised for adopting research methods that revolved around a multidisciplinary framework (Edgar and Taylor, 1996). On reflection we agree with this criticism; however, as the project has evolved a more integrated approach has grown.

We found that a recurring theme in the literature was the concept of management orientation and its causal impact upon the success of international firms. As a result of this discovery the objectives for the research were realigned, 'centricity' being a conceptual unifying dimension. A methodology has since been devised which accommodates all discipline/functional requirements.

The research aims to assess the centric profile or management approach taken within international hotel groups by studying their internal decision-making processes and the dynamics of these within each sample organisation. Because centricity may vary across functional areas, semi-structured interviews are being carried out with corporate level management in marketing, finance, human resource and strategic planning. To analyse centricity at regional and unit levels, interviews are also being carried out with regional and hotel management and staff. The findings will be evaluated in order to determine whether regional and unit level practices are in harmony with corporate-level strategies and policies, and to gain a fuller picture of the most dominant centric profile of each international hotel group.

Working as a group has not been easy and the process of refinement, summarised above, has taken a number of years. However, we are now beginning to understand the discipline-specific jargon of each other's subject area and as such have developed a type of meta-language. In the primary research process we can each be substituted, questioning executives in any functional area and with some credibility! We hope that our critics might now view our research framework as more representative of an interdisciplinary rather than a multidisciplinary approach.

role. Not only is the activity evolutionary but it is also temporal: team members may be together for only a limited and often intermittent period, and although they assume a culture of their own when together, they return to their respective habitats. However, the experience of being in such teams and part of a feedback network will have undoubtedly changed them.

As a team of researchers we have cultivated a synergistic interdisciplinary working alliance where the sum of our integral knowledge and expertise has enabled us to produce more innovative research findings than any individual or single disciplinary team could have achieved. However, we do recognise that as three white Anglo-Saxon women we have cultural limitations. The invitation to other researchers from overseas to join our project will assist some way in tackling this lack of cultural diversity.

In an applied sense, although the hospitality industry is varied and complex there is a large theme area comprising items of broad interest which transcend industry sectors or single disciplines. Ingram (1996) suggests that there is a need therefore to develop 'methodologies through which research may be made more accessible and credible to the world at large'. Interdisciplinarity is one such approach which allows for a holistic understanding of events and phenomena, particularly in the world of business.

The opinions expressed throughout this chapter have largely been our own, though informed by other academic and industrialist commentators supportive of the notion of interdisciplinarity. We would welcome comments from readers, particularly if you find that you do not share our 'mind-set' in relation to interdisciplinary research.

References

Becher T (1987) 'Disciplinary discourse', *Studies in Higher Education* **12**, 3, pp 261–274.

Becher T (1989) 'Academic disciplines', *Academic Tribes and Territories: Intellectual Enquiry and the Culture of Disciplines*, Society for Research into Higher Education: Open University Press: Milton Keynes, pp 19–51.

Belbin K M (1996) *Management Teams: Why They Succeed or Fail*, Butterworth-Heinemann: Oxford.

Benton D A (1976) 'Management and effectiveness measures for inter-disciplinary research', *SRA Journal*, Spring, pp 37–45.

CIRASS/EIRASS (1997) *Book of Abstracts*, 4th Recent Advances in Retailing and Services Science Conference, June 30–July 3, Scottsdale, Arizona, USA.

Doherty L and Roper A (1998) 'Removing our culturally tinted glasses: an approach to teaching international Master's programmes', *Journal of Hospitality and Tourism Eucation* **9**, 3, pp 82–86.

Dunning J (1989) 'The study of international business: a plea for a more interdisciplinary approach', *Journal of International Business Studies* **20**, 3, pp 411–436.

Dymsza W A (1984) 'Future international business research and multidisciplinary studies', *Journal of International Business Studies*, Spring/Summer, pp 9–13.

Edgar D and Taylor S (1996) 'Strategic management research in hospitality: from slipstream to mainstream?', *Fifth Annual CHME Research Conference*, Nottingham Trent University, Nottingham, 10–11 April, pp 264–278.

Fox M F and Faver C A (1982) 'The process of collaboration in scholarly research', *Scholarly Publishing*, July, pp 327–339.

Getty J M (1996) 'The use of peer evaluations in group projects: benefits, applications, and what students think of them', *Hospitality and Tourism Educator* **8**, 4, pp 44–46.

Gibbs G and Habeshaw T (1994) *Preparing to Teach*, Cromwell Press: Melksham.

Grau J and Borchgrevink C P (1993) 'Doing more with less: utilizing hidden resources', *Hospitality and Tourism Educator* **5**, 4, pp 67–69.

Hofstede G (1994) *Cultures and Organizations: Intercultural Cooperation and its Importance for Survival. Software of the Mind*, HarperCollins: London.

Ingram H (1996) 'Clusters and gaps in hospitality and tourism academic research', *International Journal of Contemporary Hospitality Management* **8**, 7, pp 91–95.

Jolliffe L B (1991) 'Industry's team approach to classroom projects', *Journalism Educator*, Summer, pp 15–24.

King A R and Brownell J (1966) *The Curriculum and the Disciplines of Knowledge*, John Wiley: New York.

King M, Lee R, Piper J and Whittaker J (1991) 'Researching in teams: lessons from experience' in Smith N C and Dainty P (Eds) *The Management Research Handbook*, Routledge: London.

Laverty S E and Fawcett S L (1987) 'The dynamics of a group project', *Business Education* **8**, 1, pp 36–42.

Litteljohn D (1990) 'Hospitality research: philosophies and progress' in Teare R, Moutinho L and Morgan N (Eds) *Managing and Marketing Services in the 1990's*, Cassell: London.

Przeclawski K (1993) 'Tourism as the subject of interdisciplinary research' in Pearce D G and Butler R W (Eds) *Tourism Research: Critiques and Challenges*, Routledge: London and New York.

Riddick C C, De Schriver M and Weissinger E (1984) 'A methodological review of research in the *Journal of Leisure Research* from 1978 to 1982', *Journal of Leisure Research* **16**, 4, pp 23–28.

Roper A, Brookes M and Hampton A (1997) 'The multi-cultural management of international hotel groups', *International Journal of Hospitality Management* **16**, 2, pp 147–159.

Schratz M (1993) 'Crossing the disciplinary boundaries: professional development through action research in higher education', *Higher Education Research and Development* **12**, 2, pp 131–142.

Shaw M and Nightingale M (1995) 'Scholarship reconsidered: implications for hospitality education', *Hospitality Research Journal* **19**, 1, pp 81–93.

Slattery P (1983) 'Social scientific methodology and hospitality management', *International Journal of Hospitality Management* **2**, 1, pp 9–14.

Taylor S and Edgar D (1996) 'Hospitality research: the emperor's new clothes?', *International Journal of Hospitality Management* **15**, 3, pp 211–227.

Thompson A A and Strickland A J (1996) *Strategic Management: Concepts and Cases*, Richard D. Irwin: New York.

Tomkins C, Rosenberg D and Colville I (1991) 'The social process of research: some reflections on developing a multi-disciplinary accounting project' in Smith N C and Dainty P (Eds) *The Management Research Handbook*, Routledge: London.

Toulmin S (1972) *Human Understanding*, Vol. 1, Clarendon Press: Oxford.

Usunier J C (1993) *International Marketing: A Cultural Approach*, Prentice Hall International: Hemel Hempstead.

Van Doren C and Heit M (1973) 'Where it's at: a content analysis and appraisal of the *Journal of Leisure Research*', *Journal of Leisure Research* No. 5, pp 67–73.

Webster F (1995) 'And finally... ', *Research Forum* **2**, 7, Oxford Brookes University: Oxford.

Whitley R (1984) *The Intellectual and Social Organization of the Sciences*, Clarendon Press: Oxford.

5 Survey research

ROSEMARY LUCAS

Introduction

The *Collins Concise Dictionary* (1989) lists nine definitions for the term 'survey' and two for 'research'. While six of the survey definitions can be discounted because they are associated with surveying land, vessels and buildings, this still leaves a broad range of meanings for the term 'survey' (p. 1310):

- to view or consider in a comprehensive or general way;
- to examine carefully, as or as if to appraise value;
- to run a statistical survey on (incomes, opinions, etc.);
- a comprehensive or general view;
- a critical, detailed, and formal inspection.

Research is defined in the dictionary as a 'systematic investigation to establish facts or collect information on a subject' or 'to carry out investigations into (a subject, etc.)' (p. 1098). Put simply, when the two meanings are combined, survey research is about looking and searching in order to answer a question, or a series of questions. The research question(s) can be closely focused or broadly drawn and may seek to test a hypothesis or a set of hypotheses. The main research methods or measurement tools are the questionnaire or interview, or both. Data, structured to a greater or lesser extent depending on the method and the topic, will be collected from a proportion or sample of a particular population. Results will be analysed and interpreted. If the research question(s) has/have been well framed, and the research carefully planned and executed, the findings will not only provide answers to the question(s) but will also contribute to knowledge in general.

There is a wide range of topics of an external nature that can be addressed by the survey method (Alreck and Settle, 1985; Moser and Kalton, 1986; de Vaus, 1996). Demographics, lifestyle, attitudes and images of customers are of major interest to hospitality organisations operating in highly competitive markets. Organisations need to know how age, sex, marital status and family status affect their business, both now and in the future. The lifestyle of a local population is of interest to a restaurateur planning to open a new restaurant in the city suburbs. The attitudes of children to food and particular types of meals are a necessary consideration to the producers and deliverers of school meals. Images that people have of particular resorts and holiday destinations are crucial to the successful marketing of package holidays (see also Urry, 1990).

The Handbook of Contemporary Hospitality Management Research, Edited by Bob Brotherton.
© 1999 John Wiley & Sons Ltd.

Surveys may also address internal matters. Organisations seeking to enhance their performance by improving managerial decision-making and behaviour would need to understand the process by which people evaluate things and associated behavioural patterns. Trying to improve job satisfaction and motivation among the workforce would entail finding out more about why people do, or do not do, certain things. Understanding affiliations in the workplace may hold the key to improving teamworking.

Finding out, explaining and evaluating tangible and intangible facts may be required for market research purposes, for policy and planning purposes and for academic research. The process is one of linked steps. It is crucial, regardless of the purpose for which a survey is undertaken, that information needs are closely defined and that the value of the data sought is considered (Fink, 1995c). Similarly, resources need to be assessed and the choice of data collection method must be appropriate. Using the wrong tools for a job that is not clearly understood will lead to inaccuracy and disaster, and will almost always produce data that are neither reliable (contain random error) nor valid (measure something else) (see Oppenheim, 1992).

Surveys, like any other research methods, have benefits and drawbacks (see Figure 5.1). They are efficient because a relatively small sample can elicit data about a larger population. By combining different modes of enquiry, such as telephone, postal survey and face-to-face interviewing, they are versatile (Alreck and Settle, 1985). They can be comprehensive and flexible in regard to simple or complex data requirements. Survey research can be customised to fit resource allocation (time and money). However, planning and managing the process can be difficult and time-consuming, questionnaire

Advantages

Postal survey	Face-to-face interview	Telephone interview
Can be cheap	Flexible	Cheap
Results can be generalised	Insightful	Quick
Structured process	Qualitative results	Large samples
Large samples	Interaction with respondent	Reach widely dispersed sample
Large amounts of data	Probing	Can elicit sensitive data
Data easily classifiable	Low non-response bias	Interaction with respondent
Quantifiable results	Visual stimuli	Low non-response bias

Disadvantages

Postal survey	Face-to-face interview	Telephone interview
Detailed administration	Time-consuming	Small amount of data per respondent
Potential for low response	Small samples	Partial picture
Partial picture	Interviewer training required	Some interviewer bias
May only be indicative	Interviewer bias	Some interviewer training
No interaction with respondents	Data recording and classification problematic	
	Logistical considerations	

Figure 5.1 Comparison of survey methods

surveys can be expensive, and results will never be perfect, although careful planning should prevent the occurrence of major errors and oversights. Finally, results should never dictate decisions. Rather, they should be viewed as representing another body of evidence which has to be evaluated in light of more practical, commonsense, considerations.

Methodological nature of the approach

The main principles outlined in this chapter centre on the nature of the survey method, planning the research, how to obtain samples, framing questions, choosing scaling techniques, questionnaire design and construction, the mechanics of conducting surveys, and processing and analysing the data.

The nature of the survey method

Survey research relies on the use of questionnaires and interviews, on their own or together. Each is based on a series of questions—the instruments of interrogation—which are structured and designed to gather data in order to answer the central research question which may be expressed as an aim or hypothesis (Marshall, 1997). Questionnaires are usually more structured than interviews. The interview allows for greater flexibility through the use of more open-ended questions while allowing the interviewer to probe the respondent to gain deeper insight into a particular response. Ideally, questionnaires can generate large-scale, quantitative, unbiased and readily classifiable data. Interviews are generally regarded as a more in-depth, qualitative mechanism which are more open to bias and where the classification of data is more problematic (see Figure 5.1).

As a general rule questionnaires will be issued to participants either by postal survey or directly by the researcher or a third party. In these cases respondents will be issued with instructions to aid the task of self-completion. The visual appearance, length, layout, complexity and appearance of the questionnaire will influence the response rate. Postal surveys based on random sampling rarely elicit more than a 30% response rate even where a pre-paid envelope is enclosed for return of the questionnaire (Alreck and Settle, 1985; Veal, 1992). Higher response rates would result from a questionnaire issued directly to a clustered sample, for example specific groups of households, customers or employees. Large amounts of data can be obtained relatively cheaply by the questionnaire method, although a high non-response rate will mean wasted costs.

Interviews can be conducted face-to-face in person, or over the telephone. Some personal interviews are used to administer a structured questionnaire, making them little more than an extension of the questionnaire method as relatively little interviewer discretion is required. More in-depth, semi-structured interviews both require and allow the interviewer to play a more active role, acting in effect as an interpreter. While this can lead to probing opportunities not presented by the use of questionnaire surveys, it can also introduce more bias into the data collection process. Such interviews are the most expensive method in terms of time and resources, particularly if large numbers of cases are involved. Telephone interviews are quick and cheap and can prove highly efficient and effective. Relative anonymity and reduced intimacy may make it easier to elicit sensitive information.

In practice these modes of data collection are often combined in various ways. Researchers might interview managers in an organisation in order to frame questions for a questionnaire about performance management. Non-respondents to a postal questionnaire survey might be telephoned a few weeks after distribution to remind them to respond, thus presenting the opportunity for obtaining additional semi-structured feedback. Respondents to a questionnaire survey who have indicated a willingness to be interviewed could be interviewed initially by telephone and subsequently in person. Survey research will be enhanced by a using a multi-mode approach, with the exercise of a little pragmatism and imagination.

Planning the research

While the research planning process is addressed as a series of sequential events (see Figure 5.2), in practice these events neither follow a predetermined logic, nor are they mutually exclusive. Rather they are closely interrelated and interdependent stages. Planning the research route is more circuitous than straight but, nevertheless, should always be systematic.

Having a clear purpose for the research expressed as one or more aims and objectives and/or a hypothesis or a set of hypotheses is an essential starting point. Without this driving force the research is bound to fail. Defining the high-priority information needed to answer the fundamental research question(s) will affect the choice of method. It is important to bear in mind that the survey method is simply not appropriate or, at best, inadequate in many cases. Many behavioural issues, such as ascertaining what managers and employees do, are more richly informed by participant observation.

Tangible resource constraints encompass direct costs for labour, materials and data processing, and are important determinants of the research scope and its parameters. It is very easy to underestimate the resources required, particularly where these are intangible, most particularly related to time. The survey method must be appropriate to time, cost and sample size considerations. Issues of validity and reliability are also important (Fink, 1995c). These factors will influence the choice of survey method—questionnaire or interview—and the most appropriate way of processing the data obtained.

Resources, among other things, will determine whether the survey seeks to obtain a large amount of data from a small sample or a small amount of data from a large sample. The crucial primary question has to be 'what is the size of the responding population required?'. The secondary question relates to the ability of either the questionnaire or the interview approach to encompass the types of questions, with appropriate scales of measurement, required to generate categorical or continuous data that can be classified. A cost allowance must be made for the large proportion of questionnaires that will not be returned. The feasibility of obtaining the necessary cooperation of respondents to be interviewed also has to be considered.

The planning process will entail a series of draft outlines in timetable format that will eventually become the final research plan. With the best will in the world, this will never remain absolute and will become subject to some change as the research exercise develops. The skill is in ensuring that the degree of modification is small rather than large.

FORMULATE AIM/HYPOTHESIS
↓
DEFINE INFORMATION NEEDS
↓
SELECT METHOD
↓
CHECK/ALLOCATE RESOURCES
↓
DETERMINE SAMPLE SIZE
↓
DRAW UP TIMETABLE
↓
SELECT SAMPLE
↓
FRAME QUESTIONS
↓
SELECT SCALING TECHNIQUES
↓
DESIGN RESEARCH INSTRUMENT
↓
PILOT QUESTIONNAIRE/INTERVIEW
↓
RECORD DETAILS
↓
ANALYSE DATA
↓
REFINE TOOLS
↓
CARRY OUT MAIN SURVEY
↓
PROCESS RESULTS
↓
ANALYSE RESULTS
↓
PRODUCE FINDINGS
↓
PRODUCE REPORT

Figure 5.2   The research process

How to obtain samples

Most researchers do not have the luxury of being able to sample a complete population, however defined, mainly because of high costs and resource implications. For these and other reasons, the UK Census of Population is conducted only every ten years. Other national statistical surveys in the UK take place more frequently on the basis of sampling.

The principle of sampling is to select a part of some population to represent the whole population, whatever that may be. Careful selection is necessary both to minimise bias and error, and to maximise reliability and validity (Alreck and Settle, 1985; Moser and Kalton, 1986; Marshall, 1997). If a survey is reliable it is free from random error. For a survey to be valid it must measure only what it is supposed to measure.

Where sampling error occurs there are differences between the sample data and the population data purely by random chance. Sampling bias would arise, for example, where only the views of young males were sought in relation to the desirability of women working full-time or part-time.

For statistical purposes, random sampling is most desirable (Alreck and Settle, 1985; Moser and Kalton, 1986). The researcher can compute and report confidence intervals indicating the probability that the population average is within a certain range around the sample average. It is also possible to calculate and report the statistical significance of relationships between survey items based on the probability that such relationships would result only from sampling error. Where random sampling is not used none of the statistical coefficients or values would be accurate or legitimate. The sampling frame lists all the units in the population. Random sampling could be made on the basis of selecting every tenth name on a list, for example. The actual starting point should also be chosen randomly and could be any of the first ten names on the list.

Alternatively it may be necessary to identify a particular population who possess the information sought. Stratified sampling would split the population into segments and sample a different proportion of each; for example in the hotel industry there are considerably fewer national hotel companies than independent, single proprietorships. Cluster sampling selects respondents in close proximity to one another and can save on costs. For reasons amplified below, there are many factors about the hospitality industry which point researchers to the alternatives of stratified sampling or cluster sampling.

Framing questions

Referred to above as the instruments of interrogation, questions are the core matter of survey research regardless of the mode of inquiry used. Questions necessarily have to be sufficiently focused to obtain the required answer, succinct to minimise error and bias, and uncomplicated to aid common understanding (Alreck and Settle, 1985; Oppenheim, 1992; Fink, 1995b).

If questions incorporate too much jargon or complex, multi-purpose sentences, and are not focused on the views of the respondents (as opposed to what someone else might think), the data collected will detract from the research aims. So questions must be specific, be applicable to the survey population, and avoid terms that could be ambiguous (for example, dinner can denote lunch or an evening meal).

The wording of questions can also predicate respondents of a particular predisposition to respond with bias. Structured questions, and the scaling techniques applied to them, are crucial to obtaining the required response. Response is much harder to control in interviews because of a more unstructured environment which increases the potential opportunities to deviate from a fixed notion of response.

Choosing scaling techniques

Numbers are much easier to manipulate than words. A numeric database saves both time and money as well as ensuring greater accuracy, reliability and validity. For these reasons, it is best to use questions that ask the respondent to make a choice within a category or along a spectrum. Scales are then coded with numbers, thus aiding data processing. There are techniques to manipulate responses to questions which generate unstructured answers, including ethnographic packages such as NUD.IST (available from Sage Publications) which allow data to be structured by the use of systematic indexing.

Some questions require only simple structuring in terms of a yes, no or don't know response, whereas others are more complex, requiring particular scaling techniques to be applied. There are many conventional scale types and there is seldom a clear-cut choice between them. Many are based on the principle of five, where a middle value is complemented by more extreme values (positive and negative) on either side. Scales can be used for single or multiple responses (see Alreck and Settle, 1985; Moser and Kalton, 1986).

One of the best known scaling techniques is the *Likert scale* which is used to obtain respondents' degree of agreement or disagreement to a stated opinion or attitude.

> *Example*: The introduction of a National Minimum Wage will lead to higher unemployment. (Strongly agree, agree, neutral, disagree, strongly disagree).

The *verbal frequency scale* seeks to ascertain how often people do something.

> *Example*: How often do you go to your local fast-food restaurant? (Always, often, sometimes, seldom, never).

An *ordinal scale* would list alternatives in an ordered sequence.

> *Example*: On which day(s) do you usually have a takeaway meal? (Monday, Tuesday, Wednesday, Thursday, Friday, Saturday, Sunday).

Forced ranking asks the respondent to make a choice in order of priority.

> *Example*: Please rank the beverages listed below in order of preference. 1 indicates first preference, 2 indicates second preference and so on. (Tea, coffee, water, fruit juice, carbonated soft drinks).

Paired comparison measures simple choices between alternatives.

> *Example*: For each pair of beverages listed below, please tick the one you most prefer. (Tea/coffee, tea/water, coffee/water).

The *horizontal, numeric scale* measures from extremely unimportant (1) to extremely important (5), usually on a five-point scale. The respondent is given a number of statements that relate to a topic and must allocate a score to each statement.

> *Example*: How important are the following to you when choosing wine to accompany a meal? (Price, country of origin, colour, type of meal).

Alternatively, the *comparative scale* compares one object with one or more others.

> *Example*: Compared to the last time you ate in this restaurant, how is the quality of service? (Very superior, quite superior, about the same, quite inferior, very inferior).

The *semantic differential scale* lists a series of bipolar adjectives in order to elicit an opinion. There can be more than five choices within the two extremes.

> *Example*: Please circle the number on each line to show your opinion of Glug lager. (Good 1 2 3 4 5 6 7 bad; expensive 1 2 3 4 5 6 7 inexpensive).

The *adjective checklist* selects broad information about how a topic is described and viewed.

Example: Please circle the words that describe your job. (Fulfilling, interesting, low-paid, boring, routine, challenging, dangerous, tiring).

Stapel scaling refines how well these adjectives describe the job.

Example: Please select a number on the scale (1, 2, 3, 4, 5, 6, 7) to show how well each word describes your job and write it next to the word. (Difficult, strenuous, pleasant).

The *fixed sum scale* identifies proportions of a resource or activity from several choices.

Example: In your last five visits to the fish and chip shop, how many times did you purchase the following items? Make sure the total equals five. (Plaice, haddock, cod, pie, sausage).

Questionnaire design and construction

Questionnaires contain three main sections. The opening part usually asks general questions that should not be sensitive or threatening or else the respondent may not go on. The main, and largest, part will contain sections of questions that follow a logical and meaningful sequence. The concluding part can contain more sensitive issues and biographical details. By then the respondents' trust will have been gained so they are more likely to cooperate. Even if they do not answer a few of these questions, you will still have the bulk of the data to work with.

Ordering the sections in the main body of the questionnaire will take some time, involving many drafts, and can be organised by topic, content or scaling technique. Avoid too much branching, which is where there is a subsidiary question to a main question or where a particular response requires the respondent to skip some questions. Where this is unavoidable give clear instructions either to skip questions 5, 6 and 7 or to go direct to question 8, for example. Instructions in all cases should be kept as clear and simple as possible.

It may be desirable to allow for the transcription of precoded responses onto boxes located in a separate column on the right-hand side of each page. This is usually headed 'for office use only'. This makes it easier for whoever is processing the data, although careful precoding can allow the data to be read straight from the questionnaire (see Bourque and Fielder, 1995).

The principles of questionnaire design also apply to interviews. For telephone interviews the design of the questionnaire will be similar to that used in postal surveys. For personal interviews, the questionnaire format can be semi-structured, structured or a combination of both (see Alreck and Settle, 1985; Moser and Kalton, 1986; Frey and Mertens Oishi, 1995).

The mechanics of conducting surveys

The key issue in surveys, by both questionnaire and interview, is to get the respondent to participate. You want them to complete the questionnaire promptly and not throw it in the bin or place it in the pending tray. You want them to agree to respond and then to respond freely.

In all surveys, it is good practice to pilot the questionnaire or interview (Oppenheim, 1992; Fink, 1995c). This may be necessary to test the feasibility of the research and the usefulness of the instrument. Adjustments are always almost necessary, and some fine-tuning will improve the quality of the data collected in the main survey.

In postal surveys it is easy to underestimate the time it takes to address and fill envelopes with the appropriate contents. Appearance and quality of the research packet, the envelope and contents which arrive at the office of a busy manager, are very important. The covering letter, preferably no longer than one side of letter-headed paper, should anticipate any questions the recipient might have and summarise them. The questionnaire should have an attractive front page, be well laid out and user friendly. It should contain assurances about confidentiality where this is required, and the name and telephone number of a person to contact in case of queries. Thank the respondent for his or her time and effort in helping with the research. Enclosing a pre-paid envelope will help increase the response rate.

Make a numbered checklist of participants. These numbers can be entered at the top of the questionnaire so that a record can be kept of who has responded or of those questionnaires which are returned marked 'gone away'. The timing of the survey will also affect the response rate. This is something which is particularly problematic in the hospitality industry and is discussed below. It may also be appropriate to have a cut-off date. Most of the questionnaires that are going to be returned come back within four weeks. Contacting non-respondents after a couple of weeks can help increase response rates. Keep spare questionnaires as people often claim not to have received one in the first place. Speaking to potential respondents in this way helps bind them to the process. It may be desirable to make contact in this way before the questionnaire is issued in order to obtain the name of the appropriate person (Alreck and Settle, 1985).

In the interview the role of the interviewer is axiomatic. However, acting as an interpreter can give variation to results obtained from the same set of questions which are more difficult to classify than scaled questionnaire data. Interviews can be conducted by the researcher(s) or contracted out. If the latter option is to be used, it is probably most appropriate where the data is highly structured or simple. Any experienced researcher will know that close, hands-on involvement makes a qualitative difference to a project.

Interviewers must be trained in the how and why of interviewing (Frey and Mertens Oishi, 1995). They need to know how to make contact, greet, interrogate, record and terminate proceedings. They need to know why it is important to follow instructions and procedures. Even so, error can creep in at a number of points for many reasons. The likelihood of increased response bias can occur in the recording and interpretation of the interviewees' responses. Appropriate timing, location, the avoidance of interruptions and distractions, and effective recording methods make for more effective interviewing (see Alreck and Settle, 1985; Moser and Kalton, 1986; Oppenheim, 1992).

Processing and analysing the data

With a well-structured, designed and scaled questionnaire, files for data processing can be set up in advance. There are a number of statistical packages available, among which SPSS is widely used. It is advantageous to know what statistical tools are available when designing the questionnaire. Summaries of these tools are given below in order to aid understanding of some practical research applications discussed in the next part of the chapter (see also Alreck and Settle, 1985; Fink, 1995a).

Statistical analysis makes sense of large amounts of data, assuming of course that scaling techniques are reliable and valid. Statistics can be used to describe categorical distributions, for example the sex of respondents in a frequency table. Continuous distributions, such as hourly pay rates, can be represented by the most typical value (median or mean), the amount of deviation from it (range, minimum/maximum, standard deviation) and the form of the distribution (skewness, kurtosis). Statistics can also show the relationship between independent variables (the variable causing the other to vary or be affected) and dependent variables (the variable being affected or likely to vary). Here variables must be identified as either categorical or continuous so that the appropriate statistical test can be chosen. If necessary, continuous variables can be categorised into categorical groups for analysis.

Cross-tabulation of two categorical variables is the most commonly used method of testing relationships between an independent variable (such as gender) and a dependent variable (such as work sector). Significance is measured by the chi-squared test. Analysis of variance (ANOVA) measures the statistical significance between two or more means, while the differences between two mean values are measured by the t-test. ANOVA would be used to assess the effect of an independent categorical variable (such as gender) on a dependent continuous variable (average customer spend in public houses over time). By looking at mean values alone which show a difference in spend between males and females, it would not be possible to tell if this was because the entire population of males and females differed or the sample happened to select those of one sex who spent more. Multivariate analysis of variance (MANOVA) would be used where there were multiple independent and dependent variables. Where a survey obtains ratings or continuous data from two or more variables from the *same* respondents, the paired t-test is used.

Regression and correlation analysis measure the relationship between two continuous variables. Correlation analysis between two variables generates a single value, the correlation coefficient, and the degree to which they are related. The sign (+ or −) and value (between one and zero) of the correlation coefficient unlock the nature of the relationship. In a positive (direct) relationship the variables move in the same direction, while in a negative (inverse) relationship the variables move in the opposite direction. Closer to zero shows a lesser relationship, while closer to one indicates a greater relationship. Regression analysis requires one variable to be independent and the other to be dependent. Simple linear regression is used where there is one independent variable. Multilinear regression is necessary where there is more than one independent variable, such as a survey in fast-food seeking to determine the effect of age and income on levels of customer spend.

It is quite difficult to measure the relationship between an independent continuous variable and a categorical dependent variable. ANOVA can be used where it is impossible to identify whether variables are independent or dependent. Otherwise discriminant analysis is necessary. This measures the degree and direction of influence that the independent variable has on the dependent variable and to obtain an equation that would permit the researcher to predict the category of the dependent variable when it is not known, based on the known value of the independent variable. Discriminant analysis is analogous to regression analysis except that the dependent item is in categories or groups rather than in continuous numeric form.

Applications in hospitality management research

Survey research has potentially wide-ranging application in the hospitality industry for the purposes of market research, policy and planning matters and academic study. Two aspects of survey research are considered here. The first is national surveys, in the main government sponsored statistical surveys, which provide important data about the industry and its consumers. These may be collated on an international or a European basis. Surveys conducted by academics, which may utilise one or more survey methods (telephone interviews, questionnaire surveys and face-to-face interviews) in more focused research studies, are considered in greater detail. These are not meant to be a systematic representation of all survey research, but have been chosen, mainly from recent international journals, to illustrate a variety of examples of survey research in the UK and worldwide.

Before specific examples of survey research are discussed, it is necessary to make some general observations about the industry and attendant difficulties which impinge on the survey method and process. While most of the principles of survey research outlined above are within the commonsense grasp of any researcher, there are some fundamental difficulties associated with using this method that are universal, particularly in regard to their effect on sampling organisations, management and workers. By contrast, customer research can often be more straightforward.

Some fundamental research problems

The first problem is one of definition. At a macro-level there is no consensus on what the hospitality industry represents. In Britain the industry has been divided into two sectors (Hotel and Catering Training Company (hereafter HCTC), 1994). The commercial sector, employing 1.3 million workers, includes hotels, guest houses, restaurants, cafés, snack bars, public houses, clubs and contract catering. The catering services sector, employing 1.1 million workers, includes tourism and travel catering, catering in education, medical and other health services, public administration and national defence, retail distribution, personal and domestic service, and industrial and office catering.

Is hospitality the same as hotel and catering and how do these constructs relate to tourism? At a micro-level what is an hotel? Is the provision of accommodation enough to bind a 500-room luxury hotel with extensive restaurant, retailing and leisure services, to a 50-room budget hotel without other services, or to a restaurant with ten rooms? No comprehensive membership lists exist of either hospitality or hotels even if they could be defined. There are lists of quoted hotel companies (Slattery, Feehely and Savage, 1994) and the major hotel chains (Business Ratio Plus, 1994) which make them more easily identifiable and, for other reasons, make them the most likely object of hospitality research studies.

The second problem concerns the structural characteristics of the industry and its component parts. In spite of the high public profile of organisations such as Hilton, Granada, McDonald's and Whitbread, most businesses are small, self-managed proprietorships and dispersed on a wide geographical scale. Large organisations are more visible, identifiable and influential, making them more likely to be researched, yet they often represent only the tip of the iceberg. While the commercial sector of the British hospitality industry comprised 264,500 establishments in 1991 (HCTC, 1994), McDonald's had a mere 13,000 outlets in 53 countries (Royle, 1995).

The large number of workplaces in the industry and within its main, highly diverse, subsectors creates a third difficulty. Any attempt at conducting a survey based on a random sample of the British hotel industry would be very expensive in terms of time and resources, even if it were possible to design an appropriate sampling frame. This problem has universal application. In the United States, Tse (1991: 63) noted: 'The size and diversity of the restaurant industry, with ownership from small single purpose proprietorships to strategic business units of conglomerates, makes it virtually impossible to randomly sample. In addition, there is no single published comprehensive listing of all operators in the industry.' Diversity and instability of product means, in practice, that most sampling will have to be stratified and/or clustered.

The fourth problem centres around the nature of hospitality organisations and the effect this has on the management structure and attitudes. Management is a fragmented process and largely *ad hoc* (Lucas, 1995). Many managers are 'hands-on' and active rather than administrators, and pay little attention to keeping records of data that might be required. In some units the concept of a single manager in overall charge is inappropriate because there are several shift managers to cover round-the-clock operations. Also, there often seems to be undue sensitivity about disclosing company information, for example pay, even among some of the larger concerns. All these factors contribute to the likelihood of a lower level of response in surveys because it will be difficult to find managers who are willing to cooperate and participate. It is even more difficult to obtain organisations' consent to approach members of their workforce below management levels. This has contributed to an imbalance of research evidence about managers with relatively little research being directed at, in effect, most of the hospitality workforce who are non-managerial.

A fifth problem relates to the inherent instability of the industry. Labour turnover is high; many personnel do not remain with the same organisation for long, so establishing contact points with individual general managers or personnel managers can be difficult. Numbers employed vary according to season. The life cycle of small firms is often short. Patterns of ownership among the larger concerns are also highly changeable. This makes for difficulties in conducting longitudinal studies. Some businesses open only for a particular season, or may be extremely busy at particular times of the year, making the timing of surveys difficult to put into effect.

Some of these difficulties exist outside hospitality but nowhere near to the same degree, intensity or extent. Even national government surveys may be 'incomplete' because they do not sample firms that are small, not registered for Value Added Tax (VAT), or workers who are not part of a Pay-As-You-Earn (PAYE) personal taxation scheme. In sum, researching in hospitality is more difficult and challenging than in most other employment sectors.

Using international and national statistics

A number of organisations collate national statistics on an international or European basis, including the Economist Intelligence Unit (for example, Todd and Mather, 1995) and Euromonitor (for example, Euromonitor, 1995). One particular problem is the huge variation in the definition of terms and data collection methods used at country level. Individual sources are often contradictory. Rapid changes in economies make all information quickly obsolete, rendering them, at best, only broad indicators of trends and developments.

In the UK the Office for National Statistics (ONS), formed in April 1996 from the merger of the Central Statistical Office and the Office of Population Surveys, is the government agency responsible for the collection, analysis and dissemination of many of the UK's economic, social and demographic statistics, including the Retail Price Index, trade figures and labour market data. The ONS works with others in the Government Statistical Service (GSS) located throughout many government departments.

While national statistics make possible the identification of trends, there are also problems related to obtaining a consistent, longitudinal series because there are necessarily changes to, and in, the way data are collected and manipulated (Levitas and Guy, 1996). For example, the Standard Industrial Classification has been revised four times since its inception in 1948, most recently in 1992. They can also exclude important sections of the hospitality industry. For example, it is estimated that around one-fifth of part-time workers are outside the scope of the New Earnings Survey (NES) and there are limited data on male part-time workers.

National surveys can, nevertheless, be used to answer a number of research questions about the structure of the industry, the nature of the workforce, and characteristics of consumers. They also provide national and regional control data against which the findings of other studies may be compared. Much of the data can now be accessed from databases.

The Hospitality and Training Foundation (formerly the HCTC) and its predecessors have done sterling work in analysing national data from surveys such as the Census of Employment (CE), the Labour Force Survey (LFS) and the NES in order to shed light on these points. Others have used similar data to report on pay and employment trends in hospitality (Lucas, 1995). O'Connor (1993) has used the Family Expenditure Survey (FES) to identify average household spend on meals, variations by income group and expenditure on meals out, and the UK National Accounts to chart patterns of expenditure on meals and accommodation over time. The Business Monitor catering and allied trades inquiry covers all businesses registered for VAT, and regularly collects data on financial turnover, capital expenditure and the number of businesses (as opposed to establishments).

However, the ONS does not hold a monopoly over national surveys. Other national surveys that can be used to inform hospitality research include UK Tourism Statistics (British Tourist Authority), which contain some hotel data, and the Workplace Industrial Relations Survey (WIRS) (Lucas, 1995). The British Hospitality Association (BHA) has carried out surveys of pay and benefits in conjunction with Greene Belfield-Smith, the consultancy division of Touche Ross.

Telephone interviews

At its most simple level, Marketpower, on behalf of the *Caterer and Hotelkeeper*, conducted a telephone survey of 502 respondents (92 owners and 410 non-owners) about issues that 'caterers believe need to be tackled', including a National Minimum Wage (NMW) (Huddart, 1997). The instrument was a one-page structured questionnaire incorporating four questions. These questions were simple, using yes or no, the Likert scale, the horizontal, numeric scale, and branching (should a minimum wage be set and, if so, what should the rate be?). This enabled relatively large numbers of simple data to be produced, including the proportion of those in favour of a NMW and an average acceptable figure for it.

More complex approaches are possible. Using semi-structured interviews, 200 hospitality managers were asked 'How do you determine whether you've done a good job?' (Peacock, 1995). From this a seven-fold classification was derived in order to determine what constitutes a successful hospitality manager. Peacock was able to criticise those who perceive quality and success as 'objective criteria subject to quantifiable analysis' (Peacock, 1995: 48). His argument is that these terms are grounded in the perception of the user which make them too subjective to be quantified in any meaningful way.

Jones and Ioannou (1993) interviewed managers responsible for administering guest surveys in the top 20 international hotel chains in the UK. Against their list of 11 essential criteria of guest satisfaction measurement, they were able to identify that the chains' adopted methods were 'at best unreliable and at worst actually misleading' (Jones and Ioannou, 1993: 31).

Lammont and Lucas (1997a, 1997b, 1997c) conducted semi-structured interviews lasting around 30 minutes with 200 school students who had indicated a willingness to be interviewed during a questionnaire survey. Many of the students were working part-time in hospitality, and data were collected about their work experiences, providing a valuable insight into young people's orientations to work, coping with the service encounter and (tacit) skills development. These data, interpreted ethnographically, have helped redress the dearth of data about the hospitality workforce, flexible labour strategies and the nature of the employment relationship.

Questionnaire surveys

This is by far the most common method used, often in combination with a separate interview programme. Interviews may be precursors to a questionnaire survey in order to frame the research question(s) and appropriate instrumentation (Gilpin and Kalafatis, 1995) or to refine areas for the survey (Glancey and Pettigrew, 1997). Interviews may be follow-up procedures to validate questionnaire responses (Lucas, 1997) and/or to obtain more qualitative data (Commission for Racial Equality (CRE), 1991; Hallam and Baum, 1996). Many have used existing models to guide their inquiry, such as Hofstede's four dimensions of cultural difference (Huang, Huang and Wu, 1996) or TORA (theory of reasoned action) (Buttle and Bok, 1996), while others have been more inductive with the view to developing models (Lucas, 1997).

Postal questionnaire surveys have sought to address a wide range of topics which are difficult to classify. In 1996 most of the *International Journal of Hospitality Management* and *International Journal of Contemporary Hospitality Management* articles had what may be termed an organisational focus, dealing with issues of strategy and policy. Examples include contracting out food and beverage operations (Hallam and Baum, 1996), environmental policy (Brown, 1996), franchising (Hing, 1996a, 1996b), marketing (Buttle and Bok, 1996), budgeting (Schmidgall, Borchgrevink and Zahl-Begnum, 1996), service quality (Harrington and Akehurst, 1996; Huang, Huang and Wu, 1996), labour turnover (Hartman and Yrle, 1996) and pay policy (Radiven and Lucas, 1996). Some, necessarily, drew data from customers (Buttle and Bok, 1996; Kim, 1996). Issues in small firms were addressed in a complete edition of the *International Journal of Contemporary Hospitality Management* (Volume 8, No. 5). More details of the range of subjects can be gleaned from the bibliography and references to this chapter.

Other studies have focused more specifically on managers and management practice, such as hotel financial controllers (Burgess, 1996) and transformational leadership (Tracey and Hinkin, 1996). Management education has been addressed by Purcell and Quinn (1996) and Eves *et al.* (1996). Employee surveys seem less common, but include employee commitment (Smith, Gregory and Cannon, 1996).

Questionnaires can be administered by interview (Honggen and Huyton, 1996; Huang, Huang and Wu, 1996). Self-completion surveys feature most prominently. These may be conducted by post (CRE, 1991; Tse, 1991; Bach and Pizam, 1996; Brotherton and Shaw, 1996; Harrington and Akehurst, 1996; Hing, 1996a, 1996b; Radiven and Lucas, 1996; Schmidgall, Borchgrevink and Zahl-Begnum, 1996) or in person by the researcher(s) (Brymer, Perrewe and Johns, 1991) or be distributed directly by the organisation (Hse, Smith and Finley, 1991; Gilpin and Kalafatis, 1995; Smith, Gregory and Cannon, 1996; Tracey and Hinkin,. 1996). These non-postal distribution methods may also be combined (Lucas, 1997).

In many cases, problems relating to sampling have been emphasised. Having found it impossible to sample randomly in the restaurant industry, Tse arrived at 'sample selection by necessity' (Tse, 1991: 63). In order to encompass different types of hotel, Brown (1996) used three strata to design a sampling frame, the *Caterer and Hotelkeeper*'s top and medium hotel groups plus independent hotels drawn from the English Tourist Board and Scottish Tourist Board lists. Similar attempts to stratify hotels in this way have been used by Hallam and Baum (1996), Harrington and Akehurst (1996) and Radiven and Lucas (1996).

Others have concentrated on the 'luxury' end of the hotel sector, regarding it as more likely to produce a good response. However, Brotherton and Shaw (1996) report how promises to participate from leading quoted companies were not delivered. Hotel companies tend to predominate in hospitality research, for a range of reasons, including relative ease of sampling. Lynch (1996) has noted that the bed and breakfast sector, representing one-third of serviced accommodation in England and Wales and over 50% in Scotland, has yet to become the object of a large-scale published academic research survey. Other sampling frames can be identified more easily and lend themselves to random sampling, such as colleges providing hospitality education (Eves *et al.*, 1996) and law enforcement agencies (Bach and Pizam, 1996).

The response rate of postal surveys can vary from as little as 10% in a random sample of 600 Scandinavian hotels (Schmidgall, Borchgrevink and Zahl-Begnum, 1996) to 65% in a clustered sample of small hotels in a Scottish town, where precursor interviews had been used to refine the questionnaire (Glancey and Pettigrew, 1997). The CRE's (1991) survey of the largest hotel groups about recruiting ethnic minorities, which achieved a 90% response rate, is highly unusual. Most other response rates have tended to fall between the level of 20% and 40% (Tse, 1991; Bach and Pizam. 1996; Burgess, 1996; Hing, 1996a).

By contrast, Brymer, Perrewe and Johns (1991) achieved a 100% response rate by administering questionnaires to managers during staff meetings. Similarly high response rates were achieved by Lucas (1997) by administering questionnaires to students during class contact time. Other high response rates in the order of 80% have also been reported where questionnaires were distributed by the organisation.

Sample sizes varied enormously. The two largest samples were 7504 employees at 94 lodging properties (Smith, Gregory and Cannon, 1996) and 712 alumni of all UK hospitality courses in 1989 (Purcell and Quinn, 1996). Most samples were below 100 with the smallest standing at nine (Hing, 1996a). The use of particular statistical tests requires several hundred responses if they are to be meaningful.

A wide variety of analysis techniques have been deployed, with some of the methods outlined above having been refined by particular researchers. Behavioural research requires more sophisticated analysis, and many articles contain highly complex statistical data, an approach which seems to be more frequently utilised by researchers in the USA and the Far East than in the UK.

Face-to-face interviews

The review of the two international hospitality journals found relatively few cases of interviews being used as the sole method (Baloglu and Uysal, 1996; Ineson, 1996; MacVicar and Rodger, 1996; Morrison, 1996; Watson and D'Annunzio-Green, 1996). The first of these, a German study, was a large-scale household interview of 1212 tourists possessing certain attributes in order to identify marketing opportunities for overseas pleasure travellers. The large sample size enabled the use of canonical correlation analysis using MANOVA. Watson and D'Annunzio-Green (1996) interviewed 22 staff in two hotels in order to explore implementing cultural change through human resources.

In the previous year Lashley's (1995) and Royle's (1995) use of this method was facilitated and dependent on a close relationship between the researchers and McDonald's. The McDonald's studies were about involvement and empowerment, with sample sizes of 15 (managers) and 64 (a cross-section of employees including top management).

Conclusions and issues for future research

Survey research embraces two distinct but related methods. Questionnaire research is a practical and efficient way of generating large amounts of quantitative data, and can be highly effective for market research, policy and planning purposes and academic research. Its main limitation, and where its validity is criticised by those favouring more qualitative methods, comes from the use of statistical data to try to establish causal relationships. Interviews allow more scope for interpretation, yet the more qualitative approach may produce data that is neither valid nor reliable.

Survey research remains a widely used research method in hospitality with the potential to be taken forward in academic research, particularly in mixed methodology research. Large aspects of the industry are still relatively 'uncharted waters' making 'fact finding' survey research a useful precursor to more qualitative exercises. Even so, the fundamental research problems outlined in this chapter should not be used as an excuse for inaction. Rather, they should be recognised and tackled systematically, with full and frank acknowledgment of any limitations. This may engage researchers in more innovative and imaginative survey research than is envisaged by some textbooks, but without it we cannot hope to extend knowledge, discourse and debate.

If a little contentious, it is argued that survey research as conceived above is of value. It is certainly more valuable than research which, though technically and statistically correct, does not address a meaningful research problem. Hospitality literature about high labour turnover and some other behavioural issues is becoming jaundiced by a lack of imagination that precludes the search for new approaches and perspectives. Survey research in itself will not necessarily achieve this, but it may provide the starting point for new discoveries. We should all have a shot at being empiricists.

References and bibliography

Alreck, P.L. and Settle, R.B. (1985) *The Survey Research Handbook*. Homewood, Illinois: Richard Irwin.

Bach, S. and Pizam, A. (1996) 'Crimes in hotels'. *Hospitality Research Journal* **20**, 2, 59–76.

Baloglu, S. and Uysal, M. (1996) 'Market segments of push and pull motivations: a canonical correlation approach'. *International Journal of Contemporary Hospitality Management* **8**, 3, 32–38.

Bourque, L.B. and Fielder, E.P. (1995) *How to Conduct Self-Administered and Mail Surveys*. London: Sage.

Brotherton, B. and Shaw, J. (1996) 'Towards an identification and classification of Critical Success Factors in UK Hotels Plc'. *International Journal of Hospitality Management* **15**, 2, 113–136.

Brown, M. (1996) 'Environment policy in the hotel sector: "green" strategy or stratagem?'. *International Journal of Contemporary Hospitality Management* **8**, 3, 18–23.

Brymer, R.A., Perrewe, P.L. and Johns, T.R. (1991) 'Managerial job stress in the hotel industry'. *International Journal of Hospitality Management* **10**, 1, 47–58.

Burgess, C. (1996) 'A profile of the hotel financial controller in the United Kingdom, United States and Hong Kong'. *International Journal of Hospitality Management* **15**, 1, 19–28.

Business Ratio Plus (1994) *Industry Report—the Hotel Industry*. London: ICC Group Publication.

Buttle, F. and Bok, B. (1996) 'Hotel marketing strategy and the theory of reasoned action'. *International Journal of Contemporary Hospitality Management* **8**, 3, 5–10.

Commission for Racial Equality (1991) *Working in Hotels*. London: CRE.

de Vaus, D.A. (1996) *Surveys in Social Research*, 4th edition. London: UCL Press.

Euromonitor (1995) *Consumer Catering in Eastern Europe*. London: Euromonitor.

Eves, A., Corney, M., Kipps, M. and Noble, C. (1996) 'Nutrition education of caterers in England and Wales'. *International Journal of Hospitality Management* **15**, 1, 69–86.

Fink, A. (1995a) *How to Analyze Survey Data*. London: Sage.

Fink, A. (1995b) *How to Ask Survey Questions*. London: Sage.

Fink, A. (1995c) *The Survey Handbook*. London: Sage.

Fowler, F.J. and Mangione, T.W. (1990) *Standardized Survey Interviewing*. London: Sage.

Frey, J.H. and Mertens Oishi, S. (1995) *How to Conduct Interviews by Telephone and in Person*. London: Sage.

Gilpin, S. and Kalafatis, S.P. (1995) 'Issues of product standardisation in the leisure industry'. *Service Industries Journal* **15**, 2, 186–202.

Glancey, K. and Pettigrew, M. (1997) 'Entrepreneurship in the small hotel sector'. *International Journal of Contemporary Hospitality Management* **9**, 1, 21–24.

Hallam, G. and Baum, T. (1996) 'Contracting out food and beverage operations in hotels: a comparative study of practice in North America and the United Kingdom'. *International Journal of Hospitality Management* **15**, 1, 41–50.

Harrington, D. and Akehurst, G. (1996) 'Service quality and business performance in the UK hotel industry'. *International Journal of Hospitality Management* **15**, 3, 283–298.

Hartman, S.J. and Yrle, A.C. (1996) 'Can the hobo phenomenon help explain voluntary turnover?'. *International Journal of Contemporary Hospitality Management* **8**, 4, 11–16.

Hing, N. (1996a) 'Maximizing franchisee satisfaction in the restaurant sector'. *International Journal of Contemporary Hospitality Management* **8**, 3, 24–31.

Hing, N. (1996b) 'An empirical analysis of the benefits and limitations for restaurant franchisees'. *International Journal of Hospitality Management* **15**, 2, 177–188.

Honggen, X. and Huyton, J. (1996) 'Tourism and leisure: an integrative case in China'. *International Journal of Contemporary Hospitality Management* **8**, 6, 18–24.

Hotel and Catering Training Company (1994) *Catering and Hospitality Industry—Key Facts and Figures*. London: HCTC.

Hse, C.H.C., Smith, F.M. and Finley, D.H. (1991) Restaurant managers' learning styles and their implications. *International Journal of Hospitality Management*, **10**, 1, 81–94.

Huang, J.-H., Huang, C.-T. and Wu, S. (1996) 'National character and response to unsatisfactory hotel service'. *International Journal of Hospitality Management* **15**, 3, 229–244.

Huddart, G. (1997) 'Industry says yes to minimum wage'. *Caterer and Hotelkeeper*, 2 January, p. 5.

Ineson, E.M. (1996) 'Selection for vocational courses—a consideration of the viewpoint of graduate employers'. *International Journal of Contemporary Hospitality Management* **8**, 6, 10–17.

Jones P. (1996) 'Hospitality research—where have we got to?'. *International Journal of Hospitality Management* **15**, 1, 5–10.

Jones, P. and Ioannou, A. (1993) 'Measuring guest satisfaction in UK-based international hotel chains: principles and practice'. *International Journal of Contemporary Hospitality Management* **5**, 5, 27–31.

Kim, H.-B. (1996) 'Perceptual mapping of attributes and preferences: an empirical examination of hotel F&B products in Korea'. *International Journal of Hospitality Management* **15**, 4, 373–392.

Lammont, N. and Lucas, R.E. (1997a) Tacit skills in service work. Paper presented to the 2nd Conference on Graduate Education and Graduate Students' Research in Hospitality and Tourism, Las Vegas, January 1997.

Lammont, N. and Lucas, R.E. (1997b) 'Getting by' and 'getting on' in service work. Paper presented to the 15th Annual International Labour Process Conference, University of Edinburgh, March 1997.

Lammont, N. and Lucas, R.E. (1997c) Context-dependent skills as coping mechanisms. Paper presented to the British Sociological Association Annual Conference, University of York, April 1997.

Lashley, C. (1995) 'Empowerment through delayering: a pilot study at McDonald's restaurants'. *International Journal of Contemporary Hospitality Management* **7**, 2/3, 29–35.

Levitas, R. and Guy, W. (eds) (1996) *Interpreting Official Statistics*. London: Routledge.

Lucas, R.E. (1995) *Managing Employee Relations in the Hotel and Catering Industry*. London: Cassell.

Lucas, R.E. (1997) 'Youth, gender and part-time work: students in the labour process'. *Work, Employment and Society* **11**, 4, 595–614.

Lynch, P. (1996) 'The Cinderella of hospitality management research: studying bed and breakfasts'. *International Journal of Contemporary Hospitality Management* **8**, 5, 38–40.

MacVicar, A. and Rodger, J. (1996) 'Computerized yield management systems: a comparative analysis of the human resource management implications'. *International Journal of Hospitality Management* **15**, 4, 325–332.

Marshall, P. (1997) *Research Methods*. Plymouth: How To Books Ltd.

Morrison, P. (1996) 'Menu engineering in upscale restaurants'. *International Journal of Contemporary Hospitality Management* **8**, 4, 17–24.

Moser, C.A. and Kalton, G. (1986) *Survey Methods in Social Investigation*. Aldershot: Gower.

O'Connor, J. (1993) 'A review of dining-out patterns in Britain'. *International Journal of Contemporary Hospitality Management* **5**, 5, 3–9.

Office for National Statistics (1996) *New Earnings Survey 1996 Part A*. London: ONS.

Oppenheim, A.N. (1992) *Questionnaire Design, Interviewing and Attitude Measurement*. London: Pinter Publications.

Peacock, M. (1995) '"A job well done": hospitality managers and success'. *International Journal of Contemporary Hospitality Management* **7**, 2/3, 48–51.

Phillips, P. (1996) 'Strategic planning and business performance in the quoted UK hotel sector: results of an exploratory study'. *International Journal of Hospitality Management* **15**, 4, 347–362.

Purcell, K. and Quinn, J. (1996) 'Exploring the education–employment equation in hospitality management: a comparison of graduates and HNDs'. *International Journal of Hospitality Management* **15**, 1, 51–68.

Qu, H. and Cheng, S.Y. (1996) 'Attitudes towards utilizing older workers in the Hong Kong hotel industry'. *International Journal of Hospitality Management* **15**, 3, 245–254.

Radiven, N. and Lucas, R.E. (1996) 'Wages council abolition and small hotels'. *International Journal of Contemporary Hospitality Management* **8**, 5, 10–14.

Royle, T. (1995) 'Corporate versus societal culture: a comparative study of McDonald's in Europe'. *International Journal of Contemporary Hospitality Management* **7**, 2/3, 52–56.

Salant, P. and Dillman, D.A. (1994) *How to Conduct Your Own Survey*. New York: John Wiley & Sons.

Schmidgall, R.S., Borchgrevink, C.P. and Zahl-Begnum, O.H. (1996) 'Operations budgeting practices of lodging firms in the United States and Scandinavia'. *International Journal of Hospitality Management* **15**, 2, 189–203.

Slattery, P., Feehely, G. and Savage, M. (1994) *Quoted Hotel Companies: the World Markets 1994, 8th Annual Review*. London: Kleinwort Benson Research.

Smith, K., Gregory, S.R. and Cannon, D. (1996) 'Becoming an employer of choice: assessing commitment in the hospitality workplace'. *International Journal of Contemporary Hospitality Management* **8**, 6, 3–9.

Taylor, S. and Edgar, D. (1996) 'Hospitality research: the emperor's new clothes?'. *International Journal of Hospitality Management* **15**, 3, 211–228.

Todd, G. and Mather, S. (1995) *The International Hotel Industry*. London: The Economist Intelligence Unit.

Tracey, J.B. and Hinkin, T.R. (1996) 'How transformational leaders lead in the hospitality industry'. *International Journal of Hospitality Management* **15**, 2, 165–176.

Tse, E. C.-Y. (1991) 'An empirical analysis of organizational structure and financial performance in the restaurant industry'. *International Journal of Hospitality Management* **10**, 1, 59–72.

Urry, J. (1990) *The Tourist Gaze: Leisure and Travel in Contemporary Society*. London: Sage.

Veal, A.J. (1992) *Research Methods for Leisure and Tourism*. London: Pitman.

Watson, S. and D'Annunzio-Green, N. (1996) 'Implementing cultural change through human resources: the elusive alchemy?'. *International Journal of Contemporary Hospitality Management* **8**, 2, 25–30.

6 Experimental research

PETER JONES

Introduction

Unlike many forms of research, experiments and experimentation have a high profile in popular culture. For over a century people have associated this methodology with the stereotypical 'mad scientist', such as Dr Jekyll and Dr Frankenstein exemplified in stories and films. This perception of experimentation as somehow being dangerous has been further reinforced by the disclosure that various kinds of experimental research have been conducted on humans without their knowledge. For instance, there were studies in the 1950s relating to radioactivity and biological and chemical weapons. More recently, there has been widespread popular concern about some forms of experimentation related to the use of laboratory animals for cosmetics and medical research and the so-called genetic engineering of plants and animals. Therefore, it is clear that the ethics of this type of research are of particular concern.

This chapter reviews the nature of experimentation. It identifies two basic types of experimental research, one of which tends to be used in the physical or natural sciences and the other in social sciences. It proceeds to review examples of both types of experimentation in the context of hospitality. It also discusses the role of this kind of research, and associated ethical considerations, and concludes with some reflection on the future of this particular methodology in hospitality research.

The experimental method in context

It should be remembered that there is no common agreement between scientists—both natural and social—on the nature of reality, the structure of science, and scientific values. These differences are more than those existing between researchers from different disciplines, such as biologists or chemists, psychologists or sociologists. They are fundamental philosophical differences based on alternatives. In some cases a research methodology may be used in the context of a number of such paradigms, but experimental research is firmly rooted within an 'objective–rationalistic' paradigm. This view is derived from the natural sciences and has been applied in the social sciences. This view of the world, in which experimentation is regarded as 'the' valid method, is based on the idea that reality is concrete and conforms to certain universal laws. Indeed, subjects (the 'thing' being studied) respond in predictable ways to external forces or stimuli. Hence it is possible to both observe and measure this reality. Therefore it

The Handbook of Contemporary Hospitality Management Research, Edited by Bob Brotherton.
© 1999 John Wiley & Sons Ltd.

follows that this paradigm is only concerned with 'manifest phenomena', i.e. those it is possible to observe and measure. But even within this paradigm there is some debate as to the nature of the scientific method (and hence experimentation).

Magee (1973: 37) states: 'The way scientists were supposed to proceed was first systematically described by Francis Bacon'. This method is known as induction and is summarised in Table 6.1. Magee goes on to say: 'The scientist begins by carrying out experiments … to make carefully controlled and meticulously measured observations [at the frontier of knowledge]. He [*sic*] systematically records his findings [so that] he and other workers in the field accumulate a lot of shared and reliable data. As this grows, general features begin to emerge and individuals start to formulate hypotheses—statements of a lawlike character which fit all known facts and explain how they are causally related to each other. The scientist tries to confirm his hypothesis by finding evidence which will support it'. This scientific method of induction is the 'hallmark of science … and the criterion of demarcation between science and non-science'. However, the scientific method, as conceived prior to the 1930s, has been critiqued as fundamentally flawed.

Hume was the first to provide such a critique. Firstly, this scientific method assumes that because some 'laws' have been found to hold good in the past, it does not logically follow that they will in the future. Secondly, it is not entirely logically valid to suppose that a general statement can be made on the basis of observed instances, however many there may be. Russell (1961: 699) wrote: 'Hume has proved that pure empiricism is not a sufficient basis for science'. So the whole of science is based on the principle of induction which is known to be logically flawed. Despite this, 'science delivers the goods'. To Hume's critique, Popper adds the view that it is naive to assume that scientists have no theory before they begin to observe, since 'observation is always selective. It needs a chosen object, a definite task, an interest, a point of view, a problem … [inevitably] they are interpretations in the light of theories' (Magee, 1973: 58). Magee (1973) believes that 'Popper's seminal achievement has been to offer an acceptable solution to the problem of induction'. Popper starts with the 'logical asymmetry between verification and falsification'. If, as Hume suggests, no number of observed instances proves a hypothesis beyond doubt, just one observed instance that disproves it is enough—'in logic therefore a scientific law is conclusively falsifiable although it is not conclusively verifiable'. The methodological implication of this is the view that theories should be developed as clearly as possible and be deliberately tested for refutation. Thus, Popper believed that no theory could ever be relied upon to be the final truth. Popper's method is compared with the traditional view of scientific method in Table 6.1.

Table 6.1   Alternative views of scientific method

Traditional view	*Karl Popper's view*
Observation and experiment	Problem—often rebuff to existing theory
Inductive generalisation	Proposed solution, i.e. new theory
Hypothesis	Deduction of testable propositions
Attempted verification of hypotheses	Observation tests, i.e. attempts at refutation
Proof or disproof	Provisional knowledge
Probabilistic knowledge	

Source: Based on Magee (1973: 56).

In the context of this debate about scientific method, experimental research is therefore designed either to 'prove' a theory or to 'refute' a theory. The value of experimentation in particular, compared with other methods, is that by controlling the conditions under which the research is undertaken, it should be possible to clearly demonstrate *cause* and effect. 'Experiments have the advantage, at least in principle, of permitting causal inference to be made with more confidence' (Lewis-Beck, 1993: ix). Just how experimental researchers go about designing experiments to achieve the highest possible level of confidence in the results, and hence inference about cause and effect, is explained in the next section.

The experimental research method

Experimentation entails the intervention of the researcher, usually to introduce the independent variable, with a high degree of control over the dependent variable (or subject). Two key aspects of experimentation are manipulation and control. Manipulation refers to the ability to organise and arrange the subject so that it can be measured or observed and be subjected to an external stimulus. Control is concerned with ensuring the elimination or isolation of all other stimuli (or variables) other than those being manipulated. A test of such control usually means that the experiment is designed in such a way that it may be repeated at another time or in another place and still produce the same results. Such replication of a study, both at another time and in another place, is a key aspect of *reliability*.

There are two experimental methodologies: *experimental* and *quasi-experimental*. The former tends to be used in the natural sciences, whereas the latter is mostly used in the social sciences. True experiments are essentially laboratory based due to the high level of control that good experimentation requires. This methodology is particularly suited to the physical sciences. Hence of most interest to hospitality researchers is experimental research relating to food, drink and technology. Highly controlled experiments can be conducted as many times as is necessary to ensure a high degree of reliability. However, the fact that such research is conducted under laboratory conditions may reduce some aspects of its external validity.

In the social sciences, laboratory experimentation has the weakness that population validity may be low and 'ecological validity' is weak (Gill and Johnson, 1991: 43). To overcome these weaknesses, it is possible to conduct quasi-experiments in real-life situations, albeit that doing so presents different problems. Bell (1993: 9) writes: '... the experimental style does allow conclusions to be drawn ... if the design is sound, but in social sciences generally, large groups are needed if the many variations and ambiguities involved in human behaviour are to be controlled. Such large-scale experiments are expensive to set up and take more time ...'. In most cases, quasi-experimental research in hospitality is concerned with either customer or employee behaviour.

Experimental research in laboratories is an appropriate setting for basic research seeking knowledge about nature simply for the sake of understanding it better. Quasi-experimentation in natural settings is more appropriate for applied research, which seeks knowledge to improve conditions under which people work and live. The latter can also be used to assess the external validity of laboratory-based experimental research findings.

Key features of the experimental research methodology

To ensure findings that are valid, objective and replicable, both types of experimental research design entail four basic steps (Gill and Johnson, 1991). Firstly, the *dependent variable* needs to be identified, i.e. the phenomenon whose variation the research aims to explain. Secondly, the *independent variables* need to be postulated, i.e. those factors that may cause or explain the changes in the dependent variable. Thirdly, these variables need to be operationalised so that the impact the controlled changes to the independent variables have on the dependent variable can be observed, and hence inference about cause and effect can be drawn. Finally, every effort should be made to ensure that *extraneous variables*, i.e. other factors that might cause variation in the dependent variable, are neutralised or at least controlled for. Experimental research therefore presents six challenges, three relating to definition of variables and three to observation and measurement, as follows:

- definition of dependent variable
- definition of independent variable(s)
- definition of extraneous variable(s)
- observation, manipulation and measurement of dependent variable
- observation, manipulation and measurement of independent variable(s)
- observation, manipulation and measurement of extraneous variable(s).

Clearly the simplest form of experimental design would involve the manipulation of just one independent and one dependent variable. However, in the social sciences in particular, most studies involve multiple variables. 'The multiple independent variable study is the most common, although multiple dependent variable designs have become quite popular in recent years' (Spector, 1993: 5).

All true experiments must involve at least two groups, one of which would be the 'control' group against which experimental groups could be compared. One-group designs are therefore non-experimental or quasi-experimental, although they are widely used in the social sciences. One-group and multiple group designs are compared in Figure 6.1.

A *one-group design* takes a sample of the subject or subjects, measures the characteristic under research prior to the introduction of the independent variable, introduces this external stimulus, and measures the subject afterwards to identify if any changes in the characteristic have taken place. This is illustrated in Figure 6.1(a). This simple 'test–retest' method presents the problem that it is often difficult to ensure that the changes which are measured or observed derive solely from the introduction of the stimulus, as there is no control to compare with. One-group designs can also include interrupted *time series studies*, which take measurements on more than one occasion, and *correlational studies*, which measure a number of variables. Such designs are often applied to real-world, non-laboratory-based studies, and are therefore quasi-experimental.

The simplest form of multiple-group design is the *two-group (post-test only) design* in which the sample is divided into two groups—the experimental group who will be subject to the stimulus and the control group who will not, as illustrated in Figure 6.1(b). This typical research design involves the establishment of a *control* in order to identify how the subject or dependent variable behaves without the introduction of the stimulus or independent variable, followed by the introduction of each independent

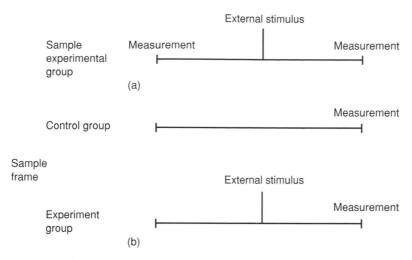

Figure 6.1 Two approaches to 'experimental' design: (a) test–retest; (b) control group design

variable being researched in order to measure its effect on the dependent variable. The argument which supports this approach is that if there is a change to the experimental group, but no change to the control group, this can only be due to the stimulus. The potential flaw in this argument (especially in social science) is the difficulty of creating two identical groups in the first place.

Throughout this process every effort would be made either to remove all extraneous variables or to ensure that they remained constant. One key aspect of this is the extent to which the subject, if human beings, may introduce extraneous variables into the study. Hence the selection of subjects is a challenge. In those studies involving human subjects, the most common experimental design—the *random groups design*—generates separate groups of subjects by randomly assigning them to groups, the control group and one or more experimental groups. This is known as an independent groups design. This random assignment into groups is meant to ensure the groups are equivalent at the start of the study, so that any change in the experimental group can be assigned to the introduction of the independent variable, rather than any inherent characteristics of the group itself.

Despite the random assignation of subjects, there is still the possibility that one group is inherently different from the other. To overcome this an alternative, a *within-subjects design*, can be adopted. In this case, all the subjects are exposed to all the treatments in the experiment. For instance, in a food-tasting experiment all participants might taste all the foods. The challenge to overcome in this design is the problem of *differential transfer*, i.e. when the preceding condition affects performance under the following condition. This concept is further explored later in this chapter when two specific examples of this, the Hawthorne effect and the Stroop effect, are discussed. There are two ways of overcoming this problem. The complete within-subjects design administers the conditions several times to each subject, changing the order in which they are administered, whilst the incomplete within-subjects design assigns one group of subjects one possible combination and other groups other combinations.

Sound experiments must be internally valid, externally valid, reliable and sensitive. An *internally valid* experiment provides an unambiguous interpretation of the outcome—usually achieved by the control of extraneous variables and the use of equivalent groups. *External validity* refers to the idea that results can be generalised. As will be seen, this is a limitation of the experimental method, usually overcome by replication or the 'continuity assumption'. To ensure *reliability* so that the results from one study are generalisable, either the study can be replicated in a number of different settings on a number of different occasions, or the continuity assumption is made that 'behaviour is continuous across time, subjects and settings unless there is a reason to believe otherwise' (Zechmeister and Shaughnessy, 1994: 84). A *sensitive* experiment is one that that is likely to detect the effect of an independent variable even when that effect is small.

There are a number of factors which may threaten the internal validity of experiments, especially quasi-experiments. These have been described by Campbell and Stanley (1966) as follows:

- *history*: the occurrence of an event other than the treatment which produces a change in subjects' behaviour
- *maturation*: changes in subjects associated with the passage of time
- *testing*: the effect of testing on subsequent tests
- *instrumentation*: changes over time in the instruments used to measure behaviour
- *selection*: differences that exist between different groups of subjects from the outset of the experiment
- *interaction between selection and history*: an event occurring in time may have a greater effect on one group than on another
- *interaction between selection and maturation*: subjects in one group may mature at a faster rate than those in another
- *interaction between selection and instrumentation*: test instruments may be less sensitive to changes in performance of one group than those of another.

The procedure that attempts to control for these threats (with the exception of the last three listed above) is *non-equivalent control group design*. This involves a comparison between control and experimental groups that have been established on some basis other than by random assignment. Nonetheless both groups should be as similar as possible.

These issues of internal validity, external validity, reliability and sensitivity have led to the development of many different experimental research designs. As will be seen, each of these has its advantages and disadvantages.

Alternative experimental designs

So far, only the two-group design measuring two variables, one independent and one dependent, has been considered. This was illustrated in Figure 6.1(b). Alternatively, it can be illustrated as follows:

$$X_1 O_1$$

$$X_2 O_1$$

where X represents the two groups and O observation of the dependent variable. However, it was stated earlier that experiments may be designed with multiple groups and be designed to measure more than one dependent or independent variable.

The *multiple-group post-test design* is an extension of the two-group design. It measures the dependent variable (O) and any number of levels of the independent variable (X), as follows:

$$X_1 O_1$$

$$X_2 O_1$$

$$...$$

$$...$$

$$X_n O_1$$

This design has the advantage that not only can more levels of independent variable be compared, but also more than one control group could be used. Measuring a number of levels of the independent variable is usually desirable if it is measured on a continuous basis rather than discretely. Where an independent variable is discrete, or no inference about an independent variable measured on a continuous scale is made beyond that which is measured in the study, the variable is said to have a *fixed effect*. If, however, the independent variable is continuous and conclusions are made concerning values not included in the design, it is said to be a *random effect*. In the case of continuous variables, the researcher can choose whether to regard the effect as fixed or random. For instance, a study might be designed to determine the effect on purchase preferences of two radio advertisements lasting ten seconds and thirty seconds. If the thirty-second advertisement were to influence preferences more than the ten-second spot, this could be treated as a fixed effect or a random effect. If fixed, the only conclusion drawn is that the thirty-second spot was more effective than the ten-second one. No inferences are drawn about the general influence of radio advertisement length on preferences. If random, such inferences would be drawn, however, and it would be suggested that a twenty-second advertisement would be more effective than a ten-second one, and so on. Since it is extremely unwise to assume a random effect on the basis of only two levels, the multiple-group post-test design enables random effects to be measured more precisely.

The *multiple-group pre-test/post-test design* addresses a different problem than the simple two-group design illustrated in Figure 6.1(b). The simple design assumed that the two groups were identical without pre-testing to check this was so. The multiple-group pre-test/post-test design measures the dependent variable before as well as after the treatment, as follows:

$$O_1 X_1 O_2$$

$$O_1 X_2 O_2$$

$$...$$

$$...$$

$$O_1 X_n O_2$$

This design clearly demonstrates the level of the dependent variable both before and after the treatment, and hence establishes a more reliable baseline for comparing alternative treatment effects.

A further extension of the pre-test/post-test design is the *multiple-group time series design*. This takes multiple measures of the dependent variable both before and after treatment. One example, for two groups and six measures, may be illustrated as follows:

$$O_1 O_2 O_3 X_1 O_4 O_5 O_6$$

$$O_1 O_2 O_3 X_2 O_4 O_5 O_6$$

The major advantage of this design is that it takes into account any trend in the dependent variable before and after treatment. It also facilitates understanding of whether treatment has a short-term or long-term effect.

So far, the designs identified have involved only a single independent variable; however, most experimental designs have several independent variables and it is their combined effect that is of interest. This requires a *factorial design*, which may also range from simple to complex.

The simplest factorial design is the *two-by-two factorial design*. This consists of two independent variables, each taking on two levels or values. The design is structured so that both levels of one independent variable are associated with the two levels of the other. This makes four such combinations possible, as follows (with post-testing only):

$$X_1 + X_a O_1$$

$$X_1 + X_a O_2$$

$$X_2 + X_a O_3$$

$$X_2 + X_a O_4$$

In such studies, it is desirable that each combination has the same number of subjects in order to simplify the analysis.

A special case example of the 2×2 factorial design is the *Solomon four-group design*. This is particularly used if there is concern about instrument reactivity, i.e. that subjects may be sensitised by pre-testing, thereby making them more receptive to the experimental treatment than they would otherwise be. In this design only half the subjects are pre-tested. It may be illustrated as:

$$O_1 X_1 O_2$$

$$X_1 O_2$$

$$O_1 X_2 O_2$$

$$X_2 O_2$$

It is generally agreed that 'this design is quite powerful and sees too little application in the social sciences' (Lewis-Beck, 1993: 54). Bryman (1989: 85) speculates that the reason for this is that 'the requirement of two additional groups simply in order to test for the effects of pre-testing necessitates the diversion of time and money which many investigators seem unprepared to countenance'.

However, for independent variables measured on continuous scales, the 2×2 factorial design can be expanded to any number of levels of this variable within practical limits. This design is referred to as the *M × N factorial design*.

Furthermore, factorial designs are not limited to two independent variables, and so *higher-order factorial designs* may be used. Theoretically any number of independent variables could be included, so long as it is possible to collect data on a sufficient number of subjects. In practice, the number of subjects is finite and interpretation of complex designs becomes extremely challenging. For instance, a four independent variable design has 16 combinations ($2 \times 2 \times 2 \times 2$), and so needs four times as many subjects as a 2×2 design. If the same four independent variable design had three levels per variable, there would be 81 combinations, needing hundreds of subjects to complete the study.

Limitations

The experimenter must always be aware of the possibility of measurement error. Measurement is the process of assigning numbers to variables in order to enable analysis. Variables may either be discrete or continuous. A *discrete variable* is one which clearly belongs to a category. For instance, gender normally has two categories—male or female. A *continuous variable* is one that may be measured along a continuum, such as length, time or a score on a test of some kind. Generally a low score for the continuous variable indicates less of the characteristic.

Measurement is taken with an *instrument*, which is a device or procedure for enabling quantification of the results. Instruments are of many kinds such as thermometers, stop watches, pencil and paper test, or a survey scale. All instruments are likely to have error associated with them. Such error can occur due to limits in the precision of the instrument, misuse by the person using the instrument, or error in the design of the instrument itself. Experimental researchers seek to minimise such errors, but cannot eliminate them altogether. Two types of error may occur. *Random error* is non-systematic and is as likely to affect results in one direction as in the other. Such error reduces the precision of measurement but does not necessarily invalidate the results. *Bias error* occurs when the error tends to be in one direction, and hence results are distorted. Bias can be removed only by redesigning the instrument or procedures.

Probably the most challenging aspect of experimental research is to ensure that the dependent variable is reacting to the independent variable, without the intervention of extraneous variables. This has been found difficult to avoid in a number of instances, which have come to be recognised as specific syndromes. For instance, there is the so-called *Hawthorne effect* deriving from the early studies conducted into work behaviour by the researcher of that name. In the first study at the Western Electric Company, an experiment was designed to investigate the influence that lighting levels would have on productivity. A control group and an experimental group were established, but output increased in both groups, with that in the experimental group increasing with no direct relationship to the lighting level. It is assumed that this effect is due to the subjects being aware of the 'experiment' and responding to this rather than the independent variable under investigation. Likewise there is the *Stroop effect*, which arises when a higher perceptual process interferes with a lower process, discovered from a within-subjects experiment (see above). This is particularly relevant to hospitality researchers interested in the sensory evaluation of foods or drinks, since a visual cue may interfere with other sensory cues such as smell and taste. For instance, Pangborn, Berg and Hansen

(1963) showed that experienced wine tasters were influenced by the colour of the wine when evaluating its sweetness. An experimental study by Blackwell (1995) set out to demonstrate this. In her abstract (1995: 24) she describes 'how 48 subjects … were first instructed to describe the odour of six fruit solutions (the dependent variable), four of which were inappropriately coloured (the independent variable) … . The results indicated that the identification of fruit odours proves significantly more difficult when the colour of the solution is inappropriate'.

A major limitation of this research method (apart from the philosophical debate summarised in Table 6.1) is that results cannot be generalised beyond the specific settings of the study, even with replication or the continuity assumption. In other words, although it is likely that the results of tests conducted under experimental conditions will match results arising from non-experimental conditions, no one can ever be entirely sure. This is because the methodology is based upon the fundamental design principle of removing all extraneous variables. In reality, our ecosystem is based upon the multiple interaction of many, many variables. The world is not a laboratory; it is a highly interactive, dynamic environment. So, for instance, it can be hypothesised that two new food additives that were separately tested in a laboratory and found to be 'safe' for human consumption could be harmful when consumed together in real life. Even results from quasi-experimental studies (those conducted in the real world) cannot be successfully generalised, since it is almost impossible in this kind of research to completely remove extraneous variables—typically the surroundings or environment in which the research was conducted. Thus a study of queuing behaviour in one context, such as a bank, might lead to some conclusions about queuing behaviour in general, but these cannot begin to be substantiated unless behaviours in a number of settings other than a bank are researched.

The experimenter must also be alert to two factors that may distort results—demand characteristics and experimenter effects. *Demand characteristics* (Orne, 1962) refers to the way information, or 'cues', may be provided to subjects which modifies their behaviour so that they do what they believe the experimenter wants rather than what they would otherwise do. *Experimenter effects* (Rosenthal, 1976) occur when the experimenter's expectations lead to bias in the way the experimenter treats subjects in different groups or records the data. Experimental research design can overcome these challenges by the use of a placebo control or by double-blind procedures. A *placebo control* can be used in experiments such as drug trials, where substances are administered to subjects. In such studies, some subjects are given the drug or other active substance whilst others are given the placebo, an inert or inactive substance, without the experimenter knowing which subjects are receiving which substance. The *double-blind experiment* is one in which both the subject and the observer are kept unaware of what treatment (or stimulus) is being administered. Thus the experimenter asks someone to observe the experimental conditions without telling them what to expect.

Applications in hospitality research

In order to explore how this methodology is applied in the hospitality context, both types of experimental research will be considered in turn.

Experimentation

In hospitality, the most likely application of experimental research is in the general area of food, food science and nutrition. Such research is both 'pure' (usually conducted in universities or research institutes) and 'applied' (often conducted in industry). This natural science research can often be extremely valuable. For instance, in 1996 there was the largest ever single outbreak of food poisoning in the UK due to *E. coli* in Scotland. Earlier that year, Phillips and Roscoe (1996) reported on their experimental study of the 'Survival of *Escherichia coli* 0157:H7 in ground beef during normal cooking procedures'. They hypothesised that the dependent variable—contamination by *E. coli*—might be influenced by two independent variables—the raw state of burgers (frozen or thawed) and the thickness of burgers (regular or 'quarter-pounder'). Under laboratory conditions, designed to eliminate extraneous variables, they set aside some regular burgers and quarter-pounders as a control and deliberately contaminated a sample of burgers of each type with the pathogen. Both uncontaminated and contaminated burgers were cooked according to the manufacturer's instructions, some from the frozen state and some after thawing. They found that burgers from the control sample were uncontaminated, as was expected. Also the cooked regular burgers were uncontaminated, irrespective of their frozen or thawed state. Likewise both types of burgers that had been deliberately contaminated were found to be so in their raw state, as was expected, along with quarter-pounders that had been cooked from frozen or thawed. This experiment clearly demonstrated that the thickness of burgers could affect the elimination of contamination during cooking.

As well as conducting experiments on food and drink, laboratory experimentation can also be conducted on materials and machines. This type of research is most suitable for testing the safety of equipment. For example, automobiles are experimentally crashed to identify the impact on human beings, simulated by crash dummies.

The range of experimental studies that investigate foods, equipment or a combination of both is numerous. Experiments have been conducted into the effect of storage time and storage equipment on both raw materials and finished products (see, for instance, Chome *et al.*, 1995); consumer acceptance of more healthy ingredients or recipes (such as the study of low-fat pizzas by Brewer *et al.*, 1993); the effect of alternative cooking methods on foodstuffs, especially meat, fish and vegetables (exemplified by the Berry and Bigner (1995) study of using alternative pieces of equipment to cook steaks); the impact on cooked yield and quality of different cooking temperatures (see Hamouz *et al.*, 1995); and so on.

Although the emphasis of laboratory experimentation has been largely focused on food and technology, it can also be used to study human behaviour. Most studies of this type are based on a design that involves monitoring human response to audio and/or visual stimuli in the form of audio-taped or video-taped events. For example, Sparks and her colleagues have conducted a number of such experiments to investigate communication in the hospitality context (Sparks, 1994; Sparks and Bradley, 1997). In Sparks' (1994) study into the most appropriate communication style for hotel reservationists, audio tapes of a hotel booking being made by 'telephone' were used as the stimulus. One female and one male actor were used, each recording six scripted interactions. Three of these were convergent styles of communication (i.e. they used customer's name, sought customer's preferences, responded to information supplied by customer) and three were maintenance style (with no use of customer name and a standard dialogue). For each style, the actor recorded one highly competent version, a moderately competent version and a poorly conducted version. In total, 96 subjects were asked to listen in small groups to the tape and then rank each version of the booking on a set of 12 bipolar rating scales relating to service quality. They were also asked to rate the reservationist against six statements concerning the performance of the receptionist. In this study the dependent variable was the degree of effectiveness of the communication and the independent variables were the communication style and level of competency of the reservationist.

This study illustrates one further issue relating to experimental research, namely *bias in the selection of subjects*. The Sparks and Bradley (1997) study used 96 subjects, all of whom were university students. This is quite common in laboratory-based research that takes place in universities as there are lots of students available and they are often willing to participate. However, they may not be a representative sample of the population as a whole, as Bryman (1989: 87) comments that 'students tend to have a highly specific cluster of personal, attitudinal and socio-economic characteristics which differ from those of the wider population'. As well as trying to ensure the representativeness of the sample, there is also the related issue of how the subjects were obtained for the research. In some cases they may be volunteers, but there is evidence to suggest that people who volunteer to participate in such studies are not representative. Rosnow and Rosenthal (1997) who conclude that 'volunteers tend to be better educated, to have greater need for approval, to score higher on IQ tests, to be less authoritarian and to be better adjusted than non-volunteers'. If this is the case, this reduces the external validity of the study. Alternatively, the researcher may offer some inducement to subjects in the form of payment. This too may result in a biased sample and hence questionable results.

Quasi-experimentation

As well as testing the laboratory testing of technology, it can also be experimentally tested in the field. In most cases, such studies are concerned with the socio-technical interface, i.e. the way in which humans interact with the technology. An example of this kind of research is that conducted by Smith and Gregory (1996) into the efficacy of customer-activated terminals in quick-service restaurants. They hypothesised that such terminals could be used to increase sales and profitability (through suggestive selling), improve productivity, and heighten customer satisfaction. To test these hypotheses they used three burger restaurants in the same chain and geographic area. One was designated as a 'control', whilst two were 'test' restaurants in which terminals were installed. In all three restaurants data was collected relating to sales figures, average spend, order times, usage and labour statistics, and customer surveys were conducted at various times to measure customer satisfaction. The study then compared the data from the two test restaurants with that from the control.

Quasi-experimental research can be used to investigate both the physical behaviour of people and their mental processes. An example of this is the research that has been conducted into the so-called 'psychology of waiting lines' (such as Davis and Vollmann, 1990; Katz, Larson and Larson, 1991). More recently, Jones and Peppiatt (1996) conducted a quasi-experiment into queuing in a retail shop. In this study, the dependent variable, i.e. the difference between actual and perceived waiting times of people queuing, was measured by selecting customers at random and timing their actual wait time with a stop watch without their knowledge. The perceived wait time was established by asking customers, after the sales transaction was complete, the simple question 'How long do you think you have been waiting in the queue?'. Respondents were not told that their actual wait time had been measured. The possible extraneous variables which may have affected this study have been suggested from previous research (Davis and Vollmann, 1990), i.e. whether location would affect demographic profile of customers, whether weekdays would be different from weekends, and time of day. Likewise, the Katz, Larson and Larson (1991) study suggested that a clock can serve as an extraneous variable, affecting the accuracy of customers' perception. In the Jones and Peppiatt (1996) study, these variables were controlled for by using only one outlet, always at the same time of day, with no clock in the premises. However, it was also hypothesised that extraneous variables might also include the individual characteristics of the queuer, as suggested by Davis and Vollmann (1990) in relation to the demographic profile of the customer base.

The other queuing studies discussed above had largely assumed that the factors such as gender, age and residency did not affect the perception of wait times. In order to ensure that this was the case, a preliminary study of 100 subjects was undertaken to identify if there were differences in perception of wait time between sub-groups made up of males and females, of different age groups, and of local residents and visitors. This preliminary study also enabled the research design to be tested in the field to identify if it was feasible to measure actual times and if customers would respond to the questions in sufficient numbers to provide an adequate sample. Finally, the three independent variables were observed and where necessary manipulated. These were the hypotheses that unoccupied time feels longer than occupied time, solo waiting feels longer than group waiting, and new users feel they wait longer than repeat users. The first of these was tested by installing a television set in the shop as a distracter. The second was tested through observation of the queuer in terms of whether they were alone or with other people. And the third was established by asking the customers after the transaction an additional question relating to their frequency of use, i.e. whether they visited the shop every day, once or more than once a week, once or more than once a month, or whether it was the first occasion.

Another obvious application of experimental research in hospitality is in the area of productivity. However, there appear to have been no such studies conducted (see, for instance, Johns, 1996), or if they have been conducted the results have not been published. Some industry firms are, however, conducting investigations based around the classic techniques of work study and method study, although their results are not being published. For instance, Horst Schulze, the Chief Executive Officer of Ritz-Carlton Hotels, describes (AHMA, 1995) how his company 're-engineered' 18 different key tasks carried out in hotels that led to significant increases in productivity and cost savings.

Ethical considerations

As was commented on at the beginning of this chapter, experimental research involves a number of ethical considerations that are specific to this methodology. Such considerations largely arise out of how the subjects of the research are treated, against a background of the need to control the experiment and avoid extraneous variables affecting results. As a result, this type of research may be subject to governmental law and regulation, as well as institutional procedures designed to maintain high ethical standards. For instance, the American Psychological Association has published principles governing the conduct of experimental research with human and animal subjects.

Laboratory-based experiments researching new foods, drugs, additives, and so on, may involve the use of animals. Rodents, especially rats and mice, are the largest group of laboratory animals, but other species such as monkeys, cats, dogs and fish may also be used. For example, research on sugar substitutes used in soft drinks was conducted in this way: a control group of mice were kept under identical conditions to the experimental group, which was administered the additive. It was found that testosterone levels in the experimental group reduced relative to the control group, suggesting that this additive if taken in enough quantities would turn men into women! The concerns arising out of this kind of research range from those who believe that it is unethical, even immoral, to use animals at all for such experiments to the view that it is acceptable to use animals if they are specially bred for this purpose and/or do not suffer as a result of the experiment. Partly to address these concerns, most countries have laws and regulations that govern the treatment and care of animal subjects, designed to protect their welfare as far as possible.

Secondly, there is concern about the threat that may arise out of experiments into phenomena which may be harmful to the people and/or the environment. For instance, it may be reasonable to assume that not all new 'food' additives or products developed in a laboratory will prove to be safe for human consumption. Hence there is occasionally public, media and scientific concern that poor laboratory procedures or ineffective waste screening could release harmful materials into the environment and the food chain.

Finally, even materials that are deemed to be safe on the basis of experimental research are of concern to some special interest groups or pressure groups. Such concerns arise out of the limitations of the experimental method (discussed above), namely that results cannot be generalised. For instance, Nelson and Poorani (1997) discuss the challenges posed by genetically altered foods. They identify a number of different groups with concerns about this development, including consumers, animal rights activists, environmentalists and celebrity chefs. The concerns include the consumers' 'right to know' that they are eating genetically altered foods, the presence of new life forms in the ecosystem, the well-being of genetically altered livestock, and the impact on the environment of increased pesticide use to support genetically modified crop growth.

Similarly, as noted earlier, quasi-experimentation often involves studies of human behaviour without the knowledge of the participants. Even in studies where people are aware of the nature of, and willing participants in, the research, they are often not told or even misinformed as to the purpose of the study. This is clearly because the research depends on people behaving in as natural a way as possible and avoiding the Hawthorne effect. The ethical considerations here relate to the acceptability of studying people without their knowledge and consent, or of deliberately misinforming willing participants of the purpose of the research. Experimental researchers therefore weigh risks to the individual against the potential benefits to society as a whole. Major ethical issues involving research with human participants include those associated with determining the nature and degree of risk to the participants, obtaining informed consent (or not), using deception (or not), safeguarding individual privacy, and evaluating the risk/benefit ratio. To exercise a degree of control in this respect, the American Psychological Association's (1992) code of conduct stipulates, with regard to informed consent, that the language used is 'reasonably understandable' by participants; participants are told that they are free to accept or decline prior to the study and to withdraw during the study; participants are also informed of 'any possible factors that may influence their willingness to participate (such as risk, discomfort, adverse effects, or limitations on confidentiality)'; and the researcher should answer any questions potential participants may have.

Subjects involved in experimental research may be exposed to a range of possible risks, including possible physical, psychological or social injury. *Physical injury* may be avoided by careful experimental design and screening of participants to ensure that no-one at a higher than average risk is included in the sample. For example, diabetics may be screened out of a study concerned with the testing or tasting of chocolate products. *Psychological injury* derives from the possible mental or emotional stress caused by participation in an experimental study. The researcher can limit such effects by providing extensive post-experimental debriefing to help subjects understand the goals of the research and their reactions to the situation. *Social injury* may arise when an individual's participation in a research study is revealed to others and leads to embarrassment or social stigma. This can be prevented by the rigorous application of anonymity in the research procedure. However, the extent to which information is regarded as private may depend on a number of factors (Diener and Crandall, 1978) such as the sensitivity of the information, the setting, and the degree of dissemination. It is for these reasons that an additional safeguard in experimental design is often a requirement of the research study to be approved by an independent committee, such as a research ethics committee or independent review board. This review would consider the aims of the research, methods of protecting confidentiality, benefits to society of the research outcome, and other important factors. As a result of this review, the researcher may be advised to use a different methodology from experimentation, such as naturalistic observation or survey methods.

Conclusions

Experimentation and experimental research has a number of advantages that make it a suitable methodology for investigating hospitality phenomena. It may be carried out in the real world. This gives it a high level of 'ecological validity'. However, hospitality research has yet to be highly valued by industrialists. Academics are still viewed as 'boffins' and universities as 'ivory towers' whose major failing is not understanding the real world. Conducting research in the real world should help to bridge this gap between industry and academia. Not only will industry colleagues understand the relevance of the research, they will also ascribe greater face validity to the findings. Secondly, experimentation is a particularly useful approach to designing research aimed at evaluating various types of innovation and policy change. In view of the fact that the hospitality industry regularly claims to be innovating rapidly, understanding this process and its implications would seem to be highly appropriate.

It has also been argued that all researchers applying any kind of deductive methodology should understand experimental research—'it is important for any researcher to be conversant with the logic that forms the basis of the "true" experiment ... because this very logic underpins many of the deductive research methodologies commonly used in management research' (Gill and Johnson, 1991: 41). There is no doubt it is a method that is time consuming and potentially difficult to organise. But this reflects the rigour of the methodology. The findings of experimental research potentially have a high degree of both validity and reliability (in the context of an 'objective–rationalistic' paradigm).

Hospitality operations are complex, rich environments which provide many opportunities for this methodology. Some operations management problems are routinely investigated using this approach. For instance, productivity has been researched through well-established techniques such as work measurement and method study. Other areas now involve simulations of the real world so that computer-generated experiments can be conducted, especially with regard to layout and design problems. But there are many other areas which would benefit from experimental study, such as boundary role stress, service recovery strategies, mystery shopper programmes, customer care initiatives, the socio-technical interface, and so on.

Future research issues

Outside the food, nutrition and technology area, a review of the hospitality literature, especially that related to operations management, reveals little academic research based on the experimental approach. For example, there were 55 papers presented at the CHME National Research Conference in 1994. Of these none reported on experimental research, one-third used survey methodology, and one-quarter were entirely conceptual, as illustrated in Table 6.2. A scan of proceedings from other conferences and of refereed journal articles suggests that CHME '94 may be regarded as typical of the type of research methods currently favoured in hospitality and tourism research.

It can be considered surprising that experimental research is not conducted by hospitality researchers for three reasons. Firstly, one of the earliest, significant experimental studies in an industrial setting is extremely well known—the Hawthorne studies in the 1930s. The methodology, and its pitfalls, can hardly fail to be drawn to hospitality

Table 6.2 CHME National Research Conference 1994 research papers

	No.	%
Questionnaire-based survey	18	33
Face-to-face structured interviews	5	9
Case study	3	5
Ethnographic	2	3
Conceptual analysis	14	25
Literature review	5	9
Research plan	7	14
Research methodology	1	2
Total	55	100

researchers' attention due to the prominence Hawthorne has in much of the literature. Secondly, operations researchers in general frequently use experimental methodology and often select hotel or catering operations in which to conduct their research, for instance the study (Davis and Vollmann, 1990) of over 700 customers conducted in a fast-food chain when researching the 'psychology of waiting lines'. Thirdly, experimental research is relatively common in industry. If non-hospitality researchers and industrialists conduct experiments in the hospitality field, a strong case can be made for hospitality researchers to utilise this methodology more.

The potential areas for experimental research span a wide spectrum. For instance, in organisational studies, experimental research has been applied to job enrichment and job enlargement, productivity, worker participation, supervisor and management style, remuneration schemes, worker resistance to change, workplace design and many other issues. In consumer studies and marketing, the experimental approach has been applied to purchasing behaviour, advertising, pricing, branding, and so on. However, to date, most of this research tends to have taken place in the context of manufacturing industry. There is no reason why this research methodology would not be more widely used in studying the hospitality phenomenon.

References

American Hotel and Motel Association (1995) *Key Notes: Horst Schulze*, INNsider Video, No. 64166

American Psychological Association (1992) 'Ethical principles of psychologists and code of conduct', *American Psychologist*, Vol. 47, pp. 1597–1611

Bell, J. (1993) *Doing Your Research Project*, Open University Press: Milton Keynes

Berry, B.W. and Bigner, M.E. (1995) 'Use of grilling and combination broiler–grilling at various temperatures for beef loin steaks differing in marbling', *Journal of Foodservice Systems*, No. 8, pp. 65–74

Blackwell, L. (1995) 'Visual cues and their effects on colour assessment', *Nutrition and Food Science*, No. 5, September/October, pp. 24–28

Brewer, M.S., Reinhard, M., Schmidt, S., Potter, S.M. and Bond, H. (1993) 'Sensory and physical characteristics of consumer-acceptable lower-fat pizza for foodservice production', *Journal of Foodservice Systems*, No. 7, pp. 149–169

Bryman, A. (1989) *Research Methods and Organisation Studies*, Routledge: London

Campbell, D.T. and Stanley, J.C. (1966) *Experimental and Quasi-Experimental Designs for Research*, Rand McNally: Chicago

Chome, F., Chinnan, M.S., Phillips, R.D. and Resurreccion, A. (1995) 'Effect of storage time and storage device on objective quality measurements of fried chicken filet sandwiches', *Journal of Foodservice Systems*, No. 8, pp. 229–241

Davis, M.M. and Vollmann, T.E. (1990) 'A framework for relating waiting time and customer satisfaction in a service operation', *Journal of Service Marketing*, Vol. 4, No. 1, Winter, pp 61–69

Diener, E. and Crandall, R. (1978) *Ethics in Social and Behavioural Research*, University of Chicago Press: Chicago

Gill, J. and Johnson, P. (1991) *Research Methods for Managers*, Paul Chapman Publishing, London

Hamouz, F.L., Mandigo, R.W., Calkins, C.R. and Janssen, T.J. (1995) 'Prediction of oven temperature effects on beef bottom round roast yield and quality', *Paper No. 11274, Journal Series*, Nebraska Agricultural Research Division, University of Nebraska

Johns, N. (1996) *Productivity Management in Hospitality and Tourism*, Cassell: London

Jones, P. and Peppiatt, E. (1996) 'Managing perceptions of waiting times in service queues', *International Journal of Service Industry Management*, Vol. 7, No. 5, pp. 47–61

Katz, K.L., Larson, B.M. and Larson, R.C. (1991) 'Prescription for waiting-in-line blues: entertain, enlighten, and engage', *Sloan Management Review*, Winter, pp. 44–53

Lewis-Beck, M.S. (1993) *Experimental Design and Methods*, Sage Publications: London

Magee, B. (1973) *Popper*, Fontana: London

Nelson, R.R. and Poorani, A.A. (1997) 'What challenges do genetically altered foods pose for the hospitality industry? The opinions of a blue chip panel of industry experts', *Hospitality Research Journal*, Vol. 20, No. 3, pp. 83–98

Orne, M.T. (1962) 'On the social psychology of the psychological experiment: with particular reference to demand characteristics and their implications', *American Psychologist*, Vol. 17, pp. 776–783

Pangborn, R.M., Berg, H.W. and Hansen, B. (1963) *American Journal of Psychology*, Vol. 76, pp. 492–495

Phillips, C.A. and Roscoe, N. (1996) 'Survival of *Escherichia coli* 0157:H7 in ground beef during normal cooking procedures', *Nutrition and Food Science*, No. 2, March/April, pp. 23–26

Rosenthal, R. (1976) *Experimenter Effects in Behavioural Research*, Irvington: New York

Rosnow, R.L. and Rosenthal, R. (1997) *People Studying People: Artifacts and Ethics in Behavioural Research*, Freeman: New York

Russell, B. (1961) *History of Western Philosophy*, 2nd Ed., Allen & Unwin: London

Smith, K. and Gregory, S. (1996) 'Customer activated terminals: technology-driven quick food-service ordering systems', *Journal of Restaurant and Foodservice Marketing*, Vol. 1, No. 3/4, pp. 107–120

Sparks, B. (1994) 'Communicative aspects of the service encounter', *Hospitality Research Journal*, Vol. 17, No. 2, pp. 39–50

Sparks, B. and Bradley, G. (1997) 'Antecedents and consequences of perceived service provider effort in the hospitality industry', *Hospitality Research Journal*, Vol. 20, No. 3, pp. 17–34

Spector, P.E. (1993) 'Research designs' in Lewis-Beck, M.S. (ed.) *Experimental Design and Methods*, Sage Publications: London, pp. 1–73

Zechmeister, E.B. and Shaughnessy, J.J. (1994) *A Practical Introduction to Research Methods in Psychology*, McGraw-Hill: New York

7 Case study research

BOB BROTHERTON

Introduction

Historically, case study research has been extremely popular in a number of 'traditional' academic disciplines, but has become less prevalent in some and/or suffered a decline and subsequent revival in others. In the eyes of many academic researchers, notably those with a positivist orientation, case study research is often viewed as completely valueless at worst and markedly inferior to other methodological choices, such as experimentation and large N surveys, at best. However, those researchers with a more phenomenological or interpretivist orientation would argue that case study research, frequently in conjunction with ethnographic and field methods, is at the very least extremely valuable for developing 'grounded' theoretical insights through an inductive process and may be seen as a type of research capable of providing valid theoretical generalisations beyond the specific case(s) considered in the study.

This chapter seeks to explore both these philosophical and methodological issues and many others associated with case study research. It addresses the fundamental issues of the nature of case study research and the problems associated with defining what a case study is; the perspectives and criteria which can be adopted to differentiate between different types of case study; the considerations relevant to the researcher's decision to choose case study research as a preferred design; and the issues which require attention at various stages of the case study research process, from research question and conceptual framework formulation through data collection, analysis and interpretation to writing up the case study results; and it reflects upon some of the key issues and demands faced by or placed on the case study researcher. Finally, the chapter concludes by commenting on the current situation facing the use of the case study approach in contemporary hospitality management research, and the issues this research community may wish to consider in relation to this approach for the future development of hospitality management research.

Within this structure the chapter utilises insights from both key methodological sources concerned with case study research *per se*, drawn from the general 'research methods' literature, and specific examples of the use and application of case study research to hospitality management research projects. The discussion of material drawn from the general case study literature sources is designed to alert and sensitise the reader both to the nature of contemporary methodological debates surrounding the value, use and implementation of case study research and to the specific issues and choices the hospitality management researcher faces in deciding to adopt this

The Handbook of Contemporary Hospitality Management Research, Edited by Bob Brotherton.
© 1999 John Wiley & Sons Ltd.

orientation for an intended research project. This latter aspect is further reinforced through reference to specific hospitality management case study research examples within the context of the methodological discussion. Hence, both the general and the particular are interwoven to meet the needs of those hospitality management researchers who may wish to consider choosing a case study research approach in preference to other alternatives.

What is a case study?

In common with any form of research it is important at the outset to define and delineate the nature of the issues to be explored. Case study research is no different in this respect from any other form of research. However, defining 'cases' and 'case studies' is not necessarily as simple as it may appear. There is a tendency for many authors and researchers to use these terms somewhat flexibly and interchangeably. As Ragin (1992: 1, 3) observes: 'the term "case" and the various terms linked to the idea of case analysis are not well defined in social science, despite their widespread usage and their centrality to social scientific discourse … . To the question "what is a case?" most social scientists would have to give multiple answers. A case may be theoretical or empirical or both; it may be a relatively bounded object or a process; and it may be generic and universal or specific in some way.' Similarly, Merriam (1988: 5) comments that: 'there is little consensus on what constitutes a case study or how one actually goes about doing this type of research … . The terms case history, case record, and case method, sometimes used in conjunction with case study, further confuse the issue'.

Some authors refer to case studies as a 'strategy' for undertaking research (McClintock, Brannen and Maynard-Moody, 1979; Robson, 1993; Hartley, 1994; Eisenhardt, 1995), some suggest it ought to be conceived as an 'approach' (Goode and Hatt, 1952; Rose, 1991; Hamel, Dufour and Fortin, 1993), and others contend that it should be regarded as a research 'method' (Merriam, 1988; Smith, 1991). Some commentators strongly contend that case study research is predominantly qualitative rather than quantitative in nature (Smith, 1991), whilst others take a more balanced perspective in claiming that there is no *a priori* reason automatically to characterise and classify case study research as one or the other (Hartley, 1994). At first sight these may appear to be, but are not, trivial issues of a semantic nature. If there is confusion over what cases, case analysis and case studies are, and whether the latter constitutes a research strategy, an approach or a design, then there exists a substantial degree of uncertainty for the researcher contemplating case study research. As Ragin (1992: 8) points out: 'answers to this question [what is a case?] affect the conduct and results of research'.

Unfortunately, the contemporary literature suggests that the production of a clear and unambiguous definition is not a simple task. A 'case' may be conceived in various ways. It may be regarded as a particular source of manipulation and/or a source of information. For example, an experimental subject may be defined as a case, as can a particular respondent (in either individual or organisational form) within a survey. An individual interviewee in an ethnographic study could equally be categorised as a 'case' within the nature of the study. Those familiar with the use of the SPSS data analysis software will be aware that its data sheet format is structured to regard the data from each individual questionnaire as a single case on each of its horizontal rows. Indeed, Ragin (1992: 2) makes a similar point by using an example of a survey of individuals conducted within the context of a country: 'A study of this type can be seen both as an extensive analysis of many cases (the sample of individuals) and as an intensive case study of the United States.' 'Cases' are also often referred to as holistic entities or, in other words, as the case study itself. Here no differentiation is made between the terms 'case' and 'case study'; they are used synonymously. On the other hand, Robson (1993: 51) suggests that cases and case studies are not synonymous: 'In a case study, the case is the situation, individual, group, organisation or whatever it is that we are interested in.'

It might be expected that the definitions proffered in the specific literature on case study research would be helpful to clarify some of these basic issues. However, this may be a rather optimistic view. Bromley (1986: 7, 8) defines a case study as 'a general term widely used, especially in the social and behavioural sciences, to refer to the description and analysis of a particular entity [which are] usually natural occurrences within definable boundaries, although they exist and function within a context of surrounding circumstances.' Robson (1993: 145) takes the view that a case study is a 'strategy for doing research which involves an empirical investigation of a particular contemporary phenomenon within its real life context using multiple sources of evidence. The "contemporary phenomenon", in other words the case, can be virtually anything.'

Bell (1993: 8) suggests that a case study is 'concerned principally with the interaction of factors and events' which are 'related to a particular instance or situation'. Hartley (1994: 208, 209) offers the view that a case study 'consists of a detailed investigation, often with data collected over a period of time, of one or more organisations, or groups within organisations, with a view to providing an analysis of the context and processes involved in the phenomenon under study. The phenomenon is not isolated from its context ... but is of interest precisely because it is in relation to its context.' Stake's (1994) contention that a case study should be viewed as an object rather than a process, and is characterised by being an integrated system, is rejected by Yin (1994) as too broad to be useful. Yin's criticism here is that the breadth of Stake's definition effectively means that anything could be defined as a case regardless of the research methodology adopted for the study. Instead Yin (1994: 13) proffers the view that: 'A case study is an empirical inquiry that investigates a contemporary phenomenon within its real-life context, especially when the boundaries between phenomenon and context are not clearly evident.' Wilson (1979: 448) takes the view that a case study essentially comprises a process 'which tries to describe and analyse some entity in qualitative, complex and comprehensive terms not infrequently as it unfolds over a period of time.'

One common theme which does appear to emerge from this range of case study definitions is that of a 'bounded system' (Rose, 1991). As both Yin (1994) and Rose (1991) point out, not only does a case study have a discrete identity in terms of both the centrality of the phenomenon under investigation and the context within which this is to be studied, but these two elements are inextricably linked. In a similar vein, Merriam (1988: 10) refers to Cronbach's (1975) 'interpretation in context' phrase, and suggests that this characterises the case study through its emphasis on 'the interaction of significant factors characteristic of the phenomenon'. This concept of a bounded entity does appear to hold some hope of salvation for the bemused case study researcher, as the phenomenon-context nexus implies that the latter is both relatively easy to identify and possesses an appropriate degree of spatial and temporal stability. However, this may not always be as straightforward as it appears. Where the case study is located within a discrete and clearly delimited context, such as an organisation, the boundaries for the case phenomenon and associated context are likely to be relatively easy to establish. For example, a case study designed to research the stress experienced by front-line, customer service employees in a fast-food unit, or one investigating the work of hotel general managers within a given hotel company, would be relatively easy to design and bound. On the other hand, a case study designed to investigate the career trajectories of senior executives would not. In this situation the 'context' becomes rather difficult to bound and incorporate in the study as it will almost certainly be extremely varied and complex, both spatially and temporally.

Thus, if the phenomenon-context nexus is central to the definition of what constitutes a case study, it may be argued that the ability to satisfactorily identify and bound both the phenomenon, or subject, and its context is the key issue. This contention is supported by Abbott (1992: 63) who suggests that the bounding of the case study is indeed a vital issue: 'Once the case is delimited, the unity of the case ... is held to require that case attributes take their meaning from the case context.' The phenomenon-context nexus also implies that the concept of 'holism' ought to feature strongly in any definition of what constitutes a case study. The inseparability of phenomenon and context in case study research presents a 'natural' opportunity to obtain holistic synergies (Gummesson, 1991). Where phenomenon and context are conceived as a single entity the case becomes a 'whole' from the outset.

However, the process of 'bounding' a case study is not without its problems. Abbott (1992) suggests that the researcher's ontological stance will have a fundamental impact upon how case studies are conceived and defined. In discussing the differing ontological positions of the positivist (population/analytic) and phenomenological (case/narrative) perspectives, he suggests that: 'The former requires rigidly delimitable cases, assigns them properties with trans-case meanings, builds cases on the foundation of simple existence, and refuses all fundamental transformations. The latter, by contrast, assumes cases will have fuzzy boundaries, takes all properties to have case-specific meanings, analyses by simplifying presumably complex cases, and allows, even focuses on, case transformation' (Abbott, 1992: 64).

Although these ontological perspectives are clearly different, both have to address the common issue of the case 'plot' to define what a case study is (Abbott, 1992). Essentially, this entails identifying and organising the events within a case study. The 'population/analytic' approach to this would be to represent the events as discrete points in variable space, at an abstract level, which have a continuity related to the causal theory being applied. This means that 'finding the plot is a matter of connecting the dots .... The plot is basically continuous' (Abbott, 1992: 65). On the other hand, the 'case/narrative' approach would treat events as having a specific, contextually-rooted, and finite duration (Abbott, 1992).

If particularism, inseparability of phenomenon and context, and holism are key elements in an attempt to create a distinctive definition of what the case study is, it would appear that the 'case/narrative' approach, with its underlying ontological assumptions, holds greater promise than the 'population/analytic' approach. Indeed, this is a view Abbott (1992: 65) would concur with: 'The move from population/analytic approach to

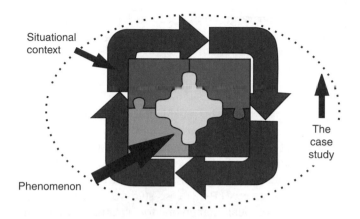

Situational context

Phenomenon

The case study

Figure 7.1   The case study

case/narrative approach is thus a move first to a new way of regarding cases—as fuzzy realities with autonomously defined complex properties—and a move second to seeing cases as engaged in a perpetual dialogue with their environment, a dialogue of action and constraint that we call plot.' However, as Abbott (1992) cautions, defining the case study in terms of its 'plot' is not without problems. Firstly, case study plots temporally intersect with the past and future (antecedents and consequences). Secondly, plots are essentially researcher cognitions and may have a questionable reality. Thirdly, case studies will tend to assume, implicitly or explicitly, that their plots 'have beginnings, middles, and ends, rather than simple endless middles' (Abbott, 1992: 66). Thus, these issues imply that the task of defining a case study, via bounding it in terms of its plot, may be fine in theory but difficult in practice.

Given the foregoing discussion the meaning of the term 'case study' to be used in this chapter is that of a discrete, bounded entity within which the phenomenon and context are inseparable facets of the study. This implies that the parameters of the study effectively bound the defined 'context' for the study and provide the empirical scope for the investigation of the phenomenon. Hence, a case study may be defined as a study of a phenomenon in its situational context. Conceptually, this is represented in Figure 7.1.

Types of case study

The prevailing literature suggests that it is possible to categorise case studies in a number of different ways, which are not necessarily mutually exclusive. Although the significance and value of such categorisations may not be immediately apparent, they can assist the researcher in selecting appropriate combinations to design an effective strategy for a given piece of case study research. This is an issue which will be explored further later in this chapter.

Case studies may be differentiated according to their primary disciplinary base, assuming of course that they have not been explicitly designed as interdisciplinary or multi-disciplinary ventures. Using this criterion it is relatively simple to classify case studies into distinct disciplinary groupings such as legal, psychological, sociological, anthropological, educational, political and so on. Although this may be of some initial assistance to the case study researcher seeking to identify prior studies in the field of interest, it is probably of little value beyond this.

Alternatively, case studies may be categorised by their theoretical orientation (Hartley, 1994). Those studies which seek to confirm or refine existing theory through the case(s) under investigation may be regarded as deductive in nature. On the other hand, where the primary purpose of the case study is to create new theory it will be inductive in nature. Muller's (1990) study of Marriott illustrates the deductive approach via its application of Porter's (1980, 1985) competitive analysis and strategy models to explain the nature and process of Marriott's decision to divest its restaurant and fast food divisions, while Overstreet's (1993) case study of Charlottesville's hotels similarly employs Porter's theoretical framework to investigate value creation. Leigh's (1989) study also illustrates the application of a competitive assessment conceptual framework to the case study company's decision to enter the economy lodging segment.

Stake (1995) makes the typological distinction between case studies on the basis of the focus or purpose of the study. Where a case is studied because of an interest in, or need to know about, its specifics he refers to this as an 'intrinsic' type. On the other hand, where a case is studied as a means to develop a wider understanding of a particular issue or phenomenon he suggests it ought to be referred to as 'instrumental'. The scope of case studies is also used to differentiate between studies which focus upon a single individual, a sub-organisational group, an organisation, a collection of organisations (such as an industry sector, or an industry itself), and national entities. Thus, the scope of case studies may range from a single individual to those with an international dimension.

It is also possible to differentiate between cases on the basis of how typical the case is as an example of the phenomena to be studied. In some senses this is self-explanatory, but the essence of this distinction is the rarity, or otherwise, of the case(s) in question. Although it is frequently argued that all cases are unique entities, some are more uniquely differentiated than others. Where either the incidence or severity of the phenomenon to be investigated is extremely limited and/or confined to a very small number of possible cases, the possibilities for case selection are also necessarily limited. Therefore, it is possible to dichotomise cases into 'typical' and 'atypical' instances of a given phenomenon.

Merriam (1988) suggests that case studies may be differentiated by the aim of the research and the nature of the final report, i.e. descriptive, interpretative, or evaluative. A descriptive case study is one designed to present a detailed account of the particular phenomenon being studied. According to Lijphart (1971) such studies are 'atheoretical' and exist in a 'theoretical vacuum'. The general or 'trade' hospitality literature abounds with such 'atheoretical' case studies which are often offered as examples of good practice. These may be described as 'journalistic'-style studies which attempt to highlight the contribution that particular individuals have made to the hospitality industry or to 'showcase' the activities of hospitality companies seen to be leaders or innovators in a particular sector or activity. Good examples of both these types of journalistic case study are provided by Pearson's (1987) account of the contribution that Tom Staed has made to the success of the Oceans Eleven company in the USA, and the 'showcase' study on the Carlson Hospitality Worldwide Group, and its constituent companies, provided as a collection of linked articles in *Hotels* (1995a–1995k).

Similarly, both general, and specific hospitality, management texts are also used as vehicles for presenting descriptive, atheoretical case studies designed to highlight particular successes or failures and what can be learned from such experience. This type of case study is typified by the Burger Chef and McDonald's studies presented by Hartley (1991). It is even possible to find such atheoretical studies in academic journals! Examples are the Bergstrom Hotels case study by Breiter, Tyink and Corey-Tuckwell (1995) and Clark's (1993) descriptive/reflective study of Holiday Inn Worldwide. In the accepted scientific sense, such studies may be seen to have relatively little value. However, Merriam (1988: 27) makes the point that even case studies of this type do have some value: 'They are useful ... in presenting basic information about areas ... where little research has been conducted .... Such studies often form a data base for future comparison and theory building .... Whatever the area of enquiry, basic description of the subject being studied comes before hypothesising or theory testing.'

Interpretative case studies also contain detailed 'rich' descriptive material, but are characterised by a greater extent and degree of abstraction and conceptualisation. This may range from suggesting possible, emergent relationships, categories, and typologies to the construction of a more formalised theoretical framework. This type of case study is also sometimes referred to as an 'analytical' case study. According to Merriam (1988: 28) interpretative case studies are 'used to develop conceptual categories or to illustrate, support, or challenge theoretical assumptions held prior to the data gathering. [Or alternatively] If there is a lack of theory, or if existing theory does not adequately explain the phenomenon, hypotheses can be developed to structure a research investigation.' For example, Oppermann, Din and Amri's (1996: 55) study of urban hotel location in Kuala Lumpur, Malaysia, is an example of a case study conducted on an under-researched issue: 'Analyses of hotel location and the evolution of the urban tourism landscape are almost non-existent.'

Evaluative case studies embrace those elements of description and explanation found in descriptive and interpretative case studies, but also incorporate the element of judgement. However, this latter element should be approached with some caution by the case study researcher, as it has the potential to generate a significant normative aspect to the work. There may be a great temptation for the researcher to venture into the highly subjective realms of what should be, rather than what is, and why. This said, evaluative case studies do provide a potentially valuable vehicle for evaluative studies, as Barsky's (1996: 17) study evaluating the success of the 'Hotel Sofitel North America' programme—'Customer Satisfaction: The Sofitel Vision'—demonstrates. However, as will be seen later in the chapter, the case study process forces the researcher to carefully 'weigh' the evidence in order to produce a robust judgement.

Finally, Yin (1994) suggests that case studies can be subdivided into single or multiple studies, with holistic or embedded units of analysis. This combination produces a 2×2 matrix which Yin uses to suggest a fourfold typology (see Figure 7.2). Type 1 studies are single cases adopting a holistic, or single, unit of analysis. This type effectively conceptualises the case and unit of analysis as the same entity. Type 2 studies are again single cases, but now have embedded, or multiple, units of analysis. Here the units of analysis are subdivisions of the case entity. Both Types 1 and 2 are independent, stand-alone case studies in their own right. However, in Types 3 and 4 each case

	Single cases	Multiple cases
Holistic	TYPE 1	TYPE 3
Embedded	TYPE 2	TYPE 4

Figure 7.2 Case study research designs (source: Yin, 1994: 39). Reprinted by permission of Sage Publications, Inc.

now becomes subordinate to the overall scope of the study. Hence, these types of case study have a somewhat different purpose from that of the single-case variety. The purpose here is to explicitly use the selected cases to undertake a comparative study, whether this be at a case-by-case (holistic) level or a unit-by-case (embedded) level.

The hospitality management literature provides numerous examples of Yin's four types of case study. What follows is a small sample of such studies which are indicative of each type. Brownell and Jameson's (1996) study of how service quality concepts are defined, understood and communicated in a single hotel is a good example of Yin's Type 1—a single case with a holistic unit of analysis. Similarly, Luchars and Hinkin's (1996) 'Service Quality Audit' (SQA) study also corresponds closely to Yin's Type 1 as it explores the SQA in a single hotel. Although this study explores the SQA process via an analysis of six different types of front-desk transaction error, its focus is on a single unit of analysis, the SQA.

By contrast the case study conducted by Morey and Dittman (1995), on benchmarking hotel general managers' performance, is a good example of Yin's Type 2. The case for this study was a single 'nationally known [hotel] chain, geographically dispersed over the continental United States' (Morey and Dittman, 1995: 31), within the context of which data was collected from 54 of the chain's owner-managed hotels in order to compare the GM's performance. Thus, the hotel chain comprised the single case, with the individual hotels (and their GMs) constituting the embedded units of analysis.

An example of Yin's Type 3 is provided by Figueiredo, Latas and Gomes' (1995) analysis of case studies of management strategies in four 'five star' hotels. Here the multiple case studies, the four hotels, are analysed via a single unit of analysis, the management strategies. Finally, the application of Yin's Type 4 is demonstrated in Moncarz and Kron's (1993) study of two hotels in financial distress. In this study the authors 'analyse the operating performance of two hotels facing varying degrees of failure by comparing them with an industry sample comprising similar operations' (Moncarz and Kron, 1993: 176). To achieve this the study compares financial performance in the two case study hotels with that of the wider sample via a set of departmental/functional level comparisons. Hence, the study uses embedded units of analysis within a multiple-case framework.

Choosing case study research

Whether case studies are regarded as a strategy, an approach or a design is not an important distinction when the researcher is facing the decision of whether it is appropriate to undertake a case study to effectively answer the research questions. The value of any research strategy, approach or design lies in its potential for assisting the researcher to meet the aims and objectives of the research in the most effective and appropriate way possible. In this sense, the decision is largely one of fitness for purpose. This, of course, begs the question: for what purpose is the adoption of case study research the most appropriate?

On this issue Yin (1993: xi) is clear: 'The method is appropriate when investigators desire to (a) define topics broadly and not narrowly, (b) cover contextual conditions and not just the phenomenon of study, and (c) rely on multiple and not singular sources of evidence.' One of the purposes strongly implied by Yin's (1993) view, and widely quoted in the literature, is that of in-depth 'particularism', often of a processural nature. Therefore case study research tends to be adopted in situations where there is a desire to research a particular phenomenon within a particular situation, and perhaps during a particular time. It is this particularism, arising from the inseparability of phenomenon and context, which Yin (1993) suggests is a key issue in deciding whether the case study should be the preferred method. Whereas other methods, i.e. experimental designs, explicitly design or 'control out' the context in order to focus exclusively on the phenomenon, in case study research the context is a vital and integral element of the research design, a feature Yin (1993: 59) claims creates a 'technically distinctive characteristic' for case study research.

This importance of the contextual dimension is echoed by Hartley (1994) who claims that case study research is especially valuable for exploring unfolding processes, via an in-depth analysis, in order to develop a deep understanding of these processes within their context of occurrence, whether this be contemporary, historical or both. Such processes may be contextually typical or atypical, established or emergent, codified or tacit. Case study research may be adopted for any or all of these. Perhaps a key issue here is the implied trade-off between breadth or scope on the one hand, and depth on the other. Case study research is widely regarded as more appropriate when the research purpose, and associated question(s), are concerned with the development of deeper understanding rather than relatively superficial description. Where the research is primarily concerned with 'why' and 'how' type questions the use of the case study method should be a consideration in the researcher's methodological decision making. As Yin (1993: 31) points out: 'Case studies are an appropriate research method when you are trying to attribute causal relationships—and not just wanting to explore or describe a situation.'

However, where case study research attempts to answer 'why' and 'how' questions it frequently encounters the problem of establishing so-called unarguable truths. Understanding the underlying mechanisms to any phenomenon involving complex human behaviour inevitably demands a degree of empathy and interpretation. Ethnographic studies adopt a 'naturalistic enquiry' approach in order to seek answers to these types of questions by developing an interpretative understanding rooted in both the reality of the situation and its human occupants. Therefore, case study research is widely used in ethnographic studies as a method which allows the researcher both to limit the scope of the enquiry and simultaneously to explore the central phenomenon within such manageable parameters. A good example of the application of the ethnographic approach to a hospitality case study is provided by Sosteric (1996) who examines 'subjectivity and the labour process' in a single night-club.

This combination of naturalistic, qualitative, field-oriented research often leads to a suggestion in the literature that case study research is an appropriate strategy where the researcher's intention is to undertake an inductive study to build new theory. For example, Hamel, Dufour and Fortin (1993: 29, 41) comment that: 'a theory must be constructed before it can be validated ... a theory or theoretical framework first emerges from the study of an empirical case or object, the approach to which is not and cannot be deductively defined .... All theories are initially based on a particular case or object ... the case study is an inductive approach, perhaps even the ideal inductive approach.'

Similarly, this combination of why/how questions and ethnographic, naturalistic enquiry tends to suggest strongly that case study research is most appropriate where the nature of the research to be conducted will be qualitative and inductive, and raises the question whether case study research is appropriate only for inductive, qualitative research. Logically the answer to this is no. There is no compelling reason to suggest that case study research could not be conducted on a quantitative basis, or that such an orientation would lack value. Indeed the collection and analysis of quantitative data may constitute a major, minor, or zero element within a case study. Where the scope and scale of a case study are large, such as those involving whole industries or countries, the quantitative element may assume a far greater prominence and importance than in individual and/or small group studies. An example of this is provided by Overstreet's (1993) study in which the need to collect and analyse a significant amount of financial performance data is an integral part of the study's design.

However, it is reasonable to suggest that the selection of case study research, as a preferred method, is far more likely in research studies having a qualitative orientation. Some authors justify this largely on the basis that studies with a qualitative orientation are concerned with the uniqueness of the particular, rather than the universality of the general. Consequently the established types of qualitative field research methods and techniques, such as those of observation and in-depth interviewing, are adopted within limited contexts. There is both a rational and a practical logic to such a view. If the research is seeking to answer why/how type questions in any meaningful level of depth, it is difficult to see how this can be effectively achieved through the use of either an experimental design or a large-scale survey. In addition, not only would experimental and/or survey methods, techniques and instruments generally be seen as poor methodological choices for such an endeavour, but the practicalities of designing and implementing such a project using these would raise serious questions about the effective use of time and resources to achieve the desired ends. Hence, it might almost be claimed that there are certain 'natural' methodological choices in relation to the nature and emphasis of the research question(s).

Other authors would suggest that decisions whether or not to adopt the case study method should be centred around the issues of representativeness and generalisation. At the heart of this argument is the 'n' (number) issue, which contends that the size and representativeness of the research, and particularly the sample, is the determining factor in influencing whether the methodological choice should be geared towards supporting small or large 'n' studies. In general this argument is based upon the issue of 'statistical' rather than 'theoretical' generalisation, with the consequent epistemological view that the positivistic, hypothetico-deductive approach to research should predominate to test existing theory. The small 'n' criticism of case study research is therefore founded on the claim that case studies cannot be regarded as representative, and are incapable of generating findings which can be validly generalised to wider instances of the phenomenon in the population at large. One obvious response to this criticism would be for the researcher to select and conduct their case study research from a more positivistic standpoint. As Smith (1991: 151) points out: 'By incorporating elements of positivist research design (sampling, quantification, etc.) they [researchers] absolve themselves from the charge that their cases are unrepresentative.'

Unfortunately, this solution may be inappropriate at best, i.e. in an individual case study, and akin to the 'tail wagging the dog' at worst. The selection of a particular case for inclusion in a study is normally purposive rather than random in nature. Thus, the basis for selection is not usually governed by the concerns of statistical probability but by theoretically informed judgement. Cases are selected to provide the best possible situations to research the phenomena in question, whether these are selected as typical or atypical situations. Statistical typicality and representativeness is therefore not a major issue for case study research. As Rose (1991: 192) notes: 'generalisability has come to mean the ability to extrapolate with statistical confidence from that sample to the population from which it was drawn … . In case-study research, by contrast, it is considered more appropriate to treat representativeness in terms of a qualitative logic for the selection of cases for study, rather than a quantitative logic of sampling from a population.' This 'qualitative logic' suggests that case selection should be theoretically directed (Burgess, 1984), and that one should seek to select cases which offer the highest level of explanatory potential (Mitchell, 1983; Platt, 1988). The goal of the case study researcher is therefore to 'expand and generalise theories (analytical generalisation) and not to enumerate frequencies (statistical generalisation)' (Yin, 1989: 21).

Thus case study research facilitates logical rather than statistical inferences. Representativeness, in the positivistic, quantitative sense, as an arguably spurious basis for claiming validity, simply becomes irrelevant. As Silverman (1985: 114) succinctly puts it: 'The claim, therefore, is not to representativeness but to faultless logic.' Similarly, the purpose of the case study researcher may be fundamentally different from, say, that of the survey researcher. For example, the case study researcher may primarily be attempting to generate new, inductive, analytical insights into the phenomenon; or may seek to create rich descriptions of the phenomenon and associated context as opposed to pursuing statistically valid correlations. Furthermore, the specificity of the case study situation(s) selected by the researcher should not necessarily be seen as a 'natural' barrier to the generation of logically valid theoretical generalisations. The detailed knowledge of the case situation(s) should permit the researcher to disentangle the case-specific conditions (contingencies) of the phenomenon from those of a more generic nature where the phenomenon will be theoretically expected to occur in the same way (Hartley, 1994). As Bassey (1981: 85, 86) points out: 'The relatability of a case study is more important than its generalisability … if they are relatable, and if by publication of the findings they extend the boundaries of existing knowledge, then they are valid.'

Indeed, it may be argued that analytic generalisation and relatability are essentially processes of analytic extension from the particular to the general, or from local to global, and that the local (the case study) is a concentrated instance of the global (Hamel, Dufour and Fortin, 1993). The connection from the local to the global is therefore made by first identifying the existence and incidence of the latter within the former, and secondly by reconstructing the global from the local. Thus, in this view, the case is conceptualised as a representative, concentrated microcosm of the global phenomenon which can be used to iterate theoretical understanding between the particular and the general.

Designing case study research

In common with most other forms of research the fundamental starting point for designing case study research is the formulation of the research question. Merriam (1988: 41, 43) suggests: 'There are three basic types of research problem: conceptual, action and value', all of which may constitute a starting point to consider the essential purpose of the research and assist in defining the nature of the case study: 'In identifying a research problem, one moves from general interest, curiosity, or doubt about a situation to a specific statement of the research problem. Translating one's general curiosity into a research problem paves the way for defining the case to be investigated.' This of course raises the question as to which type(s) of research question can be addressed by using case studies. As commented upon earlier, the case study is likely to be a particularly appropriate choice where the research questions are focused upon 'why' and 'how' issues, as case study analysis readily facilitates a relatively constrained but in-depth study of the phenomenon in question. In this respect Hartley (1994: 212) suggests that: 'The strength of case studies lies especially in their capacity to explore ... processes as they unfold in organisations ... . A case study allows for a processual, contextual and generally longitudinal analysis of the various actions and meanings which take place and which are constructed within organisations. The open-ended nature of much data gathering also allows for processes to be examined in considerable depth.'

The case study is likely to be an appropriate choice (Hartley, 1994) where:

- satisfactory answers to the research question are contingent upon developing an understanding within a context (be that historical or contemporary);
- the phenomenon is new or little understood at present;
- the intention is to explore extreme or atypical incidence of the phenomenon and/or its emergent properties;
- the dynamics of the phenomenon need to be incorporated;
- a detailed understanding of meanings is required in comparative research.

Thus, the choice to adopt case study research as the preferred option may be appropriate both under a wide range of circumstances and for varied research questions. Given a decision that case study research is the researcher's preferred choice, one key issue in designing the research is the role of theory. Yin (1993: 4) claims that theory can assist the case study researcher to:

- 'Select the cases to be studied in the first place ... ;
- specify what is being explored when you are doing exploratory case studies;
- define a complete and appropriate description when you are doing descriptive case studies;
- stipulate rival theories when you are doing explanatory case studies;
- generalise the results to other cases'

and further that this view means: 'the term *theory* covers more than causal theories. Rather *theory* means the design of research steps, according to some relationship in the literature, policy issues, or other substantive source' [original emphasis]. Yin's view of 'theory' is similar to what Robson (1993: 150) refers to as the 'conceptual framework' which 'covers the main features (aspects, dimensions, factors, variables) of a case study and their presumed relationships' and serves essentially the same purposes as 'theory' for case study design.

However, Robson (1993) tends to take a rather more pragmatic stance than Yin (1993) towards the extent to which *a priori* theoretical/conceptual frameworks can be utilised to design case study research comprehensively from the outset. In recognising that the ability conceptually to pre-structure case study research depends on the type of case study selected, i.e. whether it is exploratory or confirmatory, Robson (1993) contends that the state of extant theory, empirical realities and research practicalities are likely to generate a 'trade-off' between the 'looseness', or otherwise, of the initial conceptual framework and the flexibility the researcher is able to employ in conducting the study. Therefore, unless there are compelling reasons for utilising either a highly constrained, or a predominantly emergent, conceptual framework, the researcher may be well advised to tread an appropriate path between these extremes. As Hartley (1994: 217) states: 'some focus is needed to structure the study to avoid the twin dangers of being overwhelmed by data and being drawn into narrative—rather than theory building ... . Even the most open-ended approach to theory building—grounded theory ... —argues for an initial framework which is then tested against the data gained in the study.' Again the nature of the study's research question(s), i.e. the extent to which they are general or specific, should help the researcher determine the most appropriate type of conceptual framework to design the research. There should clearly be consistency between the research question(s) and the conceptual framework.

Yin (1993) suggests that determining the case(s) to be selected for a case study is perhaps one of the most difficult tasks in designing case study research. A parallel, and interrelated, difficulty is that of determining the appropriate unit(s) of analysis for the research. Without a clear definition of the study's central unit(s) of analysis it is difficult to see how the study can be sufficiently focused and delimited, and how the case study findings may be generalised to either extant theory or other empirical cases. On the other hand, this may not always be a straightforward task for the case study researcher. Where a substantial body of extant theory relating to the phenomenon under investigation already exists, the task of determining *a priori* the most appropriate unit(s) of analysis for the study is likely to be relatively easy. The existence of established theoretical frameworks clearly provides a validated basis for the researcher to determine the most appropriate unit(s) of analysis in relation to existing theory.

However, where such a body of theory does not exist the task of definitively identifying the appropriate unit(s) of analysis, prior to the start of the study, may be more problematic. Where extant theory does not exist or is underdeveloped the most appropriate unit(s) of analysis may not be self-evident or unambiguous. In these circumstances the case study researcher will need to proceed with caution. Initial views of what the unit(s) of analysis should be require testing, verifying, and amending if necessary, during the early stages of the research. In these circumstances the researcher must retain flexibility in the basic design of the work in order to ensure that the eventual decisions made are as optimal as possible, but also requires a basis for identifying the potential units of analysis in the first instance.

The identification of pertinent 'issues' might be a useful approach in this respect, whereby the research questions are related to each 'issue' to add more detail to the initial research design (Stake, 1995). As an identification of key issues tends to draw the researcher's attention to the major theoretical and empirical problems and concerns associated with the research, this process can help to inform the nature of observations which have to be made to answer the research question(s). Stake (1995) proposes that both 'etic' and 'emic' issues be considered in this context. According to Stake (1995) 'etic' issues are those brought in by the researcher from outside, i.e. the researcher's issues; whilst 'emic' issues are those which arise from within the case situation. In addition it is important to remember that any such 'issues' are located within a context. Hence, the researcher must also consider whether the issues are primarily related to the phenomenon (subject) of the research or the situational conditions evident within the case study.

Case selection itself is driven by both theoretical and practical considerations with, other things being equal, the former assuming primacy over the latter. Cases may be selected as *typical*, i.e. average or 'normal' instances of the phenomenon; *extreme*, i.e. where extreme characteristics of the phenomenon are evident; *unique*, i.e. where some attributes of the case are unusual or rare; *ideal*, i.e. where a case is selected to correspond to an 'ideal' theoretical model; or as a *replication* for comparative purposes, whether this be consequential or concurrent in nature. However, many hospitality case studies do not explain or justify why the particular case(s) adopted for the study have been selected (see, for example, Tse and Elwood, 1990; Morey and Dittman, 1995; Luchars and Hinkin, 1996). In these studies the rationale for case selection is not made explicit but left to the reader's imagination! In Tse and Elwood's (1990) study the use of McDonald's Corp. and Holiday Corp. for the case study is presumably made because these two organisations present suitable (ideal?) case opportunities to investigate the main issue of concern: the relationship between the management style and characteristics of leaders and business strategy in relation to the organisation's life cycle. However, the reasoning in selecting these two organisations is never made explicit! In both Morey and Dittman's (1995) and Luchars and Hinkin's (1996) studies it would appear that the reasons for selecting the cases concerned had more to do with either convenience and/or pre-existing contact and ease of access. Again both studies never make the reasons for case selection clear.

By way of contrast, Ogden's (1995) study of the relationship between strategy, structure and employee relations within public sector organisations involved in the compulsory competitive tendering process, and Moncarz and Kron's (1993) study of hotels in financial distress, provide good examples of a sound rationale for case selection which links both the nature of organisational characteristics and contextual conditions. Ogden (1995: 38) explains this rationale as follows: 'Each case study was selected for its particular characteristics using both a literal and theoretical sampling logic in order to investigate whether differing external and internal conditions would produce different case-study results .... The first [case] was selected because it was thought that the contracts in this authority were likely to be attractive to private-sector contractors .... The second ... was selected for literal replication reasons .... The third ... was selected on a theoretical replication basis.'

Moncarz and Kron (1993) also explain and justify their case selection in terms of both the particular reasons for selecting the two case study hotels, as being 'exemplary' of the type/degree of financial failure being researched, and directly comparable to other similar types of hotel in the wider sample used for this purpose. Thus, as both the Ogden (1995) and Moncarz and Kron (1993) studies succinctly point out, the issue of case selection is inextricably linked with that of sampling. This will be explored further in the following section.

Undertaking case study research

Given that the development of the initial design for the research has been undertaken with due cognisance to the issues discussed in the previous section, the case study researcher has further methodological choices to make in respect of data collection and analysis. While these are likely to be strongly influenced by the earlier design decisions there are, nevertheless, some more detailed considerations to be addressed during the study's implementation stage. One key issue is that of 'sampling'. Sampling in respect of case selection has been addressed in the previous section; here it is considered in relation to the selection of data types and sources within the defined case study. Given the rich complexity of case study situations, it is simply not possible to gather data on everything. As Robson (1993: 154, 155) suggests, the researcher has 'to come to some principled decision about:

Who   Which persons are to be observed, interviewed, etc.?
Where   In (or about) which settings are data collected?
When   At what times?
What   Which events, activities or processes are to be observed, etc.?'

In addition there will also be a need for the researcher to consider why the decisions made in response to these four 'W' questions are likely to be the most appropriate ones in a methodological sense, and also the practicalities of implementing these decisions, i.e. the 'how'. Consideration of all these issues should help to ensure that not only is the sampling strategy methodologically sound, but it is also feasible given the resources and situation at hand. However, as noted earlier, there is evidence that these issues are not being adequately considered or addressed by some hospitality management researchers undertaking case study research.

Both probability and non-probability sampling strategies may be used in case study research, depending upon the aims and nature of the study in question. However, as many case studies tend to be qualitative rather than quantitative in nature, and potential sources of information in the case study 'population' are often not equally appropriate to the phenomenon under investigation, non-probabilistic sampling strategies are often more suitable than those based upon probabilistic selection. In most instances the quality of the sources and/or respondents will be the key factor. Furthermore, as it is likely that the case study itself will have been selected for theoretical rather than statistical reasons, it would be logical for the study's sampling decisions to be based upon the same set of considerations. The most common form of non-probabilistic sampling is generally referred to as 'purposive' (Chenin, 1981) or 'purposeful' (Patton, 1987), and is based on determining criteria to make the sample selection. According to Merriam

(1988: 48) purposive sampling 'is based on the assumption that one wants to discover, understand, gain insight; therefore one needs to select a sample from which one can learn the most'. The establishment of the sample selection criteria thus enables the researcher to identify those events, processes, people, documents, etc., which could constitute the study's sample frame. From this an appropriate sample can be determined.

Clearly, given the variety of reasons for undertaking case study research in the first instance, the specific criteria for sample selection may vary widely across case studies in general and are likely to be relatively situation specific. However, as noted earlier, typical criteria referred to in the literature would include sample selections based on:

- typical or extreme instances
- those of a critical nature to the phenomenon under investigation
- a focus on unique and/or ideal types
- a desire for adequate representation via quotas
- the maximum range or variation of data/perspectives
- 'membership' of specific groups or networks
- criteria to facilitate comparative analysis in multiple case study designs.

Although in some studies it may be possible to identify the relevant criteria and make the majority of the sample selection decisions before the study begins, in others it will not. In situations where either the theoretical framework and/or the phenomenon itself can only be loosely articulated at the outset of the study, there will be a need for the case study researcher to adopt a more flexible and emergent approach to sampling decisions. Where this is necessary Glaser and Strauss (1967: 45) propose that the researcher adopts a 'theoretical sampling' strategy: 'Theoretical sampling is the process of data collection for generating theory whereby the analyst jointly collects, codes, and analyses his data and decides what data to collect next and where to find them, in order to develop his theory as it emerges.' In this strategy sampling decisions are influenced by the iteration between pre-existing and emergent theory.

Whatever the specific sampling strategy adopted, the case study researcher will almost inevitably encounter the problem of when to cease data collection. Regardless of the sampling strategy adopted most, if not all, case study research has an inherent potential for the collection of a huge amount of data. However, like many things in life this will eventually become subject to the law of diminishing returns. As the process of data collection proceeds, the case study researcher must continually question whether additional data, of varying types and from a range of different sources, is vital for achieving the purpose of the research. Hartley (1994) offers the view that the researcher can conclude that the data 'saturation point' has been reached when it is felt that further data collection will not yield 'significant' new information.

One issue the case study researcher can consider as a means to coherently link sampling and data collection decisions is the need to collect multiple types of evidence from a range of different sources. One commonly cited problem for case study researchers is a need for them to build confidence in the internal validity of the case study's methodology and findings. This is often referred to as the process of 'triangulation' (Stake, 1995; Merriam, 1988; Yin, 1994; Bonoma, 1985). As all types and sources of data or evidence have their strengths and weaknesses, a strategy which relies upon a single type and/or source is unlikely to be robust enough to stand up to potential criticism. For example, Stake (1995) refers to the 'contestability' of interpretations and conclusions based upon research procedures and evidence which are not sufficiently robust to withstand criticisms of their validity. The opportunity to use a triangulated approach may therefore be seen as a major strength of case study research (Merriam, 1988) in building a methodologically robust study: 'Ideally a researcher can simultaneously pursue high levels of data validity and generalisability by adopting triangulation strategies which provide replication and/or corroboration of findings across methods within a single research project' (Bonoma, 1985: 201). A good example of the application of triangulation in hospitality management case study research is provided by Overstreet (1993) who not only uses both quantitative and qualitative data but also employs different methods to collect and analyse the case study data.

Yin (1994: 92), in using the phrase 'sources of evidence' to mean what has been referred to here as 'types of evidence', indicates the importance of this issue: 'the most important advantage presented by using multiple sources of evidence is the development of *converging lines of enquiry* ... . Thus any finding or conclusion in a case study is likely to be much more convincing and accurate if it is based on several different sources of evidence, following a corroboratory mode' [original emphasis]. Both Yin (1994) and Stake (1995), referring to the work of Patton (1987) and Denzin (1984, 1989) respectively, indicate that 'data type/source triangulation' is a critical procedure for assuring internal validity in case study research. As Stake (1995: 113) comments, 'it is an effort to see if what we are observing and reporting carries the same meaning when found under different circumstances' in the case study. The need for triangulation also arises from the nature of case study research and the process required to determine a complete understanding of both the phenomenon and situation constituting the case in question. As Bromley (1986: 287) points out, case studies are complex, real-world investigations which require the collection of a diversity of relevant evidence: 'Such a diversity of evidence is necessary in case-studies because one does not have the abundance of direct evidence characteristic of an experimental investigation. Having evidence in a case study is like having a few pieces of a jigsaw puzzle, and trying to work out what picture the puzzle would make if all the pieces were available ... . Case studies have much in common with detective work.' Thus, triangulation is required to complete a picture, or puzzle, the form of which is not pre-specified at the outset.

As the types and sources of data which may be required to achieve triangulation within a given piece of case study research are well documented in the research literature (Merriam, 1988; Yin, 1994; Stake, 1995), and because of limited space, it is not intended to provide a detailed account of these types and sources, and the methods associated with their collection here. Both qualitative and quantitative data may be required within a case study, though, as commented earlier, there is often a leaning to the former rather than the latter in this form of research. Case studies will almost inevitably require the collection of primary data and may also utilise relevant secondary data.

The majority of both this primary and secondary data is likely to be 'internal' to the case, i.e. relating to the phenomenon and context which constitute the definition of the case study itself, but there may also be a need for the researcher to collect 'external' data relating to the study in certain circumstances. For example, a case study designed to investigate hotel company performance will clearly need 'internal' data relating to the company or companies concerned and the associated context(s). However, the researcher may also wish to incorporate 'external' primary and/or secondary data relating to views of independent financial analysts and other informed commentators into such a study in order to increase its validity. Both the Leigh (1989) and Moncarz and Kron (1993) studies referred to earlier illustrate this point. The former incorporates an 'external', industry-segment dimension to place the issues in context, and the latter embraces other, similar resort hotels to provide a meaningful context for comparisons.

Data analysis in case study research may take various forms and use a range of different methods and techniques depending on whether the purpose of the research is inductively to 'build' theory or deductively to 'test' existing theory. Similarly, it may rely on quantitative or qualitative methods, though the latter are often regarded as more appropriate to the nature and purpose of many case studies, i.e. the development of in-depth, contextually rooted descriptions and explanations. In inductive case studies the first stage of data analysis is often regarded as one involving the scanning and initial coding of the raw data in order to establish appropriate classificatory or categorisation schemes to organise the data (LeCompte and Preissle, 1993). This process invariably generates discrete 'domains', predicated on semantic relationships, which can then be aggregated into coherent 'groups'. At the next level 'taxonomies' may be identified, which enhance the internal coherence of the domains and/or groups, to facilitate an identification of emergent constructs.

Following this basic level of data organisation the analysis moves on to establish connections and confirm relationships, both within and between the constructs. This process requires the researcher to establish the chronology of incidents and develop inferences (perhaps speculatively at this stage) concerning the nature of the associations between these incidents. This whole process has been referred to as 'analytic induction' (LeCompte and Preissle, 1993) and is essentially an *ex-post* procedure. Though similar in purpose, i.e. categorical identification and relationship establishment, Glaser and Strauss' (1967) 'constant comparison' method diverges from analytic induction as it is a method designed to be applied on a more continuous basis while the earlier stages of the research are taking place. Therefore, it is significantly more iterative with, and conducted parallel to, the process of data collection.

Where the case study investigation takes a deductive form it is likely that data collection and analysis will be more concerned with enumeration in relation to the prior, theoretically informed constructs and categories, established at the outset of the work as opposed to the types of 'constructionist' data analysis methods and techniques discussed above. Given the creation of prior operationally defined categories, such enumeration will comprise the coding and allocation of data into these categories and the production of frequency counts concerning incidence. As the prior determination of categories acts to structure, quite precisely, both the data collection and analysis processes, this approach facilitates hypothesis verification. Yin (1994) suggests that 'pattern-matching' is a desirable strategy in such circumstances. This essentially involves the comparison of the empirical pattern (observed outcomes) with that predicted by the theoretical propositions (expected outcomes) in order to establish the internal validity of the findings (Trochim, 1989).

Yin (1994: 106, 108) proposes that both 'non-equivalent dependent variables as a pattern' and 'rival explanations' can serve as types of 'pattern matching' for case study data analysis. The former is particularly appropriate where multiple dependent variables (outcomes) are evident. 'If, for each outcome, the initially predicted values have been found, and at the same time alternative "patterns" of predicted values ... have not been found, strong causal inferences can be made' (Yin, 1994: 106, 107). The latter focuses on the independent rather than the dependent variables in the study. Where one or more cases exhibit a common outcome the analysis will tend to focus on the reasons how and why such an outcome has arisen. Thus, this procedure attempts to analyse the common outcome, in either one case or many, by reference to alternative theoretical explanations. As Yin (1994, 108) also points out, one important consideration in this approach is that each of the rival explanations 'involves a pattern of independent variables that is mutually exclusive: if one explanation is to be valid, the others cannot be'.

In multiple case study designs there will be a need for not only 'within-case' but also 'cross-case' data analysis. Eisenhardt (1995: 76) suggests that the purpose of 'within-case' analysis is to 'become intimately familiar with each case as a stand-alone entity. This process allows the unique patterns of each case to emerge before investigators push to generalise patterns across cases.' The need for an intensive analysis of the data in a piece of single case study research is self-evident, but clearly this is also important as a prelude to the type of comparative analysis required in multiple case study research. Eisenhardt (1995) outlines a number of tactics which may be employed to produce valid comparisons where multiple case studies are involved. First, 'within-group' similarities for the categories or dimensions are established as a basis for identifying intergroup differences. Second, pairs of case studies may be selected to establish both the similarities and differences between them. Third, the data may be subdivided by its type and/or source, i.e. a separate analysis is conducted on interview, observational, questionnaire, etc., data before it is brought back together as a whole.

Whatever the analytical method(s) chosen, it is important to remember that case study data analysis is essentially designed to produce a 'situational analysis'. Therefore, the analysis should contain both narrative and structural elements which embrace the contemporary and historical dimensions relevant to the phenomenon. Bromley (1986: 290) refers to this issue as one addressing both the 'proximal' (current) and 'distal' (historical) causes of events: 'A proximal explanation, by definition, is one which deals with causes and effects which are closely connected in time and space. A distal explanation is one which deals with causes and effects which are remote from each other.' This is an important view as it recognises the fact that actions, events, etc., are not only influenced by contemporaneous structural constraints but also derived from particular historical antecedents. Thus, data analysis within case studies should not be temporally independent but requires the researcher to establish a meaningful chronological framework which can be used to establish key antecedents, patterns and trajectories. Yin (1994) refers to this process as one which establishes, and maintains, a reliable 'chain of evidence'.

To complete the data analysis process it is necessary for the researcher to bring together the theoretical and empirical elements of the study. Eisenhardt (1995) refers to this as 'enfolding the literature'. Whether the study is inductive or deductive in nature will clearly influence the nature of this process. However, the overall purpose of the process is essentially the same: to create a more valid and robust understanding of the phenomenon in question by linking existing knowledge to the new knowledge created in the case study research. This constitutes the conceptual–empirical nexus and is highly dependent upon both the technical skills and quality of insight possessed by the case study researcher. As Hamel, Dufour and Fortin (1993: 48) succinctly state: 'The case study must not conclude in a systematisation of field information, presented as an explanation. In other words, such a study must not be a restatement of information that has been collected and arranged by the written word to give it a systematic appearance. The explanation must provide information that ... transcends this information because of the [theoretical] perspective prevailing over the case study.'

The final stage of the case study research process is that of writing up the analysis of the study. The specific format and contents of this final case study report will vary depending upon the reasons for undertaking the case study in the first place, its nature and particular emphasis, and the characteristics of the target audience. Yin (1994) suggests that there are four main varieties of case study report: the 'classic' single-case narrative, the multiple-case version of the single-case narrative, a single- or multiple-case report which is structured according to the study's research questions, and the cross-case analysis format which may be adopted in studies with multiple cases.

Whatever the type of final case study report chosen by the researcher, one particular pitfall should be recognised at an early point in the writing-up stage: the almost inevitable situation of too much case study data to put into the final report (Stake, 1995). Given the nature of the case study process, it is highly likely that the total volume of data collected during the study will significantly exceed that which is appropriate to include in the final report. This presents the case study researcher with the dilemma of what to include and which aspects to emphasise. In one sense the solution to this dilemma is straightforward. The researcher makes the decision to include or exclude material by reference to the research questions established for the study at the outset. However, in reality such decisions are seldom so clear cut. The extent to which the case's descriptive narrative should be limited, and how much detail is to be provided on the study's basic methodology and data analysis procedures, are not always easy decisions to make. The guiding principles which should be adopted in this respect are necessity and sufficiency. Clearly, material which is not fully necessary and relevant to the case report should not be included, but the researcher must ensure that sufficient material, both narrative and analytical, is present to enable the reader to fully understand and evaluate the research.

Given the case study's 'database', Yin (1994: 137, 138) proposes six possible approaches to structuring the final report as follows:

- 'Linear-Analytic
- Chronological
- Suspense
- Comparative
- Theory-Building
- Unsequenced'

The Linear-Analytic structure is essentially the 'standard' approach to presenting research findings found in most journal articles. A Comparative structure will be employed where the purpose is to make either intra- or inter-case, or both, comparisons. In the intra-case version the same case may be examined a number of times from alternative theoretical perspectives. In the inter-case version comparisons may be structured on a case-by-case or a unit-of-analysis by unit-of-analysis basis depending upon the nature of the comparative aim established for the research.

The Chronological structure may be employed in situations where it is important to produce a 'case history' in the final report. Although there is likely to be a need to identify pertinent chronological aspects within all case studies *per se*, where the study has a particularly strong focus on identifying causal sequences, i.e. in longitudinal studies, this type of structure will perhaps be a more dominant feature of the case report. In the Theory-Building structure the material is sequenced by reference to the logic employed to build the theory. Thus the case report leads the reader through the logical process used by the researcher to develop the theory.

The Suspense structure reverses the logic underlying the Linear-Analytic structure by presenting the answer or outcome at the beginning, with the remainder of the report providing a logical explanation, or defence, of this conclusion. Finally, the Unsequenced structure may be adopted where the particular order in which material is presented is of no great significance. What is important here is the need to ensure that the overall collection of material is sufficiently complete to produce a coherent description in total.

Being a case study researcher

Given that case study research is often characterised by being an emergent, fluid and iterative process, and is almost invariably a multi-faceted empirical investigation, it is not surprising that the demands placed upon the case study researcher are considerable. Indeed, Yin (1989: 62) goes as far as to suggest that 'the demands of a case study on a person's intellect, ego and emotions are far greater than those of any other research strategy.' In a similar vein, Merriam (1988: 37, 38) contends that: 'Case study research ... places the investigator in a largely uncharted ocean. For some it becomes an adventure full of promise and discovery; for others, it can be a disorienting and unproductive experience.' Robson (1993: 162, 163) suggests that case study research requires 'well trained investigators [and that] Personal qualities such as having an *open and enquiring mind*, being a *"good listener"*, general *sensitivity* and *responsiveness* to *contradictory evidence* are needed [and, in short, case study investigators] need an intelligent appreciation of what they are doing and why.'

Essentially, what these authors suggest is a need for the case study researcher to have a high tolerance for ambiguity, be resilient, flexible, and sensitive to the emergent characteristics and processes in the evolving study. Stake (1995) proposes that many of these desirable researcher characteristics may be embodied in the 'role(s)' adopted, and how they are played, by the case study researcher. According to Stake the roles that the case study researcher may adopt are as follows. The first is that of 'Teacher' in that one aim of research is to inform, educate, and facilitate further learning. Secondly, though not all case study research is explicitly evaluative in purpose, a degree of evaluation is inevitable; thus the case study researcher is also likely to occupy the role of 'Evaluator', even if this is as limited as evaluating the value of the case(s) used in the study. Thirdly, as case study analysis is invariably constructionist in nature, this demands that the case study researcher adopts an 'Interpreter' role to produce new insights. And finally, an 'Advocate' role may be assumed by the case study researcher, wherein an attempt is made to convince others that they should also accept and believe the conclusions of the study.

Clearly, these roles are not mutually exclusive and any piece of case study research may require the researcher to adopt some or all of them at different stages of the work. Which to choose, when and for what purposes are questions beyond detailed discussion here. However, Stake (1995: 103) does provide some indication of the issues which may influence the researcher's decisions to adopt a particular role stance. These include considerations concerning:

a.   'How much to participate personally in the activity of the case.
b.   How much to pose as expert, how much comprehension to reveal.
c.   Whether to be neutral observer or evaluative, critical analyst.
d.   How much to try to serve the needs of anticipated readers.
e.   How much to provide interpretations about the case.
f.   How much to advocate a position.
g.   Whether or not to tell it as a story.'

As noted earlier in this chapter, case study research, unless it is entirely based upon secondary or archival analysis, demands that the researcher is actively involved in the unfolding research process and maintains direct contact with its subject(s). Not only does this raise 'process' and 'technical' issues concerned with the ability of the researcher to establish and maintain effective roles and relationships and to utilise observational and interviewing techniques, but it also gives rise to 'emotional' and 'validity' issues associated with close involvement, subjective perceptions, and possible obtrusiveness and reactivity.

While appropriate research training can help to overcome many of these 'technical' and 'validity' issues, the 'process' and 'emotional' issues are less amenable to modification via training. With regard to negotiating access, establishing and maintaining roles and relationships, and managing the emotional aspects of involvement, the case study researcher needs to have an appropriate disposition. While this is something which can be developed and enhanced to a degree by appropriate training, it does tend to presuppose a certain type or level of personality traits and interpersonal/social relations skills which are conducive to the effective conduct of this type of research.

It has also long been recognised that the quality of research data, and consequent findings, are affected by the nature of the relationship between the researcher and the researched (Rosenthal, 1966). This is particularly the case in situations where the researcher and researched have direct, and often prolonged, contact. In case study research the researcher assumes a boundary spanning position: 'partly insider, partly stranger, partly accepted and partly not; partly understanding the culture and partly still being able to question it' (Hartley, 1994: 223). Therefore, the case study researcher must be cognisant of, and prepared to deal with, the inherent tensions which this type of situation generates. One trait which can assist greatly in this respect is that of communication: 'a good case study researcher must also be a good communicator. A good communicator empathises with respondents, establishes rapport, asks good questions, and listens intently' (Merriam, 1988: 39).

Thus, although there may be a temptation for some commentators in the research methodology literature to regard case study research as a 'softer' option than the more quantitative, experimental or survey approaches, it clearly is not. The case study researcher not only needs to possess a significantly greater range and degree of 'interactional' skills than is the case in non-interactional approaches, but must also be capable of implementing a multiple-method study in relation to data collection, analysis and interpretation. Far from being a 'soft' option it is perhaps one of the most difficult and demanding for the researcher.

Conclusions and further issues

This chapter has highlighted a number of significant general issues and concerns related to the selection, design and implementation of case study research and has related a number of hospitality management research studies which have adopted the case study approach to these general issues. What is clear from the discussion of these issues is that adoption of the case study approach to research is not the easy or 'soft' option some commentators would suggest. Case study research may be predominantly qualitative or quantitative in nature, conducted to generate new theory or test existing theory, and designed as single, 'stand-alone' or multiple, comparative pieces of research. It may be undertaken for descriptive, analytical or evaluative purposes, can cope with the widely discussed 'generalisability' issue and is likely to be the preferred methodological choice for certain types of research question; and its design and conduct invariably place significant multiple-method demands upon the researcher(s) concerned.

There arc cxamples of both good, and not so good, case study research design and implementation in the hospitality management research literature. However, the evidence as a whole seems to suggest that the application of case study research methodology in these studies is rarely sound in all its components. Although there are examples of good methodological practice, relating to specific aspects of the case study research process, contained in a number of the hospitality management studies referred to in the chapter, the general picture would appear to be one in which this good practice is not sustained throughout the various elements of many of these studies. This may indicate that hospitality management researchers adopting the case study approach either do not tend to give adequate thought to the full range of methodological issues associated with their case study design as a whole, or are not sufficiently transparent in reporting, and justifying, the decisions they have made in this respect. This often leads to studies being published which are open to considerable methodological criticism and, as a consequence, may be either undervalued or rightfully damned by other researchers!

Therefore, a key message for hospitality management researchers pursuing the case study route is the need to ensure that the study as a whole is designed and implemented on the basis of sound, comprehensive and defensible methodological decisions, which permeate the published findings. Although there is an obvious need for this feature to be present in any research study, whether it adopts a case study approach or not, there is perhaps an even greater imperative in case study research because of the willingness of many critics to regard such research as sloppy, 'poor science', or indeed 'non-science'! In addition, because case study research is often qualitative in nature and utilises multiple methods, the type of 'standard', generally accepted methodological decisions frequently used in non-case study, quantitative research projects are not applicable. Thus there is a need for the case study researcher to provide greater detail and justification where the underlying methodological rigour is not likely to be as immediately clear or straightforward as it may be in other types of study.

Perhaps partly because of these issues, and in common with many other fields of study, hospitality management research has not adopted the case study approach as extensively as it might have done. Hospitality management is still a relatively young field of academic research which has extensively borrowed concepts, methodologies and techniques from other more established fields. It is still searching for a distinctive identity and attempting to build a coherent body of knowledge within a field regarded by many of its occupants as possessing, at the very least, a degree of uniqueness. However, this claim is not strongly reflected in the body of contemporary hospitality management research as a whole. If hospitality, and hospitality management, do indeed possess such a degree of uniqueness, it should be a field where case study research has a far greater presence than it does at present.

As readers will recall from the earlier discussion, one rationale for preferring the case study approach is where the phenomenon in question, and/or its context of occurrence, is regarded as atypical or unique; another is the need to develop appropriate theoretical insights in fields which do not possess sufficient extant theory. If indeed these are features of hospitality *per se*, and hospitality management in particular, then a greater emphasis upon case study research could be seen as a vital element in the development of hospitality management research as a distinct and discrete field in its own right. In addition, a greater emphasis on the conduct of comparative case study research by hospitality management researchers could also help to address the contention that this field has its own unique properties. This contention needs to be both conceptually and empirically tested through comparative case study research designed to ascertain whether hospitality does have distinct divergent properties or is substantially the same as other phenomena and contexts it is purported to differ from.

An expansion in the quantity and quality of hospitality management-related case study research, both that taking an internal and in-depth focus on hospitality management phenomena/contexts, and that focusing upon a comparative analysis of such phenomena *vis-à-vis* other service and/or manufacturing contexts, would assist the hospitality management research community to explore more systematically claims made regarding the distinctiveness, or otherwise, of the field. Such a process may help to create the 'critical mass' of research evidence required to address these fundamental issues.

References

Abbott, A. (1992) What do cases do? Some notes on activity in sociological analysis. In Ragin, C. C. and Becker, H. S. (Eds) *What is a Case?*, Cambridge University Press, New York, pp. 53–82.

Barsky, J. D. (1996) Building a program for world-class service. *Cornell Hotel and Restaurant Administration Quarterly*, Vol. 37, No. 1, pp. 17–27.

Bassey, M. (1981) Pedagogic research on the relative merits of search for generalisation and study of single events. *Oxford Review of Education*, Vol. 7, No. 1, pp. 73–93.

Bell, J. (1993) *Doing Your Research Project* (2nd Edition). Open University Press, Milton Keynes.

Bonoma, T. V. (1985) Case research in marketing: opportunities, problems, and a process. *Journal of Marketing Research*, Vol. 22, May, pp. 199–208.

Breiter, D., Tyink, S. A. and Corey-Tuckwell, S. (1995) Bergstrom Hotels: a case study in quality. *International Journal of Contemporary Hospitality Management*, Vol. 7, No. 6, pp. 14–18.

Bromley, D. B. (1986) *The Case Study Method in Psychology and Related Disciplines*. John Wiley & Sons, Chichester.

Brownell, J. and Jameson, D. (1996) Getting quality out on the street—a case of show and tell. *Cornell Hotel and Restaurant Administration Quarterly*, Vol. 37, No. 1, pp. 28–33.

Burgess, R. G. (1984) *In the Field: An Introduction to Field Research*. Allen & Unwin, London.

Chenin, I. (1981) Appendix: An introduction to sampling. In Kidder, L. H. (Ed.) *Sellitz, Wrightsman and Cooks' Research Methods in Social Relations* (4th Edition), Holt, Rinehart & Winston, New York.

Clark, J. J. (1993) Holiday Inn: new rooms at the inn. *Cornell Hotel and Restaurant Administration Quarterly*, Vol. 34, No. 5, pp. 59–67.

Cronbach, L. J. (1975) Beyond the two disciplines of scientific psychology. *American Psychologist*, Vol. 30, pp. 116–127.

Denzin, N. (1984) *The Research Act*. Prentice-Hall, Englewood Cliffs, NJ.

Denzin, N. (1989) *Interpretive Biography*. Sage Publications, Newbury Park, CA.

Eisenhardt, K. M. (1995) Building theories from case study research. In Huber, G. P. and Van de Van, A. H. (Eds) *Longitudinal Field Research Methods: Studying Processes of Organisational Change*, Sage Publications, Thousand Oaks, CA.

Figueiredo, K., Latas, J. R. and Gomes, D. (1995) A strategic service vision in the hotel industry: some conclusions from case studies. In Teare, R. and Armistead, C. (Eds) *Services Management: New Directions, New Perspectives*, Cassell, London.

Glaser, B. G. and Strauss, A. L. (1967) *The Discovery of Grounded Theory: Theories for Qualitative Research*. Aldine Publishing Co., Chicago.

Goode, W. J. and Hatt, P. K. (1952) The case study. In *Methods in Social Research*, McGraw-Hill, New York, pp. 330–340.

Gummesson, E. (1991) *Qualitative Methods in Management Research*. Sage Publications, Newbury Park, CA.

Hamel, J., Dufour, S. and Fortin, D. (1993) *Case Study Methods*. Sage Publications, Newbury Park, CA.

Hartley, R. F. (1991) *Management Mistakes and Successes* (3rd Edition). John Wiley & Sons, New York.

Hartley, J. F. (1994) Case studies in organisational research. In Cassell, C. and Symon, G. (Eds) *Qualitative Methods in Organisational Research: A Practical Guide*, Sage Publications, London, pp. 208–229.

Hotels (1995a) Carlson Companies, Inc. harnesses the power of global synergy. *Hotels*, Vol. 29, No. 11, pp. 51–52.

Hotels (1995b) Carlson Hospitality Worldwide: the brands of choice around the globe. *Hotels*, Vol. 29, No. 11, pp. 53–55.

Hotels (1995c) Carlson Hospitality Worldwide expands aggressively. *Hotels*, Vol. 29, No. 11, pp. 56–57.

Hotels (1995d) Radisson achieves strongest growth momentum in its history. *Hotels*, Vol. 29, No. 11, pp. 57–59.

Hotels (1995e) Radisson leads the industry in astute marketing strategies. *Hotels*, Vol. 29, No. 11, p. 60.

Hotels (1995f) Superior technology puts Radisson in the winner's circle. *Hotels*, Vol. 29, No. 11, p. 61.

Hotels (1995g) Superior training creates loyal guests worldwide. *Hotels*, Vol. 29, No. 11, p. 62.

Hotels (1995h) Breakthrough growth for country inns and suites by Carlson. *Hotels*, Vol. 29, No. 11, p. 63.

Hotels (1995i) Country Kitchen hits its stride. *Hotels*, Vol. 29, No. 11, p. 64.

Hotels (1995j) Friday's turns 30 and reaches $1 billion mark. *Hotels*, Vol. 29, No. 11, pp. 65–66.

Hotels (1995k) Radisson Seven Seas Cruises—one brand with three acclaimed vessels. *Hotels*, Vol. 29, No. 11, p. 67.

LeCompte, M. D. and Preissle, J. (1993) *Ethnography and Qualitative Design in Educational Research* (2nd Edition). Academic Press, London.

Leigh, T. W. (1989) Competitive assessment in service industries: the case of entering the economy lodging segment. In Prescott, J. E. (Ed.) *Advances in Competitive Intelligence*, Society of Competitive Intelligence Professionals, Virginia.

Lijphart, A. (1971) Comparative politics and the comparative method. *American Political Science Review*, Vol. 65, No. 3, pp. 682–694.

Luchars, J. Y. and Hinkin, T. R. (1996) The service-quality audit: a hotel case study. *Cornell Hotel and Restaurant Administration Quarterly*, Vol. 37, No. 1, pp. 34–41.

McClintock, C., Brannen, D. and Maynard-Moody, S. (1979) Applying the logic of sample surveys to qualitative case studies: the case cluster method. *Administrative Science Quarterly*, Vol. 24, pp. 612–629.

Merriam, S. B. (1988) *Case Study Research in Education: A Qualitative Approach*. Jossey-Bass, San Francisco.

Mitchell, J. C. (1983) Case and situation analysis. *Sociological Review*, Vol. 31, pp. 187–211.

Moncarz, E. S. and Kron, R. N. (1993) Operational analysis: a case study of two hotels in financial distress. *International Journal of Hospitality Management*, Vol. 12, No. 2, pp. 175–196.

Morey, R. C. and Dittman, D. A. (1995) Evaluating a hotel GM's performance: a case study in benchmarking. *Cornell Hotel and Restaurant Administration Quarterly*, Vol. 36, No. 5, pp. 30–35.

Muller, C. (1990) The Marriott divestment: leaving the past behind. *Cornell Hotel and Restaurant Administration Quarterly*, Vol. 30, No. 4, pp. 7–13.

Ogden, S. (1995) Strategy, structure and employee relations: lessons from compulsory competitive tendering. *International Journal of Contemporary Hospitality Management*, Vol. 7, No. 2/3, pp. 36–41.

Oppermann, M., Din, K. H. and Amri, S. Z. (1996) Urban hotel location and evolution in a developing country: the case of Kuala Lumpur, Malaysia. *Tourism Recreation Research*, Vol. 21, No. 1, pp. 55–63.

Overstreet, G. A. (1993) Creating value in oversupplied markets: the case of Charlottesville, Virginia, hotels. *Cornell Hotel and Restaurant Administration Quarterly*, Vol. 34, No. 5, pp. 68–96.

Patton, M. Q. (1987) *How to Use Qualitative Methods in Evaluation*. Sage Publications, Newbury Park, CA.

Pearson, J. (1987) The making of a hotel great: Tom Staed. *Lodging*, December, pp. 11–28.

Platt, J. (1988) What can case studies do? *Studies in Qualitative Methodology*: Vol. 1, JAI Press, Greenwich, CT, pp. 1–23.

Porter, M. E. (1980) *Competitive Strategy: Techniques for Analysing Industries and Competitors*. Free Press/Macmillan, New York.

Porter, M. E. (1985) *Competitive Advantage: Creating and Sustaining Superior Performance*. Free Press/Macmillan, New York.

Ragin, C. C. (1992) Introduction: cases of 'What is a case?'. In Ragin, C. C. and Becker, H. S. (Eds) *What is a Case?*, Cambridge University Press, New York, pp. 1–17.

Robson, C. (1993) *Real World Research*. Blackwell, Oxford.

Rose, H. (1991) Case studies. In Allan, G. and Skinner, C. (Eds) *Handbook for Research Students in the Social Sciences*, Falmer Press, London, pp. 190–202.

Rosenthal, R. (1966) *Experimenter Effects in Behavioural Research*. Appleton-Century-Crofts, New York.

Silverman, D. (1985) *Qualitative Methodology and Sociology*. Gower, Aldershot.

Smith, N. C. (1991) The case study: a vital yet misunderstood research method for management. In Smith, N. C. and Dainty, P (Eds) *The Management Research Handbook*, Routledge, London, pp. 145–158.

Sosteric, M. (1996) Subjectivity and the labour process: a case study in the restaurant industry. *Work, Employment and Society*, Vol. 16, No. 2, pp. 297–318.

Stake, R. E. (1994) Case studies. In Denzin, N. K. and Lincoln, Y. S. (Eds) *Handbook Of Qualitative Research*, Sage Publications, Thousand Oaks, CA, pp. 236–247.

Stake, R. E. (1995) *The Art of Case Study Research*. Sage Publications, Thousand Oaks, CA.

Trochim, W. (1989) Outcome pattern matching and program theory. *Evaluation and Program Planning*, Vol. 12, pp. 355–366.

Tse, E. C.-Y. and Elwood, C. M. (1990) Synthesis of the life cycle concept with strategy and management style: a case analysis in the hospitality industry. *International Journal of Hospitality Management*, Vol. 9, No. 3, pp. 223–236.

Wilson, S. (1979) Explorations of the usefulness of case study evaluations. *Evaluation Quarterly*, Vol. 3, pp. 446–459.

Yin, R. K. (1989) *Case Study Research: Design and Methods* (Revised Edition). Sage Publications, Beverly Hills, CA.

Yin, R. K. (1993) *Applications of Case Study Research*. Sage Publications, Newbury Park, CA.

Yin, R. K. (1994) *Case Study Research—Design and Methods* (2nd Edition). Sage Publications, Thousand Oaks, CA.

8 Comparative research

BOB BROTHERTON

Introduction

Some researchers would question whether it is possible to identify comparative research as a distinct type of research in its own right, as all research embodies comparisons of various types. Experimental research will involve pre- and post-treatment effect comparisons and those made between the experimental and control groups used in the research. Survey research is likely to contain sub-sample comparisons in its data analysis. Case study and other field research will invariably embody a varied range of comparisons relating to the phenomenon of interest within the context of the research study. Indeed, as Swanson (1971: 145) succinctly pointed out many years ago, 'Thinking without comparison is unthinkable. And, in the absence of comparison, so is all scientific thought and scientific research.'

All research does therefore tend to exhibit varying degrees of comparison within its design and procedures (Lieberson, 1985). However, not all research is explicitly designed to be comparative in nature, and the occurrence of comparisons within a given piece of research does not make it comparative research. For research to be classified as *comparative* its overall aim or purpose should be explicitly comparative in nature and it should be designed with this specific outcome in mind. As Ragin (1996: 75) points out, 'there are important differences between the *orientations* of most comparativists and most noncomparativists and these differences have important methodological consequences' (emphasis in original). One such methodological issue is that of the importance given to 'contextual factors' by comparative researchers, a point succinctly made by Pearce (1993: 31) who states that, 'particular attention in comparative studies must be given to contextual factors. If one of the basic purposes of comparative studies is to test theories in, or to generalise from, a range of contexts then it follows that the contextual factors—the independent variables in such studies—need to be clearly and explicitly identified and described.'

Although there exists a strong tradition of conducting comparative research in some of the more established fields of study, for example in comparative sociology, government and politics, religion, etc., as Pearce (1993) has noted, the development of a strong and coherent body of comparative research in the tourism field has not materialised. This is a situation mirrored in hospitality management. Although, as will be seen later in the chapter, there is evidence that some hospitality management researchers have undertaken comparative studies, this type of research is largely underutilised and underdeveloped within the hospitality management field. Given the admittedly debatable

The Handbook of Contemporary Hospitality Management Research, Edited by Bob Brotherton.
© 1999 John Wiley & Sons Ltd.

claims many members of the hospitality management research community routinely make about its supposed uniqueness, this is rather a surprising situation.

As comparative research is essentially concerned with 'discovering similarities and differences among phenomena' (Warwick and Osherson, 1973: 7), it might reasonably have been expected that the hospitality management research community would have strongly embraced this type of research as a key strategy to demonstrate the validity of the uniqueness claims they frequently espouse. Could it be that the purported uniqueness of hospitality is a spurious claim, which has been blindly accepted by hospitality management researchers as an 'act of faith', or is it indeed one of significance which has not been adequately explored? Either way, as Wieviorka (1992: 170) points out, the adoption of comparative research methods could provide a route to a more satisfactory answer: 'A comparison may have at least two main functions. It may help to deconstruct what common sense [accepted wisdom?] takes to be unique or unified. On the contrary, it may construct the unity of what seems to be broken up into practical categories. It is never so useful as when it combines these two functions and thus justifies both the deconstruction of a pre-conception and the construction of a scientific category.'

More specifically, Neuman (1994: 387, 389) suggests that comparative research has a number of particular advantages over non-comparative research in that it:

- 'improves measurement and conceptualisation [because] it is difficult for a researcher to detect hidden biases, assumptions, and values until she applies a concept in different cultures or settings;
- can eliminate or offer alternative explanations for causal relationships;
- raises new questions and stimulates theory building.'

On the other hand, Neuman (1994: 389) also points to some of the disadvantages associated with comparative research in that:

- 'it is more difficult, more costly, and more time consuming than research that is not comparative;
- the types of data that can be collected and problems with equivalence ... are also frequent limitations;
- comparative researchers can rarely use random samples;
- comparative researchers can apply, not test, theory and make only limited generalisations.'

Given the enormous scope of comparative research *per se*, it is impossible for this chapter to cover the breadth of the field in detail. Therefore, it will focus on examining the key issues and approaches relating to comparative research in general, and will discuss specific considerations the hospitality management researcher would need to confront in any decision to undertake comparative research as a preferred methodology. These considerations include issues concerning the selection of entities to be used for comparative purposes and the establishment of the comparative base. The chapter also explores the nature of what may be termed the 'basic types' of comparative research, namely cross-sectional, longitudinal and replicative studies; and illustrates the usage of these basic types in hospitality management research by providing a number of examples of studies involving their application. However, what may be regarded as another 'basic type' of comparative research—meta-analysis—is not included in this chapter owing to space limitations and its limited application in contemporary hospitality management research. Finally, the chapter concludes with an indication of the key issues which hospitality management researchers need to consider in undertaking comparative research.

Issues and approaches

Comparative research is potentially a very 'broad church' which can range from studies explicitly designed to compare two individuals to cross-national studies comparing at least two countries and, as will be seen in the following section of this chapter, it may be cross-sectional or longitudinal in nature, or possibly both. Given such a potential range, it is not surprising that the central research questions, focus, phenomena of interest, aims/objectives, scope/scale, contexts and/or time frames, and methods adopted for such research, may be extremely varied (see, for example, Przeworski and Teune, 1970; Skocpol, 1984; Tilley, 1984; Stinchcombe, 1978; Lijphart, 1971). However, behind this apparent complexity, it is possible to identify some common or generic issues relating to comparative research *per se*.

Although the purpose of any particular piece of comparative research will clearly be specific to the nature of the study concerned, it is possible to identify the general purposes likely to form the basis for a decision to undertake this type of research. Antal, Dierkes and Weiler (1996: 9) suggest three general purposes for comparative research, the first being that it 'permits the stepwise and controlled falsification of hypotheses generated within a specific sectoral, regional, or national context. It defines the limits of generalisation by specifying the conditions under which hypotheses are valid.' This purpose may be implemented by the testing of 'macro-hypotheses', which reflect the possible interrelationships between the structural dimensions of total systems, or via 'micro-replications' conducted in a 'new' context to further test a proposition which has previously been validated in one or more other contexts (Rokkan, 1966). Thus, the conduct of comparative research helps to develop and strengthen theoretical insight by systematically exploring the nature of generalities and particularities.

Antal, Dierkes and Weiler's (1996: 10) second purpose is that comparative research can make a strong contribution to developing the type of knowledge base required to inform the determination of policy: 'Structured comparison provides a framework for determining those aspects of a situation which are due to unique circumstances, and those which are more generally applicable—and therefore possibly appropriate to consider transferring to other contexts.' In this sense comparative research can inform policy determination by identifying those factors which are generically causal or contextually contingent, and those which are amenable to control or otherwise. Thus it can establish the 'transferability' of the research findings (Pearce, 1993). The third purpose for comparative research proposed by Antal, Dierkes and Weiler (1996) is that this type of research explicitly recognises the generally greater degree of 'interdependence' characterising the contemporary world. Sectors, systems, industries, national and supranational entities are becoming increasingly interrelated and mutually dependent. Again, by studying the phenomenon in other contexts it becomes possible not only to disentangle its generic and contingent facets but to build a greater understanding in relation to the main context of interest to the researcher.

Despite the differences in emphasis, all Antal, Dierkes and Weiler's (1996) purposes have a clear central theme, that of identifying similarities/differences, or convergence/divergence, to further an understanding of the phenomenon in question. Regardless of whether the comparisons are being made at the level of individuals, organisations or countries, this central theme remains the same. Although Ragin (1994) makes the claim that the distinguishing feature of comparative research is its concentration on diversity, this is somewhat misleading as diversity and similarity are essentially two sides of the same coin. To identify diversity it is necessary to explore similarity, and vice versa. Diversity will be evident where dissimilarity exists, and similarity will arise where there is little or no diversity.

Kohn (1996) refers to four different types of cross-national comparative research studies, which he contends have different purposes or 'intent', where the nation is either the *object*, the *context* or the *unit of analysis*, or the work is *transnational* in nature. Although Kohn's categorisation is framed within the context of cross-national research, it is applicable to all types and levels of comparative research. In the *object* perspective the researcher's focus is on the particular context being studied, either in its totality or in relation to a clearly defined sub-part. Therefore the researcher will have a strong intrinsic interest in the particular companies, industries or countries selected as the object for the study. Each will be important for its own sake; they will not be selected merely as 'useful settings for pursuing some general hypothesis' (Kohn, 1996: 29), as they would be in the *context* perspective where each becomes little more than a convenient vehicle to test the generality of the research findings.

The distinction between Kohn's (1996) *context* and *unit of analysis* perspectives is rather a fine one, as indeed he recognises. In the latter perspective the researcher will be interested in exploring the characteristics of each company, industry, country, etc., in order to analyse the extent to which relevant structures and processes are systematically related to these characteristics. Therefore, the companies, industries, countries, etc., are classified by reference to one or more relevant dimensions to create prototypical rather than empirical entities. Finally, Kohn's (1996) *transnational* perspective may also be read as 'trans-organisational', 'trans-sectoral' or 'trans-industrial'. The issue here is the view that the particular type of entity selected for comparative purposes is itself a component of a wider system. It is not seen as an isolated and discrete entity but one which is systematically interrelated with its wider domain of existence. A good example of this issue is demonstrated in the work of Pettigrew (1989) which adopts a 'contextualist' approach to study strategic change to embrace both horizontal and vertical levels of analysis in the comparative case studies.

Rokkan (1996) suggests that comparative research may be dichotomised into two basic 'styles'. These may be regarded as 'inter' and 'intra' types of comparative studies. The former is concerned with examining the research issues across or between the particular entities selected for the study, i.e. companies, countries, cultures, etc., while the latter focuses on making comparisons between the relevant sub-units included within the single entity adopted for the study. Thus the 'inter' type of study is essentially one involving horizontal comparisons across entities, often conducted at a relatively large scale, while the 'intra' type is likely to have a greater focus on making more detailed vertical comparisons within the boundaries of the singular entity used for the study (Janoski, 1991). Although many authors (see, for example, Ragin, 1991, 1994) would contend that the 'proper' role of comparative research is that of making 'macrocomparisons' across large-scale entities, Smelser (1996: 96, 97) makes the pertinent point that the 'intra' type of study may offer greater potential than many commentators would give it: 'In some cases intraunit comparisons may prove more fruitful than interunit comparisons ... having located what appear to be the operative factors in the intraunit comparisons, it is possible to move to the interunit comparisons to see if the same differences hold in the large.'

In comparative studies adopting multiple case study designs the intraunit, or 'within-case', analysis is likely to be fairly prominent as a basis to explore comparisons across the cases at a later stage. As Eisenhardt (1995) has commented, this 'within-case' analysis allows the researcher to become familiar with the particularities of each case before seeking to establish whether these particularities may be generalised across the cases in the study. In this respect Eisenhardt (1995) advocates the use of a number of different analyses to produce valid comparisons in multiple case study projects. The first is to identify 'within-group' similarities for the relevant theoretical categories or dimensions as a foundation for considering inter-group differences. The second is to explore combinations of cases to establish the similarities or differences between them. And thirdly, the comparative analysis may be conducted by subdividing the empirical data by its type and/or source, analysing each in turn *vis-à-vis* each theoretical category, and then combining the separate analyses to determine the degree of congruence or otherwise.

However, the value of the simple dichotomy between intraunit and interunit type studies is questioned by Janoski (1991: 66) who, in supporting Ragin's (1987) call for more development of 'synthetic' strategies for comparative research, contends that 'all comparative research is synthetic in that it integrates internal and external analysis ... comparative research steps from external to internal analysis, and back again to external analysis'; but also recognises that within this iterative process 'the methods and theory in each stage may differ considerably'. The possible combinations of internal/external analysis and qualitative/quantitative methods are explored further by Janoski (1991) who suggests that seven of the nine possibilities he identifies could be regarded as synthetic strategies embracing these subdivisions of the two methodological–analytical dimensions.

Whatever the purpose for, and perspective or type of, study adopted by the comparative researcher, the comparative research literature in general invariably supports Warwick and Osherson's (1973: 52) contention that: 'Explanation or generalisation through comparative research is usually sought via one of two paths: a positive approach in which similarities are identified in independent variables associated with a common outcome, or a negative one whereby independent variables associated with divergent outcomes are identified.' This contention is generally referred to in the literature as the application of the Millian logic of analysis, which is derived from the work of John Stuart Mill who suggested that there are two basic techniques for comparative analysis: 'the *method of agreement* and the *indirect method of difference*' (Wickham-Crowley, 1991: 86) (emphasis in original). The *method of agreement* corresponds to the positive approach and seeks to identify the common factors or variables related to the convergent outcome which can then be used to infer causal generalisation across otherwise different entities. The *indirect method of difference* corresponds to the negative approach in that it takes entities which differ in terms of the final outcome of interest and seeks to identify the factor(s) or variable(s) upon which these outcomes depend. For example, the entities may share many common conditions but may be found to differ on only one of these conditions in terms of its presence, non-presence, or nature. It is this which then explains why the different outcomes have occurred.

A good example of the application of this Millian logic is provided by Ragin (1987, 1994) who uses Boolean algebra to systematise his approach to its implementation. This process proceeds in the following way. Initially each case is analysed to establish the absence or presence of the outcome the study is focused upon. This is followed by the same type of procedure for the conditions or variables thought to have produced the outcome. These two sets of information are then combined into a 'truth' table, with the hypothesised causes as columns and the cases as rows. Each case is then assigned a number to indicate whether the condition or variable is present (1) or not (0). This data structure must then be successively reduced, 'to establish which conditions are *necessary and sufficient to produce either outcome* ... . "Necessary" means that a condition must be present, or the outcome will not occur; it may, however, have that effect only in the context of other supporting conditions. "Sufficient" means that the occurrence of this condition alone will produce the outcome in question; this does not preclude the existence of other conditions, or even sets of conditions, that might also be sufficient' (Wickham-Crowley, 1991: 87) (emphasis in original). When complete this process culminates in a set of scenarios which specify the set or sets of conditions which produce the outcomes. Thus, the Boolean truth table process forces the researcher to consider closely the relationship between analytic frames and empirical evidence, in both constructing the table and interpreting its product. This has led Ragin (1994: 129, 130) to claim that: 'The construction of the truth table itself is an important part of the dialogue between ideas and evidence in comparative research because the truth table must be free of inconsistencies before it can be simplified. Evidence-based images emerge from the simplification of truth tables in the form of configurations of conditions that differentiate subsets of cases.'

While both the positive and negative approaches could embrace what Kohn (1996) refers to as 'transhistorical generalisations' or 'historically contextualised knowledge', the positive approach is perhaps more likely to reflect the former and the negative approach the latter. Although common outcomes may be generated by very different historical processes, a focus on the structural similarities within the comparative entities is likely to be 'the most efficient strategy in searching for an explanation' (Kohn, 1996: 32). This is also a view supported by Smelser (1996: 96) who contends that where two or more entities 'share some important conditions in common, it is relatively more permissible to treat these common conditions as parameters, and proceed to examine the operation of other variables as if these common conditions were not operative, because their operation is presumably similar in both cases'. On the other hand, the existence of divergent outcomes implies not only differences in structural relationships between the entities but also perhaps more profound differences in the historical processes which generated such diversity. Hence, the negative approach will be more likely to consider the influence of 'historically contextualised knowledge' in seeking to identify the causal processes associated with the divergent outcomes. Ragin (1987) contends that one of the great strengths of comparative research is its ability to deal with multiple and 'conjunctional' causation to explain common and divergent outcomes.

Both the positive and negative approaches to comparative research may be implemented by either *case-oriented* or *variable-oriented* methodologies, with Kohn's

(1996) distinction between 'transhistorical generalisations' and 'historically contextu-alised knowledge' being reflected in this case versus variable debate within the comparative research literature. The historically interpretative (case-oriented) approach, which favours a qualitative tradition, takes the view that cases are the basis for comparative research and that, while the analysis of cases may be conducted in terms of variables, they should be seen as holistic and meaningful entities (Ragin, 1996; Yin, 1993). By contrast, the transhistorical analytic (variable-oriented) approach, which favours a quantitative tradition, 'decomposes cases into variables' and treats each case as a 'mere observation' in order 'to place boundaries around the measurement of variables' (Ragin, 1991), and usually is designed to 'produce generalisations about relationships among variables, not to understand or interpret specific historical outcomes in a small number of cases or an empirically defined set of cases' (Ragin, 1996: 84).

Hence, the case-oriented approach may be seen to be one which does not easily accommodate the type of 'structural explanations' which the variable-oriented approach is more suited for (Ragin, 1987; Van de Vijver and Leung, 1997). However, while this may be a reasonable contention in relation to cross-sectional studies, it becomes distinctly more problematic when related to longitudinal studies. In the latter, even where the study is comprised of a single case, Rueschemeyer (1991) argues that the longer time span of investigation inherent within a longitudinal study will facilitate the identification of those structural conditions related to different event sequences. Also, where a cross-sectional study contains a careful selection of cases reflecting different structural conditions related to similar outcomes, it becomes possible to embrace this aspect within a case-oriented analysis. Therefore in situations where there is a desire, or imperative, to research a particular phenomenon within a particular situation, and perhaps during a particular time, the case-oriented approach is likely to be favoured as it treats phenomena and events as having a specific, contextually rooted, finite duration whereas the variable-oriented approach would represent such phenomena and events as discrete points in variable space (Abbott, 1992).

Ragin (1996: 83, 84) argues that the case-oriented approach, which he calls 'the comparative method', is superior to the variable-oriented approach for the following reasons:

- 'First, the statistical method is not combinational; each relevant condition typically is examined in a piecemeal manner.
- Second, applications of the comparative method produce explanations that account for every instance of a certain phenomenon.
- Third, the comparative method does not require the investigator to pretend that he or she has a sample ... drawn from a particular population so that tests of statistical significance can be used. The boundaries of a comparative examination are set by the investigator.
- Finally, the comparative method forces the investigator to become familiar with the cases relevant to the analysis.'

In his earlier work Ragin (1987: 49) also claimed that 'One of the most valuable features of the case-oriented approach ... is the fact that it engenders an extensive dialogue between the investigator's ideas and the data.' By way of contrast Rueschemeyer (1991: 22) indicates that the qualitative, variable-oriented approach to comparative research deserves respect in terms of its 'breadth of coverage, the objectivisation of analysis, and the quantitative testing of specific hypotheses'.

Quantitative, variable-oriented approaches to comparative research invariably focus upon identifying and analysing covariation between the variables across a large number of entities to produce generalised explanations (Ragin, 1994). Such covariation is frequently established by the use of correlation and regression techniques to describe the patterns of covariation and posit relationships from these patterns which, in turn, lead to inferences regarding the nature of causation. Covariation may be examined in cross-sectional, longitudinal and replicative studies, and be concerned with single or multiple independent or dependent variable correlations and regressions across time or space. Not surprisingly, the variable-oriented approach is more suited to testing, rather than building, theories to establish 'nomothetic relationships between variables' (Smith, 1991) and make generalisable predictions based on large databases. Although this does mean that it tends to lack the 'rich', 'contextually rooted' detail contained in case-oriented studies, it does, in contrast, have the advantage of greater parsimony. The selection of entities and samples for a variable-based study must be undertaken with care, as the entities need to be suitable for testing a given theory and the samples selected in such a way as to achieve maximum generalisability of results. Similarly, as variable-based research has a primary concern with measurement, the eventual value of this type of comparative study rests heavily upon the development of valid and reliable measurement instruments. Indeed, as Ragin (1994: 143) points out: 'Measurement is one of the most difficult and important tasks facing the quantitative researcher because so much depends on accurate measurement.'

This dichotomised case versus variable debate is typified by Ragin's (1991: 3) observation that: 'The choice, as it appears to most, is between variables and cases—between radically analytic, statistical techniques that obscure cases and qualitative–historical methods that immerse the investigator in cases.' However, as Ragin (1991: 2, 3, 4) goes on to cogently argue, such a methodological polarisation holds deficiencies in both its extremes and there is a need for a satisfactory middle ground to be found: 'Discourse on variables in the absence of discourse on cases can easily become sterile ... discourse that is too slanted toward variables degenerates into arid debates about the best way to measure variables and model their relationships without concern for the empirical events reflected in the variables or for the reconstitution of events as "data" ... discourse that is too slanted toward cases can atomise comparative social science, with each scholar attached to a seemingly unique case or set of related cases and deriving authority from knowledge that cannot be socialised or pooled in some way .... To achieve a better balance between discourse about cases and variables in comparative research, new methodological strategies are necessary.'

One such methodology referred to by Rueschemeyer (1991: 32) is that of 'analytic induction', which he contends 'breaks with the conventional view that research based on one or a few cases can at best stimulate some hypotheses, while only research on a large number of cases can test them' and that it 'builds its arguments from the under-standing of individual histories', moving to generate 'potentially generalisable theoret-ical insights capable of explaining the problematic features of each case' which are then 'tested and retested in other detailed case analyses'. This method therefore retains the importance of the historical context for causal explanation in developing more general-isable theoretical insights. Glaser and Strauss (1967) referred to this process as the 'con-stant comparative method' whereby comparisons of similarities and differences are used to help define categories and concepts. In a similar vein, Wickham-Crowley

(1991) and Griffin *et al.* (1991) suggest that the adoption of 'Qualitative Comparative Analysis' (QCA) is a useful approach to generate a better balance between the extremes of the case versus variable methodological choice. QCA is a 'holistic' approach to comparative analysis which focuses upon external analysis, i.e. the analysis of holistic entities (cases), but is sensitive to the configurational and/or temporal issues of internal analysis and is able to build bridges between qualitative and quantitative data (Ragin, 1991). Although space does not permit a detailed discussion of the QCA approach here, readers interested in exploring this approach further are referred to Wickham-Crowley (1991) and Griffin *et al.* (1991), with the latter authors (1991: 113, 131) claiming its main virtues to be that it:

- 'offers the possibility of overcoming some of the problems of the statistical–quantitative strategies without, at the same time, discarding one of their main strengths, analytic rigour;
- is both analytically formal and causal in orientation, generating inferences which are based on a data reduction logic rooted in Boolean algebra and mimicking the logic of experimental design ...;
- forces the analyst to make a number of decisions which typically are left implicit and "automatic" in quantitative analysis;
- poses the vexing issue of "theoretical generality" vs. "case particularity" so starkly that the analyst must confront it;
- pushes theoretically "general" analyses of entire populations to the specific and the particular. The results of "particular" case studies, moreover, can be incorporated back into richer, more historically- and culturally-specific and elaborated examinations of the "general". This ... represents one of the primary strengths of QCA.'

Following consideration of the relatively broad epistemological and methodological issues discussed in this section, the researcher will have to focus attention on some of the more specific methodological decisions which need to be addressed in designing a piece of comparative research. These are now addressed in the following two sections of the chapter.

Selecting the entities for comparison

Another generic issue facing the comparative researcher is how many and what type of comparisons to include in the study. In terms of generalisability it may be trite, but perhaps true, to say that the more entities used to make comparisons within the study, the better! However, in reality there is frequently a trade-off between the number of entities included in the study and the amount of data obtained. At its crudest this trade-off runs from one end of the continuum (few entities/deep data) to the other (many entities/surface data), and is akin to the distinction between case-based and variable-based strategies and the desire for contextually rooted knowledge or transhistorical generalisations. The answer to the question of how many comparisons is not simple or formulaic in nature. Kohn (1996) advises that the choice of entities, in terms of both their nature and their number, should be informed by a type of risk analysis. As the selection of entities for comparative research is always something of a gamble, the researcher needs to consider carefully whether the 'payoff is commensurate with the risk' (Kohn, 1996: 45). This can be assessed by evaluating the likely value of any possible similarities or differences in the research outcomes for informing theoretical development and understanding of the phenomenon in question.

The selection of entities for comparative research should address what some authors call the 'comparability problem' (Ragin, 1994; Smelser, 1996). Smelser (1996: 90) suggests that this problem 'arises at three distinct levels:

(a) How can we be certain that the *events* and *situations* we wish to explain are comparable from one ... context to another?
(b) How can we be sure that the general *dimensions* used to [make comparisons] do not do violence to the events and situations we wish to study?
(c) How is it possible to compare very different ... *units* (or ... systems) with one another?' (emphasis in original).

These are significant issues facing the comparative researcher and will be fully addressed in the discussion of *equivalence* contained in the next section of the chapter.

The selection of the set of entities will be informed by both the conceptual framework adopted by the researcher and the empirical relatedness of the entities, i.e. they 'share membership in a meaningful, empirically defined category ... [and] ... offer some potential for advancing ... thinking' (Ragin, 1994: 113). In addition, the comparative researcher must also be aware of what is referred to as 'Galton's Problem' (Neuman, 1994) in selecting the entities to be used for comparison. As Neuman (1994: 391, 392) points out, 'When a researcher compares units, or their characteristics, he wants the units to be distinct and separate from each other. If the units are not "really" different but are actually the subparts of a larger unit, then he will find spurious relationships ... . Galton's problem occurs when the relationship between two variables in two different units is actually due to a common origin, and they are not truly distinct units.' Essentially this is an issue of diffusion. Where the same relationship appears in different settings, it may be tempting to conclude that this has arisen independently and that this provides confirmatory evidence for suggesting that the relationship is generic in nature. However, this may be spurious in the sense that the same relationship found in different entities could share a common, rather than an independent, origin and has simply been diffused across the different entities over time.

Establishing the comparative base

As has been noted earlier there are a number of specific methodological issues associated with the conduct of comparative research. Although the specific nature of these issues does vary according to whether the research is variable- or case-based, qualitative or quantitative in design, and transhistorical or contextually rooted in nature, there is no doubt that the most significant generic methodological issue is that of *equivalence*, which is 'similar to the problems that arise with measurement validity in quantitative research' (Neuman, 1994: 396) and lies at the heart of the researcher's ability to make valid comparisons, thereby addressing the 'comparability' problem (Ragin, 1994). Any lack of equivalence gives rise to problems of bias, which Van de Vijver and Leung (1997: 10) propose is 'a generic term for all nuisance factors threatening the validity of

… comparisons. [and that] Equivalence cannot be assumed but should be established and reported in each study.' Clearly methodological differences across studies may produce consistent or inconsistent findings. Where sufficiently close similarities are found in the results from a number of studies, regardless of any methodological differences in their designs, it will be unlikely that the differences in such results arise as a consequence of any methodological differences; 'Substantive similarity in the face of methodological dissimilarity might even argue for the robustness of the findings' (Kohn, 1996: 36). On the other hand, where there are differences in the results derived from a number of studies it is not easy to determine whether these are real or merely 'methodological artefacts' (Kohn, 1996).

The problem here of course is that the researcher will not have *ex-ante* knowledge of whether the results of the intended comparative study will be similar to or different from other studies conducted on the same issue, and it also presumes that there are other studies to make this *ex-post* comparison with. Consequently, it is sound practice not to rely on chance but to address the key methodological issue of equivalence in the design of the research. The starting point for establishing equivalence in the research design is to focus attention on what some authors refer to as *conceptual equivalence* (Warwick and Osherson, 1973) and others as *construct equivalence* (Van de Vijver and Leung, 1997). This type of equivalence is concerned with establishing a commonality of meaning across the entities to be used for comparison and is an issue in both cross-sectional and longitudinal research as it applies equally to spacio-cultural and historico-temporal equivalence concerns (Neuman, 1994). Where the concept has a sufficiently similar, ideally identical, meaning within the spatio-temporal entities used for the study, there will clearly be significant degrees of construct overlap, and hence this type of equivalence is likely to be high, and vice versa. However, even where this is the case, poor domain sampling, arising from inadequate operational definitions, within the design of the data collection instrument can generate bias. This is a feature Embretson (1983) has termed 'construct under-representation'.

Although this problem is widely recognised by researchers to be particularly problematic in cross-national and cross-cultural studies (Hantrais and Mangen, 1996; Anderson, 1996), it often does not always receive the same degree of attention in comparative work which is not cross-national or cross-cultural. This frequently proves to be a significant omission on the part of the comparative researcher because even concepts and terms which appear to be unambiguous may not be so in reality. For example, the concept of 'gross profit' has a very different meaning in the hotel industry than it does in other industries. Similarly, concepts such as quality, productivity, empowerment, profitability, etc., may not be interpreted and used in exactly the same way in different firms and industries. Hence it is dangerous for the comparative researcher to make what may prove to be unwarranted assumptions about conceptual universality across the entities in the study. One approach to this issue which may prove to be of particular interest to hospitality management researchers is the descriptive concept of 'regimes' (Schunk, 1996). This approach was used by Schunk in her study of the 'welfare mix' and associated 'care options' to structure and map the patterns and characteristics of elderly patient care in England and Germany in order to enhance the validity of the desired cross-national comparisons. This 'regimes' approach could equally be applied to hospitality and/or more general service systems to enhance the validity of either cross-sectional or longitudinal comparisons in such comparative studies.

The significance of the need to establish conceptual equivalence in the research design becomes even more apparent when the issue of *measurement equivalence* is considered. Without conceptual equivalence to establish construct validity in the first place, measurement becomes meaningless. Meaningful comparisons cannot be made where the very basis of the measurement instrument has a variable meaning across different entities. Exploratory factor analysis is often a favoured technique used by researchers to establish measurement equivalence by examining the similarity in factor loadings across different samples or time periods in the study. However, Van de Vijver and Leung (1997: 9, 10) suggest that such apparent equivalence may be illusory rather than real: 'Bias that affects all stimuli of an instrument in more or less the same way cannot be detected by factor analysis.'

The issue of measurement equivalence may arise in relation to either the design of the measurement instrument or its implementation, or both. Van de Vijver and Leung (1997) refer to this as either 'item bias' or 'method bias'. They suggest that the former may arise due to differential appropriateness in item content and/or inadequate item formulation; and the latter from differences in response styles and procedures, familiarity with the stimuli, physical conditions during administration, and communication problems between the researcher and respondent. The same authors (1997: 18) also contend that both item and method bias may be 'uniform' or 'nonuniform' in nature, where uniform bias 'refers to influences of bias on scores that are more or less the same for all score levels' and therefore does not threaten measurement unit equivalence but will impact upon scalar equivalence. On the other hand, Van de Vijver and Leung (1997: 19) state that: 'Nonuniform bias will destroy equivalence to a considerable extent because the measurement units in the two groups are no longer the same.'

Even when conceptual equivalence is established the researcher is still faced with the problem of whether 'different measures are necessary in different contexts for the same concept' (Neuman, 1994: 398). The key issue here, of course, is whether the instruments used in the study measure the same concept, whether their substantive content and procedures are identical or not. Thus it is possible that the use of different instruments and indicators in different contexts may be required. As long as it is possible to compare the results derived from such different indicators, this should not pose a problem. However, in practice, this is likely to be a significant problem for measurement equivalence.

Neuman (1994: 397) also highlights the importance of *lexicon equivalence*, 'the correct translation of words or phrases, or finding a word that means the same thing as another word', a problem which is most apparent in cross-national and cross-cultural comparative research embracing entities with different languages. In these circumstances 'back translation' is often required, where the words or phrases used are translated from one language to another, and back again, by two independent bilingual people. If the second version in the original language is identical to the first then the instrument will have lexicon equivalence. However, the problem of lexicon equivalence is not limited to contemporary cross-sectional studies as the meaning of words can also clearly change over time within the same language. It is therefore also a pertinent issue for longitudinal researchers.

The issue of what Neuman (1994) refers to as *contextual equivalence*, and what other authors (Janoski, 1991; Hantrais and Mangen, 1996) tend to term *functional equivalence*, is also one which researchers need to consider in establishing a sound comparative base. This type of equivalence focuses attention on the observation that a concept either may or may not take different forms in different spatio-temporal contexts but essentially perform the same purpose, and/or that the same linguistic term may have different empirical implications in different spatio-temporal contexts. In a similar, but slightly different, vein Hantrais and Mangen (1996) also raise the issue of the 'spatial equivalence' of units of analysis for cross-sectional studies. This is essentially a subset of *contextual equivalence* and refers to the variability which may exist between spatial definitions of the unit(s) of analysis within the contexts in question. For example, studies designed to compare levels and volumes of hospitality activity on a 'regional' basis or across city or urban areas, particularly at a cross-national level, may be faced with the problem of non-standard statistical definitions of what a region or city is. If care is not taken to explore the specific nature of the definitions used to delimit these entities, there are likely to be significant implications for comparability.

Equivalence *per se* is thus concerned with the threats of bias for external validity and, as comparative research necessitates the making of valid comparisons, it is clearly a fundamental issue in establishing a valid basis for making such comparisons. In addition to the general issue of equivalence, the comparative researcher will also need to consider the issue of *transferability* in relation to the comparative base. Transferability is closely associated, though not synonymous, with issues of *generalisability* and is concerned with identifying and separating the contextual/situational and generic causal factors within the study. Some aspects of transferability may be specified in the research design for the study, and be reflected in its research questions and hypotheses, where it is possible to postulate contextual and/or generic relationships prior to implementing the empirical work. Where this is not possible or indeed desired, as in the case of inductive studies, it will need to be addressed at the data analysis stage of the work.

Although establishing transferability will assist the comparative researcher to identify which relationships are contextually dependent (contingent) and which independent (generic), this alone will not necessarily extend the *generalisability* of the study's findings. For example, where the study is limited to comparisons across two very similar entities or contexts, transferability may be high but the ability to generalise these results to more divergent contexts will be limited. Therefore, generalisability is more concerned with establishing transferability across a wider range of different contexts in order to increase the explanatory and predictive power of the underlying theory.

Thus, the issues of equivalence, transferability and generalisability are all central concerns for the comparative researcher seeking to establish a valid and consistent basis to make the desired comparisons. If these issues are not successfully addressed, the validity and value of any comparisons made may be called into question.

Cross-sectional, longitudinal and replicative studies

The two basic types of comparative research are generally regarded as *cross-sectional* and *longitudinal* studies. Essentially the difference between them is the comparative reference point. In cross-sectional studies the comparisons are temporally constrained within a limited, predetermined and typically contemporary time period. The primary focus of the study will be to examine differences in the phenomenon across different spatial contexts, whilst time is effectively held constant. In longitudinal studies the reverse is true. Here identifying and explaining changes in the phenomenon over time is a central concern. As a consequence longitudinal research invariably seeks to limit the degree of spatial or contextual variation evident within the study. Thus, in relation to the role of time, cross-sectional studies are synchronic in nature, while longitudinal studies may be described as diachronic. Any decision to select either the cross-sectional or the longitudinal type of comparative research should be informed by theoretical issues. Monge (1995: 270) clearly articulates the nature of this issue as follows: 'If theory specifies that several variables constitute a process that unfolds over time, then there is good reason to design longitudinal research to study the process. If theory specifies that two or more phenomena covary within a population at any point in time, then it makes little sense to conduct longitudinal research; a static, cross-sectional research design is preferable.'

Therefore, at least in practice, there tends to be a clear distinction between cross-sectional and longitudinal forms of comparative research. However, although this distinction may imply that the researcher is faced with a simple dichotomous choice, there is no logical reason why a piece of comparative research could not embrace both cross-sectional and longitudinal elements in its design, and some do. While there may be sound conceptual and/or practical reasons for holding either temporal or spatial variation constant, there may equally be sound reasons for the researcher to allow both to vary within a given project via the use of a synthetic strategy. Where the research is of a comparative case study nature, it is highly likely there will be a longitudinal element applied to each of the case studies included in the overall study. Similarly, if cross-sectional studies are repeated over time, or where longitudinal studies are conducted in parallel within multiple contexts, both types of variation will be reflected in such research designs.

Thus, there is no particular logical reason why the cross-sectional and longitudinal types of comparative research should be automatically regarded as mutually exclusive methodological choices. That they frequently are is a reflection of the additional complexity and cost likely to be generated in a research design combining both types. However, there are research designs which do effectively combine the two types without generating significantly greater levels of complexity and/or cost. For example, 'Pooled Cross-Sectional Analysis' (PCSA) is a type of hybrid approach which facilitates this combination and is one used extensively by economists and political scientists. PCSA operates by collecting a series of cross-sectional data over time, at either micro- or macro-levels, which may be spatially or temporally dominated depending upon the relative balance of cross-sectional and time-series data units in the pooled set (Hicks, 1994). This data may be collected from different samples drawn from the same population, or repeatedly from the same sample (panel or cohort surveys), over time. PCSA may be seen to operate in the yield management systems used in the airline and hotel industries where pricing/revenue data is collected on a regular basis over a relatively long period of time and used to identify 'temporal dependencies' as the basis for predicting future patterns.

As long as a high degree of consistency is maintained in the questions, and the variables and sampling method remain the same, 'sequences of measures may be created in *discrete* time and it is possible to incorporate a time trend into the analysis' (Davies and Dale, 1994: 7) (emphasis in original). However, this is not as straightforward and unproblematic as it may appear. The main problem with using PCSA to convert data from a temporally discrete to a continuous form is the lack of information available on the intervening periods. This has to be dealt with by logical or statistical inference, with the latter typified by the use of regression-based models. However, while such inference may be useful it is imperfect and may be subject to a number of errors (see Hicks, 1994).

Although discrete data collection will record change, or no change, on the variables at each point the data is collected, it will not indicate when any possible changes occurred in the intervening period or how many changes took place. This issue gives rise to some potentially serious problems. If the data shows no change between each of the collection points, the researcher may be unaware of whether this has arisen because there has indeed been no change in the intervening period, or because there has been either a change and movement back to the prior level recorded or compensatory changes which have cancelled each other out to generate the same level. Similarly, any change may have occurred immediately before the latest date of data collection, immediately after the previous data collection point, or at some indeterminate point in between! In view of this the researcher should approach the use of PCSA, as a quasi-longitudinal research design, with some caution. As Davies and Dale (1994: 15) pertinently comment, 'when data are recorded in continuous time, the number and sequence of events *and* the durations between them can all be calculated. Additionally, the relationship of one event to another can be analysed ... [this] ... enables the researcher to investigate not only the factors affecting outcomes but also the factors which affect the timing of the outcomes' (emphasis in original). For a more detailed discussion of the issues and techniques associated with pooling data see Janoski and Hicks (1994).

In addition to the generally accepted view that cross-sectional and longitudinal research constitute the two 'basic types' of comparative research, it could also be argued that *replication* studies constitute a third basic type. This would not be a contention supported by all comparative researchers, but is one worthy of consideration. As stated earlier in the chapter, the essence of comparative research is the identification and explanation of similarities and differences. Replication research has this goal at its heart as it seeks to confirm or refute theory by extending either the spatial or temporal boundaries of such theory. Although replication research is not generally a very popular type of comparative research amongst social scientists, including hospitality management researchers, it should receive greater attention because of the difficulties such researchers often have in successfully operationalising the variables they are investigating. Greater replication of studies would help to establish the reliability, or otherwise, of these operationalisations. Therefore, a discussion of the issues associated with replication research is included in this section of the chapter.

Cross-sectional studies

Cross-sectional studies are not usually regarded as being as useful as longitudinal designs for researching change or developmental issues, though it is possible to make some inferences about these issues by recognising the constraints inherent within this type of study (Adams and Schvaneveldt, 1991). However, case-oriented studies involving multiple-case comparisons are likely to embody a longitudinal aspect within each of the case studies and therefore are able to address such issues. As a case-orientation will invariably include a historical element in the respective case studies, and will tend to emphasise case-by-case holistic comparisons, the resultant cross-sectional analysis will be informed by longitudinal considerations from within each case. Conversely, variable-oriented studies are generally ahistorical in nature, with the contexts used for cross-sectional studies relegated to vehicles which facilitate element-by-element comparisons across the samples. Variable-oriented, cross-sectional surveys typically, but not necessarily, attempt to present a large-scale analysis within a broad context by using large, independent and randomly selected samples.

Although a wide range of methodological approaches can be used to implement cross-sectional studies, the variable-oriented, survey approach is frequently favoured by researchers with a quantitative disposition, whilst those researchers who favour a qualitative approach tend to adopt more of a case-oriented strategy involving multiple-case comparisons. Both variable and case-oriented approaches to cross-sectional studies can embrace internal and external analyses within the comparative study, and these may be conducted at single or multiple levels (Yin, 1994). In reality, however, variable- oriented studies tend to focus upon external analysis at a single level, whereas case- oriented studies invariably have a stronger internal analytical dimension and frequently involve multiple-level comparisons. For example, Yin's (1994) fourfold typology of case study research embraces multiple comparative possibilities. In Yin's typology, type 2 (a single case, with embedded units of analysis) places emphasis upon intra-case comparisons, whereas types 3 and 4 (Multiple Case/Holistic and Multiple/Case Embedded) provide for a greater focus on inter-case comparisons at either a single, case-by-case, or a multiple, element-by-element, level. Examples of the application of these 'types' may be found in the hospitality management research literature. Morey and Dittman's (1995) study on benchmarking hotel general managers' performance illustrates Yin's type 2 design; Figueiredo, Latas and Gomes' (1995) analysis of management strategies in five-star hotels is indicative of Yin's type 3; and an application of Yin's type 4 may be found in Moncarz and Kron's (1993) study of two hotels in financial distress.

Cross-sectional comparative studies, be they case- or variable-oriented in nature, may be conducted at a variety of levels, ranging from comparisons between individuals, groups, organisations, industry sectors, industries, countries, and supranational entities; and may focus on phenomena relating to structures, products, processes, systems, cultures, etc. In selecting the cases and/or samples for cross-sectional studies, care should be taken to recognise and control for what Coolican (1994) refers to as the 'Cohort Effect'. Essentially this arises where there are significant differences in one or more aspects of the independent samples' composition. For example, if one sample group is dominated by people in the age range 45–60 and another by people who are in the 20–35 age range, any direct comparisons made between the two groups are likely to be extremely suspect because of the influence of intergenerational differences on the two sets of respondents. Similarly, where there are significant variations in other factors such as gender, socio-economic group, occupation, ethnicity, etc., the cohort effect needs to be considered. Clearly, the same issue arises in cross-sectional studies using organisations or countries as the basis for the cases or samples. These considerations also raise the issue of 'matched samples'.

At face value this would appear to be a simple issue to resolve, but in reality it may be far more complex. At a simple level matching samples may be considered to be a process of ensuring that a broadly similar sample size and composition is determined to facilitate comparability (Van de Vijver and Leung, 1997). Where the entities selected for the cross-sectional study are sufficiently similar in nature, this may suffice, but it does assume that they have convergent spatio-temporal characteristics, an assumption which may not always bear close scrutiny. It also may be a reasonable strategy where the study is designed to investigate the research questions in the aggregate across the entities concerned, and where the latter exhibit sufficiently similar structural character- istics (see Kara, Kaynak and Kucukemiroglu, 1995). On the other hand, where the entities differ, more disaggregated and sophisticated forms of sample matching will be required. In some situations this may be satisfactorily accomplished by using statis- tical control procedures to stratify the samples to ensure matching in the sample sub- groups, but this is essentially an ahistorical procedure which does not take into account differences in the specific conditions applying to the samples drawn from the differing entities.

In this respect Brynner and Heinz (1991: 144) provide an example of a more detailed 'matching' strategy involving the application of their operationalised definition of the 'career trajectory' concept, to design the research in the first place, followed by the adoption of a series of 'matching controls' to 'hold constant the different distributions of the trajectories between the two countries and similarly the occupation to which they lead'; and, according to these authors, the more 'localised' and disaggregated data this strategy produced enabled them to 'separate out the effects of national systems, labour markets, structural characteristics and their interactions on the experience of individu- als'. The 'paired comparisons' this procedure generated were then claimed to have yielded 'qualitative data of exceptional value in uncovering the processes lying behind statistical differences. Cases can be selected for "interrogation" to find out what the dif- ferences mean. By locating such an "interrogation" within a statistical design we greatly enhance the value of the qualitative data the cases are able to yield' (Brynner and Heinz, 1991: 151).

As cross-sectional studies are a relatively popular form of comparative research *per se*, it is not surprising that this popularity is mirrored in the hospitality management research literature. The studies by Boger (1995) and Papadopoulou, Ineson and Wilkie (1995) provide examples of cross-sectional studies focusing on quick-service food delivery systems in airports and perceptions of high customer contact food and bever- age operatives' jobs respectively. These are relatively low scale and unit of analysis studies, with the former using observation-based measurements in four airports to investigate the food delivery systems issue, and the latter 14 interview respondents drawn from one hotel. However, the limited scope and units of analysis used in these studies allowed the researchers to undertake multiple comparisons across the systems and their characteristics in the former, and the management/supervisory and operative perceptions of the importance of a range of competencies and task categories in the latter, using multiple measures. Therefore cross-sectional studies of this type, which are limited in scope, offer strong potential for exploring the research issues in some depth.

Contemporary examples of hospitality management cross-sectional studies con- ducted on a larger scale, i.e. at cross-national level, are provided by Hallam and Baum (1996), Van Hoof, Verbeeten and Combrink (1996), Kara, Kaynak and Kucukemiroglu (1995), and Burrell *et al.* (1997). All of these studies involved the use of questionnaire surveys, applied to different issues across a variable range of countries. Hallam and Baum (1996: 46) place the comparative focus on the 'internal and external factors that may cause hotels to contract out portions or all of their food and beverage operations', within the contexts of the USA and UK, in their study. Unfortunately, this study suffers from representativeness and comparability problems arising from the small samples achieved (34 in the UK and 28 in the USA). Van Hoof, Verbeeten and Combrink (1996: 87) 'compared the perceptions of lodging managers in the United States, Canada, and the United Kingdom about computer technology and their opinions on technology needs, competency, and levels of automation'; and again the variability of the samples achieved (237 in the USA, 131 in the UK and 43 in Canada) gives rise to the same issues as in the Hallam and Baum study. The Kara, Kaynak and Kucukemiroglu (1995) study used Canada and the USA to explore consumer perceptions of fast-food restaurants in the two countries, though this cross-national comparison was limited to three specific cities in each country, a feature the authors recognised did not allow them to claim that the samples derived were representative of US and Canadian consumers as a whole. However, although the sample sizes (179 in the USA and 141 in Canada) were again relatively low and geographically restricted in this study, there was an attempt to build comparability into the work through the use of a common survey instrument and by selecting cities with 'structural similarities' to achieve a degree of contextual similarity.

The Burrell et al. (1997) study into equal opportunities for women employees in the hospitality industry in four European countries differs from the others referred to above, as it was conducted by an interdisciplinary research team and combined a significant amount of secondary data analysis with the postal questionnaire data obtained from the empirical aspect of the study. These authors comment on comparability problems arising due to variability in the availability and consistency of information contained in the secondary data sources, but surprisingly make little comment on the comparability issues associated with their empirical research. Although information is provided on the desire to select suitably matched samples for the study, no attempt is made to address the obvious issues of conceptual or lexicon equivalence associated with the design and implementation of the questionnaire. The study does not even make it clear whether the questionnaire was translated into the different languages of the countries concerned, or whether it was implemented in English alone.

This comparability issue also features in some hospitality management comparative studies designed to be cross-cultural in nature. For example, the Pizam et al. (1997) study into the relationship between national and industry cultures and managerial behaviour employs a survey questionnaire to elicit information from 192 hotel managers in Hong Kong, Japan and Korea, but does not contain any comment on whether the questionnaire was implemented in one or more languages or whether it was evaluated for conceptual equivalence prior to its use. Indeed, as the Cronbach's alpha reliability coefficients reported in the study ranged from a low of 0.32 to a high of 0.69, it might be assumed that it was not! Similarly, when Moutinho et al.'s (1995) cross-national work comparing the future development of the hotel sector, was extended beyond the predominantly English-speaking countries of Scotland, England, Wales and Ireland to be replicated in Spain, the authors offer no information about how such equivalence problems were addressed in the design or implementation of the questionnaire survey in this different context. By way of contrast Armstrong et al.'s (1997) study of cross-cultural expectations in relation to the measurement of service quality perceptions constitutes a model of good practice. Not only was the wording of the

SERVQUAL instrument adapted for the hotel industry context, to ensure contextual equivalence, but lexicon equivalence was addressed as: 'The instrument was translated and back translated from English to Japanese and Chinese by different language experts at Hong Kong based universities' (Armstrong *et al.*, 1997: 186).

Finally, Royle's (1995) study, of corporate versus societal culture in relation to McDonald's operations in the UK and Germany, provides a different example of a cross-sectional hospitality management study. This is a cross-national study focusing upon the HRM policy of a single multinational company, which was implemented primarily via the use of participant observation and semi-structured, face-to-face interviewing methods. Thus, it differs from many of the previous cross-sectional studies referred to in this section as it is essentially case- rather than variable-oriented, uses qualitative rather than quantitative methods, and is focused on a single organisation. In this sense it is a multiple-case study located within a cross-national context.

Longitudinal studies

In longitudinal studies time intervals are of primary importance because the main generic goal of this type of comparative research is to analyse change and development in relation to some process which occurs over time (Adams and Schvaneveldt, 1991). Longitudinal studies may be conducted through the use of experimental research designs, where treatment and control groups are used to make comparisons, but this type of design is not common in many fields as it complicates the issues of sample selection and maintenance. Many longitudinal studies adopt a 'cohort approach', where a single sample is selected as the cohort for the study, and the same survey instrument is applied to this sample at the desired time intervals in order to investigate how and why the successive outcomes are related to their antecedents. As Davies and Dale (1994: 2) point out: 'This provides the framework for a very powerful analysis of the processes experienced by individuals [or organisations/countries]; it enables a model to be constructed which explicitly takes into account the earlier circumstances suspected to have an effect which carries through into later life'; and, as Davies and Dale (1994: 3) go on to contend, as much individual, corporate and indeed national/cultural behaviour tends to exhibit 'strong temporal dependencies [and that]. ... Most of the factors creating such temporal dependencies generate inertial effects in behaviour [with some factors operating in reverse to this]. ... It will be evident that longitudinal data are essential if the temporal dependencies in micro-level behaviour are to be investigated in any analysis.'

This means that the longitudinal researcher needs to be concerned with the direction (trend), speed (rate), nature (permanent or temporary) and degree (magnitude) of change taking place over time. Essentially, longitudinal research attempts to map the patterns of such change and explain why they have occurred. To achieve this, attention must be focused on the sequence of incidents and events, which collectively constitute the process the researcher is interested in. Of particular interest to the longitudinal researcher seeking to investigate a given process will be the order of occurrence, temporal separation, and nature of the transitions between the sequence of events constituting the process in order to infer and analyse the dynamic causal relationships as they unfold over time. According to Monge (1995: 270, 271), 'The easiest way to design longitudinal research is on the basis of a dynamic theory and process hypotheses. A good process theory describes, at least in broad outline, plausible time parameters associated with change within and between the phenomena of interest. [and] ... in contrast to traditional theories, process hypotheses would describe the expected or observed behaviour of each variable over time as well as the interrelationships among the variables over time.' This can be accomplished by formulating hypotheses in such a way that they encompass the relevant time dimensions discussed below. Given the potential complexity of this issue, it may be that formulating a single hypothesis for each variable is not feasible and that multiple hypotheses may be required to achieve clarity.

Monge (1995) contends that it is useful to disentangle some of the complexity inherent within a longitudinal study containing multiple sequences and variables in a given process by initially focusing attention on the dynamic nature of each variable prior to any attempt to examine the nature of any interrelationships between the variables. An understanding of how individual variables behave over time is likely to assist the researcher in developing a better understanding of the relationships between them. To undertake this theorising requires the researcher to consider six dimensions of dynamic behaviour (Monge, 1995) which are summarised in Table 8.1.

Whether the variables are temporally continuous or discontinuous, plotting them over time may assist the researcher to identify more clearly the patterns they exhibit

Table 8.1 A framework for representing dynamic processes

Dimension	Definitions and issues
Continuity	This refers to whether the variable has a consistent non-zero value through time, where zero typically represents the non-existence of the variable. A continuous time variable always exists, whereas a discontinuous variable will fluctuate between a zero and non-zero value.
Magnitude	This refers to the amount of the variable at any point in time. Across time, magnitude may remain constant or vary considerably, and be negative or positive if the measurement scale allows.
Rate of change	This specifies how fast the magnitude increases or decreases per unit of time. Magnitudes can change rapidly, even instantaneously, or slowly over time and therefore exhibit different rates of change.
Trend	This refers to the long-term increase or decrease in the magnitude of a variable, and therefore can have a positive or negative value. Variables that are constant, or increase/decrease randomly, are said to be trendless.
Periodicity	This is the amount of time that transpires between the regular repetition of the values of a variable, controlling for trend. If a variable does not repeat on a regular basis it has no period. With continuous variables periods are usually measured from peaks to peaks (highest magnitude) or valleys to valleys (lowest magnitude), whereas periods for discontinuous variables are usually measured from the onset of the variable or from the point at which it reaches maximum magnitude.
Duration	This relates primarily to discontinuous time variables and refers to the length of time that a variable exists at some non-zero value. The duration of a variable may be short or long and may change over time.

Source: Based on Monge (1995: 272, 273).

with respect to each of the dimensions. A number of useful examples of this process can be found in Monge (1995). As these six time dimensions allow different combinations to be derived, it also becomes possible to develop a number of possible causal scenarios to explore the nature of the variable interrelationships. However, there is a certain linearity to this procedure which needs to be addressed by incorporating other dynamic elements such as feedforward and feedback in the case of relatively stable systems or entities, or perhaps aspects of chaos theory where the situation exhibits less stable characteristics.

While cross-sectional studies suffer from the 'comparability problem', as it is extremely difficult to be sure that the independent samples used in this type of study are sufficiently similar to allow valid comparisons to be made, longitudinal studies do not suffer from this problem to the same degree. By subjecting the same sample to repeated measures over time this problem is eliminated (Coolican, 1994). However, this does assume the absence of the 'sample attrition' and 'reactivity' problems referred to below. If either of these arise then the comparability problem will be evident in longitudinal work. In addition, the longitudinal researcher should recognise the potential impact of what Coolican (1994) terms the 'cross-generational problem'. This problem arises where a particular generation of people, organisations or countries are affected by significant events within a specific era while others are not. Thus, the pattern of change and development evident within this generation may not be applicable to other generations. For example, a longitudinal study investigating the views of HRM managers on industrial relations practices which began with a sample of such managers selected in the early 1970s is likely to encounter this problem if the researcher attempts to generalise these findings to new, young managers who entered their managerial positions only in the late 1980s.

One problem associated with longitudinal studies is the cost of maintaining contact with a population over time, which may mean that a smaller unit of analysis is adopted for practical reasons (Adams and Schvaneveldt, 1991). Longitudinal studies also tend to suffer from the 'attrition' problem in that some of the original sample will inevitably be lost over time due to respondent 'drop-out' and the repeated application of the same measures over time may give rise to reactivity effects. On the other hand, 'attrition' may not be a problem but a part of the design for a piece of longitudinal research. An interesting hospitality management example of this is given in the study by English, *et al.* (1996). In undertaking a longitudinal analysis of restaurant failures, within a geographically limited unit of analysis (El Paso, Texas), they used 'attrition' as a central strategy to track changes in the target cohort of restaurants over the five-year period of the study. In addition, there are also some practical issues which require the longitudinal researcher's attention. For example, Monge (1995) points to the issue of how often to gather data, sample selection, and the type of meta-analysis needed to analyse process phenomena across multiple cases, and Iverson (1995) to the value of forecasting to assess the adequacy of the models developed.

There is also a fundamental epistemological issue at the heart of longitudinal research which tends not to receive too much attention from researchers. This is the issue of time itself. In most longitudinal studies time is invariably taken to be clock or real time, but this is only one of a number of alternative ways of viewing or determining time. The way time is defined is likely to have a fundamental impact on how phenomena are viewed (Jacques, 1982). The nature and role of time cannot be assumed to have a universality and be viewed as only clock or real time. For example, Kelly and McGrath (1988) distinguish between real and experimental time. Greater attention to, and thought about, the different nature and meaning of how time is viewed in a research project, and how it is reflected in hypotheses and research designs, may begin to open up valuable new perspectives on the dynamic processes longitudinal research attempts to explain.

Longitudinal studies may be conducted using either qualitative (case-oriented) or quantitative (variable-oriented) strategies, or a combination of the two. Unfortunately space does not permit a detailed discussion of all the case- and variable-oriented strategies here. Therefore, only a brief introduction to the main strategies in each orientation can be provided. The comparative researcher interested in exploring a more detailed treatment of these strategies can pursue this via the references provided.

With regard to variable-oriented strategies, the use of 'straightforward' time-series analysis, or some variant on the same theme, is often a favoured strategy. Time-series regression techniques are predicated on the same basic logic as ordinary regression, but include some variations relating to the independence of variables over time and the influence of time-lag effects, and can be applied to any variable which is measured regularly and consistently over a given time frame (Janoski and Isaac, 1994). One of the strengths of time-series analysis is its ability to incorporate temporality within its modelling procedures which, in turn, helps to develop a strong basis for establishing causal inference. On the other hand, as Janoski and Isaac (1994: 33) point out, it does suffer from a number of 'thorny technical problems. Autocorrelation, lag structures, causal order and multicollinearity [are] amongst the more commonly encountered difficulties'. Such technical problems are illustrated in Iverson's (1995) study which sought to explore the effectiveness of different regression models for forecasting hotel employment in an environment (Guam) with limited data sources. Amongst the variety of 'simple' regression models which were 'posited, developed and tested', to interpret the quarterly time-series data collected over the ten-year period (1982–92), it was found that, 'Several promising models were rejected at this stage due to problems with serial correlations and poor response to efforts to correct for autocorrelation' (Iverson, 1995: 59). In addition to these 'technical' problems Iverson (1995: 61) also makes the important point that background, contextual knowledge on the part of the researcher is often important to facilitate the incorporation of 'judgmental' elements into such time-series models to help explain 'the underlying changes in a series'.

One time-series variant which has received considerable attention from sociologists and political scientists is Event History Analysis (EHA). EHA focuses upon studying the sequence and timing of events within either continuous or discrete time and seeks to 'describe and [statistically] model the underlying stochastic process that generates events' (Strang, 1994: 245) in a dynamic manner by exploring transition rates. Examples of the application of EHA to hospitality management research are rather thin on the ground, but the study by Sparrowe and Popielarz (1995) uses EHA to investigate the 'career histories' of hospitality employees in terms of the factors affecting the 'rate of promotions' for employees both 'within and across hospitality firms'. Sparrowe and Popielarz (1995: 100, 104) claim that the use of EHA was appropriate for their investigation into these issues because: 'Promotions are discrete events occurring in continuous time. Thus they are ideally studied using techniques that model the effects of independent variables upon the rate of events occurring in such time'; in turn, EHA allowed 'the effects of multiple factors on career progression [to be] estimated simultaneously in a series of nested models', to facilitate an exploration of the events defined as 'a promotion, transfer, or change in forms that nets the incumbent a minimum of 10% increase in total compensation'.

Replication studies

Some authors argue that there are important epistemological reasons for conducting replicative studies which seek to confirm or refute theory, whether the researcher takes a 'Verificationist' or a 'Popperian' stance (Lamal, 1991). Inductively derived knowledge requires more than one confirming instance to generate a sufficiently robust level of external validity and enhance confidence in the reliability of the methodology and findings. Similarly, taking the Popperian view, where hypotheses are deductively tested in a single study and found to be supported, there is still a need for these hypotheses to be tested more widely, as Miller (1980: 123) pointedly summarises: 'the fact that a theory has passed a test provides no evidence at all that it will pass a repetition of that test'.

If the epistemological reasons for the importance of replication are accepted, the researcher is then confronted by a number of issues to resolve. Firstly, what is meant by replication? Exact replication cannot be achieved because it is impossible to replicate accurately all the facets of a given research study. However, replications may be viewed in terms of their proximity to the original study across a number of relevant dimensions, i.e. as 'relative' replications (Rosenthal, 1991), with those exhibiting a high degree of proximity holding greater promise for comparative purposes. Secondly, Lamal (1991: 33) indicates that the researcher needs to consider 'which studies should be replicated … [and] … how many replications of a given study … should be replicated'. Lamal (1991) suggests that answers to the question of which studies to replicate may be to either 'replicate studies that have involved tests of important hypotheses … [and/or] … studies that not only confirm a theory or model but tend to rule out the competition'. One problem for the researcher attempting to make replicative study decisions based on Lamal's view is the definition of 'important hypotheses'. This implies that a distinction can easily be made between trivial and non-trivial hypotheses. Such a judgement may be more problematic than it would appear. On the issue of how many replications, it is clear that replicative research is likely to suffer from the problem of diminishing returns, but the exact point at which returns begin to diminish is not likely to be clear, will vary across different circumstances, and be influenced by the robustness of the original study's findings. Thus, the 'how many' question is a variable feast which calls for the researcher concerned to make a judgement about the extent to which it is worth pursuing further, successive comparative replications of a given study.

To the above considerations Rosenthal (1991) adds that the value of undertaking replicative studies will be strongly influenced by when, how and by whom the replications are conducted. The 'when' issue is largely concerned with the temporal proximity of the replication to the original study and is also regarded to be subject to diminishing returns, as replications conducted in relatively close temporal proximity to the original study will hold the highest utility, and 'Weighting all replications equally, the first replication doubles our information about the research issue, the fifth … adds 20% …

and the fiftieth adds only 2% to our information level' (Rosenthal, 1991: 2). Of course the crucial phrase here is 'weighting all replications equally' as it implies all replications of a given study hold equal value. Experience suggests that this is a view which should be approached critically by the researcher, as the nature of comparative research *per se*, with its potential multiplicity of spatio-temporal contexts, may negate this type of parameter for the extension of replicative studies.

The 'how' issue focuses upon the degree of methodological and contextual proximity in the replicative study to those conducted previously on the same question. Here the problem of replicability versus generalisability is encountered. If the results of a series of 'strict' replicated studies (Hendrick, 1991), having a high degree of methodological and contextual proximity to those being replicated, are consistent, then replication or 'reproducibility' (Amir and Sharon, 1991) has occurred but the generality of the results and the underlying theory have not been extended beyond these constraints. On the other hand, where methodological and/or contextual proximity are allowed to vary, consistent or divergent results may serve to illuminate contextually dependent or generic relationships across the entities studied by the comparative researcher. In situations where theoretical understanding is underdeveloped, comparative research which focuses primarily upon establishing verificatory evidence, via a reproducibility strategy, will be appropriate. Where theoretical understanding is more advanced, comparative research adopting a generalisability strategy would be more appropriate to extend the methodological and/or contextual validity of existing theory.

This clearly holds great promise for replicative comparative research seeking to explore similarities and differences across different contexts but, as Rosenthal (1991: 5) points out, also has the proverbial sting in the tail (see Figure. 8.1), making this a relatively high risk strategy: 'The more imprecise the replications, the greater the benefit to the external validity of the tested relationship if the results support the relationship. If the results do not support the original finding, however, we cannot tell whether that lack of support stems from the instability of the original results or from the imprecision of the replications.'

To minimise these risks Rosenthal (1991: 6) suggests consideration of a 'replicative battery' wherein the researcher selects a minimum of two replications for the study, one

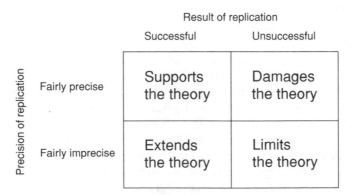

Figure 8.1. Effects on theory of the success and precision of replication (source: Rosenthal, 1991: 5). Reproduced by permission of Professor R. Rosenthal

of which is similar and 'the other is at least moderately dissimilar to the original study'. In a similar vein Hendrick (1991) proposes the use of a 'systematic replication' strategy within which certain aspects of the replicative study are replicated exactly and others varied systematically. Clearly both the 'replicative battery' and 'systematic replication' strategies are eminently suitable for comparative research, as they enable the researcher to simultaneously retain strong comparability in the conceptual and procedural elements of replication studies whilst varying the context for the study, or vice versa.

Whereas the 'when' and 'how' concerns discussed above mainly focus on external validity issues, the 'whom' question reflects upon internal validity issues. There is an assumption in the above discussion that replicative studies are conducted independently by different researcher(s) or that successive replications of study undertaken by the same researcher(s) are conducted independently of each other, but this may not always be the case. What is of concern here is the possibility of bias contaminating the replicative studies. Where a single researcher conducts a series of replications on the same phenomena, but within different contexts, it might reasonably be expected that the replications will not embody a high degree of independence. Even where a team of researchers engage in the same activity there is no guarantee that inter-researcher independence will be introduced into the study, though this may be more likely in interdisciplinary and/or inter-institutional teams, particularly where the latter are cross-national or cross-cultural in nature. The problem here is not that researcher bias is purposely introduced into the process, though of course this is possible, but that commonality of interest and expectations, methodological predisposition and the selection of specific analytical techniques are a fairly predictable conscious or unconscious consequence of replicative studies conducted under such circumstances.

Perhaps predictably, given its relatively low status in more established disciplines, there is little evidence of any substantial body of replicative studies in the hospitality management research literature. However, one study which does reflect a number of the issues discussed above is that conducted by Brotherton and Burgess (1997) on the academic research interests of hotel and restaurant companies. Following earlier replicative work by Brymer, Rousselle and Johns (1990) on this issue in the USA, Brotherton and Burgess (1997) sought to replicate the former study in the UK to provide cross-national comparative results. This study took the questionnaire survey instrument used by Brymer, Rousselle and Johns (1990) in the USA and, with only minor changes to the questionnaire to ensure validity, implemented it in the UK.

Although it cannot be claimed that the Brotherton and Burgess (1997) study constituted the use of Rosenthal's (1991) 'replicative battery' strategy, it does share a great deal in common with Hendrick's (1991) 'systematic replication' strategy wherein the substantive, conceptual and procedural aspects of the research design were held constant whilst the contextual aspects were systematically varied across the two countries used as comparative contexts. Similarly, though there is little argument that Brotherton and Burgess's (1997) study succeeded in achieving 'reproducibility', the extent to which it achieved 'generalisability' is less certain. On the one hand, the fact that the two contexts (the USA and the UK) used in the comparative study generated contextual variation suggests that the potential for generalisability was designed into the study. On the other, use of the same conceptual, instrumental and procedural elements suggests that reproducibility was a strong design influence. In terms of Rosenthal's (1991) typology, shown in Figure 8.1, it could be argued that this study was a 'fairly precise' replication which had 'successful results' and therefore was one which *supported* the original theory/findings. If the contextual variation is seen as constituting a more major divergence to the precision of the replication, a contention which perhaps would be difficult to support, then it would be viewed as a study which *extended* the theory/findings in Rosenthal's terms.

Conclusions and further research issues

This chapter has explored a number of the key issues and concerns with the nature of comparative research *per se*, and the approaches and techniques available for conducting such research, and has provided a range of comparative research examples from the hospitality management field. From the discussion of these issues and concerns, it is evident that comparative research is a very lively and evolving type of research, which has a number of ongoing epistemological and methodological debates. These debates indicate that, whether it is conducted at a relatively small or large scale, is quantitative or qualitative in nature, and is cross-sectional, longitudinal or replicative in design, there are significant issues for the comparative researcher to consider in both its design and implementation. It clearly has a distinctive focus and purpose, and faces perhaps even greater validity and reliability concerns than non-comparative research.

Comparative research is therefore often more taxing to the researcher than its non-comparative alternative. The central problem of equivalence is one not easily solved in many comparative research studies, and particularly in those which embrace significantly divergent comparative contexts. Establishing conceptual and measurement equivalence, as a basis for making valid comparisons, is notoriously difficult in cross-national and/or cross-cultural studies and those longitudinal studies which include an intergenerational time frame in their design. However, here lies the challenge. If such difficulties had been resolved a long time ago, the type of phenomena comparative research seeks to investigate would have been exhausted by previous generations of researchers. As this is not the case comparative research still holds a range of exciting possibilities for the contemporary researcher.

Indeed, it may be argued that the field of hospitality management research is one highly suitable for, and amenable to, the application of comparative research. As indicated at the beginning of this chapter, many members of the hospitality management research community subscribe to the view that hospitality is imbued with some unique characteristics which justify the claims these colleagues make regarding its 'unique' identity. Whether such a view is conceptually sustainable or empirically verifiable is open to debate. One way of seeking a resolution to this issue would clearly be for the protagonists in this debate to engage in sound comparative research designed to investigate the extent to which hospitality may be regarded as such a discrete and unique phenomenon, or vice versa. However, the available research evidence would appear to suggest that this has been a path avoided by both camps. It is, however, a path that hospitality management research must take in the near future if it is not to continue being regarded, by non-hospitality researchers, as relatively insignificant and 'out of the mainstream' of social science or business management research.

There is immense scope for researchers to explore the same phenomena in hospitality and non-hospitality contexts to ascertain whether these phenomena have convergent or divergent properties. A return to exploring some basic questions may well prove to be highly illuminating. For example, many hospitality and retail organisations share the feature of 'back and front of house' operations. Are these fundamentally the same operational types in these different contexts, or are they completely different? What is the difference, if any, in the service delivery and business support systems in a hotel and a bank? Is the very concept of hospitality the same now in the UK as it was 100 years ago, or is it the same in France and Thailand today? Does the hospitality organisation really face very different demands and structural conditions from airlines, leisure centres or multiplex cinemas, or not?

Certainly there is evidence of comparative research taking place within the generally accepted boundaries of hospitality, as the examples provided in this chapter demonstrate. But, as these examples equally show, this research is often flawed in its design and/or implementation. Hospitality management researchers need not only to develop a stronger tradition of conducting comparative research across various hospitality sectors and formats, but also to ensure that the methodological aspect of this work is sufficiently robust. The evidence would appear to suggest that there is much to be done in both respects.

References

Abbott, A. (1992) What do cases do? Some notes on activity in sociological analysis. In Ragin, C. C. and Becker, H. S. (Eds) *What is a Case?*, Cambridge University Press, New York, pp. 53–82.

Adams, G. R. and Schvaneveldt, J. D. (1991) *Understanding Research Methods* (2nd Edn). Longman, White Plains, New York.

Amir, Y. and Sharon, I. (1991) Replication research: a 'must' for the scientific advancement of psychology. In Neuliep, J. W. (Ed.) *Replication Research in the Social Sciences*, Sage Publications, Newbury Park, CA, pp. 51–69.

Anderson, R. (1996) Part three: accessing information. In Hantrais, L. and Mangen, S. (Eds) *Cross-National Research Methods in the Social Sciences*, Pinter, London, pp. 105–108.

Antal, A. B., Dierkes, M. and Weiler, H. N. (1996) Cross-national policy research: traditions, achievements, and challenges. In Inkeles, A. and Sasaki, M. (Eds) *Comparing Nations and Cultures: Readings in a Cross-disciplinary Perspective*, Prentice-Hall, Englewood Cliffs, NJ, pp. 9–17.

Armstrong, R. W., Mok, C., Go, F. M. and Chan, A. (1997) The importance of cross-cultural expectations in the measurement of service quality perceptions in the hotel industry. *International Journal of Hospitality Management*, Vol. 16, No. 2, pp. 181–190.

Boger, C. A. (1995) A comparison between different delivery systems of quick service food facilities. *Hospitality Research Journal*, Vol. 18, No. 3/Vol. 19, No. 1, pp. 111–124.

Brotherton, B. and Burgess, J. (1997) A comparative study of academic research interests In US and UK hotel and restaurant companies. *Proceedings of the Sixth Annual CHME Hospitality Research Conference*, Oxford Brookes University, Oxford, pp. 317–348.

Brymer, R. A., Rousselle, J. R. and Johns, T. R. (1990) Academic research interests of hospitality corporations. *Hospitality Research Journal*, Vol. 14, pp. 1–10.

Brynner, J. and Heinz, W. (1991) Matching samples and analysing their differences in a cross-national study of labour market entry in England and West Germany. In Ragin, C. C. (ed.) *Issues and Alternatives in Comparative Research*, Brill, Leiden, Netherlands, pp. 137–153.

Burrell, J., Manfredi, S., Rollin, H., Price, L. and Stead, L. (1997) Equal opportunities for women employees in the hospitality industry: a comparison between France, Italy, Spain and the UK. *International Journal of Hospitality Management*, Vol. 16, No. 2, pp. 161–179.

Coolican, H. (1994) *Research Methods and Statistics in Psychology* (2nd Edn). Hodder & Stoughton, London.

Davies, R. B. and Dale, A. (1994) Introduction. In Davies, R. B. and Dale, A. (Eds), *Analysing Social and Political Change: A Casebook of Methods*, Sage Publications, London, pp. 1–19.

Eisenhardt, K. M. (1995) Building theories from case study research. In Huber, G.P. and Van de Van, A. H. (Eds) *Longitudinal Field Research Methods: Studying Processes of Organisational Change*, Sage Publications, Thousand Oaks, CA.

Embretson, S. E. (1983) Construct validity: construct representation versus nomothetic span. *Psychological Bulletin*, Vol. 93, pp. 179–197.

English, W., Joslam, B., Upchurch, R. S. and Willems, J. (1996) Restaurant attrition: a longitudinal analysis of restaurant failures. *International Journal of Contemporary Hospitality Management*, Vol. 8, No. 2, pp. 17–20.

Figueiredo, K., Latas, J. R. and Gomes, D. (1995) A strategic service vision in the hotel industry: some conclusions from case studies. In Teare, R. and Armistead, C. (Eds) *Services Management: New Directions, New Perspectives*, Cassell, London.

Glaser, B. G. and Strauss, A. L. (1967) *The Discovery of Grounded Theory: Strategies for Qualitative Research*. Weidenfeld and Nicolson, London.

Griffin, L. J., Botsko, C., Wahl, A. M. and Isaac, L. W. (1991) Theoretical generality, case particularity: qualitative comparative analysis of trade union growth and decline. In Ragin, C. C. (Ed.) *Issues and Alternatives In Comparative Research*, Brill, Leiden, Netherlands, pp. 110–136.

Hallam, G. and Baum, T. (1996) Contracting out food and beverage operations in hotels: a comparative study of practice in North America and the United Kingdom. *International Journal of Hospitality Management*, Vol. 15, No. 1, pp. 41–50.

Hantrais, L. and Mangen, S. (1996) Method and management of cross-national social research. In Hantrais, L. and Mangen, S. (Eds) *Cross-National Research Methods in the Social Sciences*, Pinter, London, pp. 1–12.

Hendrick, C. (1991) Replications, strict replications, and conceptual replications: are they important? In Neuliep, J. W. (Ed.) *Replication Research in the Social Sciences*, Sage Publications, Newbury Park, CA, pp. 41–49.

Hicks, A. M. (1994) Introduction to pooling. In Janoski, T. and Hicks, A. M. (Eds) *The Comparative Political Economy of the Welfare State*, Cambridge University Press, New York, pp. 169–188.

Iverson, T. J. (1995) Forecasting hotel employment with simple time series models. *Tourism Recreation Research*, Vol. 20, No. 2, pp. 58–62.

Jacques, E. (1982) *The Form of Time*. Crane Russak, New York.

Janoski, T. (1991) Synthetic strategies in comparative research: methods and problems of internal and external analysis. In Ragin, C. C. (Ed.) *Issues and Alternatives in Comparative Research*, Brill, Leiden, Netherlands, pp. 59–81.

Janoski, T. and Hicks, A. M. (1994) *The Comparative Political Economy of the Welfare State*. Cambridge University Press, New York.

Janoski, T. and Isaac, L. W. (1994) Introduction to time-series analysis. In Janoski, T. and Hicks, A. M. (Eds) *The Comparative Political Economy of the Welfare State*, Cambridge University Press, New York, pp. 31–53.

Kara, A., Kaynak, E. and Kucukemiroglu, O. (1995) Marketing strategies for fast-food restaurants: a customer view. *International Journal of Contemporary Hospitality Management*, Vol. 7, No. 4, pp. 16–22.

Kelly, J. R. and McGrath, J. E. (1988) *On Time and Method*. Sage Publications, Newbury Park, CA.

Kohn, M. L. (1996) Cross-national research as an analytic strategy: American Sociological Association, 1987 Presidential Address. In Inkeles, A. and Sasaki, M. (Eds) *Comparing Nations and Cultures: Readings in a Cross-Disciplinary Perspective*, Prentice-Hall, Englewood Cliffs, NJ, pp. 28–53.

Lamal, P. A. (1991) On the importance of replication. In Neuliep, J. W. (Ed.) *Replication Research in the Social Sciences*, Sage Publications, Newbury Park, CA, pp. 31–35.

Lieberson, S. (1985) *Making it Count: The Improvement of Social Research and Theory.* University of California Press, Berkeley.

Lijphart, A. (1971) Comparative politics and the comparative method. *American Political Science Review,* Vol. 65, pp. 682–693.

Miller, D. (1980) Can science do without induction? In Cohen, L. J. and Hesse, M. (Eds) *Applications of Inductive Logic,* Clarenden Press, Oxford, pp. 68–98.

Moncarz, E. S. and Kron, R. N. (1993) Operational analysis: a case study of two hotels in financial distress. *International Journal of Hospitality Management,* Vol. 12, No. 2, pp. 175–196.

Monge, P. R. (1995) Theoretical and analytical issues in studying organisational processes. In Huber, G. P. and Van de Ven, A. H. (Eds) *Longitudinal Field Research Methods: Studying Processes of Organisational Change,* Sage Publications, Thousand Oaks, CA, pp. 267–298.

Morey, R. C. and Dittman, D. A. (1995) Evaluating a hotel GM's performance: a case study in benchmarking. *Cornell Hotel and Restaurant Administration Quarterly,* Vol. 36, No. 5, pp. 30–35.

Moutinho, L., McDonagh, P., Peris, S. M. and Bigne, E. (1995) The future development of the hotel sector: an international comparison. *International Journal of Contemporary Hospitality Management,* Vol. 7, No. 4, pp. 10–15.

Neuman, W. L. (1994) *Social Research Methods: Quantitative and Qualitative Approaches* (2nd Edn). Allyn and Bacon, Needham Heights, MA.

Papadopoulou, A., Ineson, E. M. and Wilkie, D. T. (1995) Convergence between sources of service job analysis data. *International Journal of Contemporary Hospitality Management,* Vol. 7, No. 2/3, pp. 42–47.

Pearce, D. G. (1993) Comparative studies in tourism research. In Pearce, D. G. and Butler, R. W. (Eds) *Tourism Research: Critiques and Challenges,* Routledge, London, pp. 20–35.

Pettigrew, A. M. (1989) Longitudinal methods to study change: theory and practice. In Mansfield, R. (Ed.) *Frontiers Of Management,* Routledge, London, pp. 21–49.

Pizam, A., Pine, R., Mok, C. and Shin, J. Y. (1997) Nationality vs industry cultures: which has a greater effect on managerial behaviour? *International Journal of Hospitality Management,* Vol. 16, No. 2, pp. 127–145.

Przeworski, A. and Teune, H. (1970) *The Logic of Comparative Social Enquiry.* John Wiley & Sons, New York.

Ragin, C. C. (1987) *The Comparative Method: Moving Beyond Qualitative and Quantitative Strategies.* University of California Press, Berkeley.

Ragin, C. C. (1991) Introduction: the problem of balancing discourse on cases and variables in comparative social science. In Ragin, C. C. (ed.) *Issues and Alternatives in Comparative Research,* Brill, Leiden, Netherlands, pp. 1–8.

Ragin, C. C. (1994) *Constructing Social Research.* Pine Forge Press (Sage Publications), Thousand Oaks, CA.

Ragin, C. C. (1996) The distinctiveness of comparative social science. In Inkeles, A. and Sasaki, M. (Eds) *Comparing Nations and Cultures: Readings in a Cross-Disciplinary Perspective,* Prentice Hall, Englewood Cliffs, NJ, pp. 74–89.

Rokkan, S. (Ed.) (1966) *Data Archives for the Social Sciences.* Mouton, Paris.

Rokkan, S. (1996) Cross-cultural, cross-societal, and cross-national research. In Inkeles, A. and Sasaki, M. (Eds) *Comparing Nations and Cultures: Readings in a Cross-Disciplinary Perspective,* Prentice-Hall, Englewood Cliffs, NJ, pp. 18–27.

Rosenthal, R. (1991) Replication in behavioural research. In Neuliep, J. W. (ed.) *Replication Research in the Social Sciences,* Sage Publications, Newbury Park, CA, pp. 1–30.

Royle, T. (1995) Corporate versus societal culture: a comparative study of McDonald's in Europe. *International Journal of Contemporary Hospitality Management,* Vol. 7, No. 2/3, pp. 52–56.

Rueschemeyer, D. (1991) Different methods—contradictory results? In Ragin, C. C. (Ed.) *Issues and Alternatives in Comparative Research,* Brill, Leiden, Netherlands, pp. 9–38.

Schunk, M. (1996) Constructing models of the welfare mix: care options of frail elders. In Hantrais, L. and Mangen, S. (Eds) *Cross-National Research Methods in the Social Sciences,* Pinter, London, pp. 84–94.

Skocpol, T. (1984) Emerging agendas and recurrent strategies in historical sociology. In Skocpol, T. (Ed.) *Vision and Method in Historical Sociology*, Cambridge University Press, New York, pp. 356–391.

Smelser, N. J. (1996) The methodology of comparative analysis of economic activity. In Inkeles, A. and Sasaki, M. (Eds) *Comparing Nations and Cultures: Readings in a Cross-Disciplinary Perspective*, Prentice-Hall, Englewood Cliffs, NJ, pp. 90–100.

Smith, D. A. (1991) Method and theory in urban studies. In Ragin, C. C. (Ed.) *Issues and Alternatives in Comparative Research*, Brill, Leiden, Netherlands, pp. 39–58.

Sparrowe, R. T. and Popielarz, P. A. (1995) Getting ahead in the hospitality industry: an event history analysis of promotions among hotel and restaurant employees. *Hospitality Research Journal*, Vol. 19, No. 3, pp. 99–118.

Stinchcombe, A. L. (1978) *Theoretical Methods in Social History*. Academic Press, New York.

Strang, D. (1994) Introduction to event history methods. In Janoski, T. and Hicks, A. M. (Eds) *The Comparative Political Economy of the Welfare State*, Cambridge University Press, New York, pp. 245–253.

Swanson, G. (1971) Frameworks for comparative research: structural anthropology and the theory of action. In Vallier, I. (Ed.) *Comparative Methods in Sociology: Essays on Trends and Applications*, University of California Press, Berkeley, pp. 141–202.

Tilley, C. (1984) *Big Structures, Large Processes, Huge Comparisons*. The Russell Sage Foundation, New York.

Van de Vijver, F. and Leung, K. (1997) *Methods and Data Analysis for Cross-Cultural Research*, Sage Publications, Thousand Oaks, CA.

Van Hoof, H. B., Verbeeten, M. J. and Combrink, T. E. (1996) Information technology revisited—international lodging-industry technology needs and perceptions: a comparative study. *Cornell Hotel and Restaurant Administration Quarterly*, Vol. 37, No. 6, pp. 86–91.

Warwick, D. P. and Osherson, S. (1973) *Comparative Research Methods*. Prentice-Hall, Englewood Cliffs, NJ.

Wickham-Crowley, T. P. (1991) A qualitative approach to Latin American revolutions. In Ragin, C. C. (Ed.) *Issues and Alternatives in Comparative Research*, Brill, Leiden, Netherlands, pp. 82–109.

Wieviorka, M. (1992) Case studies: history or sociology. In Ragin, C. C. and Becker, H. S. (Eds) *What is a Case?*, Cambridge University Press, New York, pp. 159–172.

Yin, R. K. (1993) *Applications of Case Study Research*. Sage Publications, Newbury Park, Ca.

Yin, R. K. (1994) *Case Study Research—Design and Methods* (2nd Edition). Sage Publications, Thousand Oaks, CA.

9 Action research

CONRAD LASHLEY

Introduction

This chapter argues that action research provides a valuable approach to improving professional management practice in complex hospitality situations. Even though the term itself has a variety of meanings and can involve participants differently, action research enables practitioners to analyse and intervene in their work situations in a way that improves effectiveness. It is an approach which has particular relevance in hospitality situations because of the complexity of hospitality service operations.

In these operations, traditional research, which tends to focus on single independent variables which will supposedly alter a dependent variable, does not recognise the interdependence of interfunctional and interfactoral influences in hospitality systems. Thus, with a few exceptions (Roper *et al.*, 1997), much hospitality research is monodiscipline based and rarely recognises the impacts of changes in practice on the complex socio-political organisation. The author's own research (Lashley, 1996, 1997) on employee empowerment confirms that many organisations introduce changes to employee relations under the title of empowerment without recognising the crucial importance of these changes on the feelings of the employees who are supposedly empowered, and the consequent impacts on employee performance and service quality.

Action research has much to offer hospitality organisation members. For managers it can provide a technique which assists in their own professional practice. The research activity itself involves them in systematic reflection and analysis of current practice. It provides a mechanism, which also incorporates many organisation members, drawn from all levels of the organisation, in problem definition, action and evaluation. It is an approach, therefore, which is compatible with employee empowerment, because it engages employees as organisation members and recognises the importance of employee contributions. The consequence for managers is that the quality of decisions generated is likely to be more realistic and acceptable to employees. In addition, a culture in which action research is well embedded is likely to develop higher levels of commitment because of the involvement and participation of employees. For employees, action research provides opportunities to overcome frustrations and inequalities in organisation life. Action research can be liberating and can improve the self-esteem of organisation members who are not traditionally afforded status and esteem.

Given these potential benefits, action research has important implications for educators in the design and delivery of hospitality management courses. Action research is an approach which is highly compatible with Kolb's (1984) notions of experiential

The Handbook of Contemporary Hospitality Management Research, Edited by Bob Brotherton.
© 1999 John Wiley & Sons Ltd.

learning and Schon's (1983, 1987) 'reflective practitioner', both of which are educational principles embraced by many hospitality management educators in Britain. Whilst both these writers provide ideas which have generated models to assist in the design of the hospitality management curriculum, they also assist in suggesting that approaches to research can be matched to management training and ongoing organisational learning.

The author makes no apology for the general proselytising tone to the chapter; it is intended as a contribution to a debate about the nature of hospitality management research. It is the author's belief that action research can make a significant contribution to lifting both the professionalism of hospitality management and the effectiveness of hospitality management practice. That said, action research is not uncontentious. There are a number of forms to the action research process, and there are detractors who question both its rigour as an approach to research and its practicality in generating action. The following section engages with these debates and discussions.

Action research—debates and discussions

Whilst there are a number of strands in action research which make an easy ubiquitous definition difficult to establish, there are a number of key themes in the assumptions made about the role of the researchers, the object/subject(s) of the research and the purpose of the research activity. The term itself is not shared by all those in the field. Thus for Argyris (1985) the activity is termed 'action science', whilst for others (Oja and Smulyan, 1989), action research is 'collaborative action research', though for many 'action research' (Hartley, 1994; Stringer, 1996) will suffice. These variations in terms reveal much about the nature of action research.

As the term implies, action research involves inquiry with the objective of acting on social situations. Thus both scientific reflection and intervention are key elements. 'Action research is a process by which groups of people (whether managers, academics, teachers, students or "learners" generally) work on real issues or problems, carrying real responsibility in real conditions' (Zuber-Skerritt, 1991: xiii). As stated above, this definition of action research is consistent with the concept of the 'reflective practitioner' (Schon, 1983, 1987), that is, professionals who combine professional practice and performance with reflective evaluation of their own practice with a view to improving it. There is a symbiotic relationship between models of professionalism which stress the importance of both professional competence and active reflection, and action research. Reflecting practitioners provide an important underpinning strand in definitions of action research. Processes of professional reflection imply action research and, at the same time, action research provides a mind-set and a set of procedures and techniques which can be used by practitioners aiming to improve performance. Action research, therefore, provides 'the necessary link between self evaluation and professional development' (Elliott, 1978: ii). Furthermore, the process of self-evaluation involves reflection and a deepening of understanding which in turn leads to changes in practice.

A distinguishing feature of action research according to some writers (Argyris, 1985) is that it is both capable of amending action and of generating theory which can be disseminated with others and used to inform both theorising and practice. The generation of theory, therefore, separates action research from learning through 'worka-day practice' alone (Elliott, 1978), though, as will be discussed later, there are links with the notion of 'experiential learning' (Kolb, 1984). For Kolb the cyclical link between experience, reflection, theorising and action provide an ongoing evolutionary process implicit in learning. However, for Elliott (1978: 121) action research is more than learning: '... judgement in action research is diagnostic rather than prescriptive for action, since prescriptive judgement when made reflectively arise from practical deliberation.'

Whilst the reflective practitioner strand of definitions of action research are power-ful in its current application, action research has deeply democratic and egalitarian roots. Lewin (1951) gave action research its name and advocated the approach as a means of addressing social problems—an approach which aimed to engage the people experiencing the situation or problem in the research process. Lewin was dismissive of research as an end in itself. For him research had to result in some form of action to improve social conditions, or overcome problems being experienced by a particular group or section of the community. The work produced by universities was not suffi-cient if it merely contented itself with the production of meaningful insights, and the 'social scientist had to involve practitioners at all stages of the research' (Oja and Smulyan, 1989: 3), in current terminology, empowering the subjects of research to engage in reflection with a view to overcoming the problem. Involving the subjects of the research has several benefits, not the least of which is that in complex social situa-tions it may not be possible for the traditional, disengaged researcher to fully appreci-ate and understand the subtleties of the situation. Involvement in the research process also generates more commitment and a sense of engagement with the research. Thus people are more likely to have a sense of ownership of the diagnosis of the situation and the actions needed to resolve the problems if they are more immediately involved in the action research project. Action research could demonstrate to practitioners that only through the application of social science could they 'hope to gain power to do a good job' (Lewin, 1951: 213).

The joint construction of the research project bringing together both the social sci-entist and the practitioner suggests another variation on the model outlined earlier. The practitioner needs the scientific skills of the social scientist to conduct action research. Chein, Cook and Harding (1948: 44) provide a useful insight into these early aspira-tions for action research: 'Action research is a field which developed to satisfy the need of the socio-political individual who recognised that, in science, he can find the most reliable guide to effective action, and the needs of the scientist who wants his labours to be of maximal utility as well as of theoretical significance.' Thus the interests of both those who look to social science to overcome a problem and the scientist looking for practical relevance in investigations can be met by action research.

The relationship between those concerned with social science and practical actions has proved to be a tension since the inception of action research. For all Lewin's sug-gestion that action research embraces the interests of both practitioners and social sci-entists, there were many in the scientific community who accused action research of not being 'real science'. Thus the very sense of engagement and involvement by the social scientist, seen to be the strength of action research, was seen as an anathema by those brought up in Western traditions of the detached impartial researcher striving for some universal truth. Action research was treated with suspicion by mainstream social sciences because many considered its tools and techniques as inadequate, and 'action research was condemned to a sort of orphan's role in the social sciences' (Barton-Cunningham, 1993: 4).

More recently there has been a recognition that the traditional scientific methods have limits in the study of organisational situations and development. In particular, as the social scientist is attempting to discover universal truths and establish general classifications and principles, there is a mismatch between the scientific research and problem solving in organisations. 'Scientific research methods have been accused as being unfortunate impediments to effective action' (Barton-Cunningham, 1993: 7). There has been a recognition that research into organisations needs to reflect their dynamic and complex nature. Historically much research into organisations has attempted to create experimental conditions to study the effects of changing an independent variable, 'all things being equal'; however, in most organisations, all things are not equal. Both external and internal organisational environments are constantly changing and it is impossible to control for all the influencing factors on organisational success. Much of the research which attempts to link human resource management practices and subsequent organisational performance can be criticised precisely because it is almost impossible to establish definitive causal links between the way people are managed, consulted, trained and rewarded, and the subsequent performance of the business unit in which they work. The work of Huselid (1995) provides a particularly valuable example of the elaboration to which social scientists can go in the search for positivistic and formulaic links between employment practices and increased sales revenue, profits and share values. In this view, the adoption of employment practices which improve on competitor firms will outperform them by precisely defined amounts. The problem is that the formula fails to describe in detail the specific internal and external dynamics which lead to increased effort by employees on the one hand, and the internal managerial processes together with the external circumstances on the other, which translate employee efforts into increased organisational performance.

This criticism reflects a more widespread recognition amongst practitioners and some social scientists that traditional experimental practice is limited in its ability to generate practical answers to organisational problems in time to benefit the organisation in a dynamic environment (Barton-Cunningham, 1993). Herein lies another potential tension: organisational practitioners need immediate answers which they can understand and which deal with immediate problems. This can lead to over-simplistic panaceas being advocated and applied. Lashley's (1997) work on employee empowerment shows that some initiatives like employee empowerment have a lifespan which progresses through several typical phases. The initiative is advocated with vigour by consultants and early adopters. Books and journal articles and even dedicated journals publicise the benefits to be gained from the initiative. Practitioners looking for a quick fix to organisation problems adopt the initiative without really understanding its full implications. Not surprisingly, such initiatives often fail to deliver the benefits promised if they have been inappropriately applied. To rectify this, another panacea comes along to be adopted by practitioners and the whole merry-go-round starts again. The work of Peters and Waterman (1982) is a good example of the type of generalised and dubious research which has been enormously popular with practitioners but has been severely criticised by academics (Guest, 1995).

Therefore action research can provide a means of managing the tensions between applying rigorous social science thinking to practical situations which incorporate practitioners. 'This would-be research process allows the practitioner to guarantee the methodological "rightfulness" of the research, especially where the research can be verified with those of another' (Barton-Cunningham, 1993: 9). As was shown earlier, the involvement of practitioners in the research activity also assists in ensuring that the problems are defined in a way which is meaningful to them, and subsequent action recommendations are ones which they understand and support.

Researchers in educational practice also advocate a role for action research: 'Because education is both action-oriented and practical in nature, educational research must address practical problems, rather than theoretical or context free problems' (Oja and Smulyan, 1989: 4). Co-operation between teachers and researchers will increase the perception of a need for changes in educational practice if practitioners were confident that the project which involved them revealed the need for change. Thus educators, instead of being the subjects of experiments, become the experimenters and subsequently take control of their own professional development. The problems identified, process investigation and subsequent actions are shaped by and conducted through the ownership of the educators concerned.

Action research has been described, therefore, as having the following differences when compared with traditional research. It is *practical* in that the research process is not solely concerned with theoretical outputs and the furtherance of knowledge *per se*. The production of practical improvements both during and after the research is an important objective. It is *participative* and *collaborative*: the researcher is immediately involved as a 'co-worker' doing research with the people immediately involved with the problem. Thus proximity and association with people is a distinct difference from the more traditional scientific approaches where the researcher is an external expert, detached and conducting research on 'subjects'. It is *egalitarian* in that there are no hierarchies of importance in the research process. All are equal participants, because it is recognised that the views and experiences of all contribute to an understanding of the complexity of the whole set of experiences. Action research is *interpretative*: it is not directly concerned with the testing of a predetermined research question but with analysis and solutions based on the views of various participants in the enquiry. Research validity is established through a *critical community* in which people both look to improvements in their work but also critically address the constraints which impact upon them (Zuber-Skerritt, 1991).

The action researcher is therefore a person with a particular set of skills and attitudes—a scientific mind-set with an understanding of qualitative research principles, and a strong commitment to both studying problems and formulating the practical actions required to overcome the problems. The action researcher needs to understand the processes of change and the circumstances which encourage and facilitate change, and to engage with the immediate situation and people in the context. Thus the action researcher will theorise, experiment and implement, being at once rigorous and flexible (Barton-Cunningham, 1993).

Reflection in action

The foregoing discussion has suggested that there are a number of approaches to action research which give different emphases to the 'science' or the 'practical applications' of action research. In response to criticisms from traditional social scientists, some action researchers have wanted to strengthen the science and rigour of the research process. Others, particularly practitioners, have been chiefly concerned with improving practice. It was suggested that these two traditions do not sit easily together, but for action research to be successful both have to be present in the research process. The foregoing discussion suggested that action research offers some powerful strengths in the analysis of organisational contexts and the development of solutions to problems. The following models therefore are based on approaches which enable hospitality, leisure and tourism lecturers to consider their own educational practice and models for working with hospitality practitioners. In the long term, action research provides a mechanism through which both practitioners and academics can work together to better understand organisational problems and produce actions which can help to overcome them.

Bearing in mind the variations of emphasis mentioned above, a common feature of many commentators on action research procedures is that they reflect a cyclical process. Bawden (1991) makes use of the Kolb experiential learning model (Figure 9.1) to draw parallels with both learning and research and the research, reflection, theorising and actioning elements of experiential learning. In this view, the starting point lies in the subjective nature of the world view held by each individual. The way individuals interpret the world, the way of defining reality, is subjectively and contextually specific: '... a weltanschauung of value laden, psycho-cultural, experience-modified knowledge or beliefs or assumptions which shapes the way we handle issues in our world' (Bawden, 1991: 12). In turn this reflects how individuals perceive the world and provides a predisposition to how individuals define the situations and what issues they prioritise for study.

The process of learning about the world is best explained through reference to Kolb's explanation of experiential learning, in particular, making reference to the preferences which individuals have about the way they prefer to learn and the implications this holds for what they learn. Kolb (1984) provides a model which many hospitality

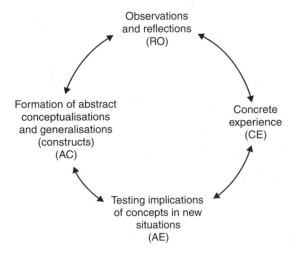

Figure 9.1 Kolb's learning styles
(Source: Bawden, 1991)

management educators use as a basis for course modelling (Lashley, 1995). The Kolb model suggests that learners tend to have learning preferences located in one of four quadrants which are produced from features of personality. The degree of introversion/extroversion and preferences towards using the left or right side of the brain are influential in producing preferred styles of learning which prioritise learning from concrete or abstract, from reflection or action. These shape students' learning styles and preferences for learning. Unpublished work being undertaken in a project at both Leeds Metropolitan University and Nottingham Trent University suggests that students on hospitality management courses have strong preferences to learn from concrete, action-based situations. These tendencies are so strong that, if not addressed, they can create difficulties in the development of reflection and theorising. Action research can be useful in underpinning learning theories which encourage reflection. Action research can move the student through forms of learning which build from personal preferences through processes which explore, assimilate findings and build findings into new ways of thinking, and shape actions in future (diverge–assimilate–converge–accommodate: Kolb, 1984).

Bawden (1991) goes on to develop the links between these ways of learning about the world by adding a third dimension which also has relevance in the hospitality, tourism and leisure context: the distinction between integration and separation in the focus of the research investigation. Each represents different ways of looking at the world. In the first case there is an assumption that it is possible to understand a situation only by studying the whole system (holism), whilst in the second case the assumption is made that the whole is far too complex and that understanding best develops from studying elements (reductionist). In much contemporary hospitality research there has been a tendency to adopt reductionist approaches, but there is a limit to the effectiveness of research which does not reflect on the impacts of changes to a systematic whole. Thus research which looks at individual elements such as service quality without a consideration of issues related to employees, customer expectations, operating systems and the whole array of factors which impact on the system will miss much. Action research provides a means of conducting such whole-system research. Similarly, any consideration by practitioners of issues which do not delve into the real practices and experiences of those who are the subjects of policies and actions will be flawed and will result in self-delusion. Lashley's (1997) research into employee empowerment confirms that initiatives which claim to be empowering, but which do not generate feelings of being empowered in employees, are treated with cynicism at best by employees. Frequently these are counter-productive because employees regard these initiatives as an imposition and stress-creating. Action research can provide a means of overcoming some of these examples of 'subject blindness' whereby practitioners omit some important elements in their analysis.

The means by which action research is conducted will reflect assumptions about the way the participants see the world, how they conceive the nature of knowledge, as well as the ethical positions they adopt. It is critically important for those engaged in action research to make explicit and share the assumptions about questions of 'reality', knowledge and the outcomes of the research activity. It is possible to define approaches which are based on rigorous experimentation, based on assumptions that there is an objective reality to be discovered through reducing situations to their elements in a manner typical of the natural sciences. In other cases approaches are shaped by notions that realities are social constructs and there are a number of truths to be discovered. For Bawden (1991: 20) both of these '… can be conceived as variations on a theme of the experiential (experienced-based, problem-based, action-based) process of learning'.

Action researchers have to operate on two levels. The first level involves the situation which is being explored and the second relates to the way in which the enquiry is being undertaken. 'We must find out; find out about finding out; take action to improve the situation; and take action to improve taking action' (Bawden, 1991: 21). At the first level action researchers:

- involve themselves directly in complex and dynamic situations;
- investigate situations from as many perspectives as possible;
- develop theories based on information gathered and integrate these with available knowledge to provide the basis for action and intervention;
- provide action in a way which is testable and capable of review.

At the second level, the action researcher has to question the processes of finding out and actioning by:

- rigorously questioning the means by which the 'facts' are defined and information is being sought;
- reflecting upon and making explicit the core assumptions behind the way the situation was defined and knowledge identified;
- theorising about theorising and theories available in the public domain;
- the way that learning and reflection is undertaken.

Bawden (1991: 23) suggests that the action researcher has many similarities with the action learner: 'The rigorous experiential or action learner, is one who is able to make conscious, critical shifts within and between these two "cycles of learning" such that there is sensible and informed sequence in the whole process of enquiry.' However, an additional requirement of the action researcher is that the outcomes of the research/learning process enter the public domain for critical review and debate. The action researcher, therefore, needs to publicly explain the research and actions so that others with interests in the subject can comment on and critically evaluate research and actions.

The relationship between the research and action aspects of action research have produced some tensions which also highlight differences in emphasis between different commentators. As was discussed earlier, early advocates of action research saw it as a technique which both empowered the subjects of social inequality and addressed problems which they faced. These early advocates were frequently criticised for the lack of rigour in the quality of the research established (Robson, 1993). In education research, for example, critics have pointed to a lack of theoretical underpinning, to research being introspective and ahistorical. On the other hand advocates have tended to dismiss the criticisms because it was not always possible to produce traditional education theory and improve practice through action research (Oja and Smulyan, 1989). These tensions between improving practitioner practice and developing a critique based on theory have produced a number of models of how the research process is initiated and managed and by whom. Whilst a defining feature of action research is that practitioners and interest groups or stakeholders are involved in the research process, there are variations in the role assigned to outside researchers. For some, professionals act reflectively and unaided by researchers from outside the group (Oja and Smulyan, 1989). In other situations, the external researcher adds to the rigour of the research and is a crucial ingredient in improving the quality and dissemination of the research outputs. Bawden (1991) offers a model of the potential relationships which build to an array of practice. This is shown diagrammatically in Figure 9.2.

By considering the role of the researcher and researcher relationships with practitioners and the context in which practitioners operate, Bawden's model suggests that there are four basic sets of relationships. In the first three cases, researchers from outside the organisation study the 'system' in either a reductionist or a holistic manner. In the first, the focus of the researcher is technical, and explores the elements in, say, the use of information technology or food nutritional/menu content. In the second model the researcher is also examining some aspect of the behaviour of organisation members, say in examining how organisation members handle food or devise menus. The focus of the researcher is that of the traditional social scientist. In the third situation, the focus shifts to a more holistic approach, to the organisation as a system. Frequently, this approach treats the organisation as a 'black box' with little reference to the relationships either within the system or between the system and its environment (Bawden, 1991). Although this third approach differs from the reductionist perspective of the first two, these three approaches have a commonality in that the researcher maintains objectivity and detachment from the object under investigation. This leads to the fourth approach, which Bawden describes as the 'action researching (soft) system'. Here the researcher is an active participant in the organisation and acts as a facilitator for 'co-researchers'. The action researcher is systemic in focus and actively participates with organisation members in the critical analysis of complex and changing situations. The focus relates to relationships between people, physical situations and environments. 'Our purpose together is to seek desirable and feasible improvements to complex, problematic situations where not only are the answers unknown, but the questions are problematic' (Bawden, 1991: 26).

The key to this approach is that it meets the requirements mentioned earlier. It is critical because the processes and outcomes, the actions implemented and conduct of the researchers are subject to critical analysis throughout. The approach is systemic: the participants are located in the situation, the processes of researching are based on experiential learning which interplays the concrete and the abstract, reflection and action, and theorising and action throughout. The actions of people within the organisation are shown to interact with the environment and the external influences on them. Above all, action research involves the critical appraisal of, and dialogue with, interested publics. This in turn results in improvements in both the researcher's and the practitioner's practice, improvements in the practitioner's situation and improvements in the practitioner's understanding of how these improvements occur.

Action research in hospitality organisations

The preceding sections have explored some of the discussions and debates about action research and established some philosophical issues relating to the nature of action research methods and the potential relationships between researchers and practitioners.

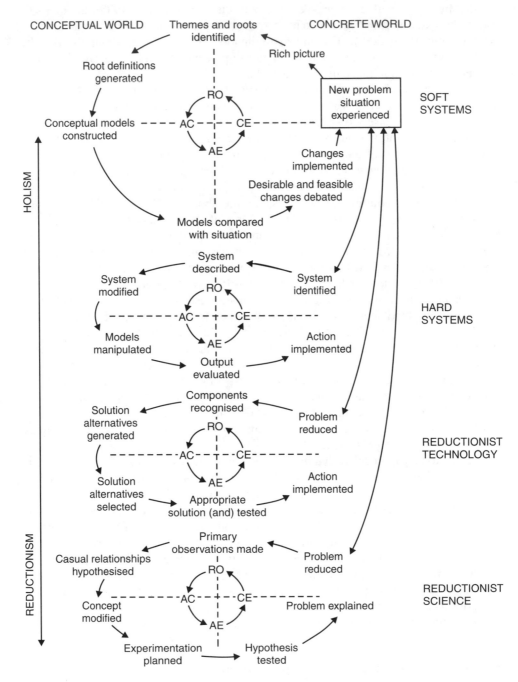

Figure 9.2   A spiral of researching systems
(Source: Bawden, 1991)

Attention is now turned to the establishment of a more practical set of procedures which need to be implemented when undertaking action research. Reinforcing some of the points made earlier, researchers have to ensure that organisation members are involved in all aspects of the experiential learning process and that effective action research is cyclical in that it encourages the 'looking, thinking and acting' (Stringer, 1996). It is also ongoing because the evaluation of results and their subsequent dissemination in turn stimulate further critical evaluation, resulting in relooking, rethinking and further action.

Action research cannot be imposed, nor will it be appropriate to every organisation. To be successful the approach requires a cultural-level commitment in which managers and others are totally committed to action research. Stringer suggests that Block's (1987) definition of entrepreneurial organisations as being based on 'enlightened self interest' has many of the elements required for action research. Entrepreneurial organisations are further defined as being based on trust, and encouraging people to take reasonable risks. Information and control are shared and contribution is measured against contribution to service users. Stringer further suggests that action research is an ideal approach to be associated with managing organisations in a more humanistic and democratic way. Certainly if these views are accepted they can be seen to be compatible with a whole array of writings suggesting that hospitality organisations of the future need to be more service driven, customer oriented and managed in a way which empowers all members to take responsibility for ensuring successful service encounters. Setting aside the somewhat simplistic, naive and unitary aspects to these assertions, action research does have a role to play in giving managers a technique for gaining information and shaping research which realistically confronts issues in a way designed to bring together the ideas, experiences and expertise of all organisation members. At its root it recognises that despite their aspirations managers are not the font of all wisdom, that in complex organisations it is unrealistic for managers to know or understand the intricacies of operational life, and that operatives are frequently better placed to analyse problems, suggest ways of overcoming them and evaluate the impacts of changes made.

In these circumstances it is necessary for researchers to understand the nature of the management style and organisation culture which are most appropriate to facilitate action research. A participative management style based on a trust culture within a 'learning organisation' committed to continuous improvement is likely to produce the best setting for action research. Participative management which encourages employee involvement in decision making fosters an organisation culture which recognises the contribution which all organisation members can make to solving problems and improving performance. Similarly, a culture based on mutual trust, a dedication to learning from experience, and continuous improvement set the context in which action research will flourish and grow. Attempts to establish action research in organisations which are driven by a short-term and exclusive preoccupation with the 'bottom line' are likely to face some considerable barriers to the effective use of action research. Very frequently these organisations are directive in management style with limited regard for the contribution made by employees. Indeed labour is frequently seen as a cost to be minimised, and the associated culture of control discourages the sense of mutuality essential for action research. Thus it is essential that managers understand the barriers and constraints in organisation management which can facilitate or hamper the development of an effective action research culture.

Hospitality organisations could benefit from action research because of the unique cluster of constraints and problems which hospitality service providers face. Many hospitality organisations have complex operational issues to manage—production and consumption of goods and services on the premises, health and safety management, the key role of employees in delivery of the core services, the interweaving of marketing, people, and operational management issues at the customer interface. These issues present a complexity which requires more of both managers and operatives on the frontline than in either a traditional manufacturing business or many other service-sector organisations. In addition, large multi-unit, branded hospitality businesses experience an added order of complexity by offering a standardised brand through chains of relatively small units located close to local markets. The logistics of attempting to manage uniformity and standardisation across hundreds or thousands of units present a difficult enough control problem, but this is made more complex by the contradictory nature of customer service needs. Frequently customers want the security of knowing what to expect from the standardised, branded service, but also want to be regarded as individuals in the service encounter. Control of operational performance then becomes extremely difficult as senior managers try to control brand integrity but allow the service deliverer some freedom of interpretation to meet both regional and individual customer differences.

Service deliverers, at both management and operative levels, have to manage the complexity of the branded offer. This requires an understanding of the nature of the brand—what customers are buying into—and a commitment to delighting the customer within the framework of the brand. As Lashley (1997) has suggested, employee empowerment, given an appropriate definition of form and fit, is a valuable way of assisting in the management of these tensions. Action research provides an important adjunct to this. Employees and managers involved in research projects can gain a great deal of self-esteem and develop the sense of personal efficacy which is essential for effective empowerment.

However, as argued above, the starting point needs to be an organisational commitment to manage the business in a more open and democratic way. A commitment by owners and/or senior managers that the business needs to be run in a way which recognises a variety of stakeholder interests, and that to be effective all members have to share common goals and purposes, is vital. These goals and purposes have to be developed in a way which both reflects the range of stakeholder interests and involves the full range of stakeholders in the goal setting. It requires managers to have a genuine understanding of organisations as reflecting a plurality of interests which must be incorporated in the research and decision-making processes. With this setting in place the following procedures need to be implemented.

Scene setting   In the first instance managers and researchers need to establish a preliminary picture of the issue(s) to be investigated. Associated with this is a need to identify all the key stakeholders who might have an interest in or a view about the study or who may be impacted by it. All these interests need to be accommodated, either with all members directly involved, or through representatives with some robust procedures for keeping in touch with the constituencies which they represent. This stage may be more complex than it seems because there may be different perceptions of the same issue. 'The aim of the inquiry is *not* to establish the "truth" or to describe what "really" is happening, but to establish the different truths and realities—constructions—held by different individuals and groups' (Stringer, 1996: 41). During this process it is important that researchers use non-autocratic language and build a consensus to which all parties can agree. The key aims at this stage are to establish a shared definition of the issues to be investigated, an agenda of actions and the legitimacy of the researcher's issues and processes.

Building a picture   The key aim of this stage is to enable the organisation members to understand and recognise what is happening. The immediacy of tasks, time limits and work pace of hospitality operations often prevent organisation members from reflecting on the nature of current work practices and the immediate context. Researchers aim to encourage members to look afresh at the organisation and to 'stand back' from it. Clearly, the full array of information-gathering techniques might be used—surveys using questionnaires and interviews, ethnographic studies involving participant observation, document searches, case studies, incident tracking, etc.; even some forms of experiments can be used to establish the nature of what is actually going on in the organisation. Apart from developing a descriptive account of who does what, how, when, where, and why, the picture needs to establish how the various stakeholders feel about what they are doing and their interactions with others. Most importantly, researchers need to ensure that their reflections and observations are congruent with those of stakeholders.

Analysis and interpretation   Once a shared picture of events has been established, the researchers need to move to processes of analysis and interpretation of the observations which have come out of the discovery stage. The key aim of this stage is to enable participants to understand their experiences not only in a way that enables them to make sense of these experiences but also in one which begins to render new actions. The researcher/facilitator builds on conceptual frameworks which stem from the experiences of the organisational members rather than on those derived from social sciences. The key here is to ensure that members are reflecting and theorising on the basis of their own experiences rather than abstractions which are externally imposed. It is important that '... interpretative accounts expose the conceptual frameworks and pragmatic working theories that people use to explain their conduct' (Stringer, 1996: 81). Through this process participants are encouraged to explore the 'taken for granted' meanings which shape everyday actions and to reshape them to bring to bear a reformulated understanding and conceptual structure to formulate future actions. Again it is important that different stakeholders are involved in the processes of interpretation and that these are shared through all stakeholders. The frameworks exposed by these processes of interpretation shape plans for future concrete action with stakeholder support.

Taking action   The stages discussed previously have been concerned with establishing consensual analysis of situations and exposing the assumptions and concepts which shape the behaviour of organisational members. Having interpreted the situation, the taking of remedial action also requires a careful consideration of various stakeholder views. Action needs to be legitimated by the people concerned and participation in formulating the desired actions needed is a crucial phase in action research. If the researchers have been successful in establishing an appropriate climate of trust and reflection during the earlier stages, actions required frequently speak for themselves.

However, there are processes to be gone through which have similarities with any action programme. In this first instance participants need to agree the priorities for action and the objectives to be set. Under a pluralistic view of organisational life it cannot be taken for granted that all stakeholders share the same objectives, though earlier stages of the action research process will have established an accommodation of different perspectives. From setting the priorities and objectives the participants consider the actions needed to implement change, the support needed to assist members to make the necessary adjustments, the resourcing implications and the consideration of potential impacts to individuals and groups both within the organisation and externally to it. Finally, participants need to review the implementation of the action and to evaluate its success or shortcomings.

In more complex organisational structures it may be necessary to elaborate some of the processes involved in implementation. Often there are a wider range of constituencies to address and the processes of building common definitions and consensual action require complex actions and negotiations. Planning and managing the introduction of change will be difficult and may require more formal and extensive arrangements which are usually unnecessary in simpler situations. In these more complex situations consensus assumes a more important role because large organisations can involve decisions, though agreed to by the majority of organisation members, which leave the agenda of marginal groups neglected. The history of solutions which suit the majority is littered with examples where unaddressed needs of the minority ultimately create problems for the whole organisation.

Evaluation   As participants work through the process of observing, reflecting, thinking about actions and then changing action, they are involved in a permanent process of review and evaluation. Referring to the earlier discussion of the 'reflective practitioner', practice is under permanent review through on-going reflection, but there may be a need to periodically evaluate the project. In some cases it may be to meet the needs of a funding body. In other cases it may be necessary to undertake some kind of cost–benefit analysis to assess whether the benefits flowing from the project are meeting the cost of undertaking it. In more complex situations there may be a need to introduce a formal stage in the process which invites evaluation. 'When people take the time to stand back from their day-to-day activities to explore and reflect on the processes in which they are engaged and to share perceptions and interpretations, they gain greater clarity about the direction of their work and efficacy of their work' (Stringer, 1996: 137). Sometimes the evaluation helps to expose gaps between purpose and activities. In situations where researchers may have been trying to improve the job competence of service workers, or the sense of self-efficacy of service workers, but where customer repeat business has not ensued, the failure to include customers in the project may be exposed. The key point is that careful management of the evaluation process can reveal weaknesses in the initial scene-setting and picture-building stages, and may require the project to be reformulated to address these gaps.

This section has attempted to demonstrate the particular benefits to hospitality organisations of using action research as an on-going process which brings together all organisation stakeholders to highlight, define and act upon organisational problems. Action research can become a permanent feature of organisational life, particularly where an organisation attempts to define itself as a 'learning company' or a 'learning organisation'. The learning organisation is one which is capable of adapting, changing and transforming itself as a result of the needs, experiences and aspirations of people both within the organisation and externally. The need to adapt and change is seen as a crucial determinant of future survival, particularly in fast-moving or highly competitive markets. Action research provides a mechanism for institutionalising the dynamics of change or where the detail and complexity of organisational life make it difficult for individual managers to foresee the consequence of their actions.

Action research is also consistent with the concept of the empowered organisation. Even allowing for the fact that empowerment is an ill-defined term which can be taken to mean a number of different things and is likely to be introduced in a variety of forms, empowerment must result in the empowered feeling a sense of personal efficacy, that they can make a difference in situations they care about (Lashley, 1997). Action research can contribute to the development of these feelings through involvement in the processes of research and action taking. At the very least it communicates the value of employee experience, job knowledge and views about the organisation, its problems and future actions.

Given the foregoing comments, action research has particular relevance to hospitality, leisure and tourism management educators. On one level it can be incorporated in the curriculum as a necessary technique for managers to develop and apply in the management of service operations. As argued earlier, it is also held in some of the management literature that future service organisations need to be learning organisations, with organisation members empowered to permanently evaluate and improve organisation activities and performance. Action research is likely to be a permanent feature of these organisations, since it is a technique through which to drive the on-going learning and empowerment of members.

At a second level, hospitality leisure and tourism management educators can themselves employ techniques of action research to improve the quality and outcome of educational programmes. There is no aspect of the educator's activities which could not benefit from action research. The stakeholders—lecturers, students, employers, university managers, parents—might all be involved in various roles and forms, depending on the issues to be investigated. The issues themselves—student learning preferences and the links to the curriculum, presentation of material, forms and expectations of assessment, the curriculum itself, work experience, etc.—are some examples where educational practice might benefit from the application of action research.

Conclusion

This chapter has argued that action research has an important contribution to make to the development of professional management practice both in the direct management of hospitality, leisure and tourism organisations and indirectly in the way that educators conduct their own professional development. Action research is furthermore entirely consistent with the conduct of learning organisations and empowered organisation members. Action research is therefore being hailed by its advocates as a technique for the millennium—it addresses the need for modern organisations to be more democratic, responsive to stakeholder interests, and adaptable to change in turbulent and competitive environments.

Action research has its origins in the post-war interest for improved social justice and egalitarianism which flowed after 1945. These origins provide action research as a technique with some of its key benefits to managers and educators. The notion that all organisation stakeholders have a contribution to make to improving organisation effectiveness is one that flows from these egalitarian origins. Similarly, the acceptance that research should result in actions to overcome some problem or difficulty also flows from these origins. In particular, the complexity of large hospitality organisations is a feature that lends itself to a research approach which attempts to model actions on systematic processes reflecting upon current practice.

In both practice and theory, action research underpins much current management education. Experiential learning (Kolb, 1984) suggests that professional development needs to encourage processes which develop both the practical skills appropriate to practitioners, and the ability to reflect and theorise. Indeed Kolb's critique of much professional education (including that of lecturers and managers) was that much educational practice focused on inappropriate theorising whilst much practitioner practice involved little reflection. Kolb's advice to educators was to model experiential learning in a way which encouraged both would-be and practising professionals to observe action, reflect on actions observed, theorise about future actions and amend action accordingly. The conceptualisation of action researching is entirely consistent with this model and the chapter has drawn links between this conceptual framework and the actions needed to implement action research.

References and bibliography

Altrichter, H. (1991) 'Do we need an alternative methodology for doing action research?', in Zuber-Skerritt, O. (ed.), *Action Research for Business Development*, Avebury, Aldershot

Altrichter, H., Kemmis, S., McTaggart, R. and Zuber-Skerritt, O. (1991) 'Defining, confining or refining action research', in Zuber-Skerritt, O. (ed.), *Action Research for Business Development*, Avebury, Aldershot

Argyris, C. (1985) *Action Science Concept Methods and Skills for Research and Intervention*, Jossey-Bass, San Francisco, CA

Barton-Cunningham, J. (1993) *Action Research and Organizational Development*, Praeger, Westport, CT

Bawden, R. (1991) 'Towards action research systems', in Zuber-Skerritt, O. (ed.), *Action Research for Business Development*, Avebury: Aldershot

Block, P. (1987) *The Empowered Manager*, Jossey-Bass: San Francisco, CA

Chein, R., Cook, T. and Harding, R. (1948) *Action Science*, Farmers: New York

Eisenhardt, K.M. (1989) 'Building theories from case study research', *Academy of Management Review*, vol. 14, no. 4, pp. 532–550

Elliott, J. (1978) 'What is action research in schools?'. *Journal of Curriculum Studies*, vol. 10, no. 4, pp. 355–7

Guest, D.E. (1995) 'Right enough to be dangerously wrong: an analysis of the *In Search of Excellence* phenomenon', in Mabey, C. and Salamon, G. (eds), *Strategic Human Resource Management*, Blackwell: Oxford

Hartley, J.F. (1994) 'Case studies in organizational research', in Cassell, C. and Symon, G. (eds), *Qualitative Methods in Organizational Research*, Sage: London

Huselid, M.A. (1995) 'The impact of human resource management practices on turnover, productivity, and corporate financial performance', *Academy of Management Journal*, vol. 38, no. 3, pp. 635–672

Kolb, D. (1984) *Experiential Learning. Experience as the Source of Learning and Development*, Prentice-Hall: Engelwood Cliffs, NJ

Lashley, C. (1995) 'Making student learning the centre piece of hospitality management education', *Innovations in Teaching and Education: a Journal for the Reflective Practitioner*, vol. 1, No. 2

Lashley, C. (1996) 'Research issues for employee empowerment in hospitality services', *International Journal of Hospitality Management*, vol. 15, no. 4, pp. 336–346

Lashley, C. (1997) *Empowering Service Excellence: Beyond the Quick Fix*, Cassell Publications.

Lewin, K. (1951) *Field Theory in Social Science*, Tavistock: London

Oja, S. and Smulyan, L. (1989) *Collaborative Action Research*, Farmers: New York

Peters, T. and Waterman, B. (1982) *In Search of Excellence*, Harper & Row: New York

Robson, C. (1993) *Real World Research*, Blackwell: Oxford

Roper, A., Brookes, M., Price, L. and Hampton, A. (1997) 'Towards an understanding of centricity: profiling international hotel groups', *6th Annual Hospitality Research Conference Proceedings*, Oxford Brookes University, Oxford

Schon, D.A. (1983) *The Reflective Practitioner*, Temple Smith: London.

Schon, D.A. (1987) *Educating the Reflective Practitioner*, Jossey-Bass: San Francisco, CA

Stringer, R. (1996) *Action Research: A Handbook for Practitioners*, Sage, London

Winter, R. (1989) *Learning from Experience: Principles and Practice in Action-Research*, Falmer, London

Zuber-Skerritt, O. (1991) *Action Research for Business Development*, Avebury: Aldershot

10 Observational research

STUART JAUNCEY

Introduction

Participant observation as a method of data collection and research provides a unique opportunity for researchers to investigate aspects of work within hospitality organisations through participating in the daily life of the operation(s). Such participation will involve the researcher in developing a first-hand understanding of the subject, and will also involve developing an awareness of the context within which the subject or focus for the study is occurring. Understanding the context of the study is particularly useful when investigating aspects of the hospitality industry, an industry which is frequently reported to be subject to specific sets of features including product and labour characteristics (Cowell, 1988; Mullins, 1993; Nailon, 1981; Wood, 1992; and many others). These features in combination may create a different technical and social environment or context than is found in other industries. Participant observation enables the researcher to investigate the chosen subject and to take account of such contextual variations which may influence the way in which the subject of investigation manifests itself, or is handled and perceived by those working within the industry.

Participant observation results in the collection of a wide range of information, some of which will be highly focused on the particular subject of the study, while other information will be contextual, looking at the relationship between the subject and other people, departments, units, markets and the wide political, economic, social and technical environment within which the subject is occurring. Such a breadth of focus or inclusiveness is both the main benefit and principal drawback of participant observation. It is the defining characteristic of participant observation which will determine if its use is appropriate within a particular study. For example, if the subject for a study were to be an assessment of the environmental performance of restaurant operations within a particular town, the researcher would want to establish specific criteria against which to assess the performance of individual restaurants. Once established (through a thorough, thematically structured literature review), such specific criteria would be tested using questionnaires, checklists, telephone or fax surveys, etc., and there would be no need for or benefit from the researcher immersing themselves as a participant observer within a limited number of operations for extended periods of time. Rather the researcher should be more interested in testing conformance across a larger sample of units. If, however, the researcher were to be interested in the job of work performed by

The Handbook of Contemporary Hospitality Management Research, Edited by Bob Brotherton.
© 1999 John Wiley & Sons Ltd.

an Assistant Restaurant Manager who had specific responsibility for environmental management, participant observation would enable the researcher to determine how much time was spent on performing work with an environmental focus, what categories or types of work this entailed, and who or what the manager consulted (both within and outside the operation); and, through proximity to the manager over a period of time, opportunities would arise for the researcher to discuss this role with the manager, to determine how he or she perceived the role and how they feel they have been supported or hindered by others within the unit, company and industry.

Participant observation allows a researcher to explore a particular subject within the context of its environment and to understand the full range of influences which impact upon it. In essence it is a process of exploring a subject rather than testing or measuring it against predetermined criteria. The results from participant observation are both quantitative and qualitative, both factual and subjective. In choosing to conduct participant observation the researcher is acknowledging that the current understanding of a subject is limited and therefore it is necessary to be receptive to all influences, circumstances, events, and even the stories which people will tell, and hope that all of this rich information may throw light upon the subject. It is an exciting methodology whose precise application will vary according to the subject under investigation, the aptitude and past experience of the researcher, and his or her ability to negotiate access and develop trust during the period of fieldwork.

In this chapter the particular relevance of participant observation for investigating the hotel and restaurant industry is discussed, along with the importance of the preparation required for fieldwork, the types of problems which may be encountered in the field and the analyses of the information collected. Throughout this chapter illustrations and examples are drawn from the author's own experience as a participant observer collecting information for a PhD thesis entitled 'The Job of the Hotel General Manager'.

The meaning of participation

In defining participant observation, Kelleher (1993: 115) focuses on what actually happens when a researcher using this method is 'in the field': '... the researcher interacts with the people that he or she is studying and makes observations in the course of these exchanges.' Moser and Kalton (1992: 245) add to this description by stating that: 'The participant observer ... shares in the life and activities of the community, observing—in the street sense—what is going on around him [*sic*] but supplementing this by conversations, interviews and studies of records.' These are important statements as they illustrate well the distinction from pure or 'complete' observation (Junkers, 1960). In complete observation the researcher objectively, and with no interaction, watches and records what is happening.

Such an approach may be appropriate for studies of the natural world (climate, astronomy, botany, etc.) or even for determining mechanistic forms of work (e.g. how 20 sommeliers open bottles of wine), but complete non-participative observation is of only limited value when looking at wider aspects of the hotel and restaurant industry, which is a people-orientated or people-moulding industry (Nailon, 1981).

Much of what happens within the hospitality industry involves complex cognitive procedures and interactions and negotiations with others. In order to understand what can be seen to be happening it is usually important to be able to ask questions, to look at documentation, to understand the financial and operational constraints of that moment in time, and to determine the range of other significant influences affecting the events being witnessed. For example, one of the managers observed by the author spent a considerable amount of time conducting the annual review of staff wages within his hotel. By watching him undertake this task it was possible to accurately record the amount of time spent on it, his use of documentation and consultation with other people, and the increments awarded. However, in order to understand why certain staff were awarded a greater pay rise than others, it was necessary to gather additional information which included developing an understanding of unionisation, performance appraisal, the manager's perception of and the value he placed on others, and the financial limits imposed by the head office. In addition, this hotel general manager was in a competitive environment for certain types of skilled labour (notably chefs) and so he was also considering the activity of competitors and alternative work technologies. Through discussion with the hotel manager and having access to relevant documentation, what at first seemed to be a simple activity of calculating wage increases turned out to be a very much more complex and interrelated process which gave a great insight into a range of factors likely to influence other aspects of this manager's job.

Participation is not simply about gaining employment in an operation and watching what happens, it is about the researcher being able to get close to the subjects, to develop a sense of trust and to glean information from a range of sources, which leads to a better understanding of events. Bryman (1989: 143) pointed out that the extent and nature of participation vary according to what is being studied, and produced three basic categories, which are based on the extent to which the researcher undertakes meaningful jobs of work within the organisation, and also on the extent to which the researcher is open and honest about his or her reasons for existing in the organisation. The first of these categories is termed 'Covert' and occurs when the researcher deliberately fails to inform members of the organisation being studied of his or her research interests. Whilst normally seen as an unethical and (owing to the usually limited access to supporting information) restricted form of data collection, this approach can and has been used within the hospitality industry, normally for the entrapment of thieves or for recording movements of people in the public areas for reasons of security. With the advent of spy cameras and additional forms of technology, the use of covert observation is increasingly possible, but participant covert observation differs from this in that the researcher is present and interacting as a fellow employee. 'Full Participant Observation' is when the researcher is employed as a full member of staff but also informs people in the organisation of the research being conducted. The third and most common category classified by Bryman is 'Indirect Participant Observation' which is '... when the researcher is constantly in and around an organisation but does not possess a work role in it' (Bryman, 1989: 143).

In his study of the lives of army soldiers, Hockey (1986) acted as a full participant observer. He was employed as a 'squaddie' and kept records of what he observed and encountered and discovered during an extended period of time. Throughout his investigation he was happy to inform others of his research interests, and his access or position in the army was approved by senior officers. Whilst this is an ideal form of participant observation, for it will and did enable Hockey to gain full information on the lives, work, ambitions and perceptions of army soldiers (and to reflect upon his findings in relation to other research and academic theory and literature in general), such an approach is not always possible. In this author's study of hotel general managers, such full participation was not possible because hotel general managers are solitary; it would be unusual to find more than one in any hotel. In addition to this obvious statement, it seemed unlikely that any hotel company or owner would have allowed one to assume such a position of authority and trust for the purpose of conducting research. For this reason it was planned to undertake indirect participant observation, to be in and around the hotels and to shadow or follow the hotel general managers at all times when possible. In the event the boundaries between these categories became blurred. One problem was that hotels as semi-public buildings contain numerous people who freely move around the public areas. Without wearing a sandwich board declaring the research interests, it would not have been possible or practical to inform everyone of what was intended. It was also quickly learnt that not everyone was interested in research, and that when the research interests were declared to quite senior members of the organisation, the topic was quickly skipped over and the conversation turned to other matters. In addition to such anonymity being imposed by the public nature of hotels, and by employees being used to meeting and talking with a wide range of visitors as an expected part of their jobs, indirect participation also on occasions switched to direct involvement in the work of the operation, as Exhibit 10.1 illustrates.

Whilst Bryman's categories are useful in thinking about the approach to take as a participant observer, and in developing an understanding of what participant observation is, the reality of undertaking fieldwork of this nature in hospitality organisations involves a constant and often unintended movement between the three forms. Other than the opportunity for the researcher to be open about the reasons for being in the organisation, and the willingness of other members of the organisation to listen to and understand this explanation, the nature of participation will also vary according to the focus of the research. For example, if the focus for the research was to be the handling

---

Exhibit 10.1

'On one memorable occasion I was standing close to the Hotel General Manager who was engaged in polite conversation with a customer, when a guest of the hotel took hold of my arm and asked for assistance in organising some travel arrangements. The hotel general manager was aware of this situation and continued in his conversation, only pausing to nod and smile at me. As I walked the customer to the reception desk and explained the arrangements to be made to a receptionist, I was aware that I had crossed over the boundary between participant observer and participant. I was also aware that the Hotel General Manager was now observing me. As I learnt to my cost on a later occasion, the balance between observer and participant is very fine. On one of the final days I spent with this manager, I was following him as he rushed through the reception area to greet a visiting VIP. As we crossed the lobby, he saw a young man in jeans standing near to the main door. "What's he doing there?" he snapped authoritatively and in such a way that I was obliged to go and find out. After dealing with the man, who had come to collect a member of staff, I realised that the hotel general manager had, in his words, "gone to ground" where he remained for about two hours, and when he re-emerged he thought the fact that he had managed to escape was incredibly amusing.' (Extract from the author's PhD thesis awaiting assessment)

of complaints by front-office staff, then direct involvement or participation (in the handling of complaints by the researcher) would detract from the researcher's ability to witness and record how front-office staff cope with such situations. If, however, the researcher is employed in another capacity behind the front desk, such as filing correspondence or performing other basic administrative duties, though still participating in a meaningful job of work the researcher will also be able to observe the event, context, content and handling of a complaint.

The nature and form of participation will then depend on various factors, including the ability of the researcher to perform a suitable job of work within the organisation which is flexible enough to allow observation to take place, and the nature of the subject being observed. If it is an insular activity (such as the job of a hotel general manager) then only indirect participation is possible on a continual basis, but the researcher may end up participating in other operational activities from time to time, and owing to their intrusion into the unit or organisation being studied, the observer is still participating in the wider environment and will be able to collect a range of contextual information. If the subject of the study is more general in nature, being performed by a range of organisational members at varying times and frequencies (such as complaint handling), then the researcher's ability to observe is governed to some extent by chance (being in the right place at the right time) and so a greater degree of participation in a normal occupational role may be an appropriate way of being in a place or department where the events, or subject, under investigation are likely to take place. Whatever the intention, some degree of involvement or participation in operations or work activities is inevitable. The members of the organisation(s) in which the research is to be conducted will be interested in the researcher's experience to date of the industry, and will want to test and involve the researcher in aspects of their work. This notion of being an 'insider', of knowing something about, and being a member of, the industry and subject being studied, raises several interesting issues which are briefly discussed later in this chapter along with other methodological issues specific to observation. The key point being made here is that the presence of an observer within a hotel or restaurant operation will invariably result in some degree of participation; this may involve the researcher in undertaking a job of work, but it will at the very least involve participation through communication, interaction and a shared awareness of what is happening.

The use of participant observation

So far this chapter has been concerned with defining participant observation and has attempted to describe the activities of the participant observer with a view to determining criteria which will help in identifying when this would be an appropriate methodology for a given study. In determining if participant observation is appropriate for a given study, the researcher needs to consider whether specific known criteria are to be investigated, or if it is wished to explore a subject in a more general sense, taking account of the context and the range of factors influencing it. If the research is asking specific questions and is not concerned with the context, then observation is not the best method to select. The researcher also needs to ask if the subject is something (an event, an activity, some form of behaviour) which can be observed. In an earlier study on decision making by hotel general managers (Jauncey, 1989) the use of observation to collect appropriate data was seriously considered. However, the behavioural or observable aspects of decision making tend to be restricted to the giving of orders, the writing of memos, or other forms of communication.

What this investigation needed to know was the basis and rationale behind the making of decisions (within the context of this study decisions were defined as resource manipulations). In order to achieve this it was eventually decided to use another method of data collection based on managers' accounts of the decisions they made over a period of time, which they recorded in the form of a decision-making diary. In the diary the managers were encouraged not only to record the resultant manipulation of categories of resource, but to also explain the need for and implication of such decisions. This approach was supplemented by semi-structured interviews conducted on either a face-to-face or telephone basis. The important point here is that observation would not have given the same insight into the cognitive processes surrounding the making of specific types of decision; it may only have enabled the behavioural results of a decision to have been recorded. By its nature observation results in a focus on behaviour. Work or subject areas which are cognitive in form are better researched through alternative methodologies which facilitate a greater degree of discussion. This distinction is not as simple as it seems, for through participation in a place of work considerable insights into the rationale behind behaviour can be gained. But if the rationale or thinking is more important than the doing and its subsequent justification, then observation is probably not the best technique to use.

In reviewing the reports and accounts of researchers who have used observation (including Whyte, 1955; Dalton, 1959; Sayles, 1964; and Lupton, 1963) other factors which also need to be considered before selecting this method are promoted. Principally participant observation is reported to be time consuming, to tend to involve or focus upon small samples, and to create considerable difficulties in both recording and analysing the collected data. That it takes time both to gain permission to undertake observation and then to settle into an organisation in such a way that the people and events being observed will accept the researcher and behave in as near normal a way as possible, should not be underestimated. It was obvious that the managers observed for week-long periods in the author's PhD study were responding to the researcher's presence. They had saved up work so that they could seem busier in that week, organised additional events, or asked for the observation to be undertaken during periods of the year that they knew would be exceptionally busy, and they tended to do additional forms of work that they would perhaps not normally undertake on so frequent a basis. As each of the one-week periods of observation progressed, and the managers became used to being observed, and as a sense of trust established itself (with the managers no longer feeling threatened by the researcher's presence) the managers' patterns of work behaviour reverted to something resembling normality. If it had been possible to extend the periods spent in the field, the likelihood of the data collected being representative of normal patterns of work behaviour would have increased.

There is an obvious relationship between the length of time spent in the field and the opportunity for the subject to manipulate or change what it is that they do. Depending upon the frequency of occurrence of the subject to be observed, this notion of time may prove to be an even more serious issue. For example, if a researcher was interested in understanding or observing such infrequent events as the management of crisis situations, the researcher may find that several incidents occurred (perhaps in the form of fire alarms or other incidents) in quite a short space of time or that no such incidents happened for many days. When deciding to undertake observation an awareness of the likely frequency of the subject occurring is a key consideration, as is the amount of time that can be spent undertaking observation. If the topic is something that is infrequent, such as the management of crises or change, then alternative methodologies (e.g. critical incident analysis, focus group discussions, key informant interviews, etc.) will prove to be better value.

Observation is better suited to the study of frequently recurring patterns of behaviour, events or roles which are performed continually. In focusing on such subject matter the researcher may be a witness to unexpected situations which add value to the research and which also add to experience as an observer. For most researchers the time-consuming nature of observation will limit the number of times observation can be undertaken. The small sample size is the price often paid for the gathering of inclusive and interrelated information. It is a question of balancing the depth or detail of information against the breadth or sample size. For this reason in the study of hotel general managers it was decided to conduct only two periods of observation, but then to test the behavioural patterns and other key findings that emerged from such detailed investigation through a second methodology (a diary study). It is the failure of past studies using observation, such as that conducted by Mintzberg (1973), to triangulate or test their findings across a more representative sample that has resulted in their criticism.

The purpose of this section of the chapter is to clarify what participant observation is, and when it is an appropriate method to use. In answer to these questions the researcher needs to consider the following:

- Is the environment or context of the subject under investigation as important as the subject itself?
- Can access to the operation (or a position within the operation) be negotiated which gives proximity to the subject and which also allows space to observe the subject as and when required?
- Is the subject of the investigation something which can be observed? That is, is it a person, event, activity or some other thing that can be seen?
- Can an adequate amount of time be allocated to be in and around the unit to collect adequate information on the subject and context within which it occurs?
- Is the subject it is intended to study likely to occur during the period allocated for conducting fieldwork?
- Will a small sample size detract from the value of the research findings? Can subsequent methods of testing key findings and theories be effectively employed using a new, larger and more representative sample?

Gaining access

Once the applicability of conducting participant observation has been assessed, the next concern of the researcher is to prepare for gaining entry to a suitable operation or organisation, and then to develop a technique for recording what is happening and relevant within it.

Gaining access to a suitable hospitality unit within which to carry out participant observation is difficult. Participant observation places particular demands and concerns upon the members of the organisation being studied, and in particular it generates concern over what it is that you will be studying, and what you will do with the information and knowledge that you will collect. Such concerns are compounded because the researcher is not usually fully able to answer these questions at the time of requesting access. By its nature participant observation is a journey, an enquiry without fully defined boundaries. The fact that at the time of applying for access to a unit the focus for the study may be 'vague' (Gill and Johnson, 1991) will not help to assure the confidence of those who manage and control the operation. Moser and Kalton (1992: 252) clarify this point when they explain that 'Participant observation is commonly used in an exploratory way, ... The participant observer's early observations help to develop his [sic] ideas.' Whilst this is almost certainly going to be the case, upon requesting permission to observe within an operation, it is essential to be able to express the key focus for the research and to explain its significance. In the case of the author's PhD study it was possible to stress the genuine educational benefits of being able to observe hotel general managers at work, and to honestly state that the findings and observations would be of great value to one's work as a teacher within a School of Hotel and Restaurant Management. Despite this, gaining access still proved to be a major stumbling block, with managers feeling either that their own operations were either atypical of traditional hotel units or that they would not be good examples.

Buchanan, Boddy and McCalman (1988: 56–57) also emphasise the problems of gaining access and state that 'Negotiating access to organisations for the purpose of research is a game of chance, not of skill.' You must be lucky to find a manager willing to support the research. They go on to offer five specific pieces of advice which are particularly pertinent to a participant observer: 'First, allow for this [negotiating access] to take time. Second, use friends and relatives wherever possible. Third, use non-threatening language when explaining the nature and purpose of your study. Fourth, deal positively with respondents' reservations with respect to time and confidentiality. Fifth, offer a report of your findings.' In addition to assuring managers of the lack of impact on the operation and of the non-threatening nature of the investigation, as a participant observer it is also possible to offer an additional benefit to a copy of the report, i.e. a willingness and ability to work within the operation. Exhibit 10.2 provides an account of how such an offer helped a researcher both to gain access, and to gain the trust and acceptance of those being observed.

Through offering to work as a full member of staff within a hotel or restaurant unit, and without the expectation of pay, it may be found that managers take the researcher's wish to learn more about the industry seriously, and also that the people

---

Exhibit 10.2

In her ethnographic study of 'Work and Social Interaction in a Manufacturing Workshop' (Purcell, 1986, unpublished PhD thesis, University of Manchester), Dr Purcell explains that: 'I worked on the shop floor full time for four months ... . My role was that of overt participant observer, permitted by management to work alongside the women, without pay ... . As far as my workmates were concerned their initial friendly suspicion was considerably defused by the fact that I clearly did mean to work as hard as I could, and any work I did could be "booked" by them, thus contributing to their piecework earning.'

worked alongside and observed feel more comfortable and confident about the researcher's presence. However, as previously discussed, such full participation in the process of work may not always be possible, depending upon the researcher's competence to work and upon the subject or focus for the investigation. In the author's own insular study of hotel general managers, such participation through assuming a full-time job of work was not possible, although it was made clear through one's behaviour that this researcher was happy to help if and when appropriate.

Promoting the fact that there was a genuine desire to learn from the hotel general managers studied proved to be the key for gaining access, for as Buchanan, Boddy and McCalman *et al.* (1988: 57) point out: 'Most people are flattered by reasonable requests to talk about themselves, and to pass on their experience, where they know it will be used in an academic context, to help with a project or educational course.' In addition, Christensen-Hughs (1997: 20) explains that 'Presenting oneself as an interested observer instead of an expert or evaluator is helpful for minimising the defensiveness of participants and putting them at ease.' At the end of the day, access will be granted if the senior managers like, trust and want to help the researcher. They must realise that the researcher wants to learn from them, to listen to what they have to say, and that there is no intention of publicly criticising or endangering in any way their position, the reputation of their unit, or the trust which they have bestowed.

Fieldwork, keeping records and analysis

Through reading accounts and methodological texts which focus (at least in part) on the process of conducting observation (Glaser and Strauss, 1967; Whyte, 1955; Leidner, 1993; Buchanan, Boddy and McCalman, 1988; Kelleher, 1993; Bryman, 1989; and others), it is apparent that there are three principal problems facing the participant observer in the field. These relate first to the technique of conducting observation and how to record data, secondly, how to analyse the data which has been recorded, and thirdly, how the researcher is to present him or herself in order to gain the greatest degree of co-operation and access to information.

Some researchers will argue that the problems of analysis should not be considered at this point, that the data should simply be collected and that, through familiarity with the data, the data itself will lead to a structure for discussing it (Glaser and Strauss, 1967). It is argued strongly here that as the mountains of data and supporting tales and information characteristic of observation accumulate, it is both necessary and good practice to analyse at least in part the data as it is unearthed. When speaking about the problems associated with the development of strategic plans, Ansoff (1969) coined the phrase 'Paralysis by Analysis'. Participant observation is an investigation without clearly defined and absolute boundaries, as it involves entering an organisation to experience it and collect information about aspects of it; there is an obvious and real danger that the researcher will become lost, having collected vast quantities of data without really knowing why or what its value will be.

In order to prevent paralysis by, or during, analysis from occurring as a result of having too much information in too unstructured a form, it is necessary to see the process of analysis as one starting before the period of observation, and being continually defined and refined during and after the time in the field. Bryman (1988) and

Martinko and Gardner (1985) would agree with this view; both promote the desirability of identifying themes, models and theories to focus and help make sense of the data as it is collected. Such theories and models will be derived from a review of relevant literature. When in the field or conducting the periods of observation, Miles and Huberman (1984) specifically suggest that the researcher should:

- look for repetition, recurring events/experiences/topics;
- note themes and patterns, look for underlying similarities between experiences;
- develop metaphors, analogies or symbols for what is happening;
- check to see if single variables/events/experiences are really several;
- connect particular events to general ones;
- note differences and similarities between events;
- note triggering, connecting or mediating variables;
- note if patterns in the data resemble theories or concepts.

This whole process of analysing and thinking about the data as it is collected is both absorbing and exhausting. It meant that the author's own days in the field were spent recording every detail of what the managers did and then the nights were spent re-reading and making notes from the data, linking it to theories of management and cross-referencing observed happenings, and other information, so that events and themes took shape.

The importance of developing and maintaining good relations and a sense of trust between the observer and those who are being observed has been mentioned earlier as one of the keys to gaining access. Whyte (1955), Bryman (1989), Kelleher (1993) and particularly Gill and Johnson (1991) also point out that this is the key to obtaining good and full information on a subject. A good relationship between the observer and the people within the organisation who are being observed will help to overcome the problems often associated with observation, those of censorship and exclusion. Buchanan, Boddy and McCalman (1988) provide some good advice on how to develop and maintain good relationships. They stress the importance of being open about the purpose and methods of the research, and promote the idea that those observed should be allowed to see what has been recorded and to censor the reports and findings generated from the data. In addition to this, it is important for the researcher to remember that he or she is a 'guest' in the organisation and that courtesy, appropriateness of dress and conduct will also have a major impact on how others perceive the researcher and the access to formal and informal information which is granted. Trust also takes time to develop. In both the hotels where the author was a participant observer, it was, at first, common to be asked to withdraw from the manager's office when staff were conducting work which they felt to be sensitive in nature (disciplinary meetings, appraisals, etc.). As the week developed in both cases this changed, and the managers tended to include the author more and more in all of their activities and to take time and care to discuss issues and give their own accounts of what was happening and why.

The process of recording information during the periods of observation will vary according to the preference of the researcher and the topic or subject being studied. Using again the example of observing the handling of complaints within a hotel, as long as the researcher is in and around the area of the premises where complaints are most likely to be lodged (normally the reception desk), it will be possible for the researcher simply to listen to and watch what happens and then to note the timing, people involved, nature of the complaint, extent of eye contact, use of resources (documents, letters, bookings forms, VDU screens, telephones, etc.) and any resultant action. In addition, the observer may be able to talk to the front-office worker concerned about how they felt in handling the complaint, how frequently they had to handle complaints of that nature, anything that they felt was unusual about that incident or that they could have done in a different way. An alternative approach might be to simply observe and record the complaint and then at a time subsequent to the period of observation return to the hotel and interview managers and front-office staff about the process, its frequency, and their thoughts and feelings. Equally informative and more exciting data will be gleaned by talking to staff during their breaks or in quiet periods of the day. In recording such data it is important to segregate the data, to be able to distinguish between things which have been witnessed and recorded as actual events and other types of information which have been related or accounted to the researcher, or which have been read. Accounts of happenings will be biased by the memory, feelings and beliefs of the informer, and whilst still providing evidence that can be used in the report, care must be taken to clearly label such data and its probable bias. In this example the researcher is able to stop their own work within the organisation to overhear and witness the event that is happening. The recording of information can take place during the event or immediately after it has occurred, and a pro-forma data collection sheet with appropriate sub-headings can be developed before the period of observation and tested and amended during the first instances of its use.

In studying the jobs of hotel general managers, the aim was to systematically collect descriptions of all work performed by the managers during the week. There were no specific types of work which were to be focused upon to the neglect of others, and this meant that the process of investigation and recording was instantaneous and continuous. As the method of recording the information was by writing, one of the major issues was to develop a method of shorthand to record what was happening as quickly as possible, accurately, and using the minimum number of words. To do this a series of codes were developed which related to areas within each of the hotels and to particular tools that the managers were likely to use. For example, telephones were represented by the capital letter T and an arrow was used to indicate the direction of the call, if the arrow pointed into the T it meant that this was an incoming call and vice versa. Lines drawn down the page were used to illustrate the presence of other people. For example, if an assistant manager were to enter the office of the hotel general manager, then the time at which he or she entered was recorded along with his or her job title. A line was then drawn down the page to the time at which this person left the office. By connecting the times at which the hotel general managers were engaged with other people, it was possible to record the presence and contributions of several people at the same time, and in fact to record the performance of more than one activity simultaneously. This problem of recording more than one happening at the same time was one of Mintzberg's (1973) main limitations, which he chose to address by concentrating on the primary activity or happening to the exclusion of other events and activities. However, Martinko and Gardner (1985: 687) point out that this was a significant failing of Mintzberg's methodology which may have resulted in a more ordered description of work than actually occurred. In the event, this simple technique of linking events and the presence of people with lines proved to be invaluable in making sense of who was where and why, and what they were doing.

These and other observational skills and techniques were first developed and practised by observing a work colleague for a few days. Such trial periods are essential in the development not only of key skills but also in building confidence and learning the variety of codes and symbols that the observer will need to be able to use in the field. Observational trials will also illustrate other problems that may be encountered, such as the need to be physically close to the person being observed in order to see and read what they can see and read. Another major problem concerned the use of telephones, which normally allow the observer to gain access to only half of a conversation. Many of these problems can be overcome once the barriers of trust and confidence have lifted, and the participants are willing to involve the researcher fully in their activities. Of particular use, and recognised by Whyte (1955) in his observational research, are breaks which occur naturally in any individual's working day. These can be used to return to episodes or events which the researcher would like to talk through, to gain further information about. When circumstances arise that are not understood or are difficult to capture and record in the detail required, the notes being taken can be marked, and when a suitable opportunity arises it is possible to flick back to that section and talk it through with the person being observed. In doing this it is important to be conscious of the need not to impose or demand too much from the person being observed, and to wait for an appropriate opening. One of the managers observed developed the habit of asking, at the end of each day, if further explanations of anything were needed. The other manager used to provide openings throughout each day to ask questions.

Conclusions and further issues

Within this chapter participant observation (in its various guises) has been presented as a research methodology which enables the context of a subject as well as the subject itself to be explored. The use of participant observation can be seen to be particularly relevant within the study of hospitality organisations, in which aspects of the context of work, its organisation and occurrence, may vary from that found in other more extensively researched industries. As a process or journey towards greater understanding, participant observation tends not to be based on the seeking of answers to specific questions, or on the collection of purely quantifiable data; its application is better suited to a more general investigation. The all-inclusive nature of the data collected, the limited sample sizes likely to be achieved, and the impact or polluting effect that the observer will have on the subject, are particular concerns which often force the use of secondary or supporting studies and methodologies, which test in a more reliable and valid form the findings, theories and propositions derived from observation. Despite these limitations and the difficulties of negotiating access and recording and analysing data, this is a methodology which provides the opportunity to gain unique insights into the industry, and in a form of baptism by fire, it enshrouds, informs and involves the researcher in a way that no other methodology can.

The key limitations which impact upon both the reliability and validity of a study using participant observation, reflect the inevitably limited sample size and the timing and location of the study. As previously mentioned, participant observation is time consuming and for this reason (especially when considered alongside the likely problems of gaining access) the size of the sample observed tends to be small. This restricts the ability to generalise from the findings. Using the earlier example of a study into complaint handling, if three front-office workers within one hotel were observed to handle complaints in a similar way, does this mean that all front-office workers in all types and sizes of hotels will adopt the same approach? In addition, there is the notion that participant observation (along with most other forms of research) is fixed in time and place, that the findings relate only to the specific organisational setting and time at which they were collected, that if the observation were to be repeated in one month's time, or if it were to be undertaken in another organisation, the findings may be different. The key to coming to terms with such limitations is to accept that participant observation is a journey, an exploration, a methodology that does not test absolute values or questions, but is rather an approach which aims to unearth findings, theories and propositions relating to a particular topic or research focus, and that it does this within a particular time and context. If generalisability is important within the study, the developed theories and propositions can be tested across a larger and more representative sample using other methodologies.

Other interesting issues concerning the use of participant observation focus on the person conducting the observation, the researcher him or herself. Moser and Kalton (1992) recognised that the researcher, as a participant, is not a passive receiver of information, but that the person's own preconceptions relating to the subject will bias the data recorded, and may even cause the researcher to be selective over what is recorded. This may be a particular issue when the subject under investigation is not new, and when the researcher has 'insider' knowledge and experience (perhaps through studying or working in the industry), which may cause the researcher to focus more on unusual events rather than the routine, taken for granted, frequent events.

This concept of being an insider, of knowing something about the industry or subject being studied, is of considerable relevance in a text of this nature. Many of the users of this book will have extensive insider knowledge and experience of the industry. Both Golding (1979) in his study of power in organisations, and Hockey (1986) whose study of army soldiers has been previously cited, investigated organisations and industrial settings of which they had considerable knowledge. Hockey, prior to undertaking his research, had been a regular soldier with the British army, and Golding's research focused upon three organisations in which he had worked as a manager. Such incidents of focusing research upon something of which the researcher has insider knowledge conflict with the traditional image of the objective academic studying a subject from a position of detraction. In the case of participant observation, however, there are advantages in studying something with which the researcher is familiar. Basically the researcher will have a good foundation for the development of trust (Paxson, 1995; Buchanan, Boddy and McCalman 1988) with the participants, and will also have a shared understanding with the participants of what is happening around them. Such shared understanding is likely to enhance the depth and quality of the data collected, for the researcher is more likely to know when and about what to ask questions. Buchanan, Boddy and McCalman (1988: 61) clarify the benefits of insider knowledge by saying: 'First, rich information is a product of close relationships .... Second, attempts to use or mislead a researcher are usually transparent .... Third, attempts to protect or distort information can be used as data, as indicating areas of particular sensitivity which require explanation.'

In addition to issues of reliability, validity, generalisability, and being an insider, participant observation is a particularly intrusive form of data collection. The participant observer is physically present in the organisation, close to and watching the subject. Those being observed may be very conscious of the researcher's presence and of the focus for the study, and may react to this by altering their behaviour and by presenting a different image and description of work and of themselves, than they would do in other circumstances. Only after very extensive periods of observation will the researcher be so taken for granted that those being observed will behave in a near-normal fashion. Even where extensive periods in the field have been possible, the researcher must recognise that by their presence, by asking questions, by focusing interest on the subject, they will change the nature of the thing they are studying. Those who have been observed and talked to will have been encouraged by this process to think in new ways about the subject; they will have had to define aspects of it, and through this process of interacting with the research they may have changed their view of the subject and their approach to it (Silverman, 1997).

In addition to this notion of the participant observer, in particular, having an impact on the subject and people observed, Kelleher (1993: 129) realises that the presence of a participant observer will have a wider impact, because: 'In our culture, people who look a lot are rarely interpreted as researchers. Rather they are signalling something sexy, menacing or curious.'

References

Ansoff, H.I. (ed.) (1969) *Business Strategy*, Penguin, Harmondsworth.

Bryman, A. (ed.) (1988) *Doing Research in Organisations*, Routledge, London.

Bryman, A. (1989) *Research Methods and Organisation Studies*, Unwin Hyman, London.

Buchanan, D., Boddy, D. and McCalman, J. (1988) 'Getting in, getting on, getting out, and getting back', in Bryman, A. (ed.) *Doing Research in Organisations*, Routledge, London.

Christensen-Hughs, J. (1997) 'Sociological paradigms and the use of ethnography in hospitality research', *Journal of Hospitality and Tourism Research*, Vol. 21, No. 1, 14–27.

Cowell, D.W. (1988) 'New service development', *Journal of Marketing Management*, Vol. 3, No. 3, 296–312.

Dalton, M. (1959) *Men Who Manage*, Wiley, New York.

Gill, J. and Johnson, P. (1991) *Research Methods for Managers*, Paul Chapman, London.

Glaser, B.G. and Strauss, A.L. (1967) 'The discovery of grounded theory: strategies for qualitative research', in Worsley P. (1970) *Modern Sociology: Introductory Readings*, Penguin, Harmondsworth, pp. 34–38.

Golding, D. (1979) *Some Symbolic Manifestations of Power in Industrial Organisations*, unpublished PhD Thesis, Sheffield City Polytechnic.

Hockey, J. (1986) *Squaddies: Portrait of a Subculture*, University of Exeter.

Jauncey, S.A. (1989) *Decision Making in British Hotels*, unpublished MSc thesis, University of Surrey.

Junkers, B.H. (1960) *Field Work: An Introduction to the Social Sciences*, University of Chicago Press.

Kelleher, A. (1993) *The Unobtrusive Researcher*, Allen and Unwin, NSW, Australia.

Leidner, R. (1993), *Fast Food, Fast Talk: Service Work and the Routinization of Everyday Life*, University of California Press, London.

Lupton, T. (1963) *On the Shop Floor*, Pergamon, Oxford.

Martinko, M. and Gardner, W. (1985) 'Beyond structured observation: methodological issues and new directions', *Academy of Management Review*, Vol. 10, No. 4, 676–695.

Miles, N. and Huberman, A. (1984) *Qualitative Data Analysis*, Sage, Beverley Hills, CA.

Mintzberg, H. (1973) *The Nature of Managerial Work*, Harper & Row, New York.

Moser, C.A. and Kalton, G. (1992) *Survey Methods in Social Investigation*, reprinted 2nd edition, Heinemann, Oxford.

Mullins, L.J. (1993) 'The hotel and the Open Systems model of organisational analysis', *Service Industries Journal*, Vol. 13, No. 1, January, 1–16.

Nailon, P. (1981) *Theory and Art in Hospitality*, an Inaugural Lecture, 4 Feb., University of Surrey.

Paxson, C. (1995) 'Increasing survey response rates' *Cornell Hotel and Restaurant Administration Quarterly*, August, 66–73.

Purcell, K.G. (1986) *Work and Social Interaction in a Manufacturing Workshop*, unpublished PhD thesis, University of Manchester.

Sayles, L.R. (1964) *Managerial Behaviour: Administration in Complex Organisations*, McGraw-Hill, New York.

Silverman, D. (ed.) (1997) *Qualitative Research: Theory, Method and Practice*, Sage, London.

Whyte, W.F. (1955) 'Participant observation', in Worsley, P. (1970) *Modern Sociology: Introductory Readings*, Penguin, Harmondsworth, pp. 103–109.

Wood, R.C. (1992) *Working in Hotels and Catering*, Routledge, London.

11 Critical incident technique

DAVID GILBERT AND ANDREW LOCKWOOD

Introduction

Critical Incident Technique, as championed by Flanagan (1954), emerged at a time when a positivist approach was the dominant paradigm for both scientific and social research. At that time, researchers saw it as one of a range of available scientific tools. In the 40 plus years of its development, there has emerged an acceptance of the validity of a wider range of approaches. The strength of CIT, as it has developed, is that in this less prescriptive age, it can feature equally effectively in either a quantitative or a qualitative research design. It is equally valid under a positivist paradigm as it is under a hermeneutic or phenomenological paradigm. The difference is in the underlying values of the overall research approach and therefore in the way that the technique is applied in practice. The procedures as described below will remain largely the same, but the outputs will vary.

Critical Incident Technique gets its name from the explicit descriptions of events and behaviours identified as incidents. The use of the incident is based upon observable human activity that is complete enough in itself to permit inferences and predictions to be made about the person acting within a specified situation. A critical incident is one that contributes to (positive), or detracts from (negative), the general aim of the activity in a significant way. A common misperception of CIT is that only incidents that are highly critical in the sense of being negative are reflected by the technique, but this is clearly untrue. The technique is essentially an incident classification method consisting of a set of procedures to capture important observations of memories of past events. From such observations it is possible to develop broad principles. However, it is important to realise that the incidents have to be of significance to the issues being studied and must meet systematically defined criteria.

The Critical Incident Technique is defined by Flanagan (1954: 327) as:

> consisting of a set of procedures for collecting direct observations of human behavior in such a way as to facilitate their potential usefulness in solving practical problems and developing broad psychological principles. The critical incident technique outlines procedures for collecting observed incidents having special significance in and meeting systematically defined criteria.

As mentioned earlier, researchers can use CIT for either quantitative or qualitative approaches to research problems; Flanagan has a positivistic, 'hard data' stance for CIT

The Handbook of Contemporary Hospitality Management Research, Edited by Bob Brotherton.
© 1999 John Wiley & Sons Ltd.

usage, which would have been the more dominant paradigm in the 1950s. This is self-evident from the following description, by Flanagan (1954: 327), of an incident:

> By an incident is meant any observable human activity that is sufficiently complete in itself to permit inferences and predictions to be made about the person performing the act. To be critical, an incident must occur in a situation where the purpose or intent of the act seems fairly clear to the observer and where its consequences are sufficiently definite to leave little doubt concerning its effects.

Flanagan explains that CIT developed from earlier studies in the aviation psychology programme of the United States Army Air Forces in World War II. One such study enabled a representative sample of actual flying incidents to be developed as a guide to selecting pilots while at training school. In another study on leadership, combat veterans described the actions of their officers and what they did. Several thousand incidents were collected from which an analysis provided the descriptive categories called the 'critical requirements of combat leadership'. After the end of World War II some of the psychologists who had participated in the USAAF studies formed the American Institute for Research where further studies were carried out related to the Civil Aeronautics Administration as well as the United States Air Force and Navy. It was here that CIT was more formally developed and given its current name. These early approaches formed the basic application of CIT, which has been used widely in a number of different fields of management.

The technique has been used extensively in diverse disciplines including management and human resources (White and Locke, 1981; Spencer, 1983; McClelland, 1976, 1987; Chell, Haworth and Brearley, 1991; Hough, 1984; Latham and Saari, 1984; Latham et al., 1980; Pursell, Campion and Gaylord, 1980); Bitner, Booms and Tetreault (1990) used critical incident technique with customers of airlines, hotels and restaurants to distinguish satisfying services from dissatisfying ones; and CIT has been used by others in the areas of tourism and hospitality (Gamble, Lockwood and Messenger, 1994; Gilbert and Morris, 1995; Lockwood, 1992), and education (Copas, 1984; Cotterell, 1982).

The examples provided demonstrate the benefit of uncovering underlying aspects of importance to the respondents in a defined situation. This is brought about by complying with a procedure of allowing respondents to identify their personal set of critical incidents, for these to be aggregated and for the results to be categorised. The procedure need not be rigid as with a set of rules. On the contrary, CIT should be used as a set of principles that should be altered and modified to match the specific research task under consideration.

The core principle of the technique is that only simple types of judgements and past reports are required of the respondent, reports from only those qualified to respond are included, and all incidents are evaluated by the researcher in terms of adherence to a clear statement of the purpose of the reported activity. The extent to which the incidents can be reported as an objective fact depends on the philosophical approach of the researcher, the quality of the chosen sample frame and the confidence in the number of individuals in the sample.

These studies and the ones described in more detail later illustrate that CIT does not consist of a single rigid set of rules governing data collection and analysis but provides a flexible set of principles that can and should be modified and adapted to reflect the specific situation being investigated.

The benefit of CIT is that a respondent is allowed to focus on those issues that are of critical importance to them. As such it provides the conscious reflections of an individual's experience, based upon deeply held attitudes, values and judgements that have affected their feelings and emotions. The technique also allows for inductive theory development if a grounded theory approach is adopted (Strauss and Corbin, 1990).

The research procedure for carrying out CIT analysis

Figure 11.1 shows an analytical framework for CIT analysis that consists of three major stages broken down into six steps. The three major stages are similar to those found in any qualitative research study—collecting and assembling the data, analysing the data so collected, and constructing explanatory frameworks. The six steps then follow the process of data collection, developing coding categories, allocating incidents or parts of incidents to categories, identifying themes and trends in the data, hypothesis testing and/or data reduction, and the explanation of underlying structure. The focus of the

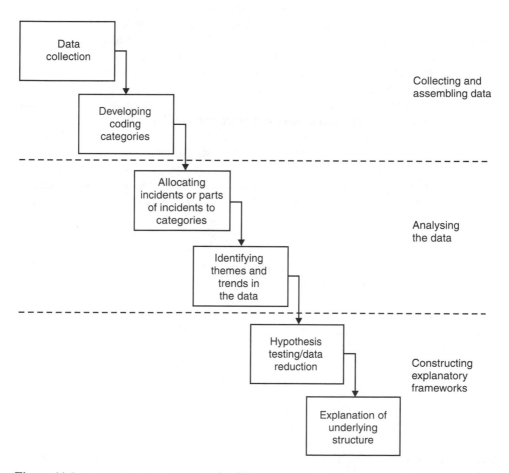

Figure 11.1 An analytical framework for CIT

discussion here will be on the first four stages that constitute the specific context of the critical incident technique.

Data collection

An incident is defined as any observable activity that is sufficiently complete in itself to permit inferences and predictions to be made about the person performing the act. A situation that is perceived as making a significant impact, either positively or negatively, to a specific task or objective is defined as critical. For example, in a study of management activity the critical incidents would be any situations in which the manager felt that their contributions or actions had made a significant difference to the outcome of a situation. By their nature, critical incidents have made an impression on the individual concerned. It has been suggested that these incidents do not, therefore, represent a true picture of a situation but only a reflection of specific major triumphs or complete disasters. Previous studies (Guerrier *et al.*, 1992; Gamble, Lockwood and Messenger, 1994; Gilbert and Morris, 1995; Bell, Gilbert and Lockwood, 1997) have, however, found this not to be the case. All aspects of a situation, both positive and negative, seem to gain appropriate coverage by this method. This is indeed supported by the experience of the current authors who in their extensive use of the technique have always found it to provide comprehensive data covering a very wide spectrum of activities.

An important step in the procedure is to clarify exactly what will constitute an incident for the purpose of a study. For example, Lockwood (1994), in describing the use of CIT in identifying service improvement points, discusses this problem. He suggests that for the purposes of his particular study an incident would be any service encounter, that is any time during which a customer directly interacts with an operation. This broad definition does not restrict the encounter to the interpersonal interactions between the customer and the service provider but encompasses all aspects of the service provision including service personnel, physical facilities and other tangible and intangible elements. A more focused study may well have been concerned with interpersonal situations only.

An example of a form that was used successfully in a previous study by Guerrier *et al.* (1992) for collecting such service incidents is shown in Figure 11.2. However, the form could be adapted to the specific requirements of any research situation to ensure that relevant incidents are collected. In addition, it is important that the researcher or the form should communicate that what is reported should be of importance (that is critical) to the respondent.

Flanagan (1954) indicated that the most crucial aspect of data collection is to ensure that the wording of any question is appropriate. He cites research where the specific question asked was 'tell me just how this employee behaved which caused ...' and how the words 'how this employee behaved' had to be changed to 'what he did' so as to provide a much broader range of incidents and not bias the results to incidents related to the employee's personality and attitudes.

Another important issue is to determine the sample to be included in the study. Decisions here will focus on the nature of the study and how representative of the population the sample is intended to be. At one end of the scale, sample selection and size can be determined along the 'classical' lines of a survey method, while at the other end

SERVICE INCIDENTS	
Setting	
People involved	
Description of the incident	
Critical points	
Positive / Negative	

Figure 11.2 Service incident report form

the sample is seen merely as a series of case examples and no overall representativeness is claimed.

There are, however, no strict rules about how many incidents need to be collected to form the basis of a useful study. In simple terms, the more there are the better the subsequent analysis is likely to be. A set of around 50 incidents will allow a researcher to go on to the category-building stage for a relatively simple piece of research, but 100 incidents will provide more reliable categories. Any further increase in the sample over 500 may not provide additional relevant incidents unless the situation being studied is highly complex.

If the incidents are going to be analysed statistically, for example to see if staff, customers and managers report different types of incidents, then a larger sample is required, probably between 300 and 500 depending on the type of analysis required. A check should be made on the initial incidents collected to judge the efficacy of the sample frame and size.

If there is no intention to carry out statistical analysis but a case example approach is being used, then it is the richness of the incidents that is crucial and not the number. The incidents collected can be used in their own right as there is no requirement to progress to the quantitative stage. The initial qualitative stage can be quite revealing if the results are written up within groupings to describe the essence of the attitudes about the incidents reported.

Once the character of the incidents and the sample frame have been defined and a clear set of questions phrased to elicit the intended responses, there are several different methods that can be used to collect the incidents.

Self-completion   Printed forms can be distributed to the selected participants and they can be asked to complete the form and return it. Experience using this approach has shown that although the responses received by this method are usually of very high quality—people have had time to think about their answer before they write it down—the response rate tends to be very low. There is also a problem that ambiguous details cannot be easily checked with the author. It is, however, an unobtrusive method that may be especially useful for customers. This technique requires a succinct introduction to the procedure so that the respondents are clear about the reporting requirements and the importance of their responses.

Interview   With this approach an individual, or a group of people depending on the scale of the study, conducts one-to-one interviews with the participants. Having asked interviewees to recount the story of their incident, the interviewer has the opportunity to ask follow-up questions to clarify any points of the story that were not clear or to elicit additional information before recording the details on the service incident form. Previous use of this method (Lockwood, 1992) has shown it to be very good at collecting detailed accounts of service incidents with little ambiguity. It is, however, time consuming for a single interviewer, whilst if a group of interviewers is used, they need to be well briefed to ensure that they do not introduce their personal bias into the data collection. Its other advantage, as with group interviews below, is that the explicit language of the respondent can be captured and assessed.

Group interviews   In this approach a group of people is brought together and then split down into pairs. The interviewer needs to introduce the purpose of the group and the procedure to be carried out. One person in the pair acts as the interviewer and elicits and records an incident from their partner. The roles are then reversed and another incident recorded. Participants continue in this way until they run out of incidents or out of time. This tends to be a very intensive and productive way of collecting incidents. At the same time it is also very enjoyable for the participants, especially if they get the opportunity of sharing incidents with other members of the group. The group could be brought together specially for this purpose or could be one of a series of regular meetings, such as quality circles or customer panels. The group could consist of just one type of respondent, such as staff members or managers, but a mixed group can also work well. Another alternative here is for the interviewer to make use of individual questionnaires and then involve the group as a whole in discussions about the incidents provided.

Developing coding categories

Once sufficient incidents have been collected, a tentative classification system can be developed by clustering the data into categories that are then further divided into sub-categories and so on. A detailed description is then developed for each category and subcategory so that any observer should be able to categorise reliably any further incidents. At this stage it is important to check the reliability of the classification descriptions by a process of inter-judge comparison. Once the classification scheme has been validated in this way, a complete classification of all the incidents collected can be completed.

The development of the categories is a largely subjective process looking for 'natural' groups within the incidents. There is no one right set of categories, only one that makes sense for a particular situation. It is the researcher who takes responsibility for abstraction and inference, not the respondent (Bitner, Booms and Tetreault, 1990). Classifying the incidents is based on repeated careful reading and sorting of the data to build groups and subgroups. These groups and subgroups should then be defined in detail to suit the principal use of the findings. The incidents are re-categorised until reliable groupings, or preferred categories, are achieved. The aim is to build category and subcategory descriptions that everyone understands. In this way different people should reliably classify the incidents into the same categories. The induction process of forming categories requires insight and judgement, which is often easier to achieve with help from others. One way of conducting this stage is to work in groups. The group or other helpers should understand the subject area to ensure their inferences and generalisations are valid.

The incidents can be divided randomly into several piles and groups can be asked to develop categories for their pile of incidents. Once this has been done, all the groups can be brought together to compare their category descriptions and agree on an overall set. It can be very interesting at this stage to split the incidents into positives and negatives and give them to different groups to see if they come up with the same or different categories.

At this stage, detailed definitive descriptions of each category and subcategory must be established to allow consistency in the classification of all incidents. If accuracy of classification is an issue for the particular research study in question then the incidents, or a random sample of the incidents in the case of a large study, should be classified by two or three separate judges and their categorisation compared. The reliability of the classification system is considered satisfactory if the percentage agreement for each category (the inter-judge reliability) is equal to or greater than 80% (Ronan and Latham, 1974).

An alternative method of classification has been used by Bitner, Booms and Tetreault (1990). The approach here is to construct a decision tree for incident classification. The researcher categorising incidents is asked to choose between two or three initial alternatives on a yes or no basis. Each of these decisions is then subdivided and can then be further divided to arrive at a final categorisation for the incident. This approach provides a very reliable but potentially constricting approach to categorisation.

It is possible to use the classification system developed for one research study as the basis for another research study. This strategy was adopted by Gremler, Bitner and

Evans (1994) where incidents concerning internal customer service encounters were classified using Bitner, Booms and Tetreault's (1990) earlier categories of external customer service encounters. They found that the original three main groups of behaviours were transferable to the later study, but that some amendments to the subgroup level were necessary by removing some and adding others to reflect better the specific nature of these types of service incidents. On the other hand, Edvardsson (1992) suggests that it does not seem to be a good idea to use a previously established set of categories because the process is inductive and partly subjective as in all qualitative research.

Allocating and analysing the incidents

Once the categories have been developed then all the incidents need to be classified and the total number of incidents in each category and subcategory established. This can be achieved with a spreadsheet or a software package such as SPSS.

The purpose of the data analysis is to summarise and describe the complexity and richness of the data in an efficient manner so that it can be effectively used for a variety of practical purposes. At this stage it is important to consider the range of demographic variables describing the sample collected. This will provide a more detailed comparison of the data and allow inferences to be drawn about the differences between certain levels of management, sectors of the industry, age groups and so on.

At the simplest level, the number of incidents in a category provides an indication of the importance of that area. The original incidents were examples of what people had found memorable and this suggests that they should also be seen as significant.

If the frequencies are calculated for positive and negative incidents, the categories can then be placed in rank order of frequency. This provides a good indication of the priority of required improvements for the negative incidents and of the most successful areas for the positive incidents. This is a simple form of Pareto or ABC analysis (Oakland, 1993). The Pareto principle suggests that 80% of the incidents will fall into 20% of the categories, although personal experience has not proved to be quite so dramatic. As such, it should be possible to identify what has been called the vital few—the few most pressing problems and the few most significant successes.

A second type of analysis can be carried out based on the relative frequency of positive and negative incidents in each of the category areas. An example of this approach is shown in Figure 11.3. Based on the work of Cadotte and Turgeon (1988), it is possible to allocate each category or subcategory to one of four quadrants of a 2 × 2 matrix. Categories that have a low score for both positive and negative incidents can be placed in the 'neutrals' quadrant. Those categories that have a high score on the negative incidents but a low score on the positive incidents would be placed in the 'dissatisfiers' quadrant. These types of incidents have a high propensity for going wrong and ending in negatives but do not seem to bring positive comments if they go right. The opposite is true of the 'satisfiers' quadrant where are placed those categories with a high score on positive incidents but a low one for negative incidents. Incidents here seem to bring positive responses but even if they go wrong it does not seem to matter all that much. The final quadrant has a high score for both positive and negative incidents. These categories of incidents will tend to result in plaudits if everything goes right but in brickbats if things go wrong. They are not surprisingly the 'criticals'. Based on this analysis

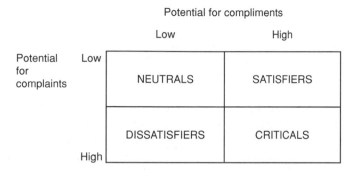

Figure 11.3   Matrix of potential for compliments and complaints

it is possible to establish some order of priority in which the incident categories could be addressed. The priority must be to ensure that the 'criticals' are looked at first and then attention can move to the 'dissatisfiers', because negative incidents are likely to have more impact than positive ones. It should then be possible to look at the 'satisfiers' to see how they might promote such positive responses.

Problems of CIT

Criticisms of CIT typically focus on issues of reliability and validity of the categories. Reliability and validity problems may arise because of the ambiguity of word meanings, category labels and coding rules of a particular study. However, research conducted by Andersson and Nilsson (1964) concluded that the data collected from the use of CIT are both reliable and valid. This was confirmed in later studies by Ronan and Latham (1974) and White and Locke (1981). As with any technique that uses small samples there will also be criticisms related to representativeness of the sample and confidence in its size. This is not borne out by the success with carefully selected qualitative samples that can demonstrate superior explanatory power over alternative methods.

Carrying out the fieldwork to collect incidents is time consuming and often expensive, as is the coding, classifying and analysis of the material collected. It should be remembered that any technique that manages to provide 'rich data' is often demanding of a researcher's time. However, CIT findings offer an opportunity to uncover those behaviours or incidents that are critical to the outcome of a service event and therefore time budgets can be judged to be efficient.

Asking for written or tape-recorded incidents can be threatening or embarrassing to a respondent, depending on the nature of the research area. Therefore, a researcher needs to ensure confidentiality for any material received so that the respondent is protected from others in their company, and from slander or misrepresentation. Moreover, the researcher needs to be sensitive to emotions and body language of the respondent who, in an interview situation, will often be reticent to convey negative incidents that reflect on others. Such situations require the interviewer to provide a mature and non-judgemental stance to establish rapport and trust with the respondent.

Using CIT in practice

The following cases show a range of applications for CIT to illustrate the approaches adopted and the type of data that emerged from the studies. The first example was a small-scale pilot study based on in-depth personal interviews looking at the perceptions of service quality of guests, staff and managers in a single hotel. It shows that even with a small number of incidents collected some very interesting and significant conclusions can be reached. The second study of service quality in food retailing shows the use of a much shorter interview structure collecting many hundreds of incidents through random sampling. The third study concerned with the influences on satisfaction with business tourism illustrates a further use of detailed personal interviews with a detailed quota sampling frame to provide representativeness. The final study is described in some detail and looks at a research project on the categorisation of management activity for the European hospitality industry conducted for the HCIMA. This example shows the complexity of the research design and analysis process that must be considered when conducting a large-scale study with nearly 2000 separate incidents.

A pilot study of hotel service quality

The results that follow are from a small pilot study used to test the technique's application to service quality in a hotel setting (Lockwood, 1994). Guest, staff and management volunteers from one hotel were interviewed by the researcher following a structured format to build up a complete picture of a series of service incidents. The interviews were conducted in the hotel and lasted between 20 and 40 minutes. Each participant was asked to recount the story of a recent positive or negative service experience they had been part of in the hotel. Although participants were asked for both positive and negative examples, not all of them were able to provide both. The 48 interviews produced a total of 70 incidents: of the 33 satisfying incidents, 12 were from guests, 11 from employees and only 10 from managers; of the 37 dissatisfying incidents, 18 were from guests, nine from employees and 10 from managers. Of the sample, 48% were men and 52% women.

The categorisation process provided nine major groupings—five positive and four negative. The positive groups were: response to guest requests, unprompted service actions, 'extra' service delivery, performance under adverse conditions, and *gestalt* evaluation. The negative groups included: system failure, lack of attention to guest, unreasonable guest demands, and *gestalt* evaluation. These nine groups were then sub-divided under a further 13 subheadings.

On the positive side, guests found unprompted service actions by staff or management as the most satisfying, while staff gave the most examples of giving 'extra' service. Management tended to see satisfaction as an overall or *gestalt* evaluation. On the negative side, guests gave most examples of inattention as a source of dissatisfaction, where staff ranked highest on the system failure category. Management showed little difference between the groups.

Despite the small exploratory scale of this study, the research findings generated some interesting insights into the different perceptions of guests, employees and managers. For example, the importance of unprompted service extras in delighting the guests (and employees) was highlighted. The danger of relying on the operation's ability to put things right after they have gone wrong was also questioned because these situations were all described as negatives. The key source of dissatisfaction was to do with failures in the service delivery system. A lack of attention paid to the guest was also seen as a strong dissatisfier. The managerial implications of this study suggested that the technical aspects of service delivery should not be neglected by managers and that there is a need to strive for customisation—adapting the service to meet more closely the individual guest's needs. Finally, the study stressed the importance of 'spontaneous' service acts that are difficult to control but seem rooted in developing a strong service orientation throughout the organisation.

A study into retail satisfaction

Bell, Gilbert and Lockwood (1997) chose CIT for research into the satisfaction of retail consumers. The authors' decision was based upon the weaknesses of earlier studies into the causes of satisfaction and dissatisfaction. Such problems were outlined by Johnston (1995) who identifies such flaws as follows:

- product focus, i.e. overlooking the service elements
- categories of service quality that are too broad
- small samples
- exploratory nature, e.g. use of student populations
- aggregation of data across industries and sectors
- a focus on negative factors only.

Taking these issues into account, CIT was identified as an appropriate method to uncover shoppers' perceptions of good and bad practice in food retailing. Other retail formats covered by CIT studies have included florists, clothing stores and hairdressers (Koelemeijer, 1995). The research design of Bell, Gilbert and Lockwood (1997) was based upon personal interviews, using a pre-prepared questionnaire, of a random sample of individuals using a large superstore. For this study the critical incidents were collected by asking the respondents to describe a recent occasion where they felt satisfied with the service from that or a similar store. Prompts for the involvement of who, what, where, when, and why were used to enlarge on the information. This process was repeated to compile the incidents for dissatisfaction. The interviews were conducted just outside the exit from the store and lasted between five and ten minutes. A range of other demographic and behavioural data was also collected.

The findings comprised a total of 792 incidents. Of these, 492 were occasions where customers had felt satisfied with the service they had received and 300 were occasions where customers had been dissatisfied. At the data entry stage, this was initially reduced to 43 separate categories. It was felt, however, that a further reduction of categories was necessary to facilitate understanding of the main issues. The critical incidents obtained were further examined by the authors and, through an iterative process, the satisfiers and dissatisfiers were agreed to fall into six distinct categories. This was achieved through the triangulation of all three researchers, where all had to agree to each reduction of the initial categories into the final boundary group of six. These were as follows: Price (offers, expectations, etc.), Process (layout of produce, systems of selection, payment, etc.), Interpersonal (staff care, empathy, etc.), Non-core (coffee shop, lottery counter, etc.), Merchandise (range of produce, freshness, quality, etc.) and Physical Environment (decor, lighting, signage, car park, etc.). From the analysis it became clear that the process dissatisfaction incidents required urgent management attention. An interesting finding was that price is not a major driver of either satisfaction or dissatisfaction and that price competition promotion may not be of key importance.

The use of CIT in tourism

Pickfords Business Travel and a recent ABC World Airways study have shown that the most important aspect of business travel is the minimisation of stress and a need to consider the dissatisfaction of employees (Curphy, 1993). Business travel and related levels of satisfaction are an under-researched area. However, to learn more of the individual traveller's likes and dislikes Gilbert and Morris (1995) sought to uncover and isolate travel satisfaction. To assess satisfaction linked to business travel arrangements, a study was made of the role of accommodation and travel in the success of overseas business trips. For the purpose of this study, critical incidents were defined as specific business trips that were especially satisfying or especially dissatisfying.

Collection of incidents   The first stage was to collect a series of business travel incidents. An incident was required to meet four criteria:

1. Involving a business trip abroad
2. Being satisfying or dissatisfying from the business traveller's point of view
3. Being a discrete episode
4. Having sufficient detail to be visualised by the business traveller being interviewed.

The sample of business travellers was derived from targeting the top 25 companies ranked by corporate travel spend found in the October 1993 issue of *Business Travel World*. Letters were written to the Travel Manager or Director of Purchasing within each company requesting interviews with three or four frequent business travellers. 'Frequent' was defined as travelling on at least five business trips a year. The sample was based upon a quota sample selection technique. Quotas were calculated using the American Express *Business Travel and Expense Management Report* (1993) which found that a 3 : 1 ratio of male to female business travellers exists within UK companies. The final sample corresponded to a 3 : 2 ratio of male to female travellers. As stated, control was made for frequent fliers and these represented senior managers in companies. Just over 50% of companies responded initially and further effort produced 92 incidents based upon 30 respondents.

To overcome non-response problems, it was decided that personal interviews would be the most appropriate data collection technique. The interviews were conducted in the respective respondent's office in an attempt to create a relaxed atmosphere in familiar surroundings. For the same reason a tape recorder was not used as it was felt that more open answers would be given. Notes were taken instead. The method was successfully piloted on three frequent business travellers to ensure the Critical Incident Technique would be successful.

The respondents were not asked to identify the underlying causes of (dis)satisfaction but rather to describe a specific instance in which a good or bad business trip occurred. Reporting events or stories in this way was found to be something most people do very easily.

Classification of incidents   Once the data were collected, the incidents were classified into a series of categories. The development of the categories was a largely subjective process looking for 'natural' groups within the incidents.

An important measure of the success of the classification descriptions is the reliability with which the incidents are classified against those descriptions by different people working independently. The authors chose someone who knew very little about the study and the results produced were more than satisfactory at the 80% agreement level.

Two key areas emerged from the findings. These were the incidents where self-esteem (88%) and time available for leisure (12%) provided the major incident groupings. These could be subdivided as follows.

- Area One: *Self-Esteem.* This area represents the business travellers who are primarily concerned with their self-image and how this is perceived by others. Factors that were perceived as being important included prestige, status, reputation, recognition and importance. The factors were based upon aspects of the method and class of travel to the destination (use of taxis, business rather than economy class), the quality of the hotel (service, comfort, and cleanliness), and the arrangement of the business side of the trip (management of the business meetings or presentations)
- Area Two: *Time Available for Leisure.* This second key area of activity includes respondents who perceived that the most significant underlying satisfaction factor of their trip was related to the spare time they had available for tourism and leisure activities.

Frequencies were calculated for positive and negative incidents. The results were 61 positive incidents representing 66% of the total, and 31 negative incidents being 34% of the total. The categories were then put together to form sets and placed in rank order for both positive and negative incidents, as shown in Table 11.1.

These results show that the category needing most improvement was the quality of the hotel and the least problematic area was the business aspects of the trip. It is interesting that neither managing the business side of the trip nor time available for leisure was referred to as a negative incident. The negative results are likely to have been dominated by the quality of the hotel because this affects the whole trip on both a personal and a work-related level. The class and quality of the travel are only a relatively small part of the trip whereas a hotel, and particularly the bedroom itself, is used every day.

Table 11.1   Classification of business travellers' experiences

Positive	Managing the business side of the trip	37%
	Method of travel to the destination	26%
	The quality of the hotel	23%
	Time available for leisure	14%
Negative	The quality of the hotel	66%
	Method of travel to the destination	34%

The critical incident technique provided for the uncovering of a number of events that could be categorised into negative or positive outcomes. It is unlikely that any other technique would have revealed this level of detail about the issues which concern business travellers. These are of benefit to organisations in the planning of business trips as well as those interested in understanding the role of job satisfaction and the performance of employees.

Management activities in the European hospitality industry: a study for the HCIMA

This research study, conducted on behalf of the Hotel and Catering International Management Association (HCIMA) by the University of Surrey (Gamble, Lockwood and Messenger, 1994), was designed to identify the types of management activities that could be seen to be typical of different sectors of the European hospitality industry.

While the focus of the two initial phases of the research, interviews with senior industry executives and focus groups with experienced managers, was very much on the view from the top, the final phase was to examine examples of current management practice. The aim of this phase of the research was to create a picture of the character of managerial work across all sectors of the hospitality industry in the UK and Europe. The objective was to build a comprehensive profile of the skills and knowledge currently used by practising managers of different levels, ages and sexes across the industry. To achieve a representative explanation of current perceptions of management strengths and weaknesses in skills and knowledge, a self-report methodology using critical incident analysis was adopted. This was designed to allow a comparison of the espoused values of the senior executives and the experienced managers with the practice of managers at all levels of responsibility and across all sectors of the industry.

For the purposes of the study, critical incidents were situations in which the manager felt that their contributions or actions had made a significant difference to the outcome of a situation. By their nature, critical incidents have made an impression on the individual concerned. It can be suggested that these incidents do not represent a true picture of a manager's job but only a reflection of major triumphs or disasters. Other studies (Guerrier et al., 1992; Gilbert and Morris, 1995; Bell, Gilbert and Lockwood, 1997) have, however, found this not to be the case. All aspects of a job, both positive and negative, seem to gain appropriate coverage by this method. This is indeed supported by the findings of this study, which covered a very wide spectrum of activities.

The incidents for this study were collected across six countries in Europe: France, Germany, Ireland, the Netherlands, Spain and the UK. Using a combination of mailed questionnaire and personal interview, approaching 2000 separate incidents were collected from managers. Once sufficient incidents had been collected, a tentative classification system was developed by clustering nearly 300 of the incidents into categories, which were then further divided into subcategories, and finally into indicative activities under each subcategory. A detailed description was then developed for each category and subcategory so that further incidents could be reliably categorised.

At this stage, the reliability of the classification descriptions was checked by a process of inter-judge comparison, achieving agreement in over 98% of cases. Once this classification scheme had been validated, a complete classification of all the incidents collected was completed.

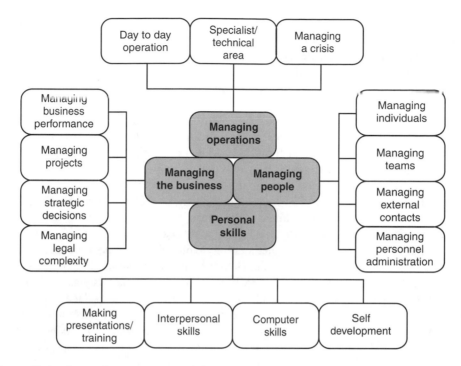

Figure 11.4   Areas of management activity

The classification system developed identified four main areas: managing operations, managing the business, managing people and personal skills. Each of these areas was further subdivided and a total of 15 categories identified (see Figure 11.4).

Collecting the incidents   The most popular method of incident collection used in critical incident studies is the personal interview. While this method is successful in those studies that are concerned primarily with a single workplace or company, it was not felt that this was a practical method for an industry-wide survey where a very wide sectoral and geographic spread was required. It was decided therefore to use a self-completion mail questionnaire that would be distributed first to all HCIMA corporate and licentiate members in the UK who represented the prime target audience for the study. Previous studies using this form of collection have reported response rates of around 20%. In addition, incidents collected by the Hotel and Catering Training Company (HCTC), who were conducting a complementary research study targeting the HCIMA fellows, were also to be made available.

The comments received from 40 pilot questionnaires were duly incorporated to produce the first version of the questionnaire. This consisted of an introductory page of description followed by four pages for incidents—one to be where the manager's skills and knowledge were used well, one where the respondents felt their skills and knowledge were lacking, and two extra pages for unclassified incidents. The final page contained the demographic profile and space for comments. Following the initial phase of the data collection, the questionnaire was revised and a second, slightly simpler version of the form was produced. This form had a slightly simpler introduction and the demographic profile was moved to the front page to start the respondent off with an easy opening. The number of incidents was reduced to two—one successful and one where skills and knowledge were lacking.

The questionnaire was mailed with a personal covering letter from the Chief Executive of the HCIMA and a freepost envelope to over 9400 corporate and licentiate members at their UK membership addresses during late August and early September 1992. The initial response rate was too low and to generate further response all the fellows of the HCIMA were then contacted by letter asking if they would be willing to participate in the critical incident survey. Several forms were sent to each fellow who agreed to accept them and pass them on to other managers within the fellows' organisations. In addition, around 500 forms were given to HCIMA branch officials for distribution at branch meetings around the country.

At the same time as this survey, the HCTC were also looking at management competencies using a slightly different methodology which favoured positive incidents and did not categorise by age of respondent. However, it was possible to incorporate some of their findings as part of the analysis. A further source of incidents was the European Caterers Association (ECA) who kindly agreed to provide address labels for all UK members who were not members of the HCIMA. In addition, students collected incidents through industrial placement connections and interviewing individuals in hospitality operations. Through this wide variety of approaches, the final response for the UK was a total of 1002 usable incidents.

Developing the categories   The initial category descriptions were based on the original 283 incidents generated by HCIMA members. Each incident was analysed to identify the key issue and a long list prepared. The first half of the sample was then used to develop tentative groups or clusters of incidents. These groups were then used as the basis for classifying the second half of the sample to ensure that all incidents could be covered by the classification system developed. These clusters formed the basis of 15 incident classes (see Figure 11.4). Within each class the incidents were further examined to identify the types of incidents or indicative activities that were to be found within this category. The categories were then grouped into four main areas and finally the detailed descriptions were developed. These represent the key categories of skills and knowledge that a manager in the hospitality industry needs to be effective.

Table 11.2 shows the definitions for the four key areas. Below this level of definition each category had its own definition and it was at this level that the major focus of the analysis was directed. For example, the description for the category of managing a crisis within the area of managing operations was:

> Faced with a crisis in the operation, which would be more serious than handling a simple operational problem and could threaten life or property or result in a serious customer complaint, the manager must be able to take charge and provide guidance for corrective action without necessarily having to do everything themselves.

These categories are further supported by a series of indicative activities that show examples of the types of events that managers may be involved in and have to deal with. These indicative activities are not intended to be a complete and comprehensive list but merely to show the range of activities covered under each category. For example, the

Table 11.2   A description of the main category areas

MANAGING OPERATIONS

This category represents those activities that form the key operational activities of the business. They are concerned with ensuring that hospitality product and services are delivered to the customer in the intended way and to the required standard. They represent that daily activity of the manager who must ensure that operations run as smoothly as possible, given the constraints of a customer-driven business.

MANAGING THE BUSINESS

This category represents those activities that are focused on controlling the current financial success of the business and determining its future strategic direction. The ability to monitor current performance must be developed and proposals for any required corrective action must be developed. On many occasions this will involve the implementation and supervision of a project-based approach to ensure that plans are carried out. Not only must managers review current performance but they must also look forward and provide a strategic direction. At all times the business must operate within legal guidelines.

MANAGING PEOPLE

The nature of the hospitality business ensures that a large part of the manager's activity will be concerned with achieving results through others, be they subordinates, colleagues or superiors. Aside from the purely interpersonal aspects of managing people dealt with in another category, managers must be able to provide a framework within which each individual or team can contribute to the best of their ability.

PERSONAL MANAGEMENT SKILLS

The skills and knowledge that a manager in the hospitality industry requires are not restricted to the technical operation of the business or the organisation of effective work activities. They must also include skills of a more personal nature which reflect not so much on what is done but more on the way things are done. Once these skills have been acquired, the manager must continue to develop to be able to deal with new situations, new technology and new challenges.

---

indicative activities for managing a crisis include taking charge of the situation, finding solutions 'on the move', and co-ordinating and initiating action.

A second example shows the category of making presentations, which is described as follows:

> Increasingly managers are required to address groups of people for a wide variety of reasons and they must therefore develop the ability to assemble, prepare and deliver effective verbal and written presentations. These presentations may be very formal and involve a large amount of advance preparation or they may be *ad hoc* training sessions conducted on the spur of the moment to respond to an identified need.

Due to the split nature of this category of activity, the indicative activities are also split into 'presentations' including formal presentations to customers/clients, preparation of written submissions, and communicating information to customers or staff; and 'training', including preparation of training packages, training others in a formal presentation, and training others in informal situations.

Validating the categories   An important measure of the success of the above classification descriptions was the reliability with which the incidents were classified against those descriptions by different judges working independently—the inter-judge reliability. The results for the first version of the category descriptions are shown in Table 11.3. As these results did not meet the 80% target (Ronan and Latham, 1974), further development was undertaken to produce a more detailed set of category descriptions. Using a different set of incidents to test the new descriptions resulted in the more than acceptable results as shown in the rightmost column of the table.

Once a reliable set of category descriptions had been determined then the complete categorisation of all the incidents could be carried out. The incidents were classified to the class level and not to the subclass or indicative activity level. The subclass level should be regarded as indicative of the range of activities that would be carried out under each category and was not designed to be an exclusive or exhaustive list.

Demographic variables   Each incident was classified under the demographic variables of industry sector, management level and gender. All incidents, other than those provided by the HCTC, were classified by age.

The industry categories used were based on the Marketpower survey (Marketpower, 1997) and were as follows: hotels—group, hotels—private, pubs, restaurants, travel catering, fast food/take away/café, entertainment/clubs, employee catering/contractors, health, education/local authority, public services, other (e.g. consultancy).

To allow for the differences in management titles and roles between industry sectors, the following management levels were used:

- Department head/junior management—managing a section within an operating unit.
- Unit manager/section manager—managing a complete unit or a section within a larger unit.
- General manager—overall control of one large unit composed of a number of sections or a collection of smaller units.

Table 11.3   Agreement in the categorisation process

Category	Description	First version % agreement	Final version % agreement
A1	Day-to-day operation	50	82
A2	Specialist/technical areas	20	100
A3	Managing a crisis	67	100
B1	Managing business performance	12	88
B2	Managing projects	28	100
B3	Managing strategic decisions	10	94
B4	Managing legal complexity	25	100
C1	Managing individuals	0	100
C2	Managing teams	30	100
C3	Managing external contacts	0	100
C4	Managing personnel administration	44	100
D1	Making presentations	44	82
D2	Interpersonal skills	66	100
D3	Computer skills	100	100
D4	First-aid skills	100	100
D5	Self-development	17	100

- Regional manager—overall responsibility for a number of separate large units or geographic areas.
- Director—responsibility for the operation and management of a complete organisation.
- Owner/proprietor/partner.

Once the categories and descriptions had been reliably agreed, the research was extended with research partners to a range of other countries across Europe, including France, Germany, Ireland, the Netherlands and Spain, using the same methodology, questionnaire and classification system. Altogether a total of nearly 2000 separate incidents were collected for subsequent analysis.

Analysis

By entering the demographic and classification data for each individual incident onto a spreadsheet, it was then possible using SPSS to extract quantitative descriptions of the categories and to investigate the data further through a range of cross-tabulations.

The following section provides a summary of some of the results collected across Europe to show the level of detail that can be achieved. There are, however, some features of the data collection process and the data analysis that should be remembered while considering these results. First, the data was collected by a process of self-report and the nature of this process may influence the results obtained. For example, it is natural that managers would rather report on incidents where they felt they had been successful and so more positive incidents are likely. Second, the incidents that were reported were chosen by the managers out of a large number of possible situations. It is reasonable to assume that the choice of the incidents reported is a reflection of the way these managers see their roles and what aspects of their jobs they consider to be important. The incidents should therefore reflect the perceptions of the respondents of the jobs they then occupied in whatever sector of the industry they were working in at the time. Third, some of the data were presented as cross-tabulations, where one variable is compared with another variable and the frequencies counted. All the chi-square tests run on each of the cross-tabulations resulted in a very high significance level of over 99% using SPSS/PC+, which indicates the significance of differences and provides strong support for the view that the number of incidents collected has been sufficiently large to ensure the reliability of the results.

Managing operations Despite moves away from an operational focus, this area recorded the second highest number of incidents across the three subcategories of managing day-to-day operations, specialist/technical areas and managing crises. The analysis by managerial level, shown in Table 11.4, as could be expected, shows a heavy emphasis in this area for the junior managers. This was greatest in day-to-day operations and specialist knowledge, but when it came to a crisis senior managers or owners were more likely to be involved.

Sector comparisons show that hotels and restaurants reported the heaviest emphasis on managing operations while employee catering had the lowest. Across the countries, managing operations was the area most often reported in France, Germany, the

Table 11.4   A cross-tabulation of level of management against the main category areas

Column % ASR*	Junior	Unit	General	Regional	Director	Owner	Total (%)
Managing operations	40.3	30.2	20.9	13.4	17.8	29.3	29.0
ASR	5.4	0.8	−3.4	−3.5	−2.2	−0.1	
Managing the business	11.8	23	32.6	41.2	41.1	32	25.2
ASR	−6.6	−1.5	3.3	3.8	3.2	2	
Managing people	10.7	16.4	15.9	19.6	12.3	9.5	14.4
ASR	−2.2	1.8	0.9	1.5	−0.5	−1.8	
Personal skills	37.2	30.4	30.6	25.8	28.8	29.3	31.5
ASR	2.6	−0.7	−0.4	−1.3	−0.5	−0.6	
Total (%)	23.2	36.5	19.6	6.3	4.8	9.6	100

*ASR: in a table of frequency data it is easy to identify that one percentage is bigger than another. It can, however, be difficult to work out how much bigger when different columns or rows may be involved. An indicator of the size of the difference that can be compared is the ASR or adjusted standardised residual. This is the difference between the expected frequency and the actual frequency standardised across the whole table to have a mean of zero and a standard deviation of one.

Netherlands and Spain but not in Ireland and the UK. In fact the pattern across all the areas for the four continental countries was remarkably similar, perhaps reflecting a more traditional operations and technical skills emphasis than in the offshore islands.

Looking at Figure 11.5, managing operations was not seen as being an area that managers are particularly comfortable in, with more incidents reported where skills were

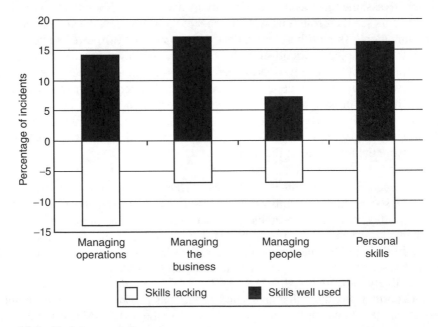

Figure 11.5   Training needs by management area

lacking than where skills were well used (33.5% to 26.7%). There is obviously a feeling that the specialist skills and knowledge in this area are still significant to hospitality operations and that it is an area where managers feel weakest.

Business orientation   The area of managing the business included aspects of managing business performance, managing projects, managing strategic decisions and managing legal complexity. Across the whole sample, this area represented 25.2% of all incidents, in third place behind personal skills at 31.5% and managing operations at 29%.

There were differences by country that are worth reporting. The UK was the only country of the six sampled to show a strong positive emphasis to these business areas; all the other countries showed a reduced number of incidents in this area. This result may be influenced by the heavier concentration ratio of corporate to independent businesses to be found in the UK. As the corporate influence matures across Europe, it is to be expected that this business orientation will emerge more strongly.

Looking at the numbers of positive and negative incidents reported in this area as an indication of possible training needs, as shown in Figure 11.5, shows that managers reported almost twice as many positive incidents as negative ones in this area. This would indicate that they are generally happy with their abilities in this direction.

Managing people   This area covered managing individuals, managing teams, managing external contacts and managing personnel administration. It was therefore surprising that, given the labour intensity of many sectors of the industry and the importance given to this area from senior executives and experienced managers, there were relatively few reported incidents in this area—only 14.4% of the total.

Personal skills   This area includes a range of generic or transferable skills that cover making verbal or written presentations, training, interpersonal skills, using computers in management, and self-development. There were more incidents reported in this area than in any other and most of these were in the interpersonal skills area (almost 23%) followed by making presentations and training. Using computers in business showed comparatively few incidents, and incidents to do with self-development were sadly, for an industry that seemingly values training highly, very sparse.

Summary

The evidence from the critical incident survey did not wholeheartedly support the views provided by the chief executives. The changes they identified did not seem to have filtered as far down the organisation as they might have expected. Relying on chief executive interviews alone would therefore have very seriously skewed the results of the study. The Critical Incident Technique has provided incontrovertible evidence of what was actually happening on the ground. For example, the move to a more business-oriented operation was in evidence but the heavy emphasis on operations and technical skills, particularly for junior managers, will not go away. In fact this was the area that received the most negative incidents, suggesting that there is still a major training gap to be filled. On the other hand, managers reported many more positive incidents in managing the business than negative ones. It would seem that the business skills developed at the universities and colleges are being put to positive use.

Another area receiving increasing emphasis on hospitality courses is that of developing interpersonal and presentation skills. This also seems to be well supported by the expressed needs of the managers surveyed across the whole of the industry. On the other hand, the chief executives' emphasis on team facilitation has not yet received the attention it may well deserve.

Conclusion

Researchers can apply the Critical Incident Technique described above over a wide range of hospitality situations. It is a simple extension of the idea of getting people to tell stories about important things that have affected or happened to them in the past. Most people enjoy recounting such stories. By formalising and recording the process, researchers collect a wealth of data that they can use, after a straightforward analysis procedure, to inform the research. The results revealed by this process are significant at two levels. Firstly, incidents provide very rich data, which can be useful at the qualitative level to identify issues and attitudes that might not otherwise be evident. Secondly, they can operate at the quantitative level to provide support for particular research priorities.

There is a tendency for researchers based firmly in the scientific tradition to question the rigour of this methodological approach, despite the body of evidence referenced throughout this paper that supports its reliability and validity. But the purpose here is not to suggest that CIT should supplant other approaches or that it is equally valid in all circumstances, rather that given the complexity, multiplicity and forever changing nature of the hospitality phenomenon, consideration should be given to all approaches that can add research value. As Lundberg (1997: 2) suggests:

> if our assumption of phenomenological complexity and changefulness seems more realistic … it suggests that for particular research projects of interest to hospitality researchers a variety of paths for discovery and understanding may be equally viable. If this is so then an awareness of and appreciation of alternative modes and means of enquiry is desirable if not requisite.

If Critical Incident Technique is to become a more widely used and respected technique for such enquiry then potential users of the approach need to address a series of questions.

First, is the technique being used from a primarily qualitative or quantitative stance? While the technique is equally valid for both, decisions about operationalising the approach will be affected. Interviews with a relatively small number of participants lasting hours rather than minutes, looking at incidents in depth, will reveal a wealth of data that can be particularly insightful and exciting. There would be little point here in carrying out detailed statistical cross-tabulations of the resulting categorisation, however. On the other hand, large-scale studies involving the collection of hundreds or thousands of separate incidents could provide some interesting statistical analysis but would say relatively little about the underlying motives or forces at play in each incident.

Second, has sufficient attention been given to the development and definition of the categories for analysis? CIT allows, if not encourages, the categories for analysis to emerge from the incident data. This allows the analysis to follow as closely as possible the perceived reality of the interviewees. It would be naive, however, to suppose that this new categorisation was without foundation. As Koestler (1975: 120) argued, 'the creative act is not an act of creation in the sense of the Old Testament. It does not create something out of nothing; it uncovers, selects, re-shuffles, combines, synthesises already existing facts, faculties, skills.' When approaching the creation of incident categories the researcher cannot be totally objective, for as Popper (1976: 57) has pointed out, 'there is no such thing as an unprejudiced observation'. The important issue here is that the researcher acknowledges and surfaces the underlying assumptions and theories that have influenced the particular categorisation scheme. There is nothing wrong in accepting an already established format to follow as long as the incident data is not being squeezed to fit it. Indeed, a comparison of two categorisation schemes based on different assumptions may provide additional insight. The key issue remains that the researcher needs to pay close attention and considerable effort in developing, clarifying and defining the categories to be used for analysis until ambiguity is removed. This iterative process may take a number of rotations to complete properly but the importance of it cannot be overstressed.

Third, has the inherent bias of the participants been acknowledged and accounted for? Again, there is an issue of underlying assumptions here. If a qualitative stance is taken then the selection and number of participants is a question of surfacing an appropriate range of issues for analysis, and the arguments over the selection of subjects for case studies (see Chapter 7) become significant. If, on the other hand, a quantitative stance is to be taken, then questions of representativeness become important and decisions about sample size and selection (see Chapter 13) take over.

A final issue arises in the presentation and use of the data collected. Do the quotations from the incidents collected accurately portray the mood of the data? There is a temptation in reporting CIT data to talk about the most interesting, exciting or humorous incidents. The danger is that these represent an extreme position and do not accurately reflect the majority of incidents that may be much less interesting and more mundane but also a more accurate reflection of the overall feel of the data. On the other hand, it is important to include real examples of incidents to give the reader a clear picture of what is involved. The selection of these incidents then remains a difficult balance between the illuminating and the distracting.

The key message that emerges from the previous paragraphs is that CIT is a serious research approach that should not be entered into lightly and which, as with all research approaches, needs to be used in a logical, careful and thoughtful way. If researchers use CIT in this way, then it provides a wealth of data that can reveal insights into a range of hospitality research issues much wider than those for which it has already been used.

References

American Express (1993) *Business Travel and Expense Management Report*, American Express UK

Andersson B E and Nilsson S G (1964) Studies in the reliability and validity of critical incident technique, *Journal of Applied Psychology* **48**, 6: 398–403

Bell J, Gilbert D and Lockwood A (1997) Service quality in food retailing operations: a critical incident analysis, *International Review of Retail, Distribution and Consumer Research* **7**, 4: 405–424

Bitner M J, Booms B H and Tetreault M S (1990) The service encounter: diagnosing favourable and unfavourable incidents, *Journal of Marketing* **54**, Jan: 71–84

Cadotte E R and Turgeon N (1988) Key factors in guest satisfaction, *Cornell Hotel and Restaurant Administration Quarterly* **28**, 4: 45–51

Chell E, Haworth J M and Brearley S (1991) *The Entrepreneurial Personality: Concepts, Cases and Categories*, London: Routledge

Copas E M (1984) Critical requirements for co-operating teachers, *Journal of Teacher Education* **35**, 6: 49–54

Cotterell J L (1982) Student experience following entry into secondary school, *Educational Research* **24**, 4: 296–302

Curphy M (1993) Businesses slash travel costs, *The Times*, 18 Nov, p 9

Edvardsson B (1992) Service breakdowns: a study of critical incidents in airlines, *International Journal of Service Industry Management* **3**, 4: 17–29

Flanagan J C (1954) The critical incident technique, *Psychological Bulletin* **51**, 4: 327–358

Gamble P, Lockwood A and Messenger S (1994) Management skills in the European hospitality industry, *48th Annual CHRIE Conference*, Palm Springs 27–30 July

Gilbert D C and Morris L (1995) The usefulness of critical incident technique analysis in isolating travel satisfactions, *International Journal of Contemporary Hospitality Management* **7**, 4: v–vii

Gremler D, Bitner M J and Evans K R (1994) The internal service encounter, *International Journal of Service Industry Management* **5**, 2: 34–41

Guerrier Y, Kipps M, Lockwood A and Sheppard J (1992) Perceptions of hygiene and quality in food service operations, *Progress in Tourism Recreation and Hospitality Management* **4**: 182–194

Hough L M (1984) Development and evaluation of the accomplishment record. Method of selecting and promoting professionals, *Journal of Applied Psychology* **69**, 1: 135–146

Johnston R (1995) The determinants of service quality: satisfiers and dissatisfiers, *International Journal of Service Industry Management* **6**, 5: 53–71

Koelemeijer K (1995) The retail service encounter: identifying critical service experiences, in Kunst P and Lemmink J (eds), *Managing Service Quality*, London: Paul Chapman

Koestler A (1975) *The Act of Creation*, London: Pan Books

Latham G, and Saari L M (1984) Do people do what they say? Further studies on the situational interview, *Journal of Applied Psychology* **69**, 4: 569–573

Latham G, Saari L M, Pursell E D and Campion M A (1980) The situational interview, *Journal of Applied Psychology* **65**, 4: 422–427

Lockwood A (1992) Maintaining the magic: Diagnosing satisfying and dissatisfying service encounters in hotel operations, Paper presented at 46th Annual CHRIE Conference, *Into the Magical Worlds of Hospitality and Tourism Education*, Orlando, Florida, 28 July–1 August

Lockwood A (1994) Using service incidents to identify quality improvement points, *International Journal of Contemporary Hospitality Management* **6**, 1/2: 75–80

Lundberg C C (1997) Widening the conduct of hospitality inquiry: toward appreciating research alternatives, *Journal of Hospitality and Tourism Research* **21**, 1: 1–13

Marketpower (1997) *The Catering Industry Population File*, London: Marketpower Ltd

McClelland D C (1976) *A Guide to Job Competency Assessment*, Boston: McBer and Co

McClelland D C (1987) Characteristics of successful entrepreneurs, *Journal of Creative Behaviour* **21**, 3

Oakland J S (1993) *Total Quality Management*, 2nd edn. Oxford: Heinemann

Popper K (1976) *Unended Quest: An Intellectual Autobiography*, London: Fontana/Collins

Pursell E D, Campion M A and Gaylord S A (1980) Structured interviewing: avoiding selection problems, *Personnel Journal*, November: 907–912

Ronan W W and Latham G P (1974) The reliability and validity of the critical incident technique: a closer look, *Studies in Personnel Psychology* **6**, 1: 53–64

Spencer L M (1983) *Soft Skill Competencies*, Scottish Council for Research in Education

Strauss A. and Corbin J (1990) *Basics of Qualitative Research: Grounded Theory Procedures and Techniques*, London: Sage

White F M and Locke E A (1981) Perceived determinants of high and low productivity in three occupational groups: a critical incident study, *Journal of Management Studies* **18**, 4: 375–387

12 Measurement

FRANCIS BUTTLE

Introduction

Most researchers view themselves as scientists. To be a scientist involves measurement. They measure tangibles such as room dimensions or the size of an audience, and intangibles such as satisfaction and stress. The process of measurement supplies the scientist with data, which, when analyzed, produces knowledge and facilitates understanding.

Measurement is founded on the idea that sensed phenomena have characteristics, properties or conditions which vary. In everyday experience, measurement often takes place unaided by precise instrumentation. We can safely claim that Venus is more distant from the Earth than the Moon. We can also make estimates of temperature, humidity, size, weight, volume. We can measure taste ('This ice-cream is sweeter than that yoghurt'). For the scientist, however, measurements such as these are subject to far too much error. Scientists need precise and stable measures of the phenomena they are studying in order to be able to develop and test theory.

This chapter examines the issue of measurement from a scientific perspective. It asks, and seeks to provide, answers to several questions. When is measurement appropriate? What can be measured? How can measures be classified? How are measures developed? The chapter concludes with a review of measurement practices used by hospitality researchers.

Measurement in positivist and constructionist traditions

Most research conducted in the hospitality, tourism and leisure environments has a positivistic flavour. Broadly, positivists believe that there is a real, immutable and ahistoric world which exists outside the person. Constructionists, in contrast, hold that knowledge of the world and beliefs about what is real are constructed socially in communication with other persons. At one time, the dominant voice, the Church, was central in creating a view that the Earth was flat. Until the voice of scientists was heard, flatness was the known reality of life on Earth. Religious and scientific groups are only two communities whose voices influence our knowledge of what is real.

The job of positivistic researchers is to reveal that reality through the rigorous application of scientific method. Four activities—conceptualization, operationalization, development of indicators and measurement—are the hallmarks of positivistic research. More is said about these later in the chapter. Clearly, measurement is one of the signs of

The Handbook of Contemporary Hospitality Management Research, Edited by Bob Brotherton.
© 1999 John Wiley & Sons Ltd.

a positivistic scientist at work. A constructionist is less interested in measurement of those concepts which are assumed, by positivists, to have some verifiable existence outside the world of the researcher, and more interested in the mechanisms by which we develop knowledge and a sense of reality. In this chapter we take a positivistic view of measurement.

What can be measured?

Attitude, Bias, Calibre, Diffusion, Energy, Force, ... , Zest. Any variable concept can be measured. Researchers distinguish between several types of variable. *Experimental* variables are those which the researcher manipulates in order to determine effects. They are also called independent or explanatory variables. *Dependent* variables are the variables which experience the effects of the experimental variables. For example, a researcher may vary the temperature of a swimming pool, and measure the effect on swimmer comfort. The experimental (independent, explanatory) variable is temperature; the dependent variable is swimmer comfort.

A further distinction is made between *controlled* and *uncontrolled* variables. Controlled variables are managed by the researcher; uncontrolled are not. In order to determine the effects of an experimental variable it is necessary to control other variables, so that the researcher can reasonably claim that the independent variable was the cause of any observed effects. For example, if we wanted to measure the impact of improved restaurant service standards on diner satisfaction, we would want to control any other possible causes such as portion sizes, dining environment and menu length. Control can be exerted in two principal ways: exclusion, and holding constant. A researcher could exclude men from a sample survey to control for the impact of gender. By holding constant all but the experimental variable, the effects of that variable are isolated and any assertion of causality can be made with some degree of confidence.

Whether measuring experimental, dependent, controlled or uncontrolled variables, scientists would seek to employ measures which are valid and reliable. A valid measuring instrument measures what it is intended to measure. A scientist would not use a foot rule to measure temperature. A reliable measure produces consistent results even though the time and place of measurement may vary. A ruler made from wood produces more reliable measures of length than one fabricated from elastic. Both, however, are prone to some degree of unreliability caused by expansion and contraction under the changing environmental conditions of temperature and humidity. More is said about these important issues later in the chapter.

Levels of measurement

Stephens (1951) developed a hierarchy of measurement levels which is very widely adopted. He wrote of four different levels of measurement: nominal, ordinal, interval and ratio. Researchers need to understand the hierarchy because it determines the types of analysis that can be performed on the data. Some statistical procedures were designed, and are therefore only suitable, for interval-level data, for example factor analysis, discriminant analysis and cluster analysis. Being hierarchical, each successive level has all the properties of the previous level and some additional properties of its own.

Nominal

Nominal measures are the lowest form of measure. They are used only to classify, identify or categorize. The numbers on hotel room doors are a form of nominal measure. Identification numbers in a guest database are also nominal measures. A successful nominal measurement system satisfies four criteria. There must be at least two categories; these must be distinct, mutually exclusive and collectively exhaustive. If there are not two categories it is not a variable. However, if there are two or more categories, the names or numbers attached to each must be distinctive to avoid confusion. The classification system must be exhaustive to capture all cases of the variable, and the categories must be mutually exclusive in that any one case should fit in only one category. Gender is a variable measured on a nominal scale. Whilst nominal measures may shed little light on the research question, they are often used in conjunction with other forms of measure. For example, gender may be used as a classificatory variable when a researcher wants to find out if men and women perceive different levels of job-related stress in a hospitality working environment.

Ordinal

Ordinal measures rank the categories being measured. If hotel groups were to be ranked by size we would be employing an ordinal measure. Ordinal measures indicate whether an observed case has more or less of some characteristic than another observed case. They do not, however, indicate the order of magnitude of difference. We would know from an ordinal scale that the first-ranked object had more of the measured characteristic than the second-ranked, but we would not know whether the latter ranked a close or distant second. Sometimes, ordinal scales feature tied places, where the objects have an equal amount of the observed characteristic.

Interval

Interval measures remedy the 'order of magnitude' problem associated with ordinal measures. Not only do interval measures identify rank orders, but the distance between categories is also known. The distance between two adjacent values at one end of the measure is the same as the distance between two adjacent values at the other end. The distance between 5 and 6 is the same as between 35 and 36. Many marketing research questionnaires use interval scales to measure attitudes and opinions. An interval measure indicates how much difference there is between observations. In interval scales there is no *fixed* zero point. If such a point appears on a scale it is arbitrary, as are the units of measurement. The Celsius and Fahrenheit temperature scales are examples of measures with arbitrary zero points. Because of this we cannot perform division or multiplication on the data. We could not, for example, say that 4°C is twice as hot as 2°C.

Ratio

Unlike interval measures, ratio measures have a fixed and absolute zero point. Ratio measures have all the properties of nominal, ordinal and interval measures also. Therefore it is possible to classify objects, rank them, and compare differences. However, because of the fixed zero point we would be able to claim that an observation at point 14 on the scale is seven times as large as an observation at point 2. These ratio calculations are not possible with interval measures. Whereas only addition and subtraction are possible on interval data, multiplication and division become possible on ratio data. Customer expenditure is measured on a ratio scale, as are age, weight and height. Ratio data would enable us to claim that a customer paying $150 for a room spent twice as much as a customer paying $75.

Developing measurements

The process of developing measurements is not always straightforward. There are some well-established measures for common variables. We measure length in metres, weight in kilograms, temperatures in degrees Celsius. Even here, though, there are conflicting traditions with the Imperial measures of feet and inches, pounds and ounces, and degrees Fahrenheit. Measurement becomes problematic where we want to measure variables which are not blessed with well-known, established and undisputed metrics. For example, if we want to measure job-related stress, quality, customer satisfaction, absenteeism, empathy or any number of other abstract variables, we might have to search the literature for measures which have been developed in the past, or may even have to develop a new measure. Measures can be developed for any variable, no matter how abstract or contentious, if the researcher follows the four-step process shown in Table 12.1.

Nominal definition

The first step is to define what it is we are trying to measure. If we are studying the impact of service quality on customer satisfaction, we have to *nominally define* what we mean by these terms. Service, quality, customer and satisfaction are the four concepts which the researcher must delimit. They are not scientific expressions like effort or volume; they do not have unambiguous meanings. Most social scientific concepts suffer from this multiplicity of meanings.

Table 12.1   Developing measurements

1. Nominal definition
↓
2. Operationalization
↓
3. Developing indicators
↓
4. Evaluating indicators

Isolating a particular meaning for a concept can in itself be a lengthy process. The first task is to develop a census of definitions of the concept. These may be derived from everyday discourse or from the specialized discourses of scientific, religious or any other community. For example, the concept 'attitude' is used in a traditional sense to mean angle of inclination. The Tower of Pisa has an attitude. In everyday English, attitude is construed as feelings. For some social psychologists attitude is more closely identified with beliefs than feelings. Researchers need to understand that the meaning of a concept lies in its use. They need to decide how the term is to be used in their research. Having inventoried the definitions, the next task is to decide which one to use. This is easier said than done, because in practice this decision is one which often emerges during the process of data collection and analysis. For example, a researcher investigating the relationship between job-related stress and absenteeism may find that absenteeism is construed by focus group participants as being not just confined to no-shows for work. It may also include certain behaviours such as arriving late, leaving early, and taking lengthy breaks.

Nominal definitions are important because they delimit the scope of the research. They establish boundaries and make the research do-able. By themselves, however, they are not sufficient for the development of measurements.

Operationalization

With concepts nominally defined, the researcher must now operationally define, or *operationalize*, the concepts. Operationalization respecifies the concepts in terms which make them measurable and testable. The first task in this process is to identify a number of dimensions of the concept. Most concepts are multidimensional. A thorough operationalization would reveal the full dimensionality of the variable. Researchers sometimes do not investigate all dimensions of the concept but limit themselves to more important or more relevant dimensions. The concept 'satisfaction', for example, could be operationally defined to possess a number of dimensions: feelings, beliefs, behaviour. A researcher could, though need not, limit herself to studying only the behavioural content of satisfaction. As variables become operationalized they become progressively less abstract. Having defined satisfaction as a three-dimensional concept (perhaps better called a construct), one of which is behaviour, the researcher might ask what we mean by behaviour. This might again be dimensionalized into volitional and non-volitional behaviours; or, differently, into behavioural intention and behavioural performance. Operationalization requires researchers to find ways of classifying or categorizing the dimensional attributes of concepts. The process of classifying imposes structure on what might otherwise be chaos.

Developing indicators

Having operationalized the concept, the next step is to *develop indicators* which might conceivably be employed to measure the variable. For example, a researcher investigating the behavioural dimension of customer satisfaction might list a number of potential indicators: actual repurchase, intention to repurchase, positive word-of-mouth, negative word-of-mouth, complaints. The two main issues facing researchers are how many indicators to employ, and how to develop the chosen indicators.

There is no clear-cut answer to the question of numbers of indicators. There are many published measurement scales which can be readily adopted by researchers. For example, the *Marketing Scales Handbook* (Bruner and Hensel, 1992) lists 588 scales with a history of use. If a published scale fits the task then the researcher could employ the scale as it is. At other times, some indicators may need to be added, omitted or edited to ensure relevance to the research objective and context of use. Such changes do affect the reliability and validity of the published scale which then needs to be reassessed (see next section). Where a new set of indicators is being developed for a new concept, the researcher might find it helpful to develop a number of sets of indicators for different operationalizations of the concept. The data they produce can then be analyzed to see which is the most useful set of indicators (and operationalization) for the purposes of the research.

The number of indicators tends to co-vary with the number of dimensions of the concept. A researcher investigating affective, cognitive and behavioural dimensions of satisfaction will clearly employ more indicators than a researcher focusing on behaviours alone. The more complex the concept the more indicators are employed. The number of indicators can be reduced through careful piloting of the instrument. Finally, administrative issues such as budget, time and measurement instrument length (e.g. questionnaire) might impact on the number of indicators.

The general rule is to use only those indicators that are necessary to measure the dimensions of the concept of interest to the researcher.

There are generally three ways of developing the indicators. First, it may be possible to adopt indicators with a history of use. There is no contention about measuring weight in kilograms. Measurement of more abstract social scientific concepts may require a deeper examination of the published literature to find an appropriate set of indicators, which often take the form of scale items listed within questionnaires. Apart from economy, these scales have further benefits. The data they generate add to a body of knowledge about the value of the instrument. Further, the results can be compared with other applications of the instrument.

If extant indicators are inadequate, the researcher will have to generate new indicators. The raw material for these is often generated in focus groups. A skilled group moderator will be able to manage group dynamics to identify indicators. If a focus group is inappropriate or difficult to assemble, then the third means of generating indicators can be employed: in-depth interviews with individual informants. For example, a researcher investigating sexual harassment in a commercial kitchen environment might want to interview potential victims privately, rather than opt for a focus group. Far more indicators than are finally employed are typically produced in focus groups and in-depth interviews. Churchill's (1979) methodological contribution to the development of the *SERVQUAL* (service quality) measurement instrument is a useful case illustration of how to generate a large number of indicators and then reduce them to a workable number.

Evaluating indicators

The final step in developing measurements is to evaluate the indicators. Researchers want to have confidence in their measurements. Confidence is reflected in the measuring instrument's ability to generate valid and reliable data. Validity addresses the issue of whether what is measured is actually what the researcher intends to measure. One would not measure satisfaction in kilograms! Sometimes it can be very difficult to obtain valid data. For instance, if a researcher wanted to investigate sexual harassment in a kitchen environment, the most valid form of data would be obtained from direct observation. However, researchers may elect to use self-report data instead, asking respondents to answer a number of indicative questions. These data are almost certainly less valid. Reliability is concerned with the consistency of the data. A highly reliable measure gives the same results over time and place. A metre rule printed on elastic tape would yield unreliable data!

An exemplary measuring instrument satisfies four validity criteria (Table 12.2). These are discussed from the perspective of items in questionnaires.

Face validity is the least demanding standard. Here, the concern is whether the instrument appears to measure what it is intended to measure. Normally researchers will want to make transparent the concepts they are investigating. Sometimes, however, they will actually want to conceal the issues, particularly if they are sensitive. Low face validity is often associated with an instrument's lack of relevance to a sample of respondents. Being socially constructed, concepts are culturally and historically situated. They do not always travel well. For example, an instrument developed in a Korean context would not necessarily make sense translated into English, unless the concepts and their dimensionality were common to both cultures. Similarly, an instrument devised for a well-educated group of hospitality researchers would make little sense to a group of nursery school children. Some questions which have face validity are unlikely to yield valid responses, for example 'Have you ever sexually harassed any of your subordinates?'.

Content validity is a somewhat more demanding standard. The concern here is whether the instrument measures all appropriate and relevant dimensions of the concept. Does it cover the entire domain? A survey into customer perceptions of the quality of hotel service which examined only the technical side of service quality would miss out on the important issue of functional quality. Technical quality is concerned with *what* service is delivered; functional quality is concerned with *how* that service is delivered. As such it is concerned with issues of attentiveness, courtesy, empathy and responsiveness. These are important components of the domain of service quality.

Criterion validity is concerned with how well the measure predicts some related behaviour or performance on some conceptually related measure. For example, a recruiter might develop a test which assesses job applicants' knowledge of hygiene regulations with a view to eliminating the risk of food-poisoning. This test would have high criterion validity if it were predictive of a reduction in alleged incidences of food-poisoning. Allegations of food-poisoning are the criterion variable. Similarly, if we

Table 12.2 Types of validity

Type	Issue
Face validity	Does the instrument appear to measure what it intends to measure?
Content validity	Does the instrument measure all dimensions of the concept?
Criterion validity	Are the data generated predictive of scores on a related variable?
Construct validity	Does the instrument satisfy theoretical expectations?

theorized that customer evaluations of service quality were linked to customer satisfaction, and measures of service quality perceptions and satisfaction were indeed highly correlated, then we could say that each measure enjoyed criterion validity from the perspective of the other.

Criterion validity takes two forms: concurrent and predictive validity. Concurrent validity would be present if two different instruments designed to measure the same concept were administered simultaneously and found to be highly correlated. Similarly, if scores on a set of indicators were predictive of the possession of some attribute (e.g. high scores on an aptitude test correlate with length of job tenure) then this would be evidence of concurrent validity. Predictive validity takes a forward-looking perspective, as in the food-poisoning example cited above.

Construct validity is the most demanding form of validity. The researcher's concern is with the theoretical substantiveness of the measure. If it works, why does it work? If it does not, why not? How does it perform against measures of theoretically related constructs? For example, one would expect that scores on a sociability index would correlate positively with scores on a gregariousness instrument. If they do not, then one or the other is probably theoretically unsound.

There are three forms of construct validity. Convergent validity is the degree to which newly developed measures of a construct correlate with established measures of the same construct. If the nominal definitions were the same, the operationalizations the same but the indicators different, one would expect there to be a high level of correlation between the scores obtained by both measures. However, if an existing measure is criticized for its lack of content validity it is unlikely that the developers of a new scale would seek convergent validity with it. Discriminant validity is the degree to which a measure does not correlate with other measures from which it is meant to differ. We would not expect to find meaningful correlations between brand equity valuations and hours of daylight. Nomological validity is the degree to which a measure correlates in theoretically predicted ways with other related measures. We might expect to find a substantial degree of correlation between the measures of brand equity and advertising expenditure, but not between brand equity and the number of computers owned by the company.

The reliability of a measure is the second major evaluative question facing researchers. Reliability is an indication of a measure's freedom from random error. Reliability is high when the same instrument administered in different circumstances produces the same results. Reliability equates to consistency. Only if there are changes in the variable being measured should the indicators generate different results. Reliability tests take three forms: test–retest reliability, alternative-forms reliability and split-half reliability (see Table 2.3).

In *test–retest* reliability, measures are taken at different points in time. For example, a sample may complete a questionnaire once, and again four weeks later. Any changes in response patterns or scores must be attributable to changes in the phenomenon being measured, not to poor reliability of the measurement. The higher the correlation between measures the higher the level of reliability. In general the longer the time interval, the lower the reliability. One major problem with this form of reliability test is that it can be prone to systematic error. The first measurement may alert the respondents to the issue being measured so that they become more sensitive to it during the period between tests. Respondents may also try to remember their first set of answers. Finally,

Table 12.3 Types of reliability

Type	Issue
Test–retest method	Do successive applications of the measure to the same sample produce the same results?
Alternative-forms method	Do two equivalent forms of the measure administered to the same sample produce the same results?
Split-half method	Are the scores obtained from one half of the measurement items the same as the scores produced from the other?

it is not always feasible to employ the test–retest method, for example, when using a measure to evaluate initial reactions to an advertising campaign. For these reasons the test–retest method is usually employed with other approaches.

In *alternative-forms* reliability, two equivalent forms of the instrument are developed (perhaps the question order in a questionnaire is altered). These are presented to the same subjects at different points in time. The higher the correlation between the scores the higher the reliability.

Unlike the foregoing two tests of reliability which are concerned with external reliability, the *split-half test* is concerned with internal reliability. It is used when testing the reliability of a summated rating scale where scores on several items are aggregated to produce a single measurement of the variable. For example, a stress indicator may employ 100 items to produce a single score. These 100 items would be split in half (say odd and even numbers, or on the basis of some other rationale) and the degree of correlation between the aggregate scores in each half measured. A convenient way of measuring split-half reliability is to employ Cronbach's alpha (α). The computerized procedure produces an average coefficient of all possible split-half combinations of the items. Alpha ranges from 0 to 1. Alphas below 0.65 are normally regarded as indicative of an unreliable instrument.

This four-step process of nominal definition (conceptualization), operationalization, development of indicators and evaluation of indicators has been presented in a stream of linear text. Research life is not like that. Should the evaluations of the selected indicators suggest that the chosen concept has been operationalized with inadequate rigour, then an iterative process is likely to begin. The concept may need to be redefined and new indicators sought.

Measurements in the hospitality industry

This part of the chapter illustrates some of these principles of measurement as they have been expressed in the hospitality industry. Published work cited here should not necessarily be taken as examples of best or even good practice. They are illustrative only.

Measurements used by hospitality researchers

All four levels of measurement—nominal, ordinal, interval and ratio—are employed in hospitality research. Here are some examples. Tas, Spalding and Getty (1989) employed gender—a *nominal* variable—to evaluate whether job satisfaction varied between male and female hospitality employees. Clements and Josiam (1995) used an *ordinal* scale to measure the psychological construct 'involvement'. The three points on the scale were low involvement, medium involvement and high involvement. Borchgrevink and Boster (1994) employed seven different batteries of *interval*-scaled items in their examination of superior–subordinate relationships. They applied to these batteries a five-point Likert scale ranging from strongly agree to strongly disagree. Morgan and Dev (1994) used a number of *ratio* scales in their research into competitive marketing strategies—the number of business nights sold per annum, the number of business trips made per annum and the room rate paid. All of these have a fixed zero point and allow for the computation of ratios.

Development of measurements

What is clear from a survey of the hospitality research literature is that very little by way of development of innovative measures has taken place. For the most part, either researchers have adopted measures which have a proven history of application in other contexts and have a satisfactory level of reliability and validity, or they have modified established instruments for application in the hospitality area.

Pizam and Neumann (1988) investigated the effect of task characteristics on hospitality employee job satisfaction and burnout. Rather than developing new instruments, they employed, without modification, the established JDS or Job Diagnostic Survey (Hackman and Oldham, 1975, 1976) and the MBI or Maslach Burnout Inventory (Maslach and Jackson, 1981). In Pizam and Neumann's (1988: 100, 101) words, the JDS 'has shown acceptable levels of stability, convergent validity and discriminant validity' and the sub-scales employed in the MBI 'have shown high levels of reliabilities [*sic*] and convergent and discriminant validity.'

By way of contrast, Knutson *et al.* (1990) have modified the well-established *SERVQUAL* model of service quality measurement for application in the lodging industry. *SERVQUAL* was developed by Parasuraman, Zeithaml and Berry (1986) and was claimed to provide a generic framework for measuring customer expectations and perceptions of service quality along five dimensions—reliability, assurance, tangibles, empathy and responsiveness (known by their initials as RATER). Knutson's adaptation, dubbed *LODGSERV*, simply adapted the wording of the original interval-scale items comprising the *SERVQUAL* scale. Knutson *et al.* (1990: 278) comment that 'since the intent of each question was maintained, the content validity of *LODGSERV* is assumed.' *LODGSERV* has achieved an overall reliability coefficient (α) of 0.92. The same team has now developed an instrument for measuring service quality in a food service context. This is branded *DINESERV* (Knutson, Stevens and Patton, 1995).

Getty and Thompson (1994) are an exception to the rule. They provide evidence of having carefully followed a process for the development of a reliable and valid instrument for measuring quality perceptions within the context of the hospitality industry. Their process was modelled on Churchill's (1979) recommendations and comprised seven stages (Table 12.4). Getty and Thompson's domain of interest was quality. As they noted, 'much confusion still exists when it comes to defining and operationalizing quality' (Getty and Thompson, 1994: 75). Through this process, which is much more rigorous than the method Knutson *et al.* (1990) followed when developing

Table 12.4 Steps in scale development process

1. Specify domain
↓
2. Generate sample of items
↓
3. Collect first data set
↓
4. Purify measure
↓
5. Collect second data set
↓
6. Assess reliability
↓
7. Assess validity

LODGSERV, Getty and Thompson devised a 25-item interval scale. These items represent three underlying dimensions—tangibility, reliability and contact—which have reliability coefficients (α) of 0.91, 0.84 and 0.97 respectively.

Getty and Thompson (1994) identified two main classes of definition of quality: producer-oriented and customer-oriented. The former focus on compliance to specification, the latter on meeting customer expectations. They discuss the problems of defining quality in a market such as hospitality where intangibility of service poses such a problem to measurement. They nominally defined quality as 'the consumer's global judgement, or attitude, relating to the perceived superiority of the lodging service provided by a given property' (Getty and Thompson, 1994: 81). They then generated a pool of possible scale items. These were obtained from the literature, case studies, and interviews with customers and hospitality management. A group of judges then examined the 68-item pool to establish whether or not they covered the domain and therefore possessed face and content validity. The pool was then administered to a group of student respondents who were asked to report their perceptions of the quality of a recent hotel experience.

The data so obtained were analyzed following steps recommended by Parasuraman, Zeithaml and Berry (1988) in order to identify redundant and less relevant items. This involved calculating Cronbach's alpha coefficient for all 68 items, computing item-to-total correlations and conducting a principal components factor analysis. This resulted in a shorter instrument comprising 28 items. The reduced scale was then administered to a fresh sample and the same analysis repeated. This check on reliability and dimensionality identified three more weak items. These were eliminated from the battery. The final battery was subjected to face, content, criterion and construct validity checks. Scores on the itemized battery correlated very highly with the single-item measure: 'How would you rate the overall quality of the property?'. The final measure, now dubbed *LODGQUAL*, is the outcome of a process designed to produce a reliable and valid measure.

Conclusions

Measurement is central to the conduct of hospitality research. Without precise measurement knowledge is precarious. Hospitality researchers employ a wide variety of measures—nominal, ordinal, interval and ratio. More often than not these measures are developed, piloted and proven in different contexts. Hospitality researchers rely on developmental efforts in the more established physical and social sciences. Adoption of these measures is frequently undertaken without due regard to the original context of their development and their relevance to the context of application.

Issues of validity and reliability are critical in the development and application of measures, yet the vast majority of published hospitality research provides no evidence of either. In the face of such weakness, data integrity becomes fragile and the decisions managers take, based upon those data, are of questionable merit. Good measures enable good research to be done which in turn enables good decisions to be made. Hospitality researchers have some way to go.

References

Borchgrevink, C. and Boster, F.J. (1994) Leader–member exchange: a test of the measurement model. *Hospitality Research Journal* **17**(3), 75–100.

Bruner II, G.C. and Hensel, P.J. (1992) *Marketing Scales Handbook: A Compilation of Multi-item Measures*. Chicago, IL: American Marketing Association.

Churchill, G.A. (1979) A paradigm for developing better measures of marketing constructs. *Journal of Marketing Research* **16**, February, 64–73.

Clements, C.J. and Josiam, B. (1995) Role of involvement in the travel decision. *Journal of Vacation Marketing* **1**(4), September, 337–347.

Getty, J.M. and Thompson, K.N. (1994) A procedure for scaling perceptions of lodging quality. *Hospitality Research Journal* **18**(2), 75–96.

Hackman, J.R. and Oldham, G.R. (1975) Development of the Job Diagnostic Survey. *Journal of Applied Psychology* **6**, 159–170.

Hackman, J.R. and Oldham, G.R. (1976) Motivation through the design of work: tests of a theory. *Organizational Behaviour and Human Performance* **16**, 250–279.

Knutson, B., Stevens, P., Wullaert, C., Patton, M. and Yokoyama, F. (1990) *LODGSERV*: a service quality index for the lodging industry. *Hospitality Research Journal* **14**(2), 277–284.

Knutson, B., Stevens, P. and Patton, M. (1995) *DINESERV*: measuring service quality in quick service, casual/theme and fine dining restaurants. *Journal of Hospitality and Leisure Marketing* **14**(2), 277–284.

Maslach, C. and Jackson, S.E. (1981) The measurement of experienced burnout. *Journal of Occupational Behaviour* **2**, 99–113.

Morgan, M.S. and Dev, C.S. (1994) Defining competitive sets of hotel brands through analysis of customer brand switching. *Journal of Hospitality and Leisure Marketing*, **2**, 2, 57–91.

Parasuraman, A., Zeithaml, V.A. and Berry, L.L. (1986) *SERVQUAL*: a multi-item scale for measuring customer perceptions of service quality. Working paper, Marketing Science Institute, Cambridge, MA.

Parasuraman, A., Zeithaml, V.A. and Berry, L.L. (1988) *SERVQUAL*: a multiple-item scale for measuring customer perceptions of service quality. *Journal of Retailing* **64**(1), 12–40.

Pizam, A. and Neumann, Y. (1988) The effect of task characteristics on hospitality employees' job satisfaction and burnout. *Hospitality Education and Research Journal* **12**(2), 99–105.

Stephens, S.S. (1951) Mathematics, measurement and psychophysics. In S.S. Stephens (ed.), *Handbook of Experimental Psychology*, New York: Wiley.

Tas, R.F., Spalding, J.B. and Getty, J. (1989) Employee job satisfaction determinants within a national restaurant company. *Hospitality Education and Research Journal* **13**(3), 129–136.

13 Sampling

NIGEL HEMMINGTON

The concept of sampling

In much business and organisational research it is impractical, in terms of cost or time, to test or interview whole target populations. For example, if we were investigating the dining-out behaviour of the adult population of Australia it is extremely unlikely that we would have the resources to interview the whole population. Similarly, in operational situations such as food production, it is rarely practical to test all the items produced, even if for no other reason than the commercial need to sell some of them!

For these reasons researchers usually select a sample of the population from which inferences about the whole population can be made. This sampling approach is not unusual in everyday life and is certainly not restricted to research. For example, when taking a shower it is normal to sample the temperature of the water with the hand before bathing. In the hospitality industry chefs constantly sample sauces through tasting. It is also common for customers to 'sample' food and drink, particularly wine, through tastings on the reasonable assumption, and expectation, that the samples will reflect the general quality of the product.

In research a similar approach is adopted. Rather than test or survey the whole population, a smaller number is selected as representative of the whole and it is from this sample that the researcher hopes to make inferences about the whole population. In the examples given above this is relatively easy because the populations (i.e. the water, the wine or the sauce) are homogeneous and all samples are the same and, therefore, are representative of the population as a whole. In these situations almost any sample could be taken to end up with results that reflect the wider population characteristics. Indeed a sample of one could be taken and it would still be representative. The issues of sampling method and sampling size are not, therefore, important in these examples and the haphazard sampling of single elements is usually acceptable.

In social scientific research, including research in hospitality management, homogeneous populations are rare and the challenge becomes one of selecting a sample that reflects the heterogeneity of the population in question. This is called representativeness and is more fully discussed in the section below. The need for representative samples of heterogeneous populations means that issues of how the sample is selected and the size of the sample become fundamental to successful research. Generalisations about the population on the basis of sample data can only be made

The Handbook of Contemporary Hospitality Management Research, Edited by Bob Brotherton.
© 1999 John Wiley & Sons Ltd.

where that sample and the data derived from it closely match the actual population in question.

In many business and management situations, therefore, the use of samples, as opposed to testing the whole population, offers advantages in terms of time, costs and logistics. Indeed it has even been argued that investigating a sample rather than a whole population is possibly more reliable because the errors associated with large volumes of data collection and processing are less likely (Zikmund, 1994; Sekaran, 1992). It is interesting to note, however, that governments continue to conduct national censuses clearly in the belief that the quality of the data generated justifies the enormous cost of administration. Indeed, where populations are very small and it is economically viable to survey the whole population it is advisable to do so. For example, in a study of employee attitudes in a small hotel with only 30 staff, there would be little point in trying to create a representative sample when surveying all the staff is clearly viable. In most business research, however, large and heterogeneous populations make sampling essential to economic viability.

Figure 13.1 shows the main steps in the sampling process. This figure also illustrates the fact that sampling is only part of any research approach and that it depends upon the clear identification of research objectives (research question) and the development of an appropriate research methodology to achieve those research objectives. Sampling then feeds into the research method by facilitating the effective and efficient gathering of data. The following sections of this chapter discuss the key issues in sampling applied to hospitality management research.

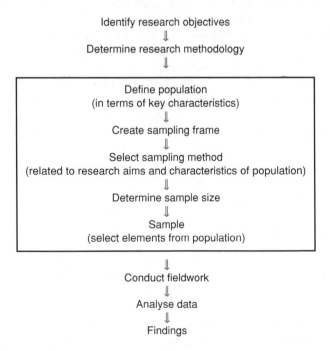

Figure 13.1   The sampling process

Some sampling terminology

Before investigating the key issues of sampling it is important that the terminology is discussed and clarified. The *population*, sometimes referred to as the *universe*, is the entire group of things being researched; it could be made up of people (customers, employees, etc.), things (hotels, restaurants, companies, etc.) or events (accidents, interviews, sales, etc.). Although these two terms are generally accepted to be synonymous, some texts distinguish between them on the basis of whether the group is finite (population) or infinite (universe).

A precise definition of the population is important. Although it will normally be determined by the focus of the research, it is important that the researcher specifies exactly what is, and what is not, included in the study. In looking at the attitudes of hotel customers, for example, the researcher would need to be clear whether the study is limited to existing customers or whether it includes all potential customers and, if it does, potential customers from where (the world or specified areas)? These considerations will clearly have implications for the definition of the population and the development of the sampling frame (discussed below).

The population will be made up of individual items which are referred to as *elements*. As discussed above, the elements could be people, things or events depending on the nature of the research. All the elements of a population will however, share, characteristics or criteria that are relevant to the study. Although the population may in fact be made up of different types of elements, a study looking at equipment usage in a kitchen, for example, may include a wide variety of types of equipment, but they would all share the key characteristic of being part of the kitchen.

A *census* is where all elements of the population are tested, surveyed or investigated. It results in an enumeration, that is, a total count of items. An example of this approach arises where national governments periodically conduct censuses of the country's population. In the UK the Office of Population Censuses and Surveys carries out the Census of Population every 10 years. A *sample* is a selected sub-group of the population designed for a specific research purpose and from which estimates of population characteristics are made.

In order to select a sample it is necessary to identify all the elements of the population being investigated. The list of these population elements is called the *sampling frame*. Sometimes there already exists a convenient list of elements that can be used. In a study of hospitality management students at a particular university, it would be relatively easy to generate a sampling frame from university records. Equally, a sampling frame of a hotel company's employees should be relatively easily created from the company's personnel records. In general, however, the creation of complete sampling frames that include all eligible members of the population is often more difficult than might be expected; see, for example, the problems faced by Ryan and Barnett (1995) in their study of conference hotels in New Zealand. Even existing lists may not reflect recent changes in the population; and in situations where there is no list available it is usually necessary to create a sampling frame from a range of sources such as telephone directories, mailing lists, guides and so on. Nevertheless, despite the researcher's best efforts in trying to create a complete list of elements, there is always likely to be some degree of discrepancy between the true population and the sampling frame. This discrepancy is the first potential source of error in the sample. Indeed, in recognising the potential problems of creating an adequate sampling frame researchers sometimes adjust the definition of the population (where it will not compromise the key focus of the research) to allow for the use of an existing list.

While the individual items in the population are called elements, the items in the sample are called *subjects*. In most approaches to sampling individuals and organisations there will be a proportion of the sample that fails to respond; those that do take part, however, are usually referred to as *respondents*.

The values of variables generated from the sample are called *statistics* whilst the true values in the population are referred to as *parameters*. Thus, in a study looking at the average marketing spend of restaurant companies in the USA, the estimate of mean percentage spend generated from the sample is a statistic and the true value in the population, which could be established through a census, is a parameter.

Representativeness and bias

The major challenge in sampling is to select a sample that mirrors as closely as possible the key characteristics of the population in question. This should then enable the sample to be used to make estimates or inferences about the population. The extent to which the sample matches the population is called representativeness. As discussed earlier, when populations are homogeneous it is relatively easy to create representative samples; indeed where a population is perfectly homogeneous a sample of one will provide accurate data about the population (e.g. taking blood tests for medical purposes). When populations are heterogeneous, however, the creation of representative samples is much more challenging.

In social scientific research heterogeneous samples are the norm and it is very difficult to make the sample exactly match the population. There are likely, therefore, to be differences between the sample statistics and the population parameters. For example, the sample mean will not be exactly the same as the population mean and the sample standard deviation is likely to be different from the population standard deviation. The extent to which the sample characteristics and the population characteristics differ is called *bias*. The whole process of selecting a sample is concerned with minimising bias and maximising representativeness. This requires the sample to be chosen very carefully using the appropriate methods as discussed below.

Statistical inference

It is possible to categorise sampling methods into two broad groups: probability sampling and non-probability sampling. In probability sampling each element in the population has a known non-zero probability of selection. Probability sampling methods are usually based on the principles of random sampling where each element has an equal probability of being selected. Where random sampling methods are used it is possible to apply the principles of statistical sampling theory to make inferences about the population parameters from the sample statistics.

The characteristics of many populations, such as weight and height, generally follow a *normal distribution*. The shape of this distribution is such that most items are located around the population mean (μ) and fewer items are located at the extremes above and below the mean, i.e. in terms of height there are relatively few people who are very tall or very short, most people being of average (mean) height (see Figure 13.2).

When a random sample is selected from a population it is hoped that it will be representative of the population; ideally, the sample distribution will reflect the population distribution and the sample mean will be the same as the population mean. In practice the mean is extremely unlikely to be exactly the same as the population mean. Indeed, if another sample were taken and its mean calculated it would almost certainly give a different value for the mean, despite the fact that the population mean is still the same. The question then arises: how close is any one sample mean likely to be to the actual population mean? The answer lies in the fact that it can be estimated that the population mean lies within a certain distance (interval) of the sample mean; this distance is called the *sampling error*.

If further random samples were to be taken from the same population, more means could be calculated until eventually another distribution could be plotted. This distribution is called the sampling distribution of the sample mean. With a large number of means this will also follow a normal distribution; it will have a mean ($\bar{x}$) equal to the population mean (μ) and its standard deviation (s) will equal the population standard deviation (σ) divided by the number in the sample (n). The standard deviation of the sampling distribution of the sample mean is usually called the *standard error* ($S_{\bar{x}}$), the formula for which is shown below. Interestingly, the sampling distribution of the sample mean will be a normal distribution irrespective of whether the population itself is normally distributed.

$$S_{\bar{x}} = \frac{\sigma}{\sqrt{n}}$$

The fact that the sampling distribution of the sample mean forms a normal distribution is very useful because a lot is known about the normal distribution. For example, with large samples (more than 30) it is known that 95% of the distribution lies within ±1.96 standard deviations of the mean and that 99% of the distribution lies within ±2.576 standard deviations of the mean. Thus, for the distribution of the sample means, 95% of them will lie within ±1.96 standard errors of the population mean. This provides an answer to the earlier question about how close the sample mean is likely to be to the

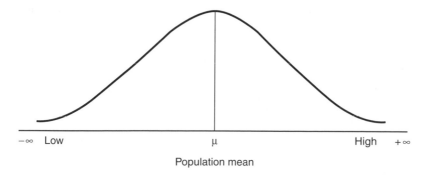

Figure 13.2   The normal distribution

population mean in the form of *confidence intervals*. At the 95% level of confidence the true population mean (μ) will lie within 1.96 standard errors of the sample mean ($\bar{x}$), as shown below:

$$\mu = \bar{x} \pm 1.96 \frac{\sigma}{\sqrt{n}}$$

The problem here, however, is that it is unlikely that the population standard deviation (σ) will be known. As a compromise the sample standard deviation (s) is used:

$$\mu = \bar{x} \pm 1.96 \frac{s}{\sqrt{n}}$$

Similarly, at the 99% level of confidence the true population mean (μ) will lie within 2.576 standard errors of the sample mean ($\bar{x}$) as shown below (again substituting s for σ);

$$\mu = \bar{x} \pm 2.576 \frac{s}{\sqrt{n}}$$

In these examples the *sampling error* is 1.96 $s/\sqrt{n}$ for the 95% level of confidence and 2.576 $s/\sqrt{n}$ for the 99% level of confidence. It is worth noting that as the level of confidence is increased the sampling error becomes larger and the confidence interval becomes wider. Thus the estimation of the population mean is less precise. This clearly illustrates the trade-off between confidence and precision. As confidence is increased the precision is reduced and vice versa.

Sampling methods

The various approaches to selecting samples can be divided into two broad groups: probability sampling and non-probability sampling. The characteristic of probability sampling is that all elements in the population have a known chance of being selected; random sampling is the most commonly used method of this type. Probability sampling methods are used where representativeness is required for generalisability to the wider population. These methods are appropriate for the application of statistical techniques as discussed above and as such are most closely allied, although not exclusively, to quantitative research methods.

In non-probability sampling the elements have an unknown probability of being selected, and selection is usually based on the researcher's judgement and expertise. In these approaches the use of statistical techniques for measuring random sampling error is not appropriate. These techniques are frequently used, although not exclusively, for qualitative research.

Probability sampling

Probability sampling methods are based on processes of random selection. As stated earlier, in probability sampling all elements in the population have a known and greater than zero chance of being selected. It should be remembered, however, that random sample selection is a formal and scientific process and does not mean an unplanned, haphazard approach to sampling.

Simple random sampling   Simple random sampling is probably the most common form of sample selection. It is sometimes referred to as unrestricted probability sampling. The principle of simple random sampling is that each element of the population has a known and equal probability, greater than zero, of being selected. To select a sample of 10 hotels from a population of 100, in random sampling each hotel would have a 10/100, or 1/10, chance of being selected. This approach is similar to a lottery or a raffle where each ticket has an equal chance of being selected. Indeed, a random sample could be drawn from a hat if all the tickets were mixed well and it was ensured that in drawing tickets there was no tendency to select from the top, the bottom or the sides of the hat. Other approaches could be used such as dice, a spinner or even a roulette wheel; but the key point is that all elements must have the same chance of selection.

In practice it is more usual for random samples to be selected using random number tables or computer-generated random numbers. The same number of random numbers is selected as the desired sample size and these numbers are then used as the basis of selecting elements from the sampling frame.

This approach to sampling should theoretically lead to the least bias, especially when large samples are used, and it offers the greatest generalisability to the original population. It is, however, rather laborious for large samples and there is the statistical possibility that important population characteristics may not be appropriately represented in a random sample. Other probability sampling approaches are designed to address these issues.

Systematic random sampling   Systematic random sampling is designed to make random sampling less laborious when large samples are being selected. The approach is based on selecting n elements from the population N. A sampling interval k is calculated as follows:

$$k = \frac{\text{Population size } (N)}{\text{Sample size } (n)}$$

A random number is then chosen between 1 and k and every kth item is selected through the sampling frame $n-1$ times. As an example, selecting a sample of 30 (n) fast-food restaurants from a population of 270 (N) would give a sampling interval (k) of 9 (270/30). If the selected random number is 4 then the fourth item in the sampling frame would be chosen and then every ninth item, 29 times (i.e. the 4th, 13th, 22nd, 31st, ... , 265th), creating a sample of 30 fast-food restaurants.

Although this approach is not strictly random, it will produce a random sample if the sampling frame is itself random. However, if the sampling frame exhibits any signs of patterns, called periodicity, these patterns could be reflected in the sample and there is a danger of systematic bias in the sample. As a very simple example, a sampling frame that lists men and women alternately could lead to a systematic random sample made up of either all men or all women, depending on whether the initial random number and the sampling interval are odd or even. If staff are listed according to the days of the week they work, sampling every seventh (or multiple of 7) day would lead to the same day being chosen throughout the sample. Clearly, this is likely to create problems and should be avoided either through restructuring the sampling frame, perhaps by alphabetical order of surname, or by using another sampling technique (simple random sampling).

In practice, however, periodicity in sampling frames is rare. Lists of people or things are usually in alphabetical order and this is very unlikely to lead to periodicity. Nevertheless, researchers should be aware of the possibility of bias arising out of periodicity and should check their sampling frames for patterns that could affect the sample.

Bojanic (1996) adopted systematic random sampling, using the local telephone directory as his sampling frame, in his study of smoking bans in restaurants in Massachusetts, USA. He was particularly concerned about the potential for bias arising from this technique combined with non-response rates. His analysis of the sample compared with government demographic statistics indicated few significant differences between the two.

Stratified sampling   Where populations have important characteristics in known proportions, such as age, sex or social class, these characteristics can be built into the sample to increase representativeness and therefore precision. Stratified sampling is an approach where the population is initially broken down into a number of mutually exclusive groups, or strata, which reflect the known characteristics of the population. Elements are then randomly selected from within these groups.

Where the proportion selected (sampling fraction) is the same for all the groups, each group will be correctly represented in the final sample, i.e. in the same proportion as in the population. This is called *proportionate stratified sampling*. By reflecting proportions in the population, stratified sampling reduces the role of chance in selecting the sample and should improve precision by reducing the standard error. Total variation in any population is made up of variation between groups (strata) and variance within groups. In proportionate stratified sampling variation between groups is removed from the standard error by the fact that it is already represented in the sample. Therefore, the standard error includes only variation within groups. Thus, the challenge in stratifying populations is to use criteria where most of the variation is between groups and the groups themselves are as homogeneous as possible.

As a simple example, imagine an investigation into environmental issues in the hotel industry. In terms of environmental management location is likely to be an important issue and the sample should reflect the locational structure of the industry. If it were known that of the 150 hotels in the population, 70 are located in urban areas, 50 are located in rural areas, 10 are located in national parks and 20 are located in resorts, the sample could be designed to reflect this structure. If it had been decided to select a sample of 30 hotels, this would represent 20% of the population and this sampling fraction could be applied to each of the different types of hotels as follows:

	Population	Sample
Urban hotels	70	14
Rural hotels	50	10
Resort hotels	20	4
Park hotels	10	2
Total	150	30

This then produces a sample that reflects that the structure of the population and any statistics that are generated should more closely reflect the true population values. Thus, proportionate stratified sampling should produce greater precision than simple random sampling as long as the criteria for stratification are relevant to the study and sampling within groups is random.

The hotel example above illustrates a problem with proportionate stratified sampling. The smaller groups such as the resort and national park hotels can produce very small sub-samples which may be too small for analysis. Where analysis of sub-groups is important to the research this is clearly a major problem. In these situations a more appropriate approach would be *disproportionate stratified sampling* which ensures adequate numbers of subjects in all sub-groups.

A second reason for using disproportionate stratified sampling is where some groups are more variable than others. The later section on sample size shows how variability is an important aspect in determining the size of the sample. Where some groups are more variable than others, therefore, it may be necessary to increase the size of these groups to ensure that their greater variability is represented in the sample.

Cluster sampling   A problem with the sampling techniques discussed so far is that they can lead to very dispersed samples that are not economically viable. A study looking at restaurants in the USA may find that any of the above techniques leads to a sample that includes restaurants as widely spread as Alaska, California and Florida. The costs associated with such research would be enormous and probably prohibitive. Cluster sampling provides an alternative where groups, or clusters, of elements are the primary sampling units and then either all the elements, or a sample of elements, is taken from within the clusters. Cluster sampling is included as a probability sampling technique because the clusters and/or the elements are selected using one of the random sampling techniques. When based on geographical clusters this approach is called *area sampling*.

Geographic cluster sampling, or area sampling, was adopted by Burrell *et al.* (1997) in their study of women's employment in four European Union countries. Having selected France, Italy, Spain and the UK as the countries for investigation, they then selected an area in each country with a sizeable regional centre and a resort area to 're-flect practices both in small, seasonal family-run hotels and in larger, chain-operated businesses with a more even spread of custom throughout the year' (Burrell *et al.*, 1997, p. 69).

Cluster sampling is also used where there are no lists available to create a sampling frame. Rather than attempting to create a sampling frame for the whole population, it is easier and more cost-effective to generate sampling frames for the selected clusters of the population. It is not appropriate, however, to select clusters on the basis of the ease with which sampling frames can be created!

Cluster sampling is most suitable where the groups of elements contain the same level of heterogeneity as the population itself and where the clusters are relatively homogeneous. If this is the case population variability will be fully represented in the clusters and will be included in the sample. Where there is variability between clusters it is usually necessary to sample larger numbers of clusters to reflect this variability.

So far, *single-stage cluster sampling* has been considered. It is also possible to sample clusters at several stages, moving from general categories to more specific categories. This approach is called *multi-stage sampling*. In area sampling this would correspond to progressively smaller geographic areas being selected at each stage. This may start by selecting national regions, then counties within the chosen regions, then districts within the chosen counties, then neighbourhoods within the chosen districts and finally the individual households in each selected neighbourhood. A similar approach might be used in a study of university students where universities are selected followed by faculties, departments, courses and finally students. It is important, however, to ensure that there is no duplication of elements in the clusters, i.e. they should be mutually exclusive.

Non-probability sampling

The second group of sampling methods are those based on non-probability techniques. In non-probability sampling the elements have an unknown probability of being selected and selection is usually based on the researcher's judgement and expertise. This means that researchers have to be very careful in their attempts at generalisations to the wider population and they must be aware that the use of statistical techniques for measuring random sampling error is not appropriate.

These approaches are most suitable for sampling people or social organisations. As such they are more akin to the phenomenological/interpretivist philosophy of research where the focus on inductive and qualitative approaches tends towards the selection of smaller samples and a focus on meanings, as opposed to quantitative research where large samples are common and there is a dependency on statistical analysis. Non-probability sampling methods such as convenience sampling, purposive sampling and theoretical sampling reflect the phenomenological philosophy in that they recognise that the world is socially constructed; they depend on the close involvement of the researcher particularly in terms of judgement and expertise; and they are more flexible and responsive to developments in the on-going research process.

Indeed, it has been argued that because social organisations are based on group activity and interaction between members, or as Prior (1997, p. 64) states, 'on forms of collective activity or praxis', social scientific research must look beyond approaches that focus on the perspectives of isolated individuals (see Taylor, 1987; Prior, 1997; for example). This view raises questions about approaches based on random sampling (which tend to lead to introspective individual responses) and provides a convincing rationale for non-probability approaches, such as purposive sampling, snowball sampling and theoretical sampling, that reflect a socially constructed perspective.

Convenience sampling   Convenience sampling is based on the collection of data from those who are readily available for investigation. As an approach for positivist research convenience sampling has been heavily criticised. It is, however, a useful approach in exploratory research and the sampling methods used in several of the more interpretive approaches such as ethnography, participant observation and case studies may be characterised as convenience sampling. That is, the sampling in these approaches is to a large extent dependent upon who is available at the location in question and at the time of the research.

An interesting approach to convenience sampling was adopted by Mihalik, Muzaffer and Ming-Chu Pan (1995) in their study of German and Japanese tourists. They generated their sample, based on households, by instructing interviewers 'who followed pre-determined walk patterns from computer selected starting points'.

Purposive sampling (judgement sampling) Purposive sampling, which is often referred to as judgement sampling, is an approach where elements are selected for their particular expertise, knowledge, experience or perspective, usually on the basis of the researcher's knowledge of people in the area of research. It is often used in research where there are a limited number of people who have the available knowledge. This approach is sometimes referred to as sampling *key informants.*

An interesting combination of purposive sampling and opportunity sampling was used in a study of the impact of environmental policy on the tourism industry in Taiwan (Lin and Hemmington, 1997). In this study, the authors identified eight categories of people with particular perspectives on the research issue and then identified individuals on the basis of 'lists of those occupying official government posts, hotel associations members' lists, personal referrals, recommendations from industry, those occupying university and college teaching posts and lists of legislators'. Those included in the final sample were selected on the basis of 'the individual's current position, experience, personal recommendation, geography and industry sector' (Lin and Hemmington, 1997, p. 39). It was through this process of sampling that the authors were able to generate findings in five key areas directly related to the objectives of the study: government policy, government administrative systems, implementation of environmental policy in the tourism industry, the effects of environmental policy on the hotel industry, and areas for further research.

Quota sampling Quota sampling is used where it is necessary to ensure that certain sub-groups are included in the sample. It is a similar approach to proportionate stratified sampling in that pre-determined proportions of the sample are selected from subgroups to reflect their presence in the population. The critical difference, however, is that whilst in stratified sampling people are selected randomly, in quota sampling they are selected on a convenience basis.

This is a technique that is often used in street and site surveys. Interviewers are given a quota of people of each type to interview and each quota is completed as people become available. For example, in a study of an industrial catering site interviewers may be given quotas that reflect the employee make-up of the site: directors, managers, supervisors, clerical staff, operational staff, manual staff, etc. The interviewers would then complete the quotas as they come across each type of person, the first question of the interview being job title to enable classification. It is very common in this approach for interviewers to have to seek out members of particular groups to enable them to fill one or two incomplete categories; often rejecting members of groups for which they already have a full quota.

Although quota sampling ensures that all important groups are included, it is important to remember that because of the use of convenience sampling, these samples are unlikely to be representative and generalisability is difficult. There are advantages, however, particularly in terms of the 100% response rate, but also more generally in terms of speed, costs and convenience that sometimes make this approach an attractive option.

Snowball sampling   Snowball sampling is an approach where an initial sample of respondents, which may be selected randomly, provide the names of additional members of the population which can then be sampled to generate further respondents. This is a useful approach where the target population is small or difficult to locate. It can also be very useful where the study is interested in reflecting the social dimensions of the issue in question (if nothing else, it can help with introductions and referrals), the resulting network of respondents reflecting social structures (Ryan, 1995). Snowball sampling may also be useful in investigating socially sensitive issues where respondents may be reticent to come forward—a study of sexual harassment at work could be a good example.

Theoretical sampling   In some forms of inductive research, particularly grounded theory, the processes of data collection, analysis and theory generation are intertwined. The researcher collects data, analyses it and on the basis of the analysis decides what data to collect next. It is through this iterative process where each stage informs the next that theory starts to emerge. The method of sampling associated with this approach is called *theoretical sampling* (Glaser and Strauss, 1967; Connell and Lowe, 1997) and it is characterised by this iterative approach where sample selection is guided by on-going analysis and the evolving theory.

Connell and Lowe (1997) used theoretical sampling in developing grounded theory in their study of franchising in the international hotel industry. They found that the opportunities for theoretical sampling can be limited by 'access restrictions' to companies and recommend that, 'researchers should try to achieve regular or sustained access agreements prior to data collection'.

Determining sample size

The most frequently asked question in sampling is: how large should the sample be? Indeed, it is quite common for novice researchers to become preoccupied by sample size to the extent that full consideration of the method of selection is neglected. Although sample size is an important consideration in research, it is not as important as the sampling method. Size is no guarantee of representativeness and even very large samples can fail to be representative if they are not selected appropriately. Consider, for example, a study looking at restaurant customers where the whole sample is selected on Mondays. No matter how large a sample is selected, it is very unlikely to be representative unless customers from other days are selected as well; clearly the sampling method is more important than the sample size.

Self-selecting samples are particularly problematic. Where samples are created solely from those who choose to respond, as in customer feedback forms, there is an inbuilt bias that is a function of the individual's motivation to respond; this is likely to result in a sample made up of those with extreme views and in customer feedback surveys usually those with complaints. In these situations increasing sample size will not improve representativeness unless attempts are made to encourage response from a wider range of potential respondents.

In general, however, it is true that, other things being equal, larger samples are better than small ones. That is, for any given sampling method the more elements that are sampled the better the statistical chance of it being more representative. There is a diminishing return in this relationship, however, and increases in sample size increase the representativeness of the sample at a reducing rate. In statistical terms the random sampling error is inversely proportional to the square root of n (sample size).

The concept of diminishing returns, in terms of accuracy and increases in sample size, is important when looking at the economics of research. Researchers, particularly in the commercial environment, inevitably have to make decisions about the cost–benefit implications of increases in sample size. Eventually a compromise has to be struck between the costs of larger samples and the marginal improvements in accuracy.

The key issues in determining sample size are:

- The variability of the population
- The acceptable error (precision required)
- The required confidence level.

In addition, two other issues should also be considered:

- Analysis of sub-samples
- Response rates.

Variability

The variability of the population, or the extent to which it is either homogeneous or heterogeneous, is measured by the standard deviation. The extent to which the population is variable or not will determine the size of the sample; homogeneous populations require only small samples, heterogeneous populations require larger samples to cover the range of different values present in the population. For example, to establish the mean height of staff in an hotel, if it is known that they are all exactly the same height (homogeneous) a sample of one would be sufficient to establish the mean. If they vary between 1.5 and 2 metres, clearly it would be necessary to take a larger sample to gain some idea of the mean. If, however, they are extremely variable (heterogeneous), say between 1 and 2.5 metres, to obtain a reasonably accurate estimate a large sample (or even a census) would have to be taken.

The only problem with this is that in practice it is unlikely that the standard deviation would be known (if it were, the mean would probably be known as well!). Sometimes researchers use their knowledge and experience of the population to guide them, or they may have the results of similar studies that can act as the basis of an estimation of the variability of the population. In many cases a pilot study is conducted and an estimate of the standard deviation can be made from the pilot data. Caution must be exercised, however, since pilot studies are normally conducted with small samples and it is likely that a small sample will underestimate the true variability of the population.

Precision

Precision is the extent to which the sample statistics accurately reflect the population parameters. In the example above, a very precise measure of the mean height of employees, to the nearest millimetre perhaps, may be needed; this would require a large sample or even a census. However, if it were necessary to know the mean height only to the nearest metre a very small sample would suffice. Indeed, if the range of heights is less than a metre (i.e. little variability) a sample of one would be sufficient!

As discussed earlier, sample statistics are actually estimates of the true population parameters and it is normal to indicate that the true population value lies within a range of the sample value. The narrower this range, the greater the precision. Precision is a function of variability as measured by the standard error ($S_{\bar{x}}$):

$$S_{\bar{x}} = \frac{\sigma}{\sqrt{n}}$$

It is important to note that in order to reduce the standard error and therefore increase precision it is necessary to increase the sample size (n), although, as mentioned earlier, the fact that the standard error is a function of $\sqrt{n}$ means that halving the standard error requires a sample four times larger. It is also significant that the standard error is a function of the variability of the population as measured by the standard deviation (σ). This confirms the fact that highly variable populations require large samples and those that are less variable can achieve the same level of precision with smaller samples.

Confidence level

The issues associated with statistical inference and the trade-off between precision and confidence levels have already been discussed. The confidence level indicates the degree of certainty in the sample estimates of the population parameters expressed in percentage terms. Business research usually operates at the 95% confidence level, usually expressed as $p \leqslant 0.05$.

Because confidence intervals are calculated as multiples of the standard error (1.96 standard errors for the 95% confidence interval and 2.576 standard errors for the 99% confidence interval), the same sample size issues apply for the level of confidence as for precision. In other words, increasing the level of confidence widens the confidence interval and reduces precision, unless the standard error is reduced by increasing the sample size.

Analysis of sub-samples

The discussion so far has concentrated on situations where the sample is analysed as a whole. It is frequently the case, however, that sub-samples of the population need to be analysed. This has important implications for the sample size (and method) in terms of the need to ensure large enough sub-samples for meaningful statistical analysis. Where there are only two or three sub-samples this may not significantly affect the overall sample size, but where there are larger numbers of sub-samples there could be a need to create a much larger sample than would have otherwise been the case.

Response rates

Finally, response rates should also be considered. The pilot study should give an indication of the likely response rate and this should be accommodated in the final sample design. This factor should not be underestimated as response rates can be as low as 20% in which case the sample would have to be increased by a factor of 5.

Conclusion and summary

This chapter has reviewed the process of sampling both in terms of the general process and through a review of methods that are suitable for quantitative and qualitative research. It is important that researchers are fully aware of the effects of sampling on the research methods that they choose. It is remarkable that many articles in refereed hospitality management journals fail to address the issue of sampling, and even those that do tend to do so in a rather cursory manner, often merely stating the characteristics of the sample obtained. This indicates a lack of understanding of the fundamental importance of sampling in research methodology and a failure to consider the implications of the sample and the sampling method on the data obtained.

It is important for all researchers to recognise the fact that all sampling is a compromise between the quality and accuracy of results and resource limitations. If unlimited resources were available it would be possible to conduct censuses and therefore generate true data about the population in question. In practice, this is rarely practical and samples have to be taken to generate data that approximates as closely as possible to the true population values. In other situations the nature of the research can make sampling very difficult in terms of access, confidentiality or the sensitivity of the issues involved. Good research acknowledges this compromise and fully explores the implications of the sampling method on the data generated and identifies the limitations or caveats that this imposes on the findings.

Table 13.1 provides a review of the sampling methods discussed in this chapter. It provides an indication of the relative costs of each method and the extent of their use and then identifies, in general terms, the strengths and weaknesses of each method. This review is, however, only a starting point for any critique of particular sampling methods, and researchers should explore fully the implications on their findings of the methods they choose, the way they have implemented them and the nature of the population that they are investigating.

Table 13.1. Review of sampling methods

Sampling method	Resource cost	Use	Strengths	Weaknesses
Probability sampling				
Simple random sampling	High; potentially very high for large, dispersed populations	Not common (in its true form)	Good generalisability; little knowledge of population required; easy to use and analyse	Inefficient; requires sampling frame; does not utilise information about the population; may lead to dispersed sample
Systematic random sampling	Moderate, although could lead to dispersed sample as above	Quite widely used	Easy to use; efficient; good generalisability	Potential for systematic bias where periodicity in sampling frame; does not use information about sample; may lead to dispersed sample
Proportionate stratified sampling	High: need sampling frame with detailed data on criteria for stratification	Moderately widely used	Very efficient; assures representation of all identified groups; increases representativeness of sample	Requires detailed information about each stratum; possible to introduce bias if inappropriate criteria used for stratification
Disproportionate stratified sampling	Moderate: less detail on strata required	Infrequently used	Ensures adequate representation of all strata	Bias in total sample and needs careful analysis
Cluster sampling	Low cost, particularly for geographic clusters (area sampling)	Frequently used	Low fieldwork costs for geographic clusters; sampling frame needed only for those clusters sampled	Greatest potential for bias of all probability methods; clusters must be mutually exclusive

Non-probability sampling

Convenience sampling	Very low cost	Very widely used (often mistaken for random sampling!)	Easy, cheap and no need for sampling frame; useful for preliminary or exploratory research	Major problems with potential bias; great care needed in generalising from data
Purposive sampling (judgement)	Low cost	Widely used	Relatively fast and cost effective; useful in forecasting	Problems of access to experts; limited pool of experts; great care needed in generalising from data
Quota sampling	Moderate cost	Widely used, particularly for opinion polls	Ensures representation of all key groups; no sampling frame required	Associated use of convenience sampling means difficult to generalise from the results
Snowball sampling	Low cost, although can be time consuming	Rarely used	Locating and gaining access to small or elusive populations; reflects social structures; useful for exploring socially sensitive issues; no sampling frame required	High potential for bias; may take time to follow up leads and gain access; depends upon the quality of those initially selected
Theoretical sampling	Usually moderate, but depends on how the research develops	Increasingly used, particularly for grounded theory	Sampling becomes an integral part of the whole research process; closely related to the development of theory; flexible; dynamic	Potential access restrictions

Sources: Sekaran (1992, pp. 237–238), Zikmund (1994, pp. 378–379).

References and bibliography

Bojanic, D. C. (1996) The smoking debate: a look at the issues surrounding smoking bans in restaurants, *Hospitality Research Journal*, Vol. 20, No. 1, pp. 27–38.

Brent-Ritchie, J. R. and Goeldner, C. R. (1994) *Travel, Tourism and Hospitality Research: A Handbook for Managers and Researchers*, John Wiley & Sons: New York.

Burrell, J., Manfredi, S., Price, L. and Rollin, H. (1997) Women's employment in hotels in France, Italy, Spain and the U.K., *Sixth Annual CHME Hospitality Research Conference*, School of Hotel and Restaurant Management, Oxford Brookes University, pp. 67–86.

Connell, J. and Lowe, A. (1997) Generating grounded theory from qualitative data: the application of inductive methods in tourism and hospitality management research, *Progress in Tourism and Hospitality Research*, vol. 3, pp. 165–173.

Curwin, J. and Slater, R. (1996) *Quantitative Methods for Business Decisions*, Thomson Business Press, pp. 49–54, 213–217.

Easterby-Smith, M., Thorpe, R. and Lowe, A. (1991) *Management Research: An Introduction*, Sage: London, pp. 34–35, 123–125.

Gill, J. and Johnson, P. (1997) *Research Methods for Managers*, Paul Chapman Publishing: London, pp. 82, 158–159.

Glaser, B. and Strauss, A. (1967) *The Discovery of Grounded Theory: Strategies for Qualitative Research*, Aldine Publishing Company: New York.

Lin, Y. and Hemmington, N. (1997) The impact of environmental policy on the tourism industry in Taiwan, *Progress in Tourism and Hospitality Research*, vol. 3, pp. 35–45.

Mihalik, B. J., Muzaffer, U. and Ming-Chu Pan (1995) A comparison of information sources used by vacationing Germans and Japanese, *Hospitality Research Journal*, Vol. 19, No. 1, pp. 39–46.

Moser, C. A. and Kalton, G. (1971) *Survey Methods in Social Investigation*, Gower: Aldershot.

Oppenheim, A. N. (1992) *Questionnaire Design, Interviewing and Attitude Measurement*, Pinter: London, pp. 38–46.

Prior, L. (1997) Following in Foucault's footsteps: text and context in qualitative research, in Silverman, D. (ed.), *Qualitative Research: Theory, Method and Practice*, Sage: London, pp. 63–79.

Rees, D. G. (1995) *Essential Statistics*, Chapman & Hall: London, pp. 84–90.

Ryan, C. (1995) *Researching Tourist Satisfaction*, Routledge: London, pp. 103–104 and 163–181.

Ryan, C. and Barnett, S. (1995) Hotel conference managers: skills and training needs in New Zealand, *Journal of Vacation Marketing*, vol. 1, no. 4, pp. 349–359.

Sekaran, U. (1992) *Research Methods for Business: A Skill Building Approach*, John Wiley & Sons: New York, pp. 223–254.

Silverman, D. (1997) *Qualitative Research: Theory, Method and Practice*, Sage: London.

Taylor, S. (1987) Interpretation and the sciences of man. In Rabinow, P. and Sullivan, M. W. (eds), *Interpretive Social Science: A Second Look*, University of California Press: London, pp. 33–81.

Zikmund, W. G. (1994) *Business Research Methods*, Dryden Press: Fort Worth, Texas, pp. 353–417.

14 Quantitative data analysis

ALAN FYALL AND RICHARD THOMAS

Introduction

The role of research in tourism and hospitality

Prior to the introduction of the various Quantitative Data Analysis techniques available to managers in the tourism and hospitality industries, and the benefits which accrue from their usage, an initial discussion of the broad role of research within tourism and hospitality will set this chapter into context.

As with the tardy introduction, application and effectiveness of a number of management techniques within the tourism and hospitality industries, the laboured adoption of many sound research practices can also best be explained by the fact that the two industries are perhaps the last to experience the change from a sellers' to a buyers' market (Calantone and Mazanec, 1991). This is substantiated by Middleton (1994) who comments that by observing the way that the two industries are conducted in many countries around the world, it would appear to be a distinctive feature of both that the use of research, and more specifically marketing research, is weaker than in any other major industry dealing with consumer products. Much of this lack of use of research can be put down, incorrectly perhaps, to the assumption made by many that research is not required when producers and customers meet face-to-face on the producers' premises and that through such contact, managers know their customers without the need for expensive research to be undertaken (Middleton, 1994). However, bearing in mind the predominance of very small businesses in the tourism and hospitality industries, this viewpoint is, perhaps, not surprising. On the contrary, the concentrated nature of the two industries suggests that some of the very large players are, and will continue to be, very active in terms of research activity. Many of the larger companies do now recognise that the lower the quality, or absence, of information used for management decision making the more likely they are to experience higher risks of failure, especially in strongly competitive markets (Middleton, 1994). Quantitative Data Analysis techniques alone cannot guarantee solutions nor ensure that correct decisions are made. All they can do is to help reduce risk and uncertainty and provide a foundation of data and information on which managers can base their decision making. Marriott International is one corporation, in particular, who put great emphasis on the collection, analysis and interpretation of management data (Camacho and Knain, 1989). Marriott have always attached a great deal of importance to their research activity. Market segmentation and market sizing, concept development and product testing, price sensitivity assessments,

The Handbook of Contemporary Hospitality Management Research, Edited by Bob Brotherton.
© 1999 John Wiley & Sons Ltd.

advertising and promotion effectiveness, market testing, facility usage, visitor trends and travel behaviour and the measurement of customer satisfaction are all marketing management areas in which Marriott are consistently applying the Quantitative Data Analysis techniques which are discussed in depth later in this chapter.

Although tourism and hospitality combined represent a powerful economic force where new destinations set out in search of the economic rewards of tourism whilst older destinations seek to protect their market share, the growth in competition from around the globe has served as a catalyst for far greater, far more accurate and far more reliable information. The onset of competition has without doubt forced a vast array of organisations, destinations, regions and countries to move away from their historical reluctance to conduct research activity and move towards a far more balanced management approach supported by accurate, timely and reliable information. In many ways, the move away from the overemphasis on advertising and promotion to product development and to the goal of maintaining competitiveness with regard to policy formulation is one that, according to March (1994), is well overdue. Whether it be governmental, profit making or non-profit making organisations in the tourism and hospitality industries, the need for accurate and timely data is greater than ever before. The need to measure visitor/guest characteristics, hotel occupancy rates, the effectiveness of advertising campaigns, the identification of trend and seasonal booking variations, economic impact studies, visitor satisfaction surveys or demand forecasting has become far more pressing in the highly competitive marketplace of the 1990s. Geo-political change, corporate takeovers and exchange rate fluctuations, to name but a few, are all factors in the dynamic external environment which are currently serving as catalysts for the need for accurate base data on which to make strategic, managerial/tactical or operational decisions. The forever increasing importance, and visibility, of hospitality and tourism on the world economic stage is, if anything, heightening the demand for quality data, something that has clearly not always been available in the past (Athiyaman, 1997).

Research dimensions

In the text, *Tourism Research: critiques and challenges*, Brent-Ritchie (1993) acquaints the reader with five distinctly different kinds of tourism and hospitality research approaches: policy, managerial, operational, action and evaluation. Taking into account the different styles of the management process (analytical, planning, execution and control) as well as the level of managerial activity taking place, whether it be strategic, managerial/tactical or operational, Brent-Ritchie relates his five approaches to research to the above two dimensions as well as to various functional areas of management activity. Thus, whether it be the long-term, broad-scale indicators required for strategic decision making, the ongoing and well-defined information requirements of managerial/ tactical decision making, or the highly frequent and structured nature of data for operational decisions to be made, it is quite evident that Quantitative Data Analysis techniques can, and do, play a vital role across the entire tourism and hospitality research spectrum. To fully benefit from the application of Quantitative Data Analysis techniques, however, Kotler, Bowen and Makens (1996) propose that the requirement of an adequate Marketing Information System (MKIS) is an absolute necessity. A Marketing

Information System, as defined by those authors, consists of people, equipment and procedures to gather, sort, analyse and distribute needed, timely and accurate information to key decision makers. In turn, the Marketing Information System sets out to balance information that managers would like to have against that which they really need (and so avoid information overload) and which is feasible to obtain. As with the example of the Marriott Corporation, Quantitative Data Analysis techniques are applicable to many marketing scenarios and cover all of the six main categories of marketing research. These are market analysis and forecasting, consumer research, product and price studies, promotions and sales research, distribution and evaluation, and performance monitoring studies.

However, prior to the establishment of any Marketing Information System it is imperative that those collating, analysing and interpreting the data are fully aware of many of the problems that impact on the validity of the data being presented. The making of incorrect assumptions, the lack of complementary qualitative information, the improper use of statistical analysis and the failure to gain true sample representation of the entire population being researched are often quoted as the main barriers to the accurate presentation of data. However, if conducted properly Quantitative Data Analysis techniques can offer many benefits. These include the provision of sound information for decision making, the maintenance of a close working relationship with customers, the identification of new markets, and the ability to monitor the performance of certain aspects of a business, draw attention to specific problems, monitor consumer reaction and reduce waste and the number of incorrect decisions being made (Latham, 1993).

The methodological nature and application of Quantitative Data Analysis techniques

The term Quantitative Data Analysis covers a wide variety of techniques which together offer a means of attaching value and meaning to raw research data. In essence it represents the means by which tourism and hospitality managers are able to summarise the results of research activity by means of tabulation and statistical analysis. In order to identify patterns, trends or even discrepancies in data, the preparation of tables showing the frequency distribution of particular events and/or the conducting of statistical analysis are efficient means by which managers can quickly get to grips with key research findings (Proctor, 1997). The following sections explore a number of key Quantitative Data Analysis techniques and provide the reader with clearly worked examples for ease of understanding. The techniques covered include the presentation of data, descriptive data analysis techniques, correlation and regression and, finally, forecasting.

Presentation of data

In many management situations involving data analysis the method of data presentation, in tabular or graphical format, is of vital importance. In particular, the application of graphical techniques can be useful in presenting management information and assisting objective decision making. This initial section includes a number of examples of the most common data presentation methods.

Example 1

The nationality of overseas visitors to a large hotel group in the UK has been recorded over a period of time. The proportion of European visitors is shown in Table 14.1. This information can be represented in the pie chart shown in Figure 14.1. The pie chart provides an easy way of presenting the data so that the proportions of individual values compared with the total are emphasised. For example, Figure 14.1 clearly indicates the dominance of the Germans, and to a lesser extent the French, in the particular market. Clearly, this may be useful for the hotel group management team in terms of formulating marketing and promotional activities.

Example 2

A survey into the destinations of tourists for their 'main holiday' has produced the results shown in Table 14.2, based on a sample of 1400 respondents. The data in Table 14.2 could be reproduced in a pie chart similar to that shown in Figure 14.1. Alternatively, a bar chart could be used to provide a better comparison of the differences between the number of visitors to each destination, as shown in Figure 14.2.

Table 14.1 Proportion of European visitors

Nationality	French	German	Dutch	Italian	Spanish	Others
Percentage	22%	36%	9%	10%	6%	17%

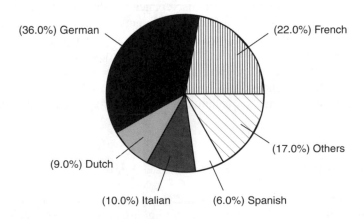

Figure 14.1 Pie chart of European visitors

Table 14.2   Holiday destinations

Destination	UK	Mediterranean	Continental Europe	North America	Others
No. of respondents	300	450	220	190	240

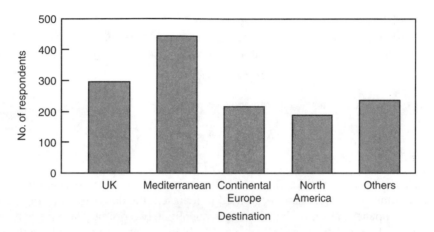

Figure 14.2   Bar chart illustrating destination statistics

Example 3

The multiple bar chart can be effectively utilised when comparing a number of data sets. For example, a report produced by NEDC entitled *Costs and Manpower Productivity in UK Hotels*, published in 1992, used such diagrams in order to compare a range of statistics such as the monthly room occupancy as shown in Figure 14.3.

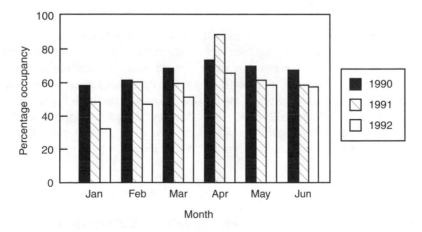

Figure 14.3   Monthly room occupancy in London hotels

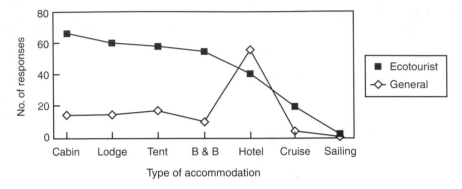

Figure 14.4 Line chart showing accommodation preferences

Example 4

The line chart (or line graph) can also be effectively used when comparing sets of data. Indeed the line chart could have been used to represent the data shown in Figure 14.3 on room occupancy. The line chart is used frequently in two primary areas: firstly in the comparison of a number of sets of data as already described, and secondly in the illustration of data over time. (Examples of the latter use can be found in the forecasting section later in this chapter.) An example of the former use is shown in Figure 14.4 and illustrates a comparison of the preferences of two sets of Canadian tourists ('experienced ecotourists' and 'general consumers') in terms of the kind of accommodation that they preferred. The information is taken from a paper by Wight (1997).

The chart given in Figure 14.4 shows a number of differences between the two tourist groups. For instance, it is not surprising to note that the general consumer prefers the hotel/motel type of accommodation whereas the ecotourist has a wider range of preferences including cabin/cottage, lodge/inn, and tent camping.

Descriptive data analysis

In many circumstances it is necessary to summarise the array of data available in order to produce a meaningful analysis. There are a wide variety of techniques used to summarise data, and in this section two important characteristics of data, namely the centre and spread, will be considered. The centre of a set of data is specified as the 'average'. This can be found in a variety of ways; the two most common methods are the *arithmetic mean* and the *median*. Both are shown in the following examples. Furthermore there are a variety of ways of measuring the spread (or dispersion) in a set of data. This section considers two important methods incorporating the *standard deviation* and *quartiles*.

Example 1

Table 14.3 shows a classification of tourists by duration of trip (number of nights) for a large West Country hotel, based on a random sample of 200 guests.

Table 14.3 Duration of trips

Duration of trip (no. of nights)	1–3	4–7	8–14	15–21	22 and over
Number of tourists	75	59	41	15	10

This distribution of the length of duration (in days) of a trip can be summarised by the *median* and the *inter-quartile range*. The median is defined as the middle value in the set of data. For instance, given the 200 guests obtained in this sample, the median would approximate to the value (duration of trip) corresponding to the 100th guest. It can be seen from Table 14.3 that there are 75 guests in the first grouping, and the second grouping (representing 4–7 nights) contains a further 59 guests. The 100th guest must therefore lie in the second grouping and thus the median is in the range 4–7. A more precise estimate can be obtained from a diagram called an *ogive* (or cumulative frequency curve) as shown in Figure 14.5.

Similarly, a measure of spread that could be used to summarise the data is the inter-quartile range. This is the distance between the *lower quartile* (i.e. a quarter of the way through the list of guests) and the *upper quartile* (three-quarters of the way through the guests). The lower quartile (denoted by Q_1) and the upper quartile (denoted by Q_3) are shown on the ogive in Figure 14.5.

The graph in Figure 14.5 is obtained by plotting the cumulative frequencies (i.e. adding up the total number of guests) against the number of nights stayed. Table 14.4 shows the cumulative frequencies used in the graph. The data in Table 14.4 show that no guests stayed for less than one night, 75 guests stayed for less than four nights, 134 guests stayed for less than seven nights, and so on. These points are plotted onto the ogive illustrated in Figure 14.5. The graph in Figure 14.5 shows that the 100th guest stays for approximately five nights, the 50th guest stays for three nights, and the 150th guest stays for 10 nights.

Thus, the data can be summarised as follows:

- Median = 5 nights
- Lower Quartile (Q_1) = 3 nights
- Upper Quartile (Q_3) = 10 nights
- Inter-Quartile Range (IQR) = $Q_3 - Q_1 = 10 - 3 = 7$ nights.

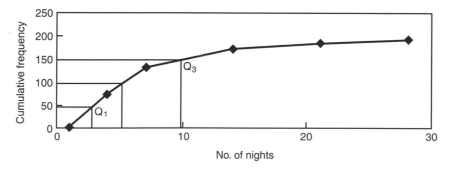

Figure 14.5 Estimation of the median and quartiles

Table 14.4 Cumulative frequencies

No. of nights	1	4	7	14	21	28
Cumulative frequency	0	75	134	175	190	200

Table 14.5 Comparison of two hotels

Area	Median	IQR
West Country	5 nights	7 nights
Lake District	12 nights	4 nights

The IQR shows that the central 50% of guests' length of stay is within seven nights of each other. In isolation this measure is not very informative, though such information can be useful when comparing sets of data.

For instance, another hotel group in the Lake District has published statistics on the length of duration of its guests. The values published are median = 12 nights with inter-quartile range = 4 nights. Such information can be used to compare the two sets of tourists, and is summarised in Table 14.5.

Comparing the medians for the two hotels, it can be seen that guests on average stay for a shorter time in the West Country than they do in the Lake District. However, comparing the inter-quartile ranges it is clear that the spread of durations is wider in the West Country than in the Lake District. This indicates that guests visiting the Lake District are much more consistent in their length of stay. Although the original data is not available, it seems that the normal length of stay in the Lake District is between one and two weeks. With this small inter-quartile range it is unlikely that many guests stay for only a few days or indeed stay for considerably longer than two weeks, unlike the guests arriving at the West Country hotel. Of course, the comments here relating to the two regions are valid only for the two hotels for which the data is available and cannot, without further work, be generalised to represent the regions as a whole.

Example 2

Table 14.6 shows the number of hotels described in terms of the number of rooms in the years 1971 and 1981. The numbers of hotels are given in hundreds (Jones and Lockwood, 1990).

Table 14.6 Comparison of hotel sizes

	No. of hotels (100s)	
Number of rooms	1971	1981
Under 15	207	95
15–49	96	84
50–200	16	17
Over 200	1	2

These data can be summarised using the arithmetic mean (usually referred to simply as the mean) and standard deviation. In general terms, given a frequency distribution of the variable x with corresponding frequencies denoted by f, the appropriate formulae are as follows:

$$\text{Mean} = \bar{x} = \frac{\Sigma fx}{\Sigma f}$$

(Note: The Σ notation is used to represent summation, i.e. Σfx can be read as 'the sum of fx'.)

$$\text{Standard deviation} = s = \sqrt{\frac{\Sigma fx^2}{\Sigma f} - (\bar{x})^2}$$

The calculation of these formulae for the data representing hotels in 1981 is shown in Table 14.7. The values of x used in the formula are the mid-values of the class intervals. For instance, the grouping 'under 15' is assumed to include all those hotels with between 6 and 14 rooms. The mid-point of the range 6–14 is 10 as shown in the table. Similarly, the range 'over 200' is assumed to be 201–400 with a mid-value of 300.5.

Table 14.7 shows the calculations of the required values. In particular, the three summations are found to be:

$$\Sigma f = 198$$
$$\Sigma fx = 6364$$
$$\Sigma fx^2 = 541\ 741$$

These values substituted into the appropriate formulae give the following:

$$\text{Mean} = \bar{x} = 32.1 \text{ rooms}$$
$$\text{Standard deviation} = s = 41.3 \text{ rooms}$$

The mean of 32.1 rooms gives an indication of the 'average' room size for the hotels in 1981. The standard deviation of 41.3 rooms shows the degree of spread in the distribution of hotel sizes. Again, as in the previous example, it is difficult to interpret this measure of spread in isolation. However, the values can be used in comparing sets of data. For instance, the room sizes in 1971 as shown in Table 14.6 yield the following statistics:

$$\text{Mean} = 23.3 \text{ rooms}$$
$$\text{Standard deviation} = 29.9 \text{ rooms}$$

Table 14.7 Tabulation of calculations

No. of rooms	Mid-point of of range (x)	f	fx	fx^2
Under 15	10	95	950	9,500
15–49	32	84	2,688	86,016
50–200	125	17	2,125	265,625
Over 200	300.5	2	601	180,600
Totals		198	6,364	541,741

The changes (if any) between the hotel sizes over the different years can now be considered. Between 1971 and 1981 the average size of hotel has increased by almost 40% (23 rooms up to 32 rooms). This is typical of a continuing trend away from smaller family-run businesses to larger modern hotels which are often part of a chain or group of companies.

The spread of hotel sizes has also increased between the years 1971 and 1981. This means that there seems to be a much greater diversity of room sizes in 1981 compared to 1971. This is largely due to the significant reduction in smaller hotels (under 15 rooms) and a much more even spread of hotels over the lower two classes, under 15 rooms and 15–49 rooms. Also the diversity of hotel sizes has been enhanced by an increase in the number of larger hotels, in the categories 50–200 rooms and over 200 rooms.

Example 3

Table 14.8 shows a summary of the statistics gathered on the age of travellers categorised into two groups. The original data was taken from the 1991 Canadian Pleasure Travel Market Survey and has been further discussed by Smith (1995). The travellers were classified according to whether they were light or heavy tourists. The definitions of these classifications are as follows. Individuals were ranked according to the number of pleasure trips (lasting at least three nights) they had been on during the past three years. Those who had been on fewer than five trips during this period were considered 'light' travellers, whereas those who had taken at least five trips were classified as 'heavy' users. Table 14.8 shows the mean and standard deviation of the ages for the two groups.

The table shows that there is little difference between the two groups of travellers. However, small variations between the two sets of data can be seen. For example, comparing the averages it is clear that on average the 'heavy' travellers are slightly older. This is not really surprising since older people are generally better off (until past a certain age, e.g. retirement) and are therefore likely to go on more pleasure trips. This has implications for the tourist industry, including the hotel trade, since this information may provide a justification for offering improved services for the older age groups. Of course, in order to consider this more carefully a more detailed breakdown of the age groups and/or the classifications of travelling frequency would be required.

The standard deviation for the age in the 'heavy' travelling group is slightly lower than for the other group. This means that there is a little more consistency in the ages of travellers in the 'heavy' category. The ages of 'light' travellers are spread over a slightly wider range. The differences in both the average and spread for these two

Table 14.8   Comparison of travellers

Statistics	*Light travellers*	*Heavy travellers*
Mean	39.9 yrs	42.2 yrs
Standard deviation	14.7 yrs	14.4 yrs

Table 14.9   Comparison of different traveller types

Statistics	Frequency of travel (no. of trips in last three years)			
	Less than 2	2–5	6–10	Over 10
Mean	26.4	38.2	45.7	41.8
Standard deviation	15.2	12.6	14.8	9.4

groups are so marginal that little can be concluded. It is likely that the similarities between the two groups mask clear differences in the travelling habits of different age groups. This could be analysed by splitting the frequency of trips down further. For instance, Table 14.9 shows a more detailed analysis which may have been helpful in the study previously quoted (the figures given are solely the invention of the author and relate to the age of travellers in each group).

Table 14.9 gives a more detailed breakdown of the travelling habits for different age groups. The mean values indicate that on average the more frequent traveller is older. However, there is a slight dip in the mean age in the most frequent travelling group (over 10 trips within three years). The reason for this reduction may be explained when considering the standard deviation in each group. The spread of ages in the 'over 10 trips' group is much less than in other groups. This shows that this group is likely to exclude most individuals at either end of the age range. For instance, the older retired person is less likely to travel as frequently, and similarly the younger person due to financial constraints is in a similar position. Therefore the spread of ages in this category is reduced. The reduction in the mean age in the most frequent traveller category is probably due to the drastic reduction in the proportion of 'older' travellers in this group. However, the increased mean (and increased spread) of the second most frequent group (6–10 trips) shows that there could be a significant number of older travellers in this category.

Correlation and regression

In the previous examples in this chapter the analysis of individual sets of data has been considered. In many business areas it is often useful to consider the relationship between these data sets. For instance, the relationship between advertising expenditure and occupancy rates in a hotel may be revealing. Other relationships such as the links between price and demand, price and length of stay, tourist expenditure and travelling costs may need to be considered. One of the ways of illustrating the relationship between two variables is by the use of a scatter diagram. To be more objective the degree of relationship between two variables can be measured by using a correlation coefficient. For instance, the strength of a 'straight line' relationship between two variables (denoted by x and y) can be calculated using the Product Moment Correlation Coefficient (r) as follows:

$$r = \frac{\sum (xy) - n\bar{x}\bar{y}}{\sqrt{(\sum x^2 - n\bar{x}^2)(\sum y^2 - n\bar{y}^2)}}$$

The value of r lies between -1 and $+1$. Values of r near -1 or $+1$ indicate a 'good' straight line relationship (or correlation) between the two variables. Values of r close to zero indicate a poor correlation between the two variables.

If two variables are correlated, then a straight line relationship exists between them. This straight line relationship can be expressed as an equation $y = ax + b$ (usually referred to as the regression equation), where the values of a and b can be found as follows:

$$a = \frac{\sum (xy) - n\bar{x}\bar{y}}{\sum x^2 - n\bar{x}^2}$$

$$b = \bar{y} - a\bar{x}$$

Using this regression equation the other values of y corresponding to specific values of x can be estimated. The following examples illustrate these techniques and how they can be applied in areas of hospitality management.

Example 1

Table 14.10 shows some results from a survey of New Zealand conference managers working in hotels as outlined in a paper by Ryan and Barnett (1995). The study looked at the importance of a range of skills in the management of conferences. A number of skills were identified and a sample of hotel staff were asked to rate the importance of these skills, and to rate how well these skills were covered in their own training. Each respondent rated these on a seven-point scale, and the averages of the responses over the total sample are given in the table.

The scatter diagram shown in Figure 14.6 illustrates the relationship between the two sets of data. The diagram shows that there is some relationship between the two variables, though the situation is not at all clear. Most of the points on the diagram lie on a narrow band stretching from the bottom left of the graph to the top right. This shows that, in general, the importance of a given skill closely relates to the level of training given. However, the relationship is not exact and there is a clear exception to this in the graph. The point on the graph relating to the lowest level of importance of the skills listed seems to have received a higher than expected level of training. This point relates to 'Marketing the venue' and it may be that senior management have concentrated on

Table 14.10   Identification of management skills

Skill	Importance	Training
1. Communication skills	6.93	5.80
2. Managing people	6.73	5.55
3. Telephone answering skills	6.59	4.89
4. Knowledge of hotel operations	6.42	5.05
5. Clear writing skills	6.15	3.79
6. Liaison with outside services	5.95	4.00
7. Marketing the venue	5.85	5.05

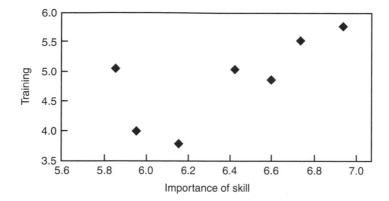

Figure 14.6 Relationship between importance of skills and training given

Table 14.11 Management skills: calculations for correlation

Skill	x	y	x^2	y^2	xy
1	6.93	5.80	48.02	33.64	40.19
2	6.73	5.55	45.29	30.80	37.35
3	6.59	4.89	43.43	23.91	32.23
4	6.42	5.05	41.22	25.50	32.42
5	6.15	3.79	37.82	14.36	23.31
6	5.95	4.00	35.40	16.00	23.80
7	5.85	5.05	34.22	25.50	29.54
Totals	44.62	34.13	285.41	16.72	218.84

marketing to the detriment of other important skills. Furthermore, it is worth noting that the level of training received in all cases lags behind the skill's importance. This may identify a 'training gap' for staff at the hotels sampled.

The degree of relationship between the two values shown can be measured by the correlation coefficient introduced earlier. The values in Table 14.11 show the required calculations involved in evaluating this coefficient. The two variables 'Importance' and 'Training' are denoted by x and y respectively.

The summations obtained from Table 14.11 are as follows:

$$\Sigma x = 44.62, \quad \Sigma y = 34.13$$

$$\Sigma x^2 = 285.41, \quad \Sigma y^2 = 169.72, \quad \Sigma (xy) = 218.84$$

Thus, the means for the values of x and y can be calculated:

$$\bar{x} = \frac{\Sigma x}{n} = \frac{44.62}{7} = 6.374$$

$$\bar{y} = \frac{\Sigma y}{n} = \frac{34.13}{7} = 4.876$$

Now, the correlation coefficient can be calculated as follows:

$$r = \frac{\Sigma\,(xy) - n\bar{x}\bar{y}}{\sqrt{(\Sigma\,x^2 - n\bar{x}^2)(\Sigma\,y^2 - n\bar{y}^2)}}$$

$$= \frac{218.84 - 7(6.374)(4.876)}{\sqrt{[285.41 - 7(6.374)^2][169.72 - 7(4.876)^2]}}$$

$$= \frac{1.2826}{\sqrt{(1.0149)(3.2924)}}$$

$$= \frac{1.2826}{1.8279}$$

$$= 0.70$$

The value of $r = 0.70$ is 'near' to +1 and seems to indicate some degree of correlation. However, further work would need to be done in order to determine whether the relationship is significant or not. A value of r close to +1 would indicate a strong relationship between the training provided and the importance of individual skills. Therefore in this instance, the correlation coefficient could be used as measure of the relevance or appropriateness of training provided. A low correlation coefficient would indicate that the training programme needs to be reviewed to take into account staff requirements.

Example 2

The data in Table 14.12 show the total worldwide air passengers during the period 1974 to 1982 (the figures are given in 10 millions).

The relationship between the year and number of airline passengers could be used to consider estimates of demand in future years. Table 14.13 shows the calculations involved in evaluating the correlation coefficient between year (x) and number of passengers (y). To simplify the calculations the years have been labelled as 1, 2, 3, etc. The

Table 14.12 Analysis of worldwide air travel (figures in 10 millions)

Year	No. of passengers
1974	52
1975	53
1976	58
1977	61
1978	68
1979	75
1980	75
1981	75
1982	76

Source: American Express (1995).

summations obtained from Table 14.13 are as follows:

$$\Sigma x = 45, \qquad \Sigma y = 593$$
$$\Sigma x^2 = 285, \qquad \Sigma y^2 = 39\,873, \qquad \Sigma (xy) = 3175$$

These values can be used to calculate the correlation coefficient which is found to be $r = 0.96$. This value of r indicates that there is a strong linear relationship between the year and total passenger numbers. Therefore the regression equation, as given by $y = ax + b$, can be determined where the values of a and b are found as below:

$$a = \frac{\Sigma (xy) - n\bar{x}\bar{y}}{\Sigma x^2 - n\bar{x}^2}$$
$$b = \bar{y} - a\bar{x}$$

Substituting the values of the summations obtained from the table, it will be found that

$$a = \frac{3175 - 9(5)(65.89)}{285 - 9(5)^2}$$
$$= \frac{210}{60}$$
$$= 3.5$$

Similarly, $b = 65.89 - 3.5(5) = 48.39$.

Therefore the regression equation relating the year (x) to the number of passengers (y) is given by $y = 3.5x + 48.39$. This can be used to forecast the demand for worldwide air travel in other years. For instance, in 1983 (when x would be equal to 10) an estimate of the number of passengers would be found by $y = 3.5(10) + 48.39 = 35 + 48.39 = 83.39$. Therefore in 1983 using this regression method it could be estimated that the number of passengers would be 83 (ten millions), i.e. 830 millions.

However, care should be taken when using a simple regression model in this way. There are a number of problems with this approach. For instance, the following points should be considered:

1. There are a limited number of previous values to work with. In this example, there are nine values, which in correlation terms is not often sufficient. However, since the

Table 14.13 Air travel: calculations for correlation

Year	x	y	x^2	y^2	xy
1974	1	52	1	2,704	52
1975	2	53	4	2,809	106
1976	3	58	9	3,364	174
1977	4	61	16	3,721	244
1978	5	68	25	4,624	340
1979	6	75	36	5,625	450
1980	7	75	49	5,625	525
1981	8	75	64	5,625	600
1982	9	76	81	5,776	684
Totals	45	593	285	39,873	3,175

values in this case represent annual demand figures it would probably not be appropriate to consider figures further back than those already given (even if they were available). Another approach would be to consider monthly or quarterly data in order to increase the number of values available for analysis.

2. It is not certain that the growth in passenger traffic does conform to a straight line, although the correlation analysis seems to confirm that it does. A scatter diagram of the data provided shows that the high growth in traffic during the early years has declined so that during the last four years (1979 to 1982) there has been very little change. Thus it may be more accurate to fit a curve to the data rather than a straight line, as shown in Figure 14.7.

3. Even assuming that the most appropriate model is chosen, forecasting based purely on historical data is still extremely problematic. There are a range of factors that could affect the demand for air travel, such as the level of economic growth. Clearly, a worldwide recession or boom would affect the demand for such travel. A number of other factors such as price, competition and advertising are also certain to affect the demand.

Example 3

Many studies have considered the effectiveness of advertising in generating additional demand from tourists. For instance, a review by Burke and Gitelson (1990) considered a number of 'conversion' studies which looked at the percentage of respondents to advertising who actually visited the specific destination. A simple approach to analysing the effectiveness of advertising is to consider the correlation between advertising expenditure and demand. For example, consider Table 14.14 giving the total advertising expenditure and revenue for a hotel chain based in the south of England.

The data in Table 14.14 could be used to consider the degree of correlation between advertising expenditure (x) and revenue (y). The correlation coefficient is found to be $r = 0.59$. Based on such a small sample (six values), this value of r is not significant and therefore it cannot be concluded that there is a linear relationship between advertising

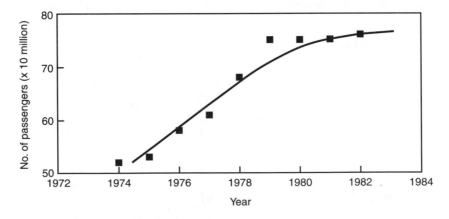

Figure 14.7   Analysis of air traffic demand

Table 14.14 Monthly hotel advertising expenditure and revenue

	Month					
	1	*2*	*3*	*4*	*5*	*6*
Advertising expenditure (£1000s)	7	9	12	10	6	4
Revenue (£100,000s)	3.1	4.3	4.7	5.1	4.9	3.3

and revenue. This may lead to a claim that the type of advertising used is not effective. However, this would really need to be investigated over a larger number of months before it could be confirmed. It should also be noted that relationships other than those of a linear nature should also be considered.

Furthermore, this analysis has not taken into account the behaviour of potential customers and their reaction to advertising. For instance, the impact of a potential 'lag' effect in this type of data should be considered. The use of advertising in a given month may not change demand immediately but may have a significant effect at a later stage. For example, the results of advertising a range of package holidays may not be seen until the following year. Thus, for this type of data there is likely to be a lag between the two variables.

In the simple example introduced above, consider a one-month lag between the variables, that is, the possibility of advertising affecting the demand in the following month. To analyse this, consider the advertising expenditure (x) with the revenue one month later (y), so that, for example, the advertising expenditure of £7000 is linked to the revenue one month later of £430,000. There would then be only five pairs of values (the advertising expenditure in month 6 cannot be used), and the correlation coefficient of these values is found to be $r = 0.90$. This value is much more significant than the previous value and shows that the advertising does affect demand a month later. This analysis could be continued to examine a two-month lag to investigate whether the effect is even greater. This, however, is not the case (the reader may wish to confirm that the correlation coefficient using a two-month lag is only 0.08).

To conclude this example, it seems as though there is a lagged relationship between advertising and revenue. Clearly, there are a range of other issues that need to be investigated before one could be certain of this. One factor not yet considered is the seasonality of demand. For example, it may be that the pattern of demand over the six-month period would have been similar to that shown with or without advertising. Further forecasting methods using the ideas of seasonality are introduced in the next section.

Forecasting

The previous section has used the techniques of correlation and regression in order to obtain basic forecasts of given values (see example 3 in previous section). In this section these ideas will be developed further to incorporate an analysis of seasonality and review basic techniques to obtain forecasts from historical data.

Forecasting models usually incorporate the elements of *trend* and *seasonal variation* into the final estimates. For instance, two simple models often used are the Additive and Multiplicative Models briefly described below.

A forecast of a variable (denoted by X_i) is a combination of the trend estimate (T_i) and the seasonal variation (S_i) as follows:

$$\text{Additive Model: } X_i = T_i + S_i$$
$$\text{Multiplicative Model: } X_i = T_i \times S_i$$

Other variations such as cyclical or irregular movements can also be incorporated into more complex models. With data involving significant seasonality, a simple approach to isolating the trend is the use of moving averages as shown in the following examples.

Example 1

Table 14.15 shows the numbers of visitors to a theme park (the figures are given in hundreds per day to the nearest hundred).

To estimate the number of visitors to the theme park during each day in week 4, the values over 21 days shown in the table can be illustrated as in Figure 14.8. The problem for forecasting this type of data is that there is a strong 'seasonal' element in the series of values. It can be seen that demand reaches a peak at the weekends, and is at its lowest during the early part of the week (Monday to Wednesday). Any forecast of future values would need to take this seasonal element into account. Such a series of data is analysed in two parts. Firstly, the data is smoothed out in order to isolate the trend. This can be achieved by 'moving averages' as shown in Table 14.16. An average of every seven values (i.e. a weekly average) is calculated. A regression analysis could then be used on these averages to obtain a forecast of future trend. The moving averages and regression line are shown on the graph in Figure 14.8. Secondly, the seasonal element is isolated by considering the differences between the moving averages and the actual figures on each day (assuming an additive model). These can then be analysed in terms of the likely seasonal element on each day in the forecasted period.

These two techniques are shown in Table 14.16. The moving averages from this table are shown on the graph and a regression line is drawn using these values. In this way estimates of the trend values in week 4 based on the regression line are found to be:

Mon	Tue	Wed	Thu	Fri	Sat	Sun
14.7	14.9	15.0	15.2	15.3	15.5	15.6

A simple procedure to estimate the likely seasonal variation in each day is to find the averages for the deviations in each period. For example, on Thursday there are three deviations: −2.0, −3.14 and −3.0. The average of these values is −2.71. This is the

Table 14.15 Theme park visitors (hundreds per day)

	Mon	*Tue*	*Wed*	*Thu*	*Fri*	*Sat*	*Sun*
Week 1	9	7	8	10	13	19	18
Week 2	9	8	10	10	15	21	19
Week 3	10	9	10	11	16	23	19

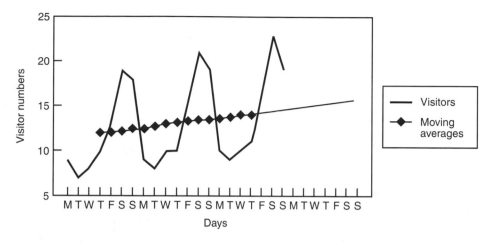

Figure 14.8 Graph of theme park visitors

estimated seasonal variation for Thursday each week. Similarly, all the seasonal variations can be found as follows:

Mon	Tue	Wed	Thu	Fri	Sat	Sun
−3.5	−4.7	−3.5	−2.7	+1.4	+7.2	+5.6

Combining the trend and seasonal variation values together provides an estimate of the week 4 figures. For instance, an estimate of the Monday figure in week 4 would be

Table 14.16 Trend and seasonal analysis

Day	No. of visitors	7-point moving averages	Deviations
Mon	9		
Tue	7		
Wed	8		
Thu	10	12.00	−2.00
Fri	13	12.00	1.00
Sat	19	12.14	6.86
Sun	18	12.43	5.57
Mon	9	12.43	−3.43
Tue	8	12.71	−4.71
Wed	10	13.00	−3.00
Thu	10	13.14	−3.14
Fri	15	13.29	1.71
Sat	21	13.43	7.57
Sun	19	13.43	5.57
Mon	10	13.57	−3.57
Tue	9	13.71	−4.71
Wed	10	14.00	−4.00
Thu	11	14.00	−3.00
Fri	16		
Sat	23		
Sun	19		

14.7 + (−3.5) = 11.2. This value would need to be rounded (to 11, i.e. 1100 visitors) since the forecasts cannot be more accurate than the original data given. The final forecasts for the number of visitors in week 4 are:

Mon	Tue	Wed	Thu	Fri	Sat	Sun
1100	1000	1200	1200	1700	2300	2100

The accuracy of this forecast depends on a range of factors including the following:

1. *The specific forecasting model used.* For instance, in this case an 'additive model' with a linear trend was used. Other models could be used, including multiplicative and/or non-linear trend models (see next example). Even when the most appropriate model is used, there can still be significant errors in forecasting due to irregular movements. In practice, a forecasting model evolves as more data become available. In addition to the trend and seasonal variation, other items may need to be included in the model. For example, there may be a cyclical variation involved which corresponds to the 'product life-cycle' (Johnson and Thomas, 1992).
2. *External factors.* The forecasting model as described above relies on historical data and the assumption that all other factors remain unchanged. However, often the situation can alter because of a range of variations in the external environment. For instance, consider the forecast of total visitors to the theme park. These figures may be affected by factors such as:

- economic recession or boom
- level of competition and price comparisons
- level of advertising (including that of competitors)
- national and international tourist trends
- currency exchange rates (particularly if there is a large proportion of overseas visitors).

Example 2

Table 14.17 shows the gross revenue for a hotel in the south of England (the figures are given in £100,000s).

The revenue data shown in Table 14.17 are illustrated in Figure 14.9. The diagram shows that there is an increasing trend for the revenue at this hotel. The trend is isolated

Table 14.17   Hotel revenue (£100,000s)

	| Quarter			
	1st	*2nd*	*3rd*	*4th*
1994	4.2	5.5	6.1	3.5
1995	4.3	5.6	6.3	3.6
1996	4.9	6.9	7.3	4.4
1997	5.6	7.7	8.4	5.0

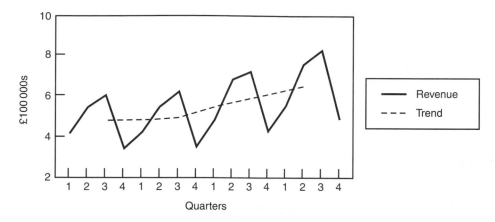

Figure 14.9 Gross revenue for hotel

by using four-point moving averages, since there is a regular seasonal component repeating itself every four values corresponding to the four quarters each year. The trend may correspond to a curve rather than a straight line and this could be incorporated into the forecast by fitting a curve to the trend values. Also it may be apparent from the graph that the seasonal variations tend to be increasing as the trend increases. This is indicative of the multiplicative model, and therefore ratios between the actual revenue and trend values are found rather than the method used in the previous example where deviations were calculated.

Thus, the two primary elements of the forecast are evaluated as follows:

1. The trend is obtained from four-point moving averages and is estimated using a curve-fitting process. Using this approach the estimates of trend are found to be:

Quarter	1st	2nd	3rd	4th
Trend	7.5	7.7	8.0	8.3

(It is interesting to note that if a straight line trend were assumed then the four trend estimates would be 7.0, 7.2, 7.3 and 7.5.)

2. Using a multiplicative model the seasonal indices are found to be:

Quarter	1st	2nd	3rd	4th
Index	0.88	1.17	1.25	0.71

These two elements are combined together to obtain a forecast of the gross revenue in £100,000s as shown:

- 1st Quarter: $7.5 \times 0.88 = 6.6$
- 2nd Quarter: $7.7 \times 1.17 = 9.0$
- 3rd Quarter: $8.0 \times 1.25 = 10.0$
- 4th Quarter: $8.3 \times 0.71 = 5.9$

The accuracy of these forecasts is again subject to the range of factors introduced in the previous example. In general terms it is notoriously difficult to obtain reliable forecasts. For instance, the estimates of tourist demand (Johnson and Thomas, 1992) are problematic and subject to unforeseen fluctuations. Nevertheless it is important, from a management decision-making perspective, that valid forecasts are obtained. Furthermore, the long-term forecasting required for strategic planning can be very unreliable. In this example on the estimation of demand, the forecasts over the next year may be reasonably reliable but will be increasingly doubtful over an extended period such as five years.

Conclusions and future research issues

This chapter has set out to provide the reader with a clear and concise understanding of Quantitative Data Analysis techniques within the wider context of tourism and hospitality. In introducing the techniques available, and their applicability to a range of management decision-making scenarios, the reader is made aware of the historical vacuum of research activity in the tourism and hospitality industries. The predominance of small, often family-run businesses in the two industries in part explains this previous lack of interest in gaining an adequate information base on which to make decisions. However, the somewhat hostile market environment of the 1990s has represented a catalytic focus for many organisations, destinations, regions and countries to adopt a far more professional and long-term approach to the collection, analysis and presentation of data.

With regard to the presentation of data, the use of tabular or graphical formats was introduced. Pie charts, bar charts, multiple bar charts and line charts were all evident in the examples given and, in many ways, demonstrate the variety of formats available for the presentation of data and research findings. In order to summarise the array of data available to produce meaningful analysis a section on descriptive data analysis was included. This section introduced the reader to the centre and spread as well as to the two most common methods of finding the average, notably the arithmetic mean and median. Furthermore, it highlighted the two most important methods of measuring the spread in a set of data: the standard deviation and quartiles. As with the preceding sections, that on correlation and regression used a number of contemporary tourism and hospitality scenarios to explain their application to the two industries in day-to-day management situations. Unlike the previous introductory techniques, both correlation and regression are highly beneficial to decision makers when considering the relationship between two sets of data such as the link between advertising expenditure and hotel occupancy rates. The final section outlining the range of Quantitative Data Analysis techniques available was on that of forecasting. This is of particular importance to those involved in tourism and hospitality planning and decision making as it incorporates an analysis of seasonality. Whether one is to use simple models such as the Additive and Multiplicative Models or more complex models, they are of significant benefit to hotel operators, theme park managers and package tour operators alike.

However, as with all tourism and hospitality decisions the taking into consideration of external factors is highly significant. Many of the techniques mentioned above are of limited use unless one considers the multiplicity of factors that linger on the decision-making horizon. These may include periods of economic boom or recession, a significant change in the nature and volume of competition, international tourist trends and changes in international exchange rates. All in all, the correct application of Quantitative Data Analysis techniques offers tourism and hospitality managers the opportunity to summarise the results of research activity by efficient means of tabulation and statistical analysis, something that Athiyaman (1997) suggests has been missing from tourism and hospitality decision making for a long time.

The remarkable ability of tourism and hospitality to survive economic downturns and their ability to expand on the back of continually improving international communication is likely to ensure that, together, they will continue to represent a significant factor in the economies of many industrialised countries, and indeed the only hope for future development in many developing countries (Witt and Moutinho, 1995). In addition to the above, the sheer dynamism of the tourism and hospitality environments and the large number of external pressures looming on the horizon suggest that the time has arrived where no longer can a manager in the fields of tourism or hospitality ignore the benefits that a sound knowledge of Quantitative Data Analysis techniques offers. Owing to the highly complex nature of the tourism and hospitality industries, very seldom would the authors recommend that the above techniques be used in isolation. In many instances the multi-disciplinary nature of tourism and hospitality suggests that a variety of research techniques should be used when solving management problems. The techniques described in this chapter have solely concentrated on the analysis of historical data in projecting forward. Other methods incorporating the ideas of regression to link variables together could also be used in this context. In reality, the authors would always recommend a balance between quantitative and qualitative techniques which, when used together, are far more likely to obtain valid estimates and more accurate forecasts of what is looming on the horizon.

References and bibliography

American Express (1995) *World Tourism Overview*, American Express Publishing, New York.

Athiyaman A (1997) Knowledge development in tourism: tourism demand research. *Tourism Management* **18**(4), pp. 221–228.

Brent-Ritchie JR (1993) Policy and managerial priorities for the 1990's and beyond, in Pearce DG and Butler RW (Eds) *Tourism Research: Critiques and Challenges*, Routledge, London, pp. 201–216.

Burke J and Gitelson R (1990) Conversion studies: assumptions, applications, accuracy, and abuse. *Journal of Travel Research*, **28**(3), pp. 46–50.

Calantone RJ and Mazanec JA (1991) Marketing management and tourism. *Annals of Tourism Research* **18**, pp. 101–119.

Camacho FE and Knain DN (1989) Listening to customers: the market research function at Marriott Corporation. *Marketing Research* (March), pp. 5–14.

Cooper C, Fletcher J, Gilbert D and Wanhill S (1993) *Tourism Principles and Practice*, Longman, Harlow.

Johnson P and Thomas B (1992) *Choice and Tourism Demand*, Mansell, London.

Jones P and Lockwood A (1990) *The Management of Hospitality Operations*, Cassell, London.

Kotler P, Bowen J and Makens J (1996) *Marketing for Hospitality and Tourism*, Prentice-Hall, Englewood Cliffs, New Jersey.

Latham J (1993) Consumer behaviour and tourism demand, in Cooper C *et al.* (Eds) *Tourism Principles and Practice*, Longman, Harlow, pp. 20–31.

March R (1994) Tourism marketing myopia. *Tourism Management* **15**(6), pp. 411–415.

Middleton V (1994) *Marketing in Travel and Tourism*, Butterworth-Heinemann, Oxford.

NEDC (1992) *Costs and Manpower Productivity in UK Hotels*, NEDO, London.

Pearce DG and Butler RW (1993) *Tourism Research: Critiques and Challenges*, Routledge, London.

Proctor T (1997) *Essentials of Marketing Research*, Pitman, London.

Ryan C and Barnett S (1995) Hotel conference managers: skills and training needs in New Zealand. *Journal of Vacation Marketing* **1**(4), pp. 349–359.

Smith SLJ (1995) *Tourism Analysis—A Handbook*, 2nd edition, Longman, Harlow.

Stewart D (1996) *Hoteliers and Hotels: Case Studies in the Growth and Development of UK Hotel Companies 1945–1989*, Search Publications, Glasgow.

Wight PA (1997) Ecotourism accommodation spectrum: does supply match demand? *Tourism Management* **18**(4), pp. 209–220.

Witt SF and Moutinho L (1995) *Tourism Marketing and Management Handbook*, Prentice Hall, London.

15 Qualitative data analysis and interpretation

ANNE HAMPTON

Introduction

This chapter will focus on the analysis of qualitative data rather than enter the general debate as to the appropriateness of qualitative research techniques. It is, however, worth reiterating the richness of data that may be collected through qualitative research techniques and the great value that may be gained from such information by developing and dynamic industries such as hospitality and tourism. Specifically this is because, in researching organisations and their customers, qualitative methods may encompass changes over time and provide more detailed or personal data, as well as being more readily understandable by the majority of people (Brunt, 1997).

The main methods for collecting qualitative data include interviewing, focus groups, observation and case studies. Each of these qualitative methods has been discussed earlier in this book and the merits and criteria for their use have been presented, although the advantage of using multiple methods within qualitative research are recognised (Mason, 1996; Marshall and Rossman, 1989). However, in considering the overall purpose of gathering qualitative data it may be concluded that it can help to develop an understanding of an otherwise unknown subject, give greater insight into reasons underlying various behaviours, practices, attitudes and decision-making processes, and provide greater depth of knowledge on a given subject. All these are pertinent to developing an understanding of the hospitality and tourism industries.

Easterby-Smith, Thorpe and Lowe (1991) recognise the contribution qualitative research may make to understanding the complexity of organisational problems, and Lowe (1992) asserts that such methods can reveal the 'texture' of organisations, this being the dynamic interaction between the activities of managers, employees and customers and, in the case of hospitality organisations, the added complexity of guests in the hotel/restaurant who may not be the customer. Thus, qualitative approaches may be appropriate at different stages of the research process and have different objectives. Whatever the purpose or method used, the aim of collecting qualitative data is to benefit from the depth and richness of the descriptive data collected. Such 'thick descriptions' provide detail of the context and meaning of events and situations for those involved and those investigating (Geertz, 1983). This begins to highlight the multiplicity of purposes for the collection of qualitative materials and also to indicate the range of objectives that may exist for the collection of such data.

The Handbook of Contemporary Hospitality Management Research, Edited by Bob Brotherton.

Similarly, qualitative data collection may be undertaken by many categories of people for many different reasons: students for assignments, major projects and thesis preparation; academics for teaching material or for other studies; managers in hospitality organisations for establishing more detailed knowledge of their customer base; and consultants for obtaining specific information for a client or project. The use of qualitative research is increasing in consultancy research and may particularly be evidenced through research into quality service delivery by consultants to supplement more traditional management measures, e.g. mystery guests and focus groups of hotel customers. These are just a few examples of those who may be involved in qualitative research work.

It must not be forgotten, however, that there is a need for careful analysis of any qualitative data if it is to provide useful, valid and meaningful information. It is simply insufficient to decide that qualitative information may be collected and interpreted without stringent and rigorous analysis. Appropriate analysis is essential if valid and reliable conclusions are to be drawn from qualitative data. It is all too easy to forget to consider how data will be analysed *prior* to undertaking the data collection stage.

Although many pieces of research may be totally quantitative by design, there are many instances where it is useful to have an element of qualitative data to provide either developmental information on which the remainder of the research is founded, or supporting information to assist in making sense of the findings. Thus, there may be a need for qualitative information and analysis at different stages in research programmes. At the beginning of a study it may be used to identify beliefs held by groups or individuals, to establish views or thought processes, or to obtain expert views informally. During the research process it may be used to gain a deeper insight or understanding of why a particular view is held, and at the end to clarify and help make sense of the underlying reasons which have led to the findings. This clearly demonstrates that quantitative and qualitative research methods may be both compatible and complementary to each other. This may be particularly obvious in considering even the simplest questionnaire design where it may be common to include open-ended questions to provide support or rationalisation for the quantitative findings. Such open-ended questions typically elicit qualitative responses which may be analysed only qualitatively.

This chapter will therefore begin with a summary of the advantages of using qualitative methods for hospitality and tourism research, and then address the issues concerning the analysis of qualitative data from the research design stage, to data collection and finally to data analysis and interpretation. Suggestions are made as to suitable approaches to analysing qualitative data and two frameworks are discussed.

Advantages of qualitative methods for hospitality and tourism research

Kelly (1980) made a plea for more qualitative research in the leisure field, arguing that qualitative research had been neglected in the field of leisure during the 1960s and 1970s. Veal (1992) bases the following arguments on Kelly's original ideas:

- The method corresponds with the nature of the phenomenon being studied, that is, leisure—*including hospitality*—is a qualitative experience.
- The method 'brings people back in' to leisure research.

- The results are more understandable to people who are not statistically trained.
- The method is more likely to be able to encompass changes over time (especially important here is the recognition of people's past life history and its strong influence on their individual views and behaviour).
- The close interaction between people which is a characteristic of leisure—*and hospitality*—and the non-verbal behaviour associated with this favours a qualitative approach which more readily allows and encourages recording of such information.
- Kelly (1980) argues that qualitative techniques are better at understanding people's needs and aspirations (although it should be recognised that many psychologists investigating these aspects may disagree on this point).

Whilst these arguments have been put forward for the tourism and leisure industries by Veal (1992), they are all equally valid for hospitality management, not only because it is a major sector of the tourism industry but also because of the need to develop a deeper understanding of hospitality organisations, their managers, employees and customers. Chacko and Nebel (1990: 383) state that 'hospitality educators and researchers have traditionally relied on quantitative research methods to "explain" this complex and multi-dimensional industry.' These same authors also advocate that qualitative research is a more appropriate methodology for hospitality researchers to use (Chacko and Nebel, 1990: 383). This is especially so when the subject of the study is concerned with behavioural issues, such as leadership, managerial skills and processes, as well as customer and employee relationship issues. All these subjects are topical for today's hospitality and tourism industries.

It is also worth noting the need to produce interpretations that are readily understood by hospitality managers (Slattery, 1983) so that they may then use the findings to develop and improve their management activities and service provisions for customers. This remains a valid comment, especially when managers in the international hospitality industry experience rapid environmental, social and technological changes '... in an increasingly complex and volatile world ...' (Olsen and Cassee, 1997: 60). The International Hotel Association (IHA) White Paper has identified 'new management' as being an essential component for the future of successful hospitality organisations. Such 'new managers' need relevant and useful research material which they can readily and efficiently assimilate for their individual and organisational needs (Olsen and Cassee, 1997). It is suggested that qualitative research will be particularly pertinent to the development of hospitality managers' knowledge and approaches to managing human relationships (customers and workforce) and in the management of cultural diversity.

Edgar and Taylor (1996) suggest a need to shift the emphasis of research into *strategy* to make hospitality research more mainstream in its methods and techniques. However, many of their arguments are relevant to hospitality management research as a whole. These authors have developed an evolutionary model of strategic management by examining the shifting emphasis of research. In strategic management terms this evolutionary model represents a shift away from strategy and strategic planning frameworks to approaches based on the organisation's core competence and organisation purpose. Edgar and Taylor purport that research approaches have softened towards being more qualitative in nature as a more holistic approach to strategic management is established. This shift in emphasis in research terms has resulted in there being greater interest in the cognitive issues of organisations and comparisons of international and intercultural dimensions of strategy.

In addition, as hospitality businesses continue to become more international, new and different decisions and situations arise. These demand explanation and understanding from both conceptual and practical perspectives. It is suggested that qualitative research may provide the most reliable and valid means of identifying the issues for the management of cultural diversity associated with internationalisation and that a holistic view of any situation is essential. As argued in Chapter 4, interdisciplinary and multi-disciplinary research may therefore be considered to be an appropriate approach to both quantitative and qualitative studies.

In an earlier paper, Taylor and Edgar (1995) argued that there was a need for hospitality management researchers to become more mainstream in their approaches and to be more familiar with mainstream research, especially those reflecting leading edge practice. They recommend hospitality management researchers to pursue research from a more interdisciplinary base and 'to embrace a broader range of methodological approaches'. It is worth noting here that they particularly emphasise the need for qualitative approaches to be included in hospitality research.

Principles of the data analysis process

This section presents the factors that affect the overall design process and suggests principles to assist in the creation of good practices to ensure rigorous qualitative analysis. It then presents two structures or frameworks developed by different authors for maintaining 'good practice' in the analysis of qualitative data. Whilst the names used for the suggested structures are different, the stages are very similar in principle.

To the novice qualitative researcher, the literature on qualitative analysis may appear confusing and contains many debates on approaches, e.g. inductive versus deductive, and 'Grounded Theory' as an alternative to the traditional positivist approaches. This may result from qualitative data analysis being rooted and developed in the social sciences, whilst management researchers have only relatively recently accepted the techniques used. However, the objective of this chapter is not to enter into such theoretical debates, but rather to provide an outline of the basic principles of good data analysis and to assist the researcher in their decision-making processes concerned with how to develop sound analysis for the data they have or are about to collect. Throughout, it is vital to be guided by the study aims.

Getting started—before the analysis begins!

Although this chapter is about the *analysis* of qualitative data, it is worth noting the importance of thinking about, and planning for, the analysis stage during the initial design process. Table 15.1 demonstrates the benefits to be gained from considering the analysis issues during the design and planning stages.

The methods and techniques to be used in the analysis will affect the type of data to be collected and the way in which it is to be collected. Design decisions are likely to

Table 15.1 Reasons for considering qualitative analysis at the design stage

Benefit	Explanation
Focuses attention on study as a whole	Ensures the researcher considers the whole study at the start of the work; helps develop a more holistic framework
Reduces any uncertainty	Robson and Foster (1989) argue that careful analysis reduces any uncertainty; encourages attention to sub-themes
Improves the descriptive data	Increases attention to detail in the analysis stage. Encourages not relying on memory or abbreviated notes alone
Prevents a purely superficial analysis	Careful design of analysis at the outset encourages careful analysis
Maintains the value of qualitative data	Analysis will reflect the objectives of the study and be appropriate to the the data collected

influence the management of the research project, such as how to store the data, how to process it and what technology is available to assist in these processes.

Miles and Huberman (1994: 16) state that 'design decisions also permit and support later analysis; they prefigure your analytic moves'. In other words, the overall research design affects the way the data collected will be analysed; if these issues are considered at the beginning of the research process, one is more likely to be guided towards the type of information that can be analysed meaningfully, and the choice of analytical technique will be suited to the data collected. If these decisions are made at the start of the research process they may then be altered as the research develops (if and when necessary), but such changes will be made in a more informed and constructive manner if they form a part of the overall research rationale. One of the advantages of qualitative research design is that it remains flexible and evolves as the data are collected and subsequently examined (Chacko and Nebel, 1990: 384).

There are a number of factors that affect the design process in respect of the type of analysis to be used. These include:

- the objectives of the study
- the time available (for both collection and analysis)
- the degree of knowledge already held about the subject being investigated
- the research instruments which are already available
- the extent of the researcher's experience of data collection methods and analytical tools available
- the sample size and method.

It is often the inability to adopt a specific technique that causes concern for researchers new to qualitative data analysis. The outline framework presented in Table 15.2 has been developed from the ideas and concepts presented by Miles and Huberman (1994) and Ritchie and Spencer (1994). Both models are similar in their conceptual principles and both take a very pragmatic approach to the analysis of qualitative data. Similarly, both methods are generic in nature and assist in the development of an analysis that is appropriate to the given data in a study; they provide a structure which will

Table 15.2   Stages in the data analysis process

Stage number	Miles and Huberman (1994)	Ritchie and Spencer (1994)
1	Early steps in analysis	Familiarisation and identification of thematic framework
2	Exploring and describing	Indexing
3	Ordering and explaining	Charting
4	Drawing and verifying conclusions	Mapping and interpretation

Source: Developed from Miles and Huberman (1994) and Ritchie and Spencer (1994).

encourage the user in the application of the model. However, this process should not be viewed as a rigid structure to be followed, but rather as a form to allow the appropriate framework for analysis to be created or developed.

This table demonstrates that the frameworks available to ensure sound data analysis are broadly similar in terms of the practical activities involved. Both models suggest stages (albeit with different titles) which emphasise the need to state the research objectives and that these will help determine the exact methods of analysis used. Adherence to the conceptual principles and practices of these frameworks will not only improve the quality and depth of the findings but also substantially increase the respectability of qualitative research. Whilst these frameworks assist in developing a holistic overview of data analysis, a different point is also worth considering. The nature of qualitative research means that data collection and analysis may, at least in part, occur simultaneously (Connell and Lowe, 1997).

Data collection methods

Whilst full details of the most popular qualitative research methods used in hospitality research are given in earlier chapters, it is worth stressing here the need to consider the method being used in terms of how it will affect the type of data being gathered. It is likely that semi-structured interviews will produce different data from participant observation techniques. This will in turn impact on the way the data is managed and analysed. For example, a series of semi-structured interviews with hotel general managers will produce significantly different material from the notes that might result from the researcher observing the same general managers. Both studies may have started with the same objective of identifying how the managers spend their time, but will produce differing styles of notes, recordings and data. Clearly, the method used to collect data will also affect how the data analysis is planned and carried out, as well as the nature of the findings.

It is at this stage that the hospitality researcher will begin to develop a real awareness of the large quantity of data they will have to manage. One 30-minute interview with a hotel's human resource manager could easily produce a 30-minute audiocassette recording, at least 10–15 pages of notes transcribed from this tape, a large pile of policy documents and an equally large number of training manuals, as well as recruitment advertisements and other documentation used by the hotel.

There are a number of principles that apply to the management of qualitative data analysis generally and are particularly important in data collection. These include:

- Be guided by the aims and objectives of the study.
- Place all data into an understandable and readable format. Avoid working from untidy notes and abbreviations that may be meaningful only to one person.
- For the findings to be useful it is important that the analysis process is *evaluative* and *critical*. It is insufficient simply to report the details of case study material in a descriptive manner or to report on how many people/interviews/statements support an idea.
- Allow ample time for the analysis stage of the work. It should be seen as equally as important as the gathering of information.

Analysing data

At the analysis stage there may be one or more differing types of data: verbal recordings, video recordings, observation notes, written notes/summaries, or case study material. It is partly this variety of data that makes the analysis of qualitative data less prescriptive than quantitative analysis, where certain statistical tests are clearly determined as appropriate for particular data types. With qualitative data it may be less obvious to the researcher as to exactly how to test or verify the data. It must always be remembered that the purpose of the qualitative research remains instrumental in determining the analysis used (Brunt, 1997). For example, if the purpose of the research was to explore individuals' ideas in a specific subject with the objective of then developing a questionnaire, the use of detailed notes in their raw form may be sufficient to enable construction of the questionnaire which would in turn be piloted prior to formal use. However, qualitative data may also be analysed to produce reports on the findings in its own right. How should an analysis which is as valid and reliable as quantitative analysis be conducted?

The following discussion outlines the principles involved in achieving sound, valid and reliable qualitative data analysis.

Preparation of data for analysis   It has already been mentioned that it is very important for the data collected to be presented in a format which more than one person could work from. This applies whatever the type of data; most commonly this means putting the data into a written document(s) that could be read or understood by anyone using the data but may also be in the form of a videocassette or other visual material. The reason for clear presentation of data is that the following stages of data reduction and analysis are much easier if the data is presented thoroughly and in an easily readable/viewable format. It is very difficult to work from abbreviated and poorly written notes and the lack of clarity of such untidy notes could mean that important data is ignored or misinterpreted.

Whilst it is not intended to be prescriptive, this section of the chapter will outline some practical activities to assist in the clear presentation of information gathered. Many students and researchers find it difficult to handle the vast amount of data that qualitative research may produce. The large amount of material is further complicated by the range of types of material collected (from video and audio recordings to written organisational documents and charts).

- *Apply the principles of good storage and retrieval systems.*   Levine (1985) outlined five general principles relating to the storage and retrieval of qualitative data. They are intended to assist in the management of large amounts of data and in developing a valid analytical process. They stress the importance of thoroughness and may be applied equally to manual or computerised records. The principles suggested by Levine (1985) are formatting, cross-retrieval, indexing or coding, abstracting and pagination. Thus, from the outset of gathering data it is essential to establish systems of note-taking and filing which enable easy access to the data. Part of this process will include clear cross-referencing of data to allow and encourage viewing data from a number of viewpoints. These points will be discussed in greater detail in the following sections of this chapter.

- *Keep detailed lists of all documentation held*, and supplementary information on this data. Material may include hotel brochures and directories, annual reports, hotel training manuals or policy documents. The record of data may usefully summarise not just the name of the documents but also the researcher's own commentary on these, such as the contents, the style of report, the type and size of manual, and sup-plementary information given by the document provider, such as the frequency of use, thus developing from the outset good formatting and retrieval systems.

- *Maintain contact summary sheets.*   Contact summary sheets are useful means of recording data on all respondents so that consistency of information is achieved. They should be specifically designed for each research project but in principle will contain some or all of the following information: contact's name, job title and posi-tion, where and when the interview took place, interviewer's initial response and thoughts about the interview (including the contribution made by the respondent, the degree of enthusiasm, comments on the personality of the person being interviewed where related to the comments made), and any new issues or ideas that have been raised. Figure 15.1 gives an example of a simple contact summary sheet.

The data analysis process in practice

Stage I: Familiarisation and discovery

This stage is concerned with beginning to familiarise oneself with the data and then to begin to identify initial or tentative themes, but really only noting ideas and statements that are easily identifiable. It makes the researcher identify new ideas, concepts or themes that may only now be seen following the completion of the original interviews or observations. Perhaps the most useful phrase that describes the activities of this stage is '*total immersion*' in the data.

It is essential to review *all* the data at this point. The researcher must therefore listen to any audiocassettes, watch any videos, read and *re-read* any material or documenta-tion. Most research into hospitality will produce formal documentation whatever the subject of research. This may take the form of policy documents, training manuals, pub-licity materials, etc. Although this may not be viewed as *central* to the study, it should nonetheless be subjected to careful analysis as it performs one or both of two functions:

Contact Summary Sheet

Respondent's name:

Date and place where interviewed:

Position and title within the organisation:

Key responsibilities:

Interest in the research:

Summary of major issues raised:

Interviewer's initial thoughts on the interview:

Points to note for research methodology:

Figure 15.1 Example of a contact summary sheet. This contact summary sheet is an outline of that currently being used in a study of senior directors in hotel companies

setting the context of the organisation and aspects of the business perceived as important and/or giving invaluable insight into pertinent issues within the organisation.

However, when using documentary evidence certain questions need to be addressed. These include: do these documents provide a complete account or perspective of the situation? Or is further information needed to make sense of them? Why, by whom and for whom were they prepared? For what purpose were they intended to be used? And, perhaps most importantly, are they reliable and accurate? (Mason, 1996).

It is also important to transcribe any cassette recordings so that a written version exists; this will enable greater information to be pulled out from the data than pure listening or watching can do. It is useful to have appropriate transcribing equipment at this stage. The sophistication of the controls on such equipment is likely to increase accuracy and detail to the transcription process.

As the material is read, a written record of the ideas that develop should be kept. This may be done in a number of ways, with the choice being made on the basis of whichever is most meaningful to the individual. Some people find it is most helpful to write notes in the margin, some prefer the use of different coloured highlighter pens, and others prefer to keep a separate log or memos of the ideas. Also write notes of possible interpretations and begin to identify emerging themes. These should be kept somewhere specific so that they can be referred back to with ease. These notes are often referred to as *memos* and their purpose and contribution to the analysis process will be discussed in detail in Stage III: Ordering and displaying. It may also prove useful to get someone else to read the information held and comment on it. Another person may be able to provide additional valuable comments or conceptual ideas that have not been seen in the first instance.

Stage II: coding and display

This phase can only be started once the researcher is totally familiar with the full information available. Many researchers complete this stage of the analysis, but do not use the terminology that has been developed by qualitative researchers over the last 20 years. One of the terms often ignored, especially by hospitality students, is 'coding'.

Coding is a 'systematic way of developing and refining interpretations of the data' (Taylor and Bogdan, 1984: 136). Coding provides an analytical extension of the work begun in Stage I. It is best to begin by listing every theme, key issue, concept or event. The objective of this exercise is to isolate 'significant incidents such as events, issues, processes or relationships' and label them using pertinent respondent or researcher terms (Connell and Lowe 1997: 169). Subsequently, the researcher should try to find ways of grouping these and developing headings which categorise each group. In continuing to refine the lists, removing any duplications and adding supplementary codes for clarity, it is important to keep clear records of all the codings and listings for cross-referral.

Coding is important because it is an efficient data labelling and retrieval device. It is time consuming to undertake but it does speed up the analysis and evaluation process in the long term. There are two different approaches to this: firstly, to work *deductively* by creating and naming such codes as would appear to be relevant to the work. Or to work more *inductively* which involves wanting to give names to codes only when the notes and analysis start suggesting possible labels (Miles and Huberman, 1994). Traditional approaches to qualitative data analysis in hospitality have led to greater use of deductive methods, but more recently the benefits of a more inductive approach (based on Grounded Theory) have been shown to be of value (Connell and Lowe, 1997). The study by Connell and Lowe (1997) uses in-depth interviews with managers of UK franchises and examines the process of internationalisation through the *experiences* of the managers and staff. Conceptual, descriptive or pattern codes were assigned only after numerical codes (representing the order in which they appeared in the interviews) had been used, descriptions applied and reviewed, and interrelationships identified.

The second part of this coding process is to review *all* the field notes, summary sheets, transcripts and other documentation, allocating codes to the various statements and sections of reports. It may be worth noting if sections of the data should be identified as a positive or negative aspect of a given code. For example, codes may represent hotel managers' approaches to managing staff: the activity of one manager may show involvement in the day-to-day running of a hotel in very positive actions but another may participate in such activities only through necessity, thus suggesting a negative coding.

Having coded the data, it is necessary to sort the codes into categories in order to group the information into useful and manageable groupings. It is also helpful to review any data that has not been coded to ensure that important and relevant information has not been excluded. For example, cultural aspects of front-line staff behaviour were not recognised as relevant to a study on service delivery by one student. The reason for this was that the study involved one nationality for managerial, supervisory and front-line employees. However, a few of the front-line employees comments' which were originally ignored were based around the communication processes of the organisation. Upon investigation, the ownership of the company, which was very different culturally from the staff and managers interviewed, was found to be fundamentally important to the service delivery issue. This point could have been missed if this questioning of the uncoded data had not been undertaken. Thus, the researcher's preconceived ideas of contributing factors may have hindered the analysis process.

This example also highlights the benefits of using a number of independent people to code the same data and then to compare the results. Chacko and Nebel (1990: 388) suggest the usefulness of having co-researchers to work with during this phase in order to discuss and debate the necessary decisions to be taken, thus validating the robustness of the coding scheme adopted. Clearly, if the coding scheme is not checked for validity the analysis which follows may be based on unsound foundations and so, arguably, could be flawed.

The coding stage of analysis is a laborious and mechanical process. However, if large quantities of data are to be managed, computer software designed specifically for sorting and categorising qualitative information may be of great value. The role of computers in qualitative research is discussed later in this chapter.

Stage III: ordering and displaying

This stage is about beginning to create order and make sense of the data held. Again, it is labour and time consuming, but requires the researcher to continue thinking and remaining intellectually involved throughout. The codes and categories are explored further, with attention being given to understanding the coded statements and their interrelationships. It is also necessary to 'discount' the data. This simply means that the researcher must view the data not only as they appear, but also within the context in which they were collected. For example, in the case of data collected by observational techniques, one must consider the influence or impact of the observer on the situations recorded. If group discussions were held, what were the relationships between the participants and did this affect the discussion or views presented in any way?

Table 15.3 demonstrates how a researcher needs to be in control of the collection of data. In the table the group structures were largely outside the control of the researcher because the participants were mostly determined by the schedules of the staff willing to participate in group discussions. This is a common problem when researching the views of staff in the hospitality industry where shift patterns are likely to determine staff availability. The dilemma may have been overcome by careful planning and communication of the group structures to the managers who had agreed to staff involvement in the research. Alternative structures are shown in Table 15.3. However, at this stage of the study it was necessary to closely review the impact of the relationships within the focus groups and explore how this may have impacted on the points and issues raised.

This clearly demonstrates that the researcher may find it helpful to draw diagrams to represent overlapping issues, or the relationships between individuals or groups of people, or even conflicting information. Charts, maps, flow diagrams, tables and other *visual* displays can be extremely useful in beginning to identify the key findings of qualitative research materials.

Memos may also assist in the process of creating order and making sense of data. Memos are comments or thoughts on incidents and linkages and are written during the coding process. They may help in the identification of patterns and propositions. 'They represent conceptual theorising about what the researcher perceives during coding'

Table 15.3 Group structures used in a study into front-line staff views of service delivery problems

Groupings used in the study	Alternative groupings
Receptionist Food service Housekeeping staff	Reception staff only
Porter Receptionist Food service	Food service staff only
Bar staff Food service Porters Housekeeping staff	Concierge staff only
Head Waiter Housekeeping staff Bar staff	Housekeeping staff only
Head Housekeeper Receptionist Food service Bar staff	Bar staff only
Head Receptionist Food service Housekeeping staff	Supervisory staff only

(Chacko and Nebel, 1990: 380). They may be likened to 'theoretical hunches' and may be of use or discarded during the analysis and interpretation process.

Stage IV: developing interpretations and verification

By the time the researcher has reached this stage, it is likely that they will have identified clear conclusions that relate to the cases or people studied. Searching for explanations and conclusions to the original research questions should be the sole aim. This is, however, not an easy stage. For meaningful and evaluative conclusions to be drawn, the researcher needs to be intuitive and reflective. Any explanations that are developed, or conclusions postulated, should be verified by cross-checking all the information. Once again, it may be necessary to review the codings and categories assigned to the data as the 'full picture' is established.

When interpreting the data, a useful and common technique is to include quotes from participants. These provide 'illuminative' statements to support the data analysis and interpretation and may help understanding as they 'tell it like it is' (Coolican, 1996: 103).

It is worth noting that whilst it may be possible to generalise causes or relationships *within* the cases, or within groups of people, care should be taken not to generalise into the broader spectrum of the world as a whole. Whilst a study may have investigated the customers of ten different hotels and established important factors as reasons for their loyalty to these establishments, it would be unwise to suggest that the same reasons would apply to all customers of all independent hotels. If, however, it was possible to broaden the reasons to specific types of loyal customers, then some generalisation may be possible. Conversely, such speculative generalisations may be of use if seen purely as speculation. Phrases such as 'it is speculated that ...', 'it could be ...' and 'it is tentatively suggested that ...' may provide useful ways to explore possible explanations. Development of such propositions may as a minimum generate possible hypotheses for testing or verification with further research.

Transferability or generalisations of qualitative studies may be achieved by a strategic approach to the overall design of the study through *triangulation*. Triangulation is the 'act of bringing more than one source of data to bear on a single point' (Marshall and Rossman, 1989: 146). Thus data from different sources, multiple cases or even multiple data collection methods may be used. For the hospitality researcher, the key questions that must be asked include 'What can each method provide in relation to the research objectives and how do these integrate and complement each other?' (Mason, 1996).

Throughout this stage, it is important for the researcher to remain sensitive to the data as well as to recognise the benefits their detailed knowledge and familiarity with the data bring.

Presentation and writing

Students often find this stage of the analysis process difficult. Whilst the suggestions made in the next chapter are invaluable at this stage, there are a number of issues which relate more specifically to qualitative analysis:

- Present the methodology clearly. Be as open as possible about how the data has been collected, the process undertaken in analysing the data and the logical development of the analysis and evaluation.
- Do not try to conceal the qualitative nature of the work. Be clear about the reasons for the appropriateness of the qualitative methods used to the design of the study as a whole.
- Remember not to apply the findings too broadly.

Suggestions for the presentation of data are given in Chapter 16.

The use of computers in qualitative data analysis

In today's increasingly computerised society it seems inevitable that computers should be able to assist in the analysis of any data. The large volume of data that qualitative approaches bring would also suggest that computerising data would be valuable. However, it should be stressed that the computer cannot replace the thoughtful and reflective approaches that characterise good qualitative analysis. However, whatever level of experience the researcher has in handling qualitative material, the use of a good word processor for the management of the textual material is invaluable. Using a word processor enables good presentation of written material and also assists in the conversion of the text into a format that can be analysed.

Miles and Huberman (1994: 44) recognise the value of the contribution that computer software packages can make in analysing data. They suggest software may be helpful in

- reducing the time taken for analysis
- reducing the drudgery of analysis
- encouraging more systematic and explicit analysis
- permitting flexibility
- allowing revision to analysis procedures

There are a number of computer software packages which have been specifically designed for the analysis of qualitative data. These include NUDIST, QUALPRO, MAX, Kwalitan, HypeRESEARCH, The Text Collector and The Ethnograph. This list is by no means exhaustive and new packages continue to be developed. It is not intended to give a commentary on the advantages and disadvantages of each package in this chapter. It is more appropriate for anyone intending to use computer software to support their analysis to investigate specific programmes with the designers and distributors as well as seeking the views of those who have used the product. Weitzmann and Miles (1993) have described useful software, as has Tesch (1990).

The most effective way of learning to use specific software is to use *real* material on it. However, because this inevitably means that the researcher is trying to learn whilst undertaking the actual analysis, it is essential to leave plenty of time for the learning process as well as the analysis of the data.

Ethical issues

If confidentiality has been promised to any respondents, such promises must be honoured. This may not be as easy to achieve in the case of studies based in specific hotels or within specific hotel chains/groups. It is perhaps best explained through the use of a recent student's thesis. The student had promised all participating human resource managers that the findings of the study would remain confidential and yet, despite fictitious names being given to the hotels, the historical and developmental summary of the hotels meant that anyone with even limited knowledge of the hotel industry would have been able to clearly identify the hotels in question. This was totally unintentional but identifies a dilemma all hospitality researchers must face when dealing with confidential information. Recognising that qualitative research is appropriate for dealing with sensitive or competitive issues, most qualitative researchers will face the complexities of how to deal with confidentiality. It is essential to uphold good ethical practice.

Secondly, if the data or findings of a piece of research have been promised to a participant, it is essential to ensure that this is provided as promised. It is all too easy, especially with student projects, to unintentionally forget to send information with the pressure to complete a study and the ensuing relief from stress on its completion. However, other students will follow the same route and need the support of hotel directors, managers and their staff if they are to be able to undertake meaningful research. Therefore, think of those future researchers, be courteous and supply the information as promised.

Conclusion and research issues

Ingram (1996) has suggested that hospitality research needs to develop methodologies that make research more accessible and credible to the world at large. It has been demonstrated here that qualitative research may indeed be more understandable for those who are not statistically trained and therefore more accessible to them. It has also been demonstrated that qualitative data may be as rigorously analysed as quantitative data and that it may therefore be viewed with as much credibility. This is particularly important for the hospitality industry where there is a need for good quality research into management practices, employee and customer issues in a dynamic and developing global industry. The value of qualitative research for the hospitality and tourism industries has been shown. Qualitative research is particularly valuable in view of the developing internationalisation of the hospitality and tourism business, as well as continuing social and technological change. The value of an in-depth understanding of management, employees and customer relationships and value systems will be important to the 'new managers'. It is suggested that qualitative data and their interpretation are of great value when explanations of new and complex situations are needed, and that the analysis of such data is likely to develop more holistic explanations. Qualitative approaches are especially pertinent when beginning initial enquiries where previous research is limited and in building theories specific to the hospitality or service setting.

The need for incorporating the appropriate data analysis approach into the overall research design process has been emphasised. It has been shown that although many of the processes involved in qualitative analysis may be viewed as practical or even mechanical tasks (coding, sorting and ordering, etc.), it is important to remain intellectually involved throughout, as this develops the researcher's ability to identify links and propositions, and thus help the interpretation process. It is essential that the analysis process is evaluative and critical, and does not simply remain *descriptive*.

For researchers considering using qualitative techniques in hospitality research, the importance of allowing sufficient time for the analysis process has been emphasised. It is suggested that the essentials for good practice in qualitative analysis are continued reference to the study objectives, good storage and retrieval systems, 'total immersion' in the data, careful and sufficient time allocations, and the development of logical and structured approaches.

It is only relatively recently that methods for qualitative analysis have been fully formatted and evidenced, and it is recognised that new solutions to methodological problems are still being developed. Like the hospitality and tourism industries, the analysis of qualitative data is dynamic and continues to be developed as its application to business research increases.

References and bibliography

Brunt P. (1997) *Market Research in Travel and Tourism*, Butterworth-Heinemann, Oxford.

Bryman A. and Burgess R.G. (eds) (1994) *Analyzing Qualitative Data*, Routledge, London.

Chacko H.E. and Nebel III E.C. (1990) 'Qualitative research: its time has come', *Hospitality Research Journal*, **14**, 2, pp 383–404.

Connell J. and Lowe A. (1997) 'Generating grounded theory from qualitative data: the application of inductive methods in tourism and hospitality management research', *Progress in Tourism and Hospitality Research*, **3**, 2, pp 165–173.

Coolican H. (1996) *Introduction to Research Methods and Statistics in Psychology* (2nd edn), Hodder and Stoughton, London.

Easterby-Smith M. Thorpe R. and Lowe A. (1991) *Management Research: An Introduction*, Sage, London.

Edgar D. and Taylor S. (1996) 'Strategic management research in hospitality: from slipstream to mainstream?', *Fifth Annual CHME Research Conference*, Nottingham Trent University, Nottingham, 10–11 April, pp 264–278.

Geertz C. (1983) *Local Knowledge: Further Essays in Interpretive Anthropology*, Basic Books, New York.

Ingram H. (1996) 'Cluster and gaps in hospitality and tourism academic research', *International Journal of Contemporary Hospitality Management* **8**, 7, pp 91–95.

Kelly J.R. (1980) 'Leisure and quality: beyond the quantitative barrier in research', in Goodale T.L. and Witt P.A. (eds) *Recreation and Leisure: Issues in an Era of Change*, State College, Pennsylvania, Venture, pp 300–314.

Levine H.G. (1985) 'Principles of data storage and retrieval for use in qualitative evaluations', *Educational Evaluation and Policy Analysis*, Random House, New York.

Lowe A. (1992) 'The Qualitative Coding Matrix—a new approach to improving the rigour of phenomenological research in service marketing', *2nd International Research Seminar in Service Management*, La Londe Les Maures, France.

Marshall C. and Rossman G.B. (1989) *Designing Qualitative Research*, Sage, Newbury Park, CA.

Mason J. (1996) *Qualitative Researching*, Sage Publications, London.

Maxwell J.A. (1996) *Qualitative Research Design: An Interactive Approach*, Applied Social Research Methods Series, Vol. 41, Sage Publications, California, London and New Delhi.

Miles M.B. and Huberman A.M. (1994) *Qualitative Data Analysis: An Expanded Sourcebook*, Sage Publications, California, London and New Delhi.

Morse J.M. (ed.) (1994) *Critical Issues in Qualitative Research Methods*, Heinemann, London.

Olsen M. and Cassee E. (1997) 'The international hotel industry in the new millennium: visioning the future', in *Into the New Millennium: A White Paper on the Global Hospitality Industry*, International Hotel Association, France.

Ritchie J. and Spencer L. (1994) 'Qualitative data analysis for applied policy research', in Bryman A. and Burgess R.G. (eds), *Analyzing Qualitative Data*, Routledge, London.

Robson S. and Foster A. (1989) *Qualitative Research in Action*, Edward Arnold, London.

Slattery P. (1983) 'Social scientific methodology and hospitality management', *International Journal of Hospitality Management* **15**, 3, pp 211–227.

Strauss A. and Corbin J. (1990) *Basics of Qualitative Research*, Sage Publications, London.

Taylor S.J. and Bogdan R. (1984) *Introduction to Qualitative Research Methods: The Search for Meanings*, John Wiley & Sons, New York.

Taylor S. and Edgar D. (1995) 'Hospitality research: the emperor's new clothes?', *IAHMS Hospitality Research Conference*, Gothenburg, Sweden, October.

Tesch R. (1990) *Qualitative Research: Analysis Types and Software Tools*, Falmer, New York.

Veal A.J. (1992) *Research Methods for Leisure and Tourism: A Practical Guide*, Longman, Harlow.

Weitzmann E.A and Miles M.B. (1993) *Computer-aided Qualitative Data Analysis: a Review of Selected Software*, Centre for Policy Research, New York.

16 Presentation of research findings

TOM BAUM

Introduction

Research findings are presented for a wide variety of reasons and the motivation behind the presentation influences the style, format and content of what is presented. It is important to bear in mind, at the onset to this chapter, that there is no single manner or method for the presentation of research findings. The presentation of research may take a number of different forms and these are all legitimate methods, although one may be more appropriate than others for particular purposes or situations. It may be decided to present the research findings in report form, as a thesis or dissertation, as a published academic journal paper or as an article for a professional or general interest magazine or newspaper, as a live presentation to a business, academic or other audience, via video, audio or other AV means, or by means of electronic distribution such as via the Internet. The choice may be to utilise a combination of the above methods.

Whatever the method, it is likely that presentation will be influenced by a number of key factors. The first of these is the audience—in other words, who the intended readership is. This may be college tutors, external examiners, a wider readership through journal publication or conference presentation, industry readers in the case of a business report or a project undertaken during work placement or internship, or the general public in the form of an information or promotional document. Each of these target groups is likely to require different treatment of the same information and data, and it would be a mistake to assume that they will require the same level of depth, emphasis and form of interpretation. Indeed, it is common to see one research study presented in a significantly different way to meet the expectations and needs of differing audiences. For example, a study on food hygiene practices may appear very differently when targeted at microbiologists, environmental health officers and chefs.

The second key factor is the overall characteristics of the research—does it represent the empirical outcomes of data collection based on an original hypothesis or set of hypotheses? Is it a replication of an existing study, utilising a tried methodology and seeking to compare outcomes with that study? Or is the study the outcome of a synthesis or analysis of secondary sources?

The third factor is the information to be presented. The form and style of presentation will depend upon the quality, quantity and characteristics of the data to be reported.

The Handbook of Contemporary Hospitality Management Research, Edited by Bob Brotherton.
© 1999 John Wiley & Sons Ltd.

This, in turn, will be a factor of methodology. Clearly, quantitative outcomes lend themselves to very different reporting approaches than qualitative information such as that derived through case study data collection or the use of methodologies such as critical incident technique or action research.

Fourthly, there are the methodological issues and methods problems faced during the conduct of the study. In part, the origins of these issues and problems will reflect the philosophical or epistemological stance adopted in the research. They will also influence both the quality and quantity of information that is available for presentation. It is also important that the reporting is limitation-sensitive, in other words that claims are not made which go beyond the validity or reliability of the available data. It is a common error of overenthusiastic research reporting to exaggerate the interpretation that can, justifiably, be placed on information obtained in limited or flawed circumstances. For example, it is often tempting to extrapolate conclusions from a small survey sample that is both statistically and conceptually suspect. Perhaps the most famous example of this was the use made by Sigmund Freud of conclusions drawn from his work with Little Albert—a sample of one! This is an area where critics are likely to look carefully for flaws in the research.

Next, the nature of the hospitality industry influences both the research process and the characteristics of those interested in the outcomes of the study. The industry is characterised by diversity in terms of its geography, the size of its operations, ownership of operations, product focus and service standards. This diversity impacts on methodological dimensions of research in hospitality and means that considerable care is required at all stages in order to ensure the validity of outcomes and conclusions.

Sixth and last, in both professional and academic senses, hospitality represents a multi-disciplinary environment and draws upon the influences of a wide variety of scientific, social scientific and humanities research traditions. As a result, it may be constrained in its approach by the reality that some of these do prescribe certain presentational parameters or conventions. These influences impact upon the approaches which different researchers adopt in presenting their studies. Likewise, hospitality, as a research environment, draws upon the traditions and practices of many operational areas (food and beverage, accommodation, conference and banqueting, entertainment, leisure) as well as mainstream business disciplines (finance, human resource management, marketing, information management, and general management). Presenters of research may choose any of these as their focus and this will have a significant influence. Similarly, the audience may take any of these areas as their experiential or conceptual starting point and evaluate research in that light. In this sense, the one audience (two tutors marking the same thesis) may also be heterogeneous and approach the work from different angles.

Having looked at the key factors likely to influence a presentation, it must be said that the multi-disciplinary nature of hospitality is such that most traditions of presentation find their way into the research outcomes of studies in the area and none has achieved primacy or necessarily dominant status. This is one of the strengths of hospitality research.

In this chapter, various approaches taken to the reporting of research findings in the context of hospitality will be examined. This examination will be supported by use of selected case studies of research reporting, drawn from published sources.

What is the purpose of presenting research findings?

Research is undertaken for a diversity of reasons and, as will have already been seen in earlier chapters of this book, by a variety of methods. Likewise, its presentation or preparation for wider access (both public and private) is the result of differing motivations. However, whatever the reasons that motivate the conduct of a particular piece of research, there are a number of common reasons for presenting the outcomes of such studies. These may include the following.

The outcomes should be of interest and value to a specific or general audience or readership. This should, of course, be the prime motivation. Good recent examples of research findings presented with this motivation include the series of three research reports on tourism published by the Department of National Heritage (1996), representing research conducted by Coopers and Lybrand and the London Business School:

1. Hotels: The Consumer View
2. Benchmarking for Small Hotels
3. People Working in Tourism and Hospitality

These studies were targeted primarily at an industry and professional readership with clear constraints on the time they would be able to devote to reading. The presentation is also intended to influence and inform practice within the tourism and hospitality sector. The outcome is a series of 'headline' findings without significant depth of detail or analysis. Such presentation would probably be unacceptable in an academic context but is entirely 'fit for purpose' with other audiences in mind. The language used is rather more informal and journalistic than is usually the case with academic studies.

It may be that the presentation of outcomes is required as part of an educational programme. This can be at undergraduate or postgraduate level in the form of a report, dissertation or thesis. It is important to bear in mind that, while the immediate audiences for such work are tutors and external examiners, many theses are placed on library shelves and are publicly accessible to a wide academic audience. Expectations of outcome are, in part, governed by academic traditions, institutional expectations and regulations, and the objectives of the study. There are clear differences between a company-based report and various levels of dissertations (Honours, Masters, Doctoral). In particular, academic presentation permits few, if any, shortcuts and researchers may be penalised for failure to include key secondary sources or full detail of their methodological rationale or methods employed, and for selectivity in the presentation of results. At the heart of academic presentation is the notion of transparency —ensuring that the reader knows exactly how and by what route the conclusions have been reached. Replication, so important to the scientific method, has a rather more limited place in hospitality research, although it may be important in allied areas such as food science. Rather, transparency in hospitality research allows the reader to assess the 'reasonableness' of the conclusions which are reached. Therefore, literature surveys should aim to show breadth of understanding in the field and how previous work has influenced the current study from both a methodological and a conceptual perspective. Likewise, the issue of originality of the work may be important and the relationship of the work to previous studies should be established in an unambiguous manner to avoid suggestions of plagiarism. Language style, in academic theses, is generally precise and formal and focuses on the full development of an argument rather than the punchy summary style which research reports destined for a wider audience might adopt.

Alternatively, the presentation of outcomes may be required by the agency or organisation commissioning or sponsoring the research. This would be the normal expectation of a consultant working for a public-sector organisation such as the European Commission, the United Nations Development Programme, the World Bank, or private-sector companies or associations. Many consulting reports adopt a style and form which is common for this genre but may be dictated by specific requirements of the commissioning agency. In general, the key component is the summary of conclusions and recommendations. This provides the client groups (funding agency, recipient country or organisation) with a clear and accessible listing of what the research found and how they might action its implications. Unlike academic presentation, where conclusions generally constitute the final chapter, here this element is front-loaded and the actual research findings and the methods employed to generate them are subservient and may be relegated to separate volumes or appendices.

Some reports of this kind may include substantial elements of analysis which has been used in almost identical form in other reports by the same organisation. For example, research for a hotel feasibility study will, in all probability, include a general analysis of the hotel sector, its performance and prospects at a national or regional level. This background material is applicable, with some modification, to a diversity of proposed hotel projects within a specified geographical area. The acceptability and normality of such practice contrasts with academic research presentation where such practice could well be deemed 'plagiarism'.

In some cases the primary motivation for the presentation will be to promote or enhance the position of an agency or organisation which has commissioned or conducted the research. Here, elements of the report and the conclusions drawn from the research findings may have a campaigning objective and, thus, may not be free from bias in the sense that academic reports purport to be. A political or charitable organisation may commission research, the findings of which, in themselves, are presented in an objective manner. The organisation, however, may reserve the right to place its own interpretation on the outcomes and draw conclusions which suit political objectives. This will frequently be in the form of an executive summary. The researcher may wish to distance himself or herself from this aspect of the report.

Finally, presentation of the research outcomes should additionally enhance the status or position of the researcher(s) who has conducted the study. This may involve any one or a combination of the above.

Stages in the presentation of a written research report

While it is impossible to generalise completely in relation to the presentation of research findings, a commonly adopted format might contain a number of key components. As the following subsections will indicate, variation from this order is common, depending on the nature and purpose of the report.

1. Title

This covers the topic title, sub-title (if any), name, date, institution or sponsor, purpose (Honours dissertation, contribution to a consultant's assessment of a specific client problem, etc.). Titles are frequently too long or contain some cryptic or 'clever' message. This is usually inappropriate in the presentation of academic theses. Simplicity is generally the most effective option.

2. Acknowledgements

It is always good practice and good etiquette to acknowledge assistance received in the conduct of the research and in the preparation of the report. This may mean thanking sponsors, those who contributed ideas and time to the conduct of the study, or those who agreed to be interviewed or completed questionnaires. Acknowledgement of the support and assistance of a supervisor (if a student report) is also conventional and diplomatic!

3. Contents

This is important as it allows readers to find exactly what they require. However, there is a need for an appropriate balance between something that is too long, with every single topic and sub-topic included, and providing insufficient information to be of use to the reader. It is important to remember that many readers decide whether to delve further into a report or to put it to one side on the basis of their initial scan of the contents page.

4. List of tables, charts and figures

These provide the reader with ready access to the statistical and visual 'heart' of the study. Again, there is a need for balance between overwhelming the reader with detail at this point and providing essential and useful information.

5. Abstract/synopsis/executive summary

This, again, is an important initial 'access point' for many readers and may be the section that is most widely read and used. It may range from 100 words for a refereed paper, a couple of pages for a PhD or even longer for a report. The aim is to summarise the report—what was done, why, how was it done, what was found, recommendations. An example of a brief journal paper abstract is given below.

> Abstract from: 'Investigation of the perceived components of the meal experience, using perceptual gap methodology', by Johns, N., Tyas, P., Ingold, T. and Hopkinson, S., *Progress in Tourism and Hospitality Research*, **2**(1), 1996, p. 15:

A differential questionnaire based upon SERVQUAL was issued to 234 customers at ten foodservice outlets. The results were subjected to factor analysis in order to identify structure within respondents' perceptions of the meal experience. In fact the complex empirical factor patterns which emerged corresponded neither with the expected SERVQUAL model, nor with two other models of the meal experience against which they were tested. Customers also appeared to perceive quality differently at different outlets. However, items concerned with food and with staff seemed to be common elements of the meal experience. The significance of these results and their value as a pointer for further research is discussed.

Presentation will vary according to purpose. An academic abstract is conventionally presented in text paragraph format while the executive summary of a consultant's report may contain a series of 'bullet' points, identifying the main findings and resultant recommendations. The executive summary may, on occasions, be prepared by a third party—for example, a sponsoring agency—and may contain material and conclusions to which the researcher may not fully subscribe. This area may require some negotiation and the possible inclusion of a disclaimer at some point.

6. Introduction to the study

This may (and frequently does) subsume stage 7 below. In addition, however, the introduction is an opportunity to place the study in a general context, to explain the origins of the research (perhaps as a contribution to organisational policy development), to explain aspects of the background to the study and the historical, social and economic backcloth to the work that is presented in the report. Introductions should be general and not too long and must avoid duplicating what follows in the literature review and in the main report of the findings.

7. Aims/purpose/objectives/hypotheses of the study

What is the study trying to achieve and why? This is very important, particularly in an academic study, but is also relevant in other contexts. It provides the reader with a clear indication of what you intended to achieve through the research and, therefore, provides the benchmark against which the outcomes of the study can be judged. If the study aspires to achieve certain things, it will be, in part, assessed on whether these aims have or have not been met. An example of research objectives, as stated in a thesis, are set out below.

Research objectives from: 'Attitudes towards utilizing older workers in the Hong Kong hotel industry', by Hailin Qu and Sheuk Yee Cheng, *International Journal of Hospitality Management*, **15**(3), 1996, p. 247:

- *To explore Hong Kong hotel personnel managers' attitudes towards employing older workers;*
- *To identify Hong Kong hotel personnel managers' perceptions of older workers and the quality of their performance;*
- *To examine Hong Kong hotel personnel managers' preference for utilizing older workers as opposed to other alternative solutions to the labor shortage problem.*

In some research studies, a degree of originality is essential (for doctoral research) and it may be a good idea to show that the aims and objectives, as stated, address a new or original approach to the subject which makes an original contribution to knowledge. This may, however, only be possible after the literature review (8 below) and, for this reason, Aims and Objectives may be located rather later than at this point in some research reports.

Some studies and their methods lend themselves to the testing of hypotheses in the manner normally associated with the scientific method. If the study reported includes the statement and testing of a hypothesis or hypotheses, these can be stated at this point, possibly in conjunction with or instead of objectives. Examples of hypotheses, taken from a recent research paper, are included below.

> Research hypotheses from: 'Promotions and purchase decisions in private clubs', by Ferreira, R.R, *Journal of Restaurant and Foodservice Marketing*, **2**(2), 1997, pp. 23–25:
>
> **H1:** *Promotion food and beverage purchases are positively related to regular priced food and beverage purchases.*
> **H2:** *Members visiting the club for the promotion are more likely to purchase one or more regular priced items than the alternative of not purchasing any regular price items.*
> **H3:** *Members visiting the club for the promotion are more likely to purchase promotion items than members who frequent the club regularly.*

8. Literature review

This is essential for all academic studies but, in a modified form and perhaps as part of the introduction, may also figure in other research reports, although without the same level of depth. The purpose of the literature review is to address and analyse relevant research and other work that has been undertaken in the same or related areas of study. It is an important vehicle by which to demonstrate a sound grasp of the field and how it relates to the research aims and objectives. The purpose of the literature review is not to demonstrate that everything ever written about a particular subject has been read. What it should do is to demonstrate to the reader that the researcher has a good and broad-based grasp of the key sources in the field and that the material used is up-to-date and appropriate to the context of the study. For example, in a study considering trends in the hotel industry in Scotland, references drawn exclusively from the North American or East Asian context would not be sufficient.

Reviewing literature should also be a critical process, one in which the quality and contribution of pieces (academic or otherwise) are analysed and their value assessed in the context of the proposed study. Poor literature reviews tend to contain summaries of published work and little else. It is also important to recognise that different literature sources do not necessarily have equal value or merit. An author presenting views or opinion on a topic will be interesting but may merit rather more cautious acceptance than a report detailing the outcome of an extended research study. A further and important purpose of the literature review, in academic work, is to place the author's own research in context. This may involve demonstrating how the study has clear epistemological, conceptual and practical precursors, studies upon which the current research is seeking to build. For example, Gabriel's (1988) seminal study of the perceptions of work in the catering industry drew, methodologically, on a tradition of similar investigation in other sectors. Likewise, Guerrier and Lockwood's (1989) study of core and peripheral work in the hospitality industry built on foundations established and published by researchers looking at other sectors of the economy. In this chapter, the consideration of how to present secondary information contains an extract from Wood's (1997) analysis of work in the hospitality industry. This book (and its precursory first edition, published in 1992) remains one of the best models for the literature review process and how to handle diverse sources in an interesting, analytical and critical manner.

9. Methodology

This is a key and critical component of most research studies and their presentation. It is frequently combined (and sometimes confused) with discussion of Methods employed (see 10 below) but may also involve fairly extended and theoretical discussion of the context in which the research is placed and how it relates to some of the main methodological traditions. The epistemological or philosophical basis which underpins research and its execution is an important issue in its own right and is the subject of extended debate within the academic research community. It does not receive much consideration in the presentation of consulting or commercial research, although epistemological considerations may well, overtly or unintentionally, influence the assumptions which underpin such studies. For example, an economic analysis of the structure of the hospitality industry may be driven by assumptions which are derived from either a free market or a Keynesian perspective and the position adopted is likely to impact upon the choice of tools and models employed. Similarly, it is frequently charged that tourism development reports, funded by international donor agencies and researched by consultants from the developed world, adopt frameworks and make assumptions which are inappropriate to the developing world environment in which they are located and where the recommendations will have to be enacted. The philosophical basis of such studies is drawn from market, political and cultural traditions which may be alien to the needs of the countries in which they are located. Prevailing economic and political orthodoxy, in many developed countries, has advocated a minimalist role for the state in the management of economic activities, and this thinking is frequently imposed on environments where there is no realistic alternative private sector in tourism to play the required lead role. At a practical level, this general issue can result in the posing of inappropriate questions within the research (and the neglect of others) and the formulation of recommendations that are irrelevant to that environment.

Discussion of epistemology, within this section of a report or thesis, is part of the process of recognition by the researcher of some of the inevitable inadequacies in hospitality research. It is the recognition and articulation of inevitable bias and the consequent destruction of the illusion of value-free research. By establishing the origins and basis of bias, within the study, whether culturally, sociologically or politically derived, the author is permitting the reader to evaluate the research and its conclusions in a transparent manner and to permit possible factoring to accommodate the researcher's starting position.

It is important that the reasons why a particular underpinning methodology was selected are clearly identified and that the implications of alternatives are discussed. Academic reports demand a fairly detailed consideration of this area, showing how the researcher has addressed the particular methodological issues which research in the hospitality field poses. As it is a multi-disciplinary area, it frequently draws on the methodological traditions of the natural and the social sciences in a fairly eclectic manner. This may need justification, as will particular methodological approaches which may have 'vogue' status at the time of writing (for example, use of grounded theory). Such detailed discussions will have less relevance in the context of non-academic research presentation, although methodology should by no means be ignored.

10. Methods

The section on methods chosen, in other words what was actually done in undertaking the research, follows closely a consideration of Methodology above and may be integrated into the same section. It relates rather more specifically to what was actually done in order to collect information/data. This section should provide details of what was done and what problems were encountered. It could include information on, for example, sampling methods used, preparation and piloting of survey instruments, structure and organisation of interviews or observation sessions, and the levels of response achieved.

Information such as this is a very important aspect of transparency and very important to the presentation of all research, because it provides the reader with some reassurances regarding the validity and reliability of the information collected and, as a result of this, the strength or otherwise of conclusions drawn and recommendations made within the report. It also permits other researchers to replicate the study with a similar or different population group. Copies of the actual instruments employed, together with supporting correspondence, can be placed as appendices to the report. Methodology and the methods employed to collect data frequently generate as much debate as the outcomes of the research study itself and, therefore, great care is required in presenting information on these areas.

It is important to recognise that few research studies will be viewed as flawless, in terms of their methodology or methods employed, by all readers. This perception may derive from epistemological differences but, more commonly, is the result of doubts about the methods employed and/or their implementation with respect to the collection of information or weaknesses regarding the quality, validity and reliability of data collected. A common problem with tourism and hospitality research relates to the level of response achieved in survey or interview studies or the comprehensiveness of information supplied (i.e. financial data may be unobtainable). It is absolutely essential that this section of the report addresses the limitations of the study from a methodological and practical perspective. Researchers can rarely be faulted if they make such limitations clear at this point and reiterate them in the context of the conclusions and recommendations that are drawn from the study.

11. Results

The results or research findings are clearly the core of any research presentation and are the central basis upon which the study will be judged. Presentation will clearly depend upon the method of data collection employed, but certain important principles should guide the organisation of this section. Clarity is essential, especially with respect to the presentation of technical or complex statistical information, and presentation methods should be employed which facilitate the reader's interpretation in so far as is possible. Therefore, illustrations in the form of graphs and charts can be very useful but their employment should be judicious, intelligent and appropriate to the information to be displayed. It can be tempting to use colourful and powerful presentation graphic techniques in order to generate charts and diagrams which misrepresent the information in question. For example, data collected through informal interviews with five hotel general managers is unlikely to generate a series of pie charts on the basis of the answers derived.

As earlier discussion, in this book, about the various data collection methods will have indicated, there can be no one correct method by which to present research results. Quantitative data may generate a considerable number of tables and accompanying charts which can make for somewhat tedious reading unless interspersed with commentary or discussion. In some contexts, their presentation may be more appropriate as an appendix to the main report or, indeed, as a separate statistical volume. By contrast, the presentation of qualitative information can become very 'wordy' and difficult to follow from a reader's perspective unless care is taken to divide information carefully into appropriate blocks by use of a section numbering system. Quotations from interviews, for example, must be clearly identified as distinct from the text and commentary. In the case of qualitative information, it can be difficult to separate the presentation of research results from discussion and analysis of their implications. If necessary this must be guarded against, as this may be inappropriate in, for example, a thesis.

An important consideration, in presenting the outcomes of research, whether qualitative or quantitative, is one of confidentiality. The study may have been possible only on the basis that full anonymity of respondents/collaborators would be maintained and that data and views expressed would not be traceable to their original source. Such commitments must be honoured and scrupulous care taken to ensure that quotes, company information or any other form of data cannot be attributed back to its source. This requirement can be met relatively readily with respect to quantitative data where aggregation tends to lose individual responses, but can be much more difficult with respect to qualitative and case study research. Care needs to be exercised in the presentation and analysis of results, and when appendices are drawn together. Illustrative material may clearly indicate the company involved and should not be included without specific permission.

Original data relating to research presented for academic purposes (thesis, dissertation, research paper) should be available for subsequent scrutiny by examiners or academic peers. Thus, completed questionnaires, computer files, print-outs, taped (audio and video) interviews and observations, transcripts and other such original sources must be retained for a reasonable period after the completion of the study. It may not be appropriate to present them alongside the report, although this may be where the outcome is in, for example, the development and testing of a computerised food and beverage management system.

12. Analysis and discussion

This provides the opportunity to bring together the outcomes of both secondary data review and original, primary research information collection. It is also the chance to interpret the outcomes and place them in the wider hospitality industry context. This is frequently the part of a report or thesis which is weakest. It is as if the researcher reaches a state of exhaustion by the time it is necessary to pull things together at the end.

The key issues are, firstly, to consider whether the objectives of the study have been met and to review whether the hypothesis has been fully tested and supported or negated by the findings of the research. The second requirement is one of interpretation and analysis of the information so that the outcomes can be assessed against the findings of other studies and their importance considered from both an academic and an applied perspective. What does the information actually mean and what lessons can future researchers and those involved in the hospitality industry learn from the findings? Finally, this section can address problems of methodology and research methods which may have arisen during the conduct of the study and consider what, if anything, these may mean for the interpretation of the findings.

It is imperative that claims and interpretations are not made which cannot be fully substantiated. If the outcomes from a survey of a small sample of hotel general managers are generalised to general managers as a group, the researcher can be rightly criticised for exceeding the extent of interpretation which is justified on the basis of the fieldwork. However, if the study is interpreted in the specific context of the limitations in the methodology or methods, the researcher will be less open to criticism. Excessive claims, which exceed what is reasonable on the basis of the evidence from either primary or secondary sources, are common in research and must be guarded against.

It can be difficult to separate the previous section, reporting research results, from this chapter considering analysis and discussion, and in some reports (especially those prepared for non-academic purposes) it may be appropriate to combine these areas.

13. Summary

This section should be succinct and focused in its presentation. It should not introduce new information but provide a clear listing of the main outcomes of the study. This section may, in effect, be very similar to an executive summary and probably should not be included if the report contains a summary at its start.

14. Recommendations and suggestions for further research

This may also include material which could be found in an executive summary. Recommendations are common in non-academic research reports but may also have a place in academic theses and dissertations. They are proposals for action on the basis of the research findings. For example, the study of hotel general managers, referred to above, may identify specific skill deficiencies among this group. Recommendations may identify training programmes which could be implemented in order to overcome these gaps. Proposals for further research may identify steps that can be taken to further test the outcomes of the study as well as pointing to lines of enquiry which may have arisen during the course of the research. The hotel management study may have identified a number of questions with respect to the finance skills which further research may help to answer.

It is possible, especially in the case of sponsored research, that the researchers will not have access to the full context within which the study has been conducted and may consequently, be unable to prepare recommendations because the 'big picture' is not available. Sponsors may choose to develop their own conclusions and recommendations or may reject those which the research study team put forward.

15. References

These are essential to most studies, especially those of an academic nature. They should be provided alphabetically, in full and in some accepted style such as Harvard. All cited works should be included, whether books, journal articles, reports, newspaper and other published sources, internet sources, television or radio broadcast sources, and other audio, video, CD-ROM and computer materials. Presentation of references can be classified by type of material, again alphabetically and as an alternative to an inclusive listing of all materials. Sources of a unique nature, such as interviews with key personnel and authorities, should probably not be included here but treated in an appendix. The determining consideration is that the purpose of a full reference is to allow the reader to verify the source in question and assess the researcher's interpretation of its significance. This usually confines sources to those published and publicly available. An excellent source of information on referencing is accessible at **http://www.unn.ac.uk/central/isd/cite**, prepared by Graham Shields and Graham Watson of the University of Northumbria.

Referencing sources from the Internet is a matter of practical concern to many researchers and students, given the wide range of material which is accessible through this source. The key principle is that articulated above: the purpose of including a reference is part of the transparency process which allows the reader to return to your source and verify the context and content of the secondary source which has been used. On this basis, the reference should include the full Web site address and any other pertinent directional information. Researchers should critically examine the status and quality of references obtained from the Internet as this type of material can be placed on the system without editorial control and may be serving unstated political or ideological purposes. Given the technological 'glitches' which can occur within the Internet, it may also be good practice for researchers to take and retain a hard or disk back-up copy of Internet sources which can be made available to key readers such as tutors and examiners.

The instability and impermanent nature of Internet sources is also a potential problem. It is possible to access a journal source published 50 years ago, while there is little guarantee that a Web site will stay in place over an extended period of time or will not be edited in some manner. Increasingly, published academic and other sources make use of Internet referencing and it is a good idea to take note of best practice in this respect. One excellent source, which uses Internet references extensively, is Gibaldi (1995). Shields and Watson's site also includes an excellent section on the referencing of electronic sources, including the Internet, and can be accessed at **http://www.unn.ac.uk/central/isd/cite/elec.htm**. For more detailed guidance, see Li and Crane (1996).

16. Appendices

These can include a variety of additional materials which would not be suitable for inclusion within the main body of the report. Such material may include questionnaires, letters, interview formats, and essential reference material not included elsewhere, as well as samples of commercial material obtained, for example, from participating hotels. It is important that such material is edited carefully for inclusion rather than included mindlessly and uncritically. Always ask what the material will contribute to the reader's understanding of the research before including it.

Questionnaires will allow the methodology to be verified and replicated and are, thus, essential. Full copies of published reports, however, can be obtained from other sources by the reader and should not be included.

Stages in the presentation of research reports in other formats

The preceding section has focused on the presentation of written research reports and identifies the key stages which can be included. In many respects, a change of format to a live presentation, audio or video medium, other electronic means or a combination of a number of these, with or without print, does not alter the main principles which have been enunciated above. While some of the more ephemeral components of a written report, such as references and appendices, may not always be appropriate for other presentation formats, it is generally good practice to include acknowledgement of elements such as

- research objectives
- key published sources
- research methodology
- key research finding
- analysis, conclusions and recommendations

within an alternative format report. Indeed, it would be difficult to satisfy transparency criteria and a wish to assess the validity and reliability of findings and conclusions without such information.

In some situations, it may be necessary to address some of the additional information requirements, such as details of methodology, methods or reference sources, in print format alongside the main presentation. In the case of a live presentation of research findings, whether to tutors or clients, it is often helpful to provide written summaries of, for example, key findings, conclusions, methodology, methods and reference sources for consideration at the time or at a later date.

Exhibit 16.1 Guidelines from *Progress in Tourism and Hospitality Research* (reproduced by kind permission of John Wiley & Sons Ltd)

NOTES FOR CONTRIBUTORS

1. Authors are requested to submit three copies of each manuscript, plus a copy of the text on disk. Please indicate on the disk the format and word processing software used.

Submissions should be addressed to—The Editors: Professor C. Cooper, Director of Research, International Centre for Tourism and Hospitality Research, School of Service Industries, Bournemouth University, Talbot Campus, Fernbarrow, Poole, BH12 5BB, UK, or Mr A. Lockwood, Department of Management Studies, University of Surrey, Guildford, Surrey, GU2 5XH UK.

2. Copyright. Because of changes in copyright laws, the change of copyright from author previously implicit in the submission of the manuscript must now be explicitly transferred to enable the publisher to ensure maximum dissemination of the author's work. A copy of the publishing agreement to be used for the *Progress in Tourism and Hospitality Research* is reproduced in each volume. Additional copies are available from the publisher: contributors may also photocopy the agreement from the journal. A signed copy of this agreement must accompany every manuscript submitted for publication.

3. Papers will be accepted for publication on the understanding that they are contributed solely to this journal, that the contents have not been published in whole or in part elsewhere and that the papers are subject to editorial revision.

4. All manuscripts are subject to double-blind review. Authors are provided with reviewers comments on their manuscripts.

5. The manuscript should be double-line spaced throughout with a minimum of one inch margins all round and printed on one side of the paper only.

Manuscripts should normally be submitted in English. The acceptance and publication of articles in languages other than English is not discouraged but will be at the discretion of the editors who should be consulted prior to submission.

Papers submitted for publication should normally be between 4,000 to 7,000 words. Papers outside these guidelines will be considered but authors should note that a part of the review process will consider the length relative to the content and clarity of the writing.

6. The first page of the manuscript should include a brief descriptive title and the author's name, affiliation, address and telephone and fax numbers. In the case of co-authors, their full details should also be included. All correspondence will be sent to the first named author, unless otherwise indicated.

7. The second page should contain the title of the paper, a summary of not more than 100 words in length, and up to six key words. The summary should provide a review of the paper and not be a simple repetition of the conclusions.

8. The paper should begin on the third page and should not relist the title or authors.

9. The paper should be sub-divided into sections to aid readability. Section headings should be in upper case and underlined. Subsection headings should be in upper and lower case and underlined.

10. References. In the text, references should be cited by the author's name and year of publication in brackets (Jones, 1994), or '… as noted by Jones (1994)'.

Where there are two or more references to one author for the same year, the following form should be used: (Jones, 1993a) or (Jones, 1993b).

Where references include three or more authors the form (Jones *et al*., 1994) should be used.

A full list of references in alphabetical order should be given at the end of the paper. All references should be written as follows:

Farber, B. M., (1994), Hotel executive teams: balance of power among department heads? *Hospitality Research Journal*, **18**, 1, 15–28.

Cooper, C., Fletcher, J., Gilbert, D. and Wanhill, S., (1993), *Tourism Principles and Practice*, London, Pitman Publishing.

Logan, A., (1994) *Quality Expectation in the European Escorted Tour Sector*, Guildford: University of Surrey, MSc Dissertation, Department of Management Studies.

Tse, E. C. and West, J. J., (1992), Development strategies for international hospitality markets, in Teare, R. and Olsen, M., (Editors), *International Hospitality Management Corporate Strategy in Practice*. New York: John Wiley and Sons, Inc., 118–134.

Note that references may not be checked by the editorial office and the responsibility for their accuracy rests solely with the author(s).

11. Charts, diagrams and figures. All charts, diagrams and figures should be numbered consecutively as 'Figure 1' etc. and should be on separate pages. Each figure should have a number, a short title and appropriate labels. In the text, the position of figures should be shown by typing on a separate line, the words 'Figure 1 about here' etc.

Each figure should be the same size as the intended printed version (so no enlargement or reduction is required), maximum width 76 mm (single column) or 160 mm and a maximum depth of 215 mm. Lettering on the artwork should be set in 8pt type. Computer-generated artwork must be submitted as laser printed output at a resolution of 600 dots per inch on high quality paper. Dot matrix printer output is unacceptable. Tints are to be avoided; hatching should be used instead. Drawn artwork should be carefully lettered and drawn in black ink. Provide copies as well as the originals. Black and white photographs should be supplied as sharp, glossy black and white prints (not photocopies or previously printed material). Laser output photographs are to be avoided. Both drawings and photographs should be clearly identified on the back with the figure number and the author's name. Artwork on disk is preferred on 3.5 inch PC or Macintosh format disk in a dedicated drawing package, such as Adobe Illustrator/Corel Draw/Macrome dia Freehand *not* presentation, spreadsheet or database packages. Each graphic should be in a separate file, should conform to the information above and be supplied as a source (original) file as well as an .EPS file, if different. Provide a hard copy print out of each figure, clearly identified.

12. Tables. Tables should be typed on a separate sheet and numbered consecutively and independently of any figures in the article. Each table should be numbered and titled. All columns should have explanatory headings. Tables should not repeat data which are available elsewhere in the paper. In the text, the position of tables should be indicated by typing on a separate line the words 'Table 1 about here' etc.

13. It is the author's responsibility to obtain written permission to quote or reproduce material which has appeared in another publication.

14. No manuscript or figures will be returned following publication unless a request for return is made when the manuscript is originally submitted.

15. Twenty-five offprints of each paper, and a copy of the journal issue in which it appears, will be provided free of charge. Additional offprints may be purchased on an order form which will accompany proofs.

16. The editors and publisher will do everything possible to ensure that the manuscripts are dealt with promptly and that those which are accepted are quickly published.

17. Electronic Submission. When a paper is in its final form and has been **accepted** for publication, it would be helpful to the publisher if you were to supply 2 disks containing the final version. These MUST be accompanied by an identical hard copy printout. The disks should be clearly labelled with: the file name; e.g. PTHMHL (The first three letters represent the Wiley journal code and the next 3 letters the author's initials—if an author only has two initials the middle letter should be X); the date; the author's name; the hardware and software package used.

The preferred medium is 5.25 or 3.5 inch disk in Macintosh or MS-DOS. We are able to deal with most standard software packages currently available, although our preference is for WordPerfect, Word or TeX (and/or one of its derivatives).

We are also able to accept line artwork graphics on disk, see details above. Again, each file should be carefully named, using the same code as for the text, but adding a reference for figures, e.g.: PTHMHL01 (the 01 representing fig. 1).

The disks must be accompanied by a hard copy printout. If the disk and paper copy differ, the paper copy will be treated as the definitive version.

Presentation style

Presentation style is clearly influenced by the context of the research information in question. To some extent, style is a matter of choice and preference and writers will adopt stylistic features which suit their purposes and disposition. However, there are perhaps some conventions of which researchers should be aware in order to enhance their presentation. Certain guidelines or requirements are specified by some universities, with respect to the presentation of research for academic purposes, or by academic journals for those seeking publication for their work. Exhibit 16.1 is an example of such guidelines, reproduced from *Progress in Tourism and Hospitality Research*.

In any case, it is important to remember that any form of presentation, including the presentation of research findings, represents a form of communication to another person or persons and that clarity and unambiguous style are critical in order to ensure that the receiver of the information (whether in written, oral or electronic form) interprets what the author is saying in the way that is intended. Therefore, a few stylistic pointers may be of value here.

- Try to write in clear, unambiguous language, avoiding excessively long and clumsy sentences or rambling, ill-defined paragraphs. Commercial reports frequently demand short, pithy paragraphs which address no more than one key point, outcome or conclusion/recommendation. Academic reports, by contrast, may include rather longer paragraphs but these should also address discrete topics where possible. In an academic context, try to avoid micro-paragraphs of, perhaps, just two to three lines.
- Ensure that what is written is grammatically correct and avoids annoying spelling errors. This may sound pedantic and 'old-fashioned' and, indeed, there are those who are tolerant or flexible in this regard. Essentially, the author cannot be faulted for being correct but may be penalised for incorrect use of language. Given that the author may not always be familiar with the target readership, caution is probably the best course of action. Common errors include incomplete sentences, constructed without verbs; failure to use commas where necessary; and difficulties with the plural form. Clearly, spelling is aided by spell-check facilities within most word-processing packages but use must be judicious and intelligent. Spell-checkers have clear limitations and make no claim to ensure the correct sense of what is written. Some words permit more than one form of spelling—for example, words which end in *ise* or *ize*, and which to use may be a matter of choice. Publishers or sponsors may specify the form they require. This may also be determined by the country of publication—the UK or the USA, for example. In any case, it is important that the form that is adopted is consistent. If English is not the author's native tongue, it can be useful to elicit assistance to check grammatical and spelling aspects of the work.
- Type-checking or proof-reading presentational material, whether a report, a thesis or posters and slides for display, is critical but also tedious and frequently undertaken poorly by researchers. Data is particularly important in this respect, especially if this involves extended tables or the presentation of calculations, accounts or similar information. It is useful to work with a partner to check the accuracy of such data when it is typed.
- It is conventional, in much research presentation, to ensure detachment and objectivity by avoiding use of the first person (i.e. I or my) in writing. A style based on the third person is the preferred approach. If it is necessary to talk about yourself, the

form 'the author' or 'the researcher' is acceptable as an alternative to the first person. In any case, it is generally prudent to avoid the overt presentation of the author's own unsubstantiated opinions in the presentation of research findings. There may be a place for a more personal assessment of the outcomes within a conclusion but, elsewhere, personal analysis is generally to be avoided.

● It is generally good practice to avoid closed or highly technical jargon, slang expressions or excessive use of acronyms, unless these are fully explained or the audience is fully conversant with the use of such terms. Remember that the reader or listener may be considerably less familiar with the field of research than the researcher is.

Presenting research findings—some case examples

Secondary source information

Many research reports consist, in whole or part, of the analysis of information culled and analysed from existing published or similar sources. Presenting such analysis, from a number of sources, is intended to identify outcomes and conclusions which the individual data or information alone may not have permitted. In other words, the researcher is not simply presenting the outcomes of the research of others, as would be the case in a conventional literature review, but is using this material in order to investigate an additional hypothesis or to postulate outcomes only possible through reference to a number of such sources. Wood's (1997) *Working in Hotels and Catering* is a book which substantially develops a series of arguments drawn exclusively from secondary sources. Case Study 16.1 is an extract from this book and illustrates how information from a number of secondary sources can be employed.

Quantitative data

Use and analysis of quantitative data is a common feature in hospitality research reports. Thus, readers seeking good examples of this form of research presentation have a wide variety of journal and other sources to which they could refer. Case Study 16.2 is taken from a study of service quality in the hotel industry, where the authors exemplify the challenges of integrating quantitative data (presented in tabular and graphical form) with analysis of their implications.

Qualitative data

Qualitative information includes, for example, the outcome of research studies based on unstructured interviews or observations of behaviour of specific hotel staff. Presenting such information involves significant selection decisions about what should be included and what should be omitted. Its presentation requires careful structuring and the use of examples and evidence drawn from the data as well as a summary of the information collected. Case Study 16.3 is taken from a study of managerial style, based on observation, and shows how it is possible to analyse qualitative research outcomes and tabulate them so as to make their interpretation rather easier for the reader.

Case Study 16.1   Fiddles and knock-offs

In addition to tips, some hotel and catering workers also benefit from 'fiddles' and 'knock-offs'. The term 'fiddles' refers to the pilferage that goes on in hotels. A 'knock-off' is a particular form of 'fiddle' involving the purloining of (usually) small items such as soap, linen and towels, though more usually it involves stealing food (Mars, 1973; Mars and Nicod, 1981). Fiddles and knock-offs tend to be institutionalised in hotel and catering operations, that is, management collude in allowing both certain monetary benefits obtained by devious means and the petty theft of physical goods. Management's concern is to set parameters beyond which pilferage will not be tolerated and will incur sanctions (Mars and Mitchell, 1976). In their various studies, Mars and his colleagues have pointed out that this gives management considerable power. For example, troublesome employees can be instantly dismissed for pilfering, despite the fact that such activity is normally tolerated within limits. The sacked employee has no recourse to the law because theft is a legally unacceptable activity though it is a normative feature of hotel and catering work.

The mechanics of pilfering small physical goods or comestibles are fairly straightforward except in organisations where security and checking systems are highly developed. Even these can be overcome however: Mars and Nicod (1984: 112) note that food can be smuggled out of establishments fairly easily, quoting the example of a waiter who helped run two restaurants of his own using supplies removed from the hotel in which he worked via the device of strapping to his leg, underneath his trousers, items such as smoked salmon and steak. The mechanisms for fiddling are more complex. In the work of Mars and his colleagues, fiddling is usually taken to refer to money fiddles, that is the means by which employees secure direct cash benefits for themselves, either at the expense of the customer or the employing organisation. The victim of a fiddle is usually defined by the location of action. Thus, in lounges and dining-rooms or restaurants, it is the employer who is usually the object of fiddling, as Mars and Nicod (1981: 66) note:

> Basically these fiddles involve first getting food and drink past a checker or control clerk and second, serving exactly what the customer has ordered, and then pocketing the payment for it. Since a waiter must eventually account for every cheque he presents to the kitchen or stillroom, his problem is to obtain food and beverages without a cheque. One solution is to introduce items which he has purchased outside the hotel so that a profit can be made when they are sold at the hotel's higher prices.

Collusion is common between waiting and kitchen staff. In the case of fiddles against the customer collaboration again is not infrequent. These fiddles are most frequently practised by bar staff and wine waiters (Mars and Nicod, 1984) and vary from simple over-charging and short-changing to product substitution. The latter can operate at two levels. First, a customer may ask for, say, a bottled beer and, providing the order can be prepared in relative secrecy, the bartender or waiter may substitute a draught product (which is usually cheaper) and pocket the difference in price (Mars and Nicod, 1981: 68). The second level at which product substitution can occur is when staff supply their own drink. Further exemplification of the variety of means of obtaining fiddles would be superfluous given the extensive literature generated. In addition to the studies by Mars (1973), Mars, Bryant and Mitchell (1979), Mars and Nicod (1981), and Mars and Nicod (1984) a variety of other works have focused directly or indirectly on fiddling and knocking-off (e.g. Spradley and Mann, 1975; Bowey, 1976). The crucial point is that these activities are regarded as a normal part of remuneration for many hotel and catering workers, though the extent to which entitlement to such rewards is universal also needs to be considered.

Mars and Nicod (1981) argue that nearly all workers in a position to have the opportunity for fiddling and knocking-off are allowed to do so. However, access to the type, quantity and quality of fiddle is highly stratified, the most important agents of stratification being membership of the core or periphery, the class of the hotel (and presumably restaurant) and the extent to which rewards are bureaucratised in the hotel in which the employee works. At a very simple level, core workers are likely to take more valuable items and be allowed greater freedom in operating money fiddles than peripherals. Core workers often operate in collusion with one another in order to secure rewards. Peripheral workers by way of contrast tend to be constrained to taking relatively inexpensive items (see also Paterson, 1981) and may not have the opportunity to run extensive money fiddles. Beyond this, the allocation of core and peripheral status depends on the type of the hotel. Mars and Nicod (1981) argue that in prestigious hotels reward allocation is based on technical skill and professional expertise and rankings are easy to devise according to these criteria, invariably leading to a pyramidal structure with a small core at the apex being allowed significant access to fiddles. In the majority of hotels however, ranking by skill is less in evidence and emphasis is instead placed on speed of service, the ability to cope during critical periods and on personal loyalty and reliability.

From: Wood, R.C. (1997), *Working in Hotels and Catering*, 2nd edn, London: International Thomson Business Press. Reproduced with permission.

Case Study 16.2 Service quality

Management by measurement

An overwhelming number of respondents (87%) emphasised the importance of measuring service quality. Measuring quality, they believed, would 'allow us to focus better on customer requirements and expectations' and would 'help the organisation plan better for future requirements'. One manager summarised general feeling on the issue when she said:

> It is extremely important to measure and monitor quality because if standards of quality deteriorate, customers won't come back.

The 'guest questionnaire' technique remains the predominant means of measuring quality at hotel unit level with almost a third (28%) of those interviewed indicating that their hotels used 'guest questionnaires' to measure service quality (see Figure 2). The predominance of the guest questionnaire technique as a means of measuring service quality (see Figure 2) in hotel organisations has been reported by other writers, most notably Johnston *et al.* (1990). The popularity of the method is, however, a matter for concern since it is for the most part unrepresentative. As Johnston *et al.* (1990) point out, participants tend to be categorised in terms of satisfaction; either extremely satisfied or highly dissatisfied. Interestingly, only 7% of managers had ever used group interviews with customers as a means of measuring quality, which lends credibility to Johnston and Morris's (1985) claim that service organisations measure that which is easy to measure.

However, despite the fact that over 87% of managers believed it important to measure quality, less than half (42%) of participant hotels had a specific department responsible for measuring service quality. In fact, almost one in three (31%) managers indicated that they had responsibility for measuring service quality. However, a significant number of participants (34%) expressed dissatisfaction with the measurement of quality at their hotels. A variety of reasons were given for expressing dissatisfaction with current initiatives – the most popular explanation being the informal manner in which quality is measured (see Table 3). A further significant explanation, however, was the insufficient time and money resources accorded to the quality process. Respondents were also critical of the lack of guest involvement and the poor delegation of responsibility in the measurement of service quality.

(continued)

Case Study 16.2   *Continued*

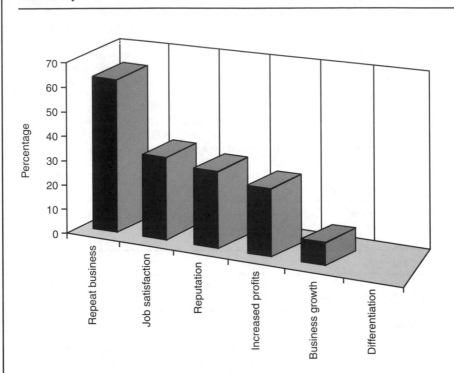

Figure 1   Benefits perceived by managers of investing in service quality

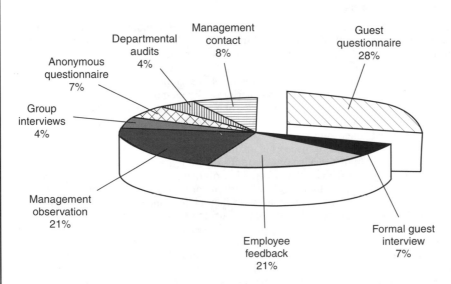

Figure 2   Procedures for evaluating service quality

Table 3 Reasons given by managers for expressing dissatisfaction with the measurement of service quality in their organisation

Reasons	Percentage (%)
Informal arrangements for measuring service quality	48
Insufficient time and money resources	24
Lack of guest involvement in measuring service quality	19
Poor delegation of responsibility for measuring service quality	10

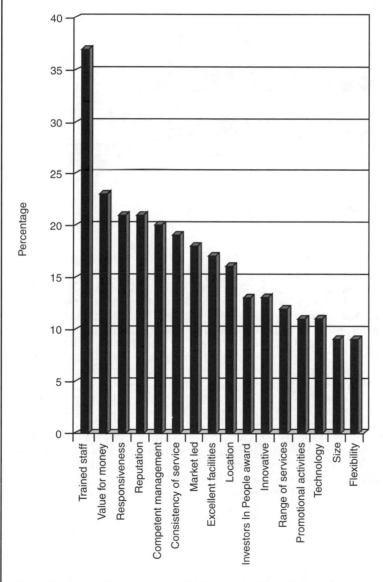

Figure 3 Competitive advantages which respondent firms feel they have over rivals in industry

(continued)

Case Study 16.2 *Continued*

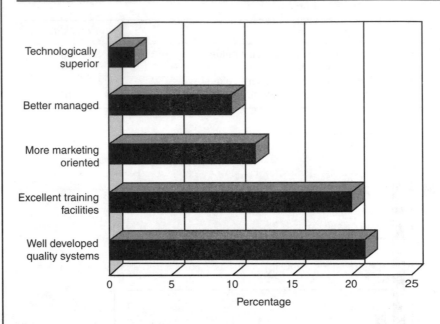

Figure 4 Reasons why competitor organisations outperform respondent firms in quality terms

Service quality and competitiveness

The managers interviewed attached much strategic importance to the concept of service quality. Of those interviewed, 87% considered quality a 'strategic concern' at their hotels. This adds weight to Tahir's proposition that quality exists for the purpose of achieving competitive advantage (Tahir, 1994). It also confirms the results of a recent study on quality which concluded that '... even where quality is already seen as important at a strategic operational level, even more importance should be attached to it' (Clark *et al.*, 1994, p. 78). Indeed, as can be seen from Figure 3, concern for quality features highly in the list of competitive advantages which general managers believed their firms had over other rivals in the industry.

Despite managerial concern with service quality, only 23% of managers held the opinion that their firms were 'very good' at offering high levels of service quality. In fact almost two thirds (62%) of respondents indicated that there were other hotel organisations who were better at providing quality service for potential customers. A number of managers mentioned that other hotels were more 'marketing oriented' (12%) and were thus better placed to deliver quality to the customer (see Figure 4). However, the majority of respondents (22%) emphasised the sophistication of competitor 'quality systems' as the reason behind them expressing dissatisfaction with current approaches to managing service quality.

From: Harrington, D. and Akehurst, G. (1996), 'Service quality and business performance in the UK hotel industry', *International Journal of Hospitality Management*, **15**(3), 283–298. Reproduced with permission.

Case Study 16.3. Managerial style

The results of this particular study show a low percentage of time allocation to the leader role and, thus agree with Ley's findings. However, the leadership style observed in the structured observation is more 'participative and achievement-oriented' than 'autocratic'. In addition, the low percentage of time allocation to this specific role signifies that the general manager who preferred 'participative and achievement-oriented' styles considered monitoring and disseminating to be the prominent roles in managing Thai hotels. The manager, as Mintzberg described, is a mediator between his network of contacts and his organisation, transferring what is received from the outside and transmitting much of it into his organisation (1973: 49). Therefore, there was a rise in the time allocations to both monitor and disseminator roles instead of the leader role as shown in Table 2. The result is very interesting not only because it is different from the previous studies but also because it reflects that the autocratic leadership style is less preferable. The hotel general managers emphasised empowerment and had less involvement in the staff's decisions. Therefore, the monitor role appeared first in rank with a high percentage of all the general managers in the sample. In this case, it could be that the monitor role is the most important role because of advanced technology. The finding also reflects the fact that there is greater competition in the Thai hotel industry than there was ten years ago. The present hotel business increasingly relies on information technology. Thus, access to data is a key to business success. There is no doubt that hotel general managers should put more emphasis on the flow of information.

The entrepreneur role is another role which yields different results to those of Mintzberg (1973). Mintzberg noted that the ten roles were common to the work of all managers and that these ten roles were an integrated whole. However, the results of the observation in this study showed that in practice there were times when a general manager did not perform all the ten roles. As shown in Table 2, General Manager 7 did not perform the entrepreneur role at all. In addition, though all the managers in the study perceived the entrepreneur role to be as important as the leader role, they spent, in fact, little time performing this role. The time allocation to the entrepreneur role ranged from 7th to 10th position, which is considered low (see Table 1). The interpretation could be that the stage of a hotel's development influences a hotel manager's entrepreneurship. The hotel general manager who works in a hotel which is well established or recently refurbished would not have many new projects to initiate. Conversely, the hotel general manager who works in the hotel which is in the transitional stage such as a change of management or a refurbishing period may, of course, have to be involved in various new initiatives and plans, as shown in the time allocations of General Managers 1, 4 and 5 (see Table 2). The results from the observation on the entrepreneur role for General Managers 1, 4 and 5 are comparatively high. This is because during the observed period there were innovations in property 1, a change of menu plan in property 4, and a change of management in property 5. In the case of General Manager 7, it could be that the observed period of five consecutive days did not represent his typical work pattern.

Overall, all general managers appeared able to judge the time spent on certain roles fairly well; for example, the mean difference in scores of General Manager 1 and General Manager 6 were both 1.7, the lowest score among all general managers (see Table 1). The results of General Manager 1 showed that he could judge the time spent on particular roles better than other general managers. There were more matched scores between perceived and actual roles. The roles which matched perceived and actual time allocations were leader, resource allocator and negotiator. Although the mean difference score of General Manager 6 was also 1.7, there were no matched scores for perceived and actual time allocation.

From: Chareanpunsirikul, S. (1997), 'Hotel General Managers' time allocations and importance to Mintzberg's framework of managerial roles', unpublished paper, The Scottish Hotel School, University of Strathclyde. Reproduced with permission.

(continued)

Table 1 Actual and perceived ranked time allocations to managerial work roles

Roles	GM1			GM2			GM3			GM4			GM5			GM6			GM7			GM8		
	Per	Act	Diff	Per	Act	Diff	Per	Act	Diff	Per	Act	Diff	Per	Act	Diff	Per	Act	Diff	Per	Act	Diff	Per	Act	Diff
Interpersonal																								
Figurehead	3	2	1	4	3	1	8	3	5	2	2	0	6	4	2	6	3	3	4	4	0	5	3	2
Leader	4	4	0	1	5	4	1	6	5	4	6	2	2	3	1	2	4	2	4	3	1	1	5	4
Liaison	6	5	1	7	4	3	4	4	0	8	4	4	7	7	0	4	6	2	6	6	0	9	4	5
Informational																								
Monitor	5	1	4	6	1	5	4	1	3	2	1	1	5	1	4	3	1	1	8	1	7	7	1	6
Disseminator	2	3	1	2	2	0	3	2	1	4	3	1	1	2	1	1	2	1	3	2	1	3	2	1
Spokesman	9	7	2	7	6	1	9	8	1	9	5	4	9	9	0	9	10	1	9	8	1	8	7	1
Decisional																								
Entrepreneur	1	8	7	2	9	7	4	9	5	1	7	6	4	8	4	7	8	1	1	10	9	4	10	6
Disturbance handler	8	9	1	9	8	1	4	5	1	7	8	1	8	10	2	7	5	2	6	9	3	5	9	4
Resource allocator	6	6	0	4	7	3	1	7	6	6	9	3	3	6	3	4	7	3	2	5	3	1	8	7
Negotiator	10	10	0	10	10	0	10	10	0	10	10	0	10	5	5	9	8	1	10	7	3	10	6	4
Total difference between actual and perceived time allocation			17			25			27			22			22			17			28			40
Mean difference			1.7			2.5			2.7			2.2			2.2			1.7			2.8			4

Note: GM – General Manager
Act – Actual ranked time allocations
Per – Perceived ranked time allocations
Diff – Difference between actual and perceived ranked time allocations
1 = most important, 10 = least important

Table 2   Actual vs perceived time allocations to managerial work roles

Roles	GM1			GM2			GM3			GM4			GM5			GM6			GM7			GM8		
	Per	Act	Diff	Per	Act	Diff	Per	Act	Diff	Per	Act	Diff	Per	Act	Diff	Per	Act	Diff	Per	Act	Diff	Per	Act	Diff
Interpersonal																								
Figurehead	13.8	15.9	-2.1	10.9	17.9	-7.9	10.4	16.3	-5.9	10.2	18.5	-8.3	10.3	9	1.3	14.2	12.7	1.5	11.2	5.9	5.3	10.6	17.5	-6.9
Leader	11.8	7.4	4.4	12.2	6.1	6.1	11.7	8	3.7	12.2	6.4	5.8	11.9	13.7	-1.8	11.5	9.8	1.7	11.2	6.3	4.9	13.7	8.3	5.4
Liaison	9.2	7.1	2.1	10	9	1	10.8	9.5	1.3	11	8.7	2.3	9.9	3.7	6.2	7.1	4.5	2.6	10.6	1.7	8.9	6.6	11.4	-4.8
Informational																								
Monitor	11.2	38.5	-27.3	10.4	35	-24.6	10.8	34.5	-23.7	11.4	34.8	-23.4	10.7	30	-19.3	14.2	43.3	-29.1	9.6	68	-58.4	9.7	32.3	-22.6
Disseminator	13.9	13.8	0.1	11.3	20.5	-9.2	11.3	17.4	-6.1	12.6	16.9	-4.3	12.3	25.7	-13.4	11.5	18.6	-7.1	12.2	14.4	-2.2	13.2	20.2	-7
Spokesman	5.3	5	0.3	10	4.4	5.6	7.4	1.9	5.5	6	7.6	-1.6	7.8	2.3	5.5	4.4	0.2	4.2	6	0.8	5.2	9.2	2.7	6.5
Decisional																								
Entrepreneur	15.1	2.5	12.6	11.3	1.3	10	10.8	0.7	10.1	9.8	3.2	6.6	11.1	3.9	7.2	15	1.5	13.5	13.8	0	13.8	11.2	0.1	11.1
Disturbance handler	6.6	2.2	4.4	9.1	1.6	7.5	10.8	8.9	1.9	9.8	2	7.8	9.5	1.6	7.9	8.8	4.7	4.1	10.6	0.4	10.2	10.6	2.3	8.3
Resource allocator	9.2	6	3.2	10.9	3.3	7.6	11.7	2.3	9.4	11	0.3	10.7	11.5	4.6	6.9	10.6	3.2	7.4	13.2	2.4	10.8	13.7	2.4	11.3
Negotiator	3.9	0.9	3	3.9	0.9	3	4.3	0.5	3.8	6	1.6	4.4	5	5.5	-0.5	2.7	1.5	1.2	1.6	0.1	1.5	1.5	2.8	-1.3

Note: GM – General Manager
Act – Actual time allocations
Per – Perceived time allocations
Diff – Difference between actual and perceived time allocations

Concluding remarks

This chapter is not intended to prescribe the form or content of research presentation, within hospitality. Such aspirations are both unrealistic and undesirable, given the diversity of research material which is studied within the area and the various methods which are employed. As has already been shown, hospitality research is also presented for a wide variety of reasons. This chapter is, rather, intended to suggest and illustrate good practice to aspiring and seasoned researchers in order that the overall quality of hospitality research presentation is enhanced and that students, in particular, are able to gain appropriate benefit and recognition through the presentation of the research which fully reflects the effort put into primary and secondary information collection.

References

Bowey, A. (1976) *The Sociology of Organisations*. London: Hodder & Stoughton.

Clark, F., Tynan, C. and Money, A. (1994) 'Senior managers' views on quality: a strategic perspective'. *Journal of Strategic Marketing*, **2**, 61–84.

Department of National Heritage (1996) *Tourism: Competing with the Best*. London: HMSO.

Gabriel, Y. (1988) *Working Lives in Catering*. London: Routledge and Kegan Paul.

Gibaldi, J. (1995) *The MLA Handbook for Writers of Research Papers*. New York: Modern Languages Association of America.

Guerrier, Y. and Lockwood, A. (1989) 'Managing flexible working'. *The Service Industries Journal*, **6**(3), pp. 406–419.

Johnston, R. and Morris, B. (1985) 'Monitoring control in service operations'. *International Journal of Operations and Production Management*, **5**, 32–38.

Johnston, R., Silvestro, R., Fitzgerald, L. and Voss, C. (1990) 'Developing the determinants of service quality', in Langeard, E. and Eiglier, P. (eds), *Marketing, Operations and Human Resource Insights into Services*, 1st International Research Seminar on Services Management, IAE, Aix-en-Provence, pp. 373, 393.

Li, X. and Crane, N.B. (1996) *Electronic Styles: An Expanded Guide for Citing Electronic Information*, 2nd edn. Medford: Information Today.

Mars, G. (1973) 'Hotel pilferage: a case study in occupational theft', in M. Warner (ed.), *The Sociology of the Workplace*. London: Allen & Unwin.

Mars G., Bryant, D. and Mitchell, P. (1979) *Manpower Problems in the Hotel and Catering Industry*. Farnborough: Gower.

Mars, G. and Mitchell, P. (1976) *Room for Reform*. Milton Keynes: Open University Press.

Mars, G. and Nicod, M. (1981) 'Hidden Rewards at Work: The Implications from a Study of British Hotels', In, Henry S. (ed) *Can I have it in cash? A Study of Informal Institutions and Unorthodox Ways of Doing Things*. London: Astragel Books.

Mars, G. and Nicod, M. (1984) *The World of Waiters*. London: Allen & Unwin.

Mintzberg, H. (1973) *The Nature of Managerial Work*. New York: Harper & Row.

Paterson, E. (1981) 'Food work: maids in a hospital kitchen', in P. Atkinson and C. Heath (eds), *Medical Work*. Farnborough: Gower.

Spradley, J.P. and Mann, B.J. (1975) *The Cocktail Waitress: Women's Work in a Man's World*. New York: John Wiley & Sons.

Tahir, M. (1994) 'Total quality management', in Baker, M. (ed.), *Perspectives on Marketing Management*, vol. 4, pp. 185–225. Chichester: John Wiley & Sons.

Wood, R.C. (1997) *Working in Hotels and Catering*, 2nd edn. London: International Thomson Business Press.

Part Two:
Perspectives, Practices and Problems

17 Quality management

NICK JOHNS

Introduction

Since the Second World War, Western nations have grown less and less dependent upon primary industries of agriculture and mineral extraction, while secondary (manufacturing) industry has increasingly moved to developing countries such as Malaysia or China, where labour is cheap. This change has left tertiary 'service' industries forming the industrial base of the West, bringing a surge of interest in 'services' from politicians, managers and academics. Since the 1980s there has been a parallel concern with service quality, mirroring previous work on the quality of manufactured output. One reflection of this has been an explosion of literature on the subject, where service and service quality appear in connection with a variety of academic disciplines.

Hospitality organizations fall within the services sector and the industry has to some extent benefited from a general increase in understanding of service operations. However, the development of 'long haul' tourism in developing countries has reinforced the need for hotels throughout the world. These include establishments of an internationally accepted standard, but there is also a growing market for small, friendly or exotic establishments. The globalisation of production and distribution of many goods has also extended the demand for hospitality services aimed at the business consumer. Thus, as well as reflecting a general Western preoccupation with service, the hospitality industry finds itself at the forefront of service quality development throughout the world.

Measuring or assessing quality is an important part of management as it is essential to obtain feedback in order to gauge the development, success or failure of the service 'product'. However, service quality is difficult to define, and further difficulties are involved in measuring and managing it. Service quality is like beauty, in that most people say they would 'know it when they see it', and yet it is also true that 'beauty is in the eye of the beholder'. Thus the paradox with service quality is to define the indefinable, and the problem is that this must be done in such a way that different observers can be persuaded to agree upon the definition. This paradox lies at the heart of all service quality research, including all aspects of its measurement or management.

Service quality is regarded as a means to differentiate hospitality brands, increase customer satisfaction, improve market share and increase staff morale (Stewart and Johns, 1996). However, this view also obscures the 'service' concept to some extent. Most services are subject to aspects such as their location and accessibility which affect the quality of 'service' extended to customers, but are not related to the service encounter itself. In addition, hospitality services also contain a high proportion of

The Handbook of Contemporary Hospitality Management Research, Edited by Bob Brotherton.
© 1999 John Wiley & Sons Ltd.

components that are unrelated to 'pure' service, most notably the tangible components: food, drink, bedrooms, the dining environment and so on. The practice of lumping all 'service industries' together under one economic catch-all term obscures the fact that different service industries play very different roles in their customers' lives. Hospitality services, in particular, often represent *experiences*, which guests may regard as a pleasure rather than an instrumental necessity. In contrast, banking, car maintenance or retail services are more concerned with utility than pleasure.

This chapter presents some general theoretical perspectives on service quality and uses these to examine the way researchers have tackled the measurement and management of service quality in the hospitality industry. It also evaluates specific methodological approaches in hospitality quality research and discusses possible future trends in this interesting field of study.

Perspectives on service quality research

Service quality and its theoretical basis

Service industries are recognised as being different from manufacturing because they exhibit three basic characteristics: time-dependence, person-dependence and customisation. These have been further elaborated by a number of authors, but basically can be summarised as shown in Table 17.1.

Table 17.1   Characteristics of services

Principal characteristic	Interpretations
Time-dependence	• Services are instant, i.e. they are produced and delivered at the same time. • Services are ultimately perishable, i.e. a hotel room or restaurant seat which fails to attract customers on one day cannot do so on another. • Service production is therefore largely dependent upon demand, because services cannot be 'stockpiled' to await future customers. • In the hospitality industry this is exacerbated by the fact that capacity is virtually fixed.
Person-dependence	• Services usually contain a considerable amount of person-to-person interaction. • Service effectiveness and quality are dependent upon the personality and behaviour of front-line service staff. • Service effectiveness and quality are also dependent upon the personality and behaviour of the customer, who is also personally involved in the service encounter.
Customisation	• Service encounters' dependence upon interpersonal interactions makes their actual style and content highly variable. • As a result there is often considerable scope for tailoring service encounters or 'service products' to the needs of specific customers or market segments.

It is generally held that service quality, like service itself, is subjective and intangible, existing only in the customer's perception. As Parasuraman, Zeithaml and Berry (1986, p. 57) put it, service quality is: 'an inference about the superiority of a product or service based on rational assessment of characteristics or attributes, or an affective judgement, an emotional response similar to an attitude'.

Both 'service' and 'quality' are fraught with conceptual problems. Some authors treat 'service' as indicating only the interpersonal aspects of the guest experience. For example in the food service industry, Martin (1986) itemises restaurant service into a series of actions and activities of service staff. This is helpful to the management of waiting staff, but clearly bears little relationship to the overall quality of the customer's experience, which might be expected to feature food, the environment, and the company in which it is eaten, at least as much as the actions of service staff. Much the same can be said of the quality of other hospitality services. The actions of service staff are certainly important, but are probably not separated from the rest of the experience in the customer's mind.

However, service quality is not simply a matter of the way customers perceive a service experience. *Expectancy-disconfirmation theory* (Oliver, 1980; Bolton and Drew, 1991) proposes that customers' expectations are also an important ingredient of service quality, as well as their actual perceptions of a particular service experience. The basis of this theory is that customer satisfaction and dissatisfaction are determined by the *disconfirmation* of customers' expectations at the 'moment of truth' when they actually receive a service. Thus service quality is considered to be a 'gap' expressed as the difference between customers' perceived service performance and their original expectations. Positive disconfirmation occurs when service performance exceeds expectations, and negative disconfirmation when the opposite is the case. Positive or zero disconfirmation is thought to indicate satisfaction, while negative disconfirmation is related to dissatisfaction.

Various authors have attempted to elaborate this model to include aspects of service quality management. Brogowicz, Delene and Lyth (1990) have summarised this work in the form of a two-cycle model, a simplified version of which is shown in Figure 17.1. According to this model, service quality can be assured by closing 'gaps' in the system, as shown in Table 17.2. Gap 5, the perception gap, is the one predicted by expectation-disconfirmation theory. The others represent areas for quality assurance and hence targets for management action.

Parasuraman, Zeithaml and Berry (1985, 1986) have attempted to measure the perception gap. After holding focus groups with a number of service customers, they identified a list of 10 key quality attributes which they considered applied to all service industries: *tangibles, reliability, responsiveness, communication, credibility, security, competence, courtesy, understanding/knowing customers* and *access*. They used this list to produce a series of standardised questions, and from these they developed a style of questionnaire known as SERVQUAL. This instrument measures customers' expectations and perceptions of service performance using two series of the standardised question items. For example, an item in the 'expectations' series might be worded 'The restaurant *should be* accessible', while a parallel 'performance' question would be 'The restaurant *is* accessible'. (Generally it is necessary to tailor the questions somewhat to fit specific service situations.) Agreement/disagreement is scored against these statements on a five- or seven-point scale, and a measure of service quality can be

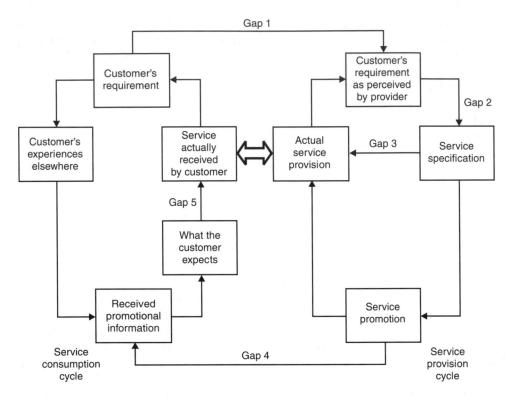

Figure 17.1   A simplified model of service quality provision showing gaps

Table 17.2   Description of the five gaps in the two-cycle model (adapted from Johns and Clark, 1993)

Conceptual gap	Description
1. The positioning gap	The gap between management's view of what the customer expects and what the customer actually expects
2. The specification gap	The gap between management's view of what the customer expects and the actual service specification
3. The delivery gap	The gap between the service that is specified and the service that is actually delivered
4. The communication gap	The gap between the service that is delivered and the service that is advertised to customers (i.e. shaping their expectations)
5. The perception gap	The gap between the service quality that customers feel they receive and the quality they expect

obtained by subtracting expectation scores from the equivalent performance scores. When Parasuraman and colleagues actually administered the SERVQUAL questionnaire, they found that they could actually identify five dimensions empirically, through factor analysis. It was possible to relate these five to the original 10, as shown in Table 17.3.

Table 17.3 Comparison of Parasuraman *et al.*'s theoretical and empirical service quality dimensions

Ten theoretical dimensions of Parasuraman, Zeithaml and Berry (1985)	Five empirical dimensions of Parasuraman, Zeithaml and Berry (1986)
Tangibles	Tangibles
Reliability	Reliability
Responsiveness	Responsiveness
Communication	Assurance
Credibility	
Security	
Competence	
Courtesy	
Understanding/knowing customers	Empathy
Access	

A substantial number of other researchers have sought to confirm this result, and although some have managed to find a five-factor pattern, many have failed. Parasuraman, Zeithaml and Berry (1991) themselves were unable to replicate their own work in a later study, which produced six factors (two apparently closely related) rather than the expected five. Assuming that customer satisfaction follows the expectancy disconfirmation model, it may be that services differ in ways which make it impossible to ask the same series of questions meaningfully of their customers. Teas (1993) questions the discriminant validity of 'expectations' questions and suggests changes to the way such items are worded. Instead of the 'should' wording he recommends that questionnaires ask questions along the lines: 'restaurants of this type are usually accessible'.

A further interesting issue is that of customer satisfaction and its relationship to service quality. Bitner and Hubbert (1994) consider *satisfaction* to be the outcome of each single, actual service experience and hence strongly influenced by the specific incidents which occurred during it. In contrast they regard service quality as the customer's overall perception of service offered by a particular company or brand. This leads to an interesting insight into the relationship between the two. Intuitively it would seem that customer satisfaction is a consequence of good or adequate service quality. However, Bitner and Hubbert's view is that the opposite is the case: customer satisfaction is a *precursor* of service quality. In their terms, a number of service incidents go to make a single customer-satisfying event, and a number of such events cause the customer to perceive high service quality. To some extent this approach reflects the persistence of a manufacturing view of service provision, where customer satisfaction is assumed to be achieved by supplying a high-quality product, often defined as such by the producer. Changing to a definition of quality as perceived by the customer gives the concept a new significance, but also profoundly affects the way service quality should be measured and evaluated.

There is a paradox inherent in service quality assessment, as follows. The purpose of measuring quality is to aid the service provider, and therefore to be of most use quality should be expressed in the provider's terms. It may also perhaps be desirable to identify partial qualities, such as the quality of the interpersonal aspect of the service encounter.

However, as has been discussed above, service quality exists only in the customer's mind, and therefore only in the customer's terms. Translating it into the provider's terms may be a problem, because customers' perceived quality is *experienced* quality, as opposed to *provided* quality. Yet the two may well be related, in ways which are as yet poorly understood.

The gap model (Figure 17.1 and Table 17.2) discussed above provides a plausible model for assuring service quality. With it in mind, a number of management activities may be proposed, as shown in Table 17.4.

Thus the gap model of service quality provision is a convenient way of understanding the roles of quality measurement and of management action. It also reinforces the need for a quality assurance stance in service provision, where quality is a matter of getting it right first time, and it is generally impossible to correct 'service errors' after they have occurred. However, it oversimplifies the problem. Real service organisations are complex systems, in which 'gaps' may appear at many locations. Each stage of the gap model—positioning, specification, delivery, etc.—is therefore made up of a series of events which interact in complex ways. In recognition of this, service organisations have tended to adopt organic management approaches, in order to assure quality.

Organic approaches to service quality management

The total quality management (TQM) concept considers a service process as a chain of events in which there is a flow of work from one employee to another. The individuals who pass on and receive work in each transaction are respectively called 'internal suppliers' and 'internal customers'. In principle the process works most efficiently (i.e. quality is optimised) when there is a good working relationship between each supplier/ customer team. Few real service situations actually reflect the simplistic picture of 'gaps' suggested by the extended service model. The TQM approach seeks to avoid unjustified assumptions about the structure of the service process or the location of service problems by regarding the service organisation as a complex 'organism' and tackling its problems systemically from within. Thus TQM programmes aim to develop

Table 17.4 Possibilities for management action suggested by the gap model of service quality provision

Conceptual gap	Potential action
1. The positioning gap	Improve feedback from customers in order to achieve the best match between the service concept and customers' expectations
2. The specification gap	Improve the match between the service concept and the quality of service which is specified
3. The delivery gap	Improve communication between those who design the service and those who deliver it
4. The communication gap	Ensure that what is advertised faithfully reflects what the guest actually receives
5. The perception gap	This gap cannot be managed except by assuring quality, i.e. by closing the other four gaps in the model

a quality-oriented organisational culture. One aspect of this is training employees to be aware of their internal customers and suppliers and to ensure that they obtain feedback about the quality of their work and give feedback about the work that is passed on to them. In service organisations employees are usually also given training in customer care (i.e. in interpersonal skills and the way they treat customers). They may also be given 'empowerment training' (i.e. to use their own initiative in order to identify what guests need and to provide it). TQM and empowerment are typical components of quality assurance programmes in hospitality and tourism organisations (see, for example, Stewart and Johns, 1996).

Continuous quality improvement (CQI) approaches attempt not only to maintain, but actually to improve, the quality of operational processes, by continuously identifying and removing defects. The majority of examples of CQI can be found in manufacturing industry, where (as discussed above) it is comparatively easy to identify defects, and hence to correct them. However, there is considerable scope for using CQI in the hospitality industry. Like TQM programmes, CQI initiatives involve re-engineering the organisational culture and climate through a well-publicised mission statement. They generally also use training to sensitise employees to internal supplier/customer relationships, but under CQI employees are also trained to identify and solve *potential* process quality defects as well as actual ones. Training programmes often feature brainstorming, mind mapping and other techniques, which enable workers to identify service problems and suggest ways of solving them. The operation of a CQI system is based around two types of 'quality team'. Management teams are generally involved in trouble-shooting defects as they are identified. Workers are often organised on a voluntary basis into quality circles: groups which meet during work time to discuss problems and look for opportunities for pro-actively improving service processes. Although some elements of CQI have been incorporated into hospitality organisations, research in the field has been more concerned to identify situations outside the hospitality industry from which lessons in quality management can be learned (see, for example, Teare, Atkinson and Westwood, 1994).

This section has outlined the theoretical structures which underpin much of our understanding of quality measurement and management in service industries. A fairly detailed conceptual basis is available for understanding the dimensions and psychological status of service quality. This provides a convenient basis for the measurement of service quality and customer satisfaction. There are also several available models for the management of service quality, though this is probably less well understood in theoretical terms. The following section discusses how research into hospitality quality has drawn upon this pool of knowledge and also contributed to it.

Practices and problems

The service quality theory discussed above represents the work of a broad spectrum of researchers, working in a number of service industries. Parallel, and to an extent overlapping, with this there has been a considerable body of research into measuring and managing hospitality quality. Because these developments can best be understood in the context of general service quality research, the present section examines the course of research into service quality specifically from the viewpoint of the hospitality industry.

Early work

A number of authors have tried to define the nature of hospitality quality, although early attempts were mainly empirical, obtaining lists of quality factors through interviewing guests, staff and managers. For instance Lewis (1984a, 1984b, 1984c) identified a list (left-hand column of Table 17.5) of quality factors which appeared to form the basis upon which guests select hotels. In an interesting series of articles, he used this list, plus a variety of multivariate statistical techniques (including factor, cluster and discriminant analysis), to differentiate US hotels on the basis of customers' perceptions of quality characteristics (Lewis, 1983–1985). His series is worthy of study, because it provides a useful overview of how statistical techniques can be applied to research in this field. At about the same time, Nightingale (1985) and Callan (1989) in the UK used comparable approaches to identify specific quality characteristics in affiliated and unaffiliated hotels respectively. These authors' results are compared with those of Lewis in Table 17.5, which demonstrates that a major problem with such approaches is the difficulty of identifying commonality between the sets of results.

Some authors have also attempted to derive theoretical frameworks upon which lists of quality attributes can be structured. For instance, Martin (1986) divided service attributes into two groups: 'procedural' (those concerned with the efficiency of the service) or 'convivial' (those to do with the interpersonal interaction itself). Shams and Hales (1989) sought to identify the theoretical roles of tangibles ('goods') and intangibles ('services') in different hospitality services. They concluded that both were integral to the hospitality experience, but were present in different proportions in each particular 'product mix'. These early approaches were quick to identify a 'service gap' which has subsequently dominated service quality research: that between the interpersonal domain and the more objective aspects such as the food or the timeliness of service. Nightingale's work has subsequently been taken up by service quality researchers in other sectors as part of the extended service model.

Impact of expectancy-disconfirmation and gap theory

Expectation-disconfirmation theory and the extended service model seem to have had little direct impact upon research into hospitality service quality. However, both have had a strong indirect effect, because they underlie the development of the SERVQUAL instrument and also underpin the notion that service quality may be assured by the correct management of 'gaps' within the service system. Both of these have had a considerable impact upon the assessment and management of hospitality quality.

Questionnaires used by practitioners to assess service quality in hotels have long been a source of concern among academics. For example, Lewis and Pizam (1982) have criticised the way many of them are worded and their general lack of formal piloting and reliability testing. Their sampling validity has also been questioned on the grounds that respondents select themselves, i.e. guests tend preferentially to complete questionnaires when they have experienced a problem, or if they happen to have time on their hands. Thus such questionnaires over-represent service failures, because dissatisfied customers tend to complete them more than satisfied ones. They also tend

Table 17.5.   Lists of hotel/service quality elements, according to three different authors

Hotel quality elements according to Lewis (1984a, 1984b, 1984c)	Hotel quality elements according to Nightingale (1985)	Service quality elements of small country hotels, according to Callan (1989)
Ambience	Availability	Efficiency of organisation and service delivery
Amenities	Smooth, fast response	Service provided with a smile
Check-in and check-out	Easy to do or use: it works	Guests receive the service they expect (anticipated by staff)
F & B facilities	Comfortable, pleasant and relaxing	Cleanliness, smartness, hygiene, appearance
Food quality	Value for money	
Housekeeping	Provision of reasonable facilities	Helpfulness, concern and understanding, willingness to learn
Luxury	Spacious	
Maintenance	Adequate choice	Courtesy, good manners, respect, civility
Modern room and bath	On your own	
Noise	Control of own time	Caring, commitment, attentiveness
Other guests	Friendly approach, greeting	Homeliness, comfort, feeling like home
Parking		Technical ability
Prices		Cheerfulness, helpfulness
Reservation system		Promptness, performance on time
Restrictive policies		Unobtrusive but available service
Room decor and comfort		Communication, articulateness, personality, charm
Room size and layout		Welcome and warmth
Security		Personal service
Service		Value for money, consistency
Staff attitude		Pride in performance, attention to detail, self-respect
Staff professionalism		Flexibility, responsiveness, ability to prioritise
		Tact and discretion
		Peaceful, unhurried, relaxing environment
		Knowledge of local services, attraction and information
		Reliability, punctuality
		Enthusiasm, eagerness to please
		Maturity and experience
		Common sense
		Provision of good tangible products, food and drink
		Remembering guests' names
		Honesty, openness, trustworthiness

to over-represent lower revenue guest segments such as leisure tourists or the elderly, rather than the lucrative business sector. These objections apply both to comment cards left in bedrooms and to one-off guest questionnaire surveys, and they have stimulated several studies aimed at improving the assessment of quality. An early example of this was that of Oberoi and Hales (1990), who conducted an empirical study of conference hotel quality in the UK. They actually used gap theory to justify and underpin their work, but rejected the SERVQUAL questionnaire itself on the grounds that its structure was too prescriptive for their study. Subsequently, Barsky (1992) has made a detailed study of quality measurement theory, which he has applied to the assessment of customer satisfaction in the US hotel industry. After interviewing a number of executives from hotel companies on the west coast of the USA, he produced a series of questions which reflected the spirit and broad aims of the SERVQUAL instrument. However, he rejected the SERVQUAL format, which specifies two parallel sets of questions, because he felt that this made the instrument too long and cumbersome for practical use in the hospitality industry. Instead Barsky used a comparative style of question, where guests were asked to rate the service they received as better or worse than expected. Barsky's approach is an interesting attempt to tailor a standardised questionnaire to the specific needs of the hospitality industry. Guest comment cards styled as he suggests can sometimes be found in use in hotels, but in general his work has not been taken up by hospitality managers or by other researchers. One problem in this respect is that the 'better/worse than' style has not been subjected to the extensive independent validity and reliability testing that has been applied to SERVQUAL.

The SERVQUAL instrument itself has also been applied to practical hospitality situations. Its most enthusiastic protagonists have been Knutson's group at Michigan State University, who have developed a series of questionnaire instruments for measuring hospitality service quality, including LODGSERV (Knutson et al., 1991) and DINE-SERV (Stevens, Knutson and Patton 1995). These represent comparatively minor modifications of SERVQUAL and have retained the double series of questions for separately assessing expectations and perceptions of quality. Lee and Hing (1995) in Hong Kong and Johns and Tyas (1996) in the UK have independently adapted the original SERVQUAL instrument of Parasuraman and colleagues for measuring satisfaction among restaurant customers. These studies have shown that the SERVQUAL style of questionnaire has utility as a means of assessing overall customer satisfaction with hospitality services. It can also be used effectively to distinguish between the quality of different hospitality outlets.

However, there are a number of problems with the use of SERVQUAL in hospitality situations, most of which centre around the five-factor structure which is supposed to underlie the questionnaire design. None of the researchers who have used SERVQUAL in hospitality situations have reported being able to demonstrate the five-factor structure. Johns et al. (1996) were unable to identify the five empirical factors in restaurant quality, but demonstrated the presence of at least two structural components concerned with food and service. Ekinci and Riley (1997) and Brotherton and Booth (1997) have also recently questioned the validity of the SERVQUAL instrument in hospitality services on the basis of its lack of an empirical factor structure. On the other hand, Knutson's group, as well as Lee and Hing, are enthusiastic about the instrument on the basis that the reliability of the expected factors (measured as Cronbach's alpha) is good. Johns and Tyas (1996) suggest that this may be because all of the questions are perceptibly related to quality, and a 'halo effect' prevails, which artificially increases the correlation between questions, and hence the alpha values.

Alternative approaches to quality assessment

Lack of an identifiable fit between empirical hospitality findings and general service quality theory has prompted some researchers to look elsewhere in an attempt to assess or measure hospitality quality. For example, Almanza, Jaffe and Lin (1994) have used a service attribute matrix to measure customer satisfaction in a college student restaurant. This technique involves identifying possible quality attributes and using a questionnaire to build up customer perceptions into a matrix. The quality attributes must be predefined and in this respect the technique is somewhat similar to other quantitative approaches. Lockwood (1994) has applied critical incident methodology to the assessment of service quality, by collecting critical incidents in hotel performance from interviews with front-line service employees. The incidents were then categorised according to their magnitude and impact and could be used to inform management action. However, the critical incident technique does not permit quantifiable measurement of service quality. Johns and Lee-Ross (1996) have developed a similar, but more customer-focused, approach which they call profile accumulation. Guests are asked to write down the best and worst aspects of the service they received, together with the reasons why these aspects are good or bad. Responses are coded and could be quantified to reveal perceived overall service quality together with the individual quality of service components. Profile accumulation has been used to differentiate between hospitality events as well as between different outlets. It has also been used to identify the dimensionality of expectations and perceptions of food-service quality (Johns and Howard, 1998).

Another way to assess hospitality quality is through service audits, a preferred approach among consultants and managers in the industry. Service quality auditing is generally presented as pragmatic, with little overt theoretical basis. However, to some extent it reflects a systems approach, and the elements of gap theory can be discerned within it. At first sight, auditing seems to make no attempt to access the customer's experience of quality, but Johns and Clark (1993) have pointed out that walk-through audits essentially reflect the customer's 'service journey' (see below). Much the same can be said of mystery guest/mystery diner programmes, which are also widely used throughout the industry. Despite the lack of a coherent theoretical basis, auditing continues to be a popular way to assess hospitality service quality (e.g. Luchars and Hinkin, 1996). The service journey model has also been used by Danaher and Mattsson (1994) to study cumulative satisfaction among conference hotel guests. In their study, guests completed questionnaires at various stages of their 'journey', through the conference—registration, introduction, coffee, lunch and so on—and the data were analysed cumulatively to show how each stage contributed to final satisfaction with the conference as a whole. It may be that studies of this kind will ultimately contribute to theoretical understanding of other service journey-related processes, such as quality auditing.

The assessment of quality is important to all segments of the international hospitality industry, including the small business sector. However, many small hospitality businesses, which make up most of the industry worldwide, generally have to rely upon grading schemes as a means of assuring quality. In a sense these are equivalent to the quality audits practised by hospitality groups. Callan (1989, 1990) has studied the value of hotel award schemes to small businesses in the UK, while Emerick and Emerick (1994) have profiled small lodging businesses in the USA.

Research in hospitality quality management

Jones and Ioannou (1993) examined the way managers measured guest satisfaction in 14 UK hotel groups. They derived a model for compiling a guest satisfaction index, consisting of 11 criteria which covered three areas: survey design, survey distribution and data processing. They found a range of practices, including one which did not assess guest satisfaction at all and one which met nine of their 11 criteria. They concluded that the majority of groups were using satisfaction measures which were at best unsatisfactory and at worst very misleading.

Boumaza (1993) studied hotel and hotel restaurant guests' perceptions of service in major Algerian hotels, and in particular the consistency of service between Algerian-managed and foreign-managed hotels. He found that there was a positive correlation between hotel and restaurant guests' attitudes towards service performance at both the Algerian-managed and the foreign-managed hotels. Staff performance at the two types of hotels and restaurants seemed to be identical.

Many researchers have been concerned with the way quality standards and principles are communicated within hospitality organisations. For instance, Brownell and Jameson (1996) found that the general manager and supervisors were the main sources of service quality information in a medium-sized US hotel, where employees tended to learn standards by watching supervisors and co-workers in action. The learning process was lengthy and often lasted six months or more. Employees whose first language was not English tended to rely more on written materials for information. Montane-Balabue (1996) found that Spanish luxury hotels' commitment to customer service was related to the proportion of customer contact employees among the total workforce. The importance accorded to training differed markedly between hotels, and most training was conducted on-the-job.

Researchers have also studied the effect of organisational strategy upon quality management. For example, Dumond (1995) investigated the relationships between internal service quality, employee satisfaction and guest satisfaction at two Californian hotels with different operational strategies. She found that three types of management/staff attitudes particularly affected internal service quality and she identified these as 'communicators of value and culture', 'supporters/enhancers of work activities' and 'supporters of hotel policies and procedures' respectively. Hartline (1993) collected data from managers, employees and guests in three US hotel chains, finding that socialisation practices had a profound impact on employee behaviour and perceived service quality. Providing employees with a precise sequence of training stages was a particularly effective way of improving behaviour and quality. Three aspects had a negative impact on perceived service quality: supervisor role conflict, job role ambiguity and low job satisfaction.

Calfas (1990) examined the failure of growing restaurant chains in the USA, using a computer simulation model. The research examined areas which impacted upon financial success, including perceived value and product quality. Failure was attributable in one case to the disastrous application of a specific management incentive programme.

Another organisation failed due to the slow erosion of market share. Both impacted through the price/quality relationship.

Conclusions and future research issues

Research into hospitality service quality reflects many of the general theoretical principles which underlie thinking in service quality as a whole. In some cases hospitality research also shows a desire to innovate and to develop new, specific theories and techniques. For instance, the SERVQUAL instrument has been modified in minor ways by researchers such as Lee and Hing (1995) and by Knutson's group (Knutson *et al.*, 1991; Stevens, Knutson and Patton, 1995). It has been adapted more extensively by Barsky (1992) and analysed in some depth by Johns and Tyas (1996), Johns *et al.* (1996) and Ekinci and Riley (1997).

Hospitality researchers have been quick to adopt new approaches towards service quality assessment, such as the service attribute matrix and critical incident technique. At least one novel technique, profile accumulation, has emerged. However, this has been employed by only a small number of researchers. A general problem with work in this area is that researchers seem generally more willing to break new ground or to import approaches from other fields of study. Few have set out to validate the techniques and approaches of other researchers in the same field.

The evidence of Jones and Ioannou (1993) suggests that the industry is also reluctant to take up the ideas of researchers in terms of measuring service quality. These authors' observations are supported by those of Brotherton and Burgess (1997), who surveyed managing directors of hospitality organisations in the UK and USA about their awareness of and interest in research. Most research interest centred around HRM, marketing and control; service quality research was not specifically mentioned at all. Even within the areas of interest an overwhelming majority of respondents in both countries (97.5% and 88.5% in the UK and USA respectively) had not adopted any of the findings of academic research.

Somewhat less theoretical underpinning is available for the management of service quality than for its measurement. The extended service model uses a basic systems view of service provision to predict where 'gaps' will occur, and it suggests management action that may be taken to close the gaps. However, it incorporates a number of assumptions that frequently do not apply to actual hospitality situations. For example, although hospitality services may be 'designed' (stage 2 of the model), in many cases they are in fact determined by tradition. The work of Brownell and Jameson (1996) suggests that the process of communicating service standards to staff is a complex one, in which different communication media may be employed with different individuals at different times.

The overall picture presented by research into hospitality service quality is a fragmented one. A variety of techniques and theoretical stances have been employed and it is challenging to rationalise them into a coherent picture. Yet a picture can be discerned, in the manner of a growing jigsaw puzzle, where only the outer rim and a few unconnected patches have been assembled. The following section attempts to identify some of the more important 'patches' upon which researchers may usefully concentrate.

An important general theoretical assumption is that service quality is subjective and intangible, existing only in the customer's perception. Although most researchers pay lip service to this principle, their attempts to measure service quality have mostly been based upon questionnaires. These are necessarily worded according to service researchers' or providers' perceptions of quality dimensions. Although a number of researchers have conducted empirical studies of hospitality quality dimensions, their results have tended to diverge, and no means has been available to reconcile them into a coherent pattern. It may be that the development of more flexible approaches such as profile accumulation will make this possible.

There is also an assumption (though increasingly challenged by some service quality researchers) that all service industries and sectors may be judged upon a single set of quality dimensions and can be measured in a similar way. This is particularly disquieting in the case of hospitality and tourism services. 'Consuming' a hospitality service inevitably seems to involve an experience, evaluated in terms of pleasure, in a way which would not be appropriate for other types of service, such as a visit to a bank. Thus there may well be some fundamental 'difference' about hospitality services that affects the way guests perceive and evaluate them. Such a difference ought also to influence the way they should be measured, and it may well be reflected in guests' predisposition to return or to recommend the service to friends and relatives. There is a generally held assumption among researchers that hospitality services are also 'different' as a result of containing a high proportion of tangible components in the service mix. In principle, therefore, the study of hospitality service quality might be expected to pinpoint new problems and questions and thus to contribute in novel ways to the general understanding of service quality. Ultimately, it might suggest ways forward for other service sectors, since it may be possible to identify and separate what is different and specific about hospitality service quality and apply it to other service industries.

The extensive body of theory that has developed around the definition and measurement of service quality makes it comparatively easy to frame studies in this area. For example, the theoretical structure includes expectancy-disconfirmation theory and an assumed relationship between service quality, customer satisfaction and repeat business. However, these assumptions also affect the style of research, predisposing it towards a positivistic, hypothetico-deductive stance, which may be detected in many recent articles and higher degree theses. Because they are concerned with the falsification of existing theory, hypothetico-deductive research approaches may in fact conceal key questions, rather than allowing them to be opened up. An alternative and perhaps preferable way forward is to use qualitative research approaches, which rely more heavily upon inductive processes. This would enable research questions to be phrased more loosely and to be freed from assumptions about the nature of service quality. However, it may also present perceived problems of academic validity and credibility.

In order to understand such systems in their full complexity it is probably most appropriate to use a qualitative research approach. Since it is unlikely that the findings can be generalised *in toto* from one situation to another, it may be best to study the way the system works as a case study, using a variety of techniques. This should ensure that the maximum of theoretical structure can be built up about the case. Soft systems methodology may provide a suitable basis for analysing the situation and managing its complexity. There is also a case to be made for the use of action research techniques, in which teams of management and staff drive the research forward under the guidance of a skilled researcher. Such approaches would probably gain the acceptance of industry more readily than the hypothesis-based studies that currently prevail in this field. However, case study method, and (even more so) action research, demand very rigorous philosophical justification and validation. In general action research is not recommended as a vehicle for academic studies in business management, and despite the work of Argyris (1985) such studies are not readily accepted as 'science'. However, it may be that hospitality research needs to develop action research as an effective way to reconcile its own specific research problems with the needs and interests of its industry.

The small business sector has been mentioned above in the context of quality grading. However, this sector has greater challenges to offer researchers into hospitality quality. It is particularly important in the hospitality field, where it is estimated that at least 80% of provision depends upon small operations. It is also a critical aspect of tourism development in unexploited or peripheral areas, where a large proportion of the provision is dependent on the small business sector. There are often specific problems of networking groups of managers together, establishing standards for very diverse provision, or drawing together hospitality and tourism provision into packages which will appeal to holiday visitors. These challenges may also be met most effectively through case studies or action research approaches. What is certain is that at present comparatively little is known about them, and there is no theoretical infrastructure upon which hypotheses might be built.

References

Almanza, B. A., Jaffe, W. and Lin, L. (1994) Use of the service attribute matrix to measure consumer satisfaction. *Hospitality Research Journal*, **17** (2): 63–76.

Argyris, C. R. (1985) *Action Science*, Jossey-Bass, San Francisco.

Barsky, J. D. (1992) Customer satisfaction in the hotel industry: meaning and measurement. *Hospitality Research Journal*, **16** (1): 51–73.

Bitner, M. J. and Hubbert, A. R. (1994) Encounter satisfaction versus service quality: the consumer's voice, in Rust, R. T. and Oliver, R. L. (Eds) *Service Quality: New Directions in Theory and Practice*, Sage Publications, Thousand Oaks, CA.

Bolton, R. N. and Drew, J. H. (1991) A multistage model of customers' assessment of service quality and value. *Journal of Consumer Research*, **17**: 375–384.

Boumaza, C. (1993) *Guests' Perceptions of Quality Service in Major Algerian Hotels*, MS Thesis, Eastern Michigan University.

Brogowicz, A. A., Delene, L. M. and Lyth, D. M. (1990) A synthesized service quality model with managerial implications. *International Journal of Service Industry Management*, **1** (1): 27–45.

Brotherton, R. and Booth, W. (1997) An application of SERVQUAL to a hotel leisure club environment. *Proceedings of the EuroCHRIE Autumn Conference*, Sheffield Hallam University.

Brotherton, R. and Burgess, J. (1997) A comparative study of academic research interests in US and UK hotel and restaurant companies. *Proceedings of the 6th Annual Hospitality Research Conference*, Oxford Brookes University: 317–349.

Brownell, J. and Jameson, D. (1996) Getting quality out on the street—a case of show and tell. *Cornell Hotel and Restaurant Administration Quarterly*, **37** (1): 28–33.

Calfas, R. A. (1990) *Why Growing Restaurant Chains Can Fail: A Computer Simulation Model*, PhD Thesis, Claremont Graduate School, USA.

Callan, R. J. (1989) Small country hotels and hotel award schemes as a measurement of service quality. *Service Industries Journal*, **9** (2): 223–246.

Callan, R. J. (1990) Hotel award schemes as a measurement of service quality—an assessment by travel industry journalists as surrogate consumers. *International Journal of Hospitality Management*, **9** (1): 45–48.

Danaher, P. J. and Mattsson, J. (1994) Cumulative encounter satisfaction in the hotel conference process. *International Journal of Service Industry Management*, **5** (4): 69–80.

Dumond, S. C. (1995) *Organizational Strategy as a Function of the Physical Environment: A Work Climate Study*, PhD Thesis, California School of Professional Psychology, Los Angeles, CA.

Ekinci, Y. and Riley, M. (1997) Examination of the SERVQUAL and LODGSERV scales performance in the case of holidaymakers' perception of resort hotel service quality. *Proceedings of the 6th Annual CHME Hospitality Research Conference*, Oxford Brookes University.

Emerick, R. E. and Emerick, C. A. (1994) Profiling American bed and breakfast accommodations. *Journal of Travel Research*, **6** (2): 20–25.

Hartline, M. D. (1993) *The Socialization of Customer-Contact Employees in Service Organizations: Effects on Employee Behaviours and Service Quality Outcomes in the Hotel Industry*, PhD Thesis, Memphis State University.

Johns, N. and Clark, S. L. (1993) The quality audit: a means of monitoring the service provided by museums and galleries. *Journal of Museum Managership and Curatorship*, **12**: 360–366.

Johns, N. and Howard, A. (1998) Customer expectations vs perceptions of service performance in the foodservice industry. *International Journal of Service Industry Management*, **9** (3) (accepted awaiting publication).

Johns, N. and Lee-Ross, D. (1996) Profile accumulation: a quality assessment technique for hospitality SMEs. *Proceedings of the First Service Industries Symposium*, Bournemouth University.

Johns, N. and Tyas, P. (1996) Use of service quality gap theory to differentiate between foodservice outlets. *Service Industries Journal*, **16** (3): 321–346.

Johns, N., Tyas, P., Hopkinson, S. and Ingold, A. (1996) Quality dimensions of the meal experience. *Progress in Tourism and Hospitality Research*, **2**: 15–26.

Jones, P. L. and Ioannou, A. (1993) Measuring guest satisfaction in UK-based hotel chains: principles and practice. *International Journal of Contemporary Hospitality Management*, **5** (5): 27–31.

Knutson, B., Stevens, P., Wullaert, C., Patton, M. and Yokoyama, F. (1991) LODGSERV: a service quality index for the lodging industry. *Hospitality Research Journal*, **14** (3): 277–284.

Lee, Y. L. and Hing, N. (1995) Measuring quality in restaurant operations: an application of the SERVQUAL instrument. *International Journal of Hospitality Management*, **14** (3): 293–310.

Lewis, R. C. and Pizam, A. (1982) The measurement of guest satisfaction, in Pizam, A., Lewis, R. C. and Manning, P. (eds) *The Practice of Hospitality Management*, AVI Publishing, New York: 189–201.

Lewis, R. C. (1983) Getting the most from marketing research. *Cornell Hotel and Restaurant Administration Quarterly*, November: 81–85.

Lewis, R. C. (1984a) Theoretical and practical considerations in research design. *Cornell Hotel and Restaurant Administration Quarterly*, February: 25–35.

Lewis, R. C. (1984b) The basis of hotel selection. *Cornell Hotel and Restaurant Administration Quarterly*, May: 54–69.

Lewis, R. C. (1984c) Isolating differences in hotel attributes. *Cornell Hotel and Restaurant Administration Quarterly*, November: 64–77.

Lewis, R. C. (1985a) Predicting hotel choice. *Cornell Hotel and Restaurant Administration Quarterly*, February, pp. 82–96.

Lewis, R. C. (1985b) The market position: mapping guests' perceptions of hotel operations. *Cornell Hotel and Restaurant Administration Quarterly*, August: 86–99.

Lockwood, A. (1994) Using service incidents to identify quality improvement points. *International Journal of Contemporary Hospitality Management*, **6** (1): 75–80.

Luchars, J. Y. and Hinkin, T. R. (1996) The service-quality audit: a hotel case study. *Cornell Hotel and Restaurant Administration Quarterly*, **37** (1): 34–41.

Martin, W. B. (1986) Defining what quality service is for you. *Cornell Hotel and Restaurant Administration Quarterly*, February: 32–38.

Montane-Balabue, M. (1996) *A Study of Training Methodology for Customer Contact Employees in Spain, and Implications on Service Quality*, MSc Thesis, University of Nevada.

Nightingale, M. (1985) The hospitality industry: defining quality for a quality assurance programme—a study of perceptions. *Service Industries Journal*, **5** (1): 9–24.

Oberoi, U. and Hales, C. (1990) Assessing the quality of the conference hotel service product: towards an empirically based model. *Service Industries Journal*, **10** (4): 700–721.

Oliver, R. L. (1980) A cognitive model of the antecedents and consequences of satisfaction decisions. *Journal of Marketing Research*, Vol. 17, pp. 460–469.

Parasuraman, A., Zeithaml, V. A. and Berry, L. (1985) A conceptual model of service quality and its implications for future research. *Journal of Marketing*, **49**: 41–50.

Parasuraman, A., Zeithaml, V. A. and Berry, L. L. (1986) SERVQUAL: a multiple-item scale for measuring customer perceptions of service quality. *Marketing Science Institute, Working Paper Report No. 86–108*, August.

Parasuraman, A., Zeithaml, V. A. and Berry, L. (1991) Refinement and reassessment of the SERVQUAL scale. *Journal of Retailing*, **67** (4): 420–450.

Shams, H. and Hales, C. (1989) Once more on goods and services: a way out of the conceptual jungle. *Quarterly Review of Marketing*, **14** (3): 1–5.

Stevens, P., Knutson, B. and Patton, M. (1995) DINESERV: a tool for measuring service quality in restaurants. *Cornell Hotel and Restaurant Administration Quarterly*, **36** (2): 56–60.

Stewart, S. and Johns, N. (1996) Total quality: an approach to managing productivity in the hotel industry, in Johns, N. (Ed.) *Productivity Management in Hospitality and Tourism*, Cassell, London: 19–37.

Teare, R., Atkinson, C. and Westwood, C. (Eds) (1994) *Achieving Quality Performance: Lessons from British Industry*, Cassell, London.

Teas, R. K. (1993) Consumer expectations and the measurement of perceived service quality. *Journal of Professional Services Marketing*, **8** (2): 33–54.

18   Strategic management

ELIZA CHING-YICK TSE AND MICHAEL OLSEN

Introduction

The list of hospitality companies that have gone bankrupt because they were no longer considered businesses with a viable concept keeps growing: Sambo's, D'Lites, Victoria Station, Fuddruckers, and Po Folks. Similarly, companies like General Motors, IBM, Sears and American Express, along with a list of other traditionally 'well-managed companies', experienced massive losses in profit and layoffs of employees in the 1980s and 1990s (Solomon, 1993). Executives of these companies learned the hard way that strategic mistakes can result in significant monetary and market share losses. An example was IBM's failure in the 1980s to maintain its leadership in the personal-computer market. Why did so many companies fail to thrive? Among the key reasons have been identity crises, failures of vision from top management, and the company's inability to adapt to changing conditions occurring in the external environment (Labich, 1994).

The hospitality industry has experienced many changes in its business environment over the course of its recent history. Prior to the introduction of franchising and chain management concepts, competition among firms in the hospitality industry was limited to the local environment. During the 1960s, 1970s and 1980s, companies expanded through franchising units and the industry enjoyed unprecedented growth. Chains such as McDonald's, Burger King and Holiday Inn grew and dominated the hospitality industry by their sheer size and customer bases. However, by the end of the 1980s, the hospitality industry in the United States started to experience the early signs of maturity with a rapid decline in growth potential, intense competition and a flat customer count.

These signs of industry maturity are most prevalent in the United States but apparent in the United Kingdom as well. Strong competition, coupled with the onset of a recession in the US economy, forced the hospitality industry to focus upon ways to compete in an increasingly volatile and dynamic business environment. Slattery and Boer (1991) discussed three phases in a 'structural theory of business travel'. The authors argued that business traveller demand is determined by the structure of an economy rather than by GDP growth. The resulting demand and development for hotels range from single-site companies in Phase I, as in Eastern Bloc countries, to multi-site companies in Phase II, as in the United Kingdom, to the plateau of Phase III, as in the case of the United States. For the US hospitality firms, the 1990s marks the entry of the industry into Phase III, a phase characterized by only marginal growth in business demand. When the corporate structure of multi-site companies and those servicing national and international

The Handbook of Contemporary Hospitality Management Research, Edited by Bob Brotherton.
© 1999 John Wiley & Sons Ltd.

markets is in place, further growth in demand for business travel is marginal. To avoid the impact of Phase III, hotel companies have the task of identifying strategies which will protect them from the effects of marginal growth. One way perhaps is to expand internationally to countries that are in Phase I and Phase II. With the limited capital available, many companies expanded internationally by management contract franchising and joint ventures in order to maintain their growth rates.

Since the 1980s, the hospitality industry has been operating in a very volatile environment. Intense competition in the domestic market has made many US firms expand their operations internationally. Many firms compete at a global level in the hope of gaining a greater market share and increased profits. As the industry is faced with increasingly demanding customers, quickly changing technology and an ever-changing workforce, there is growing interest among hospitality industry management in the concept of strategy and the practices of strategic management to anticipate changes and adapt to the challenges facing the 1990s and beyond (Feltenstein, 1992). In other words, strategy as competitive method becomes the management tool to survive and sustain growth. For instance, executives of many major companies utilized such methods as branding strategy in order to develop balanced and structured portfolios, and frequent guest programmes, greater marketing expenditures and computer reservations systems to obtain a competitive advantage. Moreover, strategy is creating fit between a company's activities. Companies need to focus on their core competencies, what they do best, and what differentiates them from the competition. Companies should search for ways to expand beyond their existing resources through licensing arrangements, strategic alliances, and supplier relationships.

The notion of strategy and strategic management in the hospitality industry is a relatively recent phenomenon. Thus, the purpose of this chapter is to provide an overview of the concept of strategy and strategic management, a review of literature reflecting different perspectives in regard to strategic management, and research studies that have been conducted in the hospitality industry. Finally, problems facing research in strategic management are discussed and future research is recommended.

Perspectives

The concept of strategy and strategic management

The concept of strategic management is a relatively young discipline and has its roots in the disciplines of business policy, organizational theory and organizational behaviour. Because of different perspectives, there is no clear-cut definition of strategy. The first modern authors to relate the concept of strategy to business were Von Neumann and Morgenstern (1947). Various researchers since then have presented different perspectives in their definitions of the concept, but with some common threads. Exhibit 18.1 shows a sample listing of strategy definitions. The differences are found in three primary areas: the breadth of the concept of business strategy, the components of strategy, and the inclusiveness of the strategy-formulation process. The similarities include a recognition that business strategy is an environmental or situational analysis used to determine a firm's posture in its field and that the firm's resources are utilized in an appropriate manner to attain its major goals.

Exhibit 18.1 A chronology of sample listings of recent definitions of strategy

Year	Contributor, source and definition
1947	Von Neumann and Morgenstern, *Theory of Games and Economic Behavior* (pp. 79–84): **Strategy** is a series of *actions* by a firm that are decided on according to the particular *situations*.
1954	Drucker, *The Practice of Management* (p. 17): **Strategy** is analyzing the present *situation* and changing it as necessary. Incorporated in this is finding out what one's *resources* are or what they should be.
1962	Chandler, *Strategy and Structure: Chapters in the History of American Industrial Enterprises* (p. 13): **Strategy** is the determinator of the basic long-term goals of an enterprise and the adoption of courses of action and the allocation of *resources* necessary for carrying of these *goals*.
1965	Ansoff, *Corporate Strategy: An Analytic Approach to Growth and Expansion* (pp. 118–122): **Strategy** is a rule for making *decisions* determined by product/market scope, growth vector, competitive advantage, and synergy.
1968	Cannon, *Business Strategy and Policy* (p. 9): **Strategy** is the *directional action decisions* which are required competitively to achieve the company's *purpose*.
1972	Schendel and Hatten, Business Policy or Strategic Management, *Academy of Management Proceedings* (p. 4): **Strategy** is defined as the basic *goals* and *objectives* of the organization, the major programs of action chosen to reach these goals and objectives, and the major pattern of *resource allocation* used to relate the organization to its environment.
1974	Ackoff, *Redesigning the Future* (p. 29): **Strategy** is concerned with long-range *objectives* and ways of pursuing them that affect the system as a whole.
1975	Glueck, *Business Policy: Strategy Formation and Management Actions,* 2nd edn (p. 3): **Strategy** is a unified, comprehensive, and integrated *plan* designed to assure that the basic *objectives* of the enterprise are achieved.
1979	Mintzberg, *The Structuring of Organizations* (p. 25): **Strategy** is the mediating force between the organization and its *environment*; consistent patterns in streams or organizational decisions to deal with the *environment*.
1979	Schendel and Hofer, *Strategic Management: A New View of Business Policy and Planning* (p. 516): **Strategy** provides directional cues to the organization that permit it to achieve its *objectives*, while responding to the opportunities and threats in its *environment*.
1980	Porter, *Competitive Strategy* (pp. 7–19): **Strategy** is the coping with competition. Porter believes there are five forces that affect the strategy a company develops: the threat of new entrants, the bargaining power of customers, the bargaining power of suppliers, the threat of substitute products or services, and the jockeying among current contestants. The collective strength of these forces helps determine the ultimate potential of an industry.
1981	Olsen and DeNoble, Strategic planning in a dynamic environment, *Cornell Hotel and Restaurant Administration Quarterly* (pp. 75–80): **Strategy** is defined as the means through which organizational *resources* are employed to meet organizational objectives and the accomplishment of an organization's *purpose*.
1983	Lawless, Ponderosa and Hart, Forces that shape restaurant demand, *Cornell Hotel and Restaurant Administration Quarterly* (pp. 7–17): **Strategy** is a systematic means by which a company becomes what it wants to be.
1985	Minor, *The Practice of Management* (p. 372): **Strategy** may be defined as the creation of *missions*, the setting of organizational *objectives* with full consideration of external and internal forces, the formulation of specific *policies* to achieve *objectives*, and the assurance of implementation—all with a view of making certain the *purposes* and *objectives* of the organization are accomplished.

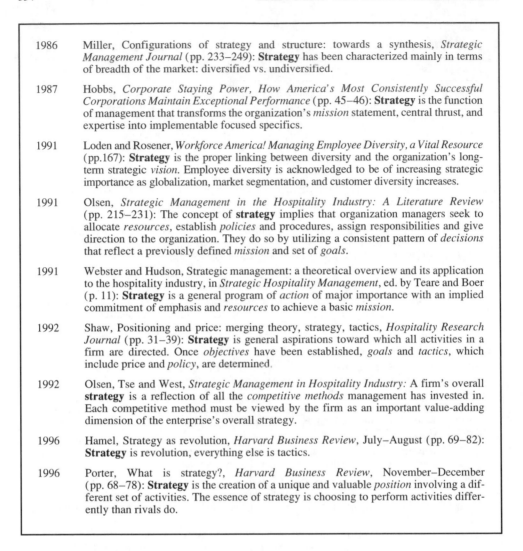

1986   Miller, Configurations of strategy and structure: towards a synthesis, *Strategic Management Journal* (pp. 233–249): **Strategy** has been characterized mainly in terms of breadth of the market: diversified vs. undiversified.

1987   Hobbs, *Corporate Staying Power, How America's Most Consistently Successful Corporations Maintain Exceptional Performance* (pp. 45–46): **Strategy** is the function of management that transforms the organization's *mission* statement, central thrust, and expertise into implementable focused specifics.

1991   Loden and Rosener, *Workforce America! Managing Employee Diversity, a Vital Resource* (pp.167): **Strategy** is the proper linking between diversity and the organization's long-term strategic *vision*. Employee diversity is acknowledged to be of increasing strategic importance as globalization, market segmentation, and customer diversity increases.

1991   Olsen, *Strategic Management in the Hospitality Industry: A Literature Review* (pp. 215–231): The concept of **strategy** implies that organization managers seek to allocate *resources*, establish *policies* and procedures, assign responsibilities and give direction to the organization. They do so by utilizing a consistent pattern of *decisions* that reflect a previously defined *mission* and set of *goals*.

1991   Webster and Hudson, Strategic management: a theoretical overview and its application to the hospitality industry, in *Strategic Hospitality Management*, ed. by Teare and Boer (p. 11): **Strategy** is a general program of *action* of major importance with an implied commitment of emphasis and *resources* to achieve a basic *mission*.

1992   Shaw, Positioning and price: merging theory, strategy, tactics, *Hospitality Research Journal* (pp. 31–39): **Strategy** is general aspirations toward which all activities in a firm are directed. Once *objectives* have been established, *goals* and *tactics*, which include price and *policy*, are determined.

1992   Olsen, Tse and West, *Strategic Management in Hospitality Industry:* A firm's overall **strategy** is a reflection of all the *competitive methods* management has invested in. Each competitive method must be viewed by the firm as an important value-adding dimension of the enterprise's overall strategy.

1996   Hamel, Strategy as revolution, *Harvard Business Review*, July–August (pp. 69–82): **Strategy** is revolution, everything else is tactics.

1996   Porter, What is strategy?, *Harvard Business Review*, November–December (pp. 68–78): **Strategy** is the creation of a unique and valuable *position* involving a different set of activities. The essence of strategy is choosing to perform activities differently than rivals do.

Strategy, from the business perspective, is defined as a course of action aimed at ensuring that the organization will achieve its objectives in sustainable advantage over competitors (Henderson, 1989). Thus, strategic management is a continuous process of analyzing the internal and external environments of a firm, investing in competitive methods which are effective, and maximizing the utilization of resources in relation to objectiveness (Bracker, 1980).

Strategic management entails a stream of decisions and actions which lead to the development and implementation of effective strategy (Mintzberg, 1979; Olsen, Tse and West, 1992; Webster and Hudson, 1991). In other words, the practice of strategic management enables the leadership to help their organization adapt continually to its changing environment. The central focus of strategy is how to deal better with competition. The basic elements of strategic competition are: (i) ability to understand competitive behaviour as a system in which competitors, customers, money, people and resources continually interact; (ii) ability to use this understanding to predict how a given strategic move will rebalance the competitive equilibrium; (iii) resources that can be permanently committed to new uses even though the benefits will be deferred; (iv) ability to predict risk and return with enough accuracy and confidence to justify that commitment; and (v) willingness to act.

The strategic management process

There are several major components in the strategic management process: strategy formulation (environmental scanning, competitive methods, core competencies), strategy implementation, and evaluation and control.

Strategy formulation   This is the process followed by organizations to develop their strategic plan. It begins with the scanning of the business environment in order to identify the threats and opportunities which exist in that environment. This effort is designed to detect both long- and short-term trends affecting the business. This step in the process is then followed by the creation/evaluation of the mission statement which defines what business the firm is in, or plans to be in, and the environmental domain in which it will compete. Following the mission statement, the firm must then decide upon the competitive methods it will choose in order to take advantage of the opportunities in its domain environment. The competitive methods are viewed as the primary value-producing activities of the business. A close match must be achieved between the opportunities in the environment and the competitive methods chosen. Bourgeois (1980) conceptualizes the relationship between strategy and environment, with primary strategy (domain definition) linked to the general environment and secondary strategy (domain navigation) linked to the task environment.

Once completed, the firm will then assess its strengths and weaknesses to determine if it has the resources and capabilities to properly implement and execute the chosen methods. This assessment will determine whether or not the firm has the core competencies to realize the overall strategy it has chosen through its selection of competitive methods (Olsen, 1998). Strategy formulation is not a linear process but a continuous process that is regularly evaluated and revised as it is carried out, with each element being interactive and interdependent.

Once the firm has identified its strengths and weaknesses, it is then ready to set long- and short-term objectives. Long-term objectives are considered to span one year or more. The objectives should be designed so as to enable the firm to overcome its weaknesses and take full advantage of its strengths. Each objective should be tied directly to a particular competitive method or set of methods. The objective must identify the physical, financial and human resources necessary to implement and execute the chosen strategy.

Throughout the organization, there are various levels of strategies: corporate, business and functional. These strategies differ in four aspects: focus, specificity, responsibility and time frame. Strategies at different levels need to be coherent to ensure competitive advantage (Hofer and Schendel, 1978). Strategy coherence is the consistency of strategic choices across business and functional levels of strategy. Nath and Sudharshan (1994) found performance differences using various performances measures between more and less coherent firms.

A corporate strategy is a master game plan for managing and operating an organization. The primary function of a corporate strategy is in deciding the scope or domain of the operation. This level of strategy provides the blueprint of the business plan in which a functional strategy can be implemented. Corporate strategies, if successfully chosen, implemented and carried out, can lead to a synergistic effect. A firm chooses a corporate strategy depending upon its mission and the goals and objectives it wants to accomplish. These strategies can guide a firm's allocation of resources among several business units and/or other ventures the firm may choose. Porter (1987), through his study of 33 large diversified US companies from 1950 to 1986, identified four concepts of corporate strategy that have been put into practice: portfolio management, restructuring, transferring skills and sharing activities. Every corporate strategy has its costs and benefits, but the main purpose for implementing a corporate strategy is to gain a greater return on investment for all its stakeholders. This can be achieved through the co-alignment principle, which involves finding the perfect corporate strategy, environment and corporate-structure fit.

For business-level strategy, Miles *et al.* (1978) proposed a typology of strategic types based on the organization's orientation toward product-market development. They suggested four strategic types: defenders, prospectors, analyzers and reactors. Porter (1980) suggested that there are three potentially successful generic competitive strategies in any industry—overall cost leadership, differentiation and focus—and a fourth, less successful, strategy stuck in the middle. Subsequently, there has been a large body of empirical research attempting to operationalize and investigate these two typologies and the sources of sustainable competitive advantage (Snow and Hrebiniak, 1980; Hambrick, 1980; Segev, 1989; Conant, Mokwa and Varadarajan, 1990). These studies generally have found support for the tendency for companies espousing the stable archetypes to perform equally well in terms of profitability and to outperform reactors or those stuck in the middle.

Strategic implementation   Once the objectives are finalized and approved and resources allocated, implementation begins. Implementation involves the actual utilization of resources for the successful execution of processes and activities associated with each competitive method.

Chandler (1962) in his classic study showed how changes in strategy require subsequent alterations in structure. Then Rumelt (1974) showed how the match between strategy and structure influences performance. Galbraith (1977) suggested that strategy implementation requires a 'fit' between strategy and organization design. Miller (1986, 1987) synthesized the relationships between common strategic and structural configurations and their implications for performance in different environments. Combining Porter's generic strategy and Mintzberg's configuration of organization design (1981), Miller proposed that differentiation (niche) strategy should be followed by simple structure, cost leadership strategy matched by machine bureaucracy structure, differentiation (innovative) strategy matched with organic structure, while conglomeration strategy is seen as supported by divisionalized structure. While most of the research on the strategy–structure fit has examined domestic organizations, Habib and Victor (1991) analyzed the strategy–structure fit and its effect on the economic performance of US manufacturing and service multinational corporations.

Similarly, Eccles and Teare (1996) reviewed the interrelationships between business strategy and organizational structure in the hospitality industry. In order to achieve a higher performance in the hotel sector, firms are required to focus development on the co-aligning effort between structure and strategy. The authors emphasize the importance of the alignment to occur at the unit level. This requires unit managers to become more strategic thinkers in order to stay competitive. These managers are in better positions than the corporate office to monitor and respond to the local environmental conditions. This calls for an organizational structure that allows the unit to be proactive, generating ideas on how best to alter the unit to meet specified objectives. This fit needs to consider the external environment to generate the most appropriate decisions. It is generally believed that without co-alignment between structure, strategy and the environment, organizations may find difficulty in achieving long-term success (Olsen, 1991; Schaffer, 1986b).

The challenge of developing or re-establishing a clear strategy is often primarily an organizational one and depends on leadership. Thus, the role of leadership is equally critical in the effective formulation and successful implementation of chosen strategy. General management is more than the stewardship of individual functions. Its core is strategy: defining and communicating the company's unique position, making trade-offs and forging fit among activities. As Leontides (1982) contends, 'Managers make strategy and strategy determines business success or failure.' Jack Welch, CEO of General Electric, stated that: 'Strategy follows people, the right person leads to the right strategy' (as quoted in Hinterhuber and Popp, 1992). It is the responsibility of the top management to ensure that these strategies are carried throughout the various levels of the organization. It is their strong commitment to resources and the fostering of an appropriate organizational culture and reward system that leads to successful strategy implementation. The leader must provide the discipline to decide which industry changes and customer needs the company will respond to, while avoiding organizational distractions and maintaining the company's distinctiveness (Porter, 1996).

Research has shown that a firm's strategy is influenced by a number of variables, including management style and characteristics of the organization's leaders, and stage of the corporate life cycle (Tsc and Elwood, 1990). Management style of the organization's leaders is believed to be one of the most critical factors in determining organizational strategy. The 'Upper Echelon' perspective examines the concept of co-alignment between specific attributes of managerial characteristics and the strategic behaviour of their firms (Hambrick and Mason, 1984; Miller, Kets de Vries and Toulouse, 1982; Miller and Toulouse, 1986). Typologies and theoretical models have been developed to explain the impact that the fit between top executive characteristics and managerial influence and strategic orientation has on organizational performance (Miles *et al.*, 1978; Porter, 1980; Leontides, 1982; Thomas, Litschert and Ramaswamy, 1991).

Moreover, it is also believed that companies with a strongly developed corporate culture usually sustain an innovative outlook and a commitment to customers and staff members. Woods and Sciarini (1996) have described cultural congruence as the extent to which its members share an organization's culture. Managers do not control their cultures but they do play important roles in them. It becomes a challenge for management to understand and appreciate the unique cultural characteristics of their own organizations and then using this information to facilitate cultural change in all organizational activities.

Evaluation and control   The implementation phase also includes evaluation and control of the strategic process against the corporate mission and long-term objectives to ensure it is functioning properly. While implementation is technically not a direct part of the formulation process, it is the link to strategy evaluation. Evaluation involves the assessment of the success of each competitive method in adding its targeted value to the firm. Results of this evaluation are used to continually cycle through the formulation process.

While the strategy field has evolved dramatically since the 1960s, theoretical models of the relationship between strategy and the control process have evolved little since then. The control system is a process which involves incentives and sanctions for business management as well as an agreement between senior and unit management on the business's objectives, the monitoring of performance against these objectives, and feedback on the results achieved (Goold and Quinn, 1990). Simons (1994) found support in his study in the notion that managers use formal control systems as a means of promoting and implementing business strategy. He identified four types of management control: belief systems (to define, communicate and reinforce the values and purposes of the organization), boundary systems (to establish explicit limits and rules), diagnostic control systems (to monitor organizational outcomes) and interactive control systems (to involve top managers in the decision activities of subordinates). He indicated that regardless of which type is adopted by top management, these systems appear to be vitally important in building credibility and selling new strategies to constituents. It is also recommended when designing a strategic control system to ensure a balance between strategy and operations, the long term and the short term.

Why do some organizations perform better than others? Studies have examined the performance consequences of formal strategic planning efforts in achieving competitive advantage (Powell, 1992). These studies provide inconclusive evidence that formalized strategic planning efforts will result in superior financial performance. Certainly, it is clear that a formal strategic planning process will not guarantee a successful formulation and implementation of strategy, nor result in a more rewarding financial performance. On the other hand, there are advantages and disadvantages of strategic management and the question remains as to whether the advantages outweigh the disadvantages.

Many executives believe that, even though it is difficult to judge the cost-effectiveness of strategic management, it is considered worthwhile even if benefits are largely intangible. They believe that explicit strategy is required to reconcile coordinated action and entrepreneurial effort as a company grows (Tiles, 1969). The major importance of strategic management is that it gives organizations a framework for analyzing their own strengths and weaknesses while identifying future opportunities and threats.

The rise and fall and rise of strategy

Strategy is a relatively new discipline and has become a buzzword in the business community in the last 30 years. Its roots can be traced back all the way to the Old Testament. The word 'strategy' comes from the Greek word *strategeo*, which means 'to plan the destruction of one's enemies through the effective use of available resources' (Bracker, 1980; Cummings, 1993). The concept of strategy has had wide application in the military and political arenas. The work by the Chinese strategist Sun Tze, *Art of the War*, is still widely read by the graduates of West Point. The adoption of the concept to the business community came after World War II. As business moved from a relatively stable environment into the rapidly changing and competitive environment of today, the need for the concept of strategy has become greater than ever. With the onset of industrial revolution, and the realization that resources are scarce, business operators realize that one cannot conduct 'business as usual'.

In academia, Harvard professors Ken Andrews and C. Roland Christensen in the early 1960s articulated the concept of strategy as a tool to link together the functions of a business and assess a company's strengths and weaknesses against competitors. In the business community, General Electric (GE) emerged as the pioneer in strategic planning. The consulting firm McKinsey & Co. helped the company to come up with the GE 9-cell approach in evaluating the performance of its portfolio. At the same time, the Boston Consulting Group became famous with such concepts as the 'experience curve' and the 'growth and market-share matrix'.

By the 1980s, as companies in the United States were challenged by the rise of global competitors, corporate America turned away from strategic planning and began to focus on operational improvement. As GE was the pioneer in embracing strategy, so was it at the forefront of its demise. In 1983, new GE Chairman Jack Welch reduced the corporate planning group. Numerous other companies followed suit as they struggled to improve quality and restructure their organizations. By the late 1980s, corporate America began massive downsizing and re-engineering of operations to increase efficiency and productivity. Executives embraced the teachings of gurus Edward Deming, father of the total quality movement, and Michael Hammer, who led the re-engineering revolution. In the hospitality industry, ITT Sheraton Corporation used the re-engineering approach to streamline its operations. The typical 300-room Sheraton Hotel had required up to 40 managers and 200 employees. By eliminating narrowly defined jobs and rethinking antiquated procedures, a re-engineered version emerged with 250 suites overseen by 14 managers and 140 employees (Byrne, 1992). Best of all, these changes produced higher customer satisfaction.

As one might expect, most of these practices target productivity and efficiency. Unfortunately, some do not generate a distinctive competitive advantage. In 1994, after 10 years of downsizing, companies begin to focus on how to grow, and strategic planning is now making a comeback in the 1990s (Byrne, 1996). At one company after another, from Sears to IBM to Hewlett-Packard to Searle, strategy is again a major focus in the quest for higher revenues and profits. Some companies are even recreating full-fledged strategic-planning groups. Many practitioners and academicians agree that business strategy is now the single most important management issue and will remain so for the next five years. While strategy has made a rebound and become a part of the main agenda of many organizations today, companies need to democratize the strategic process by involving line and staff managers from different disciplines and to include interaction with key customers and suppliers.

The comeback of strategy witnessed the emergence of a new generation of business strategists. Now, a bevy of new books are out from a new group of strategy gurus who are capturing the attention of corporate executives and redefining the process of strategy creation. Academics Gary Hamel and C.K. Prahalad have become the most influential of a new group of strategists with the publication of *Competing for the Future*

(1994). Once there were popular concepts such as value chain, experience curves, stars and dogs associated with strategic management. These are some of the new concepts: value migration (the movement of growth and profit opportunities from one industry player to another), co-evolution (the notion that by working with direct competitors, customers and suppliers, a company can create new businesses, markets and industries), business ecosystem (the creation of networks of relationships with customers, suppliers and rivals to gain greater competitive advantage) and white-space opportunity (new areas of growth possibilities that fall between the cracks because they do not naturally match the skills of existing business units).

The new perspectives on strategy

Many studies emerged after the rapid expansion of normal strategic planning in the 1960s: Thune and House (1970), Ansoff *et al.* (1970), Herold (1972) and Rhyne (1986). In explaining financial performance variance, strategic management researchers and industrial organization economists have emphasized industry factors, market share, generic strategy and strategic group membership. In contrast, organizational contingency theorists have emphasized alignments involving environment and internal structure (Powell, 1992). Porter (1980) defined strategic groups as groups of firms that follow similar strategies within a given industry. Barnett, Greve and Park (1994) suggested that the reasons why organizations vary in how well they perform can be due to differences in their strategic positions and to differences in their competitive abilities. They propose an evolutionary model in which there is a trade-off between these two sources of advantage.

In the 1980s, strategic management research on organizational performance was dominated not by the alignment approach, but by Harvard professor Michael Porter's economic-based theories. In his seminal work *Competitive Strategy* (1980), Porter introduced the concept of generic strategies, low-cost leadership, differentiation and focus. The generic strategies remain useful to characterize strategic positions at the simplest and broadest level: the base for positioning—varieties, needs and access. The implicit strategy model of the past decade includes one ideal competitive position in the industry, benchmarking of all activities and achieving best practice, aggressive outsourcing and partnering to gain efficiencies, advantages resting on a few key success factors, critical resources, core competencies, and flexibility and rapid responses to all competitive and market changes.

As the environment changes and the business community rebounds from a period of downsizing, Porter (1996) offers alternative views of strategy. Strategy is the creation of a unique and valuable position involving a different set of activities. However, choosing a unique position is not enough to guarantee a sustainable advantage. In order to create value, management must possess the knowledge of how to invest in and maintain an organization's core competencies. A valuable position will attract imitation. Thus, a strategic position is not sustainable unless there are trade-offs with other positions. Positioning trade-offs is pervasive in competition and essential to strategy. The essence of strategy is making tradeoffs in competing, choosing what not to do. Without trade-offs, there would be no need for choice and thus no need for strategy (Porter, 1996).

Porter further argued that operational effectiveness is not strategy. He maintained that operational effectiveness and strategy are both essential to superior performance. Operational effectiveness means performing similar activities better than rivals perform them. In contrast, strategic positioning means performing different activities than rivals or performing similar activities in different ways with the aim of delivering a unique mix of value. While operational effectiveness is about achieving excellence in individual activities or functions, strategy is about combining activities. As fit drives both competitive advantage and sustainability, the competitive advantage comes from the way its activities fit and reinforce one another. It is harder for a rival to match an array of interlocked activities than it is merely to imitate a particular activity.

Hamel (1996) and Hamel and Prahalad (1994a, 1994b) claimed that strategy is revolution and everything else is tactics. Strategy should not be in incremental change. They think the time is ripe for industry revolutionaries and more hostile to industry incumbents. The authors pointed out that strategic planning is not strategic. In the vast

Exhibit 18.2   Selected studies in strategic management

Topics/relationships/perspectives	Examples (author, year)
Strategy formation/perspectives	Mintzberg, 1979 Hamel, 1996 Hamel and Prahalad, 1994a Porter, 1996
Strategic planning as competitive advantage and its impact on performance	Thune and House, 1970 Ansoff et al., 1970 Herold, 1972 Rhyne, 1986 Powell, 1992
Strategy and environment	Bourgeois, 1980
Corporate-level strategy	Porter, 1987
Business-level strategic typologies/ strategic groups	Miles et al., 1978 Porter, 1980 Hambrick, 1980 Snow and Hrebiniak, 1980 Segev, 1989 Conant, Mokwa and Varadarajan, 1990 Barnett, Greve and Park, 1994
Strategy coherence across business and functional levels of strategy	Hofer and Schendel 1978 Nath and Sudharshan, 1994
Strategy and structure	Chandler, 1962 Rumelt, 1974 Galbraith, 1977 Miller, 1986, 1987 Habib and Victor, 1991
Strategy and leadership	Leontides, 1982 Hambrick and Mason, 1984 Miller, Kets de Vries and Toulouse, 1982 Miller and Toulouse, 1986 Thomas, Litschert and Ramaswamy, 1991
Organizational culture	Woods and Sciarini, 1996
Strategic control	Goold and Quinn, 1990 Simons, 1994

majority of companies, strategic planning is a calendar-driven ritual, not an exploration of the potential for revolution. The essential problem in organizations today is a failure to distinguish planning from strategizing. They proposed that strategic thinking should be seen as an opportunity to transform a corporation and change the rules of an industry to its advantage, i.e. transformational shift.

Exhibit 18.2 summarizes examples of studies that explore the perspectives of strategy and strategic management.

Practices and problems

Strategy and hospitality education

As strategy won greater acceptance in the corporate world and with the rise of strategic consulting firms such as the Boston Consulting Group, business schools in America began to incorporate strategy into their policy courses during the 1970s. Michael Porter is generally credited with revolutionizing the way in which strategy is taught at business schools. Today the capstone strategic management course is a critical component of the core curricula at the majority of American business schools (Bongiorno, 1993).

In the 1980s, strategy courses were developed and introduced to students in the hospitality majors. Tse, Meyer and Olsen (1987) conducted an extensive curriculum analysis of the hospitality programmes in the United States. Their study found that students in hospitality education develop technical skills through courses with hands-on experience and human skills through courses in human resources management, but lack the necessary conceptual skills to adapt to a changing environment. It is important for the graduates in hospitality education to have a clear understanding and appreciation for the use of strategic management as a tool to create value for hospitality firms. A book of readings devoted to strategic management was published in 1991 (edited by Teare and Boer). A number of hospitality programmes that offer a strategy course adopted *Strategic Management in the Hospitality Industry*, co-authored by Olsen, Tse and West (1992), as their textbook. Recognizing the emerging importance of the concept, the *International Journal of Hospitality Management* published a special issue in 1990 (volume 9, number 3) called 'Strategic Management in the Hospitality Industry'.

Future outlook of the hospitality industry

As we enter the new millennium, what are the forces shaping the future of the hospitality and tourism industry as well as hospitality education? How will these forces impact upon the practices and research of strategy management?

The hotel industry is extremely dynamic and in a continuous state of change. In terms of industry development and structure, the hotel industry is characterized as fragmented. While there are major chains like Holiday Inn, Hilton, Marriott and Sheraton present in the marketplace, a good proportion of hotels and motels are owned by individual proprietors. In terms of change and dynamism, competition from international hotel companies is mounting as the world quickly becomes a global economy. To identify the forces driving change in the lodging industry over the ensuing decade, the

International Hotel and Restaurant Association funded a major research effort conducted by Michael Olsen and his research team at Virginia Polytechnic Institute and State University. The study identified five major forces that will shape the future of the lodging industry for the next decade: capacity control, safety and security, assets and capital, technology, and new management (Olsen, 1995).

Capacity control   With the proliferation of the information superhighway, the hospitality industry is losing control over the sale of its stocks of hotel rooms, airline seats, car rentals, tickets to attractions, and seats in restaurants to those who own and manage global reservation systems and/or negotiate for large buying groups. How this transformation evolves will depend on several forces, such as telecommunications, software developers, the travel distribution network and government regulation, as well as the supply and demand fluctuations of the market. This complex set of forces will continue to make an impact and bring about changes in the way the industry's capacity is marketed, sold and developed. It will also create tremendous opportunities for those providers who take advantage of the technology shaping the 'Information Age'.

Safety and security   Today's travellers are increasingly confronted with potential risks to personal safety and health, from both a macro and a micro perspective. Major macro forces, which are global by nature, include terrorism, health issues and diminished government protection. While there is little the hospitality provider can do to remedy these macro problems, hoteliers should consider political stability before making decisions on investing or divesting in regard to global expansion. At the micro level, the forces include personal security, property asset security and insurance. As a result, investors and managers throughout the industry must make important strategic decisions regarding business loss insurance and investment loss protection.

Assets and capital   It is estimated that the global shift to a market economy will ultimately result in a shortage of capital worldwide to meet the existing development needs. Competing demands for capital will result in the rationing of global private capital, whether for infrastructure development in emerging nations or for competing uses elsewhere. It will put increased pressure on asset performance. The shortage of private investment capital is matched by a rationing of funds deployed by governments.

Technology   Technology represents the most significant competitive advantage hospitality firms can have for the 1990s and beyond. Hoteliers who are committed to take advantage of the technology will gain competitive advantage over those that do not. Technology will impact upon customer services, information management and hotel design, and create alternatives to existing products and services. Technology will become a major competitive method in the areas of providing decision support systems and smart hotel rooms, security management and communications technology. It becomes the responsibility of hotel management to provide an environment that ensures fully integrated, seamless systems and personnel who can interact successfully in a technological environment to provide accurate, validated information and quality service. In turn, management will be able to better concentrate on meeting the needs and wants of customers and to focus on long-range planning.

New management   Capacity control, safety and security, capital movement and an evolving technology are issues which will confront the future manager. The future manager needs to possess the ability to adapt to rapid change. One way to handle the speed of change is by becoming a 'boundary spanner', that is, having the ability to effectively run the internal operation while monitoring the opportunities and threats facing the industry that are found in the external environment. In developing conceptual skills, tomorrow's manager will become a strategist as compared to a traditional operational manager who focuses on tactical issues. To deal with the mass of information available, the manager of the future must also be technology-astute and be able to lead and manage change.

Hospitality research and studies in strategic management

A review of the literature includes both conceptual and empirical studies of strategic management in the hospitality industry.

Conceptual studies   Most of the early and some contemporary work has been conceptual (Canas, 1982; Reichel, 1982, 1986; DeNoble and Olsen, 1982; Olsen and Bellas, 1980; Reid and Olsen, 1981; Olsen and DeNoble, 1981; Zhao and Merna, 1992; Nebel and Schaffer, 1992; Tse and West, 1992; Webster and Hudson, 1991; Slattery and Boer, 1991). Some of these works were descriptive in nature, while others emphasized the use of a contingency approach for corporate strategic planning. Examples of anecdotal work that focused upon the analysis of specific companies can also be found (Langton, Bottorff and Olsen, 1992; Hazard, O'Rourke-Hayes and Olsen, 1992; Webster, 1994). Nanus and Lundberg (1988) proposed a systemic futures-research process which allows executives to examine external future trends and events that have critical implications for the organization's internal strategies and policies. Slattery and Clark (1988) pointed out the need for strategic planning to bridge the gap between the different levels of management throughout the corporation in order to enhance communication flow and to achieve the company mission and objectives. This line of work primarily addressed the application of strategy-related models developed in other sectors and applied to the hospitality industry without the actual conduct of empirical investigation (Olsen and Roper, 1998).

Empirical research   The second line of research activity has attempted to apply more empirical approaches to theory building. Success in strategy implementation depends partly on a proper match between strategy and organizational structure and this match is expected to have a positive impact on financial performance. Utilizing the underpinnings of the work of Miles *et al.* (1978) and Porter (1980), researchers such as Tse (1988a), Tse and Olsen (1988), West (1988), West and Olsen (1989, 1990), Dev and Olsen (1989), Schaffer (1986a, 1987) and Crawford-Welch (1991) have examined the multifaceted dimensions of strategy. They examined various hypotheses regarding the relationships between strategy, environmental scanning, firm structure and the impact on financial performance. Tse (1988b) examined the strategic planning activity and the degree of internal strengths and weaknesses analysis performed by restaurant firms. Parsa (1994) found that implementation plays an important role in determining performance of hospitality franchise systems. Olsen, Murthy and Teare (1994) examined the environmental scanning practices of chief executive officers of multinational hotel chains. Elwood-Williams and Tse (1995) empirically investigated the relationship between strategy and entrepreneurship in the US restaurant sector.

Attempts were made to recognize that strategy is a process that is contingent upon many variables and the difficulties of defining strategic typologies with large sample sizes. Researchers recently have begun to use the case study methodology and Delphi methods to assess strategy and its related issues. The issues addressed by these case studies include co-alignment of human resources management practices and business strategy (Ishak, 1990), exploitation of synergies between hotel brands (Weinberg, 1991), international development and modes of entry into new foreign markets (Zhao, 1992), strategy implementation (Schmelzer, 1992; Schmelzer and Olsen, 1994), and strategic alliances (Monga, 1996; Dev and Klein, 1993). Researches that used the Delphi approach include Kim's (1992) study of Asian political environments and Turnbull's (1996) study of hotel projects in the Caribbean region. These investigations have permitted in-depth analysis of several national and multinational hospitality firms. The bulk of this research was exploratory in nature and has resulted in the formulation of propositions encouraging further research and theory building (Olsen and Roper, 1998). In the study conducted by Olsen (1995), the relationships between business environmental forces driving changes in the multinational hotel industry and the competitive methods of its major hotel firms were identified. Burgess, Hampton and Roper (1995) also have looked at the factors underlying the success of international hotel groups.

Most recently, strategy research has focused upon the types of competitive methods that firms use. A typology of competitive methods in the hotel industry has been developed by Murthy (1994) and by Jogaratnam (1996) for the restaurant industry. These studies have focused upon identifying a wide range of competitive methods and some have employed factor analysis to bring about a more parsimonious classification of methods to be used in further research. In these cases the investigations further explored the relationship between these typologies and firm performance. Significant results were obtained between the choice of competitive methods and firm performance.

The latest additions to the literature have focused upon the core competencies that firms have used to seek to obtain competitive advantage. As the use of information technology (IT) has become an essential component within the commercial sector, Cho (1996) has identified it as a core competency in multinational hotel companies. Core competencies in three US casual theme restaurant concepts were studied by de Chabert (1997). Brotherton and Shaw (1996) completed work towards the identification and classification of critical success factors in UK Hotels plc, while Griffin (1994) attempted to ascertain the identity of critical success factors of yield management systems in lodging firms. Rispoli (1997) examined competitive analysis and competence-based strategies in the hotel industry. Roberts and Shea (1996) characterized core capabilities in the hotel industry. Overall the focus here has been to identify what abilities within firms or industry sectors offer competitive advantage. While the work has been primarily case study based and/or descriptive, little has been done to assess the relationships between these competencies and other constructs of the strategy paradigm (Olsen and Roper, 1998).

Exhibit 18.3 shows a summary of the studies and research of the concept of strategy and its related issues in the hospitality industry.

Exhibit 18.3   A summary of selected hospitality research studies of strategic management in the hospitality industry

Topics/relationships	Examples (author, year)	Data collection
Strategic planning	Canas, 1982	Descriptive
	Reichel, 1982	Contingency approach
	Nanus and Lundberg, 1988	QUEST
	Tse, 1988a	Telephone interviews
	Feltenstein, 1992	Descriptive
Strategic management	Webster and Hudson, 1991	Descriptive
	Olsen, 1991	Literature review
Strategy and performance	Murthy, 1994	Survey approach
Strategy and environment	West, 1988 (Porter's model)	Survey of restaurants
	Dev, 1988 (Miles *et al.*'s model)	Survey of hotels
	Crawford-Welch, 1991	Survey approach
	Jogaratnam, 1996	Survey of restaurants
Strategy implementation	Schmelzer, 1992	Case study of restaurants
	Parsa, 1994	Survey of restaurants
Strategy and structure	Schaffer, 1986a (Miles *et al.* typology)	Survey of hotels
	Tse, 1988a (Porter's model)	Survey of restaurants
	Eccles and Teare, 1996	Descriptive
Strategy and leadership	Tse and Elwood, 1990	Case study
	Ishak, 1990 (Miles *et al.* typology)	Case study of restaurants
Competitive methods	Weinberg, 1991 (synergies)	Case study of hotels
	Cho, 1996 (information technology)	Case study of hotels
	de Chabert, 1997	Case study
	Brotherton and Shaw, 1996	UK Hotels plc
	Griffin, 1994	Yield management systems, hotels
	Rispoli, 1997	Competitive analysis, hotel
	Roberts and Shea, 1996	Core competencies, hotels
Globalization	Kim, 1992	Delphi approach, hotels
	Zhao, 1992	Case study of hotels
	Olsen, 1995	Content analysis, hotels
	Burgess, Hampton and Roper, 1995	Delphi approach, hotels
	Turnbull, 1996	Delphi approach, hotels

Problems associated with service strategy research

Systematic study of strategy management in the hospitality industry has a short record because hospitality and tourism education is relatively new. The number of college and university hospitality programmes in the past 25 years has more than quadrupled. In 1978, 41 colleges and universities in the United States offered bachelor degree pro-grammes in hospitality administration; by 1990, there were as many as 160 bachelor degree programmes in the USA alone. However, not many hospitality programmes offer graduate degrees. Most of the rigorous research that has examined the practices of hospitality firms is a result of theses and dissertations emanating from a few hospitality programmes and some non-hospitality programmes.

Like many other young disciplines that are in the process of defining and cumulating their body of knowledge, study and research in the area of strategic management have exhibited the following problems:

- The concept of strategy is a multidimensional concept which makes conducting research in this field extremely challenging. The extensive number of variables to be studied and the interdependencies among them make it difficult to encompass all the variables in one study. Studies tend to oversimplify the multidimensionality of archetype constructs. As researchers cannot agree on the definition of strategy, they also cannot agree on operationalizing the constructs of strategy, measures for financial performance, choice of appropriate research design, and overall methodology.

- In the case of strategy research in the hospitality industry, the problem is further confounded by the very fragmented nature of an industry that is characterized by many thousands of business units. These units can be individually owned and/or parts of chains and management companies. This fragmentation, coupled with a wide variety of brands and segments, makes it very difficult to conduct large-scale studies that are designed to contribute important theoretical frameworks to enhance our understanding of this industry (Olsen and Roper, 1998). Furthermore, the impact of strategy is longitudinal and most studies have the constraints of time and resources and thus are cross-sectional in nature.

- As the service industry started to gain momentum in the 1980s, research studies examining the application of strategic management in the hospitality firms began to emerge. The concepts and models tested in these studies have been primarily borrowed from the proven concepts in strategy management that were developed based on the manufacturing industry, which uses product-oriented terms. However, the service industry is fundamentally different from manufacturing industry, its key elements being labour intensity, customer interaction and service customization. As some researchers have pointed out, the strategy for the service industry is different from those of manufacturing, and the characteristics of services have important implications for strategic planning (Thomas, 1978; Carmen and Langeard, 1980; Schmenner, 1986). Moreover, Habib and Victor (1991) indicated that service multinational corporations (MNCs) appear to be different from manufacturing MNCs in terms of a fit–performance relationship. Thus, the findings of these research studies leave the researchers not certain whether the theories apply. Tse and Olsen (1988) found that 'statistical analysis indicated that findings were inconclusive to validate Porter's model.' This conclusion is shared by other research studies (Schaffer, 1986a; West, 1988; Dev, 1998; Dev and Olsen, 1989). Thus, there is a gap in knowledge between the research studies in the manufacturing and service industries and a lack of theory construction in the area of strategic management.

The complex nature of the hospitality industry calls for a need to effectively manage the organizations, but the hospitality industry is generally slow to adopt good management practices (Webster and Hudson, 1991). Research in the service industry, in both volume and scope, has lagged behind similar activities in manufacturing industry. Consequently, service industry executives, along with strategy scholars, have had to rely on manufacturing sector research rather than on their own well-developed body of literature to guide their strategic efforts.

Conclusions and future research issues

Much of the research reported here has focused upon traditional constructs of the strategy paradigm such as environmental analysis, strategy formulation, strategic planning and the strategy–structure–performance relationship. These mostly unidimensional views and research in strategy offer a limited perspective on how strategy really functions in the competitive marketplace. Thus, contemporary strategic management literature attempts to offer a more dynamic viewpoint. It takes into account the fact that organizations tend to prosper in highly changeable environments when they sustain states of instability, contradiction, contention and creative tension in order to provoke new perspectives and continual learning (Hamel and Prahalad, 1994a, 1994b). It is in this direction that future research into strategy in the hospitality industry should proceed. Pursuing this direction is more complex, requiring less prescriptive fine-grained research and favouring more qualitative methods designed to reach deep into the internal workings of organizations. This will yield a more authentic, real world view of strategy in the contemporary marketplace (Olsen and Roper, 1998).

There is a need for rigorous research studies and a more speculative approach. Future research should go beyond a simple extrapolation from previous and current work in the field by suggesting alternative perspectives and approaches and proposing contemporary issues which may not have been explored in the field. In order to further the understanding of the concept of strategy, other relevant variables and the impact on performance in the service setting, efforts are needed in the area of theory construction. The aim is to develop new paradigms that would reflect the unique characteristics of the service industry. It is believed that systematic, longitudinal research on strategy and its impact on financial performance, as well as a larger sample, may show some significant differences in hypothesis testing.

Moreover, limited research has been conducted to examine the concept of strategy in the international arena. The implications for strategic management research are that firms from different countries will vary in their characteristic approaches to strategy. Future hospitality strategic management research needs to investigate firms from other cultural foundations, whose objectives and context might be more complex than the simplicities of profit maximization and perfect markets. In addition, the use of alternative strategic management frameworks will be a necessity.

Future research is also needed as there has been very little research into strategy implementation as related to firms in the hospitality industry. Studying strategy implementation in the context of the co-alignment model is one area where hospitality researchers could really contribute to mainstream strategic management literature, for it is at the regional/divisional or unit level where strategy is most often operationalized.

References

Ansoff, H., Avna, J., Brandenburg, R., Portner, F. and Radosevich, R. (1970) Does planning pay? The effect of planning on success of acquisitions in American firms, *Long Range Planning*, **3**, 2–7.

Barnett, W.P., Greve, H.R. and Park, D.Y. (1994) An evolutionary model of organizational performance, *Strategic Management Journal*, **15**, 11–28.

Bongiorno, L. (1993) Strategy is being taught in America's business schools, *Journal of Business Strategy*, **14** (5), 36–41.

Bourgeois, L.J. III (1980) Strategy and environment: a conceptual integration, *Academy of Management Review*, **5** (1), 25–39.

Bracker, J. (1980) The historical development of the strategic management concept, *Academy of Management Review*, **5(2)**, 219–224.

Brotherton, B. and Shaw, J. (1996) Towards an identification and classification of critical success factors in UK hotels plc., *International Journal of Hospitality Management*, **15**(2), 113–135.

Burgess, C., Hampton, A. and Roper, A. (1995) International hotel groups: what makes them successful?' *International Journal of Contemporary Hospitality Management*, **7**(2/3), 74–80.

Byrne, J. (1992) Management's new gurus, *Business Week*, 31 August, 44–52.

Byrne, J. (1996) Strategic planning: It's back!, *Business Week*, 26 August, 46–52.

Canas, J. (1982) Strategic corporate planning, in Lewis, R.C., Beggs, T.J., Shaw, M. and Croffoot, S.A. (eds), *The Practice of Hospitality Management II*, AVI Publishing, Westport, CT, pp. 31–36.

Carmen, J.M. and Langeard, E. (1980) Growth strategies for service firms, *Strategic Management Journal*, **1**, 7–22.

Chandler, A.D. (1962) *Strategy and Structure: Chapters in the History of American Industrial Enterprises*, MIT Press, Cambridge, MA.

Cho, W. (1996) A case study: Creating and sustaining competitive advantage through an information technology application in the lodging industry, unpublished doctoral dissertation, Virginia Polytechnic Institute and State University, Blacksburg, VA.

Conant, J.S., Mokwa, M.P. and Varadarajan, P.R. (1990) Strategic types, distinctive marketing competencies and organizational performance: a multiple measures-based study, *Strategic Management Journal*, **11**, 365–383.

Crawford-Welch, S. (1991) An empirical examination of mature service environments and high-performance strategies within those environments: the case of the lodging and restaurant industries, unpublished doctoral dissertation, Virginia Polytechnic Institute and State University, Blacksburg, VA.

Cummings, S. (1993) Brief case: the first strategists, *Long Range Planning*, **26** (3), 133–135.

de Chabert, J. (1997) Core competencies and competitive advantage in the casual theme restaurant industry: a case study, unpublished doctoral dissertation, Virginia Polytechnic Institute and State University, Blacksburg, VA.

DeNoble, A. and Olsen, M.D. (1982) The relationship between the strategic planning process and the service delivery system, in Pizam, A., Lewis, R. and Manning, P. (eds), *The Practice of Hospitality Management*, AVI Publishing, Westport, CT, pp. 229–236.

Dev, C. (1988) Environmental uncertainty, business strategy and financial performance: a study of the lodging industry, unpublished doctoral dissertation, Virginia Polytechnic Institute and State University, Blacksburg, VA.

Dev, C. and Klein, S. (1993) Strategic alliances in the hotel industry. *Cornell Hotel and Restaurant Administration Quarterly*, **34** (1), 42–45.

Dev, C.S. and Olsen, M.D. (1989) Environmental uncertainty, business strategy and financial performance: an empirical study of the US lodging industry, *Hospitality Education and Research Journal*, **13** (3), 171–186.

Dev, C., Tse, E. and West, J. (guest editors, special issue) (1990) Strategic management in the hospitality industry, *International Journal of Hospitality Management*, **9** (3).

Eccles, G. and Teare, R. (1996) Integrating strategy and structure: perspectives and challenges for hospitality managers, Chapter 6 in Kotas, R., Teare, R., Logie, J., Jayawardena, C. and Bowen, J. (eds), *The International Hospitality Business*, Cassell, London, pp. 42–51.

Elwood-Williams, C. and Tse, E.C.-Y. (1995) The relationship between strategy and entrepreneurship: the US restaurant sector, *International Journal of Contemporary Hospitality Management*, **7** (1), 22–26.

Feltenstein, T. (1992) Strategic planning for the 1990s: exploiting the inevitable, *Cornell Hotel and Restaurant Administration Quarterly*, June, 50–54.

Galbraith, J.R. (1977) *Organization Design*, Addison-Wesley, Reading, MA.

Goold, M. and Quinn, J.J. (1990) The paradox of strategic controls, *Strategic Management Journal*, **11**, 43–57.

Griffin, R.K. (1994) Critical success factors of lodging yield management systems: an empirical study, unpublished doctoral dissertation, Virginia Polytechnic Institute and State University, Blacksburg, VA.

Habib, M. and Victor, B. (1991) Strategy, structure, and performance of U.S. manufacturing and service MNCS: a comparative analysis, *Strategic Management Journal*, **12**, 589–606.

Hambrick, D.C. (1980) Operationalizing the concept of business-level strategy in research, *Academy of Management Review*, **5** (4), 567–575.

Hambrick, D.C. and Mason, P.A. (1984) Upper echelons: the organization as a reflection of its top managers, *Academy of Management Review*, **9**, 193–206.

Hamel, G. (1996) Strategy as revolution, *Harvard Business Review*, July–August, 69–82.

Hamel, G. and Prahalad, C.K. (1994a) *Competing for the Future*, Harvard Business School Press, Boston, MA.

Hamel, G. and Prahalad, C.K. (1994b) Competing for the future, *Harvard Business Review*, July–August, 122–128.

Hazard, R., O'Rourke-Hayes, L. and Olsen, M.D. (1992) Going global—acting local: the challenge of choice international, in Teare, R. and Olsen, M.D. (eds), *International Hospitality Management*, Pitman Publishing, London, pp. 91–94.

Henderson, B.D. (1989) The origin of strategy, *Harvard Business Review*, **67** (6), November–December, 139–143.

Herold, D. (1972) Long range planning and organizational performance: a cross-validation study, *Academy of Management Journal*, **15**, 91–104.

Hinterhuber, H.H. and Popp, W. (1992) Are you a strategist or just a manager?, *Harvard Business Review*, January–February, 105–113.

Hofer, C.W. and Schendel, D. (1978) *Strategy Formulation: Analytical Concepts*, West Publishing, St Paul, MN.

Ishak, N. (1990) An exploratory study of human resource management and business strategy in multiunit restaurant firms, unpublished dissertation, Virginia Polytechnic Institute and State University, Blacksburg, VA.

Jogaratnam, G. (1996) Environmental munificence, strategic posture and performance: an empirical survey of independent restaurants, unpublished doctoral dissertation, Virginia Polytechnic Institute and State University, Blacksburg, VA.

Kim, C.Y. (1992) Development of a framework for identification of political environmental issues faced by multinational hotel chains in newly industrialized countries in Asia, unpublished doctoral dissertation, Virginia Polytechnic Institute and State University, Blacksburg, VA.

Labich, K. (1994) Why companies fail, *Fortune*, 14, November, 52–68.

Langton, B.D., Bottorff, C. and Olsen, M.D. (1992) The strategy, structure, environment co-alignment, in Teare, R. and Olsen, M.D. (eds), *International Hospitality Management*, Pitman Publishing, London, pp. 31–35.

Leontides, M. (1982) Choosing the right manager to fit the strategy, *Journal of Business Strategy*, **2**, 58–69.

Miles, R.E., Snow, C.C., Meyer, A.D. and Coleman, H.J. Jr. (1978) Organizational strategy, structure, and process, *Academy of Management Review*, July, 546–562.

Miller, D. (1986) Configurations of strategy and structure: towards a synthesis, *Strategic Management Journal*, **7**, 233–249.

Miller, D. (1987) The structural and environmental correlates of business strategy, *Strategic Management Journal*, **8**, 55–76.

Miller, D., Kets de Vries, M.F.R. and Toulouse, J.M. (1982) Top executive locus of control and its relationship to strategy making, structure and environment, *Academy of Management Journal*, **25**, 237–253.

Miller, D. and Toulouse, J.M. (1986) Chief executive personality and corporate strategy and structure in small firms, *Management Science*, **32**, 1389–1409.

Mintzberg, H. (1979) *The Structuring of Organizations*, Prentice-Hall, Englewood Cliffs, NJ.

Mintzberg, H. (1981) Organization design: fashion or fit? *Harvard Business Review*, January–February, 103–116.

Monga, R. (1996) Strategic alliances in the lodging industry: a multi-case study, unpublished doctoral dissertation, Virginia Polytechnic Institute and State University, Blacksburg, VA.

Murthy, B. (1994) Measurement of the strategy construct in the lodging industry, and the strategy–performance relationship, unpublished doctoral dissertation, Virginia Polytechnic Institute and State University, Blacksburg, VA.

Nanus, B. and Lundberg, C. (1988) In quest of strategic planning, *Cornell Hotel and Restaurant Administration Quarterly*, August, 8–23.

Nath, D. and Sudharshan, D. (1994) Measuring strategy coherence through patterns of strategic choices, *Strategic Management Journal*, **15**, 43–61.

Nebel, E. and Schaffer, J.D. (1992) Hotel strategic planning at the business and unit level in the USA, in Teare, R. and Olsen, M.D. (eds), *International Hospitality Management*, Pitman Publishing, London, 228–254.

Olsen, M.D. (1991) Strategic management in the hospitality industry: a literature review, Chapter 13 in Cooper, C.P. (ed.), *Progress in Tourism, Recreation and Hospitality Management*, vol. 3, Belhaven Press, pp. 215–230.

Olsen, M.D. (1995) *Into the New Millennium: The IHA White Paper on the Global Hospitality Industry*. International Hotel Association, Paris.

Olsen, M.D. (1998) Strategic management, in Jafari, J. and Pizam, A. (eds), *Encyclopedia of Tourism*, in press.

Olsen, M.D. and Bellas, C.J. (1980) Managing growth in the 1980s: a blue print for food service survival, *Cornell Hotel and Restaurant Administration Quarterly*, **21** (2), 23–26.

Olsen, M.D. and DeNoble, A. (1981) Strategic planning in a dynamic environment, *Cornell Hotel and Restaurant Administration Quarterly*, **21** (4), 75–80.

Olsen, M.D., Murthy, B. and Teare, R. (1994) CEO perspectives on scanning the global hotel business environment, *International Journal of Contemporary Hospitality Management*, **6** (4), 3–9.

Olsen, M.D. and Roper, A. (1998) Research in strategic management in the hospitality industry, *International Journal of Hospitality Management*, **17** (2), 111–124.

Olsen, M.D., Tse, E.C.-Y. and West, J.J. (1992) *Strategic Management in the Hospitality Industry*, Van Nostrand Reinhold, New York.

Parsa, H. (1994) Exploratory investigation of organization power, and its impact on strategy implementation and firm performance: a study of the hospitality franchise systems, unpublished dissertation, Virginia Polytechnic Institute and State University, Blacksburg, VA.

Porter, M.E. (1980) *Competitive Strategy*, The Free Press, New York.

Porter, M.E. (1987) From competitive advantage to corporate strategy, *Harvard Business Review*, **65** (3), May–June, 43–59.

Porter, M.E. (1996) What is strategy? *Harvard Business Review*, November–December, 61–78.

Powell, T.C. (1992) Strategic planning as competitive advantage, *Strategic Management Journal*, **13**, 551–558.

Reichel, A. (1982) Corporate strategic planning for the hospitality industry: a contingency approach, in Pizam, A., Lewis, R.C. and Manning, P. (eds), *The Practice of Hospitality Management*, AVI Publishing, Westport, CT, pp. 49–63.

Reichel, A. (1986) Competition and barriers to entry in service industries: the case of the American lodging industry, in Pizam, A., Lewis, R.C. and Manning, P. (eds), *The Practice of Hospitality Management II*, AVI Publishing, Westport, CT, pp. 79–89.

Reid, R. and Olsen, M.D. (1981) A strategic planning model for independent food service operators, *Journal of Hospitality Education*, **6** (1), 11–24.

Rhyne, L. (1986) The relationship of strategic planning to financial performance, *Strategic Management Journal*, **7**, 423–436.

Rispoli, M. (1997) Competitive analysis and competence based strategies in the hotel industry, in Sanchez, R., Heene, A. and Thomas, H. (eds), *Dynamics of Competence Based Competition*, Pergamon, London, pp. 119–137.

Roberts, C. and Shea, L. (1996) Core capabilities in the hotel industry, *Hospitality Research Journal*, **19** (4), 141–153.

Rumelt, R.P. (1974) *Strategy, Structure, and Economic Performance*, Division of Research, Graduate School of Business Administration, Harvard University, Cambridge, MA.

Schaffer, J.D. (1986a) Competitive strategy, organization structure and performance in the lodging industry: an empirical assessment of Miles and Snow's (1978) perspectives of organizations (environment), unpublished doctoral dissertation, Virginia Polytechnic Institute and State University, Blacksburg, VA

Schaffer, J. (1986b) Structure and strategy: two sides of success, *Cornell Hotel and Restaurant Administration Quarterly*, February, 76–81.

Schaffer, J.D. (1987) Competitive strategies in the lodging industry, *International Journal of Hospitality Management*, **6** (1), 33–42.

Schmelzer, C.D. (1992) A case study investigation of strategy implementation in three multi-unit restaurant firms, unpublished doctoral dissertation, Virginia Polytechnic Institute and State University, Blacksburg, VA.

Schmelzer, C. and Olsen, M.D. (1994) A data based strategy implementation framework for companies in the restaurant industry, *International Journal of Hospitality Management*, **13** (4), 347–359.

Schmenner, R.W. (1986) How can service businesses survive and prosper?, *Sloan Management Review*, Spring, 21–32.

Segev, E. (1989) A systematic comparative analysis and synthesis of two business level strategic typologies, *Strategic Management Journal*, **10**, 487–505.

Simons, R. (1994) How new top managers use control systems as levers of strategic renewal, *Strategic Management Journal*, **15**, 169–189.

Slattery, P. and Boer, A. (1991) Strategic developments for the 1990s: implications for hotel companies, Chapter 10 in Teare, R. and Boer, A. (eds), *Strategic Hospitality Management: Theory and Practice for the 1990s*, Cassell Educational, London, pp. 161–165.

Slattery, P. and Clark A. (1988) Major variables in the corporate structure of hotel groups, *International Journal of Hospitality Management*, **7** (2), 117–130.

Snow, C.C. and Hrebiniak, L.G. (1980) Strategy, distinctive competence, and organizational performance, *Administrative Science Quarterly*, **25**, 317–366.

Solomon, J. (1993) The fall of the dinosaurs, *Newsweek*, February 8, 42–51.

Teare, R. and Boer, A. (eds) (1991) *Strategic Hospitality Management: Theory and Practice for the 1990s*, Cassell Educational, London.

Thomas, A.S., Litschert, R. J. and Ramaswamy, K. (1991) The performance impact of strategy –manager coalignment: an empirical examination, *Strategic Management Journal*, **12**, 509–522.

Thomas, D.R.E. (1978) Strategy is different in service business, *Harvard Business Review*, July–August, 158–165.

Thune, S. and House, R. (1970) Where long-range planning pays off, *Business Horizons*, August, 81–87.

Tiles, S. (1969) Making strategy explicit, in Ansoff, H.I. (ed.), *Business Strategy*, Penguin, Harmondsworth.

Tse, E.C.-Y. (1988a) An exploratory study of the impact of strategy and structure on the organizational performance of restaurant firms, unpublished doctoral dissertation, Virginia Polytechnic Institute and State University, Blacksburg, VA.

Tse, E.C.-Y. (1988b) Defining corporate strengths and weaknesses: is it essential for strategy implementation? *Hospitality Education and Research Journal*, **12** (2), 57–72.

Tse, E.C.-Y. and Elwood, C.M. (1990) Synthesis of the life cycle concept with strategy and management style: a case analysis in the hospitality industry, *International Journal of Hospitality Management*, **9** (3), 223–236.

Tse, E.C.-Y., Meyer, M.K. and Olsen, M.D. (1987) Hospitality undergraduate education: are trends in the hospitality industry reflected in our curricula?, *Journal of Hospitality Education and Research*, **11** (2), 363.

Tse, E.C.-Y. and Olsen, M.D. (1988) The impact of strategy and structure on the organizational performance of restaurant firms, *Hospitality Education and Research Journal*, **12** (2), 57–72.

Tse, E.C.-Y. and West, J. (1992) Development strategies for international markets, in Teare, R. and Olsen, M.D. (eds), *International Hospitality Management*, Pitman Publishing, London, pp. 118–134.

Turnbull, D.R. (1996) The influence of political risk events on the investment decisions of multinational hotel companies in Caribbean hotel projects (tourism), unpublished doctoral dissertation, Virginia Polytechnic Institute and State University, Blacksburg, VA.

Von Neumann, J. and Morgenstern, O. (1947) *Theory of Games and Economic Behavior* (2nd ed.), Princeton University Press, Princeton, NJ.

Webster, M.M. (1994) Strategic management in the context at Swallow hotels, *International Journal of Contemporary Hospitality Management*, **6** (5), 3–8.

Webster, M. and Hudson, T. (1991) Strategic management: a theoretical overview and its application to the hospitality industry, Chapter 2 in Teare, R. and Boer, A. (eds), *Strategic Hospitality Management: Theory and Practice for the 1990s*, Cassell Educational, London, pp. 9–30.

Weinberg, L.S. (1991) Synergy among brands of multiproduct hospitality firms, unpublished dissertation, Claremont Graduate School.

West, J.J. (1988) Strategy, environmental scanning, and their effect upon firm performance: an exploratory study of the food service industry, unpublished doctoral dissertation, Virginia Polytechnic Institute and State University, Blacksburg, VA.

West, J. and Olsen, M.D. (1989) Competitive strategies in food service: are high performers different?, *Cornell Hotel and Restaurant Administration Quarterly*, **31** (1), 68–71.

West, J. and Olsen, M.D. (1990) Grand strategy: making your restaurant a winner, *Cornell Hotel and Restaurant Administration Quarterly*, **31** (2), 72–75.

Woods, R.H. and Sciarini, M.P. (1996) The role of organizational culture in service, Chapter 14 in Kotas, R., Teare, R., Logie, J. and Jayawardena, C. (eds), *The International Hospitality Business*, Cassell Educational, London, pp. 112–121.

Zhao, J. (1992) The antecedent factors and entry mode choice of multinational lodging firms: the case of growth strategies into new international markets, unpublished doctoral dissertation, Virginia Polytechnic Institute and State University, Blacksburg, VA.

Zhao, J.L. and Merna, K. (1992) Impact analysis and the international environment, in Teare, R. and Olsen, M.D. (eds), *International Hospitality Management*, Pitman Publishing, London, pp. 3–32.

19   Human resource management

CONRAD LASHLEY AND SANDRA WATSON

Introduction

Evidence of published work which addresses issues of working in hotel and catering
has had a relatively long history. Popular books such as Orwell's (1933) *Down and Out
in Paris and London*, Whyte's (1948) *Human Relationships in the Restaurant Industry*,
and Studs Terkel's (1972) *Working*, contain many vignettes of people's working experiences in hotels, restaurants and bars. Whilst research into the hospitality industry has
developed and widened in both context and content since these early studies, there
appears to be an enduring conceptualisation that the industry is a 'people industry'.
However, this leads to particular problems when given the task of reviewing research
activity under the banner of human resource management (HRM) in the hospitality
industry. There is the need to clarify the scope of the term of human resource management. For the purpose of this chapter, research is discussed and analysed in a way which
makes no distinction between the ideology of HRM and that of personnel management,
but these matters are referred to because they impact on an agenda which researchers
in the applied field of 'people' management within the hospitality industry need to
consider.

This chapter is therefore concerned with research which addresses the management
of the labour process and employment relationships *per se*. It avoids research which is
involved in other aspects of the industry, such as operations management, information
technology, marketing and so on. However, these issues are often touched on because
of the integrated nature of hospitality operations, and the significance of 'people' in
delivering hospitality services.

According to Watson (1986) the study of employment strategy provides a useful
concept in assisting in the study of the way organisations deal with employees. In particular the study of employer strategies has a theoretical value in providing the relationships between organisational structure, organisation culture, job design, attempts to
gain employee commitment, leadership styles, recruitment, employee development and
reward systems. Although an aspiration for consistency and coherence is a key element
of the claim for a strategic role for human resource management (Sissons, 1994), the
study of employment strategy does not perforce validate the view that employment
policies are arrived at in a rational–mechanistic manner. Employment policies can be
said to emerge from internal political processes, and are shaped by managerial perceptions of the contextual factors within a cultural setting which predisposes managers to
typical responses to the phenomena which they confront (Legge, 1995). Whether

The Handbook of Contemporary Hospitality Management Research, Edited by Bob Brotherton.
© 1999 John Wiley & Sons Ltd.

employment policies emerge deliberately in a coherent and planned way, or whether they emerge as a series of incremental steps, essentially managers make choices about their employment strategies, and any attempt to understand the nature of those choices needs to be informed by the range of assumptions about the nature of business strategy and the nature and strategic role of human resource management.

Taking Watson's comments as an appropriate summation of much of the discussion, the comparison of HRM research within the applied hospitality context legitimately needs to touch on a checklist of practices in the management of people. However, researchers need to adopt an approach which sets these observations against debates about the nature of HRM and the assumption which they hold about the nature of the relationship between organisation members. The authors return to these issues when concluding the chapter and suggesting an agenda for future research within the applied field of hospitality human resource management.

Whilst recognising that the terms human resource management and personnel management have been the subject of considerable definitional debate, to be reflected upon later, we start from an inclusive approach which categorises research publications which deal with the management of people in work organisations. We were, therefore, influenced by the clusters of topics which seemed to be suggested by the material itself rather than formally accepting a human resource management or personnel position.

The work reviewed in this chapter can be located in the hospitality industry, in its broadest sense, encompassing hotels, catering, restaurants, pubs and tourism. It also clearly spans commercial and non-commercial organisations and contexts where hospitality services are either direct core organisational activities or more indirectly associated with another core business activity (Joint Hospitality Industry Congress, 1996). The main focus of the analysis explores the research on issues related to the management of people published in specialist hospitality and tourism journals, such as *The International Journal of Hospitality Management*, *The International Journal of Contemporary Hospitality Management*, *Progress in Hospitality and Tourism Research*, etc. The aim is to comment on the research published on this applied subject area in the hospitality research journals over a five-year period. However, the analysis is further developed through a comparison of research articles published over the same time period in *Personnel Review*. Whilst there are any number of generic HRM publications which might have been used, *Personnel Review* was chosen because it provided a large number of issues per volume and appeared to have a similar style of topic to those found in the specialist hospitality journals. That is, it is aimed at both academics and practitioners with a clear intent to inform the 'reflective practitioner'. Although the hospitality industry is viewed as being international in both context and nature, the authors have restricted analysis to UK-published material over the last five years. This is not intended to devalue work published elsewhere or to provide an introspective view on the HRM research which has emerged, but to provide a coherent focus for the commentary.

The articles surveyed in the study do include a list of topics which might be discussed as being either human resource management or personnel. As stated earlier, there is a need to engage in the generic debates about these terms, as they do assist in forming the conceptual backcloth to the analysis. In particular it is the authors' view that much of the applied research in hospitality HRM is restricted in its scope and focus.

Human resource management

The meaning of human resource management has also been subject to some considerable debate (Storey, 1989; Keenoy and Anthony, 1992; Legge, 1995). Whilst there are those who perceive human resource management as another (new-fangled and faddish?) name for personnel management (Armstrong, 1987) concerned with the same catalogue of issues, there are also those who define HRM, albeit in a variety of ways, as being distinctly different from personnel management. Storey's (1992: 36) well-publicised figure delineating dimensions of HRM and personnel management makes a case for differentiation and draws on the literature which emerged from the USA in the mid-1980s. Blyton and Turnbull (1992) view HRM as an 'umbrella term' describing a range of employment practices which became popular amongst both management practitioners and academics in the 1980s. Legge (1995) concludes that a comparison of personnel management and HRM reveals more similarities than differences, but that HRM provides rhetoric for corporate chief executives in the management of employees which incorporates the values of the 'enterprise culture', and in particular reflects the values of the 'New Right'. Keenoy and Anthony (1992: 238) argue that HRM is more than just a legitimisation of 'management practice which treats people as a cost' whilst articulating a rhetoric that 'people are highly valued assets'. They say (1992: 234) that HRM is a metaphor designed to reshape the social construct of the employment relationship; 'HRM reflects an attempt to redefine the meaning of work and the way individual employees relate to their employer'. In particular, it is devised to establish and legitimise a unitary perspective of work organisations, and to delegitimise employee collectives and a pluralist analysis of organisational priorities.

Guest (1987) has identified four key values or components of HRM: strategic integration of human resource and business strategies, employee commitment to organisational goals, numerical and functional flexibility of employees, and quality of product and service outputs. According to this model of HRM, these core values then should inform organisational and job design, employee empowerment, recruitment and selection, training, appraisal, reward systems, and so on, as they apply within a given organisation.

Even within this approach there are clearly different theoretical approaches which stem from different perceptions of organisational life and assumptions about the people who make up organisations. Storey's 'hard' and 'soft' models reflect different emphasis, and theoretical origins. The hard model suggests a 'utilitarian instrumentalism' (Legge, 1995), given recent voice by the Michigan School, and stresses the management of human resources as factors of production. The soft model, on the other hand, reflects a 'developmental humanism' (Legge, 1995) which emerged from the Harvard School and stresses the potential of people as a valuable resource. It is also possible to detect approaches adopted within other organisations where the strategy is to 'treat labour as a variable input and a cost to be minimised' Legge, 1995). Firms operating in cost-competitive markets, like fast-food operators, are typical of this approach. The adverse publicity about the use of variable contracts at a Burger King restaurant is typical (Bowcott, 1995). In this case individuals were formally required to attend work for a full shift period, but were required to 'clock off' when the restaurant was quiet, the result being that the labour resource was used like burger buns—purchased only when needed.

There are numerous tensions within both hard and soft aspects of the model (Noon, 1992; Legge, 1995), and the distinction between hard and soft might be two rhetorics at work in the same situation (Watson, 1994a). Legge's reference to 'tough love' (1995) suggests a preparedness to apply the hard perspective in controlling the labour cost, and to exercise care in the management of the human resource. Indeed this merging of hard and soft is further evidenced in Harvester Restaurants (Ashness and Lashley, 1995) where employees frequently decide to 'send someone home' when the business is quieter than anticipated. Here the 'hard' controls required by Burger King are delivered by 'soft' (committed?) employees themselves.

Given this range of debates and disagreements about the nature of human resource management, it is essential that analysis of the topic applied to hospitality operations reflects these debates and does not fall into the trap of assuming a single meaning for human resource management. Legge (1995) provides a range of four models in which to locate views about HRM. The *normative model* tends to state what HRM should be, or aspires to be: it provides a 'how to do' focus. The *descriptive functional model* focuses on the functions which HRM actually serves within organisations. The *critical evaluative model* locates HRM within a series of organisational and societal devices to gain commitment and win consent to managerial objectives and values, in particular in gaining support for a unitary perspective of organisational life. The *descriptive behavioural model* is concerned with examining human resource management in practice. Though not unique to the applied hospitality management field, much of the literature on management within the industry tends to discuss human resource management as though it had a single meaning and is concerned with the practices of human resource management in organisations.

Much of the current published literature on human resource management in the hospitality and tourism industries (Riley, 1992; Boella, 1992; Mullins, 1995) reflects the normative model and tends not to draw clear distinctions between human resource and personnel management. To varying degrees, all of these texts interchange the terms as though they mean the same thing. Much of the research discussed later in this chapter is framed within the normative model. It suggests that service business objectives can best be met by service organisations through the adoption of formal rational approaches to the 'problems of managing people' (Watson, 1986).

HRM as a distinctive approach expressed in normative terms has some major difficulties. It is informed by a unitary perspective of the organisation. The unitary approach takes as given a unity of interest between various organisation members. Organisation conflict, or any suggestion that stakeholders might have conflicting interests, is not considered as 'normal' and is treated as pathological. This approach provides little by way of critical analysis within the employment relationship. It frequently falls into the trap of treating the management of people as a technical process, and as a consequence fails to recognise the 'political' dimensions to management, and the uneven power relationships within organisations, or that even those with limited power find ways of resisting management power. Furthermore, attempts to establish, through empirical research, the consistent and coherent application of human resource management across industry by advocates have proved difficult (Legge, 1995).

Finally, as mentioned earlier, the normative model as expressed by writers in 'mainstream HRM' is flawed and limited in its analysis of service industries in general and the hospitality industry specifically. The service encounter and the key role of front-line staff, the recent emergence of a rhetoric espousing service quality as a now vital business strategy (Pannell Kerr Forster, 1991), and the cluster of service features, particularly the role of intangibles, is largely ignored. For example, Legge's (1995) otherwise excellent book makes just 16 references to service organisations and none at all to the hospitality industry which employs 10% of the UK workforce (Joint Hospitality Industry Congress, 1996). It is the authors' view that a thorough analysis of service organisations' HRM strategies can contribute to the wider debates about HRM by helping to establish a more rounded analysis of what HRM 'should be' against which to compare human resource management in practice. Research into the management of people applied to the hospitality industry needs to reflect these wider debates, and in the longer term shape them.

Researching the management of people at work

The aim of this research is to highlight the current trends and concerns within a literature which studies the management of people within the hospitality industry. The approach to collecting and collating data on recent research involved both electronic and manual retrieval to elicit articles, texts and electronic papers which have been produced over the last five years. The search was conducted through M.C.B's online database Emerald, the Commonwealth Agricultural Bureau's Abstracts on Rural Tourism, the Whatt hospitality database, and library catalogues using key words. The fields were restricted to 'hospitality', 'hotel and catering' and 'tourism' along with derivatives of 'employment', 'staff', 'personnel' and 'human resource management'. In total the number of references located was in the region of 200. However, when analysing further the number which fell within the boundaries of this research, the authors included 136 articles published in refereed journals.

In order to provide some structure to the discussion, each category has been subdivided into context, which identifies the location of the research in terms of 'hospitality', 'hotels', 'catering', etc. Where appropriate, research is identified as being at either a macro level or a micro level of the industry. The macro level refers to research carried out at general industry or national level, whilst the micro level locates the research at an organisational or sub-organisational level. Additionally, the level of staff which the research relates to is highlighted. Within each category the focus of the research is provided, in relation to sub-theories and perspectives.

The past five volumes of *Personnel Review* were analysed to compare trends and concerns within a publication which addresses a more generic audience. Although the title suggests a personnel perspective within the debates outlined above, this journal reflects a breadth of conceptual contributions which cover the full range of meanings of human resource management. This journal publishes eight issues per volume, though two of these provide an analysis of articles published in the management of people at work, and two are usually devoted to special editions each year. An analysis of these later articles was not included in the study because it was felt that the comparison would best benefit from articles which reflected the current research interests and trends from academics unaffected by special editions through which the editor may stimulate the production of articles around set themes. On average there are, therefore, three or four issues of the journal each year which attract articles on a wide range of topics. The analysis discussed below includes some 77 articles published in the period up to the end of 1996. Although *Personnel Review* is but one of a number of generic journals in which academic articles address issues relating to the management of people at work, it does provide some insights into trends of concern and it was felt that the journal provides an interesting 'hands on' approach which has much in common with the specialised hospitality research literature.

Published material has been categorised into the broad headings which flow from the discussions we have indicated earlier: Training and Development, Employee Behaviour, Industrial Relations, Labour Markets, Hospitality Management, Human Resource Practices, and Strategic Human Resource Management. As the analysis of the literature proceeded, both from the applied hospitality field and in *Personnel Review*, the authors reviewed another category of papers which proved to be a major theme within this latter field—Management Role and Behaviour. A slightly more detailed definition of each will be elaborated under each of the headings, but the general approach to setting up the categories was shaped by a concern to reflect both the range of issues which flow from discussions about the management of people at work, and the topics which seemed to suggest themselves from an analysis of the published articles.

Prior to discussion on each of these areas, the research can be analysed in relation to the general balance across the thematic categorisations in the two sources of material under investigation. Some interesting differences between them emerged, and these are more graphically displayed in Table 19.1. Approximately 40% of the applied hospitality research was equally located in the two themes of 'Training and Development' and 'Human Resource Practices'. A further 35% fell into the categories 'Labour Markets', 'Hospitality Management' and 'Employee Behaviour'. The smallest category was found to be in the area of 'Strategic Human Resource Management'. Less than 10% of the published articles dealt with 'Industrial Relations'.

This last category provides an interesting comparator with articles published in *Personnel Review* because 16 of the 77 (21%) articles published in this publication

Table 19.1 Comparison of HRM research papers in hospitality journals and *Personnel Review*

Research theme	Hospitality sources (number)	Hospitality sources (%)	Personnel Review (number)	Personnel Review (%)
Training and Development	31	22.8%	9	11.7%
Labour Markets	18	13.2%	2	2.6%
Human Resource Practices	26	19.1%	23	29.8%
Hospitality Management	12	8.8%	(2)*	—
Employee Behaviour	23	16.9%	2	2.6%
Industrial Relations	11	8.1%	16	20.8%
Management Role and Behaviour	10	7.3%	19	24.7%
Strategic HRM	5	3.7%	6	7.8%
Totals	136	100%	77	100%

* Not counted because the two hospitality cases were contextual and included in other themes.

related to industrial relations matters. In this journal, industrial relations represented the third largest category of themes within the articles published. Like the hospitality field, human resource procedures formed a large group of articles; 23 of the 77 (30%) covered a cluster of items dealing with recruitment, selection and appraisal. Published items specifically about the training and development of employees accounted for nine articles (12%), though a substantial number which were categorised as Management Role and Behaviour did include management development as topics for their study. In total, this latter category accounted for 19 of the 77 articles (25%). Thus, within *Personnel Review*, just three themes accounted for over 70% of the published articles.

The papers were also analysed according to their general purpose, i.e. making a conceptual or an empirical contribution. Of the 77 published papers in *Personnel Review*, 16 were conceptual in that they attempted to describe a phenomenon or suggest an analytical framework. Sixty-one papers, therefore, reported on a piece of empirical study. Two categories of research method dominated these empirical studies. Eleven papers were based on case studies, frequently the study of a single organisation. The other 50 papers used a survey style of research—15 via interviews or a combination of interviews and questionnaires and the remaining 35 reporting on the findings of research gathered through questionnaires. Though there were exceptions, the vast majority of these had been conducted through postal questionnaires.

It can be seen from Table 19.2 that the split between conceptual and empirical work within the two sources of published research is similar, with a predominance of publications which include research primary data. The methods used to collect data are also similar, with a propensity to utilise questionnaires as a primary source. The major difference to emerge is the greater use of case study methodology in the hospitality literature. The following commentary discusses key aspects of each category of research, as highlighted in Table 19.1.

Training and development

Almost half of the research has been conducted under the auspices of hospitality (Barron and Maxwell, 1993; Purcell, 1996), with six articles based in catering (e.g. Sparrow *et al.*, 1992), three in tourism (O'Neill, 1996), and the remainder in hotels (MacVicar and Brown, 1994). Fifteen specifically addressed managerial staff level, (e.g. Watson and Brotherton, 1996), three dealt with the training and development of operative staff (Collins, Sweeney and Geen, 1994) with the remaining two being non-specific (Hales *et al.*, 1996).

The focus of the majority of the research has been on educational issues, some addressing perceptions on various aspects of hospitality education (Hemmington, 1995;

Table 19.2 Research methods and focus in hospitality journals and *Personnel Review*

	Hospitality HRM research	Personnel Review
Conceptual	36 (26.4%)	16 (20.7%)
Empirical	100 (73.5%)	61 (79.2%)
Case study	26 (19.1%)	11 (14.2%)
Survey—interviews	18 (13.2%)	15 (19.4%)
Survey—questionnaires	56 (41.1%)	35 (45.4%)

Purcell, 1996) whilst others focus on the content of hospitality courses (Harris, 1995; Fawcett, 1995; Johns and Teare, 1995). Some address the role of education at a macro level and its impact/relationship with industry and/or policy development. Training research highlights service delivery (Sparrow *et al.*, 1992), skills development (Peacock, 1995b) and national training initiatives (Johnson, 1995; Hales *et al.*, 1996). Developmental research is focused on management development in the industry (Watson and Brotherton, 1996; McMahon and Quinn, 1995). The research activity is split between conceptual (14 publications) and empirical (17 publications). The methodology utilised was primarily qualitative, with predominant use made of the case study method (O'Neill, 1996; MacVicar and Brown, 1994; Fawcett, 1996). There was limited evidence of the use of comparative research (Baum, 1996b).

The training and human resource development articles within *Personnel Review* covered a range of national and international issues. Two of the nine articles examined issues in international human resource development, but no major themes seemed to dominate the topic. Two of the nine papers were conceptual, three were case studies and the remainder were interview-based surveys. It is interesting that there appears to be more concern with conceptual issues in the published applied hospitality articles, though the limited number of cases included in *Personnel Review* could be a distorting factor.

Labour markets

In contrast to the training and development theme, almost two-thirds of the research in this context was focused at the macro level of labour markets (11 articles) with almost half of the research being set in the context of tourism (Baum, 1994a; Brogan, 1994). The remainder addresses hotel and catering (Lucas, 1993a; Wood, 1992a) with only one piece of work dealing specifically with small businesses (Jameson, 1996). The focus of the research is on employment trends and labour market policy implications. Interestingly, almost 25% (four articles) of the research addressed issues surrounding age (Lucas, 1993a; Gilling, 1994). A minority of the work addressed perceptions of the industry as an employer (Ross, 1994a). The majority focused on all levels of staff, with a minority on graduate employment (Riley, 1996). Again there was strong evidence of conceptual work, taking a theoretical perspective and utilising secondary sources of data (Baum, 1994b; Jameson, 1996). There was also a strong use of survey techniques in the empirical work (Ross, 1994b; Lucas, 1995a) with less emphasis on the use of case-study/ethnography as a research medium (Burns, 1993).

The Labour Market articles in *Personnel Review* were limited in number. There were just two items which could be registered in this category. One is based on a case study of local skill markets. The second paper is conceptual, discussing a model which argued that a low skill equilibrium is created through the actions of the labour market.

Human resource practices

Almost two-thirds of this research was set in the context of hotels, for example Nankervis and Debrah (1995), with a further four publications in restaurants (Ashness and Lashley, 1995). The remainder was divided between hospitality and tourism. A total of 85% were located at a micro level of the industry (Parsons, 1995; Watson and D'Annunzio-Green, 1996). A strong emphasis of the research was on human resource management practices at a general level (Price, 1994; Lan, 1995; Baldacchino, 1994). Almost 30% of the research addressed empowerment (six publications). A further 15% investigated selection and recruitment practices (Inneson, 1996; Inneson and Brown, 1992; Mok and Luk, 1995) and 12% on labour turnover. Organisational culture seemed to be of limited interest to researchers, with some notable exceptions (Mullins, Meudell and Scott, 1993; Watson and D'Annunzio-Green, 1996). Taking the nature of the above themes, it is perhaps not surprising that the emphasis was on the managerial, rather than operative staff, level. Approximately two-thirds of all published papers dealt with management-level issues.

Seventeen publications (two-thirds) of the research utilised questionnaires and survey techniques (Mok and Luk, 1995; Anastassova and Purcell, 1995), 15% featured case study approaches, 7% interviews (Peters and Sparrow, 1994), and the remaining 15% were conceptual in nature, utilising a theoretical approach with practical applications in the research (Lashley and McGoldrick, 1994; Pye, 1994).

The papers in this category in *Personnel Review* accounted for the largest group of publications. Topics covered the full range of issues which might be expected in the study of the functional role of managing people in the workplace. These papers dealt with a range of employment and recruitment, contractual, appraisal, and redundancy subjects. Some papers explored general approaches to personnel/human resource management, and the application of information technology to the functional role.

Eight papers were conceptual and these papers tended to deal with broad brush stroke issues such as 'business process re-engineering' and organisation theory, though some attempted to develop models for the analysis of appraisal schemes. Much of the empirical work was based on surveys, though four papers were case studies. Of the nine papers using survey techniques, just one was based on interviews; the remainder all employed some form of postal questionnaire technique and were exploring the use of a variety of personnel management techniques, such as the use of occupational tests, and forms of employee consultation.

Hospitality management

Half the research was located in hospitality (Barron and Maxwell, 1993) with almost 50% in hotels (Webster, 1994; Lee-Ross, 1993). Reference to tourism was extremely limited and was encompassed under the term hospitality. Nine of the published articles featured research activity which was conducted at the macro level (Purcell and Quinn, 1996; Kim, 1994), with the remainder focusing on an organisational perspective (Webster, 1994). The research emphasis was on management career issues (Ladkin and Riley, 1995; Nebel, Braunlich and Zhang, 1994; Johns and McKechnie, 1995). The second major area was on managerial skills, 20% focusing on management styles (Lee-Ross, 1993; Messenger and Allen, 1994). Other areas included addressing specific skills and styles, e.g. listening (Brownell, 1994a), success factors (Peacock, 1995b), education (Lockwood, 1995) and graduate employment issues (Noreen, Murray and McKenna, 1992; Purcell and Quinn, 1996). Thirty per cent of the research was theoretical in nature (Messenger and Allen, 1994). Of the empirical work published in hospitality journals half used a questionnaire-based survey technique (Peacock, 1995b), and the remaining four were based on a case study method (Webster, 1994).

There were only two papers in *Personnel Review* which involved research covering hospitality industry activities. In both papers a hospitality industry firm provided the context for a case study which explored employee empowerment in one case and service quality management in the other. In this analysis the authors counted these papers under separate topic categories. The focus of the papers in question was not specifically about understanding management in the hospitality industry, but the application of an approach to managing people at work which happened to be in a hospitality industry business. Table 19.1 includes these, but counts them under topic themes.

Management role and behaviour

Articles covering the role of management and behaviour accounted for 10 of the 136 publications in the hospitality area. The majority focused on the development of key skills, for example communications and listening skills (Brownell, 1992) and decision making (Gore, 1995). There is strong evidence of research addressing the impact of management behaviour on staff (Ghei and Nebel, 1994) and factors influencing management behaviour (Pizam *et al.*, 1997; Peters and Sparrow, 1994). Fewer articles were located which addressed the role of managers. Peacock (1995a) attempts to identify success factors for hospitality managers, whilst the recent work of Hales and Tamangani (1996) investigates the relationship between organisational structure, expectations and work activities in centralised and decentralised organisations. Eight publications were empirical in nature, with the predominant methodology being questionnaires. Two of the papers in this category used a case study approach.

The papers published in *Personnel Review* covering the theme of managerial roles and behaviour represented the second largest cluster of papers. Nineteen of the 77 papers dealt with issues specifically concerned with managers, their development and careers. Ten papers featured management development, mentoring of managers or programmes of continuing professional development. A further four papers dealt with management careers, and the balance covered a range of issues from directors' pay to upward appraisal and executive stress. Two of the papers were conceptual in nature— modelling management development and human resource development. The remaining 17 covered empirical research, of which four were based on case studies and the remainder were conducted via surveys. Eight of the surveys were undertaken through the use of questionnaires and five involved some form of structured or semi-structured interview.

Employee behaviour

The research classified in the category of employee behaviour was found to be quantifiably fewer than might be expected. However, this is likely to be the result of both the research method employed and also the categorisation of located material. It could be argued that virtually all the research in HRM could be seen to fall under the banner of employee behaviour. The analysis revealed that 50% was set in the general hospitality context (Smith, Gregory and Cannon, 1996; Ross, 1992) with 45% located in hotels (Gore, 1995; Huyton and Sutton, 1996). Again there was limited evidence of research either being located in tourism or addressing tourism-related issues. The remaining 5% was found to address catering (Price, Arnould and Deibler, 1995). Considering the nature of this area it is perhaps not surprising that 95% of the activity was found to focus on micro level issues (Lee-Ross, 1995; Hobson, 1996) whilst the remainder addressed macro level issues (Wood, 1997). The seminal work by Wood (1992a, 1992b, 1994a, 1994b, 1997) provides the most comprehensive and thorough work in this area, covering a wide range of aspects of employee behaviour, built up from a sound theoretical base utilising theories and concepts from a range of disciplines.

In analysing the research activity in this area further, the following breakdown emerges: commitment/motivation (Smith, Gregory and Cannon, 1996) and skills/ attitudes (Balmer and Baum, 1993; Ross, 1992) accounted for 28% of published papers. A further 14% was concerned with issues surrounding perceptions (Clark, 1993) and stress (Ross, 1995). Crime was researched by one author (Hobson, 1996) and managerial decision making by another (Gore, 1995).

The majority of the research addressed relationships between management and staff (Lee-Ross and Boles, 1994), or the impact of practices imposed by management on employee behaviour (Price, Arnould and Deibler, 1995). Again there was a strong indication of the use of survey techniques (Harbourne, 1995) and case studies (Gore, 1995). A total of 25% of the publications were found to be theoretical/conceptual in nature (Hobson, 1996; Balmer and Baum, 1993).

In *Personnel Review*, only two papers which did not concern industrial relations issues could be located in this category. The first dealt with the factors causing employee stress which utilised an interview-based survey. The second paper reported on a questionnaire-based survey of team-working arrangements within a number of different manufacturing locations.

Industrial relations

One of the major differences between the generic and applied hospitality literature is found in the proportion of published material dealing with industrial relations issues. As Table 19.1 shows, industrial relations accounted for just 8% of the total number of papers in the hospitality research literature. Of the 11 articles located in this category, five were set in a general hospitality context (Purcell, 1996; Lucas, 1993a, 1993b, 1993c), three were in restaurant/catering contexts (Ogden, 1995; Royle, 1995), two involved studies in hotels (Jameson and Hamylton, 1992) and one in small firms (Radiven and Lucas, 1996). No research was found that related to industrial relations in tourism. The majority addressed issues at a macro level (Purcell, 1993; Jameson and Hamylton, 1992) and the minority addressed micro level issues (Ogden, 1995). The nature of the research highlighted issues to be addressed by management in most cases.

The focus of research predominantly explored equality (Jameson and Hamylton, 1992; Purcell, 1993) and payment issues (Lucas, 1992; Radiven and Lucas, 1996). Union representation and participation were additional themes for a further 20% of the publications (Wood, 1994a, 1997; Royle, 1995). Just over half of the research was found to use survey techniques with a strong emphasis on the use of questionnaires (Purcell,

1996); one in four used case study techniques (Royle, 1995). The remainder were found to be conceptual in nature, utilising secondary data to substantiate the thesis.

As stated above, the papers dealing with industrial relations matters were a significant category of published articles in *Personnel Review*, 16 papers in this category accounting for almost 21% of the total published articles. Pay and extrinsic reward schemes made a significant theme to papers (five of the 16), though disciplinary and grievance procedures and equal opportunities matters also accounted for four papers. The majority of papers reported on empirical studies, though two were conceptual. The first of these attempted to model links between pay/reward structures and quality management. The second conceptual paper dealt with the employment relationship and attempted to model both variations and change within the relationship. Two papers used case studies whilst the remainder were based on surveys. Ten of these used questionnaires whilst two included a combination of questionnaires and interviews through which to gather information.

Strategic human resource management

As indicated in Table 19.1, strategic human resource management represents the smallest category within the applied hospitality area. Only five publications were allocated within this category. Of these, three are empirical in nature and all are located within the hotel sector of the industry. Roper, Brookes and Hampton (1997) take an integrated approach to research into international hotel companies, whilst Phillips (1996) examines UK hotel-based organisations. Again this is a category which was not evident in the applied hospitality industry research into human resource management. However, a study of the *Personnel Review* publications over the period revealed six articles which appeared to deal solely with more strategic issues. Two of these papers were concerned with topics which were conceptual, exploring issues concerned with organisational competitive strategy and the role of employees. One paper reported on the role of Personnel Directors in a selection of British firms. The remaining papers were concerned with reporting on research which explored the nature of strategic human resource management—matching the management of employees with other business policies and strategies. Of the six papers in this category, two were conceptual, two were surveys based on interviews, and two were surveys based on questionnaires.

An agenda for applied HRM research?

Before discussing the nature of research into the management of human resources within the specific applications of the hospitality industry, it is necessary to engage in some of the debates and conceptual frameworks within the generic field of human resource management. This comparison of research published within the targeted 'hospitality' literature and one generic journal—*Personnel Review*—shows that there are similarities and differences in the research agenda identified in these two sets of journals. The lack of engagement with debates about human resource management is a common gap in much research within the applied hospitality field. Perhaps not surprisingly, nor is there much by way of contribution to these debates either. Apart from a few notable exceptions, most of the general field of human resource management is left untouched by examples of practice about the management of people within the industry. Nor are the models which have contributed to the development of HRM theory informed by application to the service sector in general and the hospitality industry in particular. Indeed it is fair to say that both sets of literature are impoverished by these gaps. The generic literature seems myopically concerned with practice in manufacturing and rarely discusses the specific problems of employees and employers within service industries. The applied hospitality literature continues to treat human resource management under that label but is mostly concerned with an agenda little different from personnel management. The remaining part of this chapter attempts to suggest an agenda for those engaged in research into the management of people within the hospitality industry.

A strong impression of applied research in HRM within the hospitality industry is that there are similarities and gaps when compared with generic research into the field of human resource management. Topics relating to training and development, and the 'bread and butter' topics of personnel management (recruitment and selection, appraisal, rewards, etc.), were common themes in both the literature published relating to the specifics of the industry and the articles published in *Personnel Review*. There were, however, some important differences. The amount of research in 'industrial relations' themes seemed to be lower in the hospitality literature, and there was a limited number of publications on management strategy within the hospitality industry. We will discuss this issue in more detail shortly, because it is symptomatic of a general approach to research in the hospitality industry. On a more qualitative level, two issues need to be discussed more fully as a future concern for hospitality researchers.

The unwillingness of hospitality researchers to engage in debates about the nature of human resource management has already been discussed in detail above and earlier in the chapter. At this point it is important to reiterate the key point that even amongst the generic literature theorists there is a major debate about what HRM means. Hospitality researchers, with a few exceptions, do not acknowledge that a debate exists. Much of this research starts from a view that human resource management is the same as personnel management, and several widely used books on human resource management in the hospitality industry tend to treat the topic this way. Whilst there may be a good case for this approach, there is a need to address the arguments so that this area of work does at least engage in the debates which dominate the wider literature. Indeed it could be argued that the specific features of the management of people in hospitality operations involves some unique factors which could enrich some of the more generic debates and theories.

One key assumption about the nature of human resource management, as opposed to personnel management, is that the former is said to be more strategic in its focus, the assumption being that the management of people is of fundamental importance to the management of the business. This case is made even more strongly when discussing hospitality services where the employee's performance plays such a crucial role in shaping the customer's experience of the service. The nature of the front-line employee's approach to the customer, their ability to read, match and ideally exceed customer service expectations, is said to be a fundamental requirement in generating customer satisfaction and customer repeats (Heskett *et al.*, 1994).

Whilst these aspirations for service delivery and strategic people management issues are of concern in the study of human resource management within the hospitality business, it is also essential that researchers recognise that these debates are themselves based on a set of assumptions about the role of management and the nature of strategic decision making which are but one of an array of possibilities. Thus much of the limited literature about strategic human resource management within the hospitality field tends to assume a classical view about strategic business management, namely that senior managers arrive at rational plans and cascade these, unamended and unchanged, through the organisation. Whittington (1993) has a generally critical view of this some-what limited notion about the formulation and implementation of business strategy in particular, and Legge (1995) uses the model to make a critical attack on strategic human resource management specifically. Again these decisions and debates are rarely evi-denced in the applied literature of human resource management within the hospitality industry.

On a related, though more fundamental, issue it is possible to criticise much applied hospitality research as presenting a somewhat unitary view of the organisation and deci-sions which managers make about their management. An assumption implicit in much research is that hospitality organisations are peopled by individuals who have a unity of interest in the organisation's success. Whilst this may be the case on one level of analy-sis, it is but one of several perspectives of the nature of hospitality work organisations. Fox's (1974) analysis of these perspectives suggests that it is equally important to recognise that there are likely to be conflicting needs and interests held by people in dif-ferent positions within the organisation. Thus a more pluralistic analysis suggests that managers and owners on the one hand, and employees on the other, may well find that there are quite different sets of needs from the organisation. The link between pay, costs and profits, and terms and conditions of employment, are just two examples of two sets of issues where employers and the employed have different and conflicting needs.

Similarly, a radical pluralist views conflict between those who own and manage businesses and those who work in them as endemic to the nature of employment rela-tionships in modern capitalistic economies. Under this analysis, hospitality organisa-tions and the techniques which are both advocated and introduced for their management are bound to result in conflicts between the key participants; research into the manage-ment of people within hospitality organisations should be as much concerned with con-ditions which stifle and suppress conflict as they are with techniques that are designed to win greater employee commitment.

Much of the applied research which studies the management of people within the hospitality industry can be accused of being concerned with a managerial agenda, namely with identifying current problems in the management of people within these organisations and attempting to provide answers to assist managers in being more effec-tive. The current priority given to improving customer service quality by many hospi-tality organisations suggests that this is not of itself an unworthy approach. Applied research could do much to assist managers to reduce labour turnover, improve employee performance and generally build on the strengths which individuals bring to their work in the industry. However, the research agenda also needs to consider approaches which critically question that there is a natural unity of interests between those who work in hospitality organisations and those who manage/employ them. Researchers need to be as concerned with the study *of* hospitality business practice as well as with the study *for* hospitality business practice. Philosophically this requires a more critical and analytical approach to applied research in this field. It is an approach which would be as concerned with employee resistance and compliance, as with labour turnover and employee commitment. It is an approach which needs to focus on the experiences of working in the industry, and which could well return to the boundary-breaking studies of Orwell (1933), Whyte (1948) and Terkel (1972).

References and bibliography

Anastassova, L. and Purcell, K. (1995) 'Human resource management in the Bulgarian hotel industry: from command to empowerment?', *International Journal of Hospitality Management*, **14** (2), 171–185.

Armstrong, A. (1987) 'Human resource management: a case of the emperor's new clothes?', *Personnel Management*, **19** (8), 30–35.

Ashness, D. and Lashley, C. (1995) 'Empowering service workers at Harvester Restaurants', *Personnel Review*, **24** (8), 17–32.

Baker, M., Cattet, A. and Riley, M. (1995) 'Practical food and beverage training in the UK: a study of facilities and a debate on its relevance', *International Journal of Contemporary Hospitality Management*, **7** (5), 21–24.

Baldacchino, G. (1994) 'Peculiar human resource management practices? A case study of a microstate hotel', *Tourism Management*, **15** (1), 46–52.

Baldacchino, G. (1995) 'Reception staff and the guest complaint: problem solving response styles among potential employees', *International Journal of Hospitality Management*, **14** (1), 67–68.

Ball, S. (1995) 'Enriching student learning through innovative real-life exercises', *Education and Training*, **37** (4), 18–25.

Balmer, S. and Baum, T. (1993) 'Applying Herzberg's hygiene factors to the changing accommodation environment', *International Journal of Contemporary Hospitality Management*, **5** (2).

Barron, P. and Maxwell, G. (1993) 'Hospitality management students' image of the hospitality industry', *International Journal of Contemporary Hospitality Management*, **5** (5) 5–8.

Barrows, C., Gallo, M. and Mulleady, T. (1996) 'AIDS in the US hospitality industry: recommendations for education and policy formulations', *International Journal of Contemporary Hospitality Management*, **8** (1), 5–9.

Baum, T. (1993) 'Human resource concerns in European tourism: strategic response and the EC', *International Journal of Hospitality Management*, **12** (1), 77–88.

Baum, T. (1994a) 'The development and implementation of national tourism policies', *Tourism Management*, **15** (3), 185–192.

Baum, T. (1994b) 'National tourism policies—implementing the human resource dimension', *Tourism Management*, **15** (4), 259–266.

Baum, T. (1994c) *Managing Human Resources in the European Tourism and Hospitality Industry: A Strategic Approach*, London: Chapman & Hall.

Baum, T. (1995) 'The role of the public sector in the development and implementation of human resource policies in tourism', *Tourism Recreation Research*, **20** (2), 25–31.

Baum, T. (1996a) 'Images of tourism past and present', *International Journal of Contemporary Hospitality Management*, **8** (4), 25–30.

Baum, T. (1996b) 'Unskilled work and the hospitality industry: myth or reality?', *International Journal of Hospitality Management*, **15** (3) 207–210.

Becker, C. and Olsen, M. (1995) 'Exploring the relationship between heterogeneity and generic management trends in hospitality organizations', *International Journal of Hospitality Management*, **14** (1), 39–52.

Blyton, P. and Turnbull, P. (1992) *Reassessing Human Resource Management*, London: Sage.

Blyton, P. and Turnbull, P. (1994) *The Dynamics of Employee Relations*, London: Macmillan.

Boella, M.J. (1992) *Human Resource Management in the Hospitality Industry*, Cheltenham: Stanley Thornes.

Bonn, M. and Forbinger, L. (1992) 'Reducing turnover in the hospitality industry: an overview of recruitment, selection and retention', *International Journal of Hospitality Management*, **11** (2), 47–63.

Bowcott, O. (1995) 'Burger King backs down and pays up', *The Guardian*, 19 December, p. 4.

Brogan, E. (1994) 'Human resource development in tourism: the Scottish perspective', in Seaton, A.V., Wood, R.C., Dieke, P.U.C., Bennet, M.M., Mclellan, L.R. and Smith, R. (eds), *Tourism: State of the Art*, Chichester: John Wiley & Sons, pp. 552–562.

Brownell, J. (1992) 'Hospitality managers' communication practices', *International Journal of Hospitality Management*, **11** (2), 111–128.

Brownell, J. (1994a) 'Women in hospitality management: general managers' perceptions of factors relating to career development', *International Journal of Hospitality Management*, **13** (2), 101–117.

Brownell, J. (1994b) 'Creating strong listening environments: a key hospitality management task', *International Journal of Contemporary Hospitality Management*, **6** (3), 3–10.

Bull, P.J. and Church, A. (1994) 'The geography of employment change in the hotel and catering industry of G.B. in the 1980's—a subregional perspective', *Regional Studies*, **28** (1), 13–25.

Burns, P.M. (1993) 'Sustaining tourism employment', *Journal of Sustainable Tourism*, **1** (2), 81–96.

Busby, G.D. (1995) 'The changing role of staff development for travel and tourism lecturers', *Journal of the National Association for Staff Development*, No. 33, pp. 19–26.

Clark, M. (1993) 'Communications and social skills: perceptions of hospitality managers', *Employee Relations*, **15** (2).

Clements, C.J. and Josiam, B.M. (1995) 'Training: quantifying the financial benefits', *International Journal of Contemporary Hospitality Management*, **7** (1), 10–15.

Collins, S., Sweeney, A.E. and Geen, A.G. (1994) 'Training for the UK tour operating industry: advancing current practice', *Tourism Management*, **15** (1), 5–8.

Conlin, M.V. and Baum, T. (1993) *Island Tourism: Management Principles and Practice*, Chichester: John Wiley & Sons.

Cooper, C., Scales, R. and Westlake, J. (1992) 'The anatomy of tourism and hospitality educators in the UK', *Tourism Management*, **13** (2), 234–242.

Dickinson, A. and Ineson, E.M. (1993) 'The selection of quality operative staff in the hotel sector', *International Journal of Contemporary Hospitality Management*, **5** (1), 16–21.

Dieke, P.U.C. (1993) 'Tourism policy and employment in the Gambia', *Journal of Employee Relations*, **15** (2).

Eddystone, N.C., Braunlich, C. and Zhang, Y. (1994) 'Career paths in American luxury hotels: food and beverage directors', *International Journal of Contemporary Hospitality Management*, **6** (6), 3–9.

Edwards, J. and Ingram, H. (1995) 'Food, beverage and accommodation: an integrated operations approach', *International Journal of Contemporary Hospitality Management*, **7** (5), 25–28.

Faulkner, B. and Patiar, A. (1997) 'Workplace induced stress among operative staff in the hotel industry', *International Journal of Hospitality Management*, **16** (1), 99–117.

Fawcett, L. (1995) 'The application of a US-originated computer-driven restaurant management game in the development of European hospitality managers', *Education and Training*, **37** (4), 6–12.

Fawcett, L.S. (1996) 'Fear of accounts: improving managers' competence and confidence through simulation exercises', *Journal of European Industrial Training*, **20** (2), 17–24.

Formica, S. (1996) 'European hospitality and tourism education: differences with the American model and future trends', *International Journal of Hospitality Management*, **15** (4), 317–324.

Fox, A. (1974) *Beyond Contract: Work, Power and Trust Relations*, London: Faber & Faber.

Getz, D. (1994) 'Students' work experiences, perceptions and attitudes towards careers in hospitality and tourism: a longitudinal case study in Spey Valley, Scotland', *International Journal of Hospitality Management*, **13** (1), 25–38.

Ghei, A. and Nebel, E. (1994) 'The successful manager and psychological androgyny: a conceptual and empirical investigation of hotel executives', *International Journal of Hospitality Management*, **13** (3), 247–264.

Gilbert, D. and Guerrier, Y. (1997) 'UK hospitality managers past and present', *Service Industries Journal*, **17** (1), 115–132.

Gilling, J. (1994) 'Older and wiser?', *Leisure Opportunities*, No. 126, pp. 26–27.

Go, F., Monachellao, M. and Baum, T. (1996) *Human Resource Management in the Hospitality Industry*, John Wiley & Sons.

Goldsmith, A. and Mohd Salehuddin Mohd Zahari (1994) 'Hospitality education in Malaysia: filling the skill gap', *International Journal of Contemporary Hospitality Management*, **6** (6), 27–31.

Gore, J. (1995) 'Hotel managers' decision making: can psychology help?', *International Journal of Contemporary Hospitality Management*, **7** (2), 19–23.

Guest, D.E. (1987) 'Human resource management and industrial relations', *Journal of Management Studies*, **24** (5), 503–521.

Guest, D.E. (1989) 'Personnel management and HRM: can you tell the difference?', *Personnel Management*, **21** (1), 48–51.

Guest, D.E. (1995) 'Right enough to be dangerously wrong: an analysis of the *In Search of Excellence* phenomenon', in Mabey, C. and Salamon, G. (eds), *Strategic Human Resource Management*, Oxford: Blackwell.

Hales, C. and Mercrate-Butcher, J. (1994) 'Internal marketing and human resource management in hotel consortia', *International Journal of Hospitality Management*, **13** (4), 313–326.

Hales, C. and Tamangani, Z. (1996) 'An investigation of the relationship between organizational structure, managerial role expectations and managers' work activities', *Journal of Management Studies*, **33** (6), 731–756.

Hales, C., Tamangani, Z., Walker, A. and Murphy, N. (1996) 'Factors influencing adoption of NVQ's in small hospitality businesses', *International Journal of Contemporary Hospitality Management*, **8** (5).

Harbourne, D. (1995) 'Issues in hospitality and catering', *Management Development Review*, **8** (1), 37–40.

Harris, C. and Merchant, S. (1992) 'Customised trainer training benefits top rank', *Executive Development*, **5** (1).

Harris, P.J. (1995) 'A development strategy for the hospitality operations management curriculum', *International Journal of Contemporary Hospitality Management*, **7** (5), 29–32.

Hemmington, N. (1995) 'The attitudes of students to modular hospitality management programmes', *Education and Training*, **37** (4), 32–37.

Heskett, J.L., Jones, T.O., Loveman, G.W., Sasser, W.E. and Schlesinger, L.A. (1994) 'Putting the service profit chain to work', *Harvard Business Review*, March–April, 164–174.

Hobson, P. (1996) 'Violent crime in the US hospitality workplace: facing up to the problem', *International Journal of Contemporary Hospitality Management*, **8** (4), 3–10.

Huyton, J. and Sutton, J. (1996) 'Employee perceptions of the hotel sector in the People's Republic of China', *International Journal of Contemporary Hospitality Management*, **8** (1), 22–28.

Ingram, A. and Baldwin, J. (1995) 'The new managerialism: review of human resource management; student guide to public and private organisations', *Tourism Recreation Research*, **20** (2), 46–57.

Ingram, A. and Baldwin, J. (1996) 'The new managerialism: review of human resources development and student guide to public and private organisations', *International Journal of Hospitality Management*, **15** (1), 11–18.

Inneson, E.M. (1996) 'Selection of managers: predictive model', *International Journal of Hospitality Management*, **8** (2) 25–30.

Inneson, E.M. and Brown, S.H.P. (1992) 'The use of biodata for hotel employee selection', *International Journal of Contemporary Hospitality Management*, **4** (2) 8–12.

Jameson, S.M. (1996) 'Small firms and the hospitality graduate labour market', *International Journal of Contemporary Hospitality Management*, **8** (5).

Jameson, S.M. and Hamylton, K. (1992) 'The CRE's investigation into the UK hotel industry', *International Journal of Contemporary Hospitality Management*, **4** (2), 21–26.

Johns, N. and McKechnie, M. (1995) 'Career demands and learning perceptions of hotel and catering graduates—ten years on', *International Journal of Contemporary Hospitality Management*, **7** (5), 9–12.

Johns, N. and Teare, R. (1995) 'Change, opportunity and the new operations management curriculum', *International Journal of Contemporary Hospitality Management*, **7** (5), 4–8.

Johnson, K. (1995) 'Using GNVQ core skills in a degree programme', *Education and Training*, 37 (4).

Joint Hospitality Industry Congress (1996) *The Vision for the Future*, Joint Hospitality Industry Congress, London.

Keenoy, T. and Anthony, P. (1992) 'Metaphor, meaning and morality', in Blyton, P. and Turnbull, P. (eds), *Reassessing Human Resource Management*, London: Sage.

Kim, Sang Mu (1994) 'Tourist hotel general managers in Korea: a profile', *International Journal of Hospitality Management*, **13** (1), 7–17.

Kokko, J. and Guerrier, Y. (1994) 'Overeducation, underemployment and job satisfaction: a study of Finnish hotel receptionists', *International Journal of Hospitality Management*, **13** (4), 375–386.

Ladkin, A. and Riley, M. (1995) 'Hotel management careers: research update 2', *Tourism Management*, Sept., pp. 475–476.

Ladkin, A. and Riley, M. (1996) 'Mobility and structure in the career paths of UK hotel managers: a labour market hybrid of the bureaucratic model?', *Tourism Management*, **17** (6), 443–452.

Lashley, C. (1995a) 'Towards an understanding of employee empowerment in hospitality services', *International Journal of Contemporary Hospitality Management*, **7** (1), 27–32.

Lashley, C. (1995b) 'Empowerment through delayering: a pilot study at McDonald's restaurants', *International Journal of Contemporary Hospitality Management*, **7** (2), 29–35.

Lashley, C. (1996) 'Empowering employees in hospitality retail operations', *International Journal of Hospitality Management*, **15** (1), 911–918.

Lashley, C. and McGoldrick, J. (1994) 'The limits of empowerment: a critical assessment of human resource strategy for hospitality operations', *Empowerment in Organisations*, **2** (3), 25–38.

Law, J., Pearce, P.L. and Woods, B.A. (1995) 'Stress and coping in tourist attraction employees', *Tourism Management*, **16** (4) 277–284.

Lee-Ross, D. (1993) 'Two styles of hotel manager, two styles of worker', *International Journal of Contemporary Hospitality Management*, **5** (4), 20–24.

Lee-Ross, D. (1995) 'Attitudes and work motivation of subgroups of seasonal hotel workers', *Service Industries Journal*, **15** (3), 295–313.

Lee-Ross, D. and Boles, J.S. (1994) 'Exploring the influence of workplace relationships on work-related attitudes and behaviours in the hospitality work environment', *International Journal of Hospitality Management*, **13** (2), 155–171.

Legge, K. (1989) 'Human resource management—a critical analysis', in Storey, J. (ed.), *New Perspectives in Human Resource Management*, London: Routledge.

Legge, K. (1995) *Human Resource Management: Rhetorics and Realities*, London: Macmillan.

Lennon, J. and Wood, R. (1992) 'The teaching of industrial and other sociologies in higher education: the case of hotel and catering management studies', *International Journal of Hospitality Management*, **11** (3), 239–254.

Li, L. (1995) 'Human resource management in Chinese hotels', *International Journal of Contemporary Hospitality Management*, **7** (1), 4–6.

Li, L. (1996) 'Predictors of expatriate hotel manager satisfaction in Asian Pacific countries', *International Journal of Hospitality Management*, **15** (4), 363–372.

Lockwood, A. (1995) 'Applying service quality concepts to hospitality education', *Education and Training*, **37** (4), 38–44.

Lucas, R. (1992) 'Minimum wages and the labour market—recent and contemporary issues in the British hospitality industry', *Employee Relations*, **14** (1), 33–47.

Lucas, R. (1993a) 'Ageism and the UK hospitality industry', *Employee Relations*, **15** (2).

Lucas, R.E. (1993b) 'Hospitality industry employment: emerging trends', *International Journal of Contemporary Hospitality Management*, **5** (5), 23–26.

Lucas, R. (1993c) 'The Social Charter—opportunity or threat to employment practice in the UK hospitality industry?', *International Journal of Hospitality Management*, **12** (1), 89–100.

Lucas, R. (1995a) 'Some age-related issues in hotel and catering employment', *Services Industries Journal*, **15** (2), 234–250.

Lucas, R. (1995b) *Managing Employee Relations in the Hotel and Catering Industry*, London: Cassell.

Lucas, R. and Bailey, G. (1993) 'Youth pay in catering and retailing', *Personnel Review*, **22** (7), 15–29.

Lucas, R. and Ralston, L. (1996) 'Part-time student labour: strategic choice or pragmatic response?', *International Journal of Contemporary Hospitality Management*, **8** (2), 21–24.

Lynch, P.A. (1994) 'Demand for training by bed and breakfast operators', *International Journal of Contemporary Hospitality Management*, **6** (4), 25–31.

MacVicar, A. and Brown, G. (1994) 'Investors in People at The Moat House International, Glasgow', *International Journal of Contemporary Hospitality Management*, **6** (1), 53–60.

McMahon, U. and Quinn, U. (1995) 'Maximising the hospitality management student work placement experience: a case study', *Education and Training*, **37** (4), 13–17.

Messenger, S. (1992) 'Vocational education and training', *Tourism Management*, **13**, 134–138.

Messenger, S. and Allen, R. (1994) *Management Skills: A Resource-based Approach for the Hospitality and Tourism Industries*, London: Cassell.

Mok, C. and Luk, Y. (1995) 'Exit interviews in hotels: making them a more powerful management tool', *International Journal of Hospitality Management*, **14** (2), 187–194.

Mullins, L. (1995) *Hospitality Management: A Human Resources Approach*, 2nd Edn, Harlow: Longman.

Mullins, L., Meudell, K. and Scott, H. (1993) 'Developing culture in short-life organizations', *International Journal of Contemporary Hospitality Management*, **5** (4).

Nankervis, A.R. and Debrah, Y. (1995) 'Human resource management in hotels—a comparative study', *Tourism Management*, **16** (7), 507–513.

Nebel, E.C., Braunlich, C.G. and Zhang, Y. (1994) 'Career paths in American luxury hotels; hotel food and beverage directors', *International Journal of Contemporary Hospitality Management*, **6** (6).

Noon, M. (1992) 'HRM a map, model or theory?', in Blyton, P. and Turnbull, P. (eds), *Reassessing Human Resource Management*, London: Sage.

Noreen, O.E.J., Murray, A.E. and McKenna, M.A. (1992) 'Research report: hospitality graduates and diplomates labour market experiences', *Journal of European Industrial Training*, **16** (3).

O'Connor, N. (1996) 'Rediscovering vocational education', *International Journal of Hospitality Management*, **15** (4), 307–316.

Ogden, S. (1995) 'Strategy, structure and employee relations lessons from compulsory, competitive tendering', *International Journal of Contemporary Hospitality Management*, **7** (2), 36–41.

Ohlin, J. and West, J. (1994) 'An analysis of the effect of the fringe benefit offerings on the hourly housekeeping workers in the hotel industry', *International Journal of Hospitality Management*, **12** (4), 323–336.

O'Neill, M. (1996) 'Investing in people: a perspective from Northern Ireland tourism—part 1', *Managing Service Quality*, **6** (4), 36–40.

Orr, N., Murray, A. and McKenna, M. (1992) 'Research report: Hospitality graduate and diplomat labour market experiences', *Journal of European Industrial Training*, **16** (3).

Orwell, G. (1933) *Down and Out in Paris and London*, London: Secker and Warburg.

Pannell Kerr Forster (1991) *Hotel Profitability: Critical Factors*, London: Pannell Kerr Forster Associates.

Parsons, G. (1995) 'Empowering employees—back to the future at Novotel', *Managing Service Quality*, **5** (4), 16–21.

Peacock, M. (1995a) '"A job well done": hospitality managers and success', *International Journal of Contemporary Hospitality Management*, **7** (2), 48–51.

Peacock, M. (1995b) *Information Technology in the Hospitality Industry: Managing People, Change and Computers*, London: Cassell.

Peters, S. and Sparrow, J. (1994) 'Human resource management philosophies and management action', *International Journal of Contemporary Hospitality Management*, **6** (6), 5–8.

Phillips, P. (1996) 'Strategic planning and business performance in the quoted UK hotel sector', *International Journal of Hospitality Management*, **15** (4), 347–362.

Pizam, A., Pine, R., Mok, C. and Shin, J.Y. (1997) 'National vs industry cultures: which has a greater effect on managerial behaviour?', *International Journal of Hospitality Management*, **16** (2), 127–145.

Price, L. (1994) 'Poor personnel practices in the hotel and catering industry: does it matter?', *Human Resources Management Journal*, **4** (4), 44–62.

Price, L.L., Arnould, E.J. and Deibler, S. (1995) 'Consumers' emotional responses to service encounters. The influence of the service provider', *International Journal of Service Industry Management*, **6** (3), 34–63.

Purcell, K. (1993) 'Equal opportunities in the hospitality industry: custom and credentials', *International Journal of Hospitality Management*, **12** (2), 127–140.

Purcell, K. (1996) 'The relationship between career and job opportunities: women's employment in the hospitality industry as a microcosm of women's employment', *Women in Management Review*, **11** (5), 17–24.

Purcell, K. and Quinn, J. (1996) 'Exploring the education–employment equation in hospitality management: a comparison of graduates and HNDs', *International Journal of Hospitality Management*, **15** (1), 51–68.

Pye, G. (1994) 'Customer service: a model for improvement', *International Journal of Hospitality Management*, **13** (1), 1–5.

Radiven, N. and Lucas, R. (1996) 'Wages council abolition and small hotels', *International Journal of Contemporary Hospitality Management*, **8** (5), 10–14.

Riley, M. (1992) 'Functional flexibility in hotels—is it feasible?', *Tourism Management*, **13** (4), 363–367.

Riley, M. (1996) *Human Resource Management in the Hospitality Industry*, Oxford: Butterworth-Heinemann.

Roper, A., Brookes, M. and Hampton, A. (1997) 'The multi-cultural management of international hotel groups', *International Journal of Hospitality Management*, **16** (2), 147–159.

Ross, G. (1992) 'Work attitudes and management values: the hospitality industry', *International Journal of Contemporary Hospitality Management*, **4** (3).

Ross, G.F. (1994a) 'What do Australian school leavers want of the industry?', *Tourism Management*, **15** (1), 62–66.

Ross, G.F. (1994b) 'Service quality ideals among hospitality industry employees', *Tourism Management*, **15** (4), 273–280.

Ross, G.F. (1995) 'Interpersonal stress reactions and service quality responses among hospitality industry employees', *Service Industries Journal*, **15** (3), 314–331.

Ross, G.F. (1996) 'Service quality and management: the perceptions of hospitality employees', *International Journal of Contemporary Hospitality Management*, **8** (3), 39–44.

Royle, A. (1995) 'Corporate versus societal culture: a comparative study of McDonald's in Europe', *International Journal of Contemporary Hospitality Management*, **7** (2/3), 52–56.

Simons, M. (1994) 'Hotel management contracts: some recent trends in relation to dispute resolutions in Australia', *International Journal of Hospitality Management*, **13** (2), 143–154.

Sissons, K. (ed.) (1994) *Personnel Management*, Oxford: Blackwell.

Smith, D. (1995) 'Sunday trading: an analysis of employment structures in leisure and retailing', *International Journal of Contemporary Hospitality Management*, **7** (2), 57–63.

Smith, K., Gregory, S. and Cannon, D. (1996) 'Becoming an employer of choice: assessing commitment in the hospitality workplace', *International Journal of Contemporary Hospitality Management*, **8** (6), 3–9.

Sparks, B. and Bradley, G. (1994) 'Understanding attitudes towards graduates: a marketing perspective', *International Journal of Hospitality Management*, **13** (3), 233–246.

Sparrow, J., Ingold, A., Huyton, J. and Baker, J. (1992) 'Experienced staff and tailoring food service', *International Journal of Contemporary Hospitality Management*, **4** (1), 4–10.

Storey, J. (ed.) (1989) *New Perspectives in Human Resource Management*, London: Routledge.

Storey, J. (1992) *Developments in Management of Human Resources*, Oxford: Blackwell.

Strohbehn, C. (1994) 'Graduate hospitality students' attitudes and values toward work and lifestyle factors', *International Journal of Hospitality Management*, **13** (2), 177–182.

Terkel, S. (1972) *Working*, New York: Avon.

Watson, S. and Brotherton, R. (1996) 'Hospitality management development: minimising conflict—maximising potential', *Management Development Review*, 9 (4), 13–22.

Watson, S. and D'Annunzio-Green, N. (1996) 'Implementing cultural change through human resources: the elusive organisation alchemy?', *International Journal of Contemporary Hospitality Management*, 8 (2), 25–30.

Watson, T.J. (1986) *Management Organisation and Employment Strategy: New Directions in Theory and Practice*, London: Routledge and Kegan Paul.

Watson, T.J. (1993) 'Rhetoric, strategic exchange and organisational change', conference paper to the *11th EGOS Colloquium*, Paris, July.

Watson, T.J. (1994a) *In Search of Management*, London: Routledge.

Watson, T.J. (1994b) 'Management flavours of the month: their role in managers' lives', *International Journal of Human Resource Management*, 5 (4), 893–909.

Webster, M. (1994) 'Strategic management in context at Swallow Hotels', *International Journal of Contemporary Hospitality Management*, 6 (5).

Whittington, R. (1993) *What is Strategy and Does it Matter?*, London: Routledge.

Whyte, W.F. (1948) *Human Relations in the Restaurant Industry*, New York: McGraw-Hill.

Wood, R.C. (1992a) 'Hospitality industry labour trends', *Tourism Management*, 13 (3), 297–304.

Wood, R.C. (1992b) *Working in Hotel and Catering*, London: Routledge.

Wood, R.C. (1994a) *Organisational Behaviour in Hospitality Management*, Oxford: Butterworth-Heinemann.

Wood, R.C. (1994b) 'Hotel culture and social control', *Annals of Tourism Research*, 21, 65–79.

Wood, R.C. (1997) *Working in Hotel and Catering*, 2nd Edn, London: Thomson Press.

Woods, R. (1992) 'Surfacing culture: the Northeast Restaurants' case', *International Journal of Hospitality Management*, 10 (4), 339–356.

Wynne, J. (1993) 'Power relationships and empowerment within hotels', *Employee Relations*, 15 (2), 42–50.

Yamagachi, Y. and Garley, J. (1993) 'The relationship between central life interest of restaurant managers and their level of job satisfaction', *International Journal of Hospitality Management*, 12 (4), 385–394.

20 Information Technology management

MICHAEL BAKER, SILVIA SUSSMANN AND SUSAN WELCH

Introduction

In this chapter, we have tried to identify the main streams of academic research in Information Technology management in hospitality. We illustrate each theme by reference to a number of researchers active at this time. We then go on to suggest how this research might best develop in the future. We have not attempted an exhaustive review of all research which might be defined as falling into the intersection of the Information Technology (IT), management and hospitality subjects of academic enquiry. There are good reasons not to attempt such a labour. Notably, there are sufficiently large numbers of researchers either concentrating in this area or dropping in from time to time from their more usual haunts to make an attempt at complete enumeration certain of failure.

There is also the matter of boundaries. Two issues arose. The first was the boundary with tourism, which has been difficult to delineate. This has been particularly acute in the marketing area, where the hospitality product is distributed through tourism systems.

The second question was how widely the 'management' part of our brief should be interpreted. We have interpreted it broadly, and we have taken the view that this should encompass all matters impinging on the management of hospitality, including the appropriate use of a technology and its possible impact. There is some reason for concern that hospitality IT management is not actually an identifiably separate subject. Indeed, at one time it might be argued that IT management was not a discrete business subject but this today would not be a sustainable argument, if for no other reason than the pragmatic observation that innumerable business school professors have established it as a speciality. The battle for the recognition of hospitality as a separate and definable field of study also seems to us to have been fought and won. The claim for hospitality IT management as a clearly separate subject of research seems to us to be as yet unsubstantiated. To make the claim unassailable it would be necessary to demonstrate that where IT management and hospitality intersect, the resultant subject area has emergent properties; and also to show that there is a substantial body of research to be undertaken, so that a critical mass of researchers could be kept fully occupied on it. The latter is now arguable; the former lacks proof.

However, we are happy about the unstable nature of the subject. The uncertainty about what should constitute the body of knowledge appropriate to any matter which

The Handbook of Contemporary Hospitality Management Research, Edited by Bob Brotherton.
© 1999 John Wiley & Sons Ltd.

seems to have a hospitality IT management label means that analytical tools from a wide range of impinging disciplines may be appropriate. This is all to the good. Those of us who write extensively about IT management, particularly in hospitality, are well advised to adopt an eclectic approach in our analyses; and the open nature of the borders to our patch of territory encourages marauders from other disciplines to attack problems within it, to its and our enrichment.

How much research?

In 1996 John Bowen at the University of Nevada carried out an analysis of the articles from the *Hospitality Review* published by Florida International University between 1989 and 1995 (Bowen, 1996). *The FIU Hospitality Review*'s authors include hospitality managers and educators and the articles are both empirical and conceptual. There were 113 articles in all, and Bowen identified seven main themes. Table 20.1 shows the themes and the number of articles in each.

The technology articles covered, *inter alia*, outsourcing, information systems, teleconferencing and the impact of technology on organisations. The *FIU Hospitality Review* is, of course, a US journal and tends to reflect US hospitality research. The articles on technology come mainly from the last two years of the review period, perhaps reflecting a growing interest in these issues. Nevertheless, the 'technology' theme was the least extensive, accounting for only 6% of the articles. An analysis conducted in September 1997 of papers in *Progress in Tourism and Hospitality Research* since its launch found four which discussed IT issues, out of just over 60 in total, a similar proportion, for a journal edited in the UK.

Haydn Ingram, at Surrey University, analysed the WHATT-CD Research Register of spring 1995 to gain an idea of the research being undertaken in hospitality (Ingram, 1996). WHATT-CD at that stage had 820 postgraduate research project entries (727 finished and 92 in progress), 84% of which were 'academic', with completion dates ranging from 1976 to 1999. These were put into four categories: general; hospitality—hotel or catering-related; tourism; and 'hot' issues (current areas of interest and concern). This last category was further subdivided into five: changing patterns; customers; agencies; information technology; and service/quality. However, information technology also features as a subsidiary theme in project categories other than 'hot'

Table 20.1 Analysis of articles in *FIU Hospitality Review* 1989–1995

Theme	Number of articles
People and organisations	40
Marketing	22
Environmental change, total quality management and strategy	14
Education	12
Financial analysis	10
Tourism	8
Technology	7

Source: Authors' analysis of data from Bowen, 1996.

Table 20.2   Research on IT-related subjects, 1992–1996: WHATT-CD research database

Subject	Number of projects in progress
Management attitudes and the human factor	1
Marketing (including DMS, Internet marketing, yield management, GDS)	7
Technology (including Artificial Intelligence and Virtual Reality)	6
Technological diffusion	3
Operations and human resources	2
Other (issues of organisational performance and strategic fit)	2
Total	21

issues. Regrettably, Ingram does not give the numbers in each category and sub-category, but if the 'hot' issues category comprises roughly a quarter of all entries and information technology represents about one-fifth of that, it suggests around 5%, i.e. less than half a dozen, ongoing research projects in IT at that time, including Master's dissertations.

To follow up Ingram's analysis, we looked at the current (1996) WHATT-CD, reviewing the research database, to identify all hospitality IT projects (i.e. Masters, MPhil and PhD) in work between 1992 and 1996 inclusive. The search was by WHATT-CD subject categories, and should therefore be exhaustive, catching all the information technology-related research. We obtained the results shown in Table 20.2.

Six of these were at PhD or MPhil level, so these figures (taken from the WHATT-CD one year on) are comparable to Ingram's, but suggest an increase in interest. This would correspond with our own experience, which is that interest in these research areas is growing amongst both MSc and PhD/MPhil students. Issues relating to the Internet seem to be of particular fascination. These WHATT-CD data can give a reasonable indication of the proportion of hospitality research which is in the IT field. They also indicate what aspects are of interest and how interest in IT issues is growing. They are not a good guide, however, to the total volume of research, as the WHATT-CD survey is heavily biased to UK activity.

Caution is needed in interpreting the quantitative analysis above; it can only be a guide. We also reviewed the current and earlier literature in hospitality IT management. A useful place to start is with an overview; one is provided by Cho and Connolly (1996). A picture of how IT might affect the industry by the next millennium is painted by Larry Chervenak (1993). We now turn to the various themes.

Technological diffusion

A long-standing issue of continuing interest to academics is the extent to which IT is in use in the industry. Attempts to use computers in the hospitality industry date back to the 1960s, including the unsuccessful automation of the front desk at the New York Hilton (Alvarez, Ferguson and Dunne, 1983). However, it was only during the 1980s that the use of computers became more widespread. Over the decade a number of researchers kept track of how quickly the industry was adopting IT. For instance, in the

US, O'Connor (1996b) reports a 1980 survey for the American Hotel and Motel Association by Chervenak, Keane and Co.; IBM and *Lodging Hospitality* conducted a further survey in 1991 (Watkins, 1992); and in the UK there was a survey by Whitaker (1986).

More recently, the mantle has fallen on new shoulders. In the US, the Hospitality Information Technology Association (HITA) and Pannell Kerr Forster conducted a nationwide survey of 3000 properties (Van Hoof *et al.*, 1995). In Ireland, Peter O'Connor (1991, 1996b) has been keeping track. In Wales, Main (1995a, 1995b) has surveyed independent hotels. Dimitrios Buhalis' work on independent hospitality establishments in the Aegean has enabled him and Hilary Main to compare technological diffusion in Wales and the Aegean (Buhalis and Main, 1996, 1997). This useful exercise enabled them to demonstrate similar diffusion rates and very similar issues for the hotels' management in each of these somewhat peripheral regions. Main and Ingold (1997) surveyed small and medium-sized hospitality establishments in the UK to discover the extent of their use of marketing information systems, albeit with a small telephone sample.

In an industry with a long tail of small independent establishments, rates of national diffusion will remain of continued interest. Comparisons, both longitudinal (such as the ongoing study at Napier University under Andy Frew on technology uptake and the impact of reservations networks) and cross-sectional between countries and regions, will also be of increasing value. For these reasons it would be worthwhile to see if some agreement amongst researchers about standard categories and wording of questions could be achieved perhaps through one of the interested bodies, such as HITA or the International Federation of Information Technology in Tourism (IFITT). These bodies are useful for researchers to plan joint projects such as those of Main and Buhalis. It is also to be hoped that the commercial organisations like Pannell Kerr Forster will continue to collaborate with academics through such bodies as HITA and IFITT.

Marketing

The conjunction of IT and marketing is a popular area for research, particularly for undergraduate and MSc dissertations. The tourism perspective tends to be that of the shift of strategic balance down the supply chain (for example, Poon, 1993; Reinders and Baker, 1997), whilst the hospitality industry perspective is more about the nitty-gritty of effective marketing and distribution (for example, Murphy, Forrest and Wotring, 1996a, 1996b; Marcussen, 1996, 1997). However, this may be seen as a false dichotomy, as the hospitality industry is a supplier to the other players in tourism (e.g. the operators and thus the travel agents). Dimitrios Buhalis has written extensively on the subject (for example, in Buhalis, 1993). Go and Williams (1993) and Frew and Pringle (1995) discuss the impact of technology on hospitality distribution systems. Moore and Wilkinson (1993) consider the effects of advances in communications systems on the relationship of the hotel with the frequent traveller. Similarly, the marketing debate has a number of strong and interwoven strands, including the link between the hotel Central Reservation Office (CRO) and the Global Distribution Systems (GDS); Destination Management Systems (DMS); Internet Marketing; and Yield Management Systems.

Hotels and the GDS

Larger hotel groups' development of CROs reflects their desire to realise some economies of scale in the distribution of their product, a move also emulated by marketing consortia to provide the same advantage to their members. Hotels then saw the advantage of connecting these CROs to GDS to obtain truly global distribution for their products (Beaver, 1992; Go, 1992; Lindsay, 1992; Emmet *et al.*, 1993) Because of the proliferation of proprietary systems, the hotel companies wishing to connect to GDS used a wide range of formats, resulting in the development of switches, notably THIS Co and Wizcom (Frew and Pringle, 1995). Welch (1995) discusses the use of GDS by hotels and the growth of this form of distribution.

Destination management systems

A DMS is essentially a marketing tool, concerned with the promotion of tourism products in a particular destination, which might be a nation, region, town or other recognisable geographical entity. A DMS usually has up to three components: a product database (of attractions, accommodation, travel information, etc.); a customer database (of those using, or who have used the database); and a reservation system (Baker, Sussmann and Hazelden, 1996). DMS are of particular fascination for, it would seem, three reasons. The first is that at first sight they seem to offer a conceptually simple, high-tech, potentially cheap way in which small establishments could achieve extensive (even worldwide) marketing reach. Second, over the years large sums of public money in many countries have been expended on DMS schemes. Political commitment is therefore a determinant of success (Baker, Sussmann and Hazelden, 1996); this seems to be forthcoming in Ireland, where Gulliver, the DMS developed by Bord Failte and the Northern Ireland Tourist Board, is being upgraded (O'Connor and Rafferty, 1997). Third, DMS have frequently failed, with the loss of both public and private money. Mutch (1996) gives details and reasons for one of the most recent failures, the collapse of the English Tourist Network Automation (ETNA).

The subject of DMS has attracted both academic and commercial research. Among the consultants who have written extensively on these subjects is Archdale (1992). Amongst the academic writers probably Silvia Sussmann has written or co-written as much as anyone (see, for example, Sussmann, 1994; Sussmann and Baker, 1996; Baker, Sussmann and Hazelden, 1996). An important contributor in this area is Pauline Sheldon (Sheldon, 1993, 1997).

However, the advent of the World Wide Web has probably curtailed the development of DMS which are not WWW-based. It is possible that the last great expenditure of public money will turn out to have been the Services and Applications for a World Wide Market in Tourism (SAM) trials and the predecessor projects (Byerley, 1996; Frew, Crichton and McKenzie, 1995; Maartmann-Moe, Byerley and Guinano, 1994).

Internet marketing

The Internet has tended to fascinate researchers since the inception of the WWW. This is not surprising. Hotel Internet bookings are growing at a phenomenal rate, and it is of enormous interest to managers as well as researchers to know how best to respond to this new distribution channel. For example, advice from consultants on Web-page design abounds, but there is little in the way of empirical research to support it. Recent research by Hyung-Soo Jung (personal correspondence with the authors) has determined that as yet the measurement of Website success is in a primitive phase in the hospitality-related industries. Jung is planning to make this the subject of further research.

Jamie Murphy, a PhD candidate researching this field (interactive communications) at Florida State University (Murphy, Forrest and Wotring, 1996a, 1996b), describes the potential benefits of using the WWW as a marketing tool. The first paper looks at restaurant marketing, concluding that as yet the potential is largely untapped. The second paper considers how hotels use the WWW, and concludes, *inter alia*, that the new medium brings with it the need to develop new marketing models, responding to the prospect that fashioning an offering for each customer could be cost-effective.

A regular and scholarly contributor in this field is Carl Marcussen (see, for example, Marcussen, 1996, 1997). The latter paper tackles the question, of particular interest to many, of whether the WWW will enable the smaller hotel to gain the marketing reach which up to now has only been available to those able to afford to use Global Distribution Systems (GDS) as one of their distribution channels. Frew and Dorren (1997) also consider the role of hotel companies in the WWW distribution system, in this context.

Yield management

Yield management was developed in the airline industry. More recently, 'yield management has been adopted by the hotel, rail and shipping industries, to try to help solve their problems of oversupply and increasing competition' (Ingold, Huyton and Yeoman, 1997: 48).

The quotation is taken from the editorial to the special issue (volume 9, number 2) of the *International Journal of Contemporary Hospitality Management* (*IJCHM*) devoted to yield management issues. That a significant academic hospitality journal should take this step indicated the interest and importance of the subject. In fact the papers in this edition of *IJCHM* were selected from those presented at the first international conference on this subject, held at Walton Hall in Warwickshire, attracting academic and industry delegates from Europe, North America and Australasia. The papers themselves are from teams drawn from a wide range of academic and other research institutions stretching from Australasia to Europe via Canada and Russia. The conference is to be an annual event with the second being held as a parallel stream of the Operational Research Society Conference at Bath University in September 1997. This conference should be seen as an important destination for hospitality researchers, particularly those with an interest in marketing or the use of IT in hospitality management.

Other marketing issues

There are of course other aspects of the marketing debate. Main and Ingold (1997) touch on the issue of database marketing and the development of loyalty programmes, a subject also held to be important by Peter O'Connor (personal communication with the authors). Crichton and Edgar (1995) review the strategic use of information technology in managing market complexity and environmental uncertainty in the UK short-break market. Similarly, Geographic Information Systems (GIS) could be used for a number of marketing activities. Oppermann and Brewer (1995) look at their use for choosing hotel locations, and Shribet, Muller and Inman (1995) look at how they can be used to examine the relationship between market growth and demographic change. Marketing is likely to continue to attract IT researchers. Key issues would seem to be the development and empirical testing of good theoretical models (or adaptations of old ones), particularly to explore the implications of one-to-one marketing, possibly by IT, as suggested by Murphy, Forrest and Wotring (1996b); and the development of means to help judge the effectiveness of marketing initiatives using the new technology.

Operations

The contribution of IT to the operations function in hospitality is extensive, and a wide range of topics have been taken up by authors. Of particular interest here are two questions. The first is whether the technology is used to cut costs or whether it is to help grow the business. Interesting human relations consequences can flow from this choice. The second is what contribution IT can make to service quality.

At the interface of the marketing function and the operations function lies the Property Management System (PMS). Managing the inventory is a key operational issue and the PMS is the key tool. The human element is important when specifying a PMS, a subject taken up by Collins (1990).

Michael Kasavana has written extensively on IT's application to aspects of operations, more recently, for example, on how automation can provide restaurant chain managers with competitive advantage by improving operational control (Kasavana, 1994a); how hotels can make better use of telephone call-accounting equipment (Kasavana, 1994b); and how personal computer-based register systems can help restaurant operators (Kasavana, 1995). Palmer, Kasavana and McPherson (1993) look at a model of a computer system for communication between dining room and kitchen.

In the puchasing function, EDI has attracted attention. Poorani (1995) discusses a cost–benefit analysis of EDI in the hospitality context, through a survey of 68 multi-unit food service companies, 30% of which he found to be using it. His study suggested that EDI can improve the overall performance of purchasing departments and contribute to cash flow and stockturn.

Michael Baker, Martin Wild and Silvia Sussmann have a paper in preparation on how Bass Taverns introduced their EPOS system, and the way it has enabled the empowerment of public house managers and the consequent growth of the business.

Quality

Of particular interest is the contribution IT can make to service quality. An overview of this is provided by Au and Yung (1995). Durocher and Niman (1993) consider some of the impacts of new technology on the hospitality industry. They point out that although there is continued pressure from the marketplace for improved quality, at the same time economic pressure is forcing hospitality firms to reduce their staff numbers. One of the problems of the future will be how to ensure service quality with fewer managers. The paper looks at how IT can contribute to improvements in management effectiveness and enhancement of customer services in these circumstances.

One focus for this is the use of IT in training for this purpose, a subject discussed by Graham and Lambert (1995).

Management attitudes and the human factor

It has generally been the case that surveys such as Whitaker's (1986), O'Connor's (1991, 1996b) and Main's (1995a, 1995b) have included questions aimed at investigating the factors affecting the take-up of IT. One focus of enquiry has been the attitude of managers to IT because this tends to have an important influence on both diffusion rates and on how, and how successfully, IT is used once adopted. For instance, Paul Gamble has explored this aspect of the hospitality industry (see, for example, Gamble, 1988), as has Whitaker (1987).

A related question is what determines whether, having spent money on IT, the hospitality organisation makes good use of it; this question tends to be of more interest in the case of owner-managed independent hotels and restaurants. Michael Bennett and Simon Brown have explored this issue (Bennett and Brown, 1996). Comparative studies are also interesting. Van Hoof, Verbeeten and Combrink (1996) compared technology needs and perceptions of managers in the US, Canada and the UK. They conclude that 'contrary to expectations, the perceptions of lodging managers … are not all that diverse' (p. 86).

These two questions fall into a wider theme, that of the interplay between IT and people in the organisation. One writer who has made an interesting contribution in this area is Martin Peacock, whose book (Peacock, 1995) is perceptive and useful for students who aspire to be managers in a hospitality organisation. Kasavana and David (1993) look at advances in computers which improve the human/machine interface, including touchscreen terminals and automated speech recognition systems.

There is little doubt that this is an area which could benefit from more attention. That is not to say that there is not a reasonable body of work in the area, but there could be more, and it could be more perceptive. More comparative studies would be of value. The management of change, a task inevitably going hand in hand with the introduction and effective use of IT, is little understood in the hospitality industry. Moreover, as Peacock (1995) shows, there are aspects of management styles common in hospitality which make the introduction of IT particularly uncomfortable, not least for the managers themselves. There are opportunities here for the academics to make a valuable contribution to the industry which others are not in a position to make.

What is IT?

Papers in research journals which simply describe what a particular application does are confined to experimental or speculative proposals, or emerging technology. Descriptive material on technology commonly employed in the industry tends to be the domain of textbooks. However, such descriptions are the outcome of personal research, and codify an important part of the body of knowledge for the student. A typical example of such a textbook is O'Connor's *Using Computers in Hospitality* (O'Connor, 1996a). Other books are by Kasavana (1997) and Collins and Malik (1994). However, such textbooks quickly go out of date and students need to look to the trade press for updates.

However, as indicated above, academic journals and conferences do feature papers giving straight descriptions of *emerging* IT applications. Many of Kasavana's papers have been of technology emerging at the time (for example, Kasavana, 1994a, 1994b, 1995). Three such technologies emerging now are Virtual Reality, intelligent agents and digital cash, which are described below as separate research themes.

Virtual Reality

Virtual Reality (VR) clearly potentially has some practical and valuable applications in hospitality and tourism, and the features of the travel and tourism product lend themselves to VR (Cheong, 1995). Hotels and other hospitality and leisure products are often chosen by customers who may never have seen the establishment, and realistic representations will help the customer make an informed choice. The customer's lack of knowledge of the product gives rise to anxiety on the part of the customer about the purchase which suppliers need to do their best to alleviate, a process in which various forms of information, such as brand image and brochures, for example, play their part. It is thought that the more realistic the visual representation of the product available to the customer, the less anxiety the customer will experience in choosing it. Attractions can use Virtual Reality in another way. Illustrating, for example, historical events associated with the venue without the paraphernalia of a film set would be a cost-effective way of adding to the pleasurable experiences of the consumer once he or she got there. Patrick Horan and Ciaran McDonnell, of Dublin Institute of Technology, provide a typical descriptive paper (Horan and McDonnell, 1996). Patrick Horan has continued his work on VR at Dublin Institute of Technology; also working there on VR for tourism on the World Wide Web (WWW) is Hugh McAtamney (McDonnell, personal communication with the authors). Williams and Hobson (1995) and Jacobson (1995) also discuss this subject.

Artificial Intelligence

A question of continuing interest to hospitality academics with an interest in technology is the prospect of applying Artificial Intelligence. Sunderland and O'Connor (1995), for example, describe the use of an expert system for decision support in marketing contexts for use in the Irish hospitality industry. Sanchez *et al.* (1995) describe the use of an expert system for use in food-service to forecast what has to be produced. They conclude that expert systems can be used in food service to assist both experts and non-experts.

Intelligent agents are artificial intelligences which can interface between, for instance, the consumer and a large source of data (for example the WWW) to assist in the search for, say, a holiday or a hotel. Ng and Sussmann (1996: 1), for example, describe an intelligent agent as

> a computer system that tries to fulfil its goals in a complex, dynamic environment. It is situated in the environment and interacts with the user in an autonomous manner. It operates adaptively and becomes more experienced over time in achieving its goals.

Faria Ng's work at Surrey University is ongoing. Ng and Sussmann (1996), Lenz (1996) and Steiner (1997) describe intelligent agents which help in the selection of tourism and travel products. Erni and Norrie (1997) describe an intelligent agent which provides information on the latest weather conditions to regular users such as mountain guides. Cho, Sumichrast and Olsen (1996) describe an intelligent agent application which supports or substitutes for the role of the concierge—that of advising hotel guests about nearby attractions, theatres and restaurants.

Dorren and Frew (1996) describe research on intelligent agents, specific to the hospitality industry, planned at Napier University. Claire Dorren's research was ongoing in 1997, but had become subsumed into a broader project looking at the attitudes to, and use of, technology in the industry, in the areas of electronic reservations and communications systems, the role of megamalls, the role of information intermediaries and knowledge brokers within the new tourism distribution chain, and end-user perspectives (personal communication with the authors).

Digital cash

Although potentially of interest to the hotel industry, digital cash either as a card (electronic purse) or for electronic commerce (e-cash) has not raised so much interest yet. However, Sheel and Lefeva (1996) describe the experimental use of electronic purses at the 1996 summer Olympic Games at Atlanta and the Mondex trial in Swindon, UK.

Scepticism

An interesting and welcome innovation in academic papers has been a growing scepticism. As Peacock and Shaw (1996: 1) comment:

> Any writing on technological innovation in the hospitality industry carries with it a wealth of assumptions and implications. One common assumption is that technological progress is a force for the good: a pathway to higher profits and a more successful business. This assumption can be overt or implied ….

The authors illustrate, from the literature of vendors, the trade press and academia, the tendency to take the assumption of the value of more technology on trust, but suggest that 'there seems to be a declining faith in the all-embracing power of technological change' (1996: 5). They go on to say (1996: 6): 'Perhaps the way forward lies with a more critical and incremental process to technological innovation.'

In expressing this scepticism the authors are reflecting a lively debate which has been running, particularly in the US, about the so-called 'productivity paradox'. Stephen Roach (Senior Economist, Morgan Stanley, New York) has led the debate, pointing out that service industries have had the lion's share of IT investment, but have demonstrated little growth in productivity compared to manufacturing industry, where investment in IT has been much less (Roach, 1991). Landauer (1995) has also been an influential voice attacking the poor design of IT software which affects its usefulness and usability. Baker and Li (1996), in a study of IT investment in Taiwanese hotels, raise doubts about the benefits achieved by IT investment. David, Grabski and Kasavana (1996) also look at the productivity paradox in hotels. They found that in the US, using national statistics, productivity in the hospitality industry grew on average at 1.3% per annum from 1958 through 1990 but this period included a decrease of 2.8% from 1985 to 1990, figures consistent with the 'productivity paradox'. Their study found, however, that the nine respondents to their survey of hospitality Chief Finance Officers were on the whole satisfied with the contribution their IT made to productivity and other aspects of business performance. It might be argued that given the nature of the evidence the national statistics told a more likely tale.

This is another important area which needs some of the cross-disciplinary cutting-edge analysis referred to earlier. UK hotel productivity growth is as much of a disaster area as it is for the US industry, although in the UK productivity picked up from 1984 to 1987 before collapsing back to its 1979 value in 1990 (NEDO, 1992). As NEDO (1992: 59) showed, profitability is achieved only through 'an unsatisfactory combination of low productivity and low pay'. Despite the difficulties experienced by David, Grabski and Kasavana (1996), there is no substitute for measuring productivity; asking the managers about productivity improvement gets unconvincing answers, as Baker and Li's (1996) paper shows. There is room here for some comprehensive case studies with the assistance of economists and production engineers, perhaps.

To help keep researchers sceptical (a desirable quality), case studies of failures are of inestimable value. Sussmann and Baker's (1996) and Mutch's (1996) papers are discussions of this sort. Failures of publicly owned systems, at least in the UK, are easier to research (because private sector failures are rarely allowed to emerge). This makes it all the more important that, if given the opportunity to research a case study of an IT failure, researchers grab the opportunity eagerly. We learn much more from a single failure, properly analysed, than from dozens of success stories.

Conclusions and future research directions

Where do there seem to be gaps in the body of research? At various stages in the discussion above we have made suggestions as to where it seems to us that more research would be of particular advantage. These are in areas where there is work done already but more would be a good idea. What about where there seem to be only a few papers? There seem to be only one or two obvious areas.

The first is on the implementation of IT systems. This is difficult to research because probably the most satisfactory method of research is a longitudinal study over an extended period. A carefully planned PhD research project (perhaps by a part-time student in industry) would be the most satisfactory research, given industrial co-operation. Implementation is where the deployment of change management is most crucial, and were it possible to follow more than one project the comparison would be likely to give rise to useful insights. Welch and Margerison (1997) review the issues and undertake some exploratory research based on a case study of a small group of 20 hotels.

The second area is that of Business Process Re-engineering (BPR). There have been large numbers of academic papers (one estimate is 5000 and rising) but practically none featuring hospitality. Amongst the few examples are Nebel, Rutherford and Schaffer (1994) and Baker and Sussmann (1996). Michael Baker and Silvia Sussmann, at Surrey University, are planning to launch a programme of research on this subject, and have some interesting early results. Initial studies suggest that the key to success lies in the quality of the management of the change process, with the contribution of IT being of secondary importance whose exact extent depends very much on the individual context.

The third area is the linkage between IT and strategy. Amongst the few who have tackled this subject is Paul Gamble (1991, 1994). Gamble tends to the polemic. Cho (1997) makes a contribution by considering the relevance of a resource-based view (RBV) of the hospitality firm. Connolly, Cho and Di Martino (1997) look at the task of monitoring the firm's performance in the context of the information age. Again, the need is for case studies to discover just how IT strategy is really made in the industry. Such studies would of course require the active co-operation of firms in the industry, who would need to feel confident in the researchers before they would reveal much of their strategy-making process. It goes without saying that these conditions make it difficult to mount such research.

Other areas which, as Peter O'Connor points out, have had little attention are technology planning, needs analysis and cost–benefit analysis (O'Connor, personal correspondence with the authors).

In general, what changes, if any, can be identified in hospitality IT management research? Claire Dorren (personal communication with the authors) observes that one current shift is from information storage to knowledge management. Another is the continued shift to consumer pull; i.e. the effect of IT on the strategic balance down the supply chain is shifting power further into the hands of the consumer. We would point out, however, that Reinders and Baker (1997), whilst agreeing with this, do not think the shift will be as remarkable as the increase of the bargaining power of the suppliers (including hotels) at the expense of the other players in the supply chain. However, we would agree with Dorren that this is an exciting area where big changes can be expected, and academics need to be there to chart them.

Other observable shifts, already mentioned, are the growth of scepticism about the value of IT and, correspondingly, the interest in what factors affect successful implementations; the use of the WWW as a marketing and distribution medium, and the question of whether this allows the smaller firms to gain comparatively over the larger chains; the influence of IT on relationships both between management and employees and between both of these groups and the customer; and how to manage these relationships in the context of an increasing emphasis on quality of service.

Acknowledgement

The authors would like to thank all those colleagues, in particular Peter O'Connor and Andy Frew, who offered suggestions and made comments on earlier drafts. We appreciate their help.

References

Alvarez, R., Ferguson, D. and Dunne, J. (1983) How not to automate your front office, *Cornell Hotel and Restaurant Administration Quarterly*, **24** (3), 56–62.

Archdale, G. (1992) Destination databases, *Proceedings of the 1992 PATA Destination Database Conference*, Singapore, 10–12 December.

Au, N. and Yung, J.K.F. (1995) The contribution of information technology (IT) to service quality: a quality function deployment (QFD) approach, *Proceedings of the Hospitality Information Technology Association World-wide Conference*, New Orleans, Louisiana, 24–26 June.

Baker, M.G. and Li, B. (1996) A little of what you fancy does you good? Does IT make a positive contribution to the hospitality industry?, *Proceedings of the Hospitality Information Technology Association World-wide Conference*, Edinburgh, 18–20 May.

Baker, M.G. and Sussmann, S. (1996) The ugly genie: lessons on business process re-engineering from the hospitality industry, *Proceedings, IAHMS Conference*, Leeuwarden, 6–8 November.

Baker, M.G., Sussmann, S. and Hazelden, C. (1996) Can destination management systems provide competitive advantage? A discussion of the factors affecting the survival and success of destination management systems, *Progress in Tourism and Hospitality Research*, **2** (1), 1–13.

Beaver, A. (1992) Hotel CRS—an over view, *Tourism Management*, March, 15–21.

Bennett, M. and Brown, S. (1996) An empirical study of computer usage in owner managed hotels: how can optimal benefit be achieved?, *Proceedings of the Hospitality Information Technology Association World-wide Conference*, Edinburgh, 18–20 May.

Bowen, J.T. (1996) Managing environmental change: insights from researchers and practitioners, *International Journal of Contemporary Hospitality Management*, **8** (7), 75–90.

Buhalis, D. (1993) Regional integrated computer information reservation management systems as a strategic tool for the small and medium tourism enterprises, *Tourism Management*, **14** (5), 366–378.

Buhalis, D. and Main, H. (1996) Information technology in small/independent Welsh and Aegean hotels, *Proceedings of the Hospitality Information Technology Association World-wide Conference*, Edinburgh, 18–20 May.

Buhalis, D. and Main, H. (1997) Catalysts in introducing information technology in small and medium sized hospitality organisations, in Tjoa, A.M. (ed.) *Information and Communication Technologies in Tourism, 1997, Proceedings of the International Conference in Edinburgh, Scotland*, Springer Wein, New York, pp. 275–285.

Byerley, P. (1996) SAM: past, present and future, paper presented at the *Marketing Travel over the Information Highway: the SAM Opportunity* conference, Edinburgh, 20–21 May.

Cheong, R. (1995) The virtual threat to travel and tourism, *Tourism Management*, **16** (6), 417–422.

Chervenak, L. (1993) Hotel technology at the start of the new millenium, *Hospitality Research Journal*, **17** (1), 113–120.

Cho, W. (1997) A case study: creating and sustaining competitive advantage through an IT application in the lodging industry, *Proceedings of the Hospitality Information Technology Association World-wide Conference*, Las Vegas, Nevada, 1–4 June.

Cho, W. and Connolly, D.J. (1996) The impact of information technology as an enabler on the hospitality industry, *International Journal of Contemporary Hospitality Management*, **8** (1), 33–35.

Cho, W., Sumichrast, R.T. and Olsen, M.D. (1996) Expert-system technology for hotels: concierge application, *Cornell Hotel and Restaurant Administration Quarterly*, February, 54–60.

Collins, G. (1990) Automating properties: understanding the human element, *Cornell Hotel and Restaurant Administration Quarterly*, August, 65–70.

Collins, G. and Malik, T. (1994) *Hospitality Information Technology—Learning How to Use It*, Kendall Hunt Publications, USA.

Connolly, D.J., Cho, W. and Di Martino, M.B. (1997) Developing a performance measurement framework, *Proceedings of the Hospitality Information Technology Association World-wide Conference*, Las Vegas, Nevada, 1–4 June.

Crichton, E. and Edgar, D. (1995) Managing complexity for competitive advantage: an IT perspective, *International Journal of Contemporary Hospitality Management*, **7** (2/3), 12–18.

David, J.S., Grabski, S. and Kasavana, M. (1996) The productivity paradox of hotel-industry technology, *Cornell Hotel and Restaurant Administration Quarterly*, April, 64–70.

Dorren, C. and Frew, A.J. (1996) Intelligent Agents and the UK hotel sector, *Proceedings of the Hospitality Information Technology Association World-wide Conference*, Edinburgh, 18–20 May.

Durocher, J.F. and Niman, N.B. (1993) Information technology: management effectiveness and guest services, *Hospitality Research Journal*, **17** (1), 121–131.

Emmet, R.M., Tauck, C., Wilkinson, S. and Moore, R.G. (1993) Marketing hotels: using global distribution systems, *Cornell Hotel and Restaurant Administration Quarterly*, **34** (6), December, 80–89.

Erni, A. and Norrie, M.C. (1997) SnowNet: an agent-based Internet tourist information service, in Tjoa, A.M. (ed.) *Information and Communication Technologies in Tourism, 1997, Proceedings of the International Conference in Edinburgh, Scotland*, Springer Wein, New York, pp. 29–37.

Frew, A.J., Crichton, E.K. and McKenzie, G. (1995) Multi-media marketing across ATM broadband networks: a hospitality and tourism perspective, Part 2: Global DMS?, *Proceedings of the Hospitality Information Technology Association World-wide Conference*, New Orleans, Louisiana, 24–26 June.

Frew, A.J. and Dorren, C. (1997) A qualitative analysis of hotel list providers on the World Wide Web, in Tjoa, A.M. (ed.) *Information and Communication Technologies in Tourism, 1997, Proceedings of the International Conference in Edinburgh, Scotland*, Springer Wein, New York.

Frew, A.J. and Pringle, S.M. (1995) Multi-media marketing across ATM broadband networks: a hospitality and tourism perspective, Part 1: UK hotels—reservation and distribution, *Proceedings of the Hospitality Information Technology Association World-wide Conference*, New Orleans, Louisiana, 24–26 June.

Gamble, P.R. (1988) Attitudes to computers by managers in the hotel industry, *Behaviour and Information Technology*, **7** (3) 305–321.

Gamble, P.R. (1991) An information technology strategy for the hospitality industry of the 1990s, *International Journal of Contemporary Hospitality Management*, **3** (1), 10–15.

Gamble, P.R. (1994) Strategic issues for the management of information services from the tourism to the hospitality industry—lessons for the future, *Progress in Tourism, Recreation and Hospitality Management*, **5**, 273–288.

Go, F.M. (1992) The role of computerised reservation systems in the hospitality industry, *Tourism Management*, March, 22–26.

Go, F.M. and Williams, A.P. (1993) Competing and co-operating in the changing tourism channel system, *Journal of Travel and Tourism Marketing*, **2** (2/3), 229–248.

Graham, A. and Lambert, C. (1995) Computer-aided instruction for maintaining dining room standards, *Proceedings of the Hospitality Information Technology Association World-wide Conference*, New Orleans, Louisiana, 24–26 June.

Horan, P. and McDonnell, C. (1996) An application of desktop virtual reality to the hospitality industry, *Proceedings of the Hospitality Information Technology Association World-wide Conference*, Edinburgh, 18–20 May.

Ingold, A.S., Huyton, J. and Yeoman, I. (1997) Yield management: a hospitality perspective, *International Journal of Contemporary Hospitality Management*, **9** (2), 48–49.

Ingram, H. (1996) Clusters and gaps in hospitality and tourism academic research, *International Journal of Contemporary Hospitality Management*, **8** (7), 91–95.

Jacobson, L. (1995) Mind over matter, *Tourism Management*, **16** (6), September, 417–422.

Kasavana, M.L. (1994a) Computers and multi-unit food-service operations, *Cornell Hotel and Restaurant Administration Quarterly*, **35** (3), June, 72–80.

Kasavana, M.L. (1994b) Telecommunications: dialling a better bottom line, *Cornell Hotel and Restaurant Administration Quarterly*, **35** (4), August, 23–31.

Kasavana, M.L. (1995) PC-based registers: the next generation of point-of-sale technology, *Cornell Hotel and Restaurant Administration Quarterly*, **36** (2), April, 50–55.

Kasavana, M. (1997) *Managing Computers in the Hospitality Industry*, 3rd ed., Educational Institute of the Hotel Motel Association, USA.

Kasavana, M.L. and David, J.S. (1993) Making computers 'people-literate', *Cornell Hotel and Restaurant Administration Quarterly*, **34** (2), April, 69–76.

Landauer, T.K. (1995) *The Trouble with Computers*, MIT Press, Cambridge, MA.

Lenz, M. (1996) IMTAS: Intelligent multimedia travel agent system, in Klein, S., Schmid, B., Tjoa, A.M. and Werthner, H. (eds) *Information and Communication Technologies in Tourism, Proceedings of the International Conference in Innsbruck*, Austria, Springer Wein, New York, pp. 11–17.

Lindsay, P. (1992) CRS supply and demand, *Tourism Management*, **13** (1), March, 11–14.

Maartmann-Moe, E., Byerley, P. and Guinano, R. (1994) The TIM project: tourism information and marketing, in Schertler, W., Schmid, B., Tjoa, A. and Werthner, H. (eds) *Information and Communication Technologies in Tourism, Conference Proceedings, ENTER 94*, Innsbruck, 12–14 January, Springer-Verlag, Vienna, pp. 35–42.

Main, H. (1995a) Information technology and the independent hotel—failing to make the connection, *International Journal of Contemporary Hospitality Management*, **7** (6), 30–32.

Main, H. (1995b) Independents need more of IT, *Hospitality*, April/May, 27.

Main, H. and Ingold, A. (1997) The use of marketing information systems in the hospitality industry (UK)—with particular reference to small and medium sized hospitality enterprises (SMHEs), *Proceedings of the Hospitality Information Technology Association World-wide Conference* Las Vegas, Nevada, June 1–4.

Marcussen, C.H. (1996) Hotel representation companies and the Internet, *Proceedings of the Hospitality Information Technology Association World-wide Conference*, Edinburgh, 18–20 May.

Marcussen, C.H. (1997) Electronic distribution of holiday and business hotels, in Tjoa, A.M. (ed.) *Information and Communication Technologies in Tourism, 1997, Proceedings of the International Conference in Edinburgh, Scotland*, Springer Wein, New York, pp. 190–198.

Moore, R.G. and Wilkinson, S. (1993) Communications technology, *Hospitality Research Journal*, **17** (1), 133–144.

Murphy, J., Forrest, E. and Wotring, C.E. (1996a) Restaurant marketing on the World-wide Web, *Cornell Hotel and Restaurant Administration Quarterly*, February, 61–71.

Murphy, J., Forrest, E. and Wotring, C.E. (1996b) Hotel management and marketing on the Internet, *Cornell Hotel and Restaurant Administration Quarterly*, June, 71–82.

Mutch, A. (1996) The English tourist network automation project: a case study in interorganisational system failure, *Tourism Management*, **17** (8) 603–609.

Nebel III, E.C., Rutherford, D. and Schaffer, J. (1994) Re-engineering the hotel organisation, *Cornell Hotel and Restaurant Administration Quarterly*, October, 88–95.

NEDO, 1992, *UK Tourism: Competing for Growth*, report by the National Economic Development Council's Working Party in Competitiveness in Tourism and Leisure, NEDO, London.

Ng, F.Y.Y. and Sussmann, S. (1996) A personal travel assistant for holiday selection—a learning interface agent approach, in Klein, S., Schmid, B., Tjoa, A.M. and Werthner, H. (eds) *Information and Communication Technologies in Tourism, Proceedings of the International Conference in Innsbruck, Austria*, Springer Wein, New York, pp. 1–10.

O'Connor, P. (1991) *The use of micro-computer based application generators in the design of management information systems for the Irish hotel and catering industry*, Masters Degree Thesis, University of Dublin.

O'Connor, P. (1996a) *Using Computers in Hospitality*, Cassell, New York.

O'Connor, P. (1996b) An analysis of the use of information technology in the Irish hotel industry, *Proceedings of the Hospitality Information Technology Association World-wide Conference*, Edinburgh, 18–20 May.

O'Connor, P. and Rafferty, J. (1997) Gulliver—lessons in distributing small hotels electronically, *Proceedings of the Hospitality Information Technology Association World-wide Conference*, Las Vegas, Nevada, 14 June.

Oppermann, M. and Brewer, K.P. (1995) Location decision making in hospitality using geographic information systems, *Proceedings of the Hospitality Information Technology Association World-wide Conference*, New Orleans, Louisiana, 24–26 June.

Palmer, J., Kasavana, M.L. and McPherson, R. (1993) Creating a technological circle of service, *Cornell Hotel and Restaurant Administration Quarterly*, **34** (1), February, 81–87.

Peacock, M. (1995) *Information Technology in the Hospitality Industry: Managing People, Change and Computers*, Cassell, New York.

Peacock, M. and Shaw, H. (1996) Bytes and bias: technophilia in technology writing. *Proceedings of the Hospitality Information Technology Association World-wide Conference*, Edinburgh, 18–20 May.

Poon, A. (1993) *Tourism, Technology and Competitive Strategies*, CAB International, Wallingford.

Poorani, A.A. (1995) A cost–benefit analysis of electronic data interchange (EDI), *Proceedings of the Hospitality Information Technology Association World-wide Conference*, New Orleans, Louisiana, 24–26 June.

Reinders, J. and Baker, M. (1997) The future for direct retailing of travel and tourism products: the influence of information technology, in Tjoa, A.M. (ed.) *Information and Communication Technologies in Tourism, 1997, Proceedings of the International Conference in Edinburgh, Scotland*, SpringerWein, New York, pp. 119–128.

Roach, S. (1991) Services under siege—the restructuring imperative, *Harvard Business Review*, **69** (5), September–October, 82–92.

Sanchez, N.C., Miller, J.L., Sanchez, A. and Brooks, B.L. (1995) Applying expert systems technology to the implementation of a forecasting model in food-service, *Hospitality Research Journal*, **18** (3)/**19** (1), 25–37.

Sheel, A. and Lefever, M.M. (1996) The implications of digital cash for hotels and restaurants, *Cornell Hotel and Restaurant Administration Quarterly*, December, 92–96.

Sheldon, P.J. (1993) Destination information systems, *Annals of Tourism Research*, **20** (4), 633–649.

Sheldon, P.J. (1997) *Tourism Information Technology*, CAB International, Wallingford.

Shribet, M., Muller, C. and Inman, C. (1995) Population changes and restaurant success, *Cornell Hotel and Restaurant Administration Quarterly*, **36** (3), June, 43–49.

Steiner, T. (1997) Distributed software agents for WWW-based tourism information systems (DATIS), in Tjoa, A.M., (ed.) *Information and Communication Technologies in Tourism, 1997, Proceedings of the International Conference in Edinburgh, Scotland*, Springer Wein, New York, pp. 39–46.

Sunderland, E. and O'Connor, P. (1995) The development of an expert system based marketing information system specific for the hospitality industry in Ireland, *Proceedings of the Hospitality Information Technology Association World-wide Conference*, New Orleans, Louisiana, 24–26 June.

Sussmann, S. (1994) The impact of new technological developments on destination management systems, *Progress in Tourism, Recreation and Hospitality Management*, **5**, 289–296.

Sussmann, S. and Baker, M.G. (1996) Responding to the electronic marketplace: lessons from destination management systems, *International Journal of Hospitality Management*, **15**, (2), 99–111.

Van Hoof, H.B., Collins, G.R, Combrink, T.E. and Verbeeten, M.J. (1995) Technology needs and perceptions—an assessment of the US lodging industry, *Cornell Hotel and Restaurant Administration Quarterly*, October, 64–69.

Van Hoof, H.B., Verbeeten, M.J. and Combrink, T.E. (1996) Information technology revisited: international lodging-industry needs and perceptions: a comparative study, *Cornell Hotel and Restaurant Administration Quarterly*, December, 86–91.

Watkins, E. (1992) The power of lodging technology, *Lodging Hospitality*, June, 38–40.

Welch, S.J. (1995) Room bookings via global distribution systems—the European dimension, *Proceedings of the Hospitality Information Technology Association World-wide Conference*, New Orleans, Louisiana, June 24–26.

Welch, S.J. and Margerison, J.P. (1997) An exploration of some models for systems implementation and operation in hotel groups—the case of a small UK hotel group, *Proceedings of the*

Hospitality Information Technology Association World-wide Conference, Las Vegas, Nevada, 1–4 June.

Whitaker, M. (1986) The diffusion of information technology across the hotel and catering industry (UK), *International Journal of Hospitality Management*, **5** (2), 95–96.

Whitaker, M. (1987) Overcoming the barriers to successful implementation of information technology in the hotel industry, *International Journal of Hospitality Management*, **6** (4), 225–228.

Williams, P. and Hobson, J.S.P. (1995) Virtual reality and tourism: fact or fantasy?, *Tourism Management*, **16** (6) September, 423–427.

21   Hotel operations management

ANDREW LOCKWOOD AND HAYDN INGRAM

Introduction

The aim of this chapter is to investigate the scope and dimensions of research into hotel operations, an important but somewhat neglected area of study. One difficulty in conducting a review of this nature is to identify the boundaries that determine the extent of hotel operations management. It would seem straightforward to place this review in the context of work in the wider field of operations management. Johnston (1994: 22) defines operations management as 'a body of knowledge, experience and techniques covering such topics as process design, layout, production planning, inventory control, quality management and control, capacity planning and workforce management'. Therefore, operations management is concerned with the design, operation and improvement of the processes that transform inputs into outputs, that is those processes that create the firm's primary products and services. This management function starts at the very top of the firm as part of the overall corporate strategy and proceeds through tactical levels to a concern with the day-to-day operation and the operating technology that underlies it. In the hospitality context, this conceptual framework has been explored further by Jones and Lockwood (1995) and will inform some of the discussion later in this chapter.

By its very nature, the hotel industry is fragmentary and heterogeneous where research effort is expended for very different reasons and with diverse agendas. When this is combined with the complex and diverse nature of the hotel operation itself, the prospects for a coherent approach to research are highly problematic. This chapter attempts to explore the problems facing hotel operations research, the sources of hotel research and then to discern patterns in the content of published research.

Influences on hotel operations research

The influence diagram shown in Figure 21.1 draws on a wide range of literature, from both the service operations field and the industry-specific, to identify the factors that make research in hotel operations problematic for researchers, and may partly explain why research in this area, which is fundamental to the success of hotels, is not as well developed as might be expected.

The diagram identifies three key drivers that make hotel operations research problematic. These are the complexity of hotel operations, their immediacy, and the structure of the hotel industry. These are discussed in the following paragraphs

The Handbook of Contemporary Hospitality Management Research, Edited by Bob Brotherton.
© 1999 John Wiley & Sons Ltd.

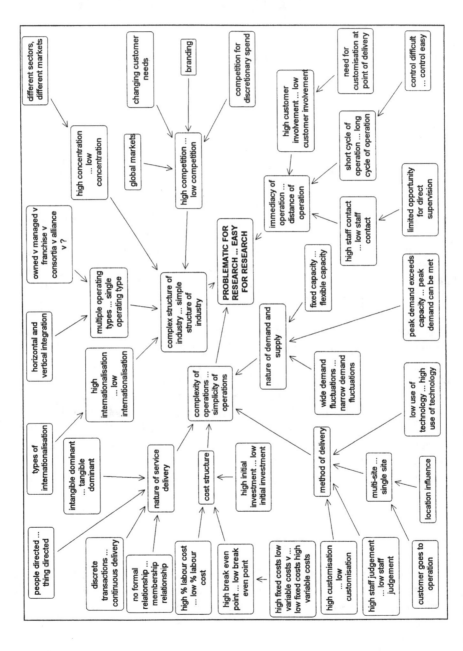

Figure 21.1 Influences on hotel operations research

The complexity of operations.   Hotel operations offer a wide range of products and services over a wide time range, potentially for 24 hours a day and 365 days a year. This in itself is a complex enough task, but it is made even more complex by the nature of demand and supply, the cost structure and the nature and method of service delivery. Hotels see wide fluctuations in demand that they need to cater for but, due to the fixed nature of hotel capacity, at peak times demand will exceed supply and potential revenue will be lost. This would be less significant if the cost structure of the operation, brought about partly by the high cost of the initial investment in the fabric of the building and the high labour cost element, leading to high fixed costs and low variable costs, did not mean that hotels need to reach a high break-even point before moving into profit. Service delivery in hotels consists of a large number of discrete transactions aimed at customers who have no membership relationship with the organisation. These customers expect a level of personal attention, which tends to make the intangible aspects of the operation more important than the tangible. At the same time, hotels offer a degree of customisation in their offer, requiring some judgement on the part of the staff who receive only limited support from the use of technology. Hotel chains have to provide this service over a number of locations with their own particular influences on operations and must endeavour to attract customers to these diverse locations.

The immediacy of operations.   Hotel operations have a short cycle. Guests often stay for only one night and the turnround time for a bedroom can be as little as 20–30 minutes. The check-in time at reception may be a matter of only a few minutes. This allows little time for controlling the standard of delivery. This is exacerbated by the high staff involvement in the interaction that gives limited opportunity for direct supervision again complicated by the customer's involvement, which may require the customisation of the service at the very point and time of delivery.

The structure of the hotel industry.   The hotel industry consists of large numbers of small operators with only a comparatively small number of chains giving relatively low industry concentration. These chains, however, have a comparatively high influence on the direction of the industry. The industry is increasingly competitive, facing a continuing battle for the customer's discretionary spending, and with an increasingly sophisticated customer with changing needs who looks to the global marketplace and the dominance of brand names as indicators of operating standards. The nature of chain operations themselves, where multiple operating types occur within the same portfolio and increasing internationalisation, brings its own complexity to an already highly fragmented picture.

The picture painted here is one of growing complexity in hotel operations, which makes the task of the researcher that much more difficult, having to take account of an increasingly diverse and conceptually complicated set of variables. At the same time, it is this inherent complexity that makes hotel operations such an exciting and rewarding area of study.

Who conducts research on hotels?

Given the scale and diversity of the hotel industry, it is not surprising that many different stakeholders are involved in hotel operations research. Research in this area may be conducted by industry or academia (Table 21.1).

Industry research

Individuals and firms   In the main, the aim of research conducted by commercial organisations is increased understanding of their operation and operating environment that will provide commercial advantage. Inevitably, there is a degree of secrecy in this type of research to avoid it falling into the hands of competitors, so it is generally produced for internal use only. Research of this type is often concerned with environmental scanning; that is the process by which organisations analyse the trends and patterns relating to their business environment (Costa, 1995). Research evidence suggests that international hotel companies are not systematic in their approach to environmental scanning and use a narrow range of secondary sources to gather information (Olsen, Murthy and Teare, 1994). Nevertheless, a survey of 200 hotels and restaurants in the USA concluded that most of the companies exert at least moderate efforts to keep abreast of academic research (Breymer, Rouselle and Johns, 1990).

Consultants   Greater understanding of emerging trends and trade patterns is provided by the general reports and surveys provided by specialist industry consultants. For example, greater market segmentation of hotels was remarked upon by Pannell Kerr Forster (1990) and this can perhaps be linked to the superior performance of larger hotel companies (Kleinwort Benson, 1994).

Many firms use consultants to investigate problems inside their organisations or to give an objective view of the future. This trend may be increasing as more large hotel

Table 21.1   The source and outcomes of research on hotels

Source	Typical outputs
Industry research	
Individuals (sole traders)	Business plans, marketing strategies, financial forecasts
Firms	Reports/evaluations of potential changes, such as the effects of new systems, units development plans, competitive analysis
Associations and consultants	Professional bodies (e.g. HCIMA, HtF) producing reports for industry use. Consultants preparing either general or commissioned studies
Academic research	
Academic institutions	Individual researchers (often studying for an academic award) or groups of researchers who access the body of literature as a basis for further study. Some undertake primary research with hotels
Published research	Books, journals, trade magazines which may be aimed at practitioners or academics. Academic theses/dissertations, conference proceedings

firms reduce the size of their head office and outsource specialist head office functions. Some consultants prepare analytical reports for general trade consumption. One example of this is a report prepared by Pannell Kerr Forster (1990) which contrasted comparable pairs of hotels in 10 different European cities. The findings suggested that successful hotels were those that applied managerial and cost control techniques consistently over every part of their operation.

Associations   Associations in the hospitality industry, which conduct research, include the Hotel and Catering International Management Association (HCIMA) and the British Hospitality Association (BHA). Many of the reports they produced in the period 1990 to 1995 addressed employee availability, remuneration and expectations. The importance of labour costs to hotel operations is reflected in reports by both the BHA (*Wages and Salaries in Hotels*, 1990, 1991) and the HCIMA (*Pay and Benefits*, 1990, 1993).

Academic research

In contrast to industry-based research, academic research is more open to the public and relies upon information that is incrementally developed. Academic researchers rely on secondary sources of literature already in the public domain on which to ground their assertions and build upon the body of knowledge. As academic researchers tend to work individually or in small research groups, their work becomes known only when they publish findings such as theses/dissertations, journal articles or book chapters, and even these tend to have a narrow audience principally composed of other academics. As so much academic research is long-term or conducted part-time by academics, these results often take years to become widely available. Recently, a central resource of completed and ongoing research into hospitality and tourism has been set up called WHATT-CD (Worldwide Hospitality and Tourism Trends) which enables researchers to share the nature of their research with like-minded people. The Research Register is available twice yearly in compact disk form which enables users to search for information quickly using a range of filters. An analysis of the Spring 1995 edition revealed that there was a total of 820 entries, 84% of which represented postgraduate research as shown in Table 21.2.

Ingram (1996a) reviewed the content of these entries and identified five themes studied by hospitality researchers:

- *Emerging patterns*. These reflect increasing concern with issues such as health and safety and disability as well as environmental awareness and healthy eating.

Table 21.2   Sources of research register entries (Ingram, 1996a)

Category	Number	Percentage
Academic	689	84
Associations	23	3
Government	41	5
Industry	67	8
Total	820	100

Reproduced by permission MCB University Press.

- *Customers*. Many researchers reflected the increasing evidence of firms adopting market-oriented approaches.
- *Agencies*. Agencies represent organisations such as consultants, government agencies and professional trade bodies that advise and control the industry.
- *Information technology (IT)*. IT is a driver of change and its impacts and applications are a major source of interest to researchers.
- *Service and quality*. These critical issues were widely studied in the Research Register.

It will be recognised in the following section that these general themes of hospitality research are reflected in the more specific domain of hotel operations. It will also be recognised that not all the research studies being conducted are available in published sources such as the journal articles, reports and books that form the basis for the following analysis.

Themes in hotel operations research

In looking to review the range of published literature relating to hotel operations, a framework has been used, based on the combination of two established conceptual models. By using this framework, it is hoped that overlaps and gaps within the research will be able to be identified. The framework, as shown in Figure 21.2, draws on the key

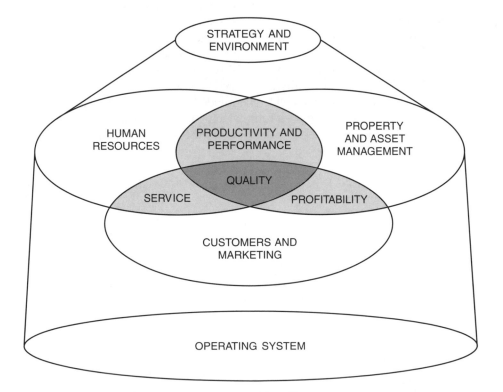

Figure 21.2   Themes in hotel operations and research

result areas model (Jones and Lockwood, 1989) which identified seven key areas or system outputs that operations managers in hotels should strive to achieve. This is combined with the systems hierarchy model drawn from Jones and Lockwood (1995) which added the strategic dimension and the operating system level to the framework.

The basis of the success of a hotel, of any size, is the determination of an effective strategy that involves long-term decisions of scope, positioning and product offering. The product offering must be made available to potential guests through marketing communication to specific customer segments. When guests arrive at the hotel, satisfaction and profitability are dependent upon operations processes (including accommodation operations, property management and service issues) and the managers and employees who deliver them. The cycle is completed when feedback from managers, staff and customers, particularly about the perceived quality and value of the offer, enables hotel strategy to be reviewed.

Strategy and business environment

Given the international scope of the hotel industry, it is not surprising that the topic of internationalisation should be a key focus for research. Litteljohn (1997) has shown a keen interest in this area over a number of years and provides an interesting insight into current developments as the introduction to a special issue of the *International Journal of Contemporary Hospitality Management* on trends in industry industrialisation. He identifies from his literature review a need for a new emphasis in internationalisation, particularly in the hotel sector as it faces a complex and fast-changing environment. The characteristics of these emerging global hotel companies are discussed by Gannon and Johnson (1995). Their research into 13 companies operating on 'five of the six economically viable continents' used an industry mapping technique based on Porter's five forces to identify groups of firms in the hotel industry following similar strategic direction. Their findings suggest groupings largely based on the companies' continent of domicile, finding a European group, an American group and an Asian group. These findings are reflected in a comparison of internationalisation in the retail and hotel sectors by Alexander and Lockwood (1996) which found strong historical differences between the strategies of European and American companies but a growing trend towards global or 'geocentric' organisations. The idea of centricity is explored by Roper *et al.* (1996) who provide an excellent literature and conceptual review as part of their ongoing investigation into international hotel groups. This investigation, using an interdisciplinary team, has already produced a number of significant outputs, for example Burgess *et al.* (1995) looking at approaches to defining the success of international companies, and Roper, Hampton and Brookes (1997) focusing on the cultural influences that impact on hotel groups.

A key decision for any hotel group concerns the most appropriate forms of business format, which again forms a clear focus for research. Business format can take a number of forms and the consequences of the choice have serious implications for the way the business will operate. Poorani and Smith (1994) explored the willingness of bed and breakfast owners in the US to become franchisees of established chains particularly to gain marketing and sales benefits. The result of the survey of a sample of 403 owners was not encouraging for the franchisors. The relationship between hotel franchisors and franchisees was also studied by Connell (1997) using grounded theory to analyse open-focus interviews with directors, managers and employees. A key factor identified here was the need for 'attunement' between the franchisor and franchisee as they come to understand each other and establish the balance between control and autonomy. This process also formed the focus for research by Gannon and Johnson (1997) who explored the nature of control and co-ordination across a range of business formats through a case study methodology of six international hotel groups. One way in which independent hotels hope to compete with hotel groups is to band together to form co-operative alliances or consortia. Research by Roper (1995) suggested, however, that consortia only partially achieved these aims and questioned their long-term survival.

A key consideration in any discussion of strategic direction must be the nature of the economic, industrial and competitive environments. Interest in environmental scanning has been reflected in a number of research studies, including Costa (1995), which despite the title offers no empirical data, Olsen, Murthy and Teare (1994) which provides the CEO's perspective, and Moutinho *et al.* (1995), who surveyed hotel managers in three European countries to examine their perceptions of the environmental factors likely to affect the industry. Phillips (1997) has explored the supply and demand factors affecting the UK hotel industry using a novel approach based on room nights rather than occupancy, which paints a bleak picture for the future. This reinforces the importance of his earlier work on strategic planning (Phillips, 1996) which identified a link between a clear and systematic approach to strategic planning and successful business performance. One factor in a systematic planning process is the provision of suitable information. This aspect was explored by Collier and Gregory (1995), who suggested that strategic management accounting, using programmes of budgeting, forward planning and analysis of market conditions, is a growing area of importance for hotels that is moving beyond the stage of infancy in the UK. The need for clear and appropriate data to assess the feasibility of hotel developments was explored by Szivas and Riley (1996) who questioned the role of financial data in the decision-making process and were particularly alarmed at the lack of impact analysis. Given that impact analysis has itself attracted research from a number of authors, notably Culligan (1995), Patel and Corgel (1995) and Roginsky (1995), this finding is all the more surprising.

Two final studies are worth reporting in this section. Callan and Fearon (1997) have identified the emergence of a new sector of hotel operations in the form of town house hotels and they provided a review of the size of the sector and its defining characteristics. This provides an interesting codification of industry practice through an academic perspective. In contrast, Hum (1997) took ideas from the academic study of strategic manufacturing operations and suggested that hotel industry practice can learn a number of lessons from that manufacturing experience.

Property and asset management

The large investment involved in and the high costs of maintenance and improvement of hotel property is a major concern for operational managers, not least because this affects the product offering and customer satisfaction. It would be expected, therefore, to be an area of keen research interest, but in fact there is comparatively little evidence of studies in this field. One area that has received attention recently is due to greater socio-cultural concern for the environment that has influenced hotels like the Botley Park to produce 'green' policies, particularly in energy conservation (McIntosh, 1991). Kirk has been at the forefront of this interest in the UK and, as well as his involvement with the HCIMA initiatives (HCIMA, 1995), his survey research (Kirk, 1995b) of hotels in Edinburgh identified the types of responses hotels were implementing and concluded that some hotels see significant benefits from adopting green policies. Brown (1996), however, was less positive about the implementation of environmental concerns and highlighted that, although there was evidence of green policies, these had not been considered at the strategic level and incorporated directly into hotel control systems or in measures of hotel manager performance. A conceptual model developed by Ayala (1995) took these issues one stage further and suggested that not only should individual hotels be involved in environmental issues, but maximum benefit will be derived from a whole-resort approach that would lead to the development of an integrated eco-resort product.

The needs for energy conservation must be built into the orginal design of a hotel to have the greatest impact. The design obviously also has a profound effect on the response of the customer. This is another area which seems of fundamental importance to hotel operations and yet has little published material. Research degrees in this field being conducted by Kemp (1995), linking customer behavioural responses to physical design features, and Saint-Claire (1994), suggesting a greater role for customers in hotel design evaluation, provide some hope for future publications.

Bach and Pizam (1996) used police records of hotel crime in Florida combined with hotel surveys of security techniques and devices to explore the approaches of hotels to security and customer safety. Although their results found only limited correlations between security and reduced levels of crime, the study highlighted an innovative way of investigating an increasingly serious concern for hotel customers. One particular group, older customers, were shown to be increasingly concerned about hotel security, according to a survey by Shortt and Ruys (1994). They identified such considerations as emergency telephones, good lighting and door chains as being important for this mature age group. Having good locks is not always a good thing, however, when, as electronic lock systems become more prevalent in hotels, Bigness (1996) suggested that lock failure can have serious implications in the case of a fire or guest illness. On another serious security issue, Hobson and Ko (1995) offer advice on ways for hotels to protect themselves and their customers against credit card fraud.

Human resources

This chapter sets out to review research in the field of hotel operations management and not human resource management, but the pivotal role of hotel employees in hotel operations encourages a considerable volume of research that cannot be ignored. The objective here, however, is to consider research that is most closely linked to operations, while a detailed review from the HRM perspective is dealt with in Chapter 19.

The role of the General Manager is seen to be a pivotal one in hotel operations and has attracted attention from a number of perspectives, including what general managers do, how they are developed and how their careers develop, their personality and leadership style, and factors affecting their success. Jauncey (1997) used a theoretical model of demands (things that must be done) and constraints (things that limit what can be done) for his PhD research of hotel managers' roles and concluded that the way these are combined influences the ability of an individual hotel general manager to do different work or to do work in a different way. The development of hotel managers was discussed somewhat critically by Guerrier and Lockwood (1989d) following case study research with a hotel chain. Hsu and Gregory (1995) used a survey instrument to identify the competencies needed by managers in Taiwan to form the basis of a hospitality management curriculum. Yu and Huat (1995) recognised that expatriate managers face particular difficulties when operating outside their own culture such as in China. This was also an issue considered by Yu and Pine (1995). The way that the careers of 114 US hotel general managers had progressed in the mid-range, up-scale and luxury sectors was investigated by Nebel, Lee and Vidakovic (1995) using a questionnaire survey. They found that the career paths of younger GMs had shifted towards operational departments, with food and beverage being the preferred option and 45% of GMs having followed this route. Maxwell (1997) used a very different methodology to explore the career paths of female general managers. Her work was based on in-depth interviews with four successful female GMs and highlighted both the positive and negative features encouraging their career success. Peacock (1995), however, found that identifying the success that could enhance a career was not a simple task and concluded that managers face a series of conflicting demands, where difficult choices have to be made and personal priorities may have to be changed. Coming from a psychological perspective, Worsfold (1989) found that effective hotel managers were more assertive, more venturesome and imaginative than other managers. This was reinforced by Stone (1988), using an almost identical methodology, who added that they were also calm, realistic, assertive, competitive, cheerful, bolder, independent, cynical, practical and had lower scholastic and mental capacity. Leadership qualities have also been the focus of work by Upchurch and Ruhland (1995) and Cichy and Schmidgall (1996) who concentrated on financial executives rather than GMs.

A key problem facing hotels is a shortage of labour. Guerrier and Lockwood (1990) used a comparison of labour shortages in England, Thailand, Cyprus and Hong Kong to identify key themes and possible solutions. Meier (1991) was also concerned with finding possible solutions, while Barrow (1991) tackled the problem from the perspective of labour turnover. An industry report by Blake Dawson Waldron and Arthur Anderson (1994) in Australia recommends greater labour flexibility and the establishment of a better-trained and committed workforce. Workforce flexibility has received considerable interest, particularly from Guerrier and Lockwood (1989a, 1989b, 1989c) following an ESRC research award. One issue that is often cited as a factor in labour shortfalls concerns the level of pay, and both the BHA and HCIMA conduct regular surveys of wages and salaries. Jones and Hall (1990) took a different angle and looked at whether hotel employment met the expectations of the unemployed in the Brighton area. In a similar vein Ross (1995) examined employee responses to stress and found higher job satisfaction in those employees with a cheerful and enthusiastic attitude to work, and that a reduction in employee stress would have a positive impact on customer perceptions. Similar relationships can be found in the work of Cannon (1991) and Lee-Ross and Johns (1995). The latter work in particular looked to evaluate the effectiveness of a particular measurement instrument applied to seasonal hotel workers. The effectiveness of personnel management and training could be expected to have an effect on employee satisfaction and yet little research in this area has been conducted. Notable exceptions are MacVicar and Brown (1994) who looked at the introduction of 'Investors in People' at the Moat House Glasgow as a case example, and Kelliher and Johnson (1997) who reported on an update of their earlier study of personnel management in hotels. They found evidence of a more sophisticated approach to personnel management being taken in large hotels, with its role being defined more broadly and emphasis being placed on employee relations and welfare. However, they found little evidence of a qualitative shift towards HRM or innovative human resource practice, but overall they were optimistic about the future.

Customers and marketing

A major preoccupation of researchers in this area is in attempting to identify the key attributes that will influence either the customers' choice of a hotel or their perceptions of it once chosen. Lewis (1985) provided a seminal influence in this field, mapping customer perceptions to provide an analysis of market positioning. However, it is Callan (1994, 1995a, 1995b, 1996, 1997) who has explored this area in the greatest detail. The first article reported here discussed the methodology for the creation of a framework to explore these characteristics using focus groups and in-depth interviews. Through this process he identified 166 attributes. His research then explored the particular attributes preferred by female customers (1995a), while a further study (1996) considered the difference in requirements of business and leisure customers. He then extended the work to include a comparison of customer attributes against hotel grading schemes (1995b). A complete review of this extensive work is planned and the first part, looking at hotel managers' perceptions of the importance of attributes, has already been published (1997). Importance of attributes was also the focus of consideration by Evans and Murriman (1989) who concentrated on personal care amenities. These items did not feature strongly in the data collected from 2712 travellers visiting information centres looking for accommodation (Greathouse et al., 1996). Factor analysis reduced the key variables to property basics (including cleanliness, friendliness and security), information (about the local area, attractions, road conditions, etc.), food and beverage (including the availability of room service) and amenities (such as cable TV and swimming pool) in rank order of importance. Kim (1996) combined factor analysis and multidimensional scaling to identify the features that customers look for in hotel food and beverage operations and to map a sample of Korean hotels and their competitive positioning. Research by Buttle and Bok (1996) also used factor analysis to relate the way that international business travellers select hotel rooms to the theory of reasoned action, concluding that the behavioural intentions of this market segment are more related to their attitudes about the satisfaction they derived from the hotel experience, and in particular the interactive quality of the guest experience, than the opinions of significant influencers. Guest satisfaction in hotels is relatively unexplored with the notable exceptions of Engeset and Heide (1996) and Gundersen, Heide and Olsson (1996).

A topic of growing importance in the marketing field in general is that of relationship marketing and, although this has not quite reached the hotel sector yet, there are signs of its emergence with work by Durr (1989) on the value to be found in the guest register as a customer database, using the Holiday Inn priority club as a case example.

This is a topic picked up by Sparks (1993) who questioned the extent to which guest history was being used in Australia and suggested that such information, accompanied with suitable training, could be a progressive step in building customer loyalty. This in turn has been taken up by Sumner and Sellars (1997) who reported on the added value that computer systems can bring to developing the usefulness of the guest history. There is also some evidence (EIU, 1995) that frequent-stay programmes, which can generate incremental income and enable a detailed database on the most valuable guests, arc appearing in the accommodation sector in a similar way to frequent-flier programmes in airlines.

There is comparatively little interest shown in the channels of distribution open to hotels. McGuffie (1990) reported on the development of computerised reservation systems and their effects on the hotel sector. Ayala (1993) identified the potential benefits of hotels forming networks to capitalise on the growing trend of hotel 'circuits' or multiple destination leisure tourism. Morrison (1995) also stresses the importance of networking in her excellent research with small UK hotels and marketing channel management. Her work was based on a detailed examination of the processes at work within a hotel consortium and provides some fascinating insights.

Profitability and yield management

As the major source of revenue and profit in most hotels derives from the provision of accommodation, the management of that function is an important activity that attracts considerable research interest, especially looking at the area of yield management. This one topic alone has probably attracted more research interest than any other. The work in this area can be divided into a number of types. First, there are a group of studies concerned with defining and clarifying the concept of yield management. These include Brotherton and Mooney (1992), IHA (1993), Lieberman (1993), Donaghy, McMahon and McDowell (1995), Donaghy (1996), and Jauncey, Mitchell and Slamet (1995). These articles usually, but not exclusively, adopt a conceptual approach and attempt to place yield management, as derived from the airlines, firmly into the hotel context. They are concerned with the definition of terms and the identification and isolation of key features—eight for Jauncey, Mitchell and Slamet (1995) but 10 for Donaghy, McMahon and McDowell (1995). This work forms a firm base upon which other researchers can build.

One way of extending understanding of the topic is to explore case studies of yield management in practice. Bradley and Ingold (1993), for example, examined the use of yield management in 11 hotels in Birmingham city centre. They found that, at this time, although all the hotels were either three or four star and part of chains, only three managers had heard of yield management and only one was using a yield management system. By the time Donaghy, McMahon-Beattie and McDowell (1997) conducted their survey of 300 group hotels in the UK, they found that 33 hotels were making extensive use of yield techniques. Their follow-up in-depth interviews with eight of these hotels' managers provided some key insights into the way that yield management could be implemented effectively in hotel operations. The process of implementation in a single unit—the Hilton National Warwick—over a 12-month transitional period was described by Peters and Reilly (1997). Savkina and Yakovlev (1997) described how the cultural, social and economic conditions in Russia make the understanding and implementation of yield management a much more complex problem.

A further extension of yield management is concerned with exploring and understanding some of the constituent parts of the yield management problem more fully. Meidan and Chiu (1995) reported on a study of hotel reservation methods in English hotels. Having rated the importance of 22 reservation practices, they used discriminant analysis to establish that hotel managers' preferences for particular reservation practices varied according to the type of hotel and the hotel's reservation policy and objectives. A study of 33 hotels in four UK cities and their discounting practices (Halcro, 1996) showed a high level of discounting overall but substantially higher levels of discount offered to independent travellers than to corporate clients. The practice of establishing very expensive rack rates, which are never used, is seriously questioned. Knowledge of overall occupancy trends is important and is provided by the English Hotel Occupancy Survey conducted on behalf of the English Tourist Board by BDO Hospitality Consulting (1994). Using this sort of data to create accurate forecasts of hotel occupancy was explored by Andrew, Cranage and Lee (1990), and the way hospitality education was teaching forecasting on their courses was considered by Miller, Miller and Horsley (1993). Forecasting techniques are moving into the more mathematical territory of operations research, and yield management in hotels has attracted interest from this field, for example from Bitran and Mondschein (1995) and Bodily and Weatherford (1995).

Yield management is not just a mathematical procedure; it has serious implications for employees. Jones and Hamilton (1992) were the first to consider the human dimension in yield management. Surprisingly their identification of key strategic concerns is not referred to by MacVicar and Rodger (1996), in their study of the human resource implications of using computerised yield management systems, or by Yeoman and Watson (1997), in their very interesting use of a systems framework to analyse the yield management human activity system into its three component parts of the forecasting system, the people system and the strategy system.

Yield management is not a technique without its critics. Kimes (1994) suggested that yield management does not necessarily appear fair to customers who may be quoted different rates for the same room on different occasions, and questioned its long-term success. Huyton, Evans and Ingold (1997) were concerned with the moral and legal implications of YM practice and suggested that most could be overcome by timely discussions with customers. They warn, however, that ethical problems of this nature are never simple. Griffin (1995, 1996, 1997) has pursued the issue of the success of yield management over several studies and has been successful in isolating from extensive survey work the critical success factors of yield management systems.

A number of researchers have started to consider how yield management can be extended through additional information or into other areas of operation. Dunn and Brooks (1990) argued that hotel yield management approaches have the aim of maximising revenue, but fail to consider the costs associated with attracting that revenue. They proposed a model in which costs were allocated first according to the cost centre (for example rooms, banquet, marketing) and second in activity centres (e.g. reservations, housekeeping, check in/out). This enabled hotels to record accurately those expenses associated with bringing in revenue from specific market segments. Without reference to this earlier study, Noone and Griffin (1997) reported along exactly the same lines, arguing that costs and guests' ancillary spend should also be taken into the customer profitability analysis. They proposed that activity-based costing offered the optimal solution to cost allocation to facilitate this approach. McEvoy (1997) suggested a two-step matrix model that would allow a hotel group to evaluate the performance of management and the implementation of its yield management system. Based on operating and financial data, the first matrix rates the hotel's performance for efficiency and return to shareholders, while the second matrix brings in the issue of risk. Van Westering (1994) suggested that if yield management worked so effectively for the rooms department in hotels then it should also be extended to the food and beverage department and suggested some ways in which this could be achieved.

The research reported here on yield management highlights a key research dilemma. The area is sufficiently mature to have attracted many research studies, which have grown away from simple descriptions and conceptualisations and been developed through significant empirical work. This is to be welcomed. At the same time, however, there is evidence that not everyone is conducting sufficiently thorough literature searches and some work that has already been completed is being largely ignored and old ground revisited.

Productivity and performance

Achieving the optimum return from the heavy capital investment that hotel developments require depends to a significant extent on the overall productivity and performance of the hotel operation. In comparing a range of the key performance variables of highly profitable hotels against those of poorly performing ones, Van-Dyke and Olsen (1989) established that five variables showed a significant relationship with profit performance. These were occupancy rate, room sales as a percentage of total sales, rooms department labour cost, food cost percentage and property tax percentage. At the same time, they highlighted that it was the rooms department that was the primary generator of profit. Roberts and Shea (1996) followed a detailed methodology starting from Delphi technique, through surveys and factor analysis to identify the core competencies or capabilities that provide a competitive advantage for a hotel organisation. They identified two asset factors and five skill factors. The two asset factors were intangible assets, comprising reputation, loyalty of customers and employees, and employee commitment; and tangible assets, comprising brand, real estate, databases and computer systems. The five skill factors were human resource management, sales, architectural design, pricing and marketing planning. Yield management did not feature here as they suggested that it had become so widely accepted that it has become a basic competitive requirement and has ceased to offer competitive advantage. They suggested that future research should concentrate on how managers could use these core capabilities to generate superior organisational performance. Brotherton and Shaw (1996) were in similar territory with their study of the critical success factors in UK hotels, concentrating on those 'must achieve' factors that are crucially important to the competitive survival/success of a company. Despite a poor response to their corporate level survey, they received responses from 15 hotels to their unit-level questions. These questions were largely open format and were then analysed with a form of content analysis. In this way they identified critical success factors and their associated critical performance indicators for front office, guest accommodation, food and beverage service, food and beverage production, conference and banqueting, leisure operations, back of house, sales and marketing, accounting and control, and human resource management. The comprehensive list that this pilot study provides should form the basis for some interesting follow-up research.

Witt and Witt (1989) looked at the key characteristics of the hotel industry and suggested how these characteristics affected efforts to improve hotel productivity, which they identified had lagged behind the improvements in other industries. They believed that a major culture shift was necessary before managers would adopt the measurement-oriented attitudes and techniques needed to monitor productivity. Johns (1993) used a case study approach to explore in detail how design and operational features could influence the management of productivity. Despite these studies, productivity remains a concern for hotel operations, in no small measure due to the difficulty of definition and measurement. Messenger and Mugomeza (1995) reported on a study of 30 hotels in Zimbabwe, looking at their awareness of performance measures and the measurement techniques they used. Awareness of performance measurement was not high, and managers considered the most important measure to be the net profit percentage; financial ratios constituted 70% of all the ratios used. They concluded that hotels should adopt standard measures across the organisation and that a systematic approach to the gathering of information was critical. One systematic approach to data collection and analysis is offered by Johns, Howcroft and Drake (1997) who investigated the applicability of the data envelopment technique to hotel productivity measurement. In their study data envelopment analysis compared the efficiency of the 15 hotels in a small chain, based on the inputs they required and the outputs they achieved. They were impressed by the technique's effectiveness as a head office tool for monitoring the performance of individual units and by its ability to incorporate 'soft' data such as those from customer satisfaction questionnaires into comparisons. Taking account of both hard and soft variables also featured in the work of Brander-Brown and McDonnell (1995) who set out to evaluate the usefulness of the balanced scorecard, which is increasingly used in other industries. Their conclusions, based on a single hotel case study, suggested that the ability of the balanced scorecard to pull together a balance of information from a variety of perspectives offered hotel managers an important new tool.

Service and quality

One of the earliest published articles on quality assurance in hotels (Willborn, 1986) recognised the crucial importance of quality and set out to describe a model of the quality management cycle, starting with customer expectations and coming round to quality audits before restarting the cycle. This article quoted no previous publications looking at quality in any aspect of hospitality. Two years later, Walker (1988) still had no references to draw on but set out to assess the success of the American Hotel and Motel Association sponsored quality assurance programmes on profit, operations, guest and employee satisfaction. Although based on a small sample, the evidence suggested that across the range of variables, and in particular employee satisfaction and labour cost, hotels that had adopted a quality assurance approach had performed better. It might be thought that from this very positive beginning, research into quality in hotels would have blossomed. In fact, there is only a limited selection to choose from. One group of research has concentrated on drawing inferences from the way in which industry has gone about introducing quality management in their operations. The research undertaken by Lockwood, Baker and Ghillyer (1996) resulted in a book of 11 case histories being produced, of which six featured hotels. The survey of hotel managers by Harrington and Akehurst (1996) indicated that although respondents understood the benefits of establishing quality in their properties, they were unaware of how this could be achieved best and the likely problems they would encounter. A case study approach was adopted by Breiter, Tyink and Corey-Tuckwell (1995) who looked at quality in a US hotel company and especially the issue of implementation. They followed the way in which Bergstrom hotels had developed their quality approach since 1989 and described the variety of tools and techniques they used, including the team process, data-based decision making and human resource support systems. Baldacchino (1995) took a more critical stance and suggested, based on an in-depth study of a single hotel, that the rhetoric of Total Quality Management may fall foul of a human resource approach, which does not support the appropriate labour relations climate needed to underpin the quality initiative. Another issue that is raised is the importance of measures that can be compared across operations, an issue which Breiter and Kline (1995) seek to address through a benchmarking approach.

One issue that researchers have considered in some detail is that of the measurement of perceptions of service quality. Getty and Thompson (1994) described in detail a procedure to follow in developing a rating scale for the measurement of customers' quality perceptions that underlies the approaches used to develop the SERVQUAL (Parasuraman, Zeithaml and Berry, 1988) and LODGQUAL (Knutson et al., 1991) scales. This approach, in particular the SERVQUAL scale, has come in for some severe criticism outside the hospitality literature, which helped to spark Johns, Lee-Ross and Ingram (1997) into a different approach using the profile accumulation technique which analysed customers' free responses to the best and worst aspects of the service they had received. The technique was piloted with 299 customers staying at eight small hotels. Armstrong et al. (1997) entered the SERVQUAL debate with an interest in whether cultural differences between customers would alter their expectations and so influence the validity of the final service quality measure based on the difference between expectations and performance. Their conclusion was that there were some significant differences in expectations between cultures but that a pure performance measure, which ignores the expectation, provided a better measure of service quality.

The classification and grading of hotels have not received wide attention, but Callan (1995c) has reviewed the major schemes operated in the UK and found considerable discrepancies between the grades allocated by different bodies. He also found, however, that many hotel managers were unaware of the grades awarded to their hotels, but were supportive of the importance of being part of the various schemes. Ingram (1996b) noted particular dissatisfaction about classification and grading schemes on the part of small hotel and guest house proprietors, due principally to the focus on facilities and to competition from unregulated properties. He suggested a major review of grading schemes, a process which at the beginning of 1998 is still going on without a clear resolution.

The final area of research in this section looks at the nature of the service delivered to the customer. Sparrow and Wood (1994) reported on the use of mapping techniques to advance the propositions that experienced food servers have a far richer picture of customers than do training manuals and that their perceptual 'maps' can assist in providing quality service. Further, they suggested that such techniques produce enhanced feelings of trust and self-worth in employees as well as reducing absenteeism and waste. Huyton and Ingold (1997) reported a study to examine whether the attitude of workers to the cultural origin of their customers was likely to affect the service they provide. The study found that one group of employees in China did clearly distinguish between Japanese, South-east Asian and local Chinese customers, who were seen as sharing negative attributes and were generally disliked, and Western customers who were looked on more positively and were made more welcome. The issue of whether these differences affect the employees' service performance is still not resolved, however. Service performance, but from a different viewpoint, was also the focus of research by Jones and Dent (1994), one of very few hotel-based articles to be found in the mainstream operations management journals. The study investigated the effect of waiting on customers' perceptions of an operation and reported on the response times found in typical hotel and restaurant operations managed by Forte plc. Based on a comparison of customer attitudes and the operations' ability to deliver, the company developed 10 key action points aimed at improving response time performance, giving examples of developments in service system design and delivery.

Given the importance of quality and service to the customer, the amount of research work published in this field is disappointing.

Operating systems

Given the practical bias of many hospitality academics, there is very little research that explores the nitty-gritty of hotel operating systems. This may be partly because the very practical nature of the problems to be addressed does not seem to be of a high academic standing. There would, however, be much to be learnt here from applying concepts and methodologies from the operations management field.

One approach advocated by a number of authors is based on a systems perspective. Kirk (1995a) concluded that it is necessary to take a holistic approach in which technical subsystems are integrated with human activity subsystems. Catering systems, for example, require technical objectives of safety, customer satisfaction and cost control as well as recognising the importance of human relationships in implementing these plans. Jones and Lockwood (1995) use systems concepts to reconcile the traditional view of hospitality operations based on operating processes with the more recent output-based approach, by identifying four levels of hospitality operations management. They concluded that process analysis is appropriate for understanding operating systems and output analysis for operational management.

The traditional view of hotel food and beverage is challenged by the work of Hallam and Baum (1996). This research addressed a significant change in the way hotels run food and beverage outlets, that is contracting them out to either individual restaurateurs or branded restaurant chains. Although this practice is regretted by many traditionalists, it is shown to be on the increase in both the US and the UK. They concluded that despite mixed responses to this process, it is a trend that will continue to prosper.

Other than this small contribution to food and beverage, the only other operating system to receive attention is that based on information technology (IT). IT is a powerful and exciting business tool, but some commentators suggest that hotels are not fully realising its potential. Cho and Connolly (1996), for example, argued that many hotel managers remain sceptical about the value of investing in IT, often because of the length of time it takes to see actual results. This view is reflected by Main (1995) who reported on a survey of the use of IT in independent hotels in South Wales. This revealed that only 50% used IT and then for essentially clerical purposes, and suggested a significant need for education, training and advice to enable independents to compete with chain operations. A similar training need was identified in research by Sumner and Sellars (1996) who examined the use of computers in the areas of guest history, reservations and yield management. They also found that computers were under-used because managers were not fully conversant with the opportunities offered by computer operations.

Gaps and potential in hotel operations research

It is perhaps inevitable that gaps should exist between the academic research that is needed and that which is carried out, because research is not strictly demand-led. Academic research is undertaken primarily for academic awards by research students mostly working alone, and the choice of subject is an individual one. Breymer, Rouselle and Johns (1990) conducted a survey of chief operating officers of hospitality corporations in the US, nearly 10 years ago, to identify their most important research interests. For lodging operations six out of 12 were in the human resource management area, two were concerned with marketing and the remainder were operations biased. These included computerised reservation systems, property management systems, productivity and property maintenance. They also indicated, however, that they were not interested in research on food and beverages. This research focus of hotel managers was confirmed in the survey of the research interests of UK and US hotel and restaurant firms by Brotherton and Burgess (1997) who found that the areas of major interest were still human resource management, marketing and, to a slightly lesser extent, control. An interest in research in food and beverage management may, however, be resurfacing.

A review of the published work described above provides the data presented in Table 21.3. These show that the most popular topic areas for hotel operations research were human resources and profitability and yield management, which each represent 21% of the work cited. The differences between these two areas are that the human resources publications show a wide spread of interests and approaches while the profitability articles are almost exclusively about yield management, and the human resources research is almost all empirically based while the work on yield management is biased towards the conceptual. This is not very surprising when human resource management is a well-developed field with a long track record of research, while yield management is a relatively new topic where definitions and models are still being developed. The third most published area concerns strategy and environment, while customers and marketing, and service and quality, take fourth and fifth place respectively. The three remaining areas—property and asset management, productivity and performance, and operating systems—each score a percentage in single figures only.

Table 21.3 An analysis of published research

Theme	No.	%	Conceptual %	Empirical %
Strategy and environment	22	16	41	59
Property and asset management	11	8	27	73
Human resources	29	21	7	93
Customers and marketing	19	13	26	74
Profitability and yield management	29	21	55	45
Productivity and performance	9	6	22	78
Service and quality	16	11	19	81
Operating systems	6	4	33	67
Total	141	100	30	70

The areas that seem under-represented, given their importance to successful hotel operations, are quality and service, which as a combined topic managed only 11% of all papers, and productivity, which reached only 6%. It is also disappointing that more attention is not paid to the serious consideration of the operating systems on which hotels rely to produce and distribute their services. This may not be the most glamorous or obviously academic of areas, but it offers a rich field of possible projects suitable for the application of operations management concepts and methodologies.

There is no doubt that the list of over 140 articles on hotel operations represents a considerable volume of research, but when compared to the over 600 academic research studies identified as ongoing by Ingram (1996a) they represent only a small part of the total research work that is being conducted. It is to be hoped that a large percentage of these research studies are converted into published papers.

The research cited above is generally of a good standard. Overall, 70% of the work is based on empirical studies and 30% is conceptual. The empirical studies show a variety of methodologies ranging from quantitative surveys, through qualitative studies to detailed case studies. Of these, however, questionnaire surveys account for the largest proportion, though unfortunately many of these are based on samples that do not allow reliable generalisations to be drawn. It is to be hoped that as this research field matures the number of very small-scale studies will decline and more large-scale studies, which can be seen as representative of the industry, will be reported.

Demetriadi (1995) noted research gaps in the budget accommodation sector and thematic gaps for quality management, health and safety, and food purchasing and production. A seminar conducted with London hotel general managers in 1997 by one of the authors highlighted their desire for more research activity into such issues as:

- the future of hotel catering
- staff retention
- pricing options
- profit enhancement through benchmarking
- outsourcing
- public relations as a means of selling the right message
- managing quality using a relevant industry-specific framework.

With such a wide range of interesting research gaps to fill and a research community that is rapidly establishing its research credentials and growing in confidence to use more complex research methodologies, the future for hotel operations research looks bright indeed.

References

Alexander N and Lockwood A (1996) Internationalisation: a comparison of the hotel and retail sectors, *Service Industries Journal* **16**, 4: 458–473

Andrew WP, Cranage DA and Lee CK (1990) Forecasting hotel occupancy rates with time series models: an empirical analysis, *Hospitality Research Journal* **14**, 2: 173–181

Armstrong RW, Mok C, Go FM and Chan A (1997) The importance of cross cultural expectations in the measurement of service quality perceptions in the hotel industry, *International Journal of Hospitality Management*, **16**, 2: 181–190

Ayala H (1993) The unresearched phenomenon of 'hotel circuits', *Hospitality Research Journal* **16**, 3: 59–74

Ayala H (1995) Ecoresort: a green masterplan for the international resort industry, *International Journal of Hospitality Management* **14**, 3–4: 351

Bach S and Pizam A (1996) Crimes in hotels, *Hospitality Research Journal* **20**, 2: 59–76

Baldacchino G (1995) Total quality management in a luxury hotel: a critique of practice, *International Journal of Hospitality Management* **14**, 1: 67

Barrow CW (1991) Employee turnover: implications for hotel managers, *Florida International University Hospitality Review* **9**, 1: 24–31

BDO Hospitality Consulting (1994) *The English Hotel Occupancy Survey*, BDO: London

Bigness J (1996) Hotel lock failures may mean no exit, *The Wall Street Europe (Netherlands)* 15 April: 4

Bitran GR and Mondschein SV (1995) An application of yield management to the hotel industry considering multiple day stays, *Operations Research* **43**, 3: 427–435

Blake Dawson Waldron and Arthur Anderson (1994) *Hotel Workplace Reform*, Tourism Task Force: Sydney

Bodily SE and Weatherford LR (1995) Perishable-asset revenue management: generic and multiple-price yield management with diversion, *Omega* **23**, 2: 173–179

Bradley A and Ingold A (1993) An investigation of yield management in Birmingham hotels, *International Journal of Contemporary Hospitality Management* **5**, 2: 13–16

Brander-Brown J and McDonnell B (1995) The balanced score-card: short-term guest or long-term resident?, *International Journal of Contemporary Hospitality Management* **7**, 2/3: 7–11

Breiter D and Kline SF (1995) Benchmarking quality management in hotels, *FIU Hospitality Review* **13**, 2: 45

Breiter D, Tyink A and Corey-Tuckwell S (1995) Bergstrom hotels: a case study in quality, *International Journal of Contemporary Hospitality Management* **7**, 6: 14–18

Breymer RA, Rouselle JR and Johns TR (1990) Academic research interests of hospitality corporations, *Hospitality Research Journal* **14**, 1: 1–10

British Hospitality Association (1990) *Wages and Salaries in Hotels*, BHA: London

British Hospitality Association (1991) *Wages and Salaries in Hotels*, BHA: London

Brotherton B and Burgess J (1997) A comparative study of academic research interests in US and UK hotel and restaurant companies, *Proceedings of the 6th Annual Hospitality Research Conference, Oxford*: 317–338

Brotherton B and Mooney S (1992) Yield management—progress and prospects, *International Journal of Hospitality Management* **11**, 1: 23–32

Brotherton B and Shaw J (1996) Towards an identification and classification of critical success factors in UK Hotels plc, *International Journal of Hospitality Management* **15**, 2: 113–136

Brown M (1996) Environmental policy in the hotel sector: green strategy or stratagem?, *International Journal of Contemporary Hospitality Management* **8**, 3: 18–23

Burgess C, Hampton A, Price L and Roper A (1995) International hotel groups: what makes them successful?, *International Journal of Contemporary Hospitality Management* **7**, 2/3: 74–80

Buttle F and Bok B (1996) Hotel marketing strategies and the theory of reasoned action, *International Journal of Contemporary Hospitality Management* **8**, 3: 5

Callan RJ (1994) Development of a framework for the determination of attributes used for hotel selection—indications from focus group and in-depth interviews, *Hospitality Research Journal* **18**, 2: 53–74

Callan RJ (1995a) Lodging preferences of female customers: an empirical study, *Progress in Tourism and Hospitality Research* **1**, 2: 99–115

Callan RJ (1995b) Hotel classification and grading schemes: a paradigm of utilization and user characteristics, *International Journal of Hospitality Management* **14**, 3–4: 271

Callan RJ (1995c) UK hotel quality grades and managers' nescience, *International Journal of Contemporary Hospitality Management* **7**, 6: vi–viii

Callan RJ (1996) An appraisement of UK business travelers' perceptions of important hotel attributes, *Hospitality Research Journal* **19**, 4: 113

Callan RJ (1997) An attributional approach to hotel selection. Part 1: The managers' perceptions, *Progress in Tourism and Hospitality Research*, **3**, 4: 351–364

Callan RJ and Fearon R (1997) Town house hotels—an emerging sector, *International Journal of Contemporary Hospitality Management* **9**, 4: 168–175

Cannon DF (1991) The relationship between job satisfaction, interferences to working and organization commitment among hotel employees, PhD thesis, Georgia State University, Atlanta, GA

Cho W and Connolly DJ (1996) The impact of information technology as an enabler in the hospitality industry, *International Journal of Contemporary Hospitality Management* **8**, 1: 33–35

Cichy RF and Schmidgall RS (1996) Leadership qualities of financial executives in the US lodging industry, *Cornell Hotel and Restaurant Administration Quarterly* **37**, 2: 56

Collier P and Gregory A (1995) Strategic management accounting: a UK hotel sector case study, *International Journal of Contemporary Hospitality Management* **7**, 1: 16

Connell J (1997) International hotel franchise relationships—UK franchisee perspectives, *International Journal of Contemporary Hospitality Management* **9**, 5/6: 215–220

Costa J (1995) An empirically-based review of the concept of environmental scanning, *International Journal of Contemporary Hospitality Management* **7**, 7: 4–9

Culligan PE (1995) Toward a new definition of impact, *Cornell Hotel and Restaurant Administration Quarterly* **36**, 4: 38

Demetriadi J (1995) Academic research in hospitality and tourism: a WHATT-CD users' view, *International Journal of Contemporary Hospitality Management* **7**, 7: iv–vi

Donaghy K (1996) Business management: understanding yield management helps, *Hospitality* **3**: 8

Donaghy K, McMahon U and McDowell D (1995) Yield management: an overview, *International Journal of Hospitality Management* **14**, 2: 139–150

Donaghy K, McMahon-Beattie U and McDowell D (1997) Implementing yield management: lessons from the hotel sector, *International Journal of Contemporary Hospitality Management* **9**, 2/3: 50–54

Dunn KD and Brooks DE (1990) Profit analysis: beyond yield management, *Cornell Hotel and Restaurant Quarterly* **31**, 3: 80–90

Durr JL (1989) The value of the guest register: customer database, *Direct Marketing* **52**, 5: 48

Economic Intelligence Unit (1995) Hotel frequent guest programmes, *Travel and Tourism Analyst* **1**: 84–96

Engeset MG and Heide M (1996) Managing hotel guest satisfaction: towards a more focused approach, *Tourism Review* **51**, 2: 23–33

Evans M and Murriman SK (1989) Personal care amenities: are they important attributes in the selection of hotels?, *Florida International University Hospitality Review* **7**, 2: 19–25

Gannon J and Johnson K (1995) The global hotel industry: the emergence of continental hotel chains, *Progress in Tourism and Hospitality Research* **1**, 1: 31–42

Gannon J and Johnson K (1997) Socialization control and market entry modes in the international hotel industry, *International Journal of Contemporary Hospitality Management* **9**, 5/6: 193–198

Getty JM and Thompson KN (1994) A procedure for scaling perceptions of lodging quality, *Hospitality Research Journal* **18**, 2: 75–96

Greathouse KR, Gregoire MB, Shanklin CW and Tri C (1996) Factors considered important in hotel accommodations by travelers stopping at visitor information centers, *Hospitality Research Journal* **19**, 4: 129

Griffin RK (1995) A categorization scheme for critical success factors of lodging yield management systems, *International Journal of Hospitality Management* **14**, 3–4: 325–338

Griffin RK (1996) Factors of successful lodging yield management systems, *Hospitality Research Journal* **19**, 4: 17–30

Griffin RK (1997) Evaluating the success of lodging yield management systems, *FIU Hospitality Review* **15**, 1: 57–61

Guerrier Y and Lockwood A (1989a) Core and peripheral employees in hotel operations, *Personnel Review* **18**, 1: 9

Guerrier Y and Lockwood A (1989b) Flexible working: current strategies and future potential, *International Journal of Contemporary Hospitality Management* **1**, 1: 11–16

Guerrier Y and Lockwood A (1989c) Managing flexible working in hotels, *Service Industries Journal* **9**, 3: 406–419

Guerrier Y and Lockwood A (1989d) Developing hotel managers—a re-appraisal, *International Journal of Hospitality Management* **8**, 2: 82–89

Guerrier Y and Lockwood A (1990) Labour shortages in the international hotel industry, *Travel and Tourism Analyst* **6**: 17–35

Gundersen MG, Heide M and Olsson UH (1996) Hotel guest satisfaction among business travelers, *Cornell Hotel and Restaurant Administration Quarterly* **37**, 2: 72

Halcro K (1996) An investigation into room price discounting, *International Journal of Contemporary Hospitality Management* **8**, 6: 34–37

Hallam G and Baum T (1996) Contracting out food and beverage operations in hotels: a comparative study of practice in North America and the United Kingdom, *International Journal of Hospitality Management* **15**, 1: 41–50

Harrington D and Akehurst G (1996) An exploratory investigation into managerial perceptions of service quality in UK hotels, *Progress in Tourism and Hospitality Research*, **2**, 2: 135–150

Hobson JSP and Ko M (1995) Counterfeit credit cards: how to protect hotel guests, *Cornell Hotel and Restaurant Administration Quarterly* **36**, 4: 48

Hotel and Catering International Management Association (1990) *Pay and Benefits*, HCIMA: London

Hotel and Catering International Management Association (1993) *Pay and Benefits*, HCIMA: London

Hotel and Catering International Management Association (1995) *HCIMA: Managing your Business in Harmony with the Environment*, HCIMA: London

Hsu JF and Gregory SR (1995) Developing future Hotel managers in Taiwan: from an industry viewpoint, *International Journal of Hospitality Management* **14**, 3–4: 261

Hum SH (1997) Strategic hotel operations: some lessons from strategic manufacturing, *International Journal of Contemporary Hospitality Management* **9**, 4/6: 176

Huyton J, Evans P and Ingold A (1997) The legal and moral issues surrounding the practice of yield management, *International Journal of Contemporary Hospitality Management* **9**, 2/3: 84–87

Huyton JR and Ingold A (1997) Some considerations of impacts of attitude to foreigners by hotel workers in the People's Republic of China on hospitality service, *Progress in Tourism and Hospitality Research* **3**, 2: 107–118

IHA (1993) IHA report: Yield management basics, *Hotels* **27**, 4: 55–58

Ingram H (1996a) Clusters and gaps in hospitality and tourism academic research, *International Journal of Contemporary Hospitality Management* **8**, 7: 91–95

Ingram H (1996b) Classification and grading of smaller hotels, guesthouses and bed and breakfast accommodation, *International Journal of Contemporary Hospitality Management* **8**, 5: 30–34

Jauncey S (1997) The job of the hotel general manager, PhD thesis in progress, Oxford Brookes University

Jauncey S, Mitchell I and Slamet P (1995) The meaning and management of yield in hotels, *International Journal of Contemporary Hospitality Management* **7**, 4: 23–26

Johns N (1993) Productivity management through design and operation: a case study, *International Journal of Contemporary Hospitality Management* **5**, 2: 20–24

Johns N, Howcroft B and Drake L (1997) The use of data envelopment analysis to monitor hotel productivity, *Progress in Tourism and Hospitality Research*, **3**, 2: 119–128

Johns N, Lee-Ross D and Ingram H (1997) A study of service quality in small hotels and guest-houses, *Progress in Tourism and Hospitality Research* **3**, 4: 351–364

Johnston R. (1994) Operations: from factory to service management, *International Journal of Service Industry Management* **5**, 1: 20–54

Jones P and Dent M (1994) Improving service: managing response time in hospitality operations, *International Journal of Operations and Production Management* **14**, 5: 52

Jones P and Hall M (1990) Do hotel operations meet the work aspirations of the unemployed?, *Hospitality Research Journal* **14**, 2: 637–639

Jones P and Hamilton D (1992) Yield management—putting people in the big picture, *Cornell Hotel and Restaurant Administration Quarterly* Feb: 89–95

Jones P and Lockwood A (1989) *The Management of Hotel Operations*, Cassell: London

Jones P and Lockwood A (1995) Hospitality operating systems, *International Journal of Contemporary Hospitality Management* **7**, 5: 17–20

Kelliher C and Johnson K (1997) Personnel management in hotels—an update: a move to human resource management, *Progress in Tourism and Hospitality Research* **3**, 4: 321–332

Kemp AJ (1995) Hotel design effectiveness: an analysis of the relationship between environment and behaviour, PhD thesis, University of Huddersfield

Kim H (1996) Perceptual mapping of attributes and preferences: an empirical examination of hotel F&B products in Korea, *International Journal of Hospitality Management* **15**, 4: 373–392

Kimes SE (1994) Perceived fairness of yield management, *Cornell Hotel and Restaurant Administration Quarterly* **35**, 1: 22–29

Kirk D (1995a) Hard and soft systems: a common paradigm for operations, *International Journal of Contemporary Hospitality Management* **7**, 5: 13–16

Kirk D (1995b) Environmental management in hotels, *International Journal of Contemporary Hospitality Management* **7**, 6: 3

Kleinwort Benson (1994) *Quoted Hotel Companies*, Kleinwort Benson: London

Knutson B, Stevens P, Wullaert C, Patton M and Yokoyama F (1991) LODGSERV: a service quality index for the lodging industry, *Hospitality Research Journal* **14**, 2: 277–284

Lee-Ross D and Johns N (1995) Dimensionality of the job diagnostic survey among distinct sub-groups of seasonal hotel workers, *Hospitality Research Journal* **19**, 2: 31

Lewis RC (1985) The market position: mapping guests' perceptions of hotel operations, *Cornell Hotel and Restaurant Administration Quarterly* **26**, 2: 86–99

Lieberman WH (1993) Debunking the myths of yield management, *Cornell Hotel and Restaurant Administration Quarterly* **34**, 1: 34–41

Litteljohn D (1997) Internationalization in hotels: current aspects and developments, *International Journal of Contemporary Hospitality Management* **9**, 5/6: 187–192

Lockwood A, Baker M and Ghillyer A (1996) *Quality in Hospitality: Best Practice in Action*, Cassell: London

MacVicar A and Brown G (1994) Investors in People at The Moat House International, Glasgow, *International Journal of Contemporary Hospitality Management* **6**, 1/2: 53–60

MacVicar A and Rodger J (1996) Computerized yield management systems: a comparative analysis of the human resource management implications, *International Journal of Hospitality Management* **15**, 4: 325–332

Main H (1995) Information technology and the independent hotel—failing to make the connection, *International Journal of Contemporary Hospitality Management* **7**, 6: 30–32

Maxwell GA (1997) Hotel general management: views from above the glass ceiling, *International Journal of Contemporary Hospitality Management* **9**, 5/6: 230–235

McEvoy BJ (1997) Integrating operational and financial perspectives using yield management techniques: an add-on matrix model, *International Journal of Contemporary Hospitality Management* **9**, 2/3: 60–65

McGuffie J (1990) CRS development and the hotel sector: Part I. *Travel and Tourism Analyst* **1**: 29–41

McIntosh M (1991) Switch the lights off, save the planet, *Director* **45**, 3: 89

Meidan A and Chiu HL (1995) Hotel reservation methods—a discriminant analysis of practices in English hotels, *International Journal of Hospitality Management* **14**, 2: 195–208

Meier JD (1991) Solutions to the hospitality industry's labour shortage, *Florida International University Hospitality Review* **9**, 2: 78–82

Messenger S and Mugomeza C (1995) An exploratory study of productivity and performance measurement in Zimbabwean hotels, *International Journal of Contemporary Hospitality Management* **7**, 5: v–vii

Miller JJ, Miller JL and Horsley S (1993) Hospitality management education: a survey of forecasting techniques, *Hospitality and Tourism Educator* **5**, 2: 58–59

Morrison A (1995) The small UK hotel firm—marketing channel management, PhD thesis, University of Strathclyde, Glasgow

Moutinho L, McDonagh P, Peris SM and Bigne E (1995) The future development of the hotel sector: an international comparison, *International Journal of Contemporary Hospitality Management* **7**, 4: 10–15

Nebel III EC, Lee JS and Vidakovic B (1995) Hotel general manager career paths in the United States, *International Journal of Hospitality Management* **14**, 3–4: 245

Noone B and Griffin P (1997) Enhancing yield management with customer profitability analysis, *International Journal of Contemporary Hospitality Management* **9**, 2/3: 75–79

Olsen M, Murthy B and Teare R (1994) CEO perspectives on scanning the global hotel business, *International Journal of Contemporary Hospitality Management* **6**, 4: 3–9

Pannell Kerr Forster (1990) Towards success and greater profits, *International Journal of Contemporary Hospitality Management* **2**, 3: i–iii

Parasuraman A, Zeithaml VA and Berry LL (1988) SERVQUAL: a multi-item scale for measuring consumer perceptions of service quality, *Journal of Retailing* **64**, 1: 12–40

Patel D and Corgel JB (1995) An analysis of hotel impact studies, *Cornell Hotel and Restaurant Administration Quarterly* **36**, 4: 27

Peacock M (1995) A job well done: hospitality managers and success, *International Journal of Contemporary Hospitality Management* **7**, 2/3: 48–56

Peters S and Reilly J (1997) Yield management transition: a case example, *International Journal of Contemporary Hospitality Management* **9**, 2/3: 89–91

Phillips PA (1996) Strategic planning and business performance in the quoted UK hotel sector: results of an exploratory study, *International Journal of Hospitality Management* **15**, 4: 347–362

Phillips PA (1997) Trouble in the UK hotel sector, *International Journal of Contemporary Hospitality Management* **9**, 4: 149–154

Poorani A and Smith DR (1994) Franchising as a business expansion strategy in the bed and breakfast industry: creating a marketing and development advantage, *Hospitality Research Journal* **18**, 2: 19–34

Roberts C and Shea L (1996) Core capabilities in the hotel industry, *Hospitality Research Journal* **19**, 4: 141–154

Roginsky RJ (1995) A critical analysis of hotel-impact issues, *Cornell Hotel and Restaurant Administration Quarterly* **36**, 4: 18

Roper A (1995) The emergence of hotel consortia as transorganizational forms, *International Journal of Contemporary Hospitality Management* **7**, 1: 4–9

Roper A, Brookes M, Price L and Hampton A (1996) Towards an understanding of centricity: profiling hotel groups, *Progress in Tourism and Hospitality Research* **3**, 3: 199–212

Roper A, Hampton A and Brookes M (1997) The multi-cultural management of international hotel groups, *International Journal of Hospitality Management* **16**, 2: 147–160

Ross GF (1995) Work stress and personality measures among hospitality industry employees, *International Journal of Contemporary Hospitality Management* **7**, 6: 9

Saint-Claire A (1994) Towards maximising value from new hotel design, MSc dissertation, School of Hotel and Catering Management, Oxford Brookes University

Savkina R and Yakovlev V (1997) Yield management in Russia: characteristics and evaluation, *International Journal of Contemporary Hospitality Management* **9**, 2/3: 91–92

Shortt G and Ruys H (1994) Hotel security: the needs of the mature age market, *International Journal of Contemporary Hospitality Management* **6**, 5: 14

Sparks B (1993) Guest history: is it being utilized?, *International Journal of Contemporary Hospitality Management* **5**, 1: 22

Sparrow J and Wood G (1994) You're stopping me from giving quality service, *International Journal of Contemporary Hospitality Management* **6**, 1/2: 61–67

Stone G (1988) Personality and effective hospitality management, *Proceedings of the International Association of Hospitality Management Schools Symposium*, Leeds Polytechnic, November

Sumner JR and Sellars T (1996) Hotel computer systems: valuable tool or missed opportunity?, *International Journal of Contemporary Hospitality Management* **8**, 2: 36–39

Sumner JR and Sellars T (1997) Investigating the value and application of guest history and computerized reservation systems as marketing tools in the UK hotel sector, *International Journal of Contemporary Hospitality Management*, **9**, 4: 180–181

Szivas E and Riley M (1996) The role of the hotel feasibility study in the development process: putting utility into perspective, *International Journal of Contemporary Hospitality Management* **8**, 6: 29–31

Upchurch RS and Ruhland SK (1995) An analysis of ethical work climate and leadership relationship in lodging operations, *Journal of Travel Research* **34**, 2: 36–42

Van-Dyke T and Olsen MD (1989) A comparison of performance variables of highly profitable mid-priced hotels and motels with marginally profitable or losing operations, *Hospitality Education and Research Journal* **13**, 1: 13–30

Van Westering J (1994) Yield management: the case for food and beverage operations, *Progress in Tourism Recreation and Hospitality Management* **6**: 139–146

Walker JR (1988) The viability of quality assurance in hotels, *Hospitality Education and Research Journal* **12**, 2: 461–470

Willborn W (1986) Quality assurance audits and hotel management, *Service Industries Journal* **6**, 3: 293–308

Witt CA and Witt SF (1989) Why productivity in the hotel sector is low, *Journal of Contemporary Hospitality Management* **1**, 2: 28–34

Worsfold P (1989) Leadership and managerial effectiveness in the hospitality industry, *International Journal of Contemporary Hospitality Management* **8**, 2: 145–155

Yeoman I and Watson S (1997) Yield management: a human activity system, *International Journal of Contemporary Hospitality Management* **9**, 2/3: 80–83

Yu L and Huat GS (1995) Perceptions of management difficulty factors by expatriate hotel professionals in China, *International Journal of Hospitality Management* **14**, 3–4: 375

Yu RWY and Pine R (1995) Use of local and expatriate hotel managers in Hong Kong, *Australian Journal of Hospitality Management* **2**, 2: 25

22 Catering operations management

PETER JONES

Introduction

It would seem that catering operations management research is not widespread. Ingram (1996: 94), in a review of 820 postgraduate research projects in the hospitality and tourism field, comments that in the hospitality area 'most relate to the leisure and hotel sectors while food and catering entries show a marketing or science focus and rarely relate to operational or service issues'. He goes on to identify that there are many key sectors of the catering industry that appear to be under-represented—pubs, hospitals, school meals, forces catering, and ferries. In another review of research, Teare (1996) provides an overview of hospitality operations management articles published in selected journals from 1989 to 1994. In his summary of the main themes and subthemes [sic], catering is not referred to at all. Finally, Green and Weaver (1993) conducted a review of the food-service system literature from 1950 to 1990 and related research techniques in the United States. They reported that 68 of the 91 articles (they reviewed) used hospital foodservice operations for the study sample, whilst schools were the second largest type of operation researched. However, it should be noted that four of the 17 journals they reviewed were specifically focused on health care, which may help to explain their findings. The research methods most used were simple description, analytical (i.e. comparing two alternative systems) or case studies. Only five out of the 91 articles were empirical, i.e. applied a scientific method in studying specific characteristics of the system.

Catering operations management research can be categorised into two types—research into catering or operations research. Research into catering refers to any kind of 'investigation' applied to the catering industry. This kind of research can be very general, cover a wide range of topics, and use a wide variety of methodologies. Operations research, on the other hand, is tightly focused research, using specific methodologies within the scientific paradigm. The systemic and systematic approach to operations research means that such studies can be easily categorised. However, in the catering operations management area most of the research conducted has been 'research into catering'. This makes the planning and structuring of this chapter highly problematic, due to the eclectic nature of such research.

The chapter will therefore begin with an overview of those journals in which catering operations research is mainly published, in order to provide some understanding of the range of studies in this field. The chapter is then divided into six main sections,

The Handbook of Contemporary Hospitality Management Research, Edited by Bob Brotherton.
© 1999 John Wiley & Sons Ltd.

based around recurrent themes in the literature. These are:

- catering operations classification
- catering systems design and technology
- operations management issues
- catering managers
- menu planning and analysis
- restaurant chain development and growth.

Orientation of research journals

There are a number of journals in which catering operations management research is reported, as well as market intelligence reports of various kinds. The journals range from the generic, i.e. covering a range of industries, to the very specific which are concerned solely with catering operations. One of the most general is the *International Journal of Service Industries Management* (*IJSIM*), which considers the service industries as a whole, with little focus on specific industry sectors. The range of articles includes those relating to operations management, service concept, service design, service delivery, and innovation.

There are four key hospitality journals in which catering operations management is reported, two published in North America and two in the UK. In the *Cornell Hotel and Restaurant Administration* (*HRA*) *Quarterly* from the years 1989 to 1997, the content of the journal covered most areas of hospitality from an American perspective. The *Quarterly* often has a specific field of interest for each issue, which includes looking at restaurants every so often. The articles in this journal tend to be focused primarily on the large restaurant chains. The *Hospitality Research Journal* (*HRJ*) is another US-based journal, although more international in its scope. Between 1988 and 1997 it has covered a general range of topics, but notably the areas of managerial skills, objectives and tasks, managerial attributes, and success factors. The *International Journal of Contemporary Hospitality Management* (*IJCHM*) has many of the features of other hospitality journals. However, it tends to emphasise publication by industry practitioners and it also regularly reviews trends and themes in hospitality research (see, for instance, Johns and Teare, 1995). Another British journal, the *International Journal of Hospitality Management* (*IJHM*), like the *IJCHM*, has special editions, often relating these to papers presented at specific hospitality conferences. The major strength of this journal tends to lie in articles relating to strategy and management.

As well as these journals there are a number of specialist journals that report on some specific aspects of catering operations management. Most of these are US-based. For instance, there is the *Journal of Foodservice Systems* which tends to routinely focus on systems, technology and catering equipment. Examples of other specialist journals include the *Journal of College and University Foodservice* and the *Journal of Nutrition in Recipe and Menu Development*.

Catering operations classification

For any kind of research to be conducted, researchers have to agree on what to call things. However, in the catering operations area there are many terms used for which there is no commonly agreed definition, such as fast food, quick service, pub, restaurant, and many others. It is also common in areas of academic study to classify complex systems by identifying and agreeing upon sub-systems. Such classification can be in the form of a 'taxonomy', which is largely concerned with the nomenclature (or 'naming') of hierarchical systems, or a 'typology', which is the categorisation of systems by type. There have been some attempts at such classification. Most of this research has been conceptual, although some has been supported by empirical measurement.

One of the earliest studies of catering systems was conducted by Cutcliffe (1971). Cutcliffe's systems model of an operation was based around the conventional restaurant. Subsequently a number of authors have demonstrated that this traditional form of operation has many variants (Jones, 1983a, 1988a). For instance, Pickworth (1988) proposed a typology which categorised the wide range of alternative service delivery systems (SDS) that exist within the whole of the catering industry. Pickworth defines a 'service delivery system' as an 'operation in which products/services are created and delivered to the customer almost simultaneously' (Pickworth, 1988: 48). In some cases a service delivery system is 'dedicated', that is to say it is an 'SDS which is designed to produce a specific range of menu items'. Pickworth uses the example of fast food chains. However, in other cases, an SDS can be 'multi-faceted', so that it is an SDS which is able to produce and serve a broad range of menu items. Thus in a dedicated SDS the expectation is that there would be one specific system, whereas in a multi-faceted operation there may exist more than one specific system operating together.

Huelin and Jones (1990) proposed a taxonomy for all kinds of catering operations, further adapted by Jones (1993). This suggests that the industry can be divided into 11 types of catering operation. This is discussed further in Jones (1994). Taxonomies and typologies have also been developed for specific types of operation, especially restaurants. Powers (1985) developed a 'restaurant typology' that was subsequently updated and developed further by Muller and Woods (1994). Their 'expanded restaurant typology' has five main categories of restaurant deriving from their menu characteristics and operational features. An alternative approach, taking more into account market segmentation, has been advocated by Goldman (1993). A taxonomy has also been proposed by Escueta, Fielder and Reisman (1986) for use in relation to catering provision in hospitals. Their classification scheme codes stages of the process as BMKPHD. This subdivides the total service delivery system into six distinct stages. They use a capital letter to signify bulk operation, and lower case to signify individual mode. Since not all six stages are essential to the catering operation, there can be two, three, four, five and six component systems, resulting in 81 different possible configurations of a hospital system.

This body of work has been largely conceptual in nature and concentrated in only some sectors of the industry, notably restaurants and hospitals. There is a need for further research to be done into how best to classify different operational types across the industry as a whole. Such research should also measure the similarities and differences between types of catering operation, so that any typology that is proposed can be tested against empirical findings. One of the main reasons this has probably not been attempted yet is that the industry is so wide ranging and large in scale. Meaningful analysis of operational types would require a major research programme. Neither the funds nor the commitment is currently available to support such a programme.

Catering systems design and technology

A key feature of the catering operations management literature is the way in which the 'craft' approach to catering is being industrialised and systematised. Taylor and Lyon (1995) in their article consider McDonald's and focus on the concepts of customisation verses standardisation in multi-unit service delivery. The focus of the article is the effect on operations management and its functional areas. Jones and Lockwood (1995) review different systems' modelling approaches in relation to hospitality operations. They give a comparison of different contemporary models and illustrate the traditional operating systems model and its evolution. Kirk (1995) reviews systems theory and emphasises some key aspects of this theory as it applies to catering. The difference between hard and soft systems is identified. Kirk also shows operations management as a hierarchy of subsystems and highlights the interrelated nature of systems.

As well as these conceptual analyses, the most common kind of empirical research in catering operations management is probably into alternative systems and their relative efficiency and effectiveness. Three studies illustrate this. Adams, Evangelos and Short (1995) conducted experimental trials of prepared meals with commercially prepared frozen meals. They found that some 'convenience foods', i.e. prepared commercially off-site, were preferred by their 764 subjects to those prepared on-site, but that this depended on the meal item. Williams and Brand Miller's (1993) study of 30 hospitals in Sydney compared the cook–chill system with the cook–hot hold system with regards to vegetable cooking. They were concerned that cook–chill methods may have had an adverse affect on nutrient retention. Finally, Hay and Stake (1988) examined the accuracy of tray assembly in hospital foodservice. They conducted a pretraining audit of 255 trays on a random basis to establish the level of variance from the performance standard. They then instituted a five-day training session and subsequently audited 198 trays, finding a significant decrease in error rate. A different type of empirical research can be conducted not into equipment but into specific aspects of catering, such as Hong and Kirk's (1995) study of edible plate waste.

The research literature into systems and technology is also concerned with how such systems and technology may change over time due to the introduction of new technologies through the process of innovation. The strategic impact of technology has been considered by Jones (1988a) who identified the impact of trends in operations management on foodservice delivery systems. Subsequently the process firms go through to proactively engage in change, through innovation, has been researched in both the fast food sector (Jones and Wan, 1993) and the flight catering industry (Jones, 1995). A sense of how technology changes is portrayed by Decareau (1992), who provides a 'historical review of microwave foodservice applications'. Likewise Kasavana (1994) considers changes in operations technology but focuses on computer assistance in multi-unit food service operations.

As is to be expected, this type of research is more empirically based than some of the other areas of catering operations research. It is relatively straightforward, either in a laboratory or in the field, to engage in studies that test the performance of items of equipment, new technology or new systems. In view of the fact that the industry is likely to become more reliant on new technologies, this work is likely to continue. This measurement of systems performance also assists with regards to developing a clearer understanding of the industry and an appropriate typology.

Operations management

Catering operations management research takes place in the context of research into operations management in general. Johnston (1994) gives the reader a definition of operations management and the scope and role of operations management within an organisation, looking at the strategic and service imperative. This article examines its common and historical past and looks at systems theory. In this context, a number of researchers consider operations management in the catering industry. Groves, Gregoire and Downey (1995) consider the relationship between operations management and service orientation. The relationship between service orientation and operational indicators is defined within the multi-unit restaurant organisation. The premise of their discussion is that good service leads to good operations. Sill (1994) in his article looks at operations engineering in chain operations and focuses on the quantitative time and method analysis of work systems. Lashley (1995) conducted a qualitative study into the restructuring of the managerial hierarchy within the McDonald's corporation and its knock-on effects in areas such as operations. The article also reviews the roles of area and unit managers. Brotherton and Coyle (1990) consider the environment of operations management. They model this as 'three Vs: variance, variability, and variety' as key components to managing operational stability.

Critical success factors or key result areas have also been considered in the catering operations literature. Two important areas are productivity and quality. Conceptually these two have been linked, by both Pickworth (1987) and Jones (1988b). Productivity is a long-standing issue in all industries. Reference to, and research in, productivity is found in the catering operations literature over a considerable number of years (see, for instance, Freshwater and Bragg, 1975; Lane, 1976; Smith and Giglio; 1979). In the UK, Ball has engaged in a major study of productivity in fast-food chains (as well as hotels) leading to a number of published articles (Pine and Ball, 1987; Ball, 1996). Rimmington and Clark (1996) discuss the inherent difficulty of measuring production in the catering context. Jones (1990) proposed, on the basis of case study research, a link between the technology of an operation and the locus of productivity management. Manning and Lieux (1995) conducted an empirical study of productivity in a commissary production system with four satellite kitchens. They found significant variation in productivity levels between the satellite kitchens and identified some variables that might account for this.

With respect to quality, a sound overview of approaches and research is provided by Johns (1993). A number of studies have been conducted into quality related issues, though few were of an empirical nature. Jones (1983b) outlines how the concept of hazard analysis and critical control points (HACCP) may be applied to catering. Other studies concerned with the implementation of approaches to quality include O'Donnell (1991) who describes the HACCP system at Orval Kent Food Company; Sawyer (1991) who reviews safety issues in relation to take-out food from US convenience stores; and Farkas and Snyder (1991) who explain how to describe a food process for quality control. There has also been limited research into statistical process control (SPC). Jones and Dent (1993) report on one study in a cafeteria, whilst Jones and Cheek (1997) have reviewed statistical process control and directly compared it conceptually with the most commonly used restaurant industry approach to quality control—the mystery shopper. There have been narrative reports of approaches to quality improvement in the industry, such as Page's (1994) report of Sutcliffe Catering's approach to quality management. There were also a number of articles advocating an assurance approach to quality in the *Cornell HRA Quarterly* in the 1980s (Wyckoff, 1984; King, 1984; Martin, 1986).

Despite the fact that catering operations research has been grouped together in an area called 'operations management', many of the studies referred to above are not grounded in generic operations management (OM) theory, do not refer to the relevant OM literature, or apply standard OM research methodologies. This reflects a tendency to rely on previous studies conducted within the catering industry as source material and inspiration for new research. Such an approach perpetuates the phenomenological approach of catering operations research. There are large areas of the OM discipline that have very largely been ignored in the catering field, specifically process design, production planning and scheduling, stock control, and capacity planning.

Catering managers

As well as research into catering management, there has also been research into catering managers. This has been focused at two levels—the unit level, usually involving restaurant managers, and the chain level, usually considering the role of area managers. Pratt and Whitney (1992) have researched the interpersonal characteristics of restaurant general managers in comparison with other groups of interest. The managers were asked to rank themselves in their abilities to do activities such as concentrate, relax or communicate; the information was compared against the other interest groups. Discussion of the findings highlighted selection and training implications among this management class. Crandall, Emenheiser and Jones (1995) have conducted a study into the link between work hours and restaurant manager intentions to leave. They surveyed 110 respondents in the US mid-south to discover the restaurant managers' demographic profile, organisational commitment, level of job and inter-role conflict, and intention to leave. Using regression analysis, they found that the four variables that impacted on managers' intentions to leave were educational level of the manager, organisational commitment, total work hours (but not late night or weekend working) and inter-role conflict. Reynolds and Tabachi (1993) conducted a study into burnout and service delivery failure in restaurant chains. The study consisted of the analysis of service delivery gained from information given by 177 unit managers in seven major US cities. The research was quantitative and used statistical tools such as non-parametric contingency data testing through chi-square analysis. There have also been a number of studies of a human resource kind that have been specifically conducted in catering operations in the USA. Hseih *et al.* (1994a) have researched employee evaluations and their effect on staff turnover and absenteeism; Vyskocil-Czajkowski and Gilmore (1992) studied job satisfaction amongst institutional foodservice supervisors; and Hseih *et al.* (1994b) considered the use of performance appraisals in non-commercial foodservice systems.

At the chain restaurant level, Umbreit (1989) researched 161 multi-unit (area) managers and their job parameters. The research compared a selection of such managers' job descriptions compared to the perceptions of the industry's senior management about these jobs. This was followed up by a questionnaire asking the managers about their actual job entailments and feelings about the job. Muller and Campbell (1995) conducted an empirical study examining the attributes and attitudes of multi-unit managers in a national quick-service restaurant firm. This analysis examined each of the discrete levels of management and the perceived level of skills and competencies required by a multi-unit manager or area manager to manage these. The research used Umbreit's five managerial dimensions as a form of analysis for this. Lefever (1989) looked at the promotion system and prospects in chain operations. This article also provided insights into industry expectations with respect to the performance of the multi-unit manager.

In this area of catering operations research there is a clear overlap with human resources management (HRM) research. The topics selected for study and the methodologies used reflect this HRM orientation. As a result, much if not all of this research is based on empirical studies, in contrast to most of the other areas of catering operations research.

Menu planning and analysis

Despite the fact that menus play a key role in catering operations, this aspect of management has been rarely researched. Some examples might include Townley (1989), who reports on market research into food and consumer trends that should have implications for new product development. Clay and Emenheiser (1995) surveyed the major US restaurant chains to identify the availability of healthy menu offerings.

The research literature identifies that menu analysis refers to a range of techniques and procedures enabling more effective decision making, with respect to both marketing and operating the menu. Jones and Atkinson (1994) review alternative approaches to menu analysis. They suggest that a review of the literature indicates that no definition exists. They consider this surprising since Kasavana and Smith (1982) have a glossary of 49 different terms with respect to this activity, but do not define the term menu analysis. There are at least three techniques used. The menu effectiveness technique advocated by Kreck (1984) is based on comparing the menu average versus the guest-check average. The frequency distribution technique proposed by Miller (1987) is based on taking the average-check calculations one step further and converting them into a frequency distribution. However, the principal technique used is menu engineering, which Kasavana and Smith (1982: 12) define as 'a quantitative model designed to provide a basis for analysing a menu's success both in terms of attracting clientele and in terms of profitability'. In practice, menu engineering adopts a portfolio analysis methodology based on the popularity of each dish on the menu and the cost/selling price relationship or contribution margin. Several variations of this approach have been proposed in the literature (Kasavana and Smith, 1982; Pavesic, 1985). Jones and Atkinson (1994) demonstrate that the outcome of applying different techniques to the same set of data produces different results. Hayes and Huffman (1985: 62) suggest that this is an inevitable consequence of using the technique of portfolio analysis. They write '[Such] methods suffer from a common flaw of matrix analysis'. Because the axes on the matrix are determined by an average ... some items must fall into the less desirable categories.' They suggest this leads to focused attention on the poor performers and ignores the impact that changes to one dish may have on other dishes. Bayou and Bennett (1992) propose using profitability analysis to overcome this inherent difficulty.

Allied to these reviews of menu analysis has been some work into alternative pricing strategies for restaurants, such as Carmin and Norkus (1990).

There has also been some research into the layout and design of menus themselves, especially with regard to whether or not sales of specific items can be promoted by their location on the menu. It is commonly believed in industry, supported by unsubstantiated reports in both the industry press and academic journals, that consumer behaviour is influenced by the physical layout and design of the menu. For instance, Lorenzini (1992) identified an 8% increase in sales as a result of menu redesign. Such opinions often quote gaze-motion studies that have demonstrated how consumers scan menus. However, Bowen and Morris' (1995) experimental study demonstrated no support for this idea. They found that increased visibility of a menu item did not cause sales of that item to increase. They conclude that such redesigns may be more effective in quick-service than in full-service restaurants.

This is an area in which there is clearly a good body of literature. However, much of the published work is conceptual. It rarely reports on actual industry practice or demonstrates empirically the effectiveness (or otherwise) of the menu analysis approach being advocated. A notable exception to this is Morrison's (1996) study of menu engineering in upscale restaurants amongst 21 establishments in Australia. He concluded that despite the range of methodologies available, no practitioners actually applied any of them systematically. This clearly demonstrates a gap between academic theorising and industry practice, which may be considered as a future research challenge in this area.

Restaurant chain development and growth

The final field of research relating to catering operations management considers the behaviour of restaurant chains and firms, especially with regard to their growth and development. Muller (1994) and Muller and Woods (1994) take a general overview of the chain restaurant industry, giving an analysis of its distinct attributes including branding, customers, characteristics and service criteria. Lombardi (1994) and Lombardi and Miner (1995) have used data from Technomic Research to analyse restaurant growth in the USA. The group have been collating and ranking the top 200 restaurant chains in North America for the last 20 years. West and Olsen (1989) took a broad look at the competitive tactics of multi-unit restaurant chains and generated an analysis into what makes the top performers different. This analysis was conducted by a study of 65 CEOs regarding their own philosophies on operations, markets, and the critical factors that govern success. Morgan (1995) takes a statistical approach in the regression analysis of intra-brand competition and operations between restaurant multi-units. Price (1993) gives analysis to chain performance in Britain through quantitative measurement. The author also highlights the changing role of multi-unit management with the increase in flexibility in the management of labour through the distancing of supervision using empowerment.

There has also been some research into the implications of alternative business formats on effective chain development and operation. In an article by Hing (1996a) satisfaction levels of franchisees in the Australian restaurant sector are identified. There is reference made to some of the management systems and criteria used when assessing viability of a new unit or site as used by chain operations. In another article by Hing

Table 22.1   Analysis of catering operations research

| Research theme | Type of research | |
	Conceptual/descriptive	Empirical
Operations classification	Escueta et al. (1986) Goldman (1993) Huelin and Jones (1990) Jones (1983a, 1988a, 1993) Muller and Woods (1994) Pickworth (1988) Powers (1985)	Cutcliffe (1971)
Systems design and technology	Decareau (1992) Jones (1988a) Jones and Lockwood (1995) Kasavana (1994) Kirk (1995) Taylor and Lyon (1995)	Adams et al. (1995) Hay and Stake (1988) Hong and Kirk (1995) Jones (1995) Jones and Wan (1993) Williams and Brand Miller (1993)
Operations management	Brotherton and Coyle (1990) Farkas and Snyder (1991) Groves et al. (1995) Johns (1993) Jones (1983b, 1988b, 1990) Jones and Cheek (1997) O'Donnell (1991) Page (1994) Sawyer (1991) Sill (1994)	Ball (1996) Jones and Dent (1993) Lashley (1995) Manning and Lieux (1995) Pine and Ball (1987) Rimmington and Clark (1996)
Catering managers		Crandall et al. (1995) Hseih et al. (1994a, 1994b) Lefever (1989) Muller and Campbell (1995) Pratt and Whitney (1992) Reynolds and Tabachi (1993) Umbreit (1989) Vyskocil-Czajkowski and Gilmore (1992)
Menu planning and analysis	Bayou and Bennett (1992) Carmin and Norkus (1990) Hayes and Huffman (1995) Jones and Atkinson (1994) Kasavana and Smith (1982) Lorenzini (1992) Miller (1987) Pavesic (1985) Townley (1989)	Bowen and Morris (1995) Clay and Emenheiser (1995) Morrison (1996)
Chain development and growth	Hing (1996b) Muller (1994) Muller and Woods (1994)	Morgan (1995) Parsa (1996) Price (1993) West and Olsen (1989)

(1996b) the author looks at the empirical benefits and limitations of restaurant franchises. Parsa (1996) uses the Technomic 200 as a basis for analysis of chain franchisee–franchisor relationships. This analysis looks at 141 unit managers and their relationships with their area managers. The research is qualitative and gives a snapshot of the situation.

It would seem likely that more research will be conducted in this area in the future. There is a trend in hospitality research in general to move away from considering individual operations towards a consideration of firms and firm behaviour. This is supported by a growing recognition of the value of interdisciplinary research into the industry.

Conclusion

The conclusions that can be drawn from this review of catering operations management research are threefold. Firstly, there is lack of specific terminology, definitions, taxonomies and typologies. This can result in researchers using the same term to describe different phenomena. American terminology is different from British terminology. For instance, Americans prefer the term 'foodservice', whilst the British term 'catering', which has a general meaning in the UK, is used in a much narrower sense in the USA, usually with reference to 'social catering'. Secondly, much of the 'research' is highly conceptual in nature. This is demonstrated by an analysis of the body of work, as illustrated in Table 22.1. This is fairly symptomatic of a relatively new field of research as researchers attempt to conceptualise their field of enquiry, establish boundaries, and develop some kind of structure. This tends to lead to the third conclusion, that much of the research is 'phenomenological' or, as it was described at the beginning of this chapter, 'research into catering'. Researchers have tended to research aspects of catering without any clear analytical framework or structured agenda. So even that research that is non-conceptual tends to be qualitative, rather than quantitative, in nature. The exceptions to this tend to be empirical studies of catering equipment and of catering managers.

Both Bowen and Morris' (1995) study of gaze-motion theory applied to menus and Morrison's (1996) study of menu analysis demonstrate the need for empirical testing of concepts. The first study demonstrated that accepted practice in industry was based on fallacious assumptions. The second showed that despite much conceptualising, in practice the industry had not adopted the approaches proposed by theorists.

Future directions

It is clear from this review that there has been very little research into some sectors of the industry such as contract foodservice and flight catering; likewise there has been little research into some aspects of operations management such as location, purchasing and procurement, or logistics. It is likely that with the emergence of some of the more specialist journals referred to earlier, these areas will be the subject of research in the future. However, there is the danger that they will be researched in the same way that catering operations management research has been conducted to date. This is an almost inevitable outcome of the way in which catering operations management researches are likely to be developed. Whereas in other aspects of hospitality research, such as HRM or marketing, it is possible that someone with a strong social science background may become interested in doing their research in hospitality, it is extremely unlikely that this will happen in the operations area. Most catering operations researchers will have probably studied for a hospitality degree. This means that if the curriculum on these degrees teaches operations as if it were unique, as opposed to being part of OM, then the appropriate theoretical and methodological foundations will not be laid.

Future research needs to be grounded very much more clearly in established OM theory. There is very little about 'catering' that makes it a unique phenomenon. Much of the empirical work that has been done has been based not on OM but on theories and methodologies developed for the study of strategic management, human resource management (HRM) or operations research. Table 22.1 illustrates this clearly. The most empirically based area of research relates to catering managers, which generally has studies based firmly on the social science methodologies used in HRM. Such grounding in relevant theory—which in the main *should be* OM theory—is needed in all areas of catering operations research. This will facilitate good quality catering research by providing clear frames of reference for research design and research methodology. It is not as if the relative failure of catering operations researchers to engage in empirical testing of models has not been recognised for some time. As long ago as 1988, Jones wrote, in relation to trends in foodservice systems, that 'there is a need for empirical research' (Jones, 1988a).

References

Adams, S.O., Evangelos, K.-L. and Short, P. (1995) Acceptability of frozen convenience foods compared to a cook and serve system, *Journal of Foodservice Systems*, **8**, 249–255.

Ball, S. (1996) Perceptions and interpretations of productivity within fast food chains: a case study of Wimpy International, in Johns, N. (ed.) *Productivity Management in Hospitality and Tourism*, Cassell: London.

Bayou, M.E. and Bennett, L.B. (1992) Profitability analysis for table service restaurants, *Cornell Hotel and Restaurant Administration Quarterly*, **33**, 1, 49–55.

Bowen, J.T. and Morris, A.J. (1995) Menu design: can menus sell?, *International Journal of Contemporary Hospitality Management*, **7**, 4, 4–9.

Brotherton, B. and Coyle, J. (1990) Managing instability in the hospitality operations environment, *International Journal of Contemporary Hospitality Management*, **2**, 4, 17–24.

Carmin, J. and Norkus, G.X. (1990) Pricing strategies for menus: magic or myth?, *Cornell Hotel and Restaurant Administration Quarterly*, November, 45–50.

Clay, J.M. and Emenheiser, D.A. (1995) Healthful menu offerings in restaurants: a survey of major US chains, *Journal of Foodservice Systems*, **8**, 91–101.

Crandall, W., Emenheiser, D.A. and Jones, C.A. (1995) Are we working our managers too hard? Examining the link between work hours and restaurant manager intentions to leave, *Journal of Foodservice Systems*, **8**, 103–113.

Cutcliffe, G. (1971) *Analysing Catering Operations*, Edward Arnold: London.

Decareau, R.V. (1992) Microwaves in foodservice, *Journal of Foodservice Systems*, **6**, 257–270.

Escueta, E.S., Fielder, K.M. and Reisman, A. (1986) A new hospital foodservice classification system, *Journal of Foodservice Systems*, **4**, 107–116.

Farkas, D.F. and Snyder, O.P. (1991) How to describe a food process for quality control, *Journal of Foodservice Systems*, **6**, 147–153.

Freshwater, J.E. and Bragg, E.R. (1975) Improving foodservice productivity, *Cornell Hotel and Restaurant Administration Quarterly*, **15**, 4, 12–18.

Goldman, K. (1993) Concept selection for the independent restaurant, *Cornell Hotel and Restaurant Administration Quarterly*, December, 59–72.

Green, C.G. and Weaver, P.A. (1993) Trends and topics in the application of statistical techniques in foodservice systems research, *Journal of Foodservice Systems*, **7**, 69–80.

Groves, J., Gregoire, M.B. and Downey, R. (1995) The relationship between the service orientation of employees and operational indicators in a multiunit restaurant corporation, *Hospitality Research Journal*, **19**, 3, 33–45.

Hay, A.L. and Stake, S.G. (1988) Tray assembly training improves accuracy in hospital food service, *Journal of Foodservice Systems*, **5**, 29–41.

Hayes, D.K. and Huffman, L. (1985) Menu analysis: a better way, *Cornell Hotel and Restaurant Administration Quarterly*, February, 64–70.

Hing, N. (1996a) Maximising franchisee satisfaction in the restaurant sector, *International Journal of Contemporary Hospitality Management*, **8**, 3, 24–31.

Hing, N. (1996b) An empirical analysis of the benefits and limitations for restaurant franchisees, *International Journal of Hospitality Management*, **15**, 2, 177–187.

Hong, W. and Kirk, D. (1995) The analysis of edible plate waste results in 11 hospitals in the UK, *Journal of Foodservice Systems*, **8**, 115–123.

Hseih, C.-F., Holdt, C.S., Zahler, L.P. and Gates, G.E. (1994a) Manager attitudes towards performance appraisals and effect of evaluations on employee absenteeism and turnover, *Journal of Foodservice Systems*, **7**, 243–254.

Hseih, C.-F., Holdt, C.S., Zahler, L.P. and Gates, G.E. (1994b) Use of performance appraisals in non-commercial foodservice systems, *Journal of Foodservice Systems*, **7**, 233–241.

Huelin, A. and Jones, P. (1990) Thinking about catering systems, *International Journal of Operations and Production Management*, **10**, 8, 42–52.

Ingram, H. (1996) Clusters and gaps in hospitality and tourism academic research, *International Journal of Contemporary Hospitality Management*, **8**, 7, 91–95.

Johns, N. (1993) Quality management in the hospitality industry: recent developments, *International Journal of Contemporary Hospitality Management*, **5**, 1, 10–15.

Johns, N. and Teare, R. (1995) Change, opportunity and the new operations curriculum, *International Journal of Contemporary Hospitality Management*, **7**, 5, 4–8.

Johnston, R. (1994) Operations; from factory to service management, *International Journal of Service Industry Management*, **5**, 1, 20–54.

Jones, P. (1983a) *Foodservice Operations*, Holt Rinehart & Winston: Eastbourne.

Jones, P.A. (1983b) The restaurant—a place for quality control and product maintenance, *International Journal of Hospitality Management*, **2**, 2, 93–100.

Jones, P. (1988a) The impact of trends in service operations on food service delivery systems, *International Journal of Operations and Production Management*, **8**, 7, 23–30.

Jones, P. (1988b) Quality, capacity and productivity in service industries, *International Journal of Hospitality Management*, **7**, 2, 104–112.

Jones, P. (1990) Managing foodservice productivity in the long term: strategy, structure and performance, *International Journal of Hospitality Management*, **9**, 2, 144–154.

Jones, P. (1993) A taxonomy of foodservice operations, *2nd CHME Research Conference*, Manchester.

Jones, P. (1994) (ed. with Merricks, P.) *The Management of Foodservice Operations*, Cassell: London.

Jones, P. (1995) Developing new products and services in flight catering, *International Journal of Contemporary Hospitality Management*, **7**, 2/3, 24–28.

Jones, P. and Atkinson, H. (1994) Menu engineering: managing the foodservice micro-marketing mix, *Journal of Restaurant and Foodservice Marketing*, **1**, 1, 37–56.

Jones, P. and Cheek, P. (1997) Service quality: an evaluation of approaches to measuring actual performance against standards in the foodservice industry, *6th CHME National Research Conference*, Oxford Brookes University.

Jones, P. and Dent, M. (1993) Lessons in consistency: statistical process control at Forte PLC, *TQM Magazine* (1).

Jones, P. and Lockwood, A. (1995) Hospitality operating systems, *International Journal of Contemporary Hospitality Management*, **7**, 5, 17–20.

Jones, P. and Wan, L. (1993) Innovation in the UK foodservice industry, *International Journal of Contemporary Hospitality Management*, **5**, 2, 32–38.

Kasavana, M.L. (1994) Computers and multiunit food-service operations, *Cornell Hotel and Restaurant Administration Quarterly*, **35**, 3, 72–80.

Kasavana, M.L. and Smith, D.I. (1982) *Menu Engineering*, Hospitality Publications.

King, C.A. (1984) Service oriented quality control, *Cornell Hotel and Restaurant Administration Quarterly*, November, 92–98.

Kirk, D. (1995) Hard and soft systems: a common paradigm for operations management, *International Journal of Contemporary Hospitality Management*, **7**, 5, 13–16.

Kreck, L.A. (1984) *Menus: Analysis and Planning*, CBI Books.

Lane, H.E. (1976) The Scanlon plan: a key to productivity and payroll costs, *Cornell Hotel and Restaurant Administration Quarterly*, **17**, 1, 76–80.

Lashley, C. (1995) Empowerment through delayering: a pilot study at McDonald's restaurants, *International Journal of Contemporary Hospitality Management*, **7**, 2/3, 29–36.

Lefever, M.M. (1989) Multi-unit management: working your way up the corporate ladder, *Cornell Hotel and Restaurant Administration Quarterly*, **30**, 1, 61–67.

Lombardi, D.J. (1994) Chain restaurant strategic planning, *Cornell Hotel and Restaurant Administration Quarterly*, **35**, 3, 38–40.

Lombardi, D.J. and Miner, T. (1995) Reengineering in the food service industry: is it just right-sizing?, *Cornell Hotel and Restaurant Administration Quarterly*, **36**, 6, 43–55.

Lorenzini, B. (1992) Menus that sell by design, *Restaurants and Institutions*, **102**, 7, 106–112.

Manning, C.K. and Lieux, E.M. (1995) Labour productivity in nutrition programs for the elderly that use a commissary-satellite production system, *Journal of Foodservice Systems*, **8**, 187–200.

Martin, W.B. (1986) Defining what quality service is for you, *Cornell Hotel and Restaurant Administration Quarterly*, February, 32–38.

Miller, J. (1987) *Menu Pricing and Strategy*, Van Nostrand Reinhold: New York.

Morgan, M.S. (1995) Assessing chain restaurant impact using linear regression, *Cornell Hotel and Restaurant Administration Quarterly*, **36**, 3, 30–33.

Morrison, P. (1996) Menu engineering in upscale restaurants, *International Journal of Contemporary Hospitality Management*, **8**, 4, 17–24.

Muller, C.C. (1994) Multi-unit restaurant management, *Cornell Hotel and Restaurant Administration Quarterly*, **35**, 3.

Muller, C.C. and Campbell, D.F. (1995) The attributes and attitudes of multi-unit managers in a national quick service restaurant firm, *Hospitality Research Journal*, **19**, 2, 3–18.

Muller, C.C. and Woods, R.H. (1994) An expanded restaurant typography, *Cornell Hotel and Restaurant Administration Quarterly*, **35**, 3, 27–37.

O'Donnell, C.D. (1991) Implementation of HACCP at Orval Kent Food Company Inc., *Journal of Foodservice Systems*, **6**, 197–207.

Page, C. (1994) Sutcliffe catering's approach to continuous improvement, *International Journal of Contemporary Hospitality Management*, **6**, 1/2, 19–24.

Parsa, H.G. (1996) Franchisor–franchisee relationships in quick-service restaurant systems, *Cornell Hotel and Restaurant Administration Quarterly*, **37**, 2.

Pavesic, D.V. (1985) Prime numbers: finding your menu's strengths, *Cornell Hotel and Restaurant Administration Quarterly*, November, 71–77.

Pickworth, J.R. (1987) Minding the Ps and Qs: linking quality and productivity, *Cornell Hotel and Restaurant Administration Quarterly*, March, 40–47.

Pickworth, J.R. (1988) Service delivery systems in the foodservice industry, *International Journal of Hospitality Management*, **7**, 1, 43–62.

Pine, R. and Ball, S. (1987) Productivity and technology in catering operations, *Food Science and Technology Today*, **1**, 3, 174–176.

Powers, T.E. (1985) A restaurant typology, *Cornell Hotel and Restaurant Administration Quarterly*, June, pp. 33–45.

Pratt, R.W. and Whitney, D.L. (1992) Attentional and interpersonal characteristics of restaurant general managers in comparison with other groups of interest, *Hospitality Research Journal*, **15**, 1, 9–24.

Price, J. (1993) Performance of fast food franchises in Britain, *International Journal of Contemporary Hospitality Management*, **5**, 3, 10–15.

Reynolds, D. and Tabachi, M. (1993) Burnout in full-service chain restaurants, *Cornell Hotel and Restaurant Administration Quarterly*, **34**, 1.

Rimmington, M. and Clark, J. (1996) Productivity measurement in foodservice systems, in Johns, N. (ed.) *Productivity Management in Hospitality and Tourism*, Cassell: London.

Sawyer, C.A. (1991) Safety issues related to use of take-out food, *Journal of Foodservice Systems*, **6**, 41–59.

Sill, B. (1994) Operations engineering: improving multi-unit operations, *Cornell Hotel and Restaurant Administration Quarterly*, **35**, 3, 64–71.

Smith, R.S. and Giglio, R.J. (1979) Reducing labour costs in foodservice operations by scheduling, in Livingstone, G.E. and Chong, C.M. (eds) *Food Service Systems*, Academic Press: New York.

Taylor, S. and Lyon, P. (1995) Paradigm lost: the rises and fall of McDonaldisation, *International Journal of Contemporary Hospitality Management*, **7**, 2/3, 64–68.

Teare, R. (1996) Hospitality operations: patterns in management, service improvement and business performance, *International Journal of Contemporary Hospitality Management*, **8**, 7, 63–74.

Townley, R.R. (1989) A survey of important trends critical for the development of new products for today's demanding foodservice consumer, *Journal of Foodservice Systems*, **5**, 113–124.

Umbreit, W.T. (1989) Multi-unit management: managing at a distance, *Cornell Hotel and Restaurant Administration Quarterly*, **30**, 1, 52–59.

Vyskocil-Czajkowski, T.L. and Gilmore, S.A. (1992) Job satisfaction of selected institutional foodservice supervisors, *Journal of Foodservice Systems*, **7**, 29–42.

West, J.J. and Olsen, M. (1989) Competitive tactics in food service: are high performers different?, *Cornell Hotel and Restaurant Administration Quarterly*, **30**, 1, 68–77.

Williams, P.G. and Brand Miller, J.C. (1993) Warm-holding of vegetables in hospitals: cook/chill versus cook/hot hold foodservice systems, *Journal of Foodservice Systems*, **7**, 117–128.

Wyckoff, D.D. (1984) New tools for achieving service quality, *Cornell Hotel and Restaurant Administration Quarterly*, November, 78–91.

23 Industry structure and strategic groups

Introduction

Developing a view of why firms act in particular ways, and the consequences of these actions, provide a fascinating area of inquiry. A major subset for research in strategic management is often taken as an industry. Much research in hospitality is, almost by definition, industry specific and confines itself to data gathering in or applying general concepts drawn from, for example, sociology to hospitality contexts.

These applications may be directed to the industry holistically (hospitality in general) or to a particular sector (e.g. contract catering) within hospitality: essentially these subdivide the industry into component sectors.

An aim of strategic group analysis is to recognise that organisations within an industry or industry sector, which may appear superficially similar, gain competitive advantage differently. Thus it can be considered a level of analysis between those which take an industry as a discrete entity and those which concentrate on the behaviour of individual firms. The notion of strategic groups hypothesises that the ways firms are structured and operate (their strategies) may result in particular circumstances in terms of market share, profitability and so on. Which attributes are considered as the strengths of a particular organisation, in comparison to the characteristics of its competitors, and the extent to which these strengths are sustainable over time require careful analysis by a strategic analyst. To this extent it is relevant to identify if there are groups of firms in an industry which appear more successful than others.

In research terms, this area of inquiry is seen by some as developing the discipline of strategic management itself (Mehera, 1996; Rumlet, Schendel and Teece, 1991). On the other hand, the approach presents a very different perspective from others which take, as their primary focus, either the behaviour of individuals within firms or the process of decision taking within individual firms. The thrust of strategic group analysis is, as its name suggests, undertaken at a strategic level and compares behaviour and performance amongst a number of firms.

To present an insight into the applications of strategic group analysis to hospitality, this chapter aims to:

- provide a background to the theoretical basis for the use of strategic group analysis;
- discuss the trends in strategic group research;

The Handbook of Contemporary Hospitality Management Research, Edited by Bob Brotherton.
© 1999 John Wiley & Sons Ltd.

- establish the use, and apply notions, of strategic group analysis to hospitality contexts and discuss possible directions for this type of analysis; and
- suggest some ways in which to progress work in the area.

Whilst strategic management essentially integrates approaches such as marketing and finance, it should be recognised that much theory underlying the study of strategic groups derives from an economic paradigm. However, no prior knowledge of economics is assumed here, though previous study of the area may prove helpful in adding depth to early sections of the chapter.

The chapter does not set out to be a definitive review in current research on strategic groups in hospitality. Neither does it deal with decisions on sample design (number, types) which some researchers may require to develop 'representative' groups for the purposes of statistical analysis. Instead the intention of the chapter is to ensure that readers who are about to embark on their projects are aware of some of the issues which may be encountered by concentrating on general theory and the conceptual development of the approach: factor analysis and other techniques, a feature of contemporary work outside hospitality, are not covered.

For the purposes of this chapter hospitality is taken to include those sectors which cover hotels, commercial food service and drink/public house sectors.

Industry and market approaches to analysing strategies

Hughes (1986: 21) states: 'firms ... can be grouped into industries: firms which produce the same good may be classified as belonging to the same industry.' The output of an industry is the total output of the firms that make it up. Different industries producing different products will have more than product differences: they could have different numbers of firms and different regulatory (government) frameworks, for example. The assumption here is that the demand and supply conditions will be different enough between industries to account for significant differences in a range of factors. Thus, the purchase of a hotel room night is subject to quite a different set of circumstances than the same consumer will face when purchasing a car.

The main source of empirical data on industry groupings is that contained in the government's Standard Industrial Classification of Economic Information. This is gathered on a regular basis on activities across the economy. Details of the hospitality component of this survey are discussed later in the chapter; meanwhile it may be noted that the Standard Industrial Classifications (SICs) provide data in such categories as agriculture, manufacturing and distribution (Central Statistical Office, 1992). These data can be important because they provide the bedrock of industry analysis through data such as sales, employment and investment within industry categories.

When analysing the actions of organisations, it may be helpful to discover the extent to which these are triggered by the conditions prevalent in their industry, as compared to the extent an organisation has fashioned a singular set of behaviours (and outcomes) for itself. For example, it might be interesting to discover whether a high level of financial return of a firm was a result of their innovative activity, as claimed by its management. If it were found that similar levels of financial return accrued to many of the firm's competitors it would seem that something more general than the management's action is at work.

There is one very practical aspect that must be taken into account when undertaking firm/industry analysis. That is the extent to which a firm is located within any single industry (or industry sub-sector). Hughes (1986: 21) makes this point when he says that ' ... because many firms produce several goods and services, identification of an industry is often difficult in practice.' For example, Granada, the UK owner of Forte Hotels, has interests in contract catering, TV entertainment production and broadcasting (media), and TV rental. Thus, while all activities may neatly fall into a general category of 'services', it is impossible to ascribe all of Granada's activities to one SIC: they would have to be spread amongst several SICs and be so identified. This type of problem will be mitigated if all firms produced their accounts in a fashion which mirrored their operations in different industry sectors. However, it is unlikely that researchers will always be able to gain this information easily.

The traditional economic approach to industrial structure

The notion of market structure is one which will be familiar to those who have studied economics, while even those who have no deep knowledge of the area will understand that some structures are considered as superior to others, in terms of either the consumer (low prices) or the supplier (high profits). The following provides a very general review of market theory and those interested should pursue these issues further with one of the texts in economics for hospitality (Hughes, 1986; Cullen, 1997) or leisure and tourism (Bull, 1991; Tribe, 1995).

Traditional economics identifies four main types of markets: Perfect Competition, Monopolistic Competition, Oligopoly and Monopoly. These stylised (or conceptual) models of market conditions are not strict reflections of reality. Instead they are intended to explain buyer/seller relationships, levels of industry profitability, etc., that exist sufficiently to allow insights on the working of markets when characterised by different numbers of buyers and sellers. Types of market, or models of market structure, are also used to predict likely outcomes when a new market arises which conforms to characteristics of one of the types. For example, if there is only one supplier of a new category of computer software, economists may look towards a model of market supply which allows them to make predictions on likely outcomes to consumers.

Table 23.1 shows the four market types related to three main variables:

1. The number of firms in the industry and their market share.
2. The firm's ability to affect price (this will depend on their levels of market share and the actions that others in the industry may take as a consequence of any changes/innovations they may make).
3. The entry barriers that may be faced by firms trying to join an industry (for example, new firms may need to reach a relatively large scale of production quickly to ensure survival because of the pricing policies existing firms pursue; on the other hand, they may need to spend large amounts on advertising where the dominant form of competition is through brand image).

These conceptual models assume that firms in an industry are relatively similar, for example in terms of motivation, and that forms of market structure are relatively permanent. Furthermore, traditional economics imposes a relatively limited number of

Table 23.1 Traditional economic approaches to market structure

Characteristics		Imperfect competition		
	Perfect competition	Monopolistic competition	Oligopoly	Monopoly
Number of firms	Many	Many	Few	One
Market share of firms	Insignificant	Relatively small	Significant for large firms	100%
Ability to affect price	None	Limited	Some	Considerable
Entry barriers	None	None	Some	Complete
Example	Fruit stalls	Corner grocer	Cars	de Beers

Source: based on Begg, Fischer and Dornbush (1987: 192).

possible structures on a large number of markets. Thus in the computer software example above, the closest parallel could be a monopoly market where there is only one supplier. Problems in this type of analysis spring from a number of sources: for example, the levels of substitutability between the products or services of one market and those of another may have considerable effects on the nature of competition between firms.

Even the theory of imperfect or monopolistic competition developed independently in the USA by Chamberlin (1933) and in the UK by Robinson (1933) to address some of the deficiencies in the other market models still does not fully address the nature of substitutability between products/services across industries. Under the assumptions of monopolistic competition firms can influence their market share by taking action in a variety of ways, including price and product differentiation. These strategies can create customer loyalty which will ensure that, within limits, customers will show a preference for the products of one company over another even when other products appear to be a better buy. Product differentiation can be implemented in a number of ways such as branding.

The industrial economics approach

A newer approach uses the analytical tools of economics and applies them to a particular grouping of firms. Termed 'industrial economics', it has been applied by Caves (1972) and Scherer (1980), amongst others. In this approach primacy is placed on the *specific* factors surrounding an industry which in turn influence, and are influenced by, the market structure, the conduct and strategies adopted by suppliers and, finally, their performance (Figure 23.1).

Demand aspects encompass product/service price elasticity, substitutes for the product/service under consideration, growth of demand, cyclical and seasonal nature of demand, purchase characteristics and so on. *Supply* conditions take into account such aspects as types of technology and their importance to the industry, labour requirements and availability, public policy scheme (e.g. training schemes, grants and loans for business start-ups), and longevity of the product or service. At the second level, *market structure* defines the numbers of buyers and sellers, the nature and extent of product

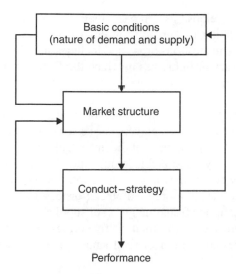

Figure 23.1 An economic structure-conduct-performance model for an industry
Source: Scherer F.M. (1980).

differentiation, industry barriers to entry, cost structures, the extent of vertical integration and other ownership variables.

At the third level, *Conduct*, the aspects to focus on are competitive behaviour areas such as as pricing, advertising, investment and product/service development. The import of this three-level analysis is to consider the performance of an industry in terms of such broad areas as employment and return on investments.

This approach has been used in services and manufacturing sectors, whilst much of its application has been directed towards the performance of firms in oligopolistic industries, particularly with questions of social equity in resource allocation: namely, whether strategies employed by companies have resulted in excess profits for firms despite lower rates of consumer satisfaction. The industrial economics approach has been less used to provide detailed comparisons at strategic levels, so that differences and similarities may be analysed in detail, though what has been termed the 'Austrian School' of economists look towards this type of analysis as they put the accent on change within an industry, and do not accept the normal economic assumptions of perfect knowledge amongst all in an industry or the tendency towards stability of market structures (e.g. Ferguson, 1988; Littlechild, 1986).

Strategic group analysis

Hunt (1972) coined the term 'strategic groups' to explain what he termed an intermediate level of analysis in competitive rivalry. He defined a strategic group as 'A group of firms within an industry that are highly symmetric ... with respect to cost structure, degree of product diversification ... formal organisation, control systems, and management rewards and punishments ... [and] the personal views and preferences for various possible outcomes' (Hunt, 1972). Thus this level of analysis lies between examining an industry as a whole and concentrating on the workings of an individual firm.

Porter (1980), who develops this approach, maintains that a principal factor in strategic success is that of relating a company to its environment. Although the relevant environment that a company relates to is broad and includes social and economic forces, the 'key aspect is the industry or industries in which the firm competes'. This focus has a strong influence in determining the competitive 'rules of the game' as well as the strategies potentially available to the firm: the key (to success or failure) is found in the differing abilities of firms to deal with outside forces affecting the industry. Any investigation must start with all the given players in a sector or industry—to eliminate any at an early stage is to cut off the richness of the investigation.

The reasons for identifying strategic groups are many. Researchers may want to *understand* an industry better; they may want to *explain* why certain conditions affect some companies' performance more than others; or they may want to *analyse* what a company needs to do to move from one group of suppliers in the industry to another.

Porter's (1980) approach is built upon the five forces model of industry competition he developed. This sees competitor or rival strategies as affected by four other main forces:

- Bargaining power of *suppliers*
- Threat of new (potential) *entrants*
- Bargaining power of *buyers*
- Threat of *substitute* products or services.

Areas of competitive rivalry may be many. Those that Porter concentrates on are shown in Table 23.2.

In implementing an analysis of this type it must not be assumed that all the factors mentioned in Table 23.2 are relevant to competitive rivalry in an industry nor that, once established, they are unchanging. Part of the necessary process in the analysis (which is aided by use of the industrial economics framework) is for the researcher to choose an appropriate set of competitive dimensions, or variables, for exploration. In this process those variables contained in Table 23.2 may act as starting point, but should not exclude the introduction of other competitive variables which may be apparent in the industry.

Industrial mapping: a tour operator example

Industry mapping as advocated by Porter (1980) is a process which helps greatly in group analysis. In this technique two important competitive dimensions (e.g. from the list in Table 23.2) are chosen. For example, in analysing the fast-food business these could be taken as importance of branding as judged by advertising spends and scale of provision, as measured by number of units. The example below is aimed to show in more detail the use of the technique. As used here it is essentially impressionistic, as opposed to the mathematical/statistical means used by some researchers.

The requirement   To establish the nature of competition amongst tour operators in the (fictitious) northern European country of Cooland.

Step one   Gather full details on all significant firms in the area of investigation, industry statistics, trends, etc. Sources may include company reports and materials,

Table 23.2   Porter's dimensions of competitive rivalry, with examples

Major strategic variable	*Example of strategic action*
1. Brand identification	Number of brands a company may have and their strength in the marketplace
2. Push vs pull	Use of distribution systems in relation to end-consumer/user focus
3. Specialisation	Extent to which a specialist niche type product is being offered
4. Channel selection	Choice of particular channels/strategies within the distribution system
5. Product quality	An emphasis on high standards in relation to the sector
6. Technological change	Investments in technology to provide a distinctive feature of strategy and operations
7. Vertical integration	Degree of being locked into/locking others into the production/distribution system through long-term/ownership relationships between organisations
8. Cost position	Cost position from an operations perspective
9. Service	Nature of service offered customer/client groups: pre-stay, duration of stay, after-stay policies
10. Price policy	Full range of pricing strategies (e.g. discounting policies)
11. Leverage	Particularly important for quoted companies (e.g. relative to price–earnings ratios)
12. Relationship to parent company	Large company variables: extent to which the holding companies allow strategic and operational autonomy
13. Relationship to host government	Extent to which companies (e.g. multinationals) develop close links with regulators in their different operating environments

Source: based on Porter (1980).

industry reports, operators' brochures, government sources, past academic articles, official/unofficial/personal contacts and so on. Ensure that the 'database' is as large and as rich as possible on the full range of industry/sector suppliers. In a group analysis it may be decided to keep all firms in the analysis or to exclude those which do not meet some given criteria (for example, that they account for at least 1% of industry sales).

Step two   Choose two important competitive dimensions by which to analyse the companies.

Amongst the 14 holiday tour operators that trade in Cooland it appears that the two important competitive dimensions are the levels of specialisation utilised by the operators, as judged firstly by the type of market focus utilised, and secondly by the extent of vertical integration which the operators have within the tourism business. This latter variable includes analysis of ownership of retail travel agencies, transport operators such as airlines, and other tourism suppliers such as hotels.

In any analysis it may be that there are more than two competitive dimensions. In this case the analyst may want to create more than one industry map, or indeed decide to pursue another line of analysis.

Step three   Operationalise the competitive dimensions so they may be scaled or mapped. The method used should allow the relative position of firms to be differentiated. There must be underlying rationale which is consistently applied to each firm and, as necessary, fully explained as the tool of analysis.

In this case the market focus axis is envisaged as a distinction between packages designed to appeal to mass markets (e.g. 'traditional' sun and sand packages) as opposed to specialist packages such as activity/hobby holidays to less popular destinations. In operationalising the second axis, that of vertical integration, decisions may be made by accounting for the extent of a firm's ownership (or contractual relations) with other tourism suppliers. A draft map (as seen in Figure 23.2 it more closely resembles a graph) can then be drawn, though it should be remembered that aspects such as the scale of the axes may need to be modified at further stages of the analysis.

Step four   Identify the position of individual firms on the map.

All operators have been plotted on the map and are represented by a dot. The position of Lozlux is arrived at through the fact that its position on the vertical axis is low—it offers few packages, all with a mass market appeal, while on the horizontal axis it has only a low level of integration in the tourism industry. Technically all firms should be named, but Figure 23.2 is used more to explain the method of analysis.

Step five   Consider the relative positions of the different firms and develop groups in terms of the chosen strategic parameters. In developing groups the important factor is the *relative* position of firms to other firms on the map: those they are close to and those they are distant from. Through careful analysis it may be possible to create groups,

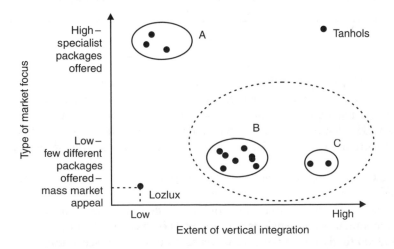

Figure 23.2   Industry map of holiday tour operators in Cooland

though decisions will not always be clear cut: for example, it is important not to create false groups.

The development of groups may not be the result of an initial plotting of the firms on the map, and may require testing with a number of different scales, etc., used to operationalise the competitive dimensions (as mentioned above, at Step three). As indicated earlier, the underlying rationale of scales, etc., should always be clear. In the example in Figure 23.2 the analyst has left Tanhols and Lozlux out of the main group structure, feeling that the analysis will be more fruitful if their positions are treated as idiosyncratic.

Step six   Relate other organisation and strategic parameters to group members to establish the existence, or otherwise, of common factors across group membership. In the Cooland example these other factors might include indications of each operator's size, distributions channels used, and advertising spend.

Step seven   Consider the implications of groups in terms of moving from one group to another and/or in relation to performance of firms in relation to group average and industry norms. Thus this could require considering the requirements of moving from one group to another: do they need to become larger organisations in terms of holidays sold, increase their promotional budgets, etc.? Alternatively (or in addition) a main variable like performance could be examined, to explore whether there existed any relationships between group membership and rates of financial performance. This might require a degree of longitudinal analysis not previously required in the mapping exercise.

The final 'results' of the 'investigation' into mapping the Cooland holiday operators are shown in Figure 23.2.

Three main groups of operators in the holiday tour market are identified in Figure 23.2. Group A, made up of three firms, is the low volume/specialist niche group. While sharing group membership, overlap between the package range offered by the operators is low. Two other groups may be noted. Group B's seven operators are distinguished from the two constituents of Group C more by their lower levels of integration than by the types of package they sell, as it appears from their position on the vertical axis that they offer similar types of packages.

Further analysis could uncover the basis of competing strategies used within the groups and, by comparison, between groups. For example, this analysis (which follows a conventional Porter line!) appears to show that Group B are 'stuck in the middle' as they offer neither the specialisms of Group A nor the potential economies available through a high degree of vertical integration (Group C). Yet, as previously remarked, the analysis also identifies two firms which appear to break the rules: Tanhols, a highly integrated operator, which yet is able to provide a high range of very specialist holidays, and Lozlux which appears to operate at the mass end of the market with very low levels of integration (and thus, potentially, low overheads).

Depending on the objectives of the project, further details of analysis could follow. For example, levels of performance could be established; the nature of change in company direction to leave their group might be considered by some Group B firms where a further level of analysis has shown the difference between them and Group C constituents.

While this type of analysis can aid in the understanding of industry dynamics, care must be taken not to accept conclusions uncritically. Two particular factors must be kept in mind. Firstly, there is a need to guard against the creation of artificial groups (Punj and Stewart, 1989; Hatten and Hatten, 1987). Secondly, performance of firms and groups must be measured reliably: this could encounter a number of different problems including, at firm level, annual accounts showing only performance data (e.g. return on capital) consolidated over a number of commercial activities in different industries.

It must also be remembered that this approach relies on being able to accumulate considerable amounts of data, finding the main competitive dimensions and operationalising them so that a map can be created. In all this the role of the analyst is key. While industry/sector knowledge is important and a creative approach to analysis is helpful, the analyst will not only have to deal with large quantities of data but be able to remain sufficiently objective and experimental to allow groups to develop which are not purely predicated by past work and/or the researcher's personal bias. Given all this it is not perhaps so unlikely that statistical factor analysis techniques are often employed in strategic group work.

Effectiveness of strategic group research

Thomas and Venkatraman (1988), Barney and Hoskisson (1990) and Reger and Huff (1993) have all reviewed work in the area. While drawing on the observations of all three, the following review concentrates on the approach used by Thomas and Venkatraman (1988) who see strategic group analysis as important as it allows multi-disciplinary analysis, thus facilitating richer investigation and data interpretation than is possible under a single or, in their terms, a uni-discipline approach. Their relatively favourable conclusions may be contrasted against the views of Barney and Hoskisson (1990) who feel that there are other ways that strategic research may be aimed.

When evaluating 20 studies in the area Thomas and Venkatraman (1988) concluded that work should be more empirically based and take into account current industry trends to a greater extent. They evaluated studies by two criteria, namely: (i) operationalisation of strategy (i.e. strategic variables examined), and (ii) the approach used for the development of these groups.

The first dimension provides a distinction between studies which specify strategy narrowly—say, focusing on one functional area—against those which view strategy in broader terms (e.g. multiple functional areas) and adopt a holistic view of strategy (Hambrick, 1980). The second dimension focused on how researchers developed views of the nature of strategic groups: specifically whether the researchers' criteria were *a priori* (based on a theoretic rationale and therefore theory driven) or *a posteriori* (based on empirical observations obtained as part of the research process and therefore data driven). By using the two dimensions to create a matrix, the authors are able to place work into one of four categories, as shown in Figure 23.3.

Work in Quadrant I uses narrow dimensions of strategy and 'imported' criteria of the nature of groups from a particular disciplinary sphere. Quadrant II work allows the narrow dimension of strategy to be developed by empirical means over the sample firms. In Quadrant III research, a broad sweep (e.g. a multi-disciplinary approach) of strategic management may be employed, though groups will be identified through

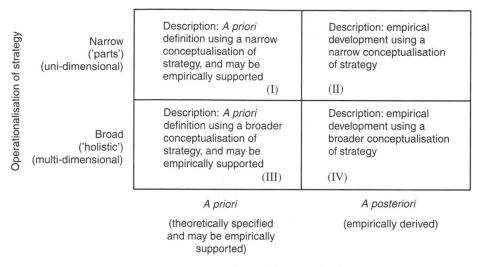

	Description: *A priori* definition using a narrow conceptualisation of strategy, and may be empirically supported (I)	Description: empirical development using a narrow conceptualisation of strategy (II)
Narrow ('parts') (uni-dimensional)		
Broad ('holistic') (multi-dimensional)	Description: *A priori* definition using a broader conceptualisation of strategy, and may be empirically supported (III)	Description: empirical development using a broader conceptualisation of strategy (IV)

A priori

(theoretically specified and may be empirically supported)

A posteriori

(empirically derived)

Approach to group development

Figure 23.3   A classificatory scheme for strategic group analysis
Source: Thomas H. and Venkatraman N. (1988).

theory-driven frames. Finally, in Quadrant IV strategic management is interpreted in a broad way and groups are derived from the empirical data gathered during the research.

A common feature of much of the work reviewed is that large (national) industries are used, comprising many different firms. In establishing strategic groups statistical techniques such as factor and cluster analysis are common. Thomas and Venkatraman (1998: 541) conclude that many studies, particularly those located in Quadrant II, are undertaken to show that firms within an industry are not homogeneous and provide 'rather *weak* interpretations of the meaning of the groups for theory and practice' (emphasis in original). They indicate that it is hardly innovative to conclude that all firms in an industry are not similar, and further observe that:

1. Industry parameters are usually predefined and use national SIC classifications.
2. There is little consistency amongst the strategic dimensions analysed across the different pieces of research. There is no common approach to examining strategic types such as those advanced by Porter (1980) or Miles and Snow (1978).
3. The construction of groups is often not detailed enough. To ensure that firms belong to a particular group, three specific factors should be certain: members should follow similar strategies; firms should show greater similarity to other group members than to any other firm in the analysis; and members should respond in a comparable form to market opportunities and threats.
4. Work surveyed supports only a weak predictive validity in establishing links between strategies employed and performance.

A weakness of the statistical approach to uncovering strategic groups is that by *merely* using statistical techniques such as cluster analysis it may be possible to identify 'groups' which have no bearing on how strategy is formulated in reality. Other reasons why the approach may be limited include the fact that not all firms may be pursuing strategies that are conscious (to the extent that they have been carefully planned and firms position themselves relative to competitors); also what Reger and Huff (1993) term overlapping group membership—firms may be in more than one group.

Amongst the suggestions that Thomas and Venkatraman (1988) make for future research is the use of more variables when structuring strategic groups. For example, they suggest examining internal factors such as the management systems employed by firms. This would allow an analysis of the strategic directions of firms (and hence group membership) by a more complex set of variables. They comment also on the popularity of secondary data sources in developing strategic group parameters and suggest that greater effort should be made to gain data directly from firms and managers.

Increasingly, too, they identify a need to carry out analysis outside the confines of an individual country, in order to take account of trends of internationalisation and global-isation. The observed tendency to focus on industries within a particular country may reflect more on the accessibility of data. It may be more productive, in the development of theory on strategic groups, to place a primacy emphasis on the nature of strategies followed, rather than using predefined industry contexts within single countries.

A particular point made by Reger and Huff (1993), enlarging on a point of Thomas and Venkatraman (1988), is that researchers must put more emphasis on the views of managers in the industry as to their strategies and rivals. With a focus on managers and their perceptions this approach is termed 'cognitive mapping'. For an indication of its development relative to strategic group analysis readers are recommended to the Reger and Huff (1993) article. For a fuller induction to the approach see Eden, Jones and Simms (1979, 1983).

It should again be stressed that much of the work reviewed is large scale and requires sophisticated statistical techniques. These are unlikely to be directly relevant to students who are just about to embark on strategic management work and who lack either knowledge of statistical techniques or the resources to carry them out. However, the analysis at least helps to provide criteria for evaluating the work of others and, more directly, to provide ground to progress new approaches for analysis in hospitality.

Foundation data for analysing industries—Standard Industry Classifications (SICs)

As previously indicated in this chapter, SICs are officially designated categories of economic activity. Government statistics provide information on the sizes and some characteristics of industries. The UK's classification system was reformed in 1992. SIC (1992) was drawn directly from the European Union's classification system —Nomenclature des Activités établies dans les Communautés Européennes (NACE)—which is an extension of a system developed by the United Nations (International Standard of Industrial Classification—ISIC).

In the UK there is a minimum list heading, which is then further subdivided into order numbers. These were first introduced in 1948 and have been regularly revised in line with the methodology of the system developed and the European Union's. In the UK hospitality activities fall under Section H, Division 55, as shown in Table 23.3. The term 'hospitality' is entirely absent from the categories, though general areas of commercial short-stay accommodation, food and drink are present.

Table 23.3   SIC section H—hotels and restaurants

Group	Class and sub-class	
55.1		**HOTELS**
	55.11	Hotels and motels, with restaurant
	55.11/1	Licensed hotels and motels
	55.11/2	Unlicensed hotels and motels
	55.12	Hotels and motels, without restaurant
55.2		**CAMPING SITES AND OTHER PROVISION OF SHORT-STAY ACCOMMODATION**
	55.21	Youth hostels and mountain refuges
	55.22	Camping sites, including caravan sites
	55.23	Other provision of lodgings not elsewhere classified
	55.23/1	Holiday centres and holiday villages
	55.23/2	Other self-catering holiday accommodation
	55.23/3	Other tourist or short-stay accommodation
55.3		**RESTAURANTS**
	55.30	Restaurants
	55.30/1	Licensed restaurants
	55.30/2	Unlicensed restaurants and cafes
	55.30/3	Take-away food shops
55.4		**BARS**
	55.40	Bars
	55.40/1	Licensed clubs with entertainment
	55.40/2	Public houses and bars
55.5		**CANTEENS AND CATERING**
	55.51	Canteens
	55.52	Catering

Source: based on Central Statistical Office (1992).

SIC divisions provide a starting place for many research projects which seek to establish the broad parameters of an industry or sector. However, they may be inadequate: as shown earlier their distinctions may be constricting in many cases (the example given earlier was that of Granada), because SICs classify organisations by their primary economic activity. Within Section H, catering at a department store or supermarket might not be included in 55.3 if it were managed by the retail establishment, though if the operation were run by a contractor such as Sutcliffe it would be covered under 55.52.

If the researcher is involved in longitudinal analysis it should be pointed out that 1992 marked a change in the SIC system—see Standard Industrial Classification of Economic Activities (Correlation between SIC (1992) and SIC(1980)) for details. Many hospitality projects dealing with related sectors may want to access Section 63 on Land Transport (divisions on railway traffic, coach services, air transport activities of travel agencies and tour operators) as well SIC Section H.

Relevant work in hospitality

Hospitality is a relatively recent area of academic interest. Much initial published work in the area concentrates on distinguishing sector constituents (e.g. hotels, restaurants

Table 23.4 Review articles including firm group analysis in the *International Journal of Contemporary Hospitality Management* (Vol. 1, No. 1–Vol. 9, No. 5/6 inclusive)

Author(s)	Nature of research	Title	Groups identified	Publication details
Ball	Conceptual/ empirical	Whither the small independent take-away?	Two different sets of groups identified: 8 groups by turnover sizes; 6 different product groups (hamburger, pizza, etc.)	Vol. 8, No. 5, 1996
Beattie	Empirical	Hospitality internationalisation: an empirical investigation	Compares hotel internationalisation by size and three types of parent groups (major hospitality orientation concentrating on hotels; hotels as one part of a wider portfolio; conglomerate interests) *vis-à-vis* extent of internationalisation by company	Vol. 3, No. 4, 1991
Chon and Sing	Empirical	Current economic issues facing the US lodging industry	Two main groups identified: 5 accommodation segments (hotel, motor hotel, B&B, etc.) and 3 organisational types (chain managed, franchised and independents)	Vol. 5, No. 3, 1993
Crawford-Welch and Tse	Empirical (secondary data)	Mergers, acquisitions and alliances in the European hospitality industry	Takeovers by origin of firms (US and non-US)	Vol. 2, No. 1, 1990
D'Annunzio-Green	Empirical	Developing international managers in the hospitality industry	Classifies recruitment strategies by categories of ethnocentricity, polycentricity, geocentricity and regiocentricity	Vol. 9, No. 5/6, 1997
Edgar, Litteljohn and Allardyce	Empirical	Strategic clusters and strategic space: the case of the short break market	4 groups: distribution; packaging; promotion; pricing strategies	Vol. 6, No. 5, 1994
English *et al.*	Conceptual/ empirical	Restaurant attrition: a longitudinal analysis of restaurant failures	3 main groups identified: independents; franchised and corporately owned	Vol. 8, No. 2, 1996
Horsburgh	Empirical and conceptual	Resources in the international hotel industry: a framework for analysis	Developed the notions of product market positions (geographic scope/brand position, differentiation) and relationships between sources of competitive advantage and strategic objectives	Vol. 3, No. 4, 1991
Jones and Lockwood	Conceptual	Hospitality operating systems	Discusses developments of published means of classifying food service operations	Vol. 7, No. 5, 1995
Kara, Kaynak and Kucukemiroglu	Empirical	Marketing strategies for fast food restaurants: a customer view	Product segmentation of suppliers coupled with empirical perception of service attributes, contrasting US and Canadian customers	Vol. 7, No. 4, 1995
Litteljohn	Empirical/ conceptual	Internationalisation in hotels: current aspects and developments	Quoted companies, international (regional analysis)	Vol. 9, No. 5/6, 1997
Litteljohn and Slattery	Empirical	Macro analysis techniques: an appraisal of Europe's main hotel markets	Implicit distinction between quoted and non-quoted hotel stock	Vol. 3, No. 4, 1991
Main	Empirical	Information Technology and the independent hotel	Core of business: three categories: rooms letting; bar/restaurant; other. Size categories also used	Vol. 7, No. 6, 1995

Table 23.4 *Continued*

Author(s)	Nature of research	Title	Groups identified	Publication details
Moutinho *et al.*	Empirical	The future development of the hotel sector: an international comparison	International differences identified (regional UK, Ireland, Spain)	Vol. 7, No. 4, 1995
Ogden	Empirical	Strategy, structure and employee relations: lessons from compulsory competitive tendering	Local authorities in Scotland	Vol. 7, No. 2/3, 1995
Olsen, Murphy and Teare	Empirical	CEO perspectives on scanning the global business environment	International Hotel Association members and, though not fully specified, comparisons made between members' status relative to size and multinational nature of operations	Vol. 6, No. 4, 1994
Peacock	Empirical	A question of size	Evolved a view of two main (perceived) competitive groups: small and large hotels (both with a geographic focus)	Vol. 5, No. 4, 1993
Phillips	Empirical/conceptual	Trouble in the UK hotel sector	Conceptual, geographic distribution	Vol. 9, No. 4, 1997
Radiven and Lucas	Empirical	Wages council abolition and small hotels	2 groups: small hotels and large (i.e. group operated) hotels	Vol. 8, No. 5, 1996
Roper	Empirical	The emergence of hotel consortia as transnational forms	5 strategic groups based on Porter's work: low cost; low cost focus; differentiation; differentiation focus; 'stuck in the middle'	Vol. 7, No. 1, 1995
Roper and Carmouche	Empirical	Budget hotels, a case of mistaken identity?	3 groups identified: new system 'budget' hotels; traditional 'budget' hotels; upper tier 'budget' hotels	Vol. 1, No. 1, 1989
Senior and Morphew	Empirical	Competitive strategies in the budget hotel sector	International comparisons on sector: 3 groups in USA—upper tier, middle tier, lower tier; 2 in France—économique and super-économique; 3 in UK—one star, two star, three star	Vol. 2, No. 3, 1990
Smith	Empirical	Sunday trading: an analysis of employment structures in leisure and retailing	Organisations in three different sectors identified: pub restaurant chain; bowling centre, bingo operator	Vol. 7, No. 2/3, 1995
Sparks	Empirical	Guest history: is it being utilised?	Responses differentiated by organisations' star classification and membership (or not) of hotel chain	Vol. 5, No. 1, 1993
Tse and Olsen	Empirical	Business strategy and organisational structure	Various corporate variables identified: 4 market segments (fast food; dinner house; coffee shop; cafeteria); 3 for geographical scope of competition (national, regional, local); also variable related to operations (size; whether franchised and numbers of concepts)	Vol. 2, No. 3, 1990
Witt and Witt	Conceptual	Why productivity in the hotel sector is low	Data presented in 6 groupings: Hotel and catering; Transport; Retail distribution; Recreation and cultural services; Other services; Whole tourism sector	Vol. 1, No. 2, 1989

and bars) from other industries. For example, much work to the mid-1980s established the area as a legitimate one for management education and research. The work made two particular points: the size and economic impact of the industry (employment, revenue creation, contribution to the balance of payments) and another emphasis on the special conditions of hospitality contexts (e.g. nature of consumption and operations) in contrast to those of other industries. The need to validate hospitality as a distinct area of activity is not surprising when the dominant management paradigm used in research (explicitly or implicitly) relates to a model of management founded on manufacturing (if not military) activity and, in many ways, a particular Western view of management.

The situation has changed somewhat since this early work was carried out. Management researchers are, in general, more aware of cultural and industry contexts in which they work. One small example is the development of an interest in service industries and services management. It was in the early 1980s, for example, when the *Service Industries Journal* started publication. As may be surmised, the significance of this work often lies in the validation and exploration of hospitality as a different, yet significant, area of research.

Differentiation in hospitality often addresses the structure of the industry, identifying its fragmented nature. For example, in analysing performance in the UK hotel industry Slattery (1992) differentiates between affiliated (groups) and non-affiliated hotels to show radically different results. To further explore the nature of strategic group analysis within hospitality, a small-scale review of literature in the field of hospitality was undertaken. Articles from the *International Journal of Contemporary Hospitality Management* (*IJCHM*) were reviewed from its inception in 1989 to mid-1997. The survey in no way attempts to apply the Thomas and Venkatraman (1988) framework (see Figure 23.3) rigorously to a hospitality context. As research in hospitality is at a relatively early stage a broad interpretation has been taken of group analysis.

Work which identified different groups of firms operating across hospitality sectors was included. Omitted from the review was work which dealt with hospitality as a homogeneous industry or which treated all firms within a sub-sector of hospitality as the same (however either of these terms was defined by the authors). Additionally, work which merely used a case study approach and provided no link back into strategic industry parameters was excluded. A more exhaustive approach would have included articles from all hospitality management journals. However, the aim here is to provide an indication of the degree to which strategic group analysis is employed in hospitality. Articles identified by the survey are itemised in Table 23.4.

That 26 articles utilise some form of group analysis indicates that, for whatever purpose, differentiation of the industry into groups is an accepted form of investigation in hospitality research. However, most group analysis is relatively cursory in nature and does not employ strategic variables to analyse data. The articles reviewed indicate that researchers who use sectoral and group analysis do so in order to:

- reveal the richness of the hospitality industry sometimes through product segmentation approaches to explore sub-sectors in the industry (e.g. budget hotels);
- address some issues in corporate internationalisation and sectoral comparisons between countries;

● account for and explore differences in types of organisation and affiliation types (e.g. geographic distribution/competition types; quoted/non-quoted companies; chain and non-chain affiliated organisations; large and small organisations).

Most of the works reviewed do not, however, develop industry groupings relative to SICs or employ the fundamental notions of strategic group analysis. Indeed, much work will never have had these as aims. In most cases, the groups identified are on the basis of *a priori* criteria. Examples of work which has adopted a strategic grouping analysis approach are those by Tse and Olsen (1990) on competition in the US restaurant industry; Beattie (1991) which uses industry mapping in relation to international hotel companies operating in Europe; Edgar, Litteljohn and Allardyce (1994) which analyses hotel strategies in the commercial short break market; and Roper (1995) which is a strategic analysis of hotel consortia. None of these works uses the factor analysis popular in the work referred to earlier. On the other hand, the use of industry-based empirical data is popular, though multi-disciplinary strategic management paradigms are less evident.

Work which uses simple classification systems of firms (e.g. quoted versus unquoted organisations, product segmentation approaches) perhaps discloses a need to describe operational differences which exist in hospitality. This type of differentiation may be appropriate in a new area of study where there exists a strong tendency to describe and categorise elements, in order to build up knowledge so that the conceptual basis of the 'discipline' (i.e. hospitality or hospitality management) may be understood. Yet, if this is merely to describe or to conclude that all firms in an industry are not similar, the result, as Thomas and Venkatraman (1988) have remarked in another context, is hardly startling. It perhaps forms a foundation for strategic level analysis, rather than a useful end in itself.

The use of existing empirical data is not necessarily always a strength. For example, the lack of statistics on hospitality sectors of the economy (rather than the sub-division in SIC Section H) has already been pointed out. If one outcome of using existing statistics is to entrench superficial divisions of industry structure and confirm conventional views of strategy (particularly if these have been generated with no reference to industries such as hospitality), the research could be severely limited. These problems point to the need for significant work to be carried out on the conceptual nature of strategic groups in hospitality fields. Thus, for example, work by Jones and Lockwood (1995) in food service and Peacock (1993) for hotels may provide some foundation for future strategic analysis in hospitality.

Suggestions for future directions in strategic group analysis in hospitality

Since the origin of the 'general' market approach of classical economics which looked at the behaviour of firms, the discipline has developed approaches which strengthen the strategic dimensions of firms. Classical economics placed an emphasis on a few models of industry structure, treated firms as homogeneous and put high value on predicting the performance and behaviour of generic market types. The industrial economics approach, introduced later, allows a more sensitive analysis of particular industry conditions and appraisal of corporate strategies/players to be made, thus allowing the behaviour of groups of firms within a given industry to be disaggregated from overall industry norms. More recently, reflecting the rise of interest in strategic management, work on strategic groups has evolved. Whilst not all commentators agree on its value, reviewers have identified several aspects to consider for future work. These include a need to consider strategic moves on an international scale; a need to provide a greater emphasis on strategic types across conventional industry boundaries; and a need for industry-based empirical data gathering, possibly through cognitive mapping techniques.

The review of a sample of hospitality literature has revealed the presence of an element of group analysis. This may reflect a need to disaggregate the industry into heterogeneous groupings and is valuable when exploring management issues from a multi-disciplinary perspective: this is particularly important in hospitality management where it has long been recognised that successful operations require a careful blend and development of a number of different management specialisms. However, in no way should hospitality be treated as an isolated part of management and strategic theory. As Thomas and Venkatraman (1988) indicate, there is a need to elevate the status of the strategic dimensions in group analysis, rather than to feel constrained by traditional industry definitions and data sources.

Given that much of strategic group analysis is large scale and statistical in nature, work will not necessarily be within the scope of a relatively constrained research project in terms of time and resources. However, there are four main areas of work which could be considered: these are discussed in the following paragraphs.

Strategic frameworks

The first area is in developing conceptual strategic frameworks for comparing hospitality organisations. Hospitality is a broad and heterogeneous industry, both horizontally (for example, hotel sector characteristics share little with those of the fast-food sector) and vertically, where a majority of operations are inevitably small businesses whilst larger chains will have very different resource bases and competitive strategies. Too much emphasis on merely identifying this type of structural characteristic of supply, may be at the expense of developing strategic frameworks and concepts that overarch these traditional divisions in industry analysis. This type of work should allow for the special circumstances and characteristics of hospitality organisations to feature in the analysis.

Strategic variables

The second area of work concentrates on strategic variables amongst hospitality and other service organisations to establish the development of competences, sustainable advantage and other strategic variables.

Work of the type of Campbell and Verbeke (1994) points to one way of addressing group analysis. In this work the sample of firms examined is confined to service multinationals. The authors validate this approach by arguing that these companies show a different pattern to internationalisation than do manufacturing multinationals. Their sample of nine companies mixes hotel companies (Sheraton, Four Seasons) together with financial services companies, data processing firms and management consultants. Their particular research interest is to explore the relative importance of centralised innovation and national responsiveness in successful multinational management.

It is essential in this type of analysis that the inclusion of industry sectors and/or sample organisations can be justified on competing criteria of 'similarity' (the organisations have a certain family resemblance) and 'comparability' (new insights to be gained). The choice of the main strategic variables will need to be grounded in a careful appraisal and knowledge of the operating and strategic variables of the operations concerned.

While the example chosen involves a small sample of organisations and identifies organisation types rather than being in the tradition of strategic group analysis, there is no reason why the approach could not in time be developed to be used on a larger scale.

Sectoral analysis

The third area concentrates on sectoral analysis in relation to organisational and strategic change. This approach was developed by Litteljohn (1993, 1994, 1996) where a sector of the industry is taken and longitudinal analysis is carried out. Under this arrangement changes in room stock and estimated turnover by the 20 largest groups in Scotland can be compared over time. This allows a number of strategic parameters such as geographical distribution of stock, room level, pricing and promotional strategies to be taken into account, as well as the nature of ownership and, as relevant, other corporate links.

To undertake this form of research it is necessary to ensure that resources exist so that valid sub-sector data (capacity, financial data) are available. Given that many new researchers will find practical difficulties in carrying out longitudinal analysis, it may be more profitable to bolt work on to existing and past studies. In a related area, it may also be interesting to conduct international comparative analysis of the information available on industry sectors and sub-sectors.

Mapping techniques

Cognitive mapping techniques can be developed amongst hospitality managers. This approach turns attention to the processes of strategic planning in organisations by gaining the views of strategy formers and decision takers in industry. Research in this area will no doubt present challenges, especially if a true multi-disciplinary approach is to be taken. Nevertheless, it may result in significant progress in the ways aspects of competition, strategic decision taking and performance are viewed in hospitality and the wider service industry.

References

Ball S D (1996) 'Whither the small independent take-away?', *International Journal of Contemporary Hospitality Management*, Vol 8, No 5, pp 25–29

Barney J and Hoskisson R E (1990) 'Strategic groups: untested assertions and research pro-
    posals', *Managerial and Decision Economics*, Vol 11, pp 187–198
Beattie R (1991) 'Hospitality internationalisation: an empirical investigation', *International
    Journal of Contemporary Hospitality Management*, Vol 3, No 4, pp 14–20
Begg D, Fischer S and Dornbush R (1987) *Economics*, Second edition, McGraw-Hill,
    Maidenhead
Bull A (1991) *The Economics of Travel and Tourism*, Longman, Cheshire
Campbell A J and Verbeke A (1994) 'The globalisation of service multinationals', *Long Range
    Planning*, Vol 27, No 2, pp 95–102
Caves R (1972) *American Industry: Structure, Conduct, Performance*, Prentice-Hall, Englewood
    Cliffs, NJ
Central Statistical Office (1992) *Standard Industrial Classification of Activities*, HMSO, London
Chamberlin E H (1933) *The Theory of Monopolistic Competition*, Harvard University Press,
    Cambridge, MA
Chon K S and Sing A (1993) 'Current economic issues facing the US lodging industry',
    International Journal of Contemporary Hospitality Management, Vol 5, No 3, pp 3–9
Crawford-Welch S and Tse E (1990) 'Mergers, acquisitions and alliances in the European hospi-
    tality industry', *International Journal of Contemporary Hospitality Management*, Vol 2,
    No 1, pp 10–16
Cullen P (1997) *Economics for Hospitality Management*, International Thomson Business Press,
    London
D'Annunzio-Green N (1997) 'Developing international managers in the hospitality industry',
    International Journal of Contemporary Hospitality Management, Vol 9, No 5/6, pp 199–208
Eden C, Jones S and Simms D (1979) *Thinking in Organisations*, Macmillan, London
Eden C, Jones S and Simms D (1983) *Messing About in Problems*, Pergamon, Elmsford, NY
Edgar D, Litteljohn D and Allardyce M (1994) 'Strategic clusters and strategic space: the case of
    the short break market', *International Journal of Contemporary Hospitality Management*,
    Vol 6, No 5, pp 20–26
English W, Josiam B, Upchurch R S and Willems J (1996) 'Restaurant attrition: a longitudinal
    analysis of restaurant failures', *International Journal of Contemporary Hospitality
    Management*, Vol 8, No 2, pp 17–20
Ferguson P R (1988) *Industrial Economics: Issues and Perspectives*, Macmillan Education,
    London
Hambrick D C (1980) 'Operationalising the concept of business-level strategy in research',
    Academy of Management Review, Vol 5, pp 567–575
Hatten K J and Hatten M L (1987) 'Strategic groups, asymmetrical mobility barriers and con-
    testability', *Strategic Management Journal*, Vol 8, pp 329–342
Horsburgh S (1991) 'Resources in the international hotel industry: a framework for analysis',
    International Journal of Contemporary Hospitality Management, Vol 3, No 4, pp 30–36
Hughes H (1986) *Economics for Hotel and Catering Students*, Second edition, Hutchinson, London
Hunt M S (1972) 'Competition in the major home appliance industry, 1960–1970', Unpublished
    doctoral dissertation, Harvard University
Jones P and Lockwood A (1995) 'Hospitality operating systems', *International Journal of
    Contemporary Hospitality Management*, Vol 7, No 5, pp 17–20
Kara A, Kaynak E and Kucukemiroglu O (1995) 'Marketing strategies for fast food restaurants:
    a customer view', *International Journal of Contemporary Hospitality Management*, Vol 7,
    No 4, pp 16–22
Litteljohn D (1993) 'The role of hotel groups in Scotland's tourism industry', *Council for
    Hospitality Management Education Research Conference*, Manchester
Litteljohn D (1994) 'Competitive strategies in Scotland's hotel industry', *Council for Hospitality
    Management Education Research Conference*, Napier University, Edinburgh
Litteljohn D (1996) 'The structure–conduct–performance model; its contribution towards an
    assessment of trends in the hotel industry', *Council for Hospitality Management Education
    Research Conference*, Nottingham, April
Litteljohn D (1997) 'Internationalisation in hotels: current aspects and developments',
    International Journal of Contemporary Hospitality Management, Vol 9, No 5/6

Litteljohn D and Slattery P (1991) 'Macro analysis techniques: an appraisal of Europe's main hotel markets', *International Journal of Contemporary Hospitality Management*, Vol 3, No 4, pp 6–13

Littlechild S C (1986) *The Fallacy of the Mixed Economy*, Second edition, Institute of Economic Affairs, London

Main H (1995) 'Information Technology and the independent hotel', *International Journal of Contemporary Hospitality Management*, Vol 7, No 6, pp 30–32

Mehera A (1996) 'Resource and market based determinants of performance in the U.S. banking industry', *Strategic Management Journal*, Vol 17, pp 307–322

Miles R E and Snow C C (1978) *Organisation, Strategy, Structure and Process*, McGraw-Hill, New York

Moutinho L, McDonagh P, Peris S M and Bigne E (1995) 'The future development of the hotel sector: an international comparison', *International Journal of Contemporary Hospitality Management*, Vol 7, No 4

Ogden S (1994) 'Strategy, structure and employee relations: lessons from compulsory competitive tendering', *International Journal of Contemporary Hospitality Management*, Vol 7, No 2/3, pp 36–41

Olsen M, Murphy B and Teare R (1994) 'CEO perspectives on scanning the global business environment', *International Journal of Contemporary Hospitality Management*, Vol 6, No 4, pp 3–9

Peacock M (1993) 'A question of size', *International Journal of Contemporary Hospitality Management*, Vol 5, No 4, pp 29–32

Phillips P (1997) 'Trouble in the UK hotel sector', *International Journal of Contemporary Hospitality Management*, Vol 9, No 4, pp 149–154

Porter M (1980) *Competitive strategy*, Free Press, New York

Punj G and Stewart D (1989) 'Cluster analysis in marketing research: review and suggestions for application', *Journal of Marketing Research*, Vol 20, pp 134–148

Radiven N and Lucas R (1996) 'Wages council abolition and small hotels', *International Journal of Contemporary Hospitality Management*, Vol 8, No 5, pp 10–14

Reger R K and Huff A S (1993) 'Strategic groups: a cognitive approach', *Strategic Management Journal*, Vol 14, No 2, pp 103–124

Robinson J (1933) *Economics of Imperfect Competition*, Macmillan, London

Roper A (1995) 'The emergence of hotel consortia as transnational forms', *International Journal of Contemporary Hospitality Management*, Vol 7, No 1, pp 4–9

Roper A and Carmouche R (1989) 'Budget hotels, a case of mistaken identity?', *International Journal of Contemporary Hospitality Management*, Vol 1, No 1, pp 25–31

Rumlet R P, Schendel D and Teece D J (1991) 'Strategic management and economics', *Strategic Management Journal*, Vol 12, Winter Special Issue, pp 1–136

Scherer F M (1980) *Industrial Market Structure and Economic Performance*, Second Edition, Rand McNally, New York

Senior M and Morphew R (1990) 'Competitive strategies in the budget hotel sector', *International Journal of Contemporary Hospitality Management*, Vol 2, No 3, pp 3–10

Slattery P (1992) 'Unaffiliated hotels in the U.K.', *Travel and Tourism Analyst*, No 1, pp 90–102

Smith D (1995) 'Sunday trading: an analysis of employment structures in leisure and retailing', *International Journal of Contemporary Hospitality Management*, Vol 7, No 2/3, pp 57–63

Sparks B (1993) 'Guest history: is it being utilized?', *International Journal of Contemporary Hospitality Management*, Vol 5, No 1, pp 22–27

Thomas H and Venkatraman N (1988) 'Research on strategic groups: progress and prognosis', *Journal of Management Studies*, Vol 25, No 6, November, pp 537–555

Tribe J (1995) *The Economics of Leisure and Tourism*, Butterworth-Heinemann, Oxford

Tse E and Olsen M (1990) 'Business strategy and organisational structure', *International Journal of Contemporary Hospitality Management*, Vol 2, No 3, pp 17–23

Witt C A and Witt S F (1989) 'Why productivity in the hotel sector is low', *International Journal of Contemporary Hospitality Management*, Vol 1, No 2, pp 28–34

24 Internationalisation

FRANK GO

Introduction

The dictionary definition of the term 'hospitality' refers to 'kindness in welcoming strangers and guests' and a place for those in need of shelter and maintenance. But in a more contemporary sense 'hospitality' encompasses a broad classification of industries, including food, beverages, shelter, entertainment and spectator sports, which render services on a profit basis and sometimes on a non-profit basis. Hospitality facilities occupy a central place in the rapidly expanding (inter)national travel and tourism sector network, that caters to the needs of business and pleasure travellers. The rendering of service should result, through personal experiences, in a bundle of benefits, including security, physical and psychological comfort, and is at the heart of any hospitality process. The service provision forms the basis for economic analysis in terms of 'why a service exists', 'to whom the service is furnished', 'how the service is performed', and 'where the service is provided'. The economic–geographic dimension of service rendering may be analysed at various scales: international, national, regional, and local. This chapter will concentrate on research into internationalisation, in relation to both general and hospitality management.

Although contemporary hospitality management is primarily domestic in nature, there is a dawning realisation, due to the globalisation of the economy, that the hospitality management process has become increasingly international in nature. The Collins dictionary defines the verb to *'internationalise'* as, 'to make international' or 'to put under international control'. According to Ansoff (1987: 125), internationalisation by producers, in strategic terms, implies 'a discontinuous move in that the customers are not the same, and that their tastes, preferences, buying habits and spending budgets are likely to be very different from those of the domestic customers'.

In future, the dynamic interaction between international hospitality management and political–economic institutions will very likely increase in significance, due, for example, to the emergence of supranational institutions, such as the single European market and the earlier mentioned globalisation of the economy. However, globalisation is not synonymous with internationalisation. The verb to 'globalise' implies 'to make global' or to organise or establish worldwide. Whilst global enterprises have not, as of yet, taken over the world, despite the acceleration of cross-border investment, it is increasingly important for managers to understand the changing international environment. This is but one reason why the increasingly complex international environment warrants the attention of researchers.

The Handbook of Contemporary Hospitality Management Research, Edited by Bob Brotherton.
© 1999 John Wiley & Sons Ltd.

This chapter attempts to provide some general theoretical perspectives on the internationalisation of management, from both a general and a hospitality dimension, as a departure point to assess what issues have been explored by researchers, who the key researchers are in selected research areas, and which new theories and findings have emerged from research in international business. It concludes with a future perspective on what questions remain unexplored and/or inadequately answered.

Perspectives on internationalisation research

Amongst the emerging research themes the internationalisation of the 'service sector', which includes hospitality management, is likely to gain in significance, due to the rising importance of services in the global economy, the emergence of the supranational arena for services, including both opportunities and barriers, specific regulations, and the increasing influence that the diffusion of new service development exerts on worldwide economic development. The subject of 'internationalisation' is studied within the realm of international business, which builds on international trade theory (Jeannet and Hennessey, 1995). The latter aims at understanding cross-border product flows or import and export activities.

There are a number of perspectives that dominate international business research. This chapter examines internationalisation following the Rotterdam School of Management research project in 'Internationalisation and Competitive Space' that is conducted at the Faculty of Management at Erasmus University. This research project aims to provide insight into the multifaceted nature of internationalisation and pinpoints relevant management models on the best strategies that should be adopted under particular circumstances. Within this framework, competitive space can be considered as the landscape within which enterprises respond or anticipate the challenges which their rivals pose to them and attempt to build and sustain a competitive advantage. Competitive space is concerned with the geographic business perspective and addressed by researchers who study the location of economic activity (Ohmae, 1995; Price and Blair, 1989) and foreign investment (Dunning, 1988).

Classical models such as Ricardo's (1971) 'comparative cost theory' and neo-classical models such as Vernon's (1971) 'international product cycle' theory, which attempted to explain international trade flows, have been circumvented by other, more interdisciplinary elaborations of organisational theory (Bain, 1959; Stinchcombe, 1965; de Jong, 1985). The latter indicates that organisational features acquired by enterprises are, to a significant extent, embedded in the national institutional environment in which they originate.

Against such a backdrop there are a number of perspectives that may be used to examine internationalisation and competitive space (van Tulder, 1997). The framework developed by the Rotterdam School of Management at Erasmus University builds on the assumption that research into internationalisation will develop along two fundamental angles of enquiry. First, social scientists might opt between an 'inside-out' or an 'outside-in' perspective in their research into internationalisation. The former concentrates on the question how enterprise strategies 'create' a particular competitive space. The latter perspective addresses the question how the competitive space influences the internationalisation strategies of enterprises.

Second, social scientists might take a comparative or an integrative analytical perspective. The comparative perspective takes the international context as given, and tends to be empirical, relatively static, and historic in nature. Most of the international business literature uses a comparative perspective and focuses on 'best practice' in international business. This 'benchmark' approach aims at examining what may be learned from 'best practice' cases and has a 'how to' orientation (e.g. Ketelhohn and Kubes, 1995). The integrative analytical perspective examines the process of internationalisation. Central to this approach are questions such as 'why enterprises internationalise', 'what determines the interaction of different strategies' and 'why differences or commonalities appear' as a basis for explaining the dynamism of international competition.

Whether enterprises opt to 'go international' depends largely on the orientation of management, that is to what extent foreign operations are perceived as complicated and risky, and on domestic market circumstances. Perlmutter's (1969) EPRG model identified four distinctive orientations associated with successive phases in the evolution of the internationalisation process of enterprises: 'ethnocentrism' or home country orientation, 'polycentrism' or host-country orientation, 'regiocentrism' with a regional orientation, and 'geocentrism' with a world orientation. The EPRG typology can be considered fundamental to comprehending internationalisation in relation to, for example, concepts such as 'globalisation', which 'refers to the world community's economic and political interdependence' (Spybey, 1996), and multinationalism, whereby competition is treated on a stand-alone basis (Yip, 1995). The EPRG orientations represent varying choices, amongst others, for a transnational enterprise's division of labour.

Against this background, the Rotterdam School of Management distinguishes three clusters for analysis: the enterprise, the network, and the environment or competitive space. In each of these clusters within the model a distinction is made between comparative approaches between nations and cultures and an integrative approach across countries. This approach gives rise to six perspectives, which shall be examined briefly: Management Styles perspective, International Management perspective, Transnational Management perspective, International Strategic Alliances perspective, Local/National Management of Competitive Space, and Inter/Supranational Management of Competitive Space.

The Management Styles perspective

Such a research perspective investigates whether management styles are national and if there are significant differences in management style according to sector, for example agrifood, computing, healthcare and hospitality/tourism (Hickson and Pugh, 1995). Whilst cultural diversity may be perceived as a 'soft' item, it is important from a research viewpoint, because culture does have a powerful impact on business. Amongst other factors culture affects relationships, how we make decisions and how status is accorded, how we manage time and relate to nature. The cross-cultural problems international managers often encounter are listed in Table 24.1.

The International Management perspective

This perspective aims to develop insights into distinct management functions, such as

Table 24.1.   Cross-cultural problems international managers encounter

Culture and definitions
Culture, cultural shock
Cultural awareness and cultural adaptation
Impact of cultural values on hospitality business practices
Anglos
Latins
Northern Europeans
East–Central Europeans
Asians
Arabs and Middle East
Developing countries

Source: Adapted from Hickson and Pugh (1995).

human resources management, organisational and staffing practices of transnational corporations, international marketing management and international finance and control. In the area of international finance the research emphasis has been on analysing the risks and opportunities which transnational corporations have to manage across national borders. The topics in this area have been primarily explored from a transnational corporate perspective, including foreign exchange management, economic and transaction exposure, political risk, transnational working capital management, financing foreign trade, foreign investment analysis, international portfolio management, and international capital budgeting (Shapiro, 1992).

The challenges of international business operations require diagnostic ability and conceptual thinking to a greater degree than in most management situations. Within this context, research into international operations focuses on whether the same should be pursued by exporting, licensing, selling to overseas distributors, franchising, management contracting or another format. In addition, research in this area would address the logic in the business objectives, strategy–tactics sequence, within single line and diversified producers (Bartlett and Ghoshal, 1992). Research from this perspective also illuminates international aspects of human resources-related issues such as the labour market, work organisation, industrial relations and human resources management within transnational corporations (Beardwell and Holden, 1994; Lessem, 1989; Evans, Doz and Laurent, 1989).

Until recently, knowledge about the home market was sufficient to survive. Today, however, managers need to ask whether their operations are comparable to the world leaders, as opposed to the domestic or regional leaders. The notion of benchmarking the best in the business concerns every aspect of the organisation from purchasing to customer service. Thus, the innovation process is critical to enterprises and, due to internationalisation, emerging information technology networks and knowledge centres, this process grows increasingly complex, as, for example, product components are simultaneously designed in different geographical locations. In relation to the growing importance of worldwide production systems, Bardaracco (1991: 17) refers to the significance of the 'globalization of knowhow'.

The Transnational Management perspective

The theory of multinational enterprise and its ability to differentiate its product is central to the analysis of international business. Bartlett and Ghoshal (1989) developed a 'transnational model' designed to incorporate a more flexible management mentality than the one that dominates the traditional hierarchy of multinational corporations (Vernon, 1977; Rugman, 1981; Caves, 1982; Porter, 1986). Their transnational model is designed to allow corporations to simultaneously cultivate three diverse and often conflicting strategic capabilities, namely the multinational flexibility to respond to diverse, local market needs; the global competitiveness to capture efficiencies of scale; and the international learning ability that results in worldwide innovation.

The International Strategic Alliances perspective

Lately, strategic alliances have become an increasingly important means of conducting business. Strategic alliances can be defined as 'organizational arrangements and operating policies through which separate organizations share administrative authority, form social links through more open-ended contractual arrangements as opposed to very specific, arms-length contracts' (Bardaracco, 1991: 17). Thus, the difference between a strategic arrangement and a joint venture is that the latter requires the formation of a new legal entity, whereas the former enables partners to benefit from the alliance without the creation of a subsidiary. The aim of the strategic alliance is to offer each an advantage that one company would be unable to achieve by itself. Within a global environment, in particular, strategic alliances can be critical instruments to meet the value-added needs of consumers (Ohmae, 1986). Whilst the dynamism behind international strategic alliances remains largely unclear (Schenk, 1995; Wassenberg, 1994), they are likely to grow in future, amongst other reasons owing to their flexible nature.

The Local/National Management of Competitive Space

Research in this area hinges around the competitive dynamism in the various countries, and specifically whether convergence or divergence might occur and what the effects thereof might be on the competitiveness of enterprises, countries and regions. One of the major consequences of the internationalisation process is that it tends to have a standardising impact in that both products and institutions originally offered domestically appear on a worldwide scale. In this regard, the omnipresence of brand-name products and services is increasingly dominating more and more sectors of society. For example, Ritzer (1993) refers to the McDonaldization of society, that is the extent to which the principles on which this American fast-food chain is operated, are changing the character of contemporary social life. In other words, the globalisation of trade, transportation, communications and travel has created a great pressure for the convergence of quality in products and services. However, rather than the single homogeneous market in which cultural differences fade away, diversity appears to be alive and well according to some research. For example, Paliwoda (1986: 92) sums this development up as follows:

'Economies come from standardisation, but the local pressures may be in favor of some degree of local modification resulting in product divergence.' Therefore what seems to be emerging is a rather paradoxical development in which cultural divergence is thriving in 'waves' of quality convergence. At the same time and perhaps as a reaction to this convergence process, there has been an increasing and visible effort on the part of many societies and cultural groups to consciously undertake efforts to strengthen and develop a clear cultural identity and supporting systems.

Other researchers have approached this question primarily from an economic and political game theory perspective. Such an approach focuses on internationalisation in the light of the international processes of restructuring and its determinants, opportunities and constraints of foreign direct investment and cross-national alliances. In addition this research perspective pays considerable attention to the position of governments in areas such as strategic trade policy, competition policy and industrial policy, and endeavours to yield an understanding of the perspectives of 'real world stakeholders' (Dicken, 1986; Ruigrok and van Tulder, 1995; Schenk, 1995) and the conduct of business enterprises based in non-Western countries such as Japan (Morgan and Morgan, 1991) and the People's Republic of China (Davies, 1995).

The Inter/Supranational Management of Competitive Space

Increasingly, the competitive space is influenced by a concern for the ecological effects of industrial activity. Accordingly, the pressure for environmental regulation is growing, and is epitomised by a number of salient factors. First, European economic integration, the North American Free Trade Association (NAFTA), the liberalisation of Central and Eastern Europe and the rise of the East Asian region present threats and opportunities. As a consequence, national environmental regulation gets 'harmonised' under the umbrella of supranational directives. Supranational institutions such as the European Union, the Free Trade Agreement (FTA), i.e. Canada, USA and Mexico, and the ASEAN, endowed with their wide competences and far-reaching powers of coordination, loom as large as ever. There is a need for greater insight into the conduct of businesses in specific regions, particularly Europe as a whole (Welchford and Prescott, 1994; Sachwald, 1994) and Central/Eastern Europe in particular, and the role and effects of supranational organisations.

Practices and problems

Hospitality companies compete, increasingly, within an international environment, even if they opt to concentrate on the 'domestic' market, because transnational corporations penetrate the 'home turf' of the former with ease. Furthermore, the 'injection' of foreign direct investment, for example by Asian multinationals, has changed the industry's game rules because Asian corporations behave strategically differently, more long-term, than Western corporations. In addition, there is a set of global industries, including financial services, banking and telecommunications, that are affecting the operation and control of specific sectors in the domestic travel and hospitality system (Go and Brent Ritchie, 1990). Lastly, international competition pressures many ethnocentric corporations to expand abroad to achieve scale economies. Such blurring of the 'domestic'/'international' distinction implies that management performance will be increasingly judged by international business standards of competitiveness and cooperation, i.e. strategic alliances and other forms of collaboration.

Put differently, the hospitality business context has changed dramatically. Within the international environment, transnational corporations are playing a major role in the restructuring of the hospitality industry. The most noticeable results of such restructuring have been the increases in the scale of businesses and their increasing functioning within international networks. This observation requires hospitality managers to obtain a new orientation, new knowledge, new thinking, new skills and new methods to operate their organisations within an international environment. Whilst there has been a rising awareness of the significance of 'internationalisation' in relation to hospitality management and tourism, as evidenced by publications by, for example, Theobald (1994), Go and Pine (1995), Teare and Olsen (1992), Witt, Brooke, and Buckley (1991) and Jones and Pizam (1993), there remains a relative dearth of research in relation to the significance of the issue of the internationalisation of hospitality management.

The international business theory examined earlier in this chapter primarily provides an overview of the interdisciplinary approach to the study primarily of international business. However, the question still remains: 'Why focus on international hospitality management?'. Since the appropriate unit of analysis is the industry in which enterprises compete, it is necessary to concentrate on a specific industry. The unit for analysis in this chapter, international hospitality, is part of the dynamic and rapidly expanding services sector that is undergoing an internationalisation which parallels the internationalisation of manufacturing. Business services continue to follow the geographic spread of transnational corporations (TNC) in manufacturing. The internationalisation of both the business services sector and manufacturing has become mutually reinforcing and has created a widespread demand for hospitality facilities. 'Such demand is being met increasingly by the development of transnational hospitality chains which offer a package of standardised facilities for their corporate clients' (Dicken, 1986: 85–88). Service industries, such as hospitality management, have been largely domestic in character and relatively little is known about international competition in services (Porter, 1990). This observation is reflected in studies which focus on the hospitality industry at the country level (De Groote, 1987; Hassan, 1986; Hankinson, 1989). In contrast, the study by Dunning and McQueen (1982) provides an international perspective on the hotel industry, which offers insights on how one might deal, for example, with configuration and coordination issues. For the purposes of understanding hospitality management as a part of the service sector, the analysis here will focus on internationalisation of hospitality management within the context of the internationalisation of services (Vandermerwe and Chadwick, 1991).

International hospitality management research appears to flow essentially from four questions researchers in this specialised field have addressed: 'Why develop abroad?', 'Where to develop?', 'How to develop?' and 'What are the effects of internationalisation?'. These four questions will form the basis for examining the practices and problems that may be encountered in researching international hospitality management.

Why develop abroad?

This first question requires insights into the 'internationalisation process' in hospitality management. Based on Porter's (1980) industry mapping technique, Beattie (1991) examined the internationalisation of the European hotel industry and categorised the sample of companies in her survey into three main groups, defined by the hospitality orientation of the corporations involved: hotels as the main interest of the company; hotels as one interest within a wider hospitality portfolio; and hotels as one interest within a wider industrial portfolio. Beattie's research findings (1991) confirm that the degree of internationalisation of hotel corporations is affected, to some extent, by size, in that smaller firms may lack the resources and corporate support required to effectively cope with the complexities of the international environment. Furthermore, parent companies have a major 'pull' effect on the internationalisation process of their affiliated hotel corporations. Finally, brand name products appear to be central to the internationalisation process and have an advantage over non-branded hotel companies as far as their international expansion is concerned (Livingston, 1982b).

Where to develop?

Research under this category typically provides insights into hospitality management strategies and practices in specified geographic areas, such as Western Europe, Central and Eastern Europe (Bell, 1992a) and China (Yu, 1992a). Not surprisingly, American researchers have paid considerable attention to investigating investment in US hotels and resorts and/or management contract expansion in the US, for example by Canadian companies (Livingston, 1982a) and by Japanese institutions (Burritt, 1991; Hara and Eyster, 1990). At the same time, they seem to have a fascination with Japan and Japanese hospitality and tourism developments (Doi, 1992; Kaven, 1992; Lin, 1990; Sharpe, 1990).

   The literature concerning hospitality developments in Pacific Asia (Choy, 1988) and other regions in Asia has grown considerably of late. Such studies often concentrate on the growth of and opportunity for tourism and the hotel industry in specific countries, including India (Dev and Kuckreja, 1989), Thailand (Chon, Singh and Mikula, 1993) and Korea (Chon and Shin, 1990), the application of market segmentation techniques in Singapore (Subhash and Vera, 1990), and the application of environmental analysis to expansion in Pacific Asia (Go and Heung, 1995).

How to develop?

Beside a comprehension of the industrial economic process, internationalisation depends, broadly, on two other management processes. The first is conceptual in nature and is addressed in terms of the way issues change as a result of internationalisation and the global economy. The second is skills-based and encompasses broadly intercultural negotiating skills and the ability to read different markets in different contexts and understand comparative politics (de Wilde, 1991) in order to be able to make sense of public policy in foreign countries. With regard to the conceptual level, researchers have investigated how to 'go global' with foodservice franchising (Go and Christensen, 1989), international profit planning (Rusth and Lefever, 1988) and the process of internationalising hospitality operations (Makens and Edgell, 1990), and have developed models for hotel development in foreign areas (Saunders and Reneghan, 1992; Kimes and Lord, 1994). The airline–hotel liaisons (Lane, 1986) which may be considered the origin of today's international hospitality industry have declined considerably in terms of their significance, whilst strategic alliances in the international hotel industry (Dev and Klein, 1993) have grown in importance. On the cross-cultural level, there is a growing list of studies regarding training for the multicultural workforce (Shames, 1986), the assessment of the implications of cultural differences upon hospitality management (Welsh and Swerdlow, 1992), and cross-cultural studies in relation to quality perception (Armstrong *et al.*, 1997).

What are the effects of internationalisation?

Internationalisation affects the industry structure and competitive dynamics at various levels. However, because of space constraints here only three of these will be addressed, namely the economic, socio-cultural and political levels. Extensive international tourism growth affects the economic development of cities, regions, countries and continents (Go and Jenkins, 1997). For example, international competition in Asia raised the question how Hong Kong's hotel industry might be able to cope with the new competitors in the region (Go, Pine and Yu, 1994). On the same level, Vallen (1989) suggested that tourism and hospitality operations would have a far-reaching impact on the economic restructuring of the former Soviet economy. In Thailand the growth of international tourism has contributed to the emergence of AIDS, the overbuilding of hotel rooms in Bangkok, pollution, infrastructure defects, and related challenges (Chon, Singh and Mikula, 1993), and questions have been raised concerning how Vietnam's tourism industry can be kept afloat.

Hospitality and tourism are a major source of intercultural contact and influence the socio-cultural structures of host countries either positively or negatively. Key research themes that have emerged in this area include host perceptions of tourism, destination choice process, and tourism planning and hospitality development. The potential conflict between continuity and change in the culture of every society is a familiar problem that most countries, regardless of their individual structures, are facing. While most countries welcome the growth of international tourism to generate income and employment, there are legitimate concerns raised about foreign influences that may irrevocably change a host country's culture. Responsible development necessitates understanding residents' perceptions of tourism impacts based on, for example, social exchange theory (Ap, 1992) or social status (Husbands, 1989) and the factors contributing to the change in attitude (Wilson, 1994).

Mansfield's (1992) review of theoretical aspects of the destination-choice process indicates a need for the application of a theoretical framework. To avoid the victimisation of a place due to tourism mismanagement (Ahmed, 1991) and to protect the fragility of resort areas such as Bali (Bell, 1992b), balanced tourism planning and hospitality development requires the input and involvement of the host community (Keogh, 1989) and understanding of the relationship between culture and tourism in a particular geographic area (Richards, 1996).

Similarly, the effects of internationalisation on the host community should be of mutual concern for citizens and entrepreneurs alike. Hospitality facilities are part of a municipality or travel destination and have the potential to contribute to the architectual style, the 'sense of place' and the 'livability' that emerges in municipalities. Within this context, researchers could utilise quality of life theory and cross-cultural research to provide important insights into whether international hospitality companies make an attempt to fit into the fabric of the host community or might be considered a form of 'neo-colonialism' (Cassee, 1995).

The research evidence also indicates that some member states have not quite grasped the seriousness of the global competition in tourism. Broadly, there are impediments imposed by governments around the world (Table 24.2) that pose economic, socio-cultural and other barriers to international travel and tourism (Theobald, 1994). The lack of urgency in this respect should be replaced by a coordinated strategic response by the Single European Market (SEM) and the tourism and hospitality industries of member states (Robinson and Mogendorff, 1993). Clearly, the European Commission's Directive on package travel, package holidays and package tours and competition law, as well as air transport deregulation, will have major implications for the tourism industry in the European Economic Community (Simons, 1992a, 1992b). Similarly, Edgell (1990) provides insights into such aspects of tourism policy and its effects from an

Table 24.2   Barriers to international travel and tourism

Economic barriers

   Currency restrictions imposed on residents/visitors
   Customs allowances for returning residents
   Restrictions on property acquisition by non-nationals
   Taxes (exit and other travel) imposed on foreign visitors
   Limitations on foreign ownership/investment/equity participation
   Currency devaluation/exchange rates
   Restrictions on imports of essential goods or services
   Restrictions on non-national personnel and employment
   Other economic barriers

Socio-cultural barriers

   Restrictions on resident overseas travel
   Entry visas, identity documents and length of stay limitations
   Work stoppages, civil unrest, terrorism and war
   Political change/government instability
   Language barriers
   Limitations on movement of foreign airline or ship passengers
   Other socio-cultural barriers

Other barriers

   Conditions and procedures for issue of travel documents
   Restrictive air transportation policies/protectionism
   Health regulations and sanitation standards/AIDS
   Fuel shortages (real and induced)
   Environmental protection requirements
   Difficulties in obtaining licences to operate

Source: Adapted from Theobald (1994).

American perspective. Whilst there is currently a considerable dependence on central government financing, the slow but sure withdrawal of government from tourism will necessitate a shift towards self-financing (Akehurst, Bland and Nevin, 1993) and suggests that the European Commission should place greater emphasis on the coordination of the efforts of member states with regard to the development of national policies. Similarly, Baum (1993) argues for a more strategic approach to human resource issues within the European Union. The impact of 'disasters' can be significant but remains scantily researched (Rues, 1989; Woods, 1991). More in-depth research is required concerning how future crises might be averted, or at least the impact thereof could be reduced by advance contingency planning (Gee and Gain, 1986).

Conclusions and future research agenda

Drawing on the literature from international business and international hospitality management, this chapter examined the approaches, methods and techniques that social scientists have applied to conduct research into the internationalisation/globalisation issues associated with business and the hospitality industry respectively. Research into internationalisation of hospitality management reflects many of the general theoretical principles which underlie thinking in international business as a whole.

Thus far, much of the research has been shallow, because most international business research studies have been characterised by a prescriptive orientation, that is, scientists have tended to emphasise 'what practitioners should do', 'how they should act' and 'which aspects they should consider when entering foreign markets'. Less emphasis has been paid to the development of specific concepts, theories, etc. (Wierenga, Pruyn and Waarts, 1995). As regards 'hospitality management research', the production of material by predominantly Anglo-American academics might possibly result in an 'excessively narrow self-interested regional focus in an innately international area of scholarship' (Burnett, Uysal and Jamrozy, 1991: 49).

From the present analysis it may be clear that the state of knowledge, in terms of both conceptual/theoretical frameworks and facts/data on internationalisation and globalisation, remains rather low. However, of late a growing number of universities have changed, or are currently in the process of changing, their programmes to respond to the internationalisation of the economy and society. It is anticipated that the key research in international business will be generated by scientists at those university business schools with an international reputation, as opposed to hospitality researchers. Whilst it is debatable which the best business schools are, a recently conducted survey may provide some insight into the 'world top ten' and the 'UK top five' such schools (Table 24.3).

Which issues need to be addressed with regard to internationalisation? In the remaining part of this chapter an attempt will be made to identify the topics, questions and key issues that remain rather unexplored and/or inadequately answered and that researchers need to address in the near future. In general, however, no priority ranking should be imputed to this 'agenda'.

First, any industry's economic significance is only as good as its data. If the hospitality industry's interests are to be seriously considered in policy making, the current system of collecting, organising and disseminating data requires improvement so that

Table 24.3   The top business schools

Worldwide	UK
1. Wharton	1. London Business School
2. INSEAD	2. Manchester Business School
3. Harvard	3. Cranfield
4. London Business School	4. Imperial College
5. Chicago	5. Warwick University
6. Stanford	
7. IMD	
8. Rotterdam	
9. Kellogg	
10. Columbia	

Source: *The Times*, 7 October 1996.

planning and development can be more effective. The diversity and non-cumulative nature of hospitality and tourism research has resulted in 'a jigsaw puzzle without a picture to refer to'. In this regard, the Worldwide Hospitality and Tourism Trends CD-ROM (WHATT-CD) initiated by Teare (1995) is an innovative technique, in that it provides a 'one-stop service approach' which facilitates the task of interpreting themes in the academic literature and provides an 'ongoing commentary on international developments in hospitality and tourism' (Teare, 1995). A question arising from the availability of the WHATT is whether it might be used as a basis to develop research that approaches internationalisation from both integrative and comparative perspectives. A European research network might be an ideal forum for theory formation and testing of internationalisation concepts. Such research would contribute considerably to the body of knowledge on internationalisation.

Second, technological innovation has become an essential element in global competitiveness. Changing technology is producing a period of discontinuous change and altering the pattern of incremental change to which society has been accustomed. The use of global distribution systems, confounding most forecasts, is narrowing economies of scale in distribution, not expanding them. These developments will lead to fundamental changes in the way corporations conduct their business. However, the industry generally does not take an active role in developing or adopting new technology. This gives rise to a series of questions which, as yet, have not been adequately explored or answered. Why are hospitality enterprises being so slow in responding to new technology? What new technologies are being adopted by the hospitality industry within the member states of the European Union? What barriers are there to the joint development and application of new technologies for the hospitality industry? How could these be overcome?

Third, product development remains an essential element of hospitality management strategy and plays a vital role in the future of the hospitality industry. Social structures, communities, enterprises and individuals around the world are experiencing profound change. Family values and lifestyles are becoming more diverse and complicated. Many Europeans are showing greater interest in the quality of life and the role a healthy lifestyle can play, including travel and hospitality, in enhancing their overall well-being. What specific changes are affecting different market segments within the European Union? And which specific needs are developing due to value and lifestyle shifts? There is a voluminous market research literature on various market segments, such as the 'seniors' market, but there are few studies which compare consumer values and lifestyles in different EU countries in relation to tourism and hospitality.

Within this context, Wierenga, Pruyn and Waarts (1995) used a framework which incorporates economics and consumer behaviour to examine the similarities and differences with respect to consumers and marketing infrastructure in the countries of the European Union. They conclude that there are tremendous differences in income levels and income spending patterns among the countries of the European Union and also major differences with respect to consumer values and lifestyles, and that the distribution and retailing environments as well as the media differ considerably from one country to another. The progressive 'greying' of society will also increasingly impact upon both the consumer and labour markets. Researchers may be able to contribute new comparative insights into changing consumer needs in the European Union, and how to create higher levels of quality service so that the hospitality industry can maintain and grow its share.

Fourth, technological developments will impact on the workplace and create both opportunities and challenges to workers. What will be the implications of the increasing demand for workers in the hospitality industry, of a changing workforce and consumer base, and of currently available education and training resources within the European Union and its member states? And what private and public sector policies will be needed to foster a balance in worker supply and demand?

Fifth, the hospitality industry is rather fragmented, and there is little cooperation between the various branches that are part of the tourism sector, including hospitality. One result is that the 'industry' is unable to speak with a united voice in Brussels. Another result is that there is little, if any, cooperation between the associations of different countries and ignorance of one another's initiatives and activities. There is, therefore, a clear need for both qualitative studies and quantitative indicators in which the multifaceted nature of the internationalisation processes of both enterprises and institutions can be tracked. Both the topic of internationalisation and that of competitive institutions deal with the question of the international coordination of activities, and can be considered a prime management research problem.

The organisational structure of the hospitality industry is characterised by a myriad of branches (foodservice, catering, beverage operations, hotels, clubs, etc.), dichotomised between a large number of small and medium-sized enterprises and a small number of large enterprises. Greater insights into the perspectives, plans and practices of different players are required to bring about more effective cooperation. Within this context, it should be helpful to conduct comparative research into the goals, philosophies, policies and practices of hospitality operations headquartered in the European Union. Greater insights into the aforementioned organisational characteristics should be helpful to stimulate greater cooperation amongst the various organisations that operate in the hospitality 'value chain'.

Sixth, given that global dominance is derived from a reputation through the power of their respective brand names, the question arises whether enterprises should maintain national brands or adopt Euro-branding. And what might be the value of a 'Euro-brand', compared to a set of national brands? (Wierenga, Pruyn and Waarts, 1995). Within this context Cassee (1995) has queried whether the European dimension in hospitality is a relic of the past. He refers to the 'colonisation' of the European hospitality industry by American companies or by American norms and values in hospitality. He signals that 'small business seems to lose the fight against the chain-type companies, both in the hotel and the restaurant sector. Variety is replaced with a limited number of formulas and management styles are based on the American way of business administration.' Whilst there is nothing wrong with this development *per se*, Cassee argues that, with the disappearance of small hospitality businesses, what makes Europe attractive, namely the collection of national identities, disappears as well. The resulting dilemma forms an important arena for research.

Particularly, more research is required on how to internationalise the curricula of educational programmes, both full-time and executive education programmes, to familiarise students and executives with the cultures of other nations and sensitise them to the cultural traditions of various groups (Pizam, 1989). Researchers can make an important contribution by explaining the significance of cultural diversity in relation to hospitality in general, what is specific and appealing about European hospitality, and how such critical factors could be preserved, perhaps by building on the obviously successful American theories (Cassee, 1995).

Finally, environmental concerns and the sustainable development of tourism have a direct impact on the quality of life for residents, the economic well-being of hospitality enterprises and the experiences of guests. If a host destination is well planned and managed, it will be able to attract visitors and create jobs, income and tax revenues. The tourism and hospitality industries are too important to local communities to be left in the hands of 'outsider' professionals (McNulty and Wafer, 1990). Moreover, the growing desire for local participation on the part of host communities and emerging new government–society interactions would suggest that research on modern governance of business might be in order (Vliet, 1993) and in keeping with an emerging vanguard of socially conscious marketers (Kotler, 1980; Fennell, 1987; Krippendorf, 1987). To make municipalities more livable in and the landscape more attractive it would be worthwhile to build on the research into the landscape conducted by Gunn (1988). For example, de Graaf and Camp (1997) researched European coastal developments, on a transnational level, thereby reflecting in particular on the relationship of architecture, hospitality and tourism development. To raise the study of internationalism to new heights, researchers should put greater emphasis on the application of an interdisciplinary approach to studying the 'internationalisation' process.

References and bibliography

Ahmed, Z.U. (1991) 'Indian tourism: a victim of mismanagement', *Cornell Hotel and Restaurant Administration Quarterly*, **32** (3): 75–83.

Akehurst, G., Bland, N. and Nevin, M. (1993) 'Tourism policies in the European Community member states', *International Journal of Hospitality Management*, **12** (1): 33–66.

Ansoff, I. (1987) *Corporate Strategy* (revised edition), London: Penguin.

Ap, J. (1992) 'Residents' perspectives on tourism impacts', *Annals of Tourism Research*, **19** (4): 665–690.

Armstrong, R.W., Mok, C., Go, F.M. and Chan, A. (1997) 'The importance of cross-cultural expectations in the measurement of service quality perceptions in the hotel industry', *International Journal of Hospitality Management*, **16** (2): 181–190.

Ascher, F. (1985) *Tourism: Transnational Corporations and Cultural Identities*, New York: Unesco.

Ashworth, G.J. and Tunbridge, J.E. (1990) *The Tourist Historic City*, London: Belhaven Press.

Ayala, H. (1991) 'International hotel ventures: back to the future', *Cornell Hotel and Restaurant Administration Quarterly*, **31** (4): 38–45.

Ayala, H. (1993) 'Mexican resorts: a blueprint with an expiration date', *Cornell Hotel and Restaurant Administration Quarterly*, **34** (4): 34–42.

Bain, J. (1959) *Industrial Organization*, New York: John Wiley.

Bardaracco, J.L. (1991) *The Knowledge Link: How Firms Compete Through Strategic Alliances*, Boston: Harvard Business School Press.

Bartlett, C.A. and Ghoshal, S. (1989) *Managing Across Borders: The Transnational Solution*, Boston: Harvard Business School Press.

Bartlett, C.A. and Ghoshal, S. (1992) *Transnational Management: Text, Cases and Readings in Cross Border Management*, Boston: Irwin.

Baum, T. (1993) 'Human resources concerns in European tourism: strategic response and the EC', *International Journal of Hospitality Management*, **12** (1): 89–100.

Beardwell, I. and Holden, L. (eds) (1994) *A Contemporary Perspective*, London: Pitman.

Beattie, R. (1991) 'Hospitality internationalisation: an empirical investigation', *International Journal of Contemporary Hospitality Management*, **3** (4): 14–20.

Bell, C.A. (1992a) 'Opening up Eastern Europe: new opportunities and new challenges', *Cornell Hotel and Restaurant Administration Quarterly*, **33** (6): 53–63.

Bell, C.A. (1992b) 'Bali: how to maintain a fragile resort', *Cornell Hotel and Restaurant Administration Quarterly*, **33** (5): 28–31.

Brownell, J. (1990) 'The symbolic/culture approach: managing transition in the service industry', *International Journal of Hospitality Management*, **9** (3): 191–206.

Burnett, G.W., Uysal, M. and Jamrozy, U. (1991) 'Articles on international themes in the *Journal of Travel Research*', *Journal of Travel Research*, **29** (3): 47–49.

Burritt, M.C. (1991) 'Japanese investment in U.S. hotels and resorts', *Cornell Hotel and Restaurant Administration Quarterly*, **32** (3): 60–66.

Cassee, E. Th. (1995) 'The European dimension in hospitality: a relic of the past?', personal communication, 29 August 1995.

Caves, R. (1982) *Multinational Enterprise and Economic Analysis*, Cambridge: Cambridge University Press.

Chandler, A.D. (1962) *Strategy and Structure: The History of American Industrial Enterprise*, Cambridge, MA: MIT Press.

Chon, K.S. and Shin, H.J. (1990) 'Korea's hotel and tourism industry', *Cornell Hotel and Restaurant Administration Quarterly*, **31** (1): 68–73.

Chon, K.S., Singh, A. and Mikula, J.R. (1993) 'Tourism and the hotel industry in Thailand', *Cornell Hotel and Restaurant Administration Quarterly*, **34** (3): 50–55.

Choy, D. (1988) 'Pacific Asia: the mass market in travel', *Cornell Hotel and Restaurant Administration Quarterly*, **28** (4): 82–88.

Clark, J.J. and Arbel, A. (1993) 'Producing global managers: the need for a new academic paradigm', *Cornell Hotel and Restaurant Administration Quarterly*, **34** (4): 83–89.

Cullen, T.P. (1981) 'Global gamesmanship: how the expatriate manager copes with cultural differences', *Cornell Hotel and Restaurant Administration Quarterly*, **22** (3): 18–24.

Cummings, L.E. (1992) 'Hospitality solid waste minimization: a global frame', *International Journal of Hospitality Management*, **11** (3): 255–267.

Davies, H. (ed.) (1995) *China Business Context and Issues*, Hong Kong: Longman.

Demko, G.J. (1992) *Why in the World: Adventures in Geography*, New York: Doubleday.

Deng, S.L., Ryan, C. and Moutinho, L. (1992) 'Canadian hoteliers and their attitudes towards environmental issues', *International Journal of Hospitality Management*, **11** (3): 225–237.

Dev, C.S and Klein, S. (1993) 'Strategic alliances in the hotel industry', *Cornell Hotel and Restaurant Administration Quarterly*, **34** (1): 42–45.

Dev, C.S. and Kuckreja, S. (1989) 'Tourism in India: growth and opportunity', *Cornell Hotel and Restaurant Administration Quarterly*, **30** (2): 71–75.

Dicken, P. (1986) *Global Shift: Industrial Change in a Turbulent World*, London: Harper & Row.

Dogan, H. (1989) 'Forms of adjustment: sociocultural impacts of tourism', *Annals of Tourism Research*, **16** (2): 216–236.

Doi, T. (1992) 'An inside look at Japanese food service', *Cornell Hotel and Restaurant Administration Quarterly*, **33** (6): 73–83.

Doz, T. and Prahalad, C.K. (1987) *The Multinational Mission*, New York: Free Press.

Dunning, J.H. (1988) *Explaining International Production*, London: Unwin Hyman.

Dunning, J.H. and McQueen, M. (1982) 'Multinational corporations in the international hotel industry', *Annals of Tourism Research*, **9**: 69–90.

Echtner, C. (1994) 'Entrepreneurial training in developing countries', *Annals of Tourism Research*, **22** (1): 119–134.

Edgell, E.D.L. Sr. (1990) *International Tourism Policy*, New York: Van Nostrand Reinhold.

Evans, P., Doz, Y. and Laurent, A. (eds) (1989) *Human Resource Management in International Firms: Change, Globalization and Innovation*, London: MacMillan Academic and Professional.

Fennell, G. (1987) 'A radical agenda for marketing science: represent the marketing concept', in *Philosophical and Radical Thought in Marketing*, Firat, A.F. (ed.), Lexington, MA: Lexington Books, pp. 289–306.

Gee, C.Y. and Gain, C. (1986) 'Coping with crisis', *Travel and Tourism Analyst*, June: 3–12.

Go, F.M. (1981) 'Hospitality and heritage—a profitable partnership', in *The Practice of Hospitality Management*, Pizam, A., Lewis, R.C. and Manning, P. (eds), Westport, CT: AVI Publishing, pp. 172–182.

Go, F. (1994) 'Emerging issues in tourism education', in *Global Tourism: The Next Decade*, Theobald, W. (ed.), Oxford: Butterworth-Heinemann, pp. 330–346.

Go, F. and Brent Ritchie, J.R. (1990) 'Transnationalism and tourism', *Tourism: Management*, **11** (4): 287–290.

Go, F. and Christensen, J. (1989) 'Going global', *Cornell Hotel and Restaurant Administration Quarterly*, **30** (3): 72–79.

Go, F., Goulding, P.J. and Litteljohn, D. (1992) 'The international hospitality industry and public policy', in *International Hospitality Management: Corporate Strategy in Practice*, Teare, B.R. and Olsen, M.D. (eds), London: Pitman, 36–66.

Go, F. and Haywood, K.M. (1990) 'Marketing of the service process: state of the art in tourism, recreation and hospitality industries', in *Progress in Tourism, Recreation and Hospitality Management*, Vol. 2, London: Belhaven.

Go, F. and Heung, V. (1995) 'Harnessing environmental analysis to expand in Asia pacific', *International Journal of Contemporary Hospitality Management*, **7** (7): i–iv.

Go, F. and Jenkins, C.L. (1997) *Tourism and Economic Development in Asia and Australasia*, London: Pinter.

Go, F.M. and Pine, R. (1995) *Globalization Strategy in the Hotel Industry*, London: Routledge.

Go, F., Pine, R. and Yu, R. (1994) 'Hong Kong: sustaining competitive advantage in Asia's hotel industry', *Cornell Hotel and Restaurant Administration Quarterly*, **35** (5): 50–61.

Go, F., Theobald, W. and Qu, H. (eds) (1996) Reducing the barriers to international tourism, *Proceedings of the International Tourism Symposium, Beijing*, organized by Purdue University, Beijing Institute of Tourism and the Hong Kong Polytechnic University.

Go, F. and Zhang, W. (1997) 'Applying importance–performance analysis to Beijing as an international meeting destination', *Journal of Travel Research*, **30** (4): 42–49.

Go, F. *et al.* (1996) Four Seasons-Regent: building a global presence in the luxury market', *Cornell Hotel and Restaurant Administration Quarterly*, **37** (4): 58–65.

Graaf, J. de and Camp, D'Laine, 1997, *Europe Coastwise: an Anthology of Reflections on Architecture and Tourism*, Rotterdam: Academy of Architecture/010 Publishers.

Griffin, T. and Briggs, S. (1994) 'Managing tourism development conflicts', in *1994 Annual Review of Travel*, New York: The American Express Annual Review of Travel International Essay Competition, pp. 37–62.

Groote, P. de (1987) *De Belgische Hotelsector: een economische–geografische analyse*, Leuven: Univeristaire Pers.

Gruber, K.J. (1988) 'Hotels of Israel: pressure and promise', *Cornell Hotel and Restaurant Administration Quarterly*, **28** (4): 36–43.

Gunn, C.A. (1988) *Tourism Planning* (2nd edition), New York: Taylor & Francis.

Hankinson, A. (1989) 'Small hotels in Britain', *Cornell Hotel and Restaurant Administration Quarterly*, **30** (3): 80–82.

Hara, T. and Eyster, J.J. (1990) 'Japanese hotel investment: a matter of tradition and reality', *Cornell Hotel and Restaurant Administration Quarterly*, **31** (3): 98–104.

Hassan, S.S. (1986) *Marketing Hotel Operations: an Investigation into the Marketing Behaviour of National and International Chain Affiliated Hotels Operating in Egypt*, Glasgow: University of Strathclyde.

Hickson, D.J. and Pugh, D.S. (1995) *Management Worldwide: The Impact of Societal Culture on Organisations around the Globe*, London: Penguin.

Hoffman, J. and Schiederjans, X. (1990) 'An international strategic management/goal programming model for structuring global expansion decisions in the hospitality industry: the case of eastern Europe', *International Journal of Hospitality Management*, **9** (3): 175–190.

Horst, H. van der (1996) 'A guest in a strange house: cultural differences and commercial hospitality', paper presented at *EuroChrie/IAHMS*, Leeuwarden, Hotel Management School, November.

Husbands, W. (1989) 'Social status and perception of tourism impacts', *Annals of Tourism Research*, **16** (2): 237–253.

Jeannet, J.P. and Hennessey, H.D. (1995) *Global Marketing Strategies* (3rd edition), Boston: Houghton Mifflin.

Johansson, J.K. and Yip, G.S. (1994) 'Exploiting globalization potential: U.S. and Japanese strategies', *Strategic Management Journal*, **15**, 579–601.

Jones, C.P. and Pizam, A. (1993) *The International Hospitality Industry: Organizational and Operational Issues*, London: Pitman, and New York: Wiley.

Jong, H.W. de (1985) *Dynamische Markttheorie* (3rd edition), Leiden: Stenfert Kroese.

Kaven, W.H. (1992) 'Japan's hotel industry: an overview', *Cornell Hotel and Restaurant Administration Quarterly*, **33** (2): 26–32.

Keegan, W.J. (1989) *Global Marketing Management* (4th edition), Englewood Cliffs, NJ: Prentice Hall.

Kennedy, P. (1989) *The Rise and Fall of the Great Powers*, New York: Vintage.

Keogh, B. (1989) 'Public participation in community tourism planning', *Annals of Tourism Research*, **17** (3): 449–465.

Ketelhohn, W. and Kubes, J. (1995) *Cases in International Business*, Oxford: Butterworth-Heinemann.

Kimes, S.E. and Lord, D.C. (1994) 'Wholesalers and Caribbean resort owners', *Cornell Hotel and Restaurant Administration Quarterly*, **35** (5): 70–75.

Knox, X. and Agnew, X. (1989) *The Geography of the World Economy*, London: Edward Arnold.

Kotler, P. (1980) *Principles of Marketing*, Englewood Cliffs, NJ: Prentice-Hall.

Krippendorf, J. (1987) *The Holiday-makers: Understanding the Impact of Travel and Tourism*, Oxford: Butterworth-Heinemann.

Lane, H.E. (1986) 'Marriages of necessity: airline–hotel liaisons', *Cornell Hotel and Restaurant Administration Quarterly*, **27** (1): 72–79.

Lee, W.K. and Ghosh, B.C. (1990) 'Korea's hotel and tourism industry', *Cornell Hotel and Restaurant Administration Quarterly*, **31** (1): 74–79.

Leslie, D. (1993) 'Higher Education for hospitality and tourism: a European dimension', *International Journal of Hospitality Management*, **12** (1): 101–107.

Lessem, R. (1989) *Global Management Principles*, New York: Prentice-Hall.

Lin, M. (1990) 'Taiwan: magnet for Japanese tourists', *Cornell Hotel and Restaurant Administration Quarterly*, **31** (1): 96–97.

Litteljohn, D. (1991) 'The European hotel industry—corporate structures and expansion strategies', paper presented at *Tourism and Hospitality Management—Established Disciplines or Ten Year Wonders?*, Surrey University, 24–27 September.

Litteljohn, D. and Beattie, R. (1985) 'Towards an economic analysis of trans-multinational hotel companies', *International Journal of Hospitality Management*, **4** (4):157–165.

Livingston, J. (1982a) 'Four seasons breaks into the U.S. market', *Cornell Hotel and Restaurant Administration Quarterly*, **22** (4): 50–53.

Livingston, J. (1982b) 'Quality Inns pursues international quantity', *Cornell Hotel and Restaurant Administration Quarterly*, **22** (4): 34–40.

Lucas, R.E. (1993) 'The Social Charter—opportunity or threat to employment practice in the U.K. hospitality industry', *International Journal of Hospitality Management*, **12** (1): 89–100.

Makens, J.C. and Edgell, D.L. (1990) 'Internationalizing your hotel's welcome mat', *Cornell Hotel and Restaurant Administration Quarterly*, **31** (3): 64–70.

Mansfield, Y. (1992) 'From motivation to actual travel', *Annals of Tourism Research*, **19** (2): 250–267.

Marquardt, M.J. and Engel, D.W. (1993) *Global Human Resource Development*, Englewood Cliffs, NJ: Prentice-Hall.

McNulty, R. and Wafer, P. (1990) 'Transnational corporations and tourism issues', *Tourism Management*, **11** (4): 291–295.

Meyer, R. and Pruyn, A. (1994) 'Nico Duin BV: a small company internationalises', in *Marketing in Europe*, Montana, J. (ed.), London: Sage.

Morgan, J.C. and Morgan, J.J. (1991) *Cracking the Japanese Market: Strategies for Success in the New Global Economy*, New York: Free Press.

Ohmae, K. (1986) 'Becoming a triad power: the new global corporation', *International Marketing Review*, **3** (3): 7–20.

Ohmae, K. (1995) 'Putting global logic first', *Harvard Business Review*, **73** (1): 119–125.

Owens, D. (1994) 'The all-season opportunity for Canada's resorts', *Cornell Hotel and Restaurant Administration Quarterly*, **35** (5): 28–41.

Paliwoda, S.J. (1986) *International Marketing*, London: Heinemann.

Perlmutter, H.V. (1969) 'The tortuous evolution of the multinational corporation', *Columbia Journal of World Business*, **4**, 9–18.

Pine, R. (1992) 'Technology transfer in the hotel industry', *International Journal of Hospitality Management*, **11** (1): 3–22.

Pitelis, Ch. N. and Dugden, R. (1991) *The Nature of the Transnational Firm*, London: Routledge.

Pizam, A. (1989) 'Ethnocentrism and the tourism industry', *Hospitality Education and Research Journal*, **13** (1): ii–iii.

Poon, G.A. (1993) *Tourism Technology and Competitive Strategies*, Wallingford, Oxon: CAB International.

Porter, M.E. (1980) *Competitive Advantage: Creating and Sustaining Superior Performance*, New York: Free Press.

Porter, M.E. (1986) *Competition in Global Industries*, Cambridge, MA: Harvard Business School Press.

Porter, M.E. (1990) *The Competitive Advantage of Nations*, New York: Free Press.

Price, D.G. and Blair, A.M. (1989) *The Changing Geography of the Service Sector*, London: Belhaven Press, Chapter 8, pp. 162–194.

Qu, H. and Li, I. (1997) 'The characteristics and satisfaction of mainland Chinese visitors to Hong Kong', *Journal of Travel Research*, **30** (4): 37–41.

Ricardo, D. (1971) *Principles of Political Economy and Taxation*, Harmondsworth: Penguin (originally published in 1817).

Richards, G. (1996) *Cultural Tourism in Europe*, Wallingford, Oxon: CAB International.

Ritzer, G. (1993) *The McDonaldization of Society*, London: Sage.

Robbins, J.A. (1985) 'Organisations and economics: some topical problems of transaction costs analysis', *Academy of Management Proceedings*, 181–185.

Robinson, G. (1993) 'Tourism and tourism policy in the European Community: an overview', *International Journal of Hospitality Management*, **12** (1): 7–20.

Robinson, G. and Mogendorff, D. (1993) The European tourism industry—ready for the single market?, *International Journal of Hospitality Management*, **12** (1): 21–31.

Rues, E.H. (1989) 'Facing the vulcano: the El Salvador Sheraton', *Cornell Hotel and Restaurant Administration Quarterly*, **30** (1) 28–39.

Rugman, A. (1981) *Inside The Multinationals*, London: Croom Helm.

Ruigrok, W. and Tulder, R. van (1995) *The Logic of International Restructuring*, London: Routledge.

Rusth, D.B. and Lefever, M.M. (1988) 'International profit planning', *Cornell Hotel and Restaurant Administration Quarterly*, **29** (3): 50–57.

Sachwald, F. (1994) *European Integration and Competitiveness*, London: Edward Elgar Publishing.

Saunders, H.A. and Reneghan, X. (1992) 'Southeast Asia: a new model for hotel development', *Cornell Hotel and Restaurant Administration Quarterly*, **33** (5): 16–23.

Schenk, H. (1995) *Industrial Policy in Bandwagon Economy Mergers, Efficient Choice, and International Competitiveness*, Rotterdam: GRASP.

Schiavone, G. (1983) *International Organizations: A Dictionary and Directory*, Chicago: St James Press.

Shames, G. (1986) 'Training for the multicultural workplace', *Cornell Hotel and Restaurant Administration Quarterly*, **26** (4): 25–31.

Shapiro, A.C. (1992) *Multifinancial Management* (4th edition), Boston: Allyn & Bacon.

Sharpe, J.L. (1990) 'Directions for the '90s: lessons from Japan', *Cornell Hotel and Restaurant Administration Quarterly*, **31** (1): 98–103.

Simons, M.S. (1992a) 'The European Commission's Directive on package travel, package holidays and package tours June 1990—II', *International Journal of Hospitality Management*, **11** (2): 83–87.

Simons, M.S. (1992b) 'Competition law, air transport deregulation and the tourism industry in the European Economic Community—I', *International Journal of Hospitality Management*, **11** (1): 33–45.

Slattery, P. (1991) 'Hotel branding in the 1980s', *EIU Travel and Tourism Analyst*, No. 1, 23–35.

Sparks, B. and Callan, V.J. (1992) 'Communication and the service encounter: the value of convergence', *International Journal of Hospitality Management*, **11** (3): 213–224.

Spybey, T. (1996) *Globalization and World Society*, Cambridge: Polity Press.

Stinchcombe, A. (1965) 'Social structures and organisations', in *Handbook of Organizations*, Marsch, J. (ed.), Chicago: Rand McNally, pp. 142–193.

Subhash, C.M. and Vera, A. (1990) 'Segmentation in Singapore', *Cornell Hotel and Restaurant Administration Quarterly*, **31** (1): 80–87.

Sung-soo Pyo (1993) 'Push pull attributes in early twenty-first century Korean tourism', *International Business Review*, **16** (June), Seoul, Korea: Kyonggi University.

Teare, R. (1995) 'The international hospitality business: a thematic perspective', *International Journal of Contemporary Hospitality Management*, **7** (7): 55–73.

Teare, B. R. and Olsen, M.D. (eds) (1992) *International Hospitality Management: Corporate Strategy in Practice*, London: Pitman and New York: Wiley.

Teichova, A., Lvey-Leboyer, X. and Nussbaum, H. (1986) *Multinational Enterprise in Historical Perspective*, Cambridge: Cambridge University Press.

Theobald, D.W. (1994) *Global Tourism: The Next Decade*, Oxford: Butterworth-Heinemann.

Theuns, H.L. (1984) *The Emergence of Research on Third World Tourism: 1945 to 1970, An Introductory Essay cum Bibliography*, Tilburg University, Research Memorandum.

Tulder, R.J.M. van (1997) 'Internationalisation and competitive space', *Erasmus Project Proposal*, Rotterdam, Erasmus University.

UNCTC (1988) *Transnational Corporations and World Development*, New York: United Nations, E88. II. A.7.

Vallen, J. (1989) 'The new Soviet tourism', *Cornell Hotel and Restaurant Administration Quarterly*, **29** (4): 73–79.

Vandermerwe, S. and Chadwick, M. (1991) 'The internationalisation of services', in *Services Marketing*, Lovelock, C. (ed.), 2nd edition, Englewood Cliffs, NJ: Prentice-Hall.

Vernon, R. (1971) *Sovereignty at Bay: The Multinational Spread of U.S. Enterprises*, New York: Basic Books.

Vernon, R. (1977) *Storm Over the Multinationals*, Cambridge, MA: Harvard University Press.

Vliet, M. (1993) 'Environmental regulation of business: options and constraints for communicative governance', in *Modern Governance, New Government–Society Interactions*, Kooiman, J. (ed.), London: Sage.

Wanhill, S.R.C. (1993) 'European regional development funds for the hospitality and tourism industries', *International Journal of Hospitality Management*, **12** (1): 67–76.

Wassenberg, A. (1994) 'European Alliances: on the art and science of directing interfirm strategies', in *Changing Business Systems in Europe. An Institutional Approach*, van Dijck, J. and Groenewegen, J. (eds), Brussels: Vubpress.

Wassenberg, A. (1995) *Strategievorming: Condities, Codes en Commitments*, Delft: Eburon.

Weekley, J.K. and Aggarwal, R. (1987) *International Business Operating in a Global Economy*, New York: CBS College Publishing.

Welchford, R. and Prescott, K. (1994) *European Business: an Issue-based Approach* (2nd edition), London: Pitman.

Wells, L. (ed.) (1972) *The Product Life Cycle and International Trade*, Cambridge, MA: Harvard University Press.

Welsh, D.H.B. and Swerdlow, S. (1992) 'Hospitality Russian style: nine communication challenges', *Cornell Hotel and Restaurant Administration Quarterly*, **33** (6): 64–72.

Wierenga, B., Pruyn, A. and Waarts, E. (1995) 'The key to successful Euromarketing: standardization or customization', *Journal of International Consumer Marketing*, **8** (3 and 4): 36–67.

Wilde, J. de. (1991) 'How to train managers for going global', *Business Quarterly*, **55** (3): 41–46.

Wilson, D. (1994) 'Unique by a thousand miles: Seychelles tourism revisited', *Annals of Tourism Research*, **21** (1): 20–45.

Witt, F.S.F., Brooke, M.Z. and Buckley, P.J. (1991) *The Management of International Tourism*, London: Unwin Hyman.

Woods, K.S. (1991) 'When the tanks rolled into town: AGMs experience in Kuwait', *Cornell Hotel and Restaurant Administration Quarterly*, **32** (1): 16–25.

World Commission on Environment and Development (1987) *Our Common Future*, Oxford: Oxford University Press.

Yip, G.S. (1989) 'Global strategy … in a world of nations', *Sloan Management Review*, **29** (fall): 29–41.

Yip, G.S. (1995) *Total Global Strategy: Managing for World Wide Comparative Advantage*, Englewood Cliffs, NJ: Prentice-Hall.

Yip, G.S. and Coundouriotis, X. (1991) 'Diagnosing global strategy potential: the world chocolate confectionery industry', *Planning Review*, **19** (1) (Jan/Feb): 4–14.

Yu, L. (1992a) 'Hotel development and structures in China', *International Journal of Hospitality Management*, **11** (2): 99–110.

Yu, L. (1992b) 'Seeing stars: China's hotel-rating system', *Cornell Hotel and Restaurant Administration Quarterly*, **33** (5): 24–27.

25 Small business management

RHODRI THOMAS, MARTIN FRIEL AND
STEPHANIE JAMESON

Introduction

The preponderance of small firms is one of the defining characteristics of the hospitality industry, both domestically and throughout the rest of the world. Although there is some debate surrounding the precise definition of a small business, there is no disagreement that the most commonly found hospitality enterprise is small, whichever definition is used. There is, however, a dissonance between this structural feature of the industry and the research interests of hospitality academics. Illustration of this observation may be made by reference to a review of articles recently published in leading hospitality journals (Teare and Bowen, 1997), where small business management barely appears as an issue. While this reflects a lack of activity in the field, it is disappointing that the publication's concluding section—'Clusters and gaps in hospitality and tourism academic research' (Ingram, 1997)—does not recognise this as an important omission.

It is possible that the apparent disregard for research conducted in small firms is accounted for by a perception that hospitality management research undertaken in large organisations may simply be transferred to the small firm context. As will be argued below, there is now sufficient empirical evidence to suggest that such a notion is misplaced; small hospitality firms are fundamentally different from large ones and, therefore, require separate and distinct analysis.

Notwithstanding these observations, there are now signs that hospitality researchers are beginning to take seriously the issue of small business management. During 1996, for example, the International Association of Hotel Management Schools (IAHMS) convened a symposium entitled 'Issues relating to small businesses in the tourism and hospitality industries'. Organised under the auspices of the Centre for the Study of Small Tourism and Hospitality Firms, Leeds, it attracted more than 30 contributions and some 70 delegates. Further, the *International Journal of Contemporary Hospitality Management* dedicated an entire issue (Volume 8, Number 5, 1996) to this theme. Textbooks on this topic are also now starting to emerge (for example Boer, Thomas and Webster, 1997). Indeed, the inclusion of a separate chapter in this volume is itself a reflection of a growing recognition of the importance of this topic.

Before reviewing the research which has been undertaken into small business management in the hospitality industry, the chapter explores how various commentators use the term 'small business' and considers the reasons for variations in usage. This is important because it tends to reflect the differing philosophical and methodological perspectives of researchers. An examination of the differences between small and large enterprises then follows. In effect, it is this section which justifies a consideration of small firms as a distinct analytical category from others. The chapter then provides a critical assessment of the methodological issues associated with estimating the number of small firms in the economy. While this discussion centres on the UK, the principles it establishes are likely to be equally applicable elsewhere. Finally, a review of recent research—in terms of both the research strategies adopted and the barriers to effective research which they reveal—is then provided. The review acts as a basis for making suggestions regarding future research in this field.

Defining a small business

In the UK, discussions about how to define small firms often begin with reference to the Committee of Inquiry Report on Small Firms (Bolton Report) which was published in 1971. This is not surprising because not only was it critical in establishing the importance of smaller enterprises in the minds of officials and academics, but its deliberations on this question remain pertinent to some extent in the 1990s.

The Bolton Committee adopted several definitions of a small firm. It argued that a small business was one which had a relatively small market share (it could not, therefore, influence market prices—it was a 'price taker'—nor could it to any significant extent affect the level of supply), was managed in a personalised way by its owners and was independent from external control. To this the Committee added a series of statistical definitions for use in different sectors. For some, such as manufacturing, a threshold number of employees (200) was used, whereas for retailing a turnover figure was adopted (Stanworth and Gray, 1991). In the case of the hospitality industry, the definition focused on the independence of the operation (Pickering, Greenwood and Hunt, 1971). The rationale for the multiplicity of definitions was that they might be used for different purposes—for example, a statistical definition would enable international comparisons to be made—and it was recognised that 'smallness' varied between sectors.

During the period since the publication of the Bolton Report, several commentators have noted its shortcomings. Stanworth and Gray (1991), for example, point out that statistical analysis is hampered by the use of varying definitions. Further, any definition which uses a financial indicator inevitably requires periodic adjustment in order to take account of inflation (Burns, 1996). To these, Storey (1994) adds two further problems of accepting the Bolton approach to defining small businesses. First, he notes the incompatibility of a definition which emphasises the personalised nature of management while *simultaneously* using statistical bands relating to numbers of employees. He argues that there is sufficient research which shows that firms employing up to 200 people would inevitably require that business decisions be taken by individuals who were not owners. Secondly, in challenging the influence which the notion of perfect competition (where small firms are price takers) had on the deliberations of the Bolton Committee, he argues that many small firms operate in niche markets where premium prices can be charged. At an anecdotal level, it would not be difficult to identify small hospitality businesses which would support his case.

In spite of the lapse of more than 25 years since the publication of the Bolton Report, there is not, to borrow Storey's (1994: 8) words, 'a single, uniformly acceptable, definition of a small firm'. This is illustrated clearly by reference to the 16 studies undertaken during the late 1980s and early 1990s which together formed the UK's largest ever small business research project (funded by the Economic and Social Research Council). The definitions used for those projects included: fewer than 10 employees, fewer than 100 employees, fewer than 200 employees, 1–500 employees, a grounded definition, users of informal venture capital (Storey, 1994: xvi–xvii). What emerges from a full review of the small business literature is a panoply of definitions which are justified by their users on the basis of their value to particular projects.

Studies of small businesses in the hospitality industry reflect a similar liberal usage of the term 'small firms' to that found in the general small business literature. Table 25.1 illustrates this by highlighting the range of definitions used by contributors to the IAHMS symposium referred to earlier. At this stage, then, there is no greater congruence among the definitions used for sector-specific studies than elsewhere.

In order to meet the perceived imperative of facilitating comparison between sectors and member states, the European Commission recently adopted a common definition of

Table 25.1   A selection of definitions used in the study of small hospitality businesses

Authors (all 1996 references)	Topic	Definition
Hales, Tamangani, Walker and Murphy	Training	Fewer than 50 employees
Morrison	Marketing	Directly managed by an individual or group in a personalised manner. Perceived to be small in terms of capacity, facilities and number of employees
Bransgrove and King	Marketing	Small market share; managed by the owners in a personalised manner; not part of a group
Ozer	Finance	Upper limit of 70–75 rooms. Managed in a personalised manner by an individual or group
Edgar and Watson	Strategic management/HRM	Privately owned with fewer than 50 rooms
Lincoln and Kusyj	Marketing	Turnover below £1m
Radiven and Lucas	Wages councils	Fewer than 25 employees
Danvers and Long	Sustainable tourism	Independence: focus on micro firms (fewer than 10 employees)
Vance, Thomas and Margerison	Consultancy	Independence, owner-managed, financed by an individual, small market share
Lynch	Bed and breakfasts	Focus on micro firms (fewer than 10 employees)

Source: IAHMS (1996).

small and medium-sized enterprises (SMEs) which emphasises numbers of employees as follows: 'micro' or 'very small enterprises' employ fewer than 10 people, 'small enterprises' employ between 10 and 49 people, 'medium-sized enterprises' employ more than 50 but fewer than 250 (Thomas, 1996: 131). Since it is more discriminating than their previous definition (which had an upper limit of fewer than 500 employees) and will be used for all EU programmes (in the past, definitions of SMEs varied according to programme), this definition will undoubtedly gain currency. It is now used, for example, by the Department of Trade and Industry (DTI) for its statistical bulletin on SMEs in the UK economy (DTI, 1997).

Some commentators have been critical of statistical definitions of small enterprises. For example, Burrows and Curran (1989) suggest that the implication of adopting what are ultimately arbitrary (employment) size bands is that too much homogeneity is ascribed to the 'small business sector'. Although their arguments are explored in a little more detail below, the essence of their case is that cross-sectoral comparisons may not be realistic, even as an aspiration.

For research to be meaningful, they promote the use of more *grounded* definitions of size, whereby sector-specific definitions are induced as a result of qualitative research in each industry. It is interesting that the research with which one of those authors was involved on small firms in the service sector—which included free houses, wine bars and restaurants—resulted in much smaller employment size categories (and emphasised independence) compared with the European Commission's definition cited above (Curran *et al.*, 1993). Peacock (1993) has also attempted to construct a grounded definition of small hotels and restaurants. Although geographically limited to London, his work is useful both for its findings and in its description of the problems encountered in undertaking such a task. Peacock suggests that the distinction between small, medium and large enterprises is unhelpful in the context of hotels and restaurants. Instead, he argues that there is greater utility in using a small/large dichotomy. Although levels of turnover are considered, Peacock ends up with a definition—based on the perceptions of practitioners—which centres on numbers of employees; his suggestion is that small restaurants employ up to 30 employees, whereas small hotels employ up to 80 people. It is perhaps disappointing that few, if any, commentators have developed his work nor utilised his findings.

Small firms as an analytical category

Given the discussion above, this chapter is necessarily flexible in its interpretation of the term 'small firm' so as not to exclude discussion of important pieces of research. Before reviewing recent studies, attention is turned to the question of the distinctiveness of small enterprises compared with their larger counterparts.

Storey (1994), in his highly regarded review of small business research, suggests that there are key differences between small and large firms. He argues, for example, that the notion of uncertainty differs between the two categories. His proposition is that smaller firms are likely to face greater uncertainty in terms of the market but will display more internal consistency in terms of their actions and motivations. Since small business owners determine their own objectives—which are often to seek a certain level of income or lifestyle—the emphasis on control, which is central to large organisations, is absent. This results in greater internal uncertainty within larger enterprises.

Storey (1994) also argues that small and large firms differ in their approach to innovation. Although small firms are unlikely to invest in research, it is suggested that they are more likely to respond to niche markets. Peacock (1993) provides an interesting polemic on the innovatory capacity of small hospitality firms, which supports Storey's position.

The third difference highlighted by Storey (1994) is the increased likelihood of change in small businesses. Here he is referring to the significant alterations to management organisation and structure if small firms grow (though it should be noted that the majority do not).

Others have also drawn attention to significant differences between small and large enterprises. For example, Burns (1996) points out that the financial constraints imposed upon small businesses imply that their strategic options are circumscribed by the availability of capital. Further, Dewhurst and Burns (1993) note that small firms will operate in a distinct manner as a result of their not having specialist managers for the various functional activities of the firm. On the basis of the above, then, it is appropriate to examine the management of small firms in a manner which recognises their distinctiveness.

Although the case for an analysis of small firms has been made, the justification for studying small *hospitality* firms remains to be explored. In a seminal review of conceptual issues associated with small business research in the service sector, Burrows and Curran (1989) argue that there are serious methodological dangers of ignoring sectoral contexts:

> Obviously size (however operationalised) *does* influence the internal and external relations of an economic unit, but other factors such as economic sector ... are likely to be just as crucial in determining whatever it is that is being investigated. (Burrows and Curran, 1989: 530)

In another paper, they advocate sectoral specificity by demonstrating that within size bands, the differences between sectors are likely to be important influences on the phenomenon being studied. To paraphrase, it is unlikely that a corner shop which employs one full-time and some part-time employees will share the same outlook, encounter similar difficulties and engage with the economy in the same manner as an owner–manager of a high-tech electronics firm employing 10 well-qualified people or a farmer with two employees supplemented by occasional casual labour (Curran and Burrows, 1989: 6).

The above, coupled with the now well-rehearsed arguments that services management and service industries are better understood if their distinctiveness from manufacturing is recognised (see, for example, Voss *et al.*, 1988), further strengthens the case for an assessment of small hospitality firms which is separate from the study of small firms in general. While it might be argued that focusing on services would be insightful, the position adopted here is that the danger of ignoring differences between, say, a small firm of solicitors and a small hotel may lead to a misunderstanding of the dynamics of such enterprises. There are, after all, established accounts of the factors which influence the demand for and supply of tourism and hospitality products (such as Cooper *et al.*, 1993) which are not transferable to all other services. This is not to suggest, of course, that the non-sector-specific literature makes no contribution to understanding these industries, merely that they need to be considered with caution.

Moreover, neither is it being suggested that small hospitality firms are homogeneous, an issue discussed further below. However, there are sufficient grounds for examining such organisations as a separate analytical category both from small firms in general and from other, larger, hospitality firms.

Methodological problems of estimating the number of small hospitality firms in the UK

Perhaps not surprisingly, the difficulties encountered when attempting to define small firms are mirrored when seeking to estimate their number. It is curious that in spite of the importance attached to the promotion of small businesses by successive governments, until recently little effort had been made by officials to accurately gauge their incidence in the economy. As will be discussed below, the situation has been slightly ameliorated as a result of developments in the Department of Trade and Industry (DTI). Prior to considering these, it is instructive to compare two prominent sector-specific publications—one from the Department of National Heritage (DNH, 1996), the other published by the Hospitality Training Foundation (HTF, 1996)—which may appear confusing, or even contradictory, to casual observers.

In commenting on the fragmentation of the industry, the DNH (1996: 16) notes that 'it is largely made up of small firms. [For example] 81% of hotels and 94% of restaurants and bars have fewer than 25 employees.' The HTF (1996: 4), however, focuses upon a broader sectoral category, namely 'small commercial establishments' (restaurants, pubs/bars, hotels, contract catering, clubs, guest-houses and take-aways which employ fewer than 10 staff). Although both sets of figures confirm an impression of fragmentation, the manner in which the information is presented (with differences in both sectors and size bands) makes comparison impossible. To complicate matters further, commercially produced reports also present varying estimates of the number of small hospitality firms in the UK (see, for example, MSI, 1991; Key Note, 1993; Wedgwood Markham, 1994). For a more comprehensive review of the various estimates relating to numbers of small firms in the hotel industry, see Morrison (1998).

There are at least two preconditions which need to be satisfied before reaching sensible judgements as to the utility of quoted statistics. First, it is important to pay careful attention to the terminology used. In the example above, the DNH uses the term 'small firm' whereas the HTF discusses 'establishments'. In an analysis of small business management, this distinction is important, for the dynamics of establishments (or units) of a large chain are likely to be quite different from those of independent owner-managed enterprises.

Second, the source of data must be noted and any inherent limitations recognised. In the case of the HTF (1996) study, for example, the principal source of data is the 1991 UK Census of Employment. On that basis, they estimate that small establishments (1–9 employees) in the hospitality industry comprise 87% of the total stock. In spite of their numerical preponderance, they suggest that this category accounts for 36% of employment, which rises to 64% when added to those establishments employing fewer than 25 people. Thus, the remaining 36% of hospitality workers are employed by those so-called large establishments (i.e. employing more than 25 staff). Although undoubtedly useful in other contexts, data from the Census of Employment has limitations for those with an interest in small *enterprises*. The Census covers Pay As You Earn (PAYE) (income tax) schemes which do not correspond precisely to firms or establishments. This is because PAYE schemes may cover employees in many locations, or there may be more than one scheme at a single site (e.g. separate schemes for monthly and weekly paid staff). Additionally, since the self-employed who do not employ others and those businesses who employ only people who are not subject to PAYE are excluded, the figures underestimate the numbers of small businesses (Bannock and Daly, 1994: 45).

Morrison (1998) reinforces this note of caution when she argues that there are several reasons why available statistics are partial in their coverage: lack of universally accepted definitions, many small businesses operating below the threshold at which they would be required to register for Value Added Tax (VAT), many accommodation units not being registered because they have too few rooms, and some small firms operating in the informal economy (Williams and Thomas, 1996).

The DTI's relatively new *Statistical Bulletin* series goes some way towards overcoming the weaknesses of using single sources of information such as the Census of Employment or VAT statistics. Their approach is to supplement the Inter-Departmental Business Register (IDBR) with estimates made of those businesses which are too small to be registered. The resulting statistics cannot be considered exact but they currently represent the most robust data on which to construct a profile of small firms. Although the DTI produces statistics for a range of hospitality-related sectors, for convenience only the hotels and restaurants data is referred to here. Obviously, considering this data alone will not provide a complete description of the structure of the hospitality industry. However, it will serve to illustrate the point that some sources of statistical information are more appropriate than others when attempting to establish how many small hospitality enterprises there are in the UK.

According to the DTI's third, and most recent, *Statistical Bulletin* (DTI, 1997), there are some 150,000 hotel and restaurant businesses in the UK. Of these, almost 99% employ fewer than 50 people. Further, as Table 25.2 indicates, very small (or micro) enterprises predominate, accounting for over 85% of firms in these sectors.

Table 25.2 Hotels and restaurants: number of businesses, employment and turnover by size (1996)

| Size (no. of employees) | Number | | | Percent | | |
	Businesses	Employment (000s)	Turnover (£m excluding VAT)	Businesses	Employment	Turnover
0	41,999	57	1,154	28.2	3.9	2.5
1–4	64,705	221	6,725	43.5	15.1	14.7
5–9	23,692	185	4,887	15.9	12.6	10.7
10–19	12,187	175	4,112	8.2	11.9	9.0
20–49	4,546	137	3,285	3.1	9.3	7.2
50–99	997	68	2,474	0.7	4.7	5.4
100–199	418	57	1,654	0.3	3.8	3.6
200–249	67	15	400	—	1.0	0.9
250–499	129	43	1,550	0.1	2.9	3.4
500+	126	511	19,547	0.1	34.8	42.7
All	148,866	1,469	45,788	100.0	100.0	100.0

Source: DTI (1997: 11). Reproduced by permission.

Those companies which employ in excess of 500 people are, however, disproportionately significant in terms of employment generation and turnover. Whereas this category accounts for only 0.1% of all hotel and restaurant businesses, it is responsible for creating 35% of employment and 43% of total sectoral turnover. Nevertheless, over 50% of those working in hotels and restaurants are employed by enterprises with fewer than 50 staff. Small businesses within this category also account for almost half of total turnover.

Although the figures above highlight the importance of small hospitality firms, they offer no insight into current trends. In the absence of long-term comprehensive and reliable statistics, tracking change is, of course, problematic. Nevertheless, the case is frequently made—from as early as Pickering, Greenwood and Hunt (1971) to, more latterly, Litteljohn (1993) and Mogendorff (1996)—that key sectors of the hospitality industry are becoming more concentrated. Moreover, it is suggested by some, notably Slattery (1994), that structural shifts in the UK economy have precipitated this development, at least as far as the hotel sector is concerned.

To some extent, the evidence—represented by the growth of multiples, especially in the fast-food and accommodation sectors over recent decades—is incontrovertible. However, the *extent* to which multiples have taken market share and will *continue* to grow at the expense of smaller operators is more questionable. The theoretical constructs which inform explanations and predictions of future changes are under-developed. Further, the measurements of concentration which are sometimes used to support propositions have been robustly challenged for their crudeness (Hughes, 1993).

There is also a suggestion that the standardisation inherent in chain operations stifles innovation (Peacock, 1993). As a consequence, dynamic small firms might continue to thrive, even in prime locations. Given the low barriers to entry, and the highly segmented nature of demand (Morrison, 1996a), such an argument is not implausible. Certainly, recent survey evidence (Thomas *et al.*, 1997)—which included a broad range of small tourism and hospitality firms—found that a majority of almost 1400 firms sampled had experienced stability or growth in revenues, profits and employment during the 12 months prior to questioning and were optimistic about the future. In addition, comparison of recent *Statistical Bulletins* suggests that in the case of hotels and restaurants, the proportion of employment and turnover accounted for by small firms has remained relatively constant (Thomas, 1998a). Clearly this is an issue which requires carefully considered research and monitoring in the years ahead.

Research methods for studying small businesses

Since research into small businesses in the hospitality industry is in its infancy, it is somewhat premature to attempt to categorise the literature in terms of various perspectives and paradigms. Instead, the emphasis will be to provide a critical review of the breadth (or narrowness) of research approaches which have been used by hospitality researchers and to consider some methodological difficulties peculiar to the study of small hospitality firms. Before this, however, it is appropriate to make some observations about the mainstream small business literature for, as in the case of other areas of enquiry, this is frequently used to inform hospitality-specific studies.

General small business research is replete with studies grounded in particular disciplines. For example, Reid's (1993) study of small firms in Scotland provides an economic analysis of small business development, whereas Goss (1991) adopts a sociological perspective for the study of these economic units. Similarly, specific—if sometimes imprecise—facets of small business ownership, such as 'entrepreneurship', have also received attention from psychologists, economists and sociologists. In spite of apparently examining the same phenomenon, their focus of study has been quite distinct. In the case of psychology, for instance, greatest effort has been expended on attempting to identify the personality traits of 'entrepreneurs'. Economists, by contrast, have tended to engage in research which examines entrepreneurs' decisions as economic actors in the market. Finally, sociologists have emphasised the importance of the social relationships which exist in different types of small businesses (Dewhurst and Horobin, 1988). This has led some commentators to argue persuasively that many studies of this topic have faltered precisely because of the constraints imposed by their disciplinary boundaries. In making a case for interdisciplinary approaches to this issue, Dewhurst and Horobin (1998) make the following observations:

> In summary, the contribution of the economists appears to indicate the existence of a distinctive set of characteristic behaviours, which serve to determine entrepreneurial acts and which provide some useful insight into the effect of the entrepreneur on the economy. However, not all business owners are entrepreneurs. Furthermore, as some economists have indicated, a psychological examination of the nature of entrepreneurship is also necessary if a more rounded understanding is to be achieved (Chell, Haworth and Brearley, 1991). The work of psychologists has resulted in some agreement as to a constellation of personality traits which might characterise entrepreneurs and enable the identification of the 'entrepreneurial personality'. The focus is again on the entrepreneur and it is acknowledged by many that links to the context in which the business is operating are necessary if a full analysis of their behaviour is to emerge. Finally, the small business owner typologies drawn up primarily by sociologists, while inherently appealing and considered useful by some, have been fundamentally challenged on methodological grounds. A by-product of this 'grail-like search for the entrepreneurial personality' (Goss, 1991: 48) by researchers from all disciplines 'has meant confusion, as writers have either used the concept in a vague and unspecified manner ..., or have constructed definitions of an extremely restricted nature' (Goss, 1991: 47) (Dewhurst and Horobin, 1998: 22–23).

As will be clear from reading earlier chapters, each discipline will generally bring with it certain theoretical and philosophical perspectives which subsequently inform the research methods adopted. This is not to suggest, of course, that there is a lack of discourse within disciplines (see, for example, Hughes 1997). Nevertheless, given its positivistic outlook, economics research, for instance, is more likely to be quantitative (see, for example, Acs and Audretsch, 1990) whereas sociological studies may involve qualitative methods such as participant observation (see, for example, Phizacklea and Ram, 1995). In this light, it is perhaps not surprising that the earlier discussion regarding how to define small businesses is influenced by the perspective—or perhaps even the disciplinary background—of the researcher: those keen to undertake quantitative analysis have an imperative to adopt a quantitative definition which may be rejected by those who emphasise the benefits of qualitative approaches to studying small businesses.

Notwithstanding the above, mainstream small business research has increasingly become interdisciplinary in nature. This has resulted in projects which use a blend of quantitative and qualitative research techniques. This may be exemplified by reference to Wynarczyk *et al.*'s (1993) study of managerial labour markets. As they point out (1993: 1):

> ... it is our intention to combine elements of industrial and labour economics ... we do not, however view the economic paradigm as the only valid perspective by which to examine these issues ... we have adopted a catholic rather than a single disciplinary approach and have incorporated, where appropriate, insights from the organisational behaviour, strategy and leadership literatures.

Further, in terms of their research approach, they note (1993: 113) that:

> ... a research study of the relationship between managerial inputs and firm performance in small firms needs to employ both a quantitative and a qualitative mode.

In turning to small business research in the hospitality industry, it is striking that a significant amount of the existing literature is either exploratory or descriptive. At this early stage of the subject's development, this is to be expected and, indeed, is probably necessary. That said, there is now a growing understanding of the characteristics and certain aspects of the behaviour of small hospitality businesses which acts as a foundation for further, more rigorous investigation. Although an appreciation of these issues is vital for those engaged in small business research, since the focus of this chapter is on research methods (rather than findings), readers are referred to Thomas (1998b) for a comprehensive review.

Table 25.3—taken from a selection of papers presented at the 1996 IAHMS small business conference—provides a sample of research methods used in the study of small hospitality firms. Naturally, this list is not a complete reflection of current activity. However, since this was the first major conference of its kind, it is considered to be a reasonable indicator of the range of methods utilised. It can be seen from the table that there is some variety in the methods used, ranging from case studies and postal surveys to matched pair research and participant observation.

The most common approaches are surveys, semi-structured interviews and case studies. While this shows a broad range of research methods being used, some papers also reveal a slightly casual approach to reporting. This is particularly noticeable in the area of quantitative studies where there is sometimes a lack of detail on important matters such as sample size, sample selection, non-response problems and statistical validity, or where there are flaws in the research procedures, most notably in not testing the research instrument(s) prior to collecting data. There is a certain amount of vagueness too in many qualitative studies where, for example, the composition of focus groups is unclear, selection procedures are not made explicit or the structure of interviews is not provided. Obviously, this presents readers—or those seeking to replicate research—with difficulties when attempting to make judgements about the validity and reliability of research projects.

Statistical analysis of data in some of the papers examined tends to be of a univariate nature, whereas multivariate analysis might offer greater insight by recognising the interplay of various variables. In addition, greater use might be made of more sophisticated statistical techniques to examine relationships and to test association between variables, such as factor, cluster and conjoint analysis. These are generally lacking in

Table 25.3   A selection of research methods used in the study of small hospitality businesses

Authors (all 1996 references)	Research topic	Research methods used
Hales, Tamangani, Walker and Murphy	Adoption of NVQs in small hospitality firms	Case studies of five small firms which involved in-depth semi-structured interviews with key informants, observation and scrutiny of internal documentation
Morrison	Marketing strategic alliances: small hotels	A multi-methods approach: organisational literature review, case studies involving in-depth interviews with key informants and participant observation, questionnaire survey. There was also a longitudinal element to this project
Bransgrove and King	Strategic marketing practice amongst small tourism and hospitality businesses	Literature search to generate questions for pilot postal survey questionnaire prior to main postal survey based on stratified random sample
Ghiselli	Cash handling and controlling employee theft in food service	Questionnaire survey developed from a literature search and preceded by a pilot survey
Edgar and Watson	Strategic success—the human touch	Focus group discussion as a basis for a structured postal survey
Russell	Innovation in small Irish tourism businesses	In-depth (two-hour) interviews with key informants and a postal questionnaire
Radiven and Lucas	Abolition of wages councils and impact on pay policy of small hotels	Postal questionnaire sent to two different sample populations (large hotels and small hotels) to allow for comparative analysis. Follow-up interviews to be conducted
Danvers and Long	Sustainability and small tourism firms	Case study of 54 small tourism firms in the Yorkshire Dales National Park which involved structured interviews
Edgar and Nisbet	Strategy in small business	Focus group discussion as a basis for structured postal survey
O'Neill, Orr and Black	Techniques to manage hotel capacity in Northern Ireland	Qualitative research study comprising semi-structured interviews informed by a pilot study
Vance, Thomas and Margerison	Subsidised consultancy schemes and the business performance of small hospitality firms	Matched pair research design with 15 participant businesses and 15 control matching businesses with semi-structured interviews to follow

Source: IAHMS (1996).

small hospitality firm research, though it is likely that as this area of study matures, so too will the methods of research and analysis.

In spite of the observations made earlier in the chapter about the fundamental differences between small and large firms, some researchers continue to use the research frameworks, methods and literature pertaining to larger firm research. Implicit in some of these studies is the assumption that small hospitality firms constitute scaled-down versions of large firms. This is probably a function of the relative infancy of research in this area. Again, it is likely that this will be remedied as more research is undertaken.

It should be noted that the rather negative observations made in this section should not be over-emphasised. Some of the papers reviewed here also reveal thorough and systematic research which takes full account of what is already understood about small hospitality firms and offer new insights. Thus, clear conceptual frameworks are offered and a variety of data collection techniques used to investigate their topics. Such studies augur well for the future understanding of the dynamics of small hospitality businesses.

Those studying the behaviour and business practices of small hospitality firms face a number of obstacles when seeking to gain access to data. The final part of this chapter explores these and considers how researchers might overcome them. Since small hospitality firms are characterised by the personalised way in which they are managed, it is frequently the case that only one person has the information sought by the researcher. The difficulty of gaining access to such key informants (because of their typically busy schedules) may be exacerbated by a perception that the findings of the research will be of little interest or value to them. Clearly, it is incumbent upon the researcher to develop appropriate networks and techniques to secure co-operation.

The reliability of some sensitive information (for example, financial) is also potentially problematic for small business researchers. Unless precision is required, it is probably more fruitful to seek general information on such matters (for example, by banding categories) and, obviously, to stress confidentiality.

Given the highly seasonal nature of demand, simply determining, say, the levels of employment of businesses is difficult. For those engaged in quantitative studies, this matter needs to be treated with care because at one time of the year a small firm may be classed as a micro enterprise, which may not be the case later in the season. Researchers, of necessity, are required to consider very carefully the extent to which such fluctuations in the scale of operations during various times of the year influence the phenomenon being studied.

Unless it is recognised, the heterogeneity of the 'small business sector' may mislead researchers. It is now well understood that the bulk of small hospitality firms do not aspire to grow and are often motivated by non-financial factors. Indeed, some commentators have argued that the majority of such enterprises should be seen as forms of consumption rather than production (Williams, Shaw and Greenwood, 1989). Consequently, alternative conceptualisations to those based on financial motivations are required if their behaviour is to be understood.

Finally, the high failure rates among small hospitality firms (Boer, 1988) suggest that longitudinal studies are not easy to execute. Again, this poses particular obstacles to small business research which are less acute for those investigating larger enterprises.

Conclusions and future research directions

Research relating to small business management in the hospitality industry is currently at a relatively early stage in its development. Thus, although it is possible to cite studies which have examined training, marketing and quality management—to name but three areas of activity—their incidence is low compared with hospitality research in large organisations. This must be considered disappointing given the structural characteristics of this industry.

As a result of this relative inactivity among hospitality researchers, there is, at the moment, little consensus even in terms of what constitutes a 'small hospitality firm'. Some commentators have suggested grounded definitions—which have yet to be accepted by others—whereas many utilise fairly arbitrary statistical definitions but which enable comparison between sectors and countries. This chapter has argued that such divergence is inevitable when researchers approach the investigation of small business management from varying theoretical and philosophical perspectives. Although a unity of understanding of the essential characteristics of small hospitality firms may be desirable—for in its absence the justification for such enterprises representing a distinct analytical category is weakened—this will only emerge as more researchers take an interest in this area. It is encouraging that there are signs that this is beginning to happen.

The chapter also explored the methodological difficulties associated with estimating the number of small firms in the economy. This is an important issue because the veracity of assertions made by some academics who point to the imminent demise of independent operators cannot be established without such data. As was argued earlier, some of the 'evidence' provided to support such claims may easily be challenged. There seems to be a need, therefore, for commentators to take a greater interest in understanding the limitations of some widely cited statistics.

The review of small business research projects revealed some strengths and weaknesses in the current literature. It found evidence of research strategies which were casually explained and which appeared to presume that the conceptual frameworks developed for large organisations might be applied in the small business context. The chapter argued that such notions were misplaced and found studies which recognised the importance of this observation. As the body of small hospitality business research develops, it is likely that there will be a growing appreciation of the need to develop alternative theoretical frameworks to explain small business behaviour.

The commentary above has, then, highlighted the need for additional research. It is clear, for example, that the defining characteristics of small hospitality firms must be examined more carefully and that rigorous means of gauging the number of such organisations—and not merely hotels and restaurants—and of understanding structural changes in this sector of the economy are urgently required. The findings of such research would then act as a solid foundation on which to examine a variety of topics which will be of value to both small business owners and those agencies engaged in supporting enterprise development. The focus of these enquiries may range from analysis of factors influencing survival rates to the impact of technology on business performance or the environmental consequences of small business growth. Given the current shortage of detailed research, the list of possibilities is almost endless.

There are, of course, numerous barriers facing researchers in this field of enquiry. Although these may militate against increased activity in this field, it is to be hoped that researchers will seek to overcome such obstacles by being creative in the design and implementation of their research strategies. If this challenge is accepted, the study of small hospitality businesses offers the opportunity of engaging in an area of research which relates to the vast majority of enterprises in this industry.

References

Acs, Z.J. and Audretsch, D.B. (eds) (1990) *The Economics of Small Firms: a European Challenge*. Kluwer, Dordrecht.

Bannock, G. and Daly, M. (1994) *Small Business Statistics*, Paul Chapman/Small Business Research Trust, London.

Boer, A. (1998) Small business failure. In Thomas, R. (ed.) *The Management of Small Tourism and Hospitality Firms*. Cassell, London, pp. 39–57.

Boer, A., Thomas, R. and Webster, M. (1997) *Small Business Management: A Resource Based Approach*. Cassell, London.

Bransgrove, C.E. and King, B.E.M. (1996) Strategic marketing practice amongst small tourism and hospitality businesses. *IAHMS Spring Symposium: Issues Relating to Small Businesses in the Hospitality and Tourism Industries*, Leeds.

Burns, P. (1996) Introduction: the significance of small firms. In Burns, P. and Dewhurst, J. (eds) *Small Business and Entrepreneurship*, 2nd edition. Macmillan, Basingstoke.

Burrows, R. and Curran, J. (1989) Sociological research on service sector small businesses: some conceptual considerations. *Work, Employment and Society*, **3** (4): 527–539.

Chell, E., Haworth, J.M. and Brearley, S.A. (1991) *The Entrepreneurial Personality: Concepts, Cases and Categories*. Routledge, London.

Cooper, C., Fletcher, J., Gilbert, D. and Wanhill, S. (1993) *Tourism: Principles and Practice*. Pitman, London.

Curran, J. and Burrows, R. (1989) Shifting the focus: problems and approaches to studying the small enterprise in the services sector. *Twelfth National Small Firms Policy and Research Conference*, London.

Curran, J., Kitching, J., Abbot, B. and Mills, V. (1993) *Employment and Employment Relations in the Small Service Sector Enterprise—A Report*. ESRC Centre for Research on Small Service Sector Enterprises, Kingston University, Surrey.

Danvers, H. and Long, J. (1996) All in the mind? The attitudes of small tourism businesses to sustainability. *IAHMS Spring Symposium: Issues Relating to Small Businesses in the Hospitality and Tourism Industries*, Leeds.

Department of National Heritage (DNH) (1996) *Tourism: Competing with the Best 3—People Working in Tourism and Hospitality*. DNH, London.

DTI (1997) *Statistical Bulletin: Small and Medium-Sized Enterprise (SME) Statistics for the United Kingdom, 1996*. DTI, Sheffield.

Dewhurst, J. and Burns, P. (1993) *Small Business Management*, 3rd edition. Macmillan, Basingstoke.

Dewhurst, P. and Horobin, H. (1998) Small business owners. In Thomas, R. (ed.) *The Management of Small Tourism and Hospitality Firms*. Cassell, London, pp. 19–38.

Edgar, D.A. and Nisbet, L. (1996) Strategy in small business—a case of sheer chaos! *IAHMS Spring Symposium: Issues Relating to Small Businesses in the Hospitality and Tourism Industries*, Leeds.

Edgar, D.A. and Watson, S. (1996) Strategic success—the human touch. *IAHMS Spring Symposium: Issues Relating to Small Businesses in the Hospitality and Tourism Industries*, Leeds.

Ghiselli, R. (1996) Cash handling procedures and controlling employee theft in food service. *IAHMS Spring Symposium: Issues Relating to Small Businesses in the Hospitality and Tourism Industries*, Leeds.

Goss, D. (1991) *Small Business and Society*. Routledge, London.

Hales, C., Tamangani, Z., Walker, A. and Murphy, N. (1996) Factors influencing adoption of NVQ's in small hospitality businesses. *IAHMS Spring Symposium: Issues Relating to Small Businesses in the Hospitality and Tourism Industries*, Leeds.

Hospitality Training Foundation (HTF) (1996) *Research Report 1996: Catering and Hospitality Industry—Key Facts and Figures*. HTF, London.

Hughes, H. (1993) The structural theory of business demand: a comment. *International Journal of Hospitality Management*, **12** (4): 309–311.

Hughes, J.C. (1997) Sociological paradigms and the use of ethnography in hospitality research. *Journal of Hospitality and Tourism Research*, **21** (1): 14–27.

Ingram, H. (1997) Clusters and gaps in hospitality and tourism academic research. In Teare, R. and Bowen, J.T. (eds) *New Directions in Hospitality and Tourism*. Cassell, London, pp. 91–95.

International Association of Hotel Management Schools (IAHMS) (1996) *Issues Relating to Small Businesses in the Hospitality and Tourism Industries*, Proceedings of the Spring Symposium, Centre for the Study of Small Tourism and Hospitality Firms, Leeds Metropolitan University.

Key Note (1993) *Fast Food and Home Delivery Outlets*. Key Note Publications, Hampton.

Lincoln, G. and Kusyj, B. (1996) Direct marketing for the small hospitality businesses. *IAHMS Spring Symposium: Issues Relating to Small Businesses in the Hospitality and Tourism Industries*, Leeds.

Litteljohn, D. (1993) Western Europe. In Jones, P. and Pizam, A. (eds) *The International Hospitality Industry*. Pitman, London, pp. 3–24.

Lynch, P. (1996) Microenterprises and micro-firms in the hospitality industry: the case of bed and breakfast enterprises. *IAHMS Spring Symposium: Issues Relating to Small Businesses in the Hospitality and Tourism Industries*, Leeds.

Mogendorff, D. (1996) The European hospitality industry. In Thomas, R. (ed.) *The Hospitality Industry, Tourism and Europe: Perspectives on Policies*. Cassell, London.

Morrison, A. (1996a) Guest houses and small hotels. In Jones, P. (ed.) *Introduction to Hospitality Operations*. Cassell, London, pp. 73–85.

Morrison, A. (1996b) Marketing strategic alliances: the small hotel firm. *IAHMS Spring Symposium: Issues Relating to Small Businesses in the Hospitality and Tourism Industries*, Leeds.

Morrison, A. (1998) Small firm statistics: a hotel sector focus. *Service Industries Journal*, **18** (1): 132–142.

MSI (1991) *Hotels: UK*. Marketing Strategies for Industry (UK) Ltd, London.

O'Neill, M.A., Orr, N. and Black, M.A. (1996) Capacity problem solving and the Northern Ireland hotel sector. *IAHMS Spring Symposium: Issues Relating to Small Businesses in the Hospitality and Tourism Industries*, Leeds.

Ozer, B. (1996) Investment analysis model for small hospitality operations. *IAHMS Spring Symposium: Issues Relating to Small Businesses in the Hospitality and Tourism Industries*, Leeds.

Peacock, M. (1993) A question of size. *International Journal of Contemporary Hospitality Management*, **5** (4): 29–32.

Phizacklea, A. and Ram, M. (1995) Ethnic entrepreneurship in comparative perspective. *International Journal of Entrepreneurial Behaviour and Research*, **1** (1): 48–58.

Pickering, J.F., Greenwood, J.A. and Hunt, D. (1971) *The Small Firm in the Hotel and Catering Industry (Committee of Inquiry on Small Firms: Research Report 14)*, HMSO, London.

Radiven, N. and Lucas, R. (1996) The abolition of wages councils and its impact on the pay policy of small businesses in the hotel industry. *IAHMS Spring Symposium: Issues Relating to Small Businesses in the Hospitality and Tourism Industries*, Leeds.

Reid, G. (1993) *Small Business Enterprise: An Economic Analysis*. Routledge, London.

Russell, B. (1996) Innovation in small Irish tourism businesses. *IAHMS Spring Symposium: Issues Relating to Small Businesses in the Hospitality and Tourism Industries*, Leeds.

Slattery, P. (1994) The structural theory of business demand: a reply to Hughes. *International Journal of Hospitality Management*, **13** (2): 173–176.

Stanworth, J. and Gray, C. (eds) (1991) *Bolton 20 Years On: The Small Firm in the 1990s*. Paul Chapman, London.

Storey, D.J. (1994) *Understanding the Small Business Sector*. Routledge, London.

Teare, R. and Bowen, J.T. (eds) (1997) *New Directions in Hospitality and Tourism*. Cassell, London.

Thomas, R. (1996) Enterprise policy. In Thomas, R. (ed.) *The Hospitality Industry, Tourism and Europe: Perspectives or Policies*. Cassell, London, pp 117–134.

Thomas, R. (1998a) An introduction to the study of small tourism and hospitality firms. In Thomas, R. (ed.) *The Management of Small Tourism and Hospitality Firms*. Cassell, London, pp. 1–16.

Thomas, R. (1998b) *The Management of Small Tourism and Hospitality Firms*. Cassell, London.

Thomas, R., Friel, M., Jameson, S. and Parsons, D. (1997) *The National Survey of Small Tourism and Hospitality Firms: Annual Report 1996–97*. Centre for the Study of Small Tourism and Hospitality Firms, Leeds Metropolitan University.

Vance, P., Thomas, R. and Margerison, J. (1996) The impact of subsidised consultancy schemes on the business performance of small hospitality firms: a framework for research. *IAHMS Spring Symposium: Issues Relating to Small Businesses in the Hospitality and Tourism Industries*, Leeds.

Voss, C., Armistead, C., Johnston, B. and Morris, B. (1988) *Operations Management in the Service Industries and Public Sector*. John Wiley & Sons, Chichester.

Wedgwood Markham (1994) *Hotels and Guest Houses*. Wedgwood Markham Associates Ltd, London.

Williams, A.M., Shaw, G. and Greenwood, J. (1989) From tourist to tourism entrepreneur, from consumption to production: evidence from Cornwall, England. *Environment and Planning A*, **21**: 1639–1653.

Williams, C. and Thomas, R. (1996) Paid informal work in the Leeds hospitality industry: unregulated or regulated work? In Haughton, G. and Williams, C. (eds) *Corporate City? Partnership, Participation and Partition in Urban Development in Leeds*. Avebury, Aldershot, pp 171–183.

Wynarczyk, P., Watson, R., Storey, D., Short, H. and Keasey, K. (1993) *Managerial Labour Markets in Small and Medium-sized Enterprises*. Routledge, London.

26 Financial management research

GERALD L. BARLOW

What is research?

The term *research* has frequently been misunderstood by those unfamiliar with the research process. Such misconceptions perceive research as a mechanical process conducted in a mystical environment by strange unrelated individuals. In reality the approach is anything but mystical or mechanical. The process of conducting any type of research, including practical accounting research, is simply a systematic investigation of an issue or problem, utilising the accountant's judgement. Research is generally classified into two primary categories: *pure research* and *applied research.*

Pure research is often labelled basic or theoretical research, involving the investigation of questions that appear interesting to the researcher. For example, a researcher may be interested in the relationship between stock returns and accounting earnings assuming that the market observes current-price information other than earnings (Lipe, 1990). This type of research has little present practical application and can be referred to as empirical research, i.e. research based upon experiment or observation. By contrast, applied research focuses on issues of immediate importance, for example an investigation into levels of working capital and the relationship with turnover and possible effects on profit within a specific hotel or operation.

Arguments about the nature of knowledge and how that knowledge is acquired are still subject to discussion and/or controversy. Rationalism represents the idea that certain knowledge (i.e., true knowledge) can be obtained only through the use of reason. This idea comes from the Greeks (especially Plato), especially those who have spent considerable time throughout their education intent on improving their powers of reasoning. Rationalism emphasises the power of logic and use of mathematics in arriving at the truth of differing theoretical arguments. The philosophical tradition is extremely suspicious of speculative method and sees logic and mathematics merely as a tool for the analysis of observations and observed knowledge. This tradition has become known as 'empiricism' and has flourished in Britain. Much has been argued and written about the merits and defects of empiricism. Much of the initial accountancy work may be considered of the rational nature, but to approach research work, as such, without the use or consideration of the appropriate empirical approach omits large sections of research and sociological considerations.

The Handbook of Contemporary Hospitality Management Research, Edited by Bob Brotherton.

An overview of the research process within accountancy

The research process, as outlined in Figures 26.1 and 26.2, in general is often defined as the scientific method of inquiry: a systematic study of a particular field of knowledge in order to discover scientific facts or principles. Thus the basic purpose of research is to obtain knowledge or information that specifically pertains to some issue or problem. An operational definition of research encompasses the following elements (Luck, Wales and Taylor, 1961):

1. There must be an orderly investigation and analysis of a clearly defined issue or problem.
2. An appropriate scientific approach must be used.

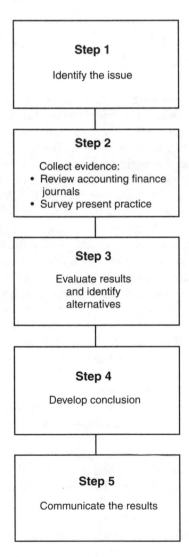

Figure 26.1   The research process

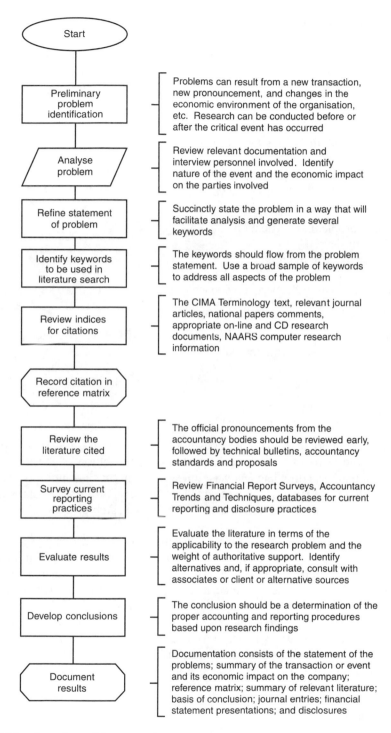

Figure 26.2   Overview of the research process

3. Adequate and representative evidence must be gathered and documented.
4. Logical reasoning must be employed in drawing conclusions.
5. The researcher must be able to support the validity or reasonableness of the conclusions.

With this basic understanding of the research process, practical *accounting research* may be defined as a systematic and logical approach to obtaining and documenting evidence underlying a conclusion relating to an accounting or financial issue or problem currently confronting the accountant/researcher.

Identify the issue or problem   Identification of the issue or problem is a vital step in the research process, though too often it is given the least attention. It can be subdivided into three stages:

1. Preliminary problem identification.
2. Problem analysis.
3. Refined statement of the problem.

Collect evidence   The collection of evidence generally involves three key components:

1. A review of related accounting literature and

   ● publications of the accountancy institutes—CA, ACCA, CIMA, etc.
   ● professional and academic journals
   ● textbooks
   ● past research publications.

2. A survey of present practice.
3. Approved practice from professional bodies.

In areas where authoritative literature does not exist on specific issues or topics, the researcher should develop a theoretical hypothesis or resolution of the issues, based upon a logical understanding and analysis. It needs noting that a solution is not always readily apparent or available. It is here that the researcher's professional skills and theoretical analysis will be of vital importance within the research process.

Evaluate results and identify alternatives   Once the collection and analysis of the evidence has been completed, the next step is to evaluate the results and identify alternatives to enable the researcher to arrive at one or more tentative conclusions to the issue under consideration. Each alternative needs to be supported by authoritative literature or a theoretical justification, with complete documentation.

It may be necessary for further analysis to be undertaken, relative to the appropriateness of the various alternatives under consideration. It is particularly at the point of evaluation that the researcher should be careful of bias entering the process, that is personal bias, or bias from outside sources such as the provider of the research information, or source of alternatives.

Develop conclusions   After the detailed analysis of the alternatives, including all possible consequences, the researcher develops a conclusion. The final conclusion selected from all the alternatives needs to be fully documented and supported with the evidence gathered. Conclusions should then be presented as a potential solution of the issues.

Communicate the results   The most important point in communicating the results reached is that the wording used must be objective and unbiased. The report should contain a clear statement of the issues researched, a statement of fact, a brief and precise discussion of the issues, and a straightforward conclusion based upon the supported and identified authoritative literature or the theoretical justification. In the production of such documents, areas to avoid include excessive discussion of the issue and facts which indicate lack of precision; excessive citations of authoritative sources—cite only the main support for the conclusions reached; appearing to avoid a conclusion by referring to the need for additional facts; and the inclusion of time-consuming research which has proved wholly irrelevant to the actual issues.

Any serious weakness in any part of the research process threatens the worth of the entire research effort. Therefore, each area of the research process should be addressed with equal seriousness as to the impact it might have on the entire research project.

'Fieldwork' is a term often used in connection with research work. Fieldwork is usually taken to mean studies of social practices in the field of activities in which they take place. In the accountancy area this may be a study of a single company or a number of companies. Hence the term 'fieldwork' today is often used in connection with that of case study research.

Case study research

> Case study research is remarkably hard, even though case studies have traditionally been considered to be 'soft' research. Paradoxically, the 'softer' a research technique, the harder it is to do. (Yin, 1984)

Case studies are becoming increasingly popular in accountancy research. Over the past 10 years a succession of writers have called on researchers to study accounting, especially management accounting, in its practical setting.

Types of accounting case studies

1. *Descriptive case studies.*   These case studies describe accounting systems, techniques and procedures currently used in practice. This type of case study is good for determining the extent of the gap between accountancy theory and practice. Professional accountancy bodies often support them because they appear to offer the possibility of determining 'best' practice.
2. *Illustrative case studies.*   Here the case study attempts to illustrate new and possibly innovative practices developed by particular companies. There can be weaknesses in the interpretation of these case studies, in that there is an implied assumption in many cases that the practices of these 'innovative' companies are, in some way, superior to the practices of other companies.
3. *Experimental case studies.*   These are used where accounting researchers have developed new accounting procedures and techniques, intended to be helpful for accounting practitioners. The cases are used to indicate what should or might be done in practice.

4. *Exploratory case studies.* This type of case study is used to explore the reasons for a particular accounting practice. They can be used to create and test hypotheses, and are often seen as the first step in research issues.
5. *Expiatory case studies.* These case studies are used to explain the reasons for observed accounting practices. Theory is used to understand and explain the specific, rather than to produce generalisations.

Weaknesses and problems of case study research

There are a number of traditional prejudices against researchers who use case studies. Critics do not regard them as acceptable methods for social scientific research. They believe that case studies lack academic rigour and cannot be generalised. These writers, however, often overlook the biases and assumptions made in their own preferred research methods. In case study research, as in any research, it is vital to give due care and attention to the collection and evaluation of data being used in the process. But this is not to say that there are no weaknesses or problems with the case study approach. It is generally acknowledged that there are three areas of difficulty that can lead to weaknesses in the use of case study research.

1. The difficulty in drawing boundaries. Case study researchers must recognise the limitations of subject matter, even with the holistic approach that this method uses.
2. The ethics of the researcher, the subject and the organisation. Many accountancy case studies require access to an organisation's information which might be of a sensitive or confidential nature. In fact access might be assured only if confidentiality is

Table 26.1   The research process

Basic steps	Specific components
1. Define the issue or problems	(a) Preliminary problem identification (b) Problem analysis (c) Refined statement of the problem
2. Collect evidence, review related literature	(a) Identification of keywords to be used in the literature search (b) Review of appropriate citations
3. Survey present practice	(a) Review of publications or computer-based services (b) Consultation with other professionals
4. Evaluate results and identify alternatives	(a) Identification of alternative principles or procedures (b) Evaluation of authoritative support for the alternatives identified (c) Consultation with other professionals
5. Develop conclusion	Selection of the appropriate principle or procedure
6. Communicate result	Preparation of memo summarising the research process, results, and the conclusion and underlying support or justification

guaranteed. This naturally raises particular problems in the writing of case reports, which can result in conflicts. For example, it may be necessary to change or disguise the identity of the organisation studied. This could well limit the value of the content and research undertaken.

3. The final problem is the nature of social reality, which is being, or is going to be, researched. It is generally accepted that social systems are not natural phenomena. They cannot be understood separately from human beings and therefore a researcher cannot be regarded as a neutral independent observer. In fact the researcher must interpret the social reality, therefore case studies must represent their interpretations of the social reality. An objective case study is therefore not possible.

A summary of the whole research process is set out in Table 26.1.

Sources of accounting research

The tools specifically available for those researching issues in the accountancy field are divided into two categories: manual sources and computerised research tools.

Manual research tools

Clearly the first sources of these are the professional bodies: the Institute of Chartered Accountants (of England, Wales and Scotland—separate bodies) (CA), the Association of Chartered Certified Accountants (ACCA), the Chartered Institute of Management Accountants (CIMA) and the British Association of Hotel Accountants (BAHA). The professional journals include:

Accountancy Age
Accountant's Digest
Accountant's Magazine
Accounting and Business Research
Accounting Horizons
Accounting Review
Accounting, Auditing and Accountability
Accounting, Organisations and Society
Accountancy Ireland
British Accounting Review (IDEAL)
CA Magazine (Canadian Chartered Accountants)
Cash Management News
Certified Accountant (ACCA)
Certified Accountant Students' Newsletter (ACCA)
Company Accountant
Company Reporting
EDI Update International
Executive Accountant
Financial Accountability and Management
Financial Accountant

Financial Analysts' Journal
Internal Journal of Accounting
International Accounting Standards Committee Insight
International Financial Statistics (statistical data)
Issues in Accounting Education
Journal of Accountancy
Journal of Accounting Research
Management Accounting (CIMA)
Management Accounting Research
Managerial Auditing
Stock Exchange Economic and Market Information Service
The Accountant

This names but some of the journals generally available in the UK in this area. The following are sources of accounting, financial and management reference text: the Chartered Institute of Accountants publishing division (Accountancy Books) publishes books with reference to all statutory standards of accountancy; ACCA publishes an annual accountancy handbook with all standards included; Ernst Young publishes the UK's leading reference text, UK GAAP (Generally Accepted Accounting Principles); and the Chartered Institute of Management Accountants (CIMA) publishes Management Accounting Official Terminology.

Computer-based research tools

- *ABI/Inform (CD-ROM)* is a 10-year compilation of articles taken from over 1000 business and management journals. Many are American and may be of little use to European researchers, but the research is current. The subject thesaurus is especially useful.
- *Anbar Management Intelligence* scans over 400 management and business journals to select the most important articles. The journals reflect the holding policy of some of the major international business schools.
- *Financial Journals Index.* Fully covers over 100 titles specific to insurance, pensions, banking and financial services.
- *PAIS International* is a monthly listing of books, articles, reports and government publications, emphasising contemporary economic and political issues, especially the making of public policy.
- *Social Sciences Citation Index* is a large multi-disciplinary database loaded at the University of Bath and available from Bath Information and Data Services (BIDS) via JANET (the Joint Academic Network) or the Internet.
- *Accounting Trends & Techniques.* The American Institute of Certified Public Accountants (AICPA) publishes two annual surveys of accounting practices: *Accounting Trends & Techniques* and *Local Governmental Accounting Trends & Techniques.*
- *Financial Report Surveys.* The AICPA produces *Financial Report Surveys*, which is a continuing series of studies designed to show in detail how specific accounting and reporting questions are actually being handled in the financial reports of companies in a wide range of industries.

- *Professional libraries.* All the professional bodies have a full professional library available for research, as do all the major accounting firms.

Computerised research tools

National Automated Accounting Research System   NAARS is a computerised information retrieval system developed by the AICPA and Mead Data Central, Inc. (see Figure 26.3). This research system has revolutionised the research function that supports the accounting profession and is the primary research system currently being utilised by accountants. Presently, the NAARS library consists of the following active files:

- *Annual Report Files.* This includes reports on corporations whose stock is traded on the New York and American Stock Exchange. Information included consists of financial statements; *Fortune* ranking; auditors' reports; Balance sheet data, including net income, current assets and equity; interim data; foreign currency exchange gains and losses.
- *Literature File.* All current and superseded authoritative and semi-authoritative accounting literature is readily available. This includes International Accounting Standards, Statements and interpretation of US accounting regulations and accounting releases.

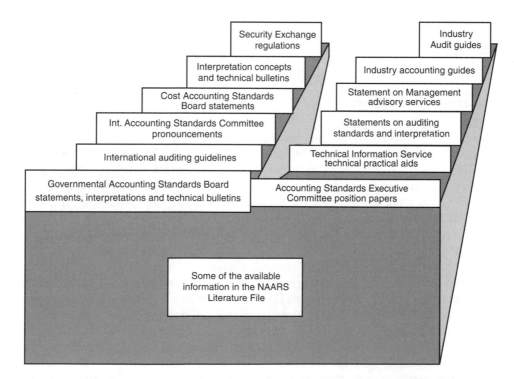

Figure 26.3   Information available in the NAARS literature file
Source: *Journal of Accountancy* – AICPSA.

- *Proxy File.* This file contains selected information from proxy statements of *Fortune*-ranked companies. This information includes prerequisites, non-audit accounting fees, legal procedures and related-party transactions, and corporate board structure.

Information access company databases

There are a number of on-line and CD-based databases such as Fame and Datastream. The major databases contain information regarding current accounts, interim earnings, dividends, ratio analysis, contract awards, management information and contracts, and so on. The following is a selection:

- *Magazine indexes.* A general research tool that covers current affairs, business education, consumer information, home and leisure activities, performing arts, science and travel.
- *Trade and Industry Index.* An invaluable source of information on business and technological developments for all major industries. The Index provides information on new products, company mergers, personnel, management, technological innovations, the regulatory environment, industry trends, forecasts and statistics.
- *National Newspaper Index.* A leading source for news from leading nationally distributed newspapers. Business information includes contracts, mergers, products, companies, current affairs, people, social conditions, scientific developments and consumer issues.
- *Industry data sources.* These databases give access to sources of marketing, financial and statistical data.

Practices and problems

Over the past 15 to 20 years there has been a considerable increase in the amount of research conducted into finance and management accounting. This research has tended to develop along two separate paths: the development of behavioural and organisational views of the actions and functions of accounting systems in general (Scapens, 1980) and the creation of quantitative decision-making or decision support activities and techniques. These two approaches have seen the behavioural approach attempt to describe the existing processes and practices, whilst the quantitative techniques have looked at methods aimed at improving the accounting practices. Both have been criticised by the accountancy professions, the quantitative techniques because of the nature of the assumptions often needed and/or the nature of the data requirements, whilst the behavioural approach often lacks realism and prescriptive contents. Whatever shortcomings these approaches have, they are still light-years ahead of much of the work done related to the hospitality industry, where what little research has been carried out has tended to be related to financial investment and return, exploration of management accounting systems and controls (Collier and Gregory, 1995c), existing costing systems and the like. Of the associated hospitality journals over the past five years, Table 26.2 outlines the number and areas of financial and management accounting contribution.

Table 26.2 Number of accountancy articles in recent hospitality journals

Subject areas

Source	Investment/ valuation					Conventional management accounting					Pricing performance and profit					Control, planning					Education and training, others				
	97	96	95	94	93	97	96	95	94	93	97	96	95	94	93	97	96	95	94	93	97	96	95	94	93
Cornell Hotel and Restaurant Administration Quarterly	2	1	2	1	1			1		1	1	3		1	1	1	1		1	1	1	1	2		2
International Journal of Contemporary Hospitality Management		1		2		1	1					1		1	1				1		1				
International Journal of Hospitality Management	1	1	2	1		1	1	2	1	1	1		1		1	1							1		1
International Journal of Service Industries					2		1			1		1	1	1	3							1			
CHME research conferences	1		1								2	2	1	1		2					1	5	1		2

Whether the relative lack of recent research is because the area is felt to have been over-researched already, with areas such as uniform accounting and standard costing techniques having been widely researched in the 1960s and early 1970s, it is difficult to imagine, because there are many potential areas of basic research open, such as the potential for techniques like Activity Based Costing in the industry, performance measures and methods of assessing their effects, possible value of issues like JIT, MRP 1, and so on.

Accounting is a mixture of many areas, topics and issues, but these are naturally divided into two main areas:

- Financial accounting
- Management accounting.

Financial accounting/management

This is one of the areas more often covered in research issues, which may be because one can hardly doubt that the hospitality industry, and in particular the hotel sector, is highly fixed-asset intensive (Parkinson, 1995), with issues like new build, acquisitions, refurbishment, extensions and rebuilds. The main issues involved in this area are often seen as being common to most capital investment situations, utilising a range of appraisal techniques, where the investment is based around an initial negative cashflow, with slowly and then increasing amounts of positive cashflows (Collier and Gregory, 1995a). Most of the standard accounting texts suggest the best approach for such issues is the use of discounted cash flow, this being common to most industries, not simply the hospitality industry.

One approach that has been employed within the industry to help resolve the problems has been the increasing use and development of the management contract. Eyster (1988a) has defined this as '... a formal arrangement under which the owner of a hotel employs the services of an operator to act as his agent to provide professional management of the hotel, in return for a fee ...'. Since the problems arising from the oil crisis of the 1970s and the slump of the 1980s and early 1990s the growth of such contracts has increased. Not just the traditional owner, but also a range of new investors uninterested in the operation have created a new market for management contract situations. The specific terms of such management contracts will typically cover the concerns of both the owners and operators, covering such areas as length of contract, performance targets, dispute arrangements, the rights of both sides, and termination arrangements (Field, 1995). The aims of these contracts are to avoid later problems and to unite the aims of both sides. Research into such contracts (Baum, 1993; Eyster, 1988a, 1988b) indicates that the early contracts favoured management issues and their side over the investors but as the process matures then the investors acquire more power, maybe because of the greater competition of the contracts, or the impact of the recession encouraging the investor/owner to have more understanding and interest in the performance of such contracts. Recent legal action in the US regarding management contract instruments and agreements may be seen as having caused the development of management contracts incorporating a lower base fee, more performance-based incentives, shorter terms and more financial involvement of the operator (Eyster, 1988b; Field, 1995).

In terms of the future of hospitality management contracts, it is expected that not only will they continue but they will increase. The range will widen following the US model of contracts for services, such as restaurant contracts within hotels, and the bargaining power of the owners and investors will similarly continue to change and grow (Eyster, 1988b, 1997a, 1997b). It is suggested that this could be accompanied by an increase in the number of mergers, acquisitions and consolidations among existing management companies, which in turn it is suggested (Eyster, 1997a, 1997b) will lead to an increase in the importance of brand affiliation and greater sharing of responsibilities between the parties, where payment will be based upon the balance of performance goals (Trice, 1992), that is, payment paid to both or all parties.

Performance measurement

An important area of development for the hospitality industry occurred as early as 1926, with the development of uniform accounting systems for key sectors of the industry, now mainly hotels, restaurants and clubs in the United States. In 1969 the first UK system for the hotel and catering sectors was created through the government's National Economic Development Office (Hotel and Catering EDC 1969 and 1971). The development and adoption within the UK and European hotel groups owes much to the growth of US chains of hotels within the UK and Europe (Chin, Barney and O'Sullivan, 1995). This also resulted in the widespread adoption of US terminology within the area of management contract agreements (Field, 1995).

Management accounting

A sample of 28 Management accounting textbooks published over the past decade (compiled from hospitality and general accounting texts) has been used to help identify the range and depth of management accounting. The areas included within these textbooks were perceived as reflecting the key areas currently conveyed to industry's management accountants, current and future. A comparison of the current and previous editions of a number of these books suggests that there have been no significant changes in these areas over the past decade or more.

A central argument used against specifically accounting research (Otley, 1988) '... is that it has no area of interest that is uniquely its own, and that it is covered by academic disciplines such as management economics, organisational theory, communication theory and social psychology (to name but four).'

Caws (1972) asks whether accounting is a science in search of a methodology or a methodology in search of a science, and favours the latter point of view. Despite this there was a remarkable consensus of commonality in the material covered by all the textbooks, as can be seen in the summary in Table 26.3.

Planning The phrase 'different costs for different purposes' became a cornerstone of management accounting literature, especially in the area of decision making, more specifically short-term decision making. The term is due to a US economist, J.M. Clark, who in 1923 investigated cost accounting and argued that there can be no unique concept of cost.

Table 26.3 The major topics in the field of management accounting

1. Planning
   - Relevant cost for decision making
   - Cost–volume–profit analysis
   - Product mix decisions
   - Capital investment decisions
   - Other relevant decisions, e.g. working capital

2. Cost classifications
   - Fixed and variable costs
   - Cost estimation techniques
   - Forecasting techniques and costs
   - Learning curve

3. Control
   - Budgeting
   - Variance analysis
   - Investigation of variance and techniques for standard costing

4. Costing
   - Job costing, process costing
   - Variable and absorption costing
   - Cost allocation
   - ABC costing

5. Divisionalisation of organisations
   - Transfer pricing
   - Performance evaluation

Most management accounting textbooks identify the relevant costs for each decision within the neo-classical economic framework, which is based on the assumption that decision-makers are profit maximisers. For this reason, the profit maximisation objectives are pursued through marginal economic analysis, which gives rise to the concept of incremental cash flows.

Cost–volume–profit (CVP) analysis techniques basically underpin most of the decisions involving profit planning. Harris (1992) indicates how seldom CVP is used, or how it is not used to its full potential in the practical issues of hotel and restaurant situations. A small survey of junior front-office management at 12 London four- and five-star hotels confirmed this: 10 of them did not know what the fixed cost of one night's accommodation was (author's survey, September 1997). Horngren (1977) reflects that the use of CVP is seen by many companies as an extremely useful tool in decision making. The straightforward relationships within CVP analysis create an excellent base for understanding the more complex relationships that exist within costs and cost drivers.

Control   This area has provided much of the recent research in the area of budgetary control and planning, with work from Brander Brown (1995), Kosturakis and Eyster (1979), Moutinho (1987), Schmidgall and Ninemeirer (1986, 1987), and Schmidgall, Borchgrevink and Zahl-Begnum (1996). This area offers much scope for research, from basic methodology and operational issues to the behavioural and psychological aspects of budgeting and its behavioural control usage (Argyris, 1953; Brander Brown, 1994, 1995). The development of newer techniques like flexible budgeting, zero-based budgeting and variance analysis (Kotas, 1977; Harris, 1992) offers other areas for today's researcher to investigate.

Pricing profit and sales mix   The most recent development in this area has been the technique of yield management, a technique developed for and by, and now widely used within, the airline industry. In the hospitality industry it involves more effective management of inventory, namely that of rooms. Orkin (1988) outlined the basics of yield management, namely that of effectively managing price and demand, and went on to propose that the yield management percentage was a measurement, or ratio, which hotels need to use to be effective. (It was to replace the occupancy percentage and average room rate as a more effective tool, being in fact a combination of the two.) Relihan (1989) argues that 'Yield management is not a systematic approach to abusing customers. The practice only attempts to bring hotel room prices into alignment with actual market forces.' Other writers, including Dunn and Brooks (1990), have been and are warning that yield management is a short-term technique, and that long-term pricing is still based on more traditional processes of thorough analysis that includes profit margins. They propose the use, or at least consideration, of techniques like activity-based costing (ABC costing). Pricing is naturally a crucial area of finance and accounting, with its basic desire to create the optimum levels of profit throughout an organisation, more so in market-based industries. Rogers (1976) studied the method of price creation in hotels, criticised the extensive use of cost-based pricing procedures and proposed the use of a contribution-based approach. Pricing relationships and dependencies have been researched by such people as Orkin (1978), Kreul (1982), Hayes and Huffman (1985), Miller (1988), Jones and Lockwood (1989) and Bayou and Bennett (1992), whilst the psychological aspects of pricing have been researched by Rogers (1977) and Pavesic (1989).

This review of these areas and some of the writers within them shows what has been covered, and perhaps more so the areas that have not been covered or have had little coverage, areas such as cost–benefit analysis to name but one.

Future review issues

Perhaps one issue that needs considering for research is why so many of the current undergraduate students are choosing to avoid research in this area for their final year dissertation. A quick, if unscientific, survey of four UK academic hospitality programmes revealed that fewer than 4% of over 150 students chose this area for their final year dissertations during the 1996–97 academic year. Basic areas that could be considered for research have been discussed earlier, but there are other areas directly related to issues like zero-based budgeting, the possible value and use of ABC costing, cost–benefit analysis, and the development of perhaps a more suited ratio analysis system. The current ratio analysis format has been developed from other industries and is based upon those designed for manufacturing and not service industries. There are some issues specific to the hospitality industry such as occupancy and yield, but there has been little research into the whole area.

More interesting, perhaps, would be linkages with other disciplines such as operations, human resource management, quality management, and so on. For example, there has been extensive research into empowerment within the industry, but what about the costs and cost–benefit analysis? A similar question arises with reference to the Investors in People initiative, or the true cost of quality. There seems to be great scope for research in joint areas of this nature for today's and future researchers to investigate, which would be of benefit to both the academic and industrial worlds alike.

Other areas which have seen little research are related to issues such as stock control and costing, or purchasing systems and the benefits available from more effective systems, all having direct linkages with financial and accounting areas.

References

Argyris, C. (1953) Human problems with budgets. *Harvard Business Review*, January–February, 105–120.

Baum, C. (1993) Management companies face tough times: as owners demand more control, management companies become more flexible on fees, incentives. *Hotel*, **23**, 4, 50–52.

Bayou, M.E. and Bennett, L.B. (1992) Profitability analysis: for table-service restaurants. *Cornell Hotel and Restaurant Administration Quarterly*, **33**, 2, 49–55.

Brander Brown, J. (1994) Effective management control in the UK hotel sector. *International Journal of Contemporary Hospitality Management*, **6**, 5, i–iii.

Brander Brown, J. (1995) Management control in the hospitality industry: behavioural implications, in Harris, P.J. (ed.) *Accounting and Finance for the International Hospitality Industry*. Butterworth-Heinemann, Oxford.

Caws, P. (1972) Accounting research—science or methodology, in Sterling, R. (ed.) *Research Methodology in Accounting*. Scholars Book Co.

Chin, J., Barney, W. and O'Sullivan, H. (1995) Best accounting practice in hotels: a guide to other industries. *Management Accounting*, December, 57–58.

Collier, P. and Gregory, A. (1995a) Investment appraisal in service industries: a field study analysis of the UK hotel sector. *Management Accounting Research*, **6**, 33–57.

Collier, P. and Gregory, A. (1995b) The practice of management accounting in hotel groups, in Harris, P.J. (ed.) *Accounting and Finance for the International Hospitality Industry*. Butterworth-Heinemann, Oxford, pp 137–159.

Collier, P. and Gregory, A. (1995c) *Management Accounting in Hotel Groups*. CIMA: London.

Dunn, K.D. and Brooks, D.E. (1990) Profit analysis: beyond yield management. *Cornell Hotel and Restaurant Administration Quarterly*, **31**, 3, 80–90.

Eyster, J.J. (1988a) Sharing risks and decision making: recent trends in the negotiation of management contracts. *Cornell Hotel and Restaurant Administration Quarterly*, **29**, 1, 43–55.

Eyster, J.J. (1988b) Recent trends in the negotiation of hotel management contracts: terms and termination. *Cornell Hotel and Restaurant Administration Quarterly*, **29**, 2, 81–90.

Eyster, J.J. (1997a) Hotel contracts in the US: the revolution continues. *Cornell Hotel and Restaurant Administration Quarterly*, **34**, 2, 14–20.

Eyster, J.J. (1997b) Hotel contracts in the US: twelve areas of concern. *Cornell Hotel and Restaurant Administration Quarterly*, **34**, 2, 21–33.

Field, H.M. (1995) Financial management implications of hotel management contract agreements; a UK perspective, in Harris P.J. (ed.) *Accounting and Finance for the International Hospitality Industry*. Butterworth-Heinemann, Oxford, pp 137–159.

Harris, P.J. (1992) *Profit Planning*. Butterworth-Heinemann, Oxford.

Hayes, D.K. and Huffman, L. (1985) Menu analysis; a better way. *Cornell Hotel and Restaurant Administration Quarterly*, **25**, 4, 65–70.

Horngren, C.T. (1997) *Cost Accounting: A Management Emphasis*, 4th edn. Prentice-Hall: London.

Horngren, C.T., Foster, G. and Datar, S. (1994) *Cost Accounting: A Managerial Emphasis*, 8th edn. Prentice-Hall, Englewood Cliffs, NJ.

Jones, P. and Lockwood, A. (1989) *The Management of Hotel Operations*. Cassell, London.

Kosturakis, J.G. and Eyster, J.J. (1979) Operational budgeting in small hotel companies. *Cornell Hotel and Restaurant Administration Quarterly*, **19**, 4, 80–84.

Kotas, R. (1977) *Management Accounting for Hotels and Restaurants*. Surrey University Press, London.

Kreul, L.M. (1982) Magic numbers; psychological aspects of menu pricing. *Cornell Hotel and Restaurant Administration Quarterly*, **23**, 2, 70–75.

Lipe, R. (1990) The relation between stock returns and accounting earnings given alternative information. *Accounting Review*, **65**, 1, 49–71.

Luck, D.J., Wales, H.C. and Taylor, D.A. (1961) *Marketing Research*. Prentice-Hall: Englewood Cliffs, NJ.

Miller, S.G. (1988) Fine-tuning your menu with frequent distributions. *Cornell Hotel and Restaurant Administration Quarterly*, **29**, 3, 86–92.

Moutinho, L. (1987) The role of budgeting in planning, implementing, and monitoring hotel marketing strategies. *International Journal of Hospitality Management*, **6**, 1, 15–22.

Orkin, E.B. (1978) An integrated menu pricing system. *Cornell Hotel and Restaurant Administration Quarterly* **19**, 2, 8–13.

Orkin, E.B. (1988) Boosting your bottom line with yield management. *Cornell Hotel and Restaurant Administration Quarterly*, **28**, 4, 52–56.

Otley, D.F. (1980) 'The Contingency Theory of Management Accounting: Achievement and Prognosis'. *Accounting, Organisations and Society*, pp 413–428.

Parkinson, G.S. (1995) Risk assessment in capital investment, in Harris, P.J. (ed.) *Accounting and Finance for the International Hospitality Industry*. Butterworth-Heinemann: Oxford.

Pavesic, D.V. (1989) Psychological aspects of menu pricing. *International Journal of Hospitality Management*, **8**, 1, 43–49.

Relihan, W.J. (1989) The yield management approach to hotel-room pricing. *Cornell Hotel and Restaurant Administration Quarterly*, **30**, 1, 40–45.

Rogers, A.N. (1976) Price formation in hotels. *Hotel, Catering and Institutional Management Journal*, **4**, spring, 227–237.

Rogers, A.N. (1977) Psychological aspects of pricing. *Hotel, Catering and Institutional Management Journal*, January, 15–16.

Scapens, R. (1980) Overview of current trends and directions for the future, in Arnold, J., Carsberg, B. and Scapens, R. (eds) *Topics in Management Accounting*. Philip Allen: London.

Schmidgall, R.S. and Ninemeirer, J.D. (1986) Food-service budgeting: how the chains do it. *Cornell Hotel and Restaurant Administration Quarterly*, **26**, 4, 51–57.

Schmidgall, R.S. and Ninemeirer, J.D. (1987) Budgeting in hotel chains: co-ordination and control. *Cornell Hotel and Restaurant Administration Quarterly*, **28**, 1, 79–84.

Schmidgall, R.S., Borchgrevink, C.P. and Zahl-Begnum, O.D. (1996) Operations budgeting practices of lodging firms in the United States and Scandinavia. *Cornell Hotel and Restaurant Administration Quarterly*, **15**, 2, 189–203.

Trice, D.R. (1992) A new partnership for the hotel industry. *Cornell Hotel and Restaurant Administration Quarterly*, **33**, 3, 15–19.

Yin, R.K. (1984) *Case Study Research Design and Methods*. Sage Publications: Beverly Hills, CA.

27 Hospitality management research: towards the future?

BOB BROTHERTON

Introduction

Writing a chapter of this nature is always fraught with difficulties, and has a high potential to make the author a hostage of fortune! It is also an exercise likely to be strongly influenced by personal preferences, priorities, and 'hobby horses'. In this sense there is probably little doubt that the views expressed here have been influenced by such considerations. On the other hand, any such personal subjectivity is hopefully balanced in this chapter through it being informed by the views of the authors who have contributed to this volume.

The aim of this chapter is to highlight a number of issues and questions which the hospitality management research community need to seriously consider if hospitality management research is to progress and achieve the recognition that many believe it deserves but has not yet achieved. The chapter does not seek to offer a series of prescriptions concerning what the current author believes should happen in the future, but focuses on the issues, questions and options which, in some cases, require further debate to seek a satisfactory resolution, and in others more immediate action. This is achieved through a synopsis of many of these issues raised by colleagues who have contributed the chapters to this text and is also informed by additional comment from the wider literature where appropriate.

Although it is perhaps somewhat artificial to subdivide the issues discussed in this chapter, such a format is adopted to help the reader focus upon the salient points raised. The issues and aspects are categorised under three main headings: Philosophical, Methodological/Technical, and Hospitality Specialisms.

Philosophical issues

Perhaps one of the key philosophical questions faced by hospitality management researchers is 'What is hospitality?'. As Roy Wood (Chapter 1), Stephen Taylor and David Edgar (Chapter 2) and Brotherton (1998) elsewhere point out, the term, let alone the concept, of hospitality is defined and used by many hospitality management researchers in a quite indistinct and unsatisfactory manner. Precisely what different researchers mean when they use the term hospitality is rarely defined or explained in

The Handbook of Contemporary Hospitality Management Research, Edited by Bob Brotherton.
© 1999 John Wiley & Sons Ltd.

either a clear or an acceptable manner. Indeed, its common usage by this research community is a relatively recent phenomenon, and one which most seem to have drifted into from the prior focus of hotel and catering in the UK or of lodging and foodservice in the USA. It is also rarely clear where the boundaries of hospitality are drawn in relation to 'near neighbours' such as tourism and leisure (Brotherton, 1989), or the structural and behavioural characteristics of other service industries such as retailing, financial services, and so on, and whether hospitality should be conceived as a product, a process, an experience, or all three! Thus, hospitality management researchers face a fundamental problem: how can the epistemological and ontological aspects of the field be developed and strengthened if the field has not been adequately defined and delimited in the first place? (Taylor and Edgar, 1996). In short, how can we have a theory of hospitality management knowledge if we are unclear over what the term hospitality constitutes?

As we approach the millennium perhaps what is even more surprising about this fundamental shortcoming is that it is hardly a new revelation. Other commentators as far back as the early 1980s, such as Nailon (1982) and Slattery (1983), have raised similar questions. Similarly, Cassee (1983: xvi) ventured: 'What we need is a sound theory of hospitality based on research'; with others such as Middleton (1983: 51) pointing out that: 'There is a definitional problem from the term "hospitality industry" [and] it may be surprising that, in the 1980s, one must contemplate educational programmes for the hospitality industry without agreement on what the industry comprises.' Towards the end of the 1980s a number of authors (Lewis, 1988; Khan and Olsen, 1988; Edgar and Umbreit, 1988; Litteljohn, 1990) also called for the hospitality management research community to raise the profile and importance of hospitality management research.

More recently Evans (1992: 58) has observed that: 'Hospitality and tourism research may be reaching a critical cross-roads in the 1990s', and Jones (1996: 6, 7) has suggested that 'there is certainly no commonly shared paradigm of what we mean by "hospitality" .... Reference to the research literature would indicate that there has been little or no discussion of what we mean by hospitality.... I would propose that the idea of hospitality research exists more in form than in substance.' Similarly, Taylor and Edgar (1996: 218, 215), in reflecting on the current state of development of hospitality management research, have pointed out: 'An essential first step ... is to decide what the scope of hospitality research should be [and] If academic research in hospitality is to develop *satisfactorily* it is our view that it must do so within a coherent framework' [emphasis in original].

In the light of the available evidence it would therefore seem clear that the hospitality management research community has been content to promulgate the supposed, but rarely successfully articulated, 'mystical' qualities of hospitality in very much a 'head-in-the-sand' manner to both the wider academic and hospitality practitioner communities it interfaces with. If hospitality is indeed distinct and has unique properties, a definition to reflect these must be urgently developed in order that its essence be identified and the field delimited, or the mythical creature be laid to rest.

As Roy Wood (Chapter 1) succinctly points out, the view that hospitality is imbued with unique properties implies a need for particular epistemological and methodological configurations to be developed and adopted in order that its characteristics and activities may be effectively researched. This view of 'uniqueness' he categorically rejects and contends that its acceptance by many hospitality management researchers has not only led to a dangerous insularity within this research community but also severely limited both the epistemological and methodological development of hospitality management research. Furthermore, Wood claims that a major consequence of hospitality management researchers accepting the 'uniqueness' issue on the one hand, whilst simultaneously seeking to emulate the dominant epistemology and methods of research traditions in the natural sciences on the other, is both epistemologically and ontologically illogical. Positivistic, quantitatively oriented studies invariably strip the phenomenon from its context in the interests of enhancing external validity and generalisability, and are seen as important components within a research strategy ultimately designed to seek legitimacy and credibility for the 'discipline' of hospitality. Thus, contemporary hospitality management research *per se* does not have a complete epistemology because it is dominated by a primary concern with methodological priorities rather than conceptual development, a feature which inhibits the creation of a coherent body of theory to guide empirical research.

This issue Stephen Taylor and David Edgar refer to in Chapter 2 as 'Conceptual Malnutrition', where they argue that philosophical questions are not resolved by additional empirical enquiry but by sound reasoning based on fundamental beliefs and logic. Hence, they propose that hospitality management research needs to develop appropriate 'Enquiry Paradigms' which not only address the implementation aspects of research, i.e. the methodological issues, but also focus more strongly on the methodological drivers of epistemology and ontology constituting the strategic aspects of research design. Without such changes in emphasis these authors argue, in common with Jones (1996), that hospitality management research will continue to be plagued by a significant vagueness concerning its objectives and scope and that, drawing on Shaw and Nightingale (1995), it will never progress beyond being a 'scholarship of application' which simply adopts epistemological stances, conceptual frameworks, and methodological techniques previously developed in other disciplines or fields of enquiry. Furthermore, Taylor and Edgar contend that this feature has forced much hospitality management research to be not only shaped by generic philosophical and methodological concerns but also driven by a perceived need to undertake research having immediate relevance, often of a normative/prescriptive nature, to the hospitality industry in order to justify its 'value'!

Methodological and technical issues

Given the inherent difficulties involved in resolving the type of philosophical issues and questions discussed in the previous section, it is not surprising that many hospitality management researchers have tended to concentrate their attention on methodological, or perhaps more accurately method, concerns. However, even here there is evidence of a less than rigorous attention to detail on the part of many such researchers (Jones, 1996). Juxtaposed with the scarcity of philosophical discourse referred to above, such methodological weaknesses pose a serious threat to the legitimacy and credibility of hospitality management research at both individual and collective levels.

Indeed there are numerous examples of the paucity of methodological thought given to research projects by hospitality management researchers in this text. It has already been noted earlier in this chapter that the literature indicates that the dominant approach taken to hospitality management research, especially in the USA, is one of a quantitative nature, based on a positivistic philosophy. On the other hand, despite this apparent wide-spread adoption of a positivistic orientation within the hospitality management research community, Peter Jones (Chapter 6) makes the observation that, paradoxically, utilisation of the 'ultimate' positivist methodology, experimental research, is conspicuously absent in the literature. Although it is found in some areas of hospitality research, i.e. food science, nutrition, cooking methods, etc., it is not a commonly adopted methodology elsewhere in hospitality management research. Perhaps this is because many researchers do not have academic traditions rooted in the natural/physical sciences, where it is the method *qua* method, but this can only be part of the explanation. Other researchers who deal with occupationally or industrially specific issues in psychology, marketing, operational and systems research, and so on, routinely adopt experimental methodologies as a matter of course. How many such studies in hospitality management research mirror this situation? Very few is the answer. The follow-up question is why?

Is it because the hospitality industry and/or hospitality management is so unique compared to other occupational/industrial contexts? Clearly not. Possibly then it is due to an inability on the part of hospitality management researchers to contemplate the use of alternative methodologies to the ubiquitous survey! Alternatively it may have arisen from a perception that experimental research is more difficult to design and conduct than questionnaire surveys, and/or is an inappropriate choice for the research questions being explored. The latter would of course be justifiable, the former misinformed.

At present it appears that experimental methodologies rarely feature in the academic hospitality management researcher's methodological choice set. However, as Jones points out this is not the case in industry where the experimental method *per se* is frequently adopted as the preferred research method. Test marketing, new product concept evaluations, pilot implementations of new methods and procedures, and menu innovations are all routinely investigated by true and/or quasi-experiments in the real world. Therefore, apart from a few scattered examples of the use of experimental methods in hospitality management research, it would appear that academic researchers do not share their practitioner colleagues' enthusiasm for experimentation. Jones argues that this apparent avoidance of experimental designs by hospitality management researchers is unfortunate, as adoption of the experimental method may help to strengthen both the conceptual and technical aspects of hospitality management research in general.

It is equally evident that the methodological foundations of hospitality management research based on the utilisation of methods other than experimental research are often suspect, to say the least. For example, Rosemary Lucas (Chapter 5) stresses the importance of methodological rigour for survey design in order that error and bias are minimised to maximise the validity and reliability of the empirical data collected. She also points to one of the major 'Achilles' Heels' frequently encountered in hospitality management survey research: sampling. In common with Nigel Hemmington (Chapter 13), Lucas identifies the enormous sampling frame, selection, access and size variations to be found in much contemporary hospitality management research, the implications of which are often ignored by the researcher(s) who proceed to utilise statistical tests designed for large N studies on very small samples. In addition, as Bob Brotherton points out (Chapter 8), such sampling deficiencies are also to be found in the 'comparative' hospitality management research literature where the use of small and potentially unrepresentative samples is rife.

Similarly the methodological issue of measurement does not escape criticism in relation to contemporary hospitality management research. Francis Buttle (Chapter 12) comments that the hospitality management research literature is characterised by a virtual absence of researchers developing innovative measures related to the specific, contingent characteristics of the hospitality context(s) being researched, the predominant *modus operandi* being for hospitality management researchers to either adopt, often unquestioningly, or adapt, often inadequately, operational definitions and measures previously developed in other contexts. As he pointedly comments, current practices amongst hospitality management researchers in this respect seem to be characterised by a general lack of concern for the integrity of the empirical data collected in many research projects. In short, the fundamentally important task of validating the measurement instrument is generally less than adequately dealt with by many hospitality management researchers. Again, as Bob Brotherton discusses (Chapter 8), this problem is also endemic within comparative hospitality management research where, especially in cross-national/cultural studies, inadequate attention is paid to the development of valid measurement instruments and procedures. This invariably leads to serious questions regarding the validity and robustness of the comparisons being made.

Bob Brotherton (Chapter 7) also identifies a number of methodological weaknesses in current case study-based hospitality management research. The hospitality management research literature on these types of studies often reveals researchers providing poor rationales for the selection of cases in the first place and apparently encountering problems in being able to define and delimit the case(s) under investigation. There is also frequently, and perhaps surprisingly, a tendency for hospitality management researchers undertaking case study research to ignore the specific, contingent aspects of the study in their attempts to conduct cross-sectional, variable-oriented, survey-type studies to demonstrate the external validity and generalisability of the results, a feature which not only betrays their positivistic philosophical roots but also illuminates a lack of thought given to the suitability of the methodological choices made.

This is a contention further evidenced by the observation that the use of qualitative approaches in hospitality management case study research is extremely limited. As Brotherton identifies (Chapter 8), although the potential value of qualitative case study research for exploring the 'uniqueness', or otherwise, of the phenomenon–context nexus is considerable, the literature indicates this is not currently a favoured methodological choice amongst hospitality management researchers in general. Similarly, although methodological and data source/type triangulation, is often claimed to be a particular methodological strength of the case study approach (Stake, 1994; Yin, 1994), it would appear to be largely absent from this type of research.

David Litteljohn and Angela Roper (Chapter 3) adopt a different and interesting conversational style to present their material on 'Researching organisations from the outside' and introduce a discussion of the more practical aspects of research. The strong theme of informed pragmatism which characterises the methodological discussions of the protagonists in this chapter raises a number of methodological concerns relating to researcher access, acceptance, observation, triangulation of data sources/types, and the ethical considerations impinging on many of these activities. Although such methodological pragmatism may be scorned by the purist, there is not necessarily a strong justification for such condemnation. For example, Stuart Jauncey's discussion

(Chapter 10) not only explores the methodological advantages and disadvantages of participant observation but also reflects on a number of the practical issues and problems likely to be encountered by a researcher adopting this approach to research. In particular, Jauncey refers to difficulties relating to both the theoretical and practical aspects of data collection, recording and interpretation, and the potential data integrity enhancement to be gained from both the type of methodological and data triangulation referred to above.

In pursuing this general theme of pragmatism and practicality, Conrad Lashley (Chapter 9) highlights the practical orientation and purported real-world value of action research and stresses the importance of viewing theory and practice as symbiotic partners. However, action research *per se* presents significant methodological problems for hospitality management and other researchers alike, as its design and conduct conflict with the dominant, positivistic tradition. As Lashley comments, action research is essentially anti-positivistic in philosophy, as it emphasises a constructionist and interpretative philosophical stance, and places researcher involvement and reflection at the heart of its design and implementation. Consequently it is not surprising that, on the basis of published studies, Lashley concludes that action research has not been widely adopted by hospitality management researchers. Once again this may be seen as yet another paradox. On the one hand, hospitality management researchers make constant reference to the 'uniqueness' of hospitality and hospitality research, whether this is accepted or not, whilst on the other they would appear to be rejecting methodological choices which have a greater potential to confirm or disconfirm such contentions. This paradox Lashley, Brotherton and Jauncey all record in relation to action, case study, comparative, and participative observation research respectively.

Maureen Brookes, Anne Hampton and Angela Roper (Chapter 4) suggest that adoption of a multi- or interdisciplinary approach, and associated methodologies, can effectively help to overcome the methodological weaknesses associated with the type of mono-disciplinary studies which tend to characterise the literature. Though this may be an arguable contention, with its success often being heavily dependent upon a number of problematic compromises for the researchers concerned, it does raise the possibility of a greater degree of methodological discourse taking place during the design and conduct of the research. On the other hand, it also offers the possibility that the regularly purported rigour and depth of mono-disciplinary research may be compromised. This of course assumes that the mono-disciplinary researchers have a strong disciplinary base to begin with, an assumption which may be challenged by many on the basis of the published evidence! Even if the jury is still out on the mono versus multidisciplinary research debate there is little doubt that the literature indicates both options continue to suffer from methodological weaknesses in hospitality management research.

Finally, Alan Fyall and Richard Thomas (Chapter 14) and Anne Hampton (Chapter 15), in reflecting on issues concerned with quantitative and qualitative data analysis respectively, draw attention not only to a number of the key methodological aspects of these areas but also to a need for hospitality management researchers to demonstrate technical competency in their use. There is evidence in the literature that some hospitality management researchers give inadequate attention to selecting and implementing appropriate data analysis techniques for the nature of the data they have collected. This occurs not only in relation to the type of sample size/composition issues identified by

Rosemary Lucas and Nigel Hemmington (Chapters 5 and 13) but also in terms of ensuring an appropriate fit between the type of data collected, the techniques selected for analysing it, and how well such techniques are implemented.

Hospitality specialisms

As hospitality management is self-evidently a very broad and diverse field of study, any attempt to try to cover the detail within the breadth of specialisms contained in Chapters 17–26 would be an enormous exercise and clearly beyond the scope of this particular chapter. Therefore, the aim of this section is largely to identify a number of issues and themes which would appear to arise out of the chapters on these specialisms. One general conclusion these chapters tend to suggest is that the research effort in many, if not all, the specialisms covered is rather eclectic and fragmented. This is generally the case in terms of the range of methodological choices hospitality management researchers have made, the type of research conducted (conceptual versus empirical), and the coverage and coherence of the research effort in relation to particular specialisms and their more specific subsets. In one sense this is not surprising as some of the specialisms, within the context of hospitality, may be regarded as emergent in nature and as such are seeking to develop their identity and critical mass.

This is the case in IT management, as Michael Baker, Silvia Sussmann and Susan Welch (Chapter 20) identify. In this rapidly evolving area it is evident that not only are the boundaries somewhat fuzzy but its substance exists in an almost permanent state of flux, reflecting the extremely fast pace of change in information technologies and their applications. Thus it is not surprising that research in this field is characterised by eclecticism in relation to both the nature of the approaches and type of studies undertaken. A similar picture is identified by Rhodri Thomas, Martin Friel and Stephanie Jameson (Chapter 25) in the Small Business Management specialism. These authors indicate the existence of definitional problems relating to small firms *per se*, the associated methodological problems of estimating the number of small firms, and the boundary-setting difficulties concerning the delimitation of small firms as a distinct analytic category. Their general view of this specialism is very much that of an emergent field currently characterised by a body of research which tends towards the exploratory and descriptive rather than the confirmatory and analytical.

However, in both these and other hospitality management specialisms there are other issues of greater concern, particularly where there is a distinct dissonance between more substantial 'generic' bodies of research relating to the issue or phenomenon and those which have been conducted to date within the context of hospitality management. In the Small Business Management field Thomas, Friel and Jameson reflect the view that while much of the 'mainstream' small business research has increasingly become interdisciplinary in nature, with a blend of quantitative and qualitative approaches being adopted, for hospitality management researchers it largely remains a monodisciplinary venture based on a choice of either quantitative or qualitative approaches. Gerald Barlow's analysis of the state of play in Financial Management research (Chapter 26) to some extent echoes some of these issues. Barlow comments that the body of generic accounting and financial management research is 'light-years ahead' of the small amount of similar research which has been conducted within the context of the hospitality industry and that there is a need not only for more research *per se* in this field, but for more of an interdisciplinary nature.

On a related, but slightly different, track, Peter Jones (Chapter 22) accurately makes the point that much of the contemporary Catering Operations Management research is not strongly rooted in, or indeed linked to, the large body of generic operations management literature, theory or methodologies developed in non-hospitality contexts, a feature which leads him to comment that much of this catering operations' management research is empirically interesting but frequently conceptually weak. This observation accords with Taylor and Edgar's accusation, referred to earlier in this chapter, that hospitality management research suffers from 'conceptual malnutrition'.

Even where hospitality management researchers do explicitly and systematically seek to incorporate wider extant literature, conceptual frameworks and empirical results from previous work in other contexts, there is invariably a lack of consideration given to the issues of contingency and validation. The uncritical importation of perspectives, models, instruments and techniques would appear to be a problem of almost epidemic proportions within the hospitality management research community. As Thomas, Friel and Jameson (Chapter 25) point out, the Small Business Management specialism has suffered because many researchers have tended to use the literature base, concepts, models, and so on, derived from the analysis of large firms. Furthermore, even though much of the small business research based on this intellectual premise has utilised 'scaled down' versions of such concepts and methodologies, this customisation cannot always be defended as valid or reliable.

On this issue of intellectual transfer Nick Johns (Chapter 17) highlights the enthusiasm hospitality management researchers have shown for applying service quality models, and associated instruments, to hospitality, often without adequately validating such transfers. Similarly, Conrad Lashley and Sandra Watson (Chapter 19) point to the conceptual and empirical problems arising from hospitality management researchers attempting to utilise 'mainstream' HRM models in hospitality HRM research.

On the other hand, a number of the authors point to a need not only for the appropriate validation of imported perspectives, models and techniques but also for the development of more specific conceptual frameworks, instruments and measures for hospitality management research. David Litteljohn (Chapter 23) suggests that there is a need for researchers to engage in more conceptual work on the nature of strategic groups within hospitality contexts in order to facilitate a greater degree of intersectoral comparative research. Eliza Ching-Yick Tse and Michael Olsen (Chapter 18) observe that much contemporary Strategic Hospitality Management research relies heavily on models originally developed within the context of manufacturing industry and that theory construction in relation to hospitality is still underdeveloped in this area. In particular, they contend that there is a need for new paradigms to be established in the context of international strategy, a contention supported by Frank Go in Chapter 24.

Another theme which emerges from many of the authors is a need for more comparative research, and in particular longitudinal studies. Tse and Olsen (Strategic Management), Litteljohn (Industry Structure and Strategic Group Analysis), Go (Internationalisation), and Baker, Sussmann and Welch (IT Management), all call for more research of this nature within their particular specialisms. As longitudinal studies are eminently suitable for researching change processes and their associated dynamics, there is a clear rationale for advocating this type of research in these areas. On the other hand, Thomas, Friel and Jameson make the observation that, while longitudinal studies could be valuable in the Small Business Management specialism, the problem of high failure rates amongst small firms in general tends to mitigate against an expansion of this type of research in this field.

In the earlier sections of this chapter it was noted that the hospitality management research community in general is predisposed towards adopting a positivistic philosophy, and hypothetico-deductive, quantitatively based approaches to research. This is a view generally supported by the hospitality specialism chapters where use of the questionnaire survey, often based on suspect sample selection, is legion. In particular, Johns (Chapter 17), Lashley and Watson (Chapter 19), and Lockwood and Ingram (Chapter 21), identify a strong hypothetico-deductive tradition in Quality Management, HRM, and Hotel Operations' Management research where they argue there is a need for more inductive, case study research to explore the qualitative aspects of these specialisms in hospitality contexts to develop more robust theoretical insights. Similarly, Baker, Sussmann and Welch (Chapter 20) also suggest a need for more case study research, involving a cross-disciplinary analysis, in the IT Management specialism.

On the issue of whether the specialisms require more emphasis to be placed on conceptual or empirical work there is, as might be expected, a fairly mixed picture. Some are seen to require an expansion of both in different subsets, whilst others are viewed as needing a greater emphasis on one or the other, either in general or in relation to specific topic areas. According to Peter Jones (Chapter 22) research into catering operations and menu analysis/planning tends to be mainly conceptual, whereas research concerned with catering systems design and technology, catering managers and operations management has a bias towards empirical work. David Litteljohn (Chapter 23) records that much of the industry structure and strategic group analysis research is empirically based, but is often of a descriptive rather than analytical nature and in need of greater theoretical sophistication.

Conclusions and future issues

As the contributions to this text indicate, there is little doubt that the quantity, and to a certain extent the sophistication (Lundberg, 1997), of hospitality management research has expanded greatly over the last 10 to 15 years. This is a significant achievement for the hospitality management research community which should be recognised. Despite many conflicting pressures, hospitality management researchers have proved to be a determined and resilient body of people in their quest to expand and raise the profile of hospitality management research. However, although the general profile of hospitality management research today is far more encouraging than it was a decade ago, the community needs to take stock of the benefits obtained thus far from the quantitative growth which has occurred. Indeed, it may well be that rather than seeking to continue in the same way the hospitality management research community should pause, reflect, consolidate and capitalise on the gains made to date to develop more systematic strategies for the future. This demands discourse and debate relating to a number of key issues.

Firstly, considerable vagueness remains over what constitutes hospitality *per se*, the nature of hospitality management, and the boundaries of the hospitality industry. Many researchers have sought to avoid these crucial issues either by implicitly or explicitly regarding the hotel/lodging and catering/foodservice industry and its management as being synonymous with the hospitality industry and hospitality management, or by seeking refuge in the view that the hospitality industry is merely a subset of the wider service sector, and that hospitality management is a branch of service operations management. However, at the same time there has also been a strong tendency amongst hospitality management researchers to claim that hospitality is at the very least different, and in more extreme views unique.

Whilst these may, or may not, be defensible assertions, the key issue is that the hospitality management research community has not paid sufficient attention to resolving some of its basic dilemmas. Though this may be understandable in some respects, this general lack of intellectual 'navel gazing' has undoubtedly contributed to the quantitative expansion referred to above. On the other hand, it does contain an inherent weakness which threatens the further development of hospitality management research. As many of the contributors to this text identify, the conceptual and methodological eclecticism, frequently based on dubiously valid importations and customisations from other disciplines and fields of enquiry, which characterises the totality of the research output in most of the hospitality management specialisms, invariably arises from inadequate epistemological, conceptual and/or methodological development within hospitality management research *per se*. This is a deficiency which must be addressed, both in general and within particular specialisms, if hospitality management research is to progress further. There is a need for the hospitality management research community to engage in more basic research on these issues.

Secondly, there is a general need for hospitality management researchers to improve the level of professional 'craft' applied to their research. Some, but by no means all, contemporary hospitality management researchers do not come from strong disciplinary backgrounds and/or have not received sufficient research training. This is often reflected in poor methodological choices, underutilisation of generic extant literature, inadequate operationalisation of existing concepts and validation of associated measures when transferred into hospitality management contexts, a relative paucity of new concept and/or measure development, and the production of unreliable generalisations. It is also reflected in the widespread adoption of epistemological and methodological stances based on those dominant in the natural and physical sciences, which are apparently seen by many to offer the best chance for hospitality management research to attain credibility and legitimacy.

Essentially this is a quality issue. If hospitality management research is to be taken more seriously by other academics and industrial practitioners outside its relatively small internal community, then it must build greater confidence among such constituencies. Any such increase in confidence is likely to be directly related to the robustness of its design and conduct. Research activity in, and output from, established disciplines and fields is generally accepted as legitimate because its supporters and recipients alike have confidence in the credibility of its basic design and implementation processes. In addition, confidence in such research is invariably enhanced by a perception, justified or otherwise, that these research communities have well-developed, rigorous internal quality assurance/control procedures which establish and maintain high standards. This is a feature the hospitality management research community has yet to convince others it has, and one which requires urgent discourse and action.

Thirdly, given that most of the research effort conducted to date in many of the hospitality specialisms is fragmented, and characterised by gaps and imbalances across the various specialism themes and subsets, there is a need for researchers operating within each of the specialist areas both to establish an enhanced level of internal coherence and to determine the specialism's future agenda(s). At present there would appear to be a general lack of organisation, vision and leadership within the specialisms arising from their eclectic evolution. Thus, there is considerable scope for leading researchers to stimulate the required debate amongst their colleagues, and to initiate the process of determining priorities and setting agendas for both the individual specialism *per se* and its subsets. Such agendas and priorities will need to reflect not only the key issues/themes in relation to the more substantive research issues but also those concerning the development of appropriate conceptual, methodological and technical innovations.

Fourthly, and related to the issues discussed above, there is a need for the hospitality management research community as a whole to engage in more substantive, agenda setting, conceptual research. Regardless of specialist boundaries the development of distinctive schools of thought, embracing all the philosophical, methodological and technical aspects of the research process, would constitute a significant step forward for hospitality management research. More established disciplines and fields of enquiry generally exhibit clear subdivisions based on well-articulated schools of thought which stimulate debate within and between the advocates of the various schools. Such debate, ranging from the ideological to the technical aspects of research, tends to provide a major stimulus for advancement in those research fields where it occurs. Schools of thought also provide 'homes' for nomadic researchers searching for a common intellectual identity and bring at least a semblance of order to an otherwise rather anomic existence.

In this sense the development of schools of thought within hospitality management research may ultimately help individuals in this community to establish a clearer, more coherent, and definitive, critical mass of research not only within each particular school of thought but also across the specialisms and field of enquiry as a whole. However, in the more immediate future a move in this direction may stimulate greater internal fragmentation as the protagonists within different camps begin the battle for dominance across the field as a whole. Although this clearly embodies a destructive potential, it nevertheless is a process capable of delivering potentially enormous benefits over time and one which may be required to ensure that hospitality management research does not suffer from atrophy.

Finally, many of the authors contributing to this text suggest there is a need for a greater emphasis to be placed on research of an inter/multi-disciplinary and/or comparative nature, and that conducted through cross-national/cultural teams. The general view appears to be that many of the issues which have been researched to date, and a number of those on the more immediate horizon, could have been or will be explored more effectively by using one or more of these approaches. Although the reasons why these types of research do not have a higher profile in the contemporary hospitality management research literature are understandable, i.e. they tend to be more complex to design and implement, and costly to do, they are likely to be important types in helping to further the development of research in this field.

Inter/multi-disciplinary research, by definition, promotes philosophical and methodological dialogue between the members of the research team which should help to generate more innovative and robust approaches to the research question(s) under consideration. The use of cross-national/cultural research teams would help to reduce the degree of ethnicity bias found in many contemporary studies and bring new insights to these issues, especially those being researched within an international context. An increase in the amount of comparative research being undertaken would not only be beneficial in those specialisms where it is needed to explore the specialism's particular issues and concerns more effectively but would also be invaluable for exploring the claims of hospitality management's 'uniqueness' currently made by many of the researchers in this community.

Here lie the issues, challenges and choices facing the hospitality management research community. If hospitality management research is to progress, develop its legitimacy and evolve into a more credible field of enquiry, its community has to be more critical and proactive. In many respects hospitality management research, in the aggregate, has arrived at this point by accident. It exhibits considerable progress in some areas but significantly less in others, and has a rather fragmented profile. Although it is light-years ahead of where it was 10 to 15 years ago, especially in terms of the volume of output, it now faces a watershed and some fundamental choices. If the achievements secured, and lessons learned, to date are not to be wasted the community, both individually and collectively, must be more proactive and strategic in developing the agenda(s) and priorities required to drive hospitality management research forward.

Bibliography

Brotherton, B. (1989) Defining hospitality, tourism and leisure: perspectives, problems and implications. *Proceedings of the IAHMS Autumn Symposium*, The Queen's College, Glasgow.

Brotherton, B. (1998) The nature of hospitality and hospitality management: a definitive view to inform research and practice for the new millennium? *The Hospitality and Tourism Global Forum* (Millennial Retrospective Conference), http://www.mcb.co.uk/htgf/current/millenial.htm, MCB Publications.

Cassee, E. H. (1983) Introduction. In Cassee, E. H. and Reuland, R. (Eds) *The Management of Hospitality*, Pergamon, Oxford, pp. xiii–xxii.

Edgar, R. and Umbreit, W. (1988) Hospitality research: re-assessing our strategy. *Cornell Hotel and Restaurant Administration Quarterly*, Vol. 29, No. 2, pp. 51–56.

Evans, M. R. (1992) The emerging role of hospitality and tourism research. *Hospitality and Tourism Educator*, Vol. 4, No. 4, pp. 57–59.

Jones, P. (1996) Hospitality research—where have we got to? *International Journal of Hospitality Management*, Vol. 15, No. 1, pp. 5–10.

Khan, M. and Olsen, M. (1988) An overview of research in hospitality education. *Cornell Hotel and Restaurant Administration Quarterly*, Vol. 29, No. 2, pp. 54–55.

Lewis, R. (1988) Uses and abuses of hospitality research. *Cornell Hotel and Restaurant Administration Quarterly*, Vol. 29, No. 3, pp. 11–12.

Litteljohn, D. (1990) Hospitality research: philosophies and progress. In Teare, R., Moutinho, L. and Morgan, N. (Eds) *Managing and Marketing Services in the 1990's*, Cassell, London.

Lundberg, C. C. (1997) Widening the conduct of hospitality inquiry: toward appreciating research alternatives. *Journal of Hospitality and Tourism Research*, Vol. 21, No. 1, pp. 1–13.

Middleton, V. T. (1983) Marketing in the hospitality industry. In Cassee, E. H. and Reuland, R. (Eds) *The Management of Hospitality*, Pergamon, Oxford, pp. 51–68.

Nailon, P. (1982) Theory in hospitality management. *International Journal of Hospitality Management*, Vol. 1, No. 3, pp. 135–143.

Shaw, M. and Nightingale, M. (1995) Scholarship reconsidered: implications for hospitality education. *Hospitality Research Journal*, Vol. 18/19, No. 3/1, pp. 81–93.

Slattery, P. (1983) Social scientific methodology and hospitality management. *International Journal of Hospitality Management*, Vol. 2, No. 1, pp. 9–14.

Stake, R. E. (1994) Case studies. In Denzin, N. K. and Lincoln, Y. S. (Eds) *Handbook of Qualitative Research*, Sage Publications, Thousand Oaks, CA, pp. 236–247.

Taylor, S. and Edgar, D. (1996) Hospitality research: the emperor's new clothes? *International Journal of Hospitality Management*, Vol. 15, No. 3, pp. 211–227.

Yin, R. K. (1994) *Case Study Research—Design and Methods* (2nd edition), Sage Publications, Thousand Oaks, CA.

Index